Under the Editorship of LUCIUS GARVIN

UNIVERSITY OF MARYLAND

The STRUCTURE OF

EDWARD H. MADDEN

The Riverside Press Cambridge

SCIENTIFIC THOUGHT

An Introduction to Philosophy of Science

SAN JOSE STATE COLLEGE

HOUGHTON MIFFLIN COMPANY · BOSTON

THE RIVERSIDE PRESS
CAMBRIDGE, MASSACHUSETTS
PRINTED IN THE U.S.A.

PREFACE

Alice asks "What is a Caucus-Race?" and the Dodo replies, "The best way to explain it is to do it." Teachers and textbook writers would do well to heed the Dodo's words. Nothing is more discouraging than to have a teacher or a textbook writer tell you in a thin anticipatory way, yet laboriously, what his subject is and how he is going to present it. How much more satisfying it is when, like the Dodo, he simply does it! Let me, then, in this Preface limit myself to a few needful practical comments and acknowledgments.

First, to the student: In my introductory essays I have followed a convention in the use of quotation marks quite common among logicians. I use single quotes around a word or sentence whenever I say something about the word or sentence itself – for example, 'Paris' has five letters; 'Brother' means male sibling; 'It will rain tomorrow' is probably true. I use double quotes in all the ordinary ways, as in direct quotations and in "quarantining" a word which is used vaguely, uncritically, or in an unusual sense.

Teachers may find the following remarks about the book helpful. The text materials at the beginning of each chapter are not simply introductions to the selections that follow; they are, rather, self-contained essays which taken together are a complete first approach to the main problems of the philosophy of science, although, to be sure, they also point out the relations among the selections. I cannot emphasize enough that the selections *are* carefully related – a basic requirement too often overlooked in books of this sort. I have related the chapters into a careful pattern, although the chapters are, to a great extent, units which can be shifted into different patterns. You may, for example, prefer to do Chapter 2 last, or use only part of it in sequence. The last two selections in each chapter are usually more difficult reading than the earlier ones, although this is not always the case.

I am indebted to many people: to my teachers and students for their past and present mental prodding; to Professor Ernest Nagel for aid in the early stages of preparing this book and to Professor John W. Lenz for help from beginning to end; to Lord Russell and Professor Lenz for permitting me to use material of theirs not previously published; to Professor Lucius Garvin for his editorial work; to numerous friends for help with typing and proofreading; and to Marian Madden for many of these things and so much more.

E. H. M.

CONTENTS

3. *BIOLOGY AND THE SCIENCES OF MAN*

4. *THE MEANING OF 'CAUSE' AND 'LAW'*

5. *PROBABILITY NOTIONS*

6. THE RIDDLE OF INDUCTION

7. SCIENCE AND VALUES

1

MAKING SENSE OF SCIENCE

Introduction

To understand the sort of thing a scientist does, it is not necessary to plunge into the depths of the most recent or most abstruse scientific thought; indeed some of the simplest and historically earliest episodes of modern science are the most valuable for making sense of science and clarifying its structure. Moreover, these episodes help to elicit the proper image of science as an ongoing, exciting enterprise in place of the all-finished, museum-piece image we get from some textbooks of science.

Consequently, I shall begin our study of the philosophy of science by describing briefly the work of Torricelli, Pascal, and Boyle on atmospheric pressure – a familiar early episode, to be sure, appearing in almost every elementary book of science – and shall proceed by pointing out how it is representative of the structure and methods of *all* science, without neglecting, of course, when necessary, to show how it is unrepresentative, too.[1] By this procedure I hope to introduce you to a new subject in a straightforward way and to fix in your minds an over-all view of science which will help clarify the nature and relations of the essays which follow.

1.

Evangelista Torricelli, one of Galileo's disciples, like his master was puzzled by the well-known fact that a simple suction pump cannot raise water more than thirty-four feet. Torricelli, unlike most others, was unwilling to accept this as a brute fact and, seeing it in a new light, so to speak, was able to suggest an explanation for it. He knew well that all objects under the surface of a sea are subjected to water pressure. Why not assume that air has weight and conceive of a "sea of air" which exerts pressure on all objects "immersed" in it? Why not, indeed, Torricelli argued, since this new way of looking at things would explain the nature of a suction pump and why it cannot raise water more than thirty-four feet. Because a moving piston creates a vacuum in the cylindrical shaft of a pump, there is no atmospheric pressure to oppose that which presses down on the reservoir of water. Consequently, this pressure "pushes" the water up the shaft of the pump. It pushes up the water only thirty-four feet because the pressure is only that great – another way of saying, of course, *that this figure measures the amount of atmospheric pressure.*

While the "sea of air" concept makes the limit of thirty-four feet understandable – or, at least, makes *some* limit understandable – this one success certainly did not establish the new hypothesis either as a fruitful or a true one. However, Torricelli himself, Pascal, and Boyle all deduced further consequences from it, checked them by experiment, and found that they squared with observable fact. Consequently, they not only showed the hypothesis to be a fruitful one, since it related, in an understandable way, a number of facts, but they also showed that it must be the true account of these facts since

[1] The best discussions of this episode are James B. Conant's "Robert Boyle's Experiments in Pneumatics," *Harvard Case Histories in Experimental Science,* Vol. I (Cambridge: Harvard University Press, 1957); and Everett W. Hall's "The Revolution in Physics in the Seventeenth Century," *Modern Science and Human Values,* Chapter 3 (Princeton, New Jersey: D. Van Nostrand Company, 1956). I have profited from both discussions.

no other hypothesis could account for all of them together.

Let us look further into Torricelli's early work before investigating these consequences and their experimental check. It was his construction of an entirely new scientific instrument, the barometer, which made it possible to test the consequences of his "sea of air" hypothesis. His early barometer was a simple instrument, to be sure. It consisted of a thin glass tube closed at one end and open at the other and filled with liquid mercury. The open end was submerged in a reservoir of mercury, and a vacuum was thus produced in the tube between the top of the mercury column and the closed end. Now, Torricelli argued, according to his hypothesis the atmospheric pressure on the reservoir without any pressure in the vacuum tube to equalize it "pushes up" or "holds up" the column of mercury.

Torricelli, with his new instrument, was now in a position to check a deductive consequence of his new hypothesis. Since mercury is nearly fourteen times as heavy as water, and since atmospheric pressure presumably holds up a thirty-four feet high column of water, then, he argued, it follows that atmospheric pressure should hold up a column of mercury proportionately smaller, namely, only $\frac{34}{14}$ or $2\frac{3}{7}$ feet. Torricelli, using his new instrument, tested this consequence and found it to hold true in fact.

Blaise Pascal thought out a further consequence of Torricelli's hypothesis and in a famous experiment had his brother-in-law Périer check his deduction with the facts. Pascal reasoned in this fashion: If the concept 'sea of air' is anything more than a metaphor, then this "sea," like a sea of water, should exert different pressures at different depths. Closer to the top of the atmospheric sea, as in a sea of water, the pressure should be less; closer to the bottom, greater. Périer tested this consequence by carrying a barometer to different heights on a mountain, the Puy-de-Dôme, in central France; and the results upheld the expectation. At the bottom of the Puy-de-Dôme the height of the mercury column in the tube was about three inches higher than at the top of the mountain, with appropriate gradations between. Thus Pascal and Périer had further confirmed the truth of Torricelli's hypothesis.

Périer's experiment seems simple indeed; it is, in fact, deceptively simple. It appears as if he simply went to the proper place and made straightforward observations, which, of course, he did, but not without careful attention to, and control of, other factors which might have affected the results. The whole experiment would be pointless, say, if the pressure varied radically from time to time at the base of the mountain. So Périer, as one might expect, kept an observer with a barometer at the bottom of the Puy-de-Dôme who reported that there were no radical changes in pressure at this control point. Périer also tested the barometer readings at various points and times on the top of the mountain – inside an enclosure and outside, in sunlight and shade, etc. – to be certain that the readings did not depend upon some local feature of a particular point of observation.

Otto von Guericke offered perhaps the most spectacular confirmation of the new hypothesis. He invented a vacuum pump which would evacuate air from a closed container; but he quickly found that any container except a spherical metal one collapsed when the air was taken out. This collapse, of course, could be predicted or explained perfectly by the new hypothesis: the atmospheric pressure on the outside of the container pushed in the sides of the container because there was no longer any such pressure on the inside to oppose it. However, there was still a more spectacular side to von Guericke's experiment. He reasoned in the following way: If two large hemispheres are held together but not joined in any way, and if air is evacuated from the spherical container thus formed, then the two hemispheres should remain together when no longer held in this position since the atmosphere would exert pressure inward while there would be no pressure inside to oppose it. Von Guericke tested this consequence of the new hypothesis, and it was dramatically confirmed. The atmospheric pressure held his hemispheres, having a diameter of three feet, so tightly together that it took a team of sixteen horses to pull them apart! However, whenever air was re-admitted to the spherical container the hemispheres simply fell apart.

Robert Boyle saw still another way to check Torricelli's hypothesis, this time by using von Guericke's pump in a different way. Look for a moment at the following diagram.

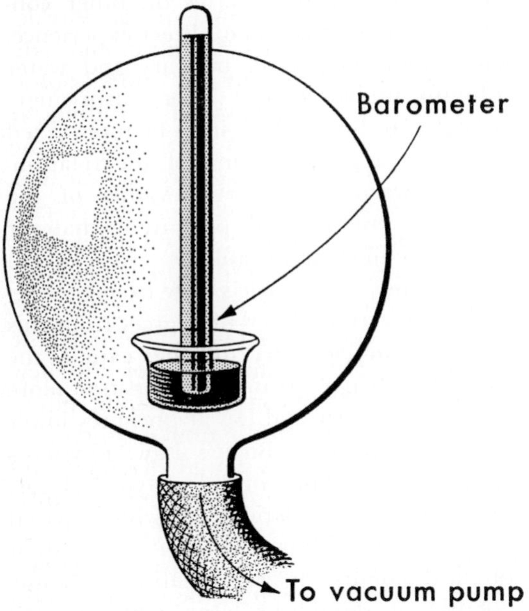

Boyle simply put the bottom part of a barometer into a spherical container from which he could evacuate the air with his vacuum pump. Now, Boyle argued, if the atmospheric pressure pushes up the mercury in the tube by pushing down on the mercury in the reservoir, then the column of mercury will fall if the air is removed from the container. When he evacuated the air from the container, the mercury column fell, as expected. To be sure, it did not fall to the level of the mercury in the reservoir, but Boyle explained away this anomaly simply by saying his pump was not efficient enough to get out all the air.

One might object, and justifiably so, that Boyle's experiment was not an independent confirmation of Torricelli's hypothesis for, after all, it is similar to Périer's experiment on the Puy-de-Dôme. Instead of varying atmospheric pressure by going to various heights and depths in the actual atmosphere, Boyle artificially produced various different pressures and watched their effects. True, Boyle's experiment is not an essentially new confirmation of the hypothesis, but it is corroborative and, most important of all, a great advance in experimentation. No longer did one have to investigate atmospheric pressure in its natural state, where it is difficult to control variables (although Périer did well enough); one could now bring "nature" into the laboratory under highly controlled conditions. In this way, Boyle's results were not simply corroborative but crucially so since they were more reliable.

Boyle was far from content, however, simply to draw a consequence from Torricelli's hypothesis and to confirm it experimentally. He was interested in finding, if possible, a quantitative relationship between this new concept of air pressure and some other concept — or some other variable, as the scientist usually says. After several false tries he finally tried to relate volume of air to pressure. To be sure, he saw, like Torricelli and Pascal, a qualitative relationship between the volume and pressure of air. Like any material, air presumably will try to "spring" back when compressed into a smaller volume. But is there any mathematical relationship between this "effort to spring back" — pressure — and volume? Boyle considered as a hypothesis a straightforward mathematical relationship; namely, that the volume of air is inversely proportional to the pressure, which means simply that if the volume is doubled the pressure is halved, or if the volume is halved (by compressing the air) the pressure is doubled. (The usual notation for this relationship is $P_1V_1 = P_2V_2$; that is to say, the product PV is a constant.) But how was Boyle to test his mathematical hypothesis? As you might expect, something new in the way of an instrument was required. Boyle met the challenge by creating an instrument like this:

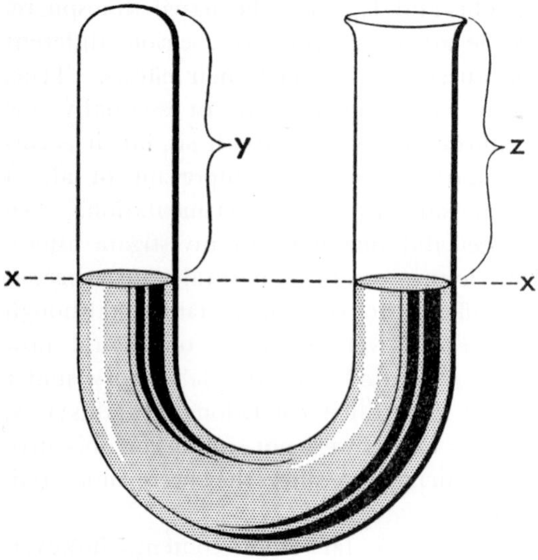

X represents the mercury level at the beginning of Boyle's experiment and *y* represents the volume of air in the closed leg of the tube. Boyle proceeded to pour liquid mercury into the open leg of the tube, which, of course, added more pressure to the original atmospheric pressure. Now what was the mathematical relation between the measure of this total pressure and the measure of the volume of air in *y?* He discovered that doubling this pressure approximately halved the volume *y*, that increasing it four times reduced the volume one-fourth, and so on. In short, his mathematical hypothesis was experimentally confirmed, and Boyle's Law thus came into being.

A thoughtful reader may well ask at this point if the scientist usually proceeds in this way. Could not Boyle have conducted his experiment first, observed the data, and then directly formulated a mathematical function to fit them?

This view of scientific procedure is a common one, but it is faulty for several reasons. We must first distinguish between variables and laws; let us say, as a simple approximation, that a law is a functional relationship between two independently meaningful variables. Now the point is this: neither the concepts in Boyle's Law nor the Law itself are matters of direct observation. Remember that Boyle took over Torricelli's new notions, the most fundamental one of which was that air has weight. The weight of air, however, is not a directly experienced concept or variable; it is, rather, a function of, and is formulated in terms of, other concepts which are matters of direct experience, namely, the heights of mercury and water columns in barometers. Nor, surprisingly enough, can Boyle's Law itself be interpreted simply as a generalization of the relationship between the observed values of the variables, volume and pressure – whatever the nature of these variables is – since actual gases do not obey Boyle's Law exactly! Actual gases vary in different degrees from this law, but they all vary to some extent, the variations being greater at pressures more than atmospheric and less at pressures lower than atmospheric. Boyle's Law, physicists came to say, defines an "ideal type" of gas; it specifies the relationship which actual gases would exhibit if certain non-existent physical conditions were realized. Consequently, it should be clear, while Boyle's Law might be characterized as an extrapolation of the relationship between the observed values of variables, it could never be characterized simply as a generalization of them.

Note, finally, the important relation of Boyle's work generally to that previously done. Boyle not only helped to confirm further Torricelli's hypothesis, but in addition he formulated a law *within the conceptual framework of this new hypothesis.* This capacity to use concepts and theories already accepted to state and elaborate others related to them is the touchstone of the success of modern science, and a lively appreciation of this factor is fundamental to understanding its structure. I should add, for proper appreciation of this example, that Boyle's new concept of 'ideal gas,' in turn, played an important role in the subsequent proliferation of the new idea of Torricelli – himself student of the master, Galileo, who, in an important sense, began the whole new scientific enterprise!

2.

The sample of science I have presented is simple indeed, but this very simplicity makes the nature of scientific inference stand out in bold relief. The sample clearly exemplifies the following pattern: formation of a relevant hypothesis, deductive elaboration of its consequences, and testing, by observation or experiment, whether or not these consequences occur in fact. Torricelli framed the 'sea of air' hypothesis; he and others deduced consequences, of which we have examined three; and they all tested these consequences – Périer by observation and Boyle by experiment – and found them to hold true in fact as well as in theory. In what follows I will examine each part of this pattern in turn.

Two of the most important problems about scientific hypotheses concern their *origin* and their *logical form.* And since the question of their origin has caused a good deal of trouble in the past, we must be clear at the outset that a hypothesis can come from any source whatever–from intuition, trial and error, past experience, accident, imagination, even a dream! The only restrictions put upon a hypothesis are these: whatever its origin, it will become a part of the fabric of science only if it yields deductive consequences which are tested by experience and found to be true in fact.

Unhappily, philosophers and scientists in the past have wasted a good deal of time insisting upon what the origin of a concept or hypothesis *must* be. For example, some philosophers – called empiricists because of their emphasis on experience – spent a great deal of time and effort trying to prove that concepts must all arise from the originator's past experience with specific objects, events, and their relations. As you will see at once, however, these empiricists inevitably run into difficulty in explaining the origin of mathematical concepts and physical ones like space and time. For such concepts do not refer to any concrete experience of objects or events, even when their experienced relations are conceived in the most refined and extended fashion. Empiricists nowadays generally agree that a scientific hypothesis need not have an experiential pedigree but insist, only, as I have done, that it must be fruitful and confirmable.

Let us look closely now at the logical form of scientific hypotheses. Consider first, though, this simple hypothetical inference from ordinary life:

1. If Mr. Jones is sick, then he will leave the office early.
2. He left the office early.

―――――――――――――――

3. He is sick.

This inference, unfortunately, is not admissible since it might also be the case that Mr. Jones will leave the office early because he has an appointment or because he promised his wife to cut the lawn before dinner. If all I know is that he left the office early, I cannot tell whether it was because he was sick, had an appointment, or had to cut the grass. Clearly all three are simple hypotheses which would explain why he left the office early, so any judgment about which one is true depends upon deducing further consequences from all the hypotheses to see which one alone can account for all the facts. Now suppose we know that Jones always takes his brief case home to do work at night. We might, then, argue in this fashion:

1. If Mr. Jones is sick, then he will leave his brief case in the office.
2. He left his brief case in the office.
3. He is sick.

We have now developed further the sickness hypothesis and confirmed another consequence, but if we develop further the appointment and grass-cutting hypotheses we see that they do not account for leaving his brief case in the office. Apparently, then, even though no one of the separate deductive tests of an hypothesis is cogent or strictly admissible, the general strategy of confirmation is sound. That is, if all competitive hypotheses, except one, are eliminated because they do not account for all the facts, while this one explains them all, it is, so to speak, left standing in the field of combat as the only acceptable winner!

Now the application of this example to science should be clear immediately. While any separate confirmation of Torricelli's hypothesis – say Périer's or Boyle's – is not cogent on strict logical grounds, the general strategy for confirming it seems perfectly admissible. There were, in Torricelli's day, competitive hypotheses to explain why water could not be pumped higher than thirty-four feet but none of them explained or organized a whole group of facts as Torricelli's so beautifully did. They were eliminated because they could not account for all the facts, while the 'sea of air,' since it did explain them, was left holding the field. Galileo saw this logic of scientific inference as clearly as anyone since his day. The Copernican hypothesis, he wrote, although it accounts for all the facts of astronomy, has a genuine rival in the Ptolemaic viewpoint. Consequently, "it is not the same thing to show that the supposition that the earth moves and the sun stands still saves the appearances [accounts for all the facts], and to demonstrate that such hypotheses are really true in nature." Nevertheless, he added, "it is quite as much and even more true that by means of [the Ptolemaic system] it is impossible to account for these appearances. This system is undoubtedly false, just as it is clear that the other, which fits the appearances most excellently, can be true, and that no other greater truth can or ought to be sought in a hypothesis than its correspondence with the particular appearances."

There is, however, a qualification which some philosophers would want to add to this analysis of scientific inference. Why, after all, they would say, should we assume that the known competitive hypotheses are the only possible ones; perhaps there is one which would account for all the facts just as well as Torricelli's does, and perhaps more economically and simply, if only one could discover it. Consequently, since we cannot be certain that Torricelli's hypothesis is *really* left alone in the field, it remains only probably, not necessarily, true. The same would hold true, of course, of all scientific knowledge: it is only probably, not necessarily, true.

We may well agree with this qualification while noting at the same time that it simply reminds us that science is not in its parts or its entirety deductively cogent. But by now this point hardly comes as a surprise. Moreover, it may well be misleading. If I say that Torricelli's, or Galileo's, or Einstein's theory is only probable, I tend to blur the distinction between those hypotheses which *are* well grounded and other ones which are still only tentative, undeveloped, or partly tested, and so in the ordinary use of the word "only probable."

There are other qualifications of my analysis of scientific inference which you should be able to discover for yourself. In fact, since my analysis presents an idealized case, there are many complications. Sometimes no one competing hypothesis will explain the whole set of relevant facts but two of them, say, will explain different parts of the set. Neither hypothesis, then, is wholly acceptable and, worse yet, they may be mutually incompatible and so cannot be combined into a more general hypothesis which will explain the whole set. (This predicament, as we shall see, occurs in the quantum theory of modern physics.) But at other times there may be an opposite difficulty. We may, for example, be confronted with two hypotheses each of which, as far as we can tell, explains the whole of a given set of relevant facts, yet both of which cannot be true since there are more than verbal differences between them. It is sometimes said, although not wholly accurately, that the Ptolemaic and Copernican systems are each able to "save all the appearances" in astronomy, so we must decide between them on other grounds. In cases where this predicament arises, the decision must be made in terms of *logical simplicity.* We will choose that hypothesis which, so to speak, explains the facts with the least difficulty; that is, explains the same number of facts with fewer undefined terms and unproved physical assumptions. This logical simplicity, however, must not be confused with psychological simplicity: the former refers to the elements of a theory, while the latter refers to the familiarity of a person with these elements. "Those not trained in physics and mathematics doubtless find a geocentric theory of the heavens simpler than a heliocentric theory, since in the latter case we must revise habitual interpretations of what it is we are supposed to see with our eyes. The theory that the earth is flat is simpler than the theory that it is round, because the untutored man finds it difficult to conceive of people at the antipodes walking on the surface of the earth without falling off. But 'simplicity' so understood can be no guide for choosing between rival hypotheses. A new and therefore unfamiliar hypothesis would never be chosen for its simplicity. . . . To say that Einstein's theory of relativity is simpler (in this sense) than Newton's physics is clearly absurd." [2]

Assuming that we are reasonably clear now about the nature of scientific hypotheses, we can profitably turn our attention to the next part of the pattern of scientific inference, namely, their deductive development. First, it is important to see this part of the pattern in the right way. The point is not that it is desirable, whenever possible, to develop a hypothesis so that one may account for new facts, but rather that development is absolutely necessary for discovering whether or not a hypothesis itself is *true.* Hypotheses are never directly verifiable (if a statement is directly verifiable, why call it a hypothesis?) ; the only way they can show their credentials for entering the sanctums of science is through the development and test of their consequences.

Hypotheses may, of course, be elaborated by verbal means alone; Torricelli's was developed in this fashion, and many of the hypotheses of biology and the social sciences still are. Nevertheless, it is difficult to overemphasize the importance of mathematics for the development of hypotheses in a highly articulated science like physics. Mathematics in all its branches and divisions is a deductive science; hence it is a perfect tool for the deductive elaboration of a new hypothesis, provided, of course, that concepts of the hypothesis are quantifiable. Boyle, as we saw, hypothesized an inverse relation between the quantifiable concepts, pressure and volume, and was thus enabled to predict innumerable consequences of a quantitative sort about the values of these variables when either one varied in any degree. Boyle's Law, needless to say, is not representative of the great mathematical sophistication of science today; for that matter, it is not even

[2] Morris Cohen and Ernest Nagel, *Introduction to Logic and Scientific Method* (New York: Harcourt, Brace and Company, 1934) , p. 213.

representative of the mathematical sophistication of seventeenth-century science, for that century produced Galileo's and Newton's work in mechanics where already complex mathematical notions were involved. Stated more elaborately, the great successes of Galileo and Newton consisted in their mathematical analysis of physical events, the combination of them into physical postulates, or "axioms," and the deductive development, from the postulates and definitions of new concepts, of theorems which, since they stated consequences about the physical world, could be tested.

To state his position as to inertial motion, Galileo found it necessary to define "uniform motion" (that is, "constant velocity"). His definition was: "By steady or uniform motion, I mean one in which the distances traversed by the moving particle during any equal intervals of time, are themselves equal." It should be clear that the uniform motion of a body was not something itself directly observable; rather one observed distances traversed and times consumed by a moving body and subsequently *figured out* whether or not it was in uniform motion. From his concept of uniform motion thus defined together with certain "axioms" which he thought followed from it Galileo deduced a number of "theorems"; for example, "If a moving particle, carried uniformly at a constant speed, traverses two distances the time-intervals required are to each other in the ratio of these distances." Thus, he was able to construct a miniature geometry of uniform motion. His deductive procedure was made possible by his definition of uniform motion, for his theorems were essentially just elaborations of what was contained in the definition; yet the whole system could be applied to observed motions, for the elements of the definition ("equal distances," "equal times") could be determined by appropriate measurements.[3]

Mathematics, however, is not a cure-all, as some people think, for all the aches and pains of science. There is no mathematically mechanical way of advancing science. The quantification of a concept in no way insures its scientific fruitfulness. Consider the following concept: A "b coefficient" is the number of hairs on anybody's head divided by the number of years he has lived, raised to the fourth power. This concept is perfectly precise and quantitative but as far as I know no one has claimed for it any scientific significance. It simply doesn't lend itself to any relation, functional or otherwise, with any other concept. It does not, in short, occur in any scientific law or hypothesis. The scientist needs mathematics, to be sure, but he needs even more a scientific genius for the formation of useful hypotheses.

The last step in scientific thinking, we saw, is the observational and experimental test of a hypothesis to see whether or not predicted and actual consequences coincide. These tests, it should be clear, must be public and repeatable ones, like the tests of Torricelli's hypothesis. A new hypothesis is not likely to enter the pandects of science if only some scientists, and then only sometimes, are able to confirm it! This unhappy situation actually existed in the early days of psychology. The early psychologist examined the properties of consciousness by introspectively analyzing the contents of his own conscious experience. The result of this introspection, one might say, was an inventory of the mind; psychologists discovered, for example, the number of colors and degrees of brightness which can be distinguished, the number of "affective elements" and emotions which can be distinguished, and so on. They investigated "mental images" and "thought contents," but here disagreement began to arise (although it was not altogether lacking previously). Some psychologists always discovered a mental image present and operative in their thought processes; others did not. The latter, then, insisted that some thought, at any rate, is imageless. The former, however, replied, not too graciously, that an image is always there if you are skill-

[3] Everett W. Hall, *op. cit.*, p. 101.

ful enough in introspective analysis to discover it! Psychology, it seemed to some, had come upon evil times: the observational or experimental results you got seemed to depend on who did the observing. So psychologists, like other scientists, came to insist that an observational or experimental test will be acceptable if and only if it can be repeated by *any* scientist competent in the area in which the hypothesis occurs. "It is required that any individual observation must be capable of confirmation by *any* qualified observer – that is, anybody who is in a position, through training, to understand the conditions of the alleged experience, manipulate the tools and instruments required to produce it, and respond to tests certifying him as a 'normal' observer."[4] In short, one might say, the conditions and results of an experiment must be sufficiently precise and specific to make the test testable!

In testing a hypothesis, whether by observation or experiment, the most important problem, and chief difficulty, is the control of relevant variables. Périer, you recall, kept an observer with a barometer at the bottom of the Puy-de-Dôme to exclude the possibility that some variable other than height caused the drop in the barometer which was carried up the mountain. He also tested the barometric reading in different spots and at different times on the mountain top to be certain that the result was not dependent on the local characteristics of particular points of observation. The logician of science would describe Périer's procedure in the following way. He indirectly controlled the variables by varying the circumstances in which the consequence occurs (falling of barometer reading) until he discovered one variable (height), suggested by Torricelli's hypothesis, to be the only one always present, and never absent, when the consequence is observed.

[4] Max Black, *Critical Thinking,* second edition (Englewood Cliffs, New Jersey: Prentice-Hall, Inc., 1952), p. 359.

Experiment, however, is superior to observation in the control of variables; the whole point of an experiment is to set up an artificial situation in which the control of variables is greater than it is in the ordinary course of natural events. In an experiment there are, ideally, two situations, one called "experimental" and the other "control." The two situations are "equated," which means that the variables of the two are identically paired off with each other except that the experimental set-up has one variable which the control one lacks. If the predicted consequence of a hypothesis occurs in the experimental set-up but not in the control one, presumably the one way and the only way in which the two set-ups differ is responsible for the difference. But the "equating" of set-ups is not an easy matter: the elements of the two must have *identical* characteristics except in one respect. The best way to be sure of identity of characteristics would be to have the elements of the control and experimental set-ups literally identical; the same one functioning, successively, as control and as experimental set-ups. Of course, if this procedure is followed, there must be good evidence that the time interval itself is not causally operative. Boyle's simple experimental set-up, you will see for yourself, is a good example of this ideal type of experiment.

Finally, there is no *a priori* way of knowing that all relevant variables have been taken into account; the only criterion, rather, is the pragmatic one that a hypothesis successfully predicts and explains a wide range of facts. Only if a prediction goes awry, or an explanation becomes inadequate without additional assumptions, do we assume there is an uncontrolled variable and proceed to look for it or make informed guesses about its nature. Again, we will think we have found it, and *now* have taken into account all relevant variables, if we can again successfully predict and explain.

Instruments are often necessary and crucial in the experimental testing of hypotheses. Torricelli's new idea, as we saw, could not have been tested in any convincing way without the creation of the barometer. The important point, however, is not to conceive the use of a scientific instrument in the wrong way. It is not simply a piece of apparatus conveniently at hand, outside the realm of theoretical science, which makes it possible to check hypotheses with which it has otherwise no intimate connection. It should be clear that the barometer and Torricelli's hypothesis are thoroughly bound up together; the barometer was suggested and required by the hypothesis, just as, say, the tangent galvanometer is suggested and required by the electromagnetic theory of Laplace and Ampère. And the barometer and galvanometer are not unique in this respect; the point holds for all scientific instruments, even the simplest. Take the case of a magnifying glass or the more complicated one of a microscope. They do not simply reveal what was hitherto hidden in a straightforward or unproblematic way; they too must be interpreted in a theoretical frame of reference before they can even function as scientific instruments. Pierre Duhem, who saw this point most clearly, wrote: "The objects seen through the magnifying glass appear circled by colors of the rainbow; is it not the theory of dispersion which teaches us to regard these colors as created by the instrument, and to disregard them when we describe the object observed? And how much more important this remark is when it is no longer a matter of a simple magnifying glass but of a powerful microscope! To what strange errors we should be exposed at times . . . if a discussion drawn from optical theories did not allow us to distinguish the role of appearances from that of realities!" [5]

[5] Pierre Duhem, *The Aim and Structure of Physical Theory* (Princeton, New Jersey: Princeton University Press, 1954), p. 154.

3.

You have by now, I hope, become well enough acquainted with the logical outlines of modern science to profit from a closer friendship. The selections that follow in this chapter carry out in detail the analysis which I have only begun. By and large the selections present a unified view of science, although I do not wish to suggest that there are no disagreements. The development of disagreement, you may be sure, takes a more prominent place in chapters to come; but, after all, we have to know some things clearly before we can profitably disagree about others.

Chauncey Wright analyzes the structure of modern science to see if there are any elements which uniquely set it off from the science of the ancients. He finds all the elements which we have discussed — "appeals to observation under the guidance of deduction by steps which are indeed correlative parts of one method" — but points out that ancient sciences, too, exhibit every aspect of this "scientific method." The sudden surge in science in the seventeenth century, Wright concludes, was caused by new psychological motivation, not by new logical techniques.

Carl Hempel and Paul Oppenheim consider the question, "What does it mean to explain the occurrence of anything?" or, more specifically, "What is the nature of *scientific* explanation?" The answer they suggest has come to be called the "deductive model of explanation," for reasons which will be quite obvious once you have read their essay. Having read it, you might ask yourself this question, "Is there any other possible model of explanation besides this deductive one and the teleological kind which explains the behavior of both physical and living bodies in terms of goals or final causes?"

Irving Copi, in his analysis of the notion of crucial experiment, shows that it is a gross oversimplification to think that every scientific hypothesis, independent of its relations to others, can be either established or refuted in a straightforward way simply by submitting it to experiment. The hypotheses of science form a web, and it is possible to do a lot of shifting of the strands of the web in order to "save appearances"!

Morris R. Cohen and Ernest Nagel, in their discussion of measurement, explain the nature of mathematics in the development of science, showing clearly how quantitative notions grew out of, and are related to, the ordinary notions of everyday life. And the distinction between fundamental and derived measurement, which they explicate in detail, is the key to understanding the nature of scientific lawfulness.

Alfred North Whitehead, finally, provides a historical background in which the concepts and logic of the new science become clearer than they ever could be when studied, as they usually are, in an intellectual vacuum. Physics has come so far by now that we fail to see how shocking it must have been to the common sense of Renaissance men for Galileo to ask why moving objects ever stop. This question must have seemed like sheer effrontery since anyone could plainly see that rest was the natural state of a body, a state which a body sought to recover as soon as it was put in motion. But Galileo insisted, quite to the contrary, that a ball in motion in a straight line, if unmolested by any other force, would continue in motion forever! Common sense rather than religion, one might almost say, was the real enemy of the new science. But the new science prevailed, and now it is a moot question whether common sense became adjusted to it or it re-made common sense! Whitehead discusses these fascinating beginnings of the new science; and if you do not read his essay with a good deal of enjoyment, even smiling now and then, you may guess you are being too heavy-handed in your study, and eventually will be heavy-lidded, too. Read the following selections, not only in this chapter but in all the book, for what they are — exciting and fascinating adventures in the world of ideas.

The Origins of Modern Science

CHAUNCEY WRIGHT

Why the inductive and mathematical sciences, after their first rapid development at the culmination of Greek civilization, advanced so slowly for two thousand years — and why in the following two hundred years a knowledge of natural and mathematical science has accumulated which so vastly exceeds all that was previously known that these sciences may be justly regarded as the

From Edward H. Madden (Ed.), *The Philosophical Writings of Chauncey Wright* (The American Heritage Series No. 23, New York, 1958). Reprinted by permission of the publishers, The Liberal Arts Press, Inc.

products of our own times — are questions which have interested the modern philosopher not less than the objects with which these sciences are more immediately conversant.[1] Was it in the employment of a new method of research, or in the exercise of greater virtue in the use of old methods, that this singular modern phenomenon had its origin? Was the long period one of arrested development, and is the modern era one of a normal growth? Or should we ascribe the characteristics of both periods to inexplicable historical accidents — to the influence of conjunctions in circumstances of which no explanation is possible save in the omnipotence and wisdom of a guiding Providence?

The explanation which has become commonplace, that the ancients employed deduction chiefly in their scientific inquiries while the moderns employ induction, proves to be too narrow, and fails upon close examination to point with sufficient distinctness the contrast that is evident between ancient and modern scientific doctrines and inquiries. For all knowledge is founded on observation, and proceeds from this by analysis and synthesis, by synthesis and analysis, by induction and deduction, and if possible by verification, or by new appeals to observation under the guidance of deduction — by steps which are indeed correlative parts of one method; and the ancient sciences afford examples of every one of these methods, or parts of the one complete method, which have been generalized from the examples of science.

A failure to employ or to employ adequately any one of these partial methods, an imperfection in the arts and resources of observation and experiment, carelessness in observation, neglect of relevant facts, vagueness and carelessness in reasoning, and the failure to draw the consequences of theory and test them by appeal to experiment and observation — these are the faults which cause all failures to ascertain truth, whether among the ancients or the moderns; but they do not explain why the modern is possessed of a greater virtue, and by what means he attained to his superiority. Much less do they explain the sudden growth of science in recent times.

The attempt to discover the explanation of this phenomenon in the antithesis of "facts" and "theories" or "facts" and "ideas" — in the neglect among the ancients of the former, and their too exclusive attention to the latter — proves also to be too narrow, as well as open to the charge of vagueness. For, in the first place, the antithesis is not complete. Facts and theories are not co-ordinate species. Theories, if true, are facts — a particular class of facts indeed, generally complex ones, but still facts. Facts, on the other hand, even in the narrowest signification of the word, if they be at all complex and if a logical connection subsists between their constituents, have all the positive attributes of theories.

Nevertheless, this distinction, however inadequate it may be to explain the source of true method in science, is well founded, and connotes an important character in true method. A fact is a proposition of which the verification by an appeal to the primary sources of our knowledge or to experience is direct and simple. A theory, on the other hand, if true, has all the characteristics of a fact except that its verification is possible only by indirect, remote, and difficult means. To convert theories into facts is to add *simple verification,* and the theory thus acquires the full characteristics of a fact. When Pascal caused the Torricellian tube[2] to be car-

[1] Cf. *North American Review,* C, 1865, pp. 423–432.

[2] [Blaise Pascal (1623–1662), French philosopher, mathematician, and scientist. "The idea of the pressure of the air and the invention of the instrument for measuring it were both new when he made his famous experiment, showing that the height of the mercury column in a barometer decreases when it is carried upwards through the atmosphere. This experiment was made by himself in a tower at Paris, and was carried out on a grand scale under his instructions by his brother-in-law Florin Périer on the

ried up the Puy de Dôme, and thus showed that the mercurial column was sustained by the weight of the atmosphere, he brought the theory of atmospheric pressure nearly down to the level of a fact of observation. But even in this most remarkable instance of scientific discovery theory was not wholly reduced to fact, since the verification, though easy, was not entirely simple, and was incomplete until further observations showed that the quantity of the fall in the Torricellian tube agreed with deductions from the combined theories of atmospherical pressure and elasticity. In the same way the theory of universal gravitation fails to become a fact in the proper sense of this word, however complete its verification, because this verification is not simple and direct, or through the spontaneous activity of our perceptive powers.

Modern science deals, then, no less with theories than with facts, but always as much as possible with the verification of theories – if not to make them facts by *simple* verification through experiment and observation, at least to prove their truth by indirect verification.

The distinction of fact and theory thus yields an important principle, of which M. Comte[3] and his followers have made much account. It is in the employment of verification, they say, and in the possibility of it, that the superiority of modern inductive research consists; and it is because the ancients did not, or could not, verify their theories that they made such insignificant progress in science. It is indisputable that verification is essential to the completeness of scientific method; but there is still room for debate as to what constitutes verification in the various departments of philosophical inquiry. So long as the philosophy of method fails to give a complete inventory of our primary sources of knowledge and cannot decide authoritatively what are the origins of first truths or the truths of observation, so long will it remain uncertain what is a legitimate appeal to observation or what is a real verification. The Platonists or the rationalists may equally with the empiricists claim verification for their theories; for do they not appeal to the reason for confirmation of deductions from their theories, which they regard as founded on observation of what the reason reveals to them?

The positivists' principle of verification comes, then, only to this – that, inasmuch as mankind are nearly unanimous about the testimony and trustworthiness of their senses, but are divided about the validity of all other kinds of authority, which they in a word call the reason or internal sense, therefore verification by the senses produces absolute conviction while verification by the reason settles nothing, but is liable to the same uncertainty which attends the primary appeals to this authority for the data of speculative knowledge.

But not only does the so-called metaphysical philosophy employ a species of verification by appealing to the testimony of reason, consciousness, or internal sense, but the ancient physical sciences afford examples of the confirmation of theory by observation proper. The Ptolemaic system of astronomy was an instance of the employment of every one of the partial steps of true method; and the theory of epicycles not only sought to represent the facts of observation but also by the prediction of astronomical phenomena to verify the truth of its representation. Modern astronomy does not proceed otherwise, except that its theories represent a much greater number of facts of observation and are confirmed by much more efficient experimental tests.

Puy de Dôme in Auvergne. Its success greatly helped . . . to bring home to the minds of ordinary men the truth of the new ideas propounded by Galileo and Torricelli." *Encyclopaedia Britannica,* Vol. 17, 1957, p. 351.]

[3] [Auguste Comte (1798–1857), French philosopher and mathematician. See his major work, *Course of Positive Philosophy,* an influential work in nineteenth century philosophy, for the ideas to which Wright refers.]

The difference, then, between ancient and modern science is not truly characterized by any of the several explanations which have been proposed. The explanation which, in our opinion, comes nearer to the true solution, and yet fails to designate the real point of difference, is that which the positivists find in the distinction between "objective method" and "subjective method." The objective method is verification by sensuous tests, tests of sensible experience – a deduction from theory to consequences, of which we may have sensible experiences if they be true. The subjective method, on the other hand, appeals to the tests of internal evidence, tests of reason, and the data of self-consciousness – authorities on which, as the history of philosophy shows, there is little unanimity among philosophers. But whatever be the origin of the theories of science, whether from a systematic examination of empirical facts by conscious induction or from the natural biases of the mind, the so-called intuitions of reason, what seems probable without a distinct survey of our experiences – whatever the origin, real or ideal, the *value* of these theories can only be tested, say the positivists, by an appeal to sensible experience, by deductions from them of consequences which we can confirm by the undoubted testimony of the senses. Thus, while ideal or transcendental elements are admitted into scientific researches, though in themselves insusceptible of simple verification, they must still show credentials from the senses, either by affording from themselves consequences capable of sensuous verification or by yielding such consequences in conjunction with ideas which by themselves are verifiable.

It is undoubtedly true that one of the leading traits of modern scientific research is this reduction of ideas to the tests of experience. The systematic development of ideas through induction from the first and simplest facts of observation is by no means so obvious a characteristic. Inductions are still performed for the most part unconsciously and unsystematically. Ideas are developed by the sagacity of the expert rather than by the systematic procedures of the philosopher. But when and however ideas are developed science cares nothing, for it is only by subsequent tests of sensible experience that ideas are admitted into the pandects of science.

It is of no consequence to scientific astronomy whence the theory of gravitation arose, whether as an induction from the theories of attractions and the law of radiations or from the rational simplicity of this law itself as the most natural supposition which could be made. Science asks no questions about the ontological pedigree or a priori character of a theory, but is content to judge it by its performance; and it is thus that a knowledge of nature, having all the certainty which the senses are competent to inspire, has been attained – a knowledge which maintains a strict neutrality toward all philosophical systems and concerns itself not at all with the genesis or a priori grounds of ideas.

This mode of philosophizing is not, however, exclusively found in modern scientific research. Ptolemy[4] claimed for his epicycles only that "they saved the appearances"; and he might have said, with as much propriety as Newton,[5] *Hypotheses non fingo,* for it was the aim of his research to represent abstractly, and by the most general formulas, the characteristics of the movements of the planets – an aim which modern astronomy,

[4] [Ptolemy of Alexandria (second century A.D.), astronomer, mathematician, and geographer. For a straightforward explanation of "epicycle," "eccentric," and "equant," fundamental concepts in his geocentric astronomical theory, see *Encyclopaedia Britannica,* Vol. 2, 1957, p. 582. His major astronomical work is the *Syntaxis* or *Almagest*.]

[5] [Sir Isaac Newton (1642–1727), English physicist and mathematician. For an analysis of Newton's philosophy of science, including his famous dictum *Hypotheses non fingo,* see Chapter 6 of *Theories of Scientific Method from the Renaissance to the Nineteenth Century,* R. W. Blake, C. J. Ducasse, and E. H. Madden, University of Washington Press, 1959.]

with a much simpler hypothesis and with immensely increased facilities, still pursues.

We find, therefore, that while moderns follow a true method of investigation with greater facilities and greater fidelity than the ancients, and with a clearer apprehension of its elements and conditions, yet that no new discoveries in method have been made, and no general sources of truth have been pointed out, which were not patent and known to the ancients; and we have so far failed to discover any solution to the problem with which we began. We have seen that it was not by the employment of a new method of research, but in the exercise of greater virtue in the use of old methods, that modern scientific researches have succeeded. But whence this greater virtue? What vivifying, energizing influence awakened the sixteenth century to the movement which has continued down to the present day to engross, and even to create, the energies of philosophic thought in the study of natural phenomena? Obviously some interest was awakened which had before been powerless or had influenced only men of rare and extraordinary genius, or else some opposing interest had ceased to exercise a preponderating influence.

We have now arrived at a new order of inquiries. We ask no longer what are the differences of *method* between ancient and modern scientific researches, but we seek the difference in the *motives* which actuated the philosophic inquiries of the two periods. We seek for the interests which in modern times have so powerfully drawn men of all orders of intelligence to the pursuit of science and to an observance of the conditions requisite for its successful prosecution. This inquiry will, we think, lead to more profitable conclusions than the course we have pursued in review of the theories which have been put forward on this subject. But we have little space in these introductory pages to develop this aspect of the history of science, or to do more than indicate the conclusions we have reached in the classification and history of the dominant motives and the sources of the questions which have determined and directed the pursuit of science. We ask no longer what course has led to successful answers in science but what motives have prompted the pertinent questions.

In place of the positivists' phraseology, that the ancients followed "the subjective method," or appealed for the verification of their theories to natural beliefs, while the moderns follow "the objective method," or appeal to new and independent experimental evidence — if we substitute the word "motive" for "method," we have the terms of one of the conclusions on which we wish to insist. But these require explanation.

By a subjective motive we mean one having its origin in natural universal human interests and emotions, which existed before philosophy was born, which continue to exist in the maturity of philosophy, and determine the character of an important and by no means defunct order of human speculations. By an objective motive we mean one having an empirical origin, arising in the course of an inquiry, springing from interests which are defined by what we already know and not by what we have always felt — interests which depend on acquired knowledge and not on natural desires and emotions. Among the latter we must include the natural desire for knowledge or the primitive, undisciplined sentiment of curiosity. An objective motive is what this becomes when it ceases to be associated with our fears, our respects, our aspirations — our emotional nature; when it ceases to prompt questions as to what relates to our personal destiny, our ambitions, our moral worth; when it ceases to have man, his personal and social nature, as its central and controlling objects. A curiosity which is determined chiefly or solely by the felt imperfections of knowledge as such, and without reference to the uses this knowledge may subserve, is prompted by what we call an objective motive.

A spirit of inquiry which is freed from the influence of our active powers and the interests that gave birth to theological and metaphysical philosophies – which yields passively and easily to the direction of objective motives, to the felt imperfections of knowledge as such – is necessarily, at all times, a weak feeling; and before a body of systematic, well digested, and well ascertained scientific truth had been generated, could hardly have had any persistent influence on the direction of inquiry.

The motives to theological and metaphysical speculation exist from the beginning of civilized human life in the active emotional nature of man. Curiosity as a love of the marvelous or as a love of facts – new facts, prized because they are new and stimulating – also dates back of civilized life. These motives find play in human nature as it emerges from a semianimal state; but they also persist and determine the growth of the human mind in its most advanced development.

The questions of philosophy proper are human desires and fears and aspirations – human emotions – taking an intellectual form. Science follows, but does not supersede, this philosophy. The three phases which the positivists assign to the development of the human mind – the Theological, the Metaphysical, and the Positive or Scientific – are not in reality successive except in their beginnings. They coexist in all the highest developments of civilization and mental activity. They coexisted in the golden age of Greek civilization, in the intense mental activity of the Middle Ages. They move on together in this marvelous modern era. But until this latest epoch positive science was always the inferior philosophy – hardly a distinct philosophy at all – not yet born. But at the beginning of the modern era its gestation was completed. A body of knowledge existed, sufficiently extensive, coherent, and varied, to bear within it a life of its own – an independent life – which was able to collect to itself, by its own determinations, the materials of a continued, new, and ever-increasing mental activity – an activity determined solely by an objective curiosity, or by curiosity in its purest, fullest, and highest energy.

We are probably indebted to the few men of scientific genius who lived during the slow advancement of modern civilization for the foundation of this culture – for the accumulation of the knowledge requisite for this subsequent growth. These men were doubtless, for the most part, the products of their own times and civilization, as indeed all great men have been, but still originators, by concentrating and making productive the energies, tendencies, and knowledges which, but for them, would have remained inert and unfruitful. It is to such men, born at long intervals in the slow progress of civilization, each carrying forward a little the work of his predecessor, that we probably owe our modern science, rather than to the influence of any single mind, like Bacon, who was, like his predecessors, but the lens which collected the light of his times – who prophesied rather than inaugurated the new era. And we owe science to the combined energies of individual men of genius rather than to any tendency to progress inherent in civilization.

We find, then, the explanation of the modern development of science in the accumulation of a body of certified knowledge, sufficiently extensive to engage and discipline a rational scientific curiosity and stimulate it to act independently of other philosophical motives. It is doubtless true that other motives have influenced this development, and especially that motives of material utility have had a powerful effect in stimulating inquiry. Ancient schools of philosophy despised narrow material utilities, the servile arts, and sought no instruction in what moderns dignify by the name of useful arts; but modern science finds in the requirements of the material arts the safest guide to exact knowledge. A theory which is utilized receives the highest possible certificate of truth. Navigation by the aid of astronomical tables, the magnetic telegraph, the innumerable utilities of mechanical and chemical science, are constant and perfect tests of scientific theories, and afford the standard of certitude which science has been able to apply so extensively in its interpretations of natural phenomena. . . .

Studies in the Logic of Explanation

CARL G. HEMPEL and PAUL OPPENHEIM[1]

1. *Introduction.* To explain the phenomena in the world of our experience, to answer the question "why?" rather than only the question "what?", is one of the foremost objectives of all rational inquiry; and especially, scientific research in its various branches strives to go beyond a mere description of its subject matter by providing an explanation of the phenomena it investigates. While there is rather general agreement about this chief objective of science, there exists considerable difference of opinion as to the function and the essential characteristics of scientific explanation. In the present essay, an attempt will be made to shed some light on these issues by means of an elementary survey of the basic pattern of scientific explanation and a subsequent more rigorous analysis of the concept of law and of the logical structure of explanatory arguments. . . .

Elementary Survey of Scientific Explanation

2. *Some Illustrations.* A mercury thermometer is rapidly immersed in hot water; there occurs a temporary drop of the mercury column, which is then followed by a swift rise. How is this phenomenon to be explained? The increase in temperature affects at first only the glass tube of the thermometer; it expands and thus provides a larger space for the mercury inside, whose surface therefore drops. As soon as by heat conduction the rise in temperature reaches

1 This paper represents the outcome of a series of discussions among the authors; their individual contributions cannot be separated in detail. The technical developments contained in Part IV, however, are due to the first author, who also put the article into its final form.

Some of the ideas presented in Part II were suggested by our common friend, Kurt Grelling, who, together with his wife, became a victim of Nazi terror during the war. Those ideas were developed by Grelling, in a discussion by correspondence with the present authors, of emergence and related concepts. By including at least some of that material, which is indicated in the text, in the present paper, we feel that we are realizing the hope expressed by Grelling that his contributions might not entirely fall into oblivion.

We wish to express our thanks to Dr. Rudolf Carnap, Dr. Herbert Feigl, Dr. Nelson Goodman, and Dr. W. V. Quine for stimulating discussions and constructive criticism.

Originally published in *Philosophy of Science,* Vol. 15, No. 2, 1948, pp. 135–175. Pp. 135–146 reprinted by permission of the authors and the editor.

the mercury, however, the latter expands, and as its coefficient of expansion is considerably larger than that of glass, a rise of the mercury level results. — This account consists of statements of two kinds. Those of the first kind indicate certain conditions which are realized prior to, or at the same time as, the phenomenon to be explained; we shall refer to them briefly as antecedent conditions. In our illustration, the antecedent conditions include, among others, the fact that the thermometer consists of a glass tube which is partly filled with mercury, and that it is immersed into hot water. The statements of the second kind express certain general laws; in our case, these include the laws of the thermic expansion of mercury and of glass, and a statement about the small thermic conductivity of glass. The two sets of statements, if adequately and completely formulated, explain the phenomenon under consideration: They entail the consequence that the mercury will first drop, then rise. Thus, the event under discussion is explained by subsuming it under general laws, i.e., by showing that it occurred in accordance with those laws, by virtue of the realization of certain specified antecedent conditions.

Consider another illustration. To an observer in a row boat, that part of an oar which is under water appears to be bent upwards. The phenomenon is explained by means of general laws — mainly the law of refraction and the law that water is an optically denser medium than air — and by reference to certain antecedent conditions — especially the facts that part of the oar is in the water, part in the air, and that the oar is practically a straight piece of wood. — Thus, here again, the question "*Why* does the phenomenon happen?" is construed as meaning "according to what general laws, and by virtue of what antecedent conditions does the phenomenon occur?"

So far, we have considered exclusively the explanation of particular events occurring at a certain time and place. But the question "Why?" may be raised also in regard to general laws. Thus, in our last illustration, the question might be asked: Why does the propagation of light conform to the law of refraction? Classical physics answers in terms of the undulatory theory of light, i.e. by stating that the propagation of light is a wave phenomenon of a certain general type, and that all wave phenomena of that type satisfy the law of refraction. Thus, the explanation of a general regularity consists in subsuming it under another, more comprehensive regularity, under a more general law. — Similarly, the validity of Galileo's law for the free fall of bodies near the earth's surface can be explained by deducing it from a more comprehensive set of laws, namely Newton's laws of motion and his law of gravitation, together with some statements about particular facts, namely the mass and the radius of the earth.

3. *The Basic Pattern of Scientific Explanation.* From the preceding sample cases let us now abstract some general characteristics of scientific explanation. We divide an explanation into two major constituents, the explanandum and the explanans.[2] By the explanandum, we understand the sentence describing the phenomenon to be explained (not that phenomenon itself); by the explanans, the class of those sentences which are adduced to account for the phenomenon. As was noted before, the explanans falls into two subclasses; one of these contains certain sentences $C_1, C_2, \cdots, C_k$ which state specific antecedent conditions; the other is a set of sentences $L_1, L_2, \cdots L_r$ which represent general laws.

If a proposed explanation is to be sound,

[2] These two expressions, derived from the Latin *explanare,* were adopted in preference to the perhaps more customary terms "explicandum" and "explicans" in order to reserve the latter for use in the context of explication of meaning, or analysis. On explication in this sense, cf. Carnap, "The Two Concepts of Probability," *Philosophy and Phenomenological Research,* Vol. 5, 1945, p. 513.

its constituents have to satisfy certain conditions of adequacy, which may be divided into logical and empirical conditions. For the following discussion, it will be sufficient to formulate these requirements in a slightly vague manner; in Part III, a more rigorous analysis and a more precise restatement of these criteria will be presented.

I. *Logical Conditions of Adequacy.*

(R1) The explanandum must be a logical consequence of the explanans; in other words, the explanandum must be logically deducible from the information contained in the explanans, for otherwise, the explanans would not constitute adequate grounds for the explanandum.

(R2) The explanans must contain general laws, and these must actually be required for the derivation of the explanandum. — We shall not make it a necessary condition for a sound explanation, however, that the explanans must contain at least one statement which is not a law; for, to mention just one reason, we would surely want to consider as an explanation the derivation of the general regularities governing the motion of double stars from the laws of celestial mechanics, even though all the statements in the explanans are general laws.

(R3) The explanans must have empirical content; i.e., it must be capable, at least in principle, of test by experiment or observation. — This condition is implicit in (R1); for since the explanandum is assumed to describe some empirical phenomenon, it follows from (R1) that the explanans entails at least one consequence of empirical character, and this fact confers upon it testability and empirical content. But the point deserves special mention because, as will be seen in §4, certain arguments which have been offered as explanations in the natural and in the social sciences violate this requirement.

II. *Empirical Condition of Adequacy.*

(R4) The sentences constituting the explanans must be true.

That in a sound explanation, the statements constituting the explanans have to satisfy some condition of factual correctness is obvious. But it might seem more appropriate to stipulate that the explanans has to be highly confirmed by all the relevant evidence available rather than that it should be true. This stipulation however, leads to awkward consequences. Suppose that a certain phenomenon was explained at an earlier stage of science, by means of an explanans which was well supported by the evidence then at hand, but which had been highly disconfirmed by more recent empirical findings. In such a case, we would have to say that originally the explanatory account was a correct explanation, but that it ceased to be one later, when unfavorable evidence was discovered. This does not appear to accord with sound common usage, which directs us to say that on the basis of the limited initial evidence, the truth of the explanans, and thus the soundness of the explanation, had been quite probable, but that the ampler evidence now available made it highly probable that the explanans was not true, and hence that the account in question was not — and had never been — a correct explanation. (A similar point will be made and illustrated, with respect to the requirement of truth for laws, in the beginning of §6.)

Some of the characteristics of an explanation which have been indicated so far may be summarized in the following schema:

Logical deduction	$C_1, C_2, \ldots, C_k$	Statements of antecedent conditions	Explanans
	$L_1, L_2, \ldots, L_r$	General Laws	
	E	Description of the empirical phenomenon to be explained	Explanandum

Let us note here that the same formal analysis, including the four necessary conditions, applies to scientific prediction as well as to explanation. The difference between the two is of a pragmatic character. If E is given, i.e. if we know that the phenomenon described by E has occurred, and a suitable set of statements $C_1, C_2, \ldots C_k, L_1, L_2, \ldots L_r$ is provided afterwards, we speak of an explanation of the phenomenon in question. If the latter statements are given and E is derived prior to the occurrence of the phenomenon it describes, we speak of a prediction. It may be said, therefore, that an explanation is not fully adequate unless its explanans, if taken account of in time, could have served as a basis for predicting the phenomenon under consideration.[2a] – Consequently, whatever will be said in this article concerning the logical characteristics of explanation or prediction will be applicable to either, even if only one of them should be mentioned.

It is this potential predictive force which gives scientific explanation its importance: only to the extent that we are able to explain empirical facts can we attain the major objective of scientific research, namely not merely to record the phenomena of our experience, but to learn from them, by basing upon them theoretical generalizations which enable us to anticipate new occurrences and to control, at least to some extent, the changes in our environment.

Many explanations which are customarily offered, especially in pre-scientific discourse, lack this predictive character, however. Thus, it may be explained that a car turned over on the road "because" one of its tires blew out while the car was travelling at high speed. Clearly, on the basis of just this information, the accident could not have been predicted, for the explanans provides no explicit general laws by means of which the prediction might be effected, nor does it state adequately the antecedent conditions which would be needed for the prediction. – The same point may be illustrated by reference to W. S. Jevons's view that every explanation consists in pointing out a resemblance between facts, and that in some cases this process may require no reference to laws at all and "may involve nothing more than a single identity, as when we explain the appearance of shooting stars by showing that they are identical with portions of a comet." [3] But clearly, this identity does not provide an explanation of the phenomenon of shooting stars unless we presuppose the laws governing the development of heat and light as the effect of friction. The observation of similarities has explanatory value only if it involves at least tacit reference to general laws.

In some cases, incomplete explanatory arguments of the kind here illustrated sup-

[2a] The logical similarity of explanation and prediction, and the fact that one is directed towards past occurrences, the other towards future ones, is well expressed in the terms "postdictability" and "predictability" used by Reichenbach in *Philosophic Foundations of Quantum Mechanics* (University of California Press, 1944), p. 13.

[3] *The Principles of Science* (London, 1924; 1st ed. 1874), p. 533.

press parts of the explanans simply as "obvious"; in other cases, they seem to involve the assumption that while the missing parts are not obvious, the incomplete explanans could at least, with appropriate effort, be so supplemented as to make a strict derivation of the explanandum possible. This assumption may be justifiable in some cases, as when we say that a lump of sugar disappeared "because" it was put into hot tea, but it is surely not satisfied in many other cases. Thus, when certain peculiarities in the work of an artist are explained as outgrowths of a specific type of neurosis, this observation may contain significant clues, but in general it does not afford a sufficient basis for a potential prediction of those peculiarities. In cases of this kind, an incomplete explanation may at best be considered as indicating some positive correlation between the antecedent conditions adduced and the type of phenomenon to be explained, and as pointing out a direction in which further research might be carried on in order to complete the explanatory account.

The type of explanation which has been considered here so far is often referred to as causal explanation. If E describes a particular event, then the antecedent circumstances described in the sentences C_1, C_2, . . . , C_k may be said jointly to "cause" that event, in the sense that there are certain empirical regularities, expressed by the laws L_1, L_2, . . . , L_r, which imply that whenever conditions of the kind indicated by C_1, C_2, . . . , C_k occur, an event of the kind described in E will take place. Statements such as L_1, L_2, . . . , L_r, which assert general and unexceptional connections between specified characteristics of events, are customarily called causal, or deterministic, laws. They are to be distinguished from the so-called statistical laws which assert that in the long run, an explicitly stated percentage of all cases satisfying a given set of conditions are accompanied by an event of a certain specified kind. Certain cases of scientific explanation involve "subsumption" of the explanandum under a set of laws of which at least some are statistical in character. Analysis of the peculiar logical structure of that type of subsumption involves difficult special problems. The present essay will be restricted to an examination of the causal type of explanation, which has retained its significance in large segments of contemporary science, and even in some areas where a more adequate account calls for reference to statistical laws.[4]

4. *Explanation in the Non-physical Sci-*

[4] The account given above of the general characteristics of explanation and prediction in science is by no means novel; it merely summarizes and states explicitly some fundamental points which have been recognized by many scientists and methodologists.

Thus, e.g., Mill says: "An individual fact is said to be explained by pointing out its cause, that is, by stating the law or laws of causation of which its production is an instance," and "a law of uniformity in nature is said to be explained when another law or laws are pointed out, of which that law itself is but a case, and from which it could be deduced." (*A System of Logic,* Book III, Chapter XII, section 1.) Similarly, Jevons, whose general characterization of explanation was critically discussed above, stresses that "the most important process of explanation consists in showing that an observed fact is one case of a general law or tendency." (*Principles of Science,* p. 533.) Ducasse states the same point as follows: "Explanation essentially consists in the offering of a hypothesis of fact, standing to the fact to be explained as case of antecedent to case of consequent of some already known law of connection." ("Explanation, Mechanism, and Teleology," *The Journal of Philosophy,* Vol. 22, 1925, pp. 150–151.) A lucid analysis of the fundamental structure of explanation and prediction was given by Karl Popper in *Logik der Forschung* (Wien, 1935), section 12, and, in an improved version, in his work *The Open Society and Its Enemies* (London, 1945), especially in Chapter 25 and in note 7 referring to that chapter. —For a recent characterization of explanation as subsumption under general theories, cf., for example, Hull's concise discussion in *Principles of Behavior* (New York, 1943), chapter I. A clear elementary examination of certain aspects of explanation is given in Hospers, "On Explanation" (*The Journal of Philosophy,* Vol. 43, 1946), and a concise survey of many of the essentials of scientific explanation which are considered in the first two parts of the present study may be found in Feigl, "Operationism and Scientific Method" (*Psychological Review,* Vol. 52, 1945), pp. 284 ff.

ences. Motivational and Teleological Approaches. Our characterization of scientific explanation is so far based on a study of cases taken from the physical sciences. But the general principles thus obtained apply also outside this area.[5] Thus, various types of behavior in laboratory animals and in human subjects are explained in psychology by subsumption under laws or even general theories of learning or conditioning; and while frequently, the regularities invoked cannot be stated with the same generality and precision as in physics or chemistry, it is clear, at least, that the general character of those explanations conforms to our earlier characterization.

Let us now consider an illustration involving sociological and economic factors. In the fall of 1946, there occurred at the cotton exchanges of the United States a price drop which was so severe that the exchanges in New York, New Orleans, and Chicago had to suspend their activities temporarily. In an attempt to explain this occurrence, newspapers traced it back to a large-scale speculator in New Orleans who had feared his holdings were too large and had therefore begun to liquidate his stocks; smaller speculators had then followed his example in a panic and had thus touched off the critical decline. Without attempting to assess the merits of the argument, let us note that the explanation here suggested again involves statements about antecedent conditions and the assumption of general regularities. The former include the facts that the first speculator had large stocks of cotton, that there were smaller speculators with considerable holdings, that there existed the institution of the cotton exchanges with their specific mode of operation, etc. The general regularities referred to are — as often in semipopular explanations — not explicitly mentioned; but there is obviously implied some form of the law of supply and demand to account for the drop in cotton prices in terms of the greatly increased supply under conditions of practically unchanged demand; besides, reliance is necessary on certain regularities in the behavior of individuals who are trying to preserve or improve their economic position. Such laws cannot be formulated at present with satisfactory precision and generality, and therefore, the suggested explanation is surely incomplete, but its intention is unmistakably to account for the phenomenon by integrating it into a general pattern of economic and socio-psychological regularities.

We turn to an explanatory argument taken from the field of linguistics.[6] In Northern France, there exist a large variety of words synonymous with the English "bee," whereas in Southern France, essentially only one such word is in existence. For this discrepancy, the explanation has been suggested that in the Latin epoch, the South of France used the word "apicula," the North the word "apis." The latter, because of a process of phonologic decay in Northern France, became the monosyllabic word "é"; and monosyllables tend to be eliminated, especially if they contain few consonantic elements, for they are apt to give rise to misunderstandings. Thus, to avoid confusion, other words were selected. But "apicula," which was reduced to "abelho," remained clear enough and was retained, and finally it

[5] On the subject of explanation in the social sciences, especially in history, cf. also the following publications, which may serve to supplement and amplify the brief discussion to be presented here: Hempel, "The Function of General Laws in History," *The Journal of Philosophy,* Vol. 39, 1942, pp. 35–48; Popper, *The Open Society and Its Enemies;* Morton G. White, "Historical Explanation," *Mind,* Vol. 52, 1943, pp. 212–229; and the articles "Cause" and "Understanding" in Charles A. Beard and Sidney Hook, "Problems of Terminology in Historical Writing," Chapter IV of *Theory and Practice in Historical Study: A Report of the Committee on Historiography,* Social Science Research Council, New York, 1946.

[6] The illustration is taken from G. Bonfante, "Semantics, Language" (an article in P. L. Harriman, ed., *The Encyclopedia of Psychology,* Philosophical Library, New York, 1946), section 3.

even entered into the standard language, in the form "abbeille." While the explanation here described is incomplete in the sense characterized in the previous section, it clearly exhibits reference to specific antecedent conditions as well as to general laws.[7]

While illustrations of this kind tend to support the view that explanation in biology, psychology, and the social sciences has the same structure as in the physical sciences, the opinion is rather widely held that in many instances, the causal type of explanation is essentially inadequate in fields other than physics and chemistry, and especially in the study of purposive behavior. Let us examine briefly some of the reasons which have been adduced in support of this view.

One of the most familiar among them is the idea that events involving the activities of humans singly or in groups have a peculiar uniqueness and irrepeatability which makes them inaccessible to causal explanation because the latter, with its reliance upon uniformities, presupposes repeatability of the phenomena under consideration. This argument which, incidentally, has also been used in support of the contention that the experimental method is inapplicable in psychology and the social sciences, involves a misunderstanding of the logical character of causal explanation. Every individual event, in the physical sciences no less than in psychology or the social sciences, is unique in the sense that it, with all its peculiar characteristics, does not repeat itself. Nevertheless, individual events may conform to, and thus be explainable by means of, general laws of the causal type. For all that a causal law asserts is that any event of a specified kind, i.e. any event having certain specified characteristics, is accompanied by another event which in turn has certain specified characteristics; for example, that in any event involving friction, heat is developed. And all that is needed for the testability and applicability of such laws is the recurrence of events with the antecedent characteristics, i.e. the repetition of those characteristics, but not of their individual instances. Thus, the argument is inconclusive. It gives occasion, however, to emphasize an important point concerning our earlier analysis: When we spoke of the explanation of a single event, the term "event" referred to the occurrence of some more or less complex characteristic in a specific spatio-temporal location or in a certain individual object, and not to *all* the characteristics of that object, or to all that goes on in that space-time region.

A second argument that should be mentioned here[8] contends that the establishment of scientific generalizations — and thus of explanatory principles — for human behavior is impossible because the reactions of an individual in a given situation depend not only upon that situation, but also upon the previous history of the individual. — But surely, there is no a priori reason why generalizations should not be attainable which take into account this dependence of behavior on the past history of the agent. That indeed the given argument "proves" too much, and is therefore a non sequitur, is made evident by the existence of certain physical phenomena, such as magnetic hysteresis and elastic fatigue, in which the magnitude of a specific physical effect depends upon the past history of the system involved,

[7] While in each of the last two illustrations, certain regularities are unquestionably relied upon in the explanatory argument, it is not possible to argue convincingly that the intended laws, which at present cannot all be stated explicitly, are of a causal rather than a statistical character. It is quite possible that most or all of the regularities which will be discovered as sociology develops will be of a statistical type. Cf., on this point, the suggestive observations by Edgar Zilsel, "Problems of Empiricism" (*International Encyclopedia of Unified Science,* Vol. II, no. 8, The University of Chicago Press, 1941), section 8, and "Physics and the Problem of Historico-Sociological Laws" (*Philosophy of Science,* Vol. 8, 1941, pp. 567–579).

[8] Cf., for example, F. H. Knight's presentation of this argument in "The Limitations of Scientific Method in Economics" (in R. Tugwell, Ed., *The Trend of Economics,* New York, 1924), pp. 251–252.

and for which nevertheless certain general regularities have been established.

A third argument insists that the explanation of any phenomenon involving purposive behavior calls for reference to motivations and thus for teleological rather than causal analysis. Thus, for example, a fuller statement of the suggested explanation for the break in the cotton prices would have to indicate the large-scale speculator's motivations as one of the factors determining the event in question. Thus, we have to refer to goals sought, and this, so the argument runs, introduces a type of explanation alien to the physical sciences. Unquestionably, many of the – frequently incomplete – explanations which are offered for human actions involve reference to goals and motives; but does this make them essentially different from the causal explanations of physics and chemistry? One difference which suggests itself lies in the circumstance that in motivated behavior, the future appears to affect the present in a manner which is not found in the causal explanations of the physical sciences. But clearly, when the action of a person is motivated, say, by the desire to reach a certain objective, then it is not the as yet unrealized future event of attaining that goal which can be said to determine his present behavior, for indeed the goal may never be actually reached; rather – to put it in crude terms – it is (a) his desire, present before the action, to attain that particular objective, and (b) his belief, likewise present before the action, that such and such a course of action is most likely to have the desired effect. The determining motives and beliefs, therefore, have to be classified among the antecedent conditions of a motivational explanation, and there is no formal difference on this account between motivational and causal explanation.

Neither does the fact that motives are not accessible to direct observation by an outside observer constitute an essential difference between the two kinds of explanation; for also the determining factors adduced in physical explanations are very frequently inaccessible to direct observation. This is the case, for instance, when opposite electric charges are adduced in explanation of the mutual attraction of two metal spheres. The presence of those charges, while eluding all direct observation, can be ascertained by various kinds of indirect test, and that is sufficient to guarantee the empirical character of the explanatory statement. Similarly, the presence of certain motivations may be ascertainable only by indirect methods, which may include reference to linguistic utterances of the subject in question, slips of the pen or of the tongue, etc.; but as long as these methods are "operationally determined" with reasonable clarity and precision, there is no essential difference in this respect between motivational explanation and causal explanation in physics.

A potential danger of explanation by motives lies in the fact that the method lends itself to the facile construction of ex-post-facto accounts without predictive force. It is a widespread tendency to "explain" an action by ascribing it to motives conjectured only after the action has taken place. While this procedure is not in itself objectionable, its soundness requires that (1) the motivational assumptions in question be capable of test, and (2) that suitable general laws be available to lend explanatory power to the assumed motives. Disregard of these requirements frequently deprives alleged motivational explanations of their cognitive significance.

The explanation of an action in terms of the motives of the agent is sometimes considered as a special kind of teleological explanation. As was pointed out above, motivational explanation, if adequately formulated, conforms to the conditions for causal explanation, so that the term "teleological" is a misnomer if it is meant to imply either a non-causal character of the explanation or a peculiar determination of the present by the future. If this is borne in mind, however, the term "teleological" may be viewed, in this context, as referring to causal explanations in which some of the antecedent conditions are motives of the agent whose actions are to be explained.[9]

Teleological explanations of this kind have to be distinguished from a much more sweeping type, which has been claimed by certain schools of thought to be indispensable especially in biology. It consists in explaining characteristics of an organism by reference to certain ends or purposes which the characteristics are said to serve. In contradistinction to the cases examined before, the ends are not assumed here to be consciously or subconsciously pursued by the organism in question. Thus, for the phenomenon of mimicry, the explanation is sometimes offered that it serves the purpose of protecting the animals endowed with it from detection by its pursuers and thus tends to preserve the species. – Before teleological hypotheses of this kind can be appraised as to their potential explanatory power, their meaning has to be clarified. If they are intended somehow to express the idea that the purposes they refer to are inherent in the design of the universe, then clearly they are not capable of empirical test and thus violate the requirement (R3) stated in §3. In certain cases, however, assertions about the purposes of biological characteristics may be translatable into statements in non-teleological terminology which assert that those characteristics function in a specific manner which is essential to keeping the organism alive or to preserving the species.[10] An attempt to state precisely what is meant by this latter assertion – or by the similar one that without those characteristics, and other things being equal, the organism or the species would not survive – encounters considerable difficulties. But these need not be discussed here. For even if we assume that biological statements in teleological form can be adequately translated into descriptive statements about the life-preserving function of certain biological characteristics, it is clear that (1) the use of the concept of purpose is not essential in these contexts, since the term "purpose" can be completely eliminated from the statements in question, and (2) teleological assumptions, while now endowed with empirical content, cannot serve as explanatory principles in the customary contexts. Thus, e.g., the fact that a given species of butterflies displays a particular kind of coloring cannot be inferred from – and therefore cannot be explained by means of – the statement that this type of coloring has the effect of protecting the butterflies from detection by pursuing birds, nor can the presence of red corpuscles in the human blood be inferred from the statement that those corpuscles have a specific function in assimilating oxygen and that this function is essential for the maintenance of life.

One of the reasons for the perseverance of teleological considerations in biology probably lies in the fruitfulness of the teleologi-

[9] For a detailed logical analysis of the character and the function of the motivation concept in psychological theory, see Sigmund Koch, "The Logical Character of the Motivation Concept," *Psychological Review,* Vol. 48, 1941. Part I: pp. 15–38, Part II: pp. 127–154. – A stimulating discussion of teleological behavior from the standpoint of contemporary physics and biology is contained in the article "Behavior, Purpose, and Teleology" (*Philosophy of Science,* Vol. 10, 1943, pp. 18–24) by A. Rosenblueth, N. Wiener, and J. Bigelow. The authors propose an interpretation of the concept of purpose which is free from metaphysical connotations, and they stress the importance of the concept thus obtained for a behavioristic analysis of machines and living organisms. While our formulations above intentionally use the crude terminology frequently applied in philosophical arguments concerning the applicability of causal explanation to purposive behavior, the analysis presented in the article referred to is couched in behavioristic terms and avoids reference to "motives" and the like.

[10] An analysis of teleological statements in biology along these lines may be found in J. H. Woodger, *Biological Principles* (New York, 1929), especially pp. 432 ff.; essentially the same interpretation is advocated by Felix Kaufmann in *Methodology of the Social Sciences* (New York, 1944), chapter 8.

cal approach as a heuristic device: Biological research which was psychologically motivated by a telelogical orientation, by an interest in purposes in nature, has frequently led to important results which can be stated in non-teleological terminology and which increase our scientific knowledge of the causal connections between biological phenomena.

Another aspect that lends appeal to teleological considerations is their anthropomorphic character. A teleological explanation tends to make us feel that we really "understand" the phenomenon in question, because it is accounted for in terms of purposes, with which we are familiar from our own experience of purposive behavior. But it is important to distinguish here understanding in the psychological sense of a feeling of empathic familiarity from understanding in the theoretical, or cognitive, sense of exhibiting the phenomenon to be explained as a special case of some general regularity. The frequent insistence that explanation means the reduction of something unfamiliar to ideas or experiences already familiar to us is indeed misleading. For while some scientific explanations do have this psychological effect, it is by no means universal: The free fall of a physical body may well be said to be a more familiar phenomenon than the law of gravitation, by means of which it can be explained; and surely the basic ideas of the theory of relativity will appear to many to be far less familiar than the phenomena for which the theory accounts.

"Familiarity" of the explicans is not only not necessary for a sound explanation — as we have just tried to show —, but it is not sufficient either. This is shown by the many cases in which a proposed explicans sounds suggestively familiar, but upon closer inspection proves to be a mere metaphor, or an account lacking testability, or a set of statements which includes no general laws and therefore lacks explanatory power. A case in point is the neovitalistic attempt to explain biological phenomena by reference to an entelechy or vital force. The crucial point here is not — as it is sometimes made out to be — that entelechies cannot be seen or otherwise directly observed; for that is true also of gravitational fields, and yet, reference to such fields is essential in the explanation of various physical phenomena. The decisive difference between the two cases is that the physical explanation provides (1) methods of testing, albeit indirectly, assertions about gravitational fields, and (2) general laws concerning the strength of gravitational fields, and the behavior of objects moving in them. Explanations by entelechies satisfy the analogue of neither of these two conditions. Failure to satisfy the first condition represents a violation of (R3); it renders all statements about entelechies inaccessible to empirical test and thus devoid of empirical meaning. Failure to comply with the second condition involves a violation of (R2). It deprives the concept of entelechy of all explanatory import; for explanatory power never resides in a concept, but always in the general laws in which it functions. Therefore, notwithstanding the flavor of familiarity of the metaphor it invokes, the neovitalistic approach cannot provide theoretical understanding.

The preceding observations about familiarity and understanding can be applied, in a similar manner, to the view held by some scholars that the explanation, or the understanding, of human actions requires an empathic understanding of the personalities of the agents.[11] This understanding of another person in terms of one's own psychological functioning may prove a useful heuristic device in the search for general psychological principles which might provide a theoretical explanation; but the existence of empathy on the part of the scientist is neither a neces-

[11] For a more detailed discussion of this view on the basis of the general principles outlined above, cf. E. Zilsel, *Problems of Empiricism, op. cit.*, sections 7 and 8, and C. Hempel, "The Function of General Laws in History," *op. cit.*, section 6.

sary nor a sufficient condition for the explanation, or the scientific understanding, of any human action. It is not necessary, for the behavior of psychotics or of people belonging to a culture very different from that of the scientist may sometimes be explainable and predictable in terms of general principles even though the scientist who establishes or applies those principles may not be able to understand his subjects empathically. And empathy is not sufficient to guarantee a sound explanation, for a strong feeling of empathy may exist even in cases where we completely misjudge a given personality. Moreover, as the late Dr. Zilsel has pointed out, empathy leads with ease to incompatible results; thus, when the population of a town has long been subjected to heavy bombing attacks, we can understand, in the empathic sense, that its morale should have broken down completely, but we can understand with the same ease also that it should have developed a defiant spirit of resistance. Arguments of this kind often appear quite convincing; but they are of an *ex post facto* character and lack cognitive significance unless they are supplemented by testable explanatory principles in the form of laws or theories.

Familiarity of the explanans, therefore, no matter whether it is achieved through the use of teleological terminology, through neovitalistic metaphors, or through other means, is no indication of the cognitive import and the predictive force of a proposed explanation. Besides, the extent to which an idea will be considered as familiar varies from person to person and from time to time, and a psychological factor of this kind certainly cannot serve as a standard in assessing the worth of a proposed explanation. The decisive requirement for every sound explanation remains that it subsume the explanandum under general laws. . . .

Crucial Experiments

IRVING M. COPI

It might appear that, given any problem, all one needs to do is set down all relevant hypotheses and then perform a series of crucial experiments to eliminate all but one of them. The surviving hypothesis is then "the answer," and we are ready to go on to the next problem. But no opinion could possibly be more mistaken.

It has already been insisted that formulating or discovering relevant hypotheses is not a mechanical process but a creative one, some hypotheses requiring genius for their discovery. It has been observed further that crucial experiments may not always be possible, either because no different observable consequences are deducible from the alternative hypotheses, or because we lack the power to arrange the experimental circumstances in which different consequences would manifest themselves. We wish at this time to point out a more pervasive theoretical difficulty with the program of deciding between rival hypotheses by means of crucial experiments. It may be well to illus-

From *Introduction to Logic,* pp. 417–425. New York: The Macmillan Company, 1953. Reprinted by permission of the author and the publisher.

trate our discussion by means of a fairly simple example. One that is familiar to all of us concerns the shape of the earth.

During the Middle Ages and the Renaissance the prevailing opinion was that the earth was flat. Most readers will remember that Christopher Columbus was looked upon as a madman for his belief that the earth is round – or rather, spherical. One of Colum-

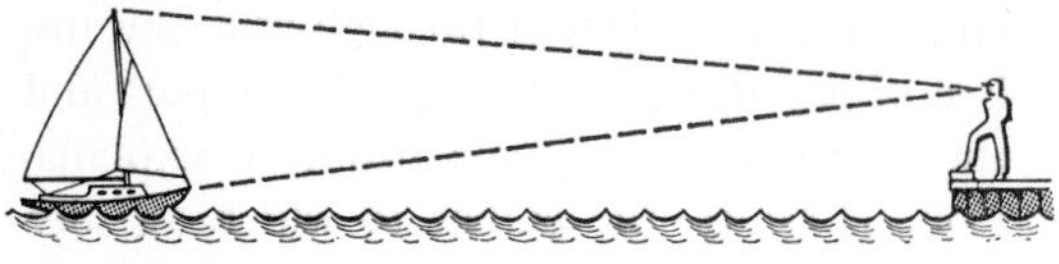

a

bus' arguments was that as a ship sails away from shore, the upper portions of it remain visible to a watcher on land long after its lower parts have disappeared from view. A slightly different version of the same argument was included by Nikolaus Copernicus in his epoch-making treatise *On the Revolutions of the Heavenly Spheres.* In Section II of Book I of that work, entitled "That the Earth also is Spherical," he presented a number of arguments intended to establish the truth of that view. Of the many found there we quote the following:

> That the seas take a spherical form is perceived by navigators. For when land is still not discernible from a vessel's deck, it is from the masthead. And if, when a ship sails from land, a torch be fastened from the masthead, it appears to watchers on the land to go downward little by little until it entirely disappears, like a heavenly body setting.[1]

As between these two rival hypotheses about the earth's shape, we might regard the foregoing as a description of a crucial experiment. The general pattern is clear. From the hypothesis that the earth is flat, H_f, it follows that if a ship gradually recedes from view, then neither its masthead nor its decks should remain visible after the other has vanished. On the other hand, from the hypothesis that the earth is spherical, H_s, it follows that if a ship gradually recedes from view, its masthead should remain visible after its decks have vanished from sight. The rationale involved here is nicely represented by a diagram.

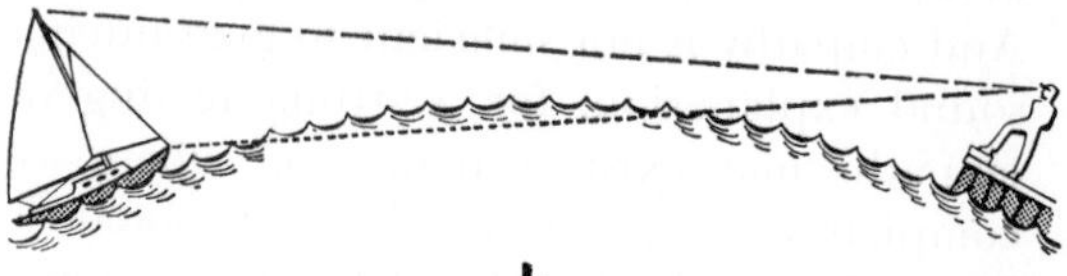

b

In the figure, *a* represents the situation which would obtain if H_f were true. It is clear that *if* the earth is flat there is no reason why any one portion of the ship should disappear from sight before any other portion. The figure *b* represents the situation corresponding to H_s. As the ship recedes, the curvature of the earth rises between the observer and the ship, blocking out his view of the decks while the masthead still remains visible. In each case the rays of light passing from ship to observer are represented by dotted lines. Now the experiment is performed, a receding ship is watched attentively, and the masthead *does* remain visible after the decks have disappeared. Our experiment may not have demonstrated the truth of H_s, it can be admitted, but surely it has established the falsehood of H_f. It is as clear an example of a crucial experiment as it is possible to obtain.

But the experiment described is *not* crucial. It is entirely possible to accept the observed facts and still maintain that the earth is flat. The experiment has considerable value as evidence, but it is not decisive. It is not crucial because the various testable predictions were not inferred from the stated hypotheses H_f and H_s alone, but from them *plus* the additional hypothesis that *light travels in straight lines.* The diagrams show clearly that this additional assumption is es-

[1] Reprinted from *On the Revolutions of the Heavenly Spheres* by Nikolaus Copernicus, as contained in *Masterworks of Science, Digests of 13 Great Classics,* edited by John Warren Knedler, Jr. Copyright, 1947, Doubleday and Company, Inc.

sential to the argument. That the decks disappear before the masthead does is not deducible from H_s alone but requires the additional premiss that light rays follow a rectilinear path (H_r). And that the decks do *not* disappear before the masthead does is not deducible from H_f alone but requires the same additional premiss: that light rays follow a rectilinear path (H_r). The latter argument may be formulated as:

The earth is flat (H_f).
Light rays follow a rectilinear path (H_r).
Therefore the decks of a receding ship will *not* disappear from view before the masthead.

Here is a perfectly good argument whose conclusion is observed to be false. Its premisses can not both be true; at least one of them must be false. But which one? We can maintain the truth of the first premiss, H_f, if we are willing to reject the second premiss, H_r. The second premiss, after all, is not a truth of logic but a contingent statement which is easily conceived to be false. If we adopt the contrary hypothesis that light rays follow a *curved* path, concave upwards, (H_c), what follows as conclusion now? Here we can infer the *denial* of the conclusion of the former argument. From H_f and H_c it follows that the decks of a receding ship *will* disappear before its masthead does. The accompanying figure explains the reasoning involved here.

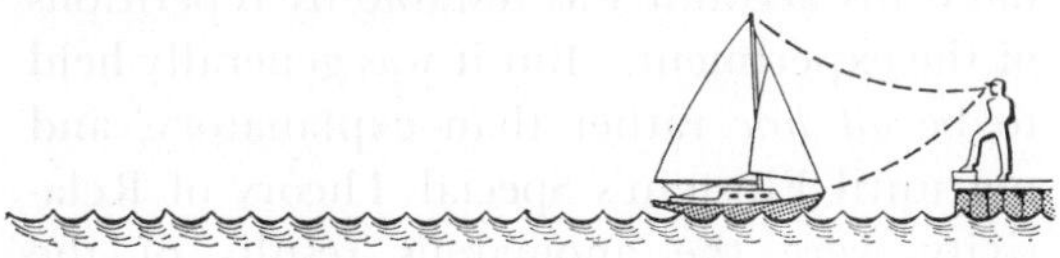

a

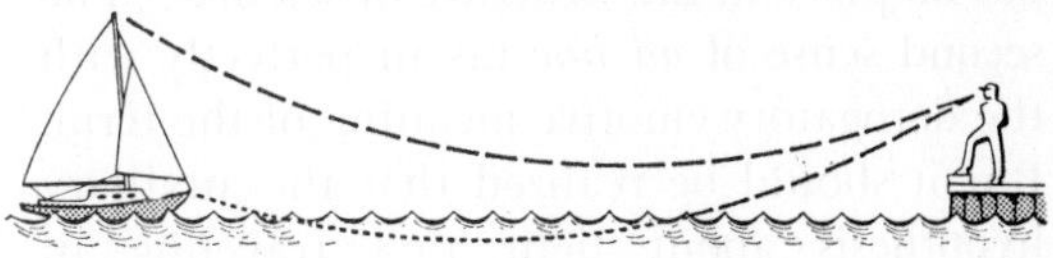

b

In this figure, *a* represents the situation when the ship is near the shore, while *b* shows that as the ship recedes, the earth (even though flat) blocks out the view of the decks while the masthead still remains visible. The light rays in this diagram too are represented by dotted lines, but in this case curved rather than rectilinear. The same experiment is performed, the decks *do* disappear before the masthead, and the observed fact is perfectly compatible with this group of hypotheses which includes H_f, the claim that the earth is flat. The experiment, therefore, is not *crucial* with respect to H_f, for that hypothesis can be maintained as true regardless of the experiment's outcome.[2]

The point is that where hypotheses of a fairly high level of abstractness or generality are involved, no observable or directly testable prediction can be deducted from just a single one of them. A whole group of hypotheses must be used as premisses, and if the observed facts are other than those predicted, *at least one* of the hypotheses in the group is false. But we have not established which one is in error. An experiment *can* be crucial in showing the untenability of a *group* of hypotheses. But such a group will usually contain a considerable number of separate hypotheses, the truth of any one of which can be maintained in the teeth of *any* experimental result, however, "unfavorable," by the simple expedient of rejecting some *other* hypothesis of the group. The conclusion to be drawn from these considerations is that no individual hypothesis can ever be subjected to a crucial experiment.

The preceding discussion may be objected to strenuously. It may be urged that the experiment in question "really does" refute the hypothesis that the earth is flat. It may be charged that the argument to the contrary is guilty of making an *ad hoc* hypothesis to obscure and get around the plain facts of the case. It may be felt that only the invention

[2] This illustration was first suggested to me by my colleague, Professor C. L. Stevenson.

of *ad hoc* hypotheses right and left can prevent some experiments from being crucial and decisively refuting single hypotheses. This reaction is perfectly natural and deserves careful attention.

The crux of the objection would seem to lie in the phrase *"ad hoc,"* which is a highly charged term of abuse. Of its emotive significance there can be little doubt, but its literal meaning is somewhat ambiguous. There are three different senses in which the term *"ad hoc"* is often used. Its first and etymological meaning would seem to be that an *ad hoc* hypothesis is one which is specially made up to account for some fact *after* that fact had been established. In this sense, however, *all* hypotheses are *ad hoc,* since it makes no sense to speak of a hypothesis which has not been devised to account for *some* antecedently established fact or other. Hence the first sense does not fit in very well with the derogatory emotive significance of the term. We must consider its other meanings.

The term *"ad hoc"* is often used to characterize a hypothesis which accounts *only* for the particular fact or facts it was invented to explain and has no other explanatory power, that is, no other testable consequences. No *scientific* hypothesis is *ad hoc* in this second sense of the term, although *every* hypothesis is *ad hoc* in the first sense explained. An hypothesis which is *ad hoc* in the second sense is unscientific; since it is not testable it has no place in the structure of science. The second sense of *ad hoc* fits in perfectly with the derogatory emotive meaning of the term. But it should be realized that the auxiliary hypothesis about light rays traveling in curved paths, which was sufficient to save the hypothesis that the earth is flat from being definitely refuted by the experiment described, is *ad hoc* only in the first sense, not the second. For it does have a considerable number of empirically testable consequences.

There is a third sense of the term *"ad hoc,"* in which it is used to denote a mere descriptive generalization. Such a descriptive hypothesis will assert only that all facts of a particular sort occur in just some particular kinds of circumstances and will have no explanatory power or theoretical scope. For example, limiting their diet to polished rice was found by Eijkman to cause polyneuritis in the small group of chickens with which he was working. . . . Eijkman's hypothesis to account for this fact was *ad hoc* in the third sense: he simply drew the generalization that a diet limited to polished rice will cause polyneuritis in *any* group of chickens. His hypothesis accounts for more than just the particular facts observed; it is testable by controlling the diets of *other* groups of chickens. But it is descriptive rather than explanatory, *merely* empirical rather than theoretical. The science of nutrition has come a long way since Eijkman's contribution. The identification of vitamins and their analysis are required for a more adequate account of the facts first observed by Eijkman. Science seeks to explain rather than merely to describe, and hypotheses which consist of bare generalizations of the facts observed are said to be *ad hoc.*

The classical example of an *ad hoc* hypothesis, in this third sense, is the Fitzgerald Contraction Effect introduced to account for the results of the Michelson-Morley experiment on the velocity of light. By affirming that bodies moving at extremely high velocities contract, Fitzgerald accounted for the given data; his account was testable by repetitions of the experiment. But it was generally held to be *ad hoc* rather than explanatory, and not until Einstein's Special Theory of Relativity were the anomalous results of the Michelson-Morley experiment given an adequate, that is, a theoretical explanation. It should be noted that the auxiliary hypothesis about the curved path of light rays is not *ad hoc* in this third sense either, since it is not a mere generalization of observed facts. (It is, in fact, an essential ingredient in the General Theory of Relativity.)

The general situation seems to be that it is not necessary to invoke *ad hoc* hypotheses — in either the second or third senses of the term, which are the derogatory ones — to prevent experiments from being crucial. Even if we confine our attention to theoretically significant hypotheses, and never invoke any *ad hoc* hypotheses whatsoever, since hypotheses are testable only in groups, no experiments are ever crucial for individual hypotheses. Our limitation here serves to illuminate again the *systematic* character of science. Scientific progress consists in building ever more adequate theories to account for the facts of experience. True enough, it is of value to collect or verify isolated particular facts, for the ultimate basis of science is factual. But the theoretical structure of science grows in a more organic fashion. In the realm of theory, piecemeal progress, one step at a time advances, *can* be accomplished, but only *within* the framework of a generally accepted body of scientific theory. The notion that scientific hypotheses, theories, or laws are wholly discrete and independent is a naive and outdated view.

The term "crucial experiment" is not a useless one, however. Within the framework of accepted scientific theory which we are not concerned to question, a hypothesis *can* be subjected to a crucial experiment. If a negative result is obtained, that is, if some phenomenon fails to occur which had been predicted on the basis of the single dubious hypothesis together with accepted parts of scientific theory, then the experiment is crucial and the hypothesis is rejected. But there is nothing absolute about such a procedure, for even well-accepted scientific theories tend to be changed in the face of new and contrary evidence. Science is not monolithic, either in its practices or in its aims.

Perhaps the most significant lesson to be learned from the preceding discussion is the importance to scientific progress of dragging "hidden assumptions" into the open. That light travels in straight lines was assumed in the arguments of Columbus and Copernicus, but it was a hidden assumption. Because they are hidden, there is no chance to examine such assumptions critically and to decide intelligently whether they are true or false. Progress is often achieved by formulating explicitly an assumption which had previously been hidden and then scrutinizing and rejecting it. An important and dramatic instance of this occurred when Einstein challenged the universally accepted assumption that it always makes sense to say of two events that they occurred *at the same time*. In considering how an observer could discover whether or not two distant events occurred "at the same time," Einstein was led to the conclusion that two events could be simultaneous for one observer but not for another, depending upon their locations and velocities relative to the events in question. Rejecting the assumption led to the Special Theory of Relativity, which constituted a tremendous step forward in explaining such phenomena as those revealed by the Michelson-Morley experiment. It is clear that an assumption must be *recognized* before it can be challenged, and this fact indicates the importance to scientific progress of formulating explicitly all relevant assumptions in any hypothesis, allowing none of them to remain hidden.

Measurement

MORRIS R. COHEN and ERNEST NAGEL

1. The Purpose of Measurement

Many of the common affairs we conduct daily depend on our being able to distinguish only qualities or characters which are fairly sharply demarcated from one another. This day is "cold," therefore we put on our coats; that day is "warm," therefore we leave them off. This pillow is "hard"; we exchange it for one that is "soft." Some foods are "sweet," others are "sour"; we choose them in accordance with our preferences.

However, it is frequently necessary, even in daily life, to make judgments upon qualities which are not so sharply demarcated from one another. "Take Professor A's course, instead of Professor B's," we may be told; "Professor A is *easier* than Professor B." "Travel by the elevated trains; they are *less crowded* than the subways." "Buy coffee of brand X; it is *fresher* than brand Y." Such injunctions are significant for us because, in spite of the absence of clearly marked distinctions, we nevertheless readily apprehend the difference between "being easy" and "being difficult," between "a crowded train" and "a train not crowded," between "being fresh" and "being stale." In the sciences, too, propositions affirming *qualitative* differences are the first fruits of inquiry. That the planets move among the fixed stars, that iron expands when heated, or that children resemble their blood relatives – these are examples of such qualitative propositions.

Both in daily life and in the sciences, however, it is often essential to replace propositions simply affirming or denying qualitative differences by propositions indicating in a more precise way the *degree* of such differences. It is essential to do so in the interest of *accuracy* of statement, as well as in the interest of discovering *comprehensive principles* in terms of which the subject matter can be conceived as systematically related. Thus we may believe that there is more unemployment this year than last, or that the winters during our childhood were more severe than those during the past few years. But it may be important to know *how much* more unemployment there is, or *how much* less severe the winters have become; for if we can state the differences in terms of degrees of differences, we not only guard ourselves against the errors of hasty, untutored impressions, but also lay the foundation for an adequately grounded control of the indicated changes. Similarly, in the sciences we wish to know *how far* the planets are away from us, *how rapidly* they are moving, *how much* iron expands under known conditions of heating, and *how great* is the degree of resemblance between different members of a blood kinship. Such information gives us great practical control over the subject studied; it also makes possible a formulation for it of principles that are capable of *unambiguous* confirmation or refutation.

Theoretical and practical considerations lead us, therefore, to replace *qualitative* distinctions by *quantitative* ones. Quantitative

From *An Introduction to Logic and Scientific Method,* pp. 289–301. New York: Harcourt, Brace and Company, 1934. Reprinted by permission of Ernest Nagel and the publisher.

distinctions are employed by many people who would be unable to offer an adequate analysis of what such distinctions mean, or to explain how they may be justified. The mother who says to her friend, "My Johnny is a head taller than your Frankie," very likely has never reflected on the difficulties of analyzing the meaning of her judgment. If pressed to offer the grounds for her assertion, she may stand the boys back to back and note by "looking" that Johnny does top Frankie by a head. But the same mother will be totally at a loss to interpret what she means when she says, "Johnny is twice as good as Frankie in arithmetic."

The employment of numbers to indicate qualitative differences requires a careful examination if it is not to lead us into error and absurdity. If our daily life and the sciences dealt with matters no more complex than that of comparing the heights of children, complicated methods of registering differences would never be used. Measurement, calculation, and the often difficult deduction of consequences from premises, would not require the elaborate techniques which they in fact do require. In every quarter, however, we find it necessary to employ a more intricate machinery of stating, gathering, and estimating evidence than that which is supplied by an untrained look or touch. Very few investigations can be carried through without the introduction of quantitative methods at some point. A study of the method of science must not, therefore, omit the study of the foundations of *applied mathematics.*

2. The Nature of Counting

What, then, are the ways of introducing precision into the judgments we make? In many inquiries, *counting* the individuals who possess a certain character is the only possible method of avoiding vague ideas. Are there more children under ten years of age in New York City than in London? Were there more industrial establishments in the United States employing less than ten people in 1900 than in 1920? "General impressions" on such questions are too vague to be reliable. It would be very unsafe to develop a comprehensive social theory (to assert, for example, that the progressive industrialization of a country is accompanied by the elimination of small-sized industries) if no empirical check upon our speculations were possible other than that supplied by vague impressions. But an unambiguous answer can be given to questions such as those cited by making an *actual count* of the individuals who belong to the respective classes.

Counting is undertaken not for its own sake, but because we suspect significant connections between the groups counted. Therefore we do not make a numerical inventory of all the groups of individuals we can find. Enumeration is undertaken on the basis of hypotheses expressing our sense of relevance. Such hypotheses play a controlling rôle at every stage of inquiry. It is clear, moreover, that the comparison of groups by enumerating their members can be made only if the groups are themselves unambiguously distinct from one another. We therefore employ counting to make precise our ideas, *subsequent* to our having acquired sufficient knowledge about a subject to permit us to distinguish various features in it.

Counting is subject to the limitation that only a discrete group, or a subject matter which may be manipulated so as to take on the form of a discrete group, may be counted. We can count the inhabitants of a city, because each inhabitant is distinct from every other inhabitant. We cannot count the drops in a glass of water unless we find some way of separating the drops from one another, and unless we introduce some convention as to what we shall regard as a drop.

The great importance of counting as a method of clarifying our ideas arises from the fact that the *number* of individuals in a group represents an *invariant property* of that group. For suppose we wish to count the apples in a bag. We take out the apples one by one, and place each apple in correspondence with a distinct number of a series of standard objects like our fingers, the numerals, or the letters of the alphabet. Suppose the first apple in the bag is placed in correspondence with the letter *A,* the second with the letter *B,* the third with *C,* and the remaining apple with *D.* We then say that there are *four* apples. The important property of this number is that had we taken out the apples from the bag in a different order and matched them with the letters, the last apple would nevertheless have still been matched with the letter *D.* The number of a collection obtained by counting is, therefore, a *constant* character of that collection; it does not depend on who does the counting, or on the order in which the objects are counted. Applied arithmetic is in part a collection of rules by means of which this invariant property can be most easily found.

Many of the difficulties that accompany the enumeration of groups arise from the difficulty of interpreting *what* it is that is counted. In many inquiries counting can be performed easily and without ambiguity, because the groups enumerated are readily distinguished. We can count the number of men and the number of women in a community, because the different biological functions of men and women make it impossible to confuse them. But where the lines of cleavage between groups is not so distinct, the interpretation of the numbers obtained by counting is uncertain. Thus it is not easy to draw the line between skilled workers and the unskilled; and while we may count the number of individuals in each group, the result will be infected with all the ambiguity that attaches to the notion of a "skilled worker."

The gathering and interpretation of information about many important social matters is attended by difficulties of a special kind. Such information is generally obtained from written or oral questionnaires submitted to only a part of the population; and it must never be forgotten that the accuracy of the tabulated form of such information cannot exceed the accuracy with which the questionnaires are answered. Allowance must be made for ignorance, dishonesty, and vanity. No amount of mathematical manipulation of the results of counting can eliminate the incalculable inaccuracies in the replies. Thus the United States census for 1890 called for the color of the respondee: whether he or she was black, mulatto, quadroon, or octoroon. Since most people are ignorant as to the *meaning* of these distinctions, and many more are not in a position to know in what classification they themselves belong, it is safe to say that the answers, even if honestly given, were unreliable. The questions asked in a census must be drawn up with great care: they must not appertain to matters about which most people are not accurately informed. Information obtained by means of questionnaires concerning the number of days the respondent has been employed, or concerning the itemized account of his yearly expenditures, is in most cases worthless. A similar evaluation must be made of the growing practice of submitting questionnaires to insufficiently trained students on problems of sex, economics, or politics.

Personal vanity and dishonesty are factors often as important as ignorance. In one British census, information was requested whether the respondent was an employer or an employee. A surprisingly large number of employers was reported, a larger number than was consistent with information based on independent sources. This discrepancy was explained, plausibly at any rate, as arising from the unwillingness of the respondent to suffer the humiliation of appearing before the census-taker as merely an employee. Most enumerations based on answers to questionnaires regarding religious and social beliefs, or the prevalence of physical or mental disorders, are sure to be unreliable, because the answers given are very likely to be influenced by the fear or sense of shame of the respondents.

If the groups we are investigating are large in numbers, or difficult to examine exhaustively, it may be impossible or financially prohibitive to undertake an enumeration of their members. In such cases we resort to taking samples. The limitations of the procedure of sampling we shall consider later. The distinctive feature of this process consists in concluding that the proportion of characters found in the sample is the same as the proportion in the entire collection. It involves the type of argument we have called reasoning from samples, or statistical inference.

3. The Measurement of Intensive Qualities

Comparisons based upon counting, as we have seen, depend on our ability to distinguish clearly between different groups or different characters. Frequently, however, characters cannot be sharply distinguished because they form a continuous series with one another. Thus we may wish to distinguish different knives on the basis of their "sharpness," different woods on the basis of their "hardness," different children on the basis of their "alertness." For some purposes it is sufficient to know that one piece of wood is harder than another, employing such rough criteria of the hardness of a wood as the ease with which we can drive a nail into it. But we often want to know just how hard one piece of wood is as compared with any other kind of wood, and we then require a more certain and uniform criterion than the one suggested. We wish, if possible, to assign numbers to indicate the different *degrees* of hardness; and we often do so. The numbers so assigned are said to *measure* the varying degrees of the quality. What principles must we observe in using numbers to denote such differences in qualities?

We must be on guard against a common error. It is often believed that because we can assign numbers to different degrees of a quality, the different degrees always bear to each other the same ratio as do the numbers we have assigned to them. This is a serious mistake, and arises because it is supposed that measurement requires nothing more than the assigning of numbers. As we shall see, not all qualities can be "measured" in the same sense. Thus when we say that one tank contains 100 quarts of water and another 50 quarts, it is legitimate to say, as we shall soon find, that the first tank contains *twice as much* water as the second. In this case, the ratio of the volumes is the same as the ratio of the numbers. But when we say that the temperature one day is 100° and on another 50°, is it permissible to say that the temperature on the first day was *twice as much* as on the second? Or when we find that one student has an I.Q. of 100 and another an I.Q. of 50, is it correct to say that the first student is *twice as intelligent* as the second? An analysis of the conditions of measurement will show that the last two assertions are strictly without meaning.

We must note that numbers may have at least three distinct uses: (1) as tags, or identification marks; (2) as signs to indicate the *position* of the degree of a quality in a *series* of degrees; and (3) as signs indicating the *quantitative* relations between qualities. On some occasions numbers may fulfill all three functions at once.

(1) The numbers given to prisoners or railroad cars serve only as convenient ways of *naming* these objects. Numbers are more convenient than verbal names, because a "name" can be found for any new individual brought into the group by simply taking the number one greater than the last number that has been so employed. When numbers are used for this purpose, most people rec-

ognize that no relation between the objects numbered corresponds to the numerical relation between the numbers assigned. The prisoner numbered 500 is not five times as dangerous or wicked as the one numbered 100. It is not even always true that Convict No. 500 entered the prison later than Convict No. 100, since the same number can be assigned several times without confusion.

(2) A scientifically more important use of numbers is when the *order* of numerical magnitude is the same as the *order* of the position of the character studied in a scale or ladder of qualities. Suppose we wish to distinguish bodies from one another with respect to their being harder or softer. We may then accept the following definition of what it means for one body to be harder than another: Diamond is harder than glass if diamond can scratch glass but glass cannot scratch diamond; and one body will be said to be just as hard as a second body if neither can scratch nor be scratched by the other. We may then arrange bodies in a scale of hardness, if we can show experimentally that relations like the following hold between every triplet of unequally hard bodies: Diamond is harder than glass, glass is harder than pine wood, diamond is harder than pine wood. The relational property of "being harder than" is then shown to be asymmetrical (if B_1 is harder than B_2, B_2 is not harder than B_1) ; and transitive (if B_1 is harder than B_2, and B_2 is harder than B_3, then B_1 is harder than B_3.) We can then arrange bodies in a linear series of hardness and thus get a scale or "ladder" of this quality.

Suppose now we have 100 different unequally hard bodies B_1, B_2, . . . B_{100} arranged so that B_1 is the hardest and B_{100} is the softest body, in conformity with the above conditions. We may wish to assign numbers to them to indicate their relative hardness in such a way that the order of numerical magnitude is the same as the order of relative degrees of hardness. (This can be done, since the relation of magnitude of numbers is asymmetrical and transitive.) But what number shall we assign to body B_1? We may decide to assign to it the number 0, or 1, or 25, or in fact any number we please. Suppose we decide on 1 for B_1, and also on 100 for B_{100}, and agree moreover to designate 2 as the hardness of B_2, 3 as the hardness of B_3, and so on.

These choices, however, were in no way forced upon us. We may have decided on 1 for B_1, 5 for B_2, 10 for B_3, and so on. *In terms of the procedure* we have followed in arranging the bodies in a scale of hardness, no meaning can be attached, therefore, to the statement that B_{50} is *twice as soft* as B_{25}. This statement has no meaning because the only relations we have defined, in arranging the bodies in the scale, are the relations of transitivity and asymmetry with respect to being capable of scratching. The statement falsely suggests that because one body is "higher up" the scale than another, it "contains more" of something called "hardness." And it falsely suggests, because one body is supposed to contain more of this something, that it contains a unit amount of it *a certain number of times.* Both of these suggestions must be ruthlessly eliminated. They arise from the mistaken idea that hardness is something which can be *added.* But there is nothing in the process of constructing the scale which can justify this. Hardness and softness, like temperature, shape, density, intelligence, courtesy, are *nonadditive* qualities. Such qualities are frequently called *intensive.* They can be "measured" only in the sense that the different degrees of the quality may be arranged in a *series.* Concerning them, questions of *how much* or *how many times* are meaningless.

4. The Measurement of Extensive Qualities

We turn to the third use of numbers. They can sometimes be employed to measure quantitative relations in the strict sense, so that answers to the questions, "How much?" and, "How many?" can be given in terms of them. Suppose we consider a set of bodies and that we wish to measure their weights. In order to do this, we must be able, in the first place, to construct a scale or ladder of weights in a manner similar to establishing a scale of hardness. We will agree, for example, that one body, R, is heavier than another body, S, if when R and S are placed in the opposite pans of a beam balance, the pan containing R sinks. We must then establish experimentally that the relation of "heavier than" is transitive and asymmetrical. We will also agree that body R is *equal in weight to* (or is as heavy as) R' if R is not heavier than R' and R' is not heavier than R; this means that neither pan of the balance will sink when R and R' are placed in opposite pans.

We are able not only to construct a scale of degrees of weights. We can also find an interpretation *in terms of some operation upon bodies* for such a statement as that one body is three times another in weight. An interpretation is possible because weights can be *added.* The physical process of addition is *the placing of two or more weights together* in the same pan of the balance. Let us now find three bodies, B, B', B'', which are equally heavy, and place them in one pan; place another body, C, in the other pan so that the beam will balance. The body C is then as heavy as the three bodies B, B', B'' combined, and is *three times* as heavy as any one of them. This procedure can be extended to define a series of standard weights. In terms of this procedure it becomes significant to say that one object is n times as heavy or $1/n$th as heavy as another.

But we have not yet done enough to be sure that numbers assigned by such a process have all their familiar meanings. We have shown that weight is an additive property as contrasted with hardness, which is not. We must also show, again by experiment, that the numbers so assigned to weights are consistent with themselves. We must make sure that we do not allow *different* numbers to be assigned to the same object. Thus suppose the weight of object A is regarded as the unit or 1, and that we can assign weights to other objects by this process so that A_2 will have weight 2, A_4 weight 4, and A_6 weight 6. Can we be sure that A_2 and A_4 placed together in one pan will just balance A_6 placed in the other? It is very important to note that we cannot be certain of this until we perform the experiment. The proposition that $2 + 4 = 6$ can be demonstrated in *pure arithmetic* without experiment. But until we perform the proper experiments we cannot be certain that the *physical operation* of addition of weights does conform to the familiar properties of pure arithmetical addition. The physical operation of addition of weight possesses the usual formal properties of arithmetical addition only in *some* cases, not in *all:* the beam balance must be well constructed, its arms must be of equal length, and so on.

The method of measuring weights can be employed to measure other properties as well. Lengths, time intervals, areas, angles, electric current, electric resistance, can be measured in the same way. These properties are additive: we can find a process such that combining two objects having a property we obtain an object with an increased degree of that property. Properties which are additive are frequently called *extensive.* They can be measured in accordance with the processes indicated in this section. Such measurement we shall call *fundamental.*

5. The Formal Conditions for Measurement

We may now state the conditions for measurement in abstract language. The minimum requirements for employing numbers in order to "measure" (in the loosest sense of the word) qualitative differences, are stated in the first two conditions.

1. Given a set of n bodies, $B_1, B_2, \ldots B_n$, we must be able to arrange them in a series with respect to a certain quality so that between any two bodies one and only one of the following relations holds: (a) $B_i > B_j$; (b) $B_i < B_j$; (c) $B_i = B_j$. The sign $>$ and its converse $<$ symbolize the relation on the basis of which the bodies can be distinguished as differing in the quality studied. The relation $>$ must be asymmetrical.

2. If $B_i > B_j$, and $B_j > B_k$, then $B_i > B_k$. This condition expresses the transitivity of the relation.

These two conditions are sufficient for the measurement of intensive qualities, such as temperature or density. They are necessary but not sufficient for extensive measurement. For the latter we require some physical process of addition, symbolized by +, which must be shown by experiment to possess the following formal properties:

3. If $B_e + B_f = B_g$, then $B_f + B_e = B_g$.

4. If $B_i = B_i'$, then $B_i + B_j > B_i'$.

5. If $B_i = B_i'$ and $B_j = B_j'$, then $B_i + B_j = B_i' + B_j'$.

6. $(B_i + B_j) + B_k = B_i + (B_j + B_k)$.

Measurement in the strict sense is possible only if all these conditions are satisfied. When only the first two conditions are satisfied, it is nonsense to make statements which imply that all six have been shown to hold. When we assert that one man has an I.Q. of 150 and another one of 75, all that we can mean is that in a *specific* scale of performance (requiring certain specialized abilities) one man stands "higher" than the other. It is nonsense to say that the first man has twice the intelligence or the training the other has, because no operation for adding intelligence or training has been discovered which conforms to the last four conditions necessary to make such a statement meaningful.

6. Numerical Laws and Derived Measurement

When we have once established a standard series of measures for any quality of bodies, we measure any further instance of that quality by comparing it with some member of the standard series. A standard series of lengths, for example, is embodied in a platinum meter kept at Paris under certain physical conditions. More or less exact duplications of it are distributed throughout the world. If anyone wishes to know how long a piece of cloth is, he will juxtapose in known ways the cloth and a meter measure or a yardstick. Direct judgments of comparison are therefore required to evaluate the length of the cloth. Similar processes are used for other measurable qualities.

But measurements of qualities are rarely performed for their own sake. They are made in order that precise relations between different properties of bodies may be established. Measurements in laboratories are carried on for the sole purpose of discovering the numerical laws which connect physical properties.

Let us examine one such numerical law. Most people are familiar with the property of liquids and solids which is called their "density." They know in general that it is the density which determines their buoyancies in water. It is not always known, however, what the relation of density is to the other properties of a body. Suppose we wished to measure the densities of the following five liquids: gasoline, alcohol, water, hydrochloric acid, mercury. We will agree to call one liquid, say mercury, more dense than water if we can find some solid body which will float on mercury but sink in water. By experiment we can then show that density so defined is an asymmetric, transitive relation, and that the liquids can therefore be arranged in a series of increasing density. The order of densities will in fact be the order in which we have written down the names of the liquids. We discover, however, that density is not an additive property of a liquid, and that we can measure it only as an intensive quality. We can then assign the numbers 1, 2, 3, 4, 5 to designate the positions of the liquids in the density scale. These numbers, as we have already pointed out, are arbitrary.

The reader may know, however, that altogether different numbers are usually assigned for the densities, numbers which are not arbitrarily chosen. The reason for this is that many intensive qualities can be measured in another way than by simply arranging them serially. And density is one of them.

This other way is fairly well known. It depends on the existence of a numerical law between other properties of the liquids, with which their density property is invariably related. For when we weigh different volumes of a liquid, say water, we discover experimentally that the *ratio* of the numbers measuring the weights and volumes of this liquid is the *same,* no matter how large or small the volume we measure. We thus establish a *numerical law* between the properties of weight and volume of a liquid. This law is that $W = cV$, where W is the measure of the weight, V that of the corresponding volume, and c is a constant for *all* samples of the same liquid but is a different constant for other liquids. By a proper choice of the units of weight and volume, we find that c has the value .75 for gasoline, .79 for alcohol, 1 for water, 1.27 for hydrochloric acid, and 13.6 for mercury. We also make the important discovery that the *order* of these ratios is the same as the order of the density of the liquids when this is determined in the way we did above. This ratio, which is constant for all samples of a homogeneous liquid, can therefore be taken as measuring its density. But we must be on our guard not to say that the density of mercury is 13.6 "times" that of water. For density, no matter how measured, is a nonadditive property. It can be measured precisely, and numbers assigned without arbitrariness to different degrees of it, only in virtue of a connection between weight and volume. This connection can be expressed as a *numerical law* between properties which can be measured by a *fundamental* process. Density can be measured only by a *derivative* method.

Numerical laws play a very important rôle in scientific inquiries. The discovery of numerical laws between qualities which can be measured in the strict sense, that is, by a fundamental process, enables us to measure carefully many intensive properties, such as temperature, density, buoyancy, elasticity, or efficiency of machines. Only by the aid of numerical laws can we measure the temperatures of the distant stars, or the blood pressure in the arteries of living things. But it is important to note that unless some properties were measurable by a fundamental process, numerical laws would be impossible, and the derivative measurement of intensive qualities could not be performed. (However, properties which are measurable by a fundamental process may also be measurable derivatively.) This explains, in part, some of the difficulties in the way of the social sciences. Precise estimates of intensive properties cannot be made because fundamental measurements in social matters are difficult, and because few numerical laws can be found which connect such intensive properties with extensive ones.

Numerical laws represent certain invariable relations between physical properties. Science aims not only at establishing such laws singly, but also at finding how different numerical laws are themselves connected with one another.

Suppose, for example, we let two circular cylinders roll down on two different inclined planes. The cylinders differ in the radii of their right sections, and the planes are inclined to the horizontal at different angles. If we wish to find the law connecting the distance traveled by each cylinder with the time, we may discover that for the first cylinder the law is $d = .20t^2$ and for the second it is $d = .35t^2$. These laws have the same "form." But the numerical constants in them are different, and *seem* to be unrelated to one another.

The science of physics tries to discover some other numerical law which will explain the variation of these numerical constants, as we employ different cylinders and different inclined planes. And physics is remarkably successful. It shows that the numerical law for the behavior of the rolling cylinder can be expressed in the form $d = ft^2$, where f itself is connected with the gravitational constant, the inclination of the plane, the coefficient of friction, the radius of the section of the cylinder, and the distribution of matter in the cylinder. Thus the sciences seek more and more general invariant laws which will account for many special features in a complicated phenomenon. But such search can meet with success only when the different properties of bodies have been distinguished by processes of measurement.

The First Physical Synthesis

ALFRED NORTH WHITEHEAD

There are in the history of civilization certain dates which stand out as marking either the boundaries or the culminations of critical epochs. It is true that no epoch either commences, ends, or sums itself up in one definite moment. It is brought upon the stage of reality in the arms of its predecessors, and only yields to its successor by reason of a slow process of transformation. Its terminals are conventional. Wherever you choose to fix them, you can be confronted with good reasons for an extension or contraction of your period. But the meridian culmination is sometimes unmistakable, and it is often marked by some striking events which lend an almost mystic symbolism to their exact date. Such a date is the year 1642 of our epoch, the year in which occurred the death of Galileo and the birth of Newton. This date marks the centre of that period of about 100 years during which the scientific intellect of Europe was framing that First Physical Synthesis which has remained down to our own times as the basis of science. The development of modern Europe from the world of the Renaissance and the Reformation is unintelligible in its unique importance without an understanding of the achievements of these two men. The great civilizations of Asia and of the classical times in the Mediterranean had their epochs of artistic and literary triumph, of religious reformation, and of active scientific speculation. But it was the fortune of modern Europe that during the seventeenth century, amid a ferment of scientific speculation, two men, one after the other, appeared, each with a supreme gift of physical intuition, with magnificent powers of ab-

From F. S. Marvin (Ed.), *Science and Civilization,* New York: Oxford University Press, 1923. Reprinted by permission of the publisher and Mrs. Alfred North Whitehead.

stract generalization, and each with subsidiary endowments exactly suited to the immediate circumstances of the scientific problem, this one a supreme experimentalist and enough of a mathematician, and that one a supreme mathematician and enough of an experimentalist. Archimedes left no successor. But our modern civilization is due to the fact that in the year when Galileo died, Newton was born. Think for a moment of the possible course of history supposing that the life's work of these two men were absent. At the commencement of the eighteenth century many curious and baffling facts of physical science would have been observed, vaguely connected by detached and obscure hypotheses. But in the absence of a clear physical synthesis, with its overwhelming success in the solution of problems which from the most remote antiquity had excited attention, the motive for the next advance would have been absent. All epochs pass, and the scientific ferment of the seventeenth century would have died down. Locke's philosophy would never have been written; and Voltaire when he visited England would have carried back to France merely a story of expanding commerce and of the political rivalries between aristocratic factions. Europe might then have lacked the French intellectual movement. But the Fates do not always offer the same gifts twice, and it is possible that the eighteenth century might then have prepared for the western races an intellectual sleep of a thousand years, prosperous with the quiet slow exploitation of the American continent, as manual labour slowly subdued its rivers, its forests, and its prairies. I am not concerned to deny that the result might have been happier, for the chariot of Phœbus is a dangerous vehicle. My only immediate thesis is that it would have been very different.

The forms of the great works by which the minds of Galileo and Newton are best known to us bear plain evidence of the contrast between their situations. In his book entitled, *The Two Systems of the World in Four Dialogues,* and published in 1632, Galileo is arguing with the past; whilst in his *Mathematical Principles of Natural Philosophy,* published in 1687, Newton ignores old adversaries and discussions, and, looking wholly to the future, calmly enunciates definitions, principles, and proofs which have ever since formed the basis of physical science. Galileo represents the assault and Newton the victory. There can be no doubt but that Galileo is the better reading. It is a real flesh and blood document of human nature which has wedged itself between the two austere epochs of Aristotelian Logic and Applied Mathematics. It was paid for also in the heart's blood of the author.

The catastrophe happened in this way: most unfortunately His Holiness, the reigning pope, in an entirely friendly interview after the Inquisition had forbidden the expression of Copernican opinions, made use of the irrefutable argument that, God being omnipotent, it was as easy for him to send the sun and the planets round the earth as to send the earth and the planets round the sun. How unfortunate it is that even an infallible pontiff and the greatest of men of science, with the most earnest desire to understand each other, cannot rid themselves of their presuppositions. The pope was trembling on the verge of the enunciation of the relativity of motion and of space, and in his Dialogues there are passages in which Galileo plainly expresses that same doctrine. But neither of them was sufficiently aware of the full emphasis to be laid upon that truth. Accordingly the next precious ten minutes of the conversation in which Galileo might have cleared away the little misunderstanding were wasted, and as a result there ensued for the world's edification the persecution of Galileo and a clear illustration of the limits of infallibility. The true moral of the incident is the importance of great men keeping their tempers. Galileo was annoyed – and very naturally so, for it was an irritating sort of argument with which to counter a great and saving formulation of scientific ideas. Unfortunately he went away and put the pope's argument into the mouth of Simplicius, the man in the Dialogues who always advances the foolish objections. It is welcomed in the following speech by the leading interlocutor, Salviatus – I give it in the seventeenth-century translation of Thomas Salusbury:

"This of yours is admirable, and truly angelical doctrine, to which very exactly that other accords in like manner divine, which whilst it giveth us leave to dispute, touching the constitution of the world, addeth withall (perhaps to the end that the exercise of the minds of men might neither be discouraged nor made bold) that we cannot find out the works made by his hands. Let therefore the Disquisition permitted and ordained us by God, assist us in the knowing, and so much more admiring his greatness, by how much less we find ourselves too dull to penetrate the profound abysses of his infinite wisdom."

At this point the Dialogues end. Galileo always protested that he had meant no discourtesy. But the pope, even if his infallibility tottered, was here assisted by the gift of prophecy and smelt Voltaire. Anyhow in his turn he lost his temper and afterwards remained the bitter enemy of Galileo.

Galileo's supreme experimental genius is shown by the way in which every hint which reached him is turned to account and immediately made to be of importance. He hears of the telescope as a curiosity discovered by a Dutch optician. It might have remained a toy, but in his hands it created a revolution. He at once thought out the principles on which it was based, improved upon its design so as to obviate the inversion of objects, and immediately applied it to a systematic survey of the heavens. The results were startling. It was not a few details that were altered, but an almost sacred sentiment which fell before it. I have often thought that the calmness with which the Church accepted Copernicus and its savage hostility to Galileo can only be accounted for by measuring the ravages made by the telescope on the sacred doctrine of the heavens. It was then seen too late that the Copernican doctrine was the key to the position. But Galileo's Dialogues plainly show that it was not the movement of the earth but the glory of the heavens which was the point at issue. It must be remembered that the heaven, which Christ had taught is within us, was by the popular sentiment of mediæval times placed above us. Accordingly when the telescope revealed the moon and other planets reduced to the measure of the earth, and the sun with evanescent spots, the shock to sentiment was profound. It is the characteristic of shocked sentiment in the case of men whose learning surpasses their genius that they begin to quote Aristotle. Accordingly Aristotle was hurled at Galileo.

The Dialogues are the record of the contemporary dispute between Galileo and the current Aristotelian tradition, and the end of the discussion was the creation of the modern scientific outlook of which Galileo was the first perfect representative – somewhat choleric but entirely whole-hearted.

So far we have been endeavouring to appreciate the climate of opinions amid which Galileo's life was passed – and you will remember that no climate is composed of a succession of uniform days, especially in its spring-time. A judicious selection could affix almost any label to the thought of the seventeenth century. What we have to keep in our minds is that at its beginning, so far as science was concerned, men knew hardly more than Aristotle and less than Archimedes, while at its end the main positions of modern science were firmly established.

I will now endeavour to explain the main revolutionary ideas which Galileo impressed upon his contemporaries. The first one was the doctrine of the uniformity of the material universe. This doctrine is now so obvious to us that we can only think of it in the attenuated form of discussions on miracles or on the relations of mind and matter. But in Galileo's time the denial of uniformity went much deeper than that. The different regions of Nature were supposed to function in entirely different ways. This presupposition led to a style of argument which is foreign to our ears. For example, here is a short speech of Simplicius, the upholder of the old Aristotelian tradition in Galileo's Dialogues, chosen almost at random: —

Aristotle, though of a very perspicacious wit, would not strain it further than needed: holding in all his argumentations, that sensible experiments were to be preferred before any reasons founded upon strength of wit, and said those which should deny the testimony of sense deserved to be punished with the loss of that sense; now who is so blind, that sees not the parts of the Earth and Water to move, as being grave, naturally downwards, namely, towards the centre of the Universe, assigned by nature herself for the end and term of right motion *deorsum;* and doth not likewise see the Fire and Air to move right upwards towards the Concave of the Lunar Orb, as to the natural end of motion *sursum?* And this being so manifestly seen, and we being certain, that *eadem est ratio totius et partium,* why may we not assert it for a true and manifest proposition, that the natural motion of the Earth is the right motion *ad medium,* and that of the Fire, the right *a medio?*

In this passage we note that different functions are assigned to the Centre of the Universe to which the Earth or any part of it naturally moves in a straight line, and to the Concave of the Lunar Orb (to which Fire naturally moves in a straight line). The idea of the neutrality of situation and the universality of physical laws, regulating casual occurrences and holding indifferently in every part, is entirely absent. On the contrary, each local part of nature has its one peculiar function in the scheme of things. It is a fine conception: the only objection to it is that it does not seem to be true. I am not sure, however, that the Einstein conception of the physical forces as being due to the contortions of space-time is not in some respects a return to it.

But let us see how Galileo in the person of the interlocutor, Salviatus, answers this speech of Simplicius. His answer is somewhat long, and I only give the relevant part: —

. . . Now, like as from the consentaneous conspiration of all the parts of the Earth to form its whole, doth follow, that they with equal inclination concur thither from all parts; and to unite themselves as much as is possible together, they there physically adapt themselves; why may we not believe that the Sun, Moon, and other mundane Bodies, be also of a round figure, not by other than a concordant instinct, and natural concourse of all the parts composing them? Of which, if any, at any time, by any violence were separated from the whole, is it not reasonable to think, that they would spontaneously and by natural instinct return? and in this manner to infer, that the right motion agreeth with all mundane bodies alike.

Note that in this answer Galileo, in the person of Salviatus, entirely ignores any peculiar function or property to be assigned to a Centre of the Universe or to a Concave of the Lunar Orb. He has in his mind the conceptions of modern science, in that the Earth, the Moon, the Sun, and the other planets are all bodies moving in an indifferent neutral space, and each attracting its own parts to form its whole — or, as Salviatus puts it, "the consentaneous conspiration of all the parts of the Earth to form its whole."

Evidently Galileo is very near to the Newtonian doctrine of Universal Gravitation. But he is not quite there. Newton enunciates the doctrine that every particle of matter attracts every other particle of matter in a certain definite way. Galileo — as children say in the game of Hide-and-Seek — is very hot in respect to this doctrine. But he does not seem, at least in this passage, to have made the final generalization. He is thinking particularly of the Earth, the Sun, the

Moon, and other planets – and his guardian angel does not appear to have whispered to him the generalization "any material body." Newton probably knew Galileo's Dialogues nearly by heart. They were standard works in his time. Cannot we imagine him sitting in his rooms between the gateway and the chapel of Trinity College, or in the orchard watching the apple fall, and with this passage of Galileo's Dialogue running in his mind, perhaps the very words of Salusbury's translation which I have quoted, "the consentaneous conspiration of all the parts of the Earth to form its whole." Suddenly the idea flashes on him – "What are the Earth and the Sun and the Moon? Why, they are any bodies! We should say therefore that any bodies attract. But if this be the case, the Earth and the Sun and the Moon attract each other, and we have the cause maintaining the planets in their orbits." In this course of thought Newton would have been assisted by his third law of motion. For by it if the Earth attracts the apple, then the apple attracts the Earth.

By this conjectural reconstruction of Newton's state of mind we see that, given a genius with adequate mathematical faculties, Newton's Principia is the next step in science after Galileo's Dialogues. Probably Galileo himself would have gone farther in this direction if his imagination had not been hampered by the necessity of arguing with the Conservative Party. It is in general a mistake to waste time in discussions with people who have the wrong ideas in their heads. But in Galileo's time and country the Conservative Party had thumb-screws at its service and could thereby enforce a certain amount of attention to its ideas.

Undoubtedly the whole implication of the answer of Salviatus is that the Earth, Sun, &c., are mere bits of matter. It is difficult for us to estimate how great an advance Galileo made in adumbrating this position. Consider, for example, this statement by Simplicius, made in another connexion, enforcing a doctrine which he upholds throughout the whole of the Dialogues: –

See here for a beginning, two most convincing arguments to demonstrate the Earth to be most different from the Cælestial bodies. First, the bodies that are generable, corruptible, alterable, &c., are quite different from those that are ingenerable, incorruptible, unalterable, &c. But the Earth is generable, corruptible, alterable, &c., and the Cælestial bodies ingenerable, incorruptible, unalterable, &c. Therefore the Earth is quite different from the Cælestial bodies.

That is the sort of thing that Galileo was up against, not as a mere casual idea occurring to a subtle reasoner, but as the very texture of current notions. The primary achievement of the first physical synthesis was to clear all this away. Galileo with his telescope, his trenchant, bold intellect, and his magnificent physical intuition was the man who did it.

But we have not nearly exhausted Galileo's contributions to the general ideas of science. We owe to Galileo the First Law of Motion. Probably most of us have in our minds Newton's enunciation of this law, "Every body continues in its state of rest or of uniform motion in a straight line except so far as it is compelled by impressed force to change that state." This is the first article of the creed of science; and like the Church's creeds it is more than a mere statement of belief: it is a pæan of triumph over defeated heretics. It should be set to music and chanted in the halls of Universities. The defeated adversaries are the Aristotelians who for two thousand years imposed on Dynamics the search for a physical cause of motion, whereas the true doctrine conceives uniform motion in a straight line as a state in which every body will naturally continue except so far as it is compelled by impressed force to change that state. Accordingly in Dynamics we search for a cause of the change of motion, namely either a change in respect to speed or a change in respect to direction of motion. For example, an Aristotelian investigating the motion of the planets in their orbits would seek for tangential forces to keep the planets moving; but a follower of Galileo seeks for normal forces to deflect the direction of motion along the curved orbit. This is why Newton, at the moment which we pictured him as he sat in his rooms in Trinity College thinking about gravitation, at once saw that the attraction of the Sun was the required force. It was nearly normal to the orbits of the planets. Here again we see how immediately Newton's physical ideas follow from those of Galileo. One genius completes the work of the other.

It has been stated by Whewell that in his Dialogues on the Two Principal Systems of the World Galileo does not enunciate the first law of motion, and that it only appears in his subsequent Dialogues on Mechanics. This may be formally true so far as a neat decisive statement is concerned. But in essence the first law of motion is presupposed in the argumentation of the earlier dialogues. The whole explanation why loose things are not left behind as the Earth moves depends upon it.

Galileo also prepared the way for Newton's final enunciation of the Laws of Motion by his masterly investigation of the uniform acceleration of falling bodies on the Earth's surface and his demonstration that this acceleration is independent of the relative weights of the bodies, except so far as extraneous retarding forces are concerned. He swept away the old classification of natural and violent motions as founded on trivial unessential differences, and left the way entirely open for Newton's final generalizations. Newton conceived explicitly the idea of a neutral absolute space within which all motion is to be construed, and of mass as a permanent intrinsic physical quantity associated with matter, unalterable except by the destruction of matter. He phrased this concept in the definition, mass is quantity of matter. He then conceived the true measure of force as being the product of the mass of the body into its rate of change of velocity. The importance of this conception lies in the fact that force as thus conceived is found to depend on simple physical conditions, such as mass, electric and magnetic charges, electric currents, and distances. We owe to Newton the final formulation of the basic physical ideas which have served science so well during these last two centuries. They comprise the foundations of the science of Dynamics, and Law of Gravitation. We also owe to Galileo's experimental genius the telescope and its first systematic use in science, the pendulum clock (subsequently perfected by Huyghens) and the experimental demonstration of the laws of falling bodies. To Newton's mathematical genius we owe the deduction of the properties of the planetary orbits from dynamical principles. To Galileo and Newton we must add the name of Kepler so far as astronomy is concerned, and of Stevinus of Bruges so far as mechanics is concerned. He discovered the famous triangle of forces. But in one lecture lasting one hour you will not expect me to give a detailed account of the science of the seventeenth century.

In like manner we must add the name of Huyghens in mentioning the services of Galileo and Newton to the science of Optics. Huyghens first suggested the undulatory theory of light, to be revived at the beginning of the nineteenth century by Thomas Young and Fresnel. But the immediately fruitful work was due to Galileo with his studies on the theory of the telescope, and to Newton with his studies on the theory of colour. Both Dynamics and Optics reached Galileo as a series of detached truths (or falsehoods) loosely connected. After the work of Galileo and Newton they emerged as well-knit sciences on firm foundations.

Galileo's preoccupation with Optics doubtless helped him to another great idea which has coloured all modern thought. Light is transmitted through space from its origin by paths which may be devious and broken. What you see depends on the light as it enters your eye. You may see a green leaf behind the looking-glass; but the leaf is really behind your head and you are really looking at its image in the mirror. Thus the green which you see is not the property of the leaf, but it is the result of the stimulation of the nerves of the retina by the light which enters the eye. These considerations led Descartes and Locke to elaborate the idea of external nature consisting of matter moving in space and with merely primary qualities. These primary qualities are its shape, its degree of hardness and cohesiveness, its massiveness, and its attractive effects and its resilience. Our perceptions of nature such as colour, sound, taste and smell, and sensations of heat and cold form the secondary qualities. These secondary qualities are merely mental projections which are the result of the stimulation of the brain by the appropriate nerves. Such in outline is the famous theory of primary and secondary qualities in the form in which it has held the field during the modern period of science. It has been of essential service in directing scientific investigation into fruitful fields both of physics and physiology. Now the credit for its first sketch is due to Galileo. Here is an extract from Galileo's work, *Il Saggiatore,* published in 1624. I take it from the English life of Galileo by J. J. Fahie: –

"I have now only to fulfil my promise of declaring my opinions on the proposition that motion is the cause of heat, and to explain in what manner it appears to me that it may be true. But I must first make some remarks on that which we call heat, since I strongly suspect that a notion of it prevails which is very remote from the truth; for it is believed that there is a true accident, affection, or quality, really inherent in the substance by which we feel ourselves heated. This much I have to say, that as soon as I form a conception of a material or corporeal substance, I simultaneously feel the necessity of conceiving that it has boundaries, and is of some shape or other; that relatively to others it is great or small; that it is in this or that place, in this or that time; that it is in motion or at rest; that it touches, or does not touch another body; that it is unique, rare, or common; nor can I, by any act of imagination, disjoin it from these qualities; but I do not find myself absolutely compelled to apprehend it as necessarily accompanied by such conditions as that it must be white or red, bitter or sweet, sonorous or silent, smelling sweetly or disagreeably; and if the senses had not pointed out these qualities, it is probable that language and imagination alone could never have arrived at them. Therefore I am inclined to think that these tastes, smells, colours, &c., with regard to the object in which they appear to reside, are nothing more than mere names, and exist only in the sensitive body; insomuch that when the living creature is removed, all these qualities are carried off and annihilated; although we have imposed particular names upon them (different from those other and real accidents), and would fain persuade ourselves that they truly and in fact exist. But I do not believe that there exists anything in external bodies for exciting tastes, smells and sounds, but size, shape, quantity, and motion, swift or slow; and if ears, tongues, and noses were removed, I am of opinion that shape, quantity, and motion would remain, but there would be an end of smells, tastes, and sounds, which, abstractedly from the living creature, I take to be mere words."

If we knew nothing else about Galileo except that in the October of the year 1623 he published this extract, we should know for certain that a man of the highest philosophic genius then existed. On the subject of this extract, he leaves nothing for Descartes and Locke to do, except to repeat his statement in their own language, and to emphasize its philosophic importance. Indeed in many ways this original statement by Galileo is, as I believe, more accurately and carefully drawn than the usual formulations of modern times which I followed in my introductory remark.

I will now quit the special consideration of Galileo and Newton. I hope that I have with sufficient clearness given my reasons for holding that they are to be considered as the parents of modern science and as the joint authors of the first physical synthesis. You cannot disentangle their work. There would have been no Newton without Galileo; and it is hardly a paradox to say, that there would have been no Galileo without Newton. Galileo was the Julius Cæsar and Newton the Augustus Cæsar of the empire of science.

But these men did not work in a vacuum. It was an age of ferment, and they had as contemporaries men with genius all but equal to theirs. Francis Bacon was a contemporary of Galileo, somewhat older (1561–1626). I need not remind you that Bacon was the apostle of the experimental method. He especially emphasized the importance of keeping our minds open throughout a careful and prolonged examination of the facts. Like all apostles he somewhat exaggerated his message, and perhaps undervalued the importance of provisional theories. But the main point is perfectly correct and particularly important in view of the tradition of the preceding 1500 years, during which experiment had languished. Aristotle had discovered the importance of classification, and neither he nor his followers had realized the danger of classification proceeding on slight and trivial grounds. The greatest curse to the progress of science is a hasty classification based on trivialities. An example of what I mean is Aristotle's classification of motions into violent and natural. Bacon's writings were a continual protest against this pitfall. Again the active life of Descartes lies between those of Galileo and Newton. He published his *Principia Philosophiae* in 1644, just two years after the date which I have assigned as the symbolic centre of the epoch. The general concepts of space and matter, body and spirit, as they have permeated the scientific world, are largely in accordance with the way in which he fashioned them. He viewed space as a property of matter and therefore rejected the idea of purely empty space. This conception of space as an essential plenum led him to speculate on the other physical characteristics of the stuff whose extension is space. He thus hit on the idea of the vortices which carry along the heavenly bodies. These vortices are a failure. For one thing, they show that Descartes had not really assimilated the full import of Galileo's work in his discovery of the first law of motion. The planets do not want anything to carry them along, and that is just what Descartes provides. But for all that I hold that Descartes with his plenum was groping towards a very important truth which I will endeavour to explain before I finish this lecture. Newton's formulation of gravitation led Newton's followers to insist on the possibility of a vacuum, but the nineteenth century again filled space with an ether. Finally Einstein has recurred to the inversion of Descartes' doctrine and has made matter a property of space. The Newtonian vacuum and the Cartesian plenum have fought a very equal duel during the last few centuries. Leibniz, Newton's contemporary, emphasized the relativity of space.

This mention of relativity leads me to my last topic, which is to ask, how to-day we would criticize this First Physical Synthesis which we owe to the seventeenth century.

In the first place, if we are wise, before criticizing it we will stop to admire it, and to note its essential services to science, and (in its main outlines) its continuing value to-day. We must do honour to the century of genius to which we owe it — a century which will compare with the greatest that Greece can show.

By a criticism of the great physical synthesis which is the legacy of this century to science I do not mean a mere enumeration of the additions since made, for example, the rise of the concept of energy, of the atomic theory, or of the theory of various chemical elements. Such homogeneous additions leave the concept undisturbed. In this way, Kelvin made it the mainspring of all his scientific speculations. But for the last thirty years or so, the great ideas of the seventeenth century have, so to speak, been losing their dominating grip on physical science.

Clerk-Maxwell probably thought that he had finally established its ascendancy. In truth, he had set going trains of thought which in the hands of his followers have caused it to totter. Galileo and his followers thought in terms of time, space, and matter. They were in fact more Aristotelian than they knew—though they wore their Aristotle with a difference. Clerk-Maxwell emphasized the importance of the electromagnetic field as an interplay of relations between various electromagnetic quantities. Maxwell himself looked on this field as merely expressing strains, stresses, and motions of the ether, a point of view quite in the Galilean tradition. But recently the field itself has come to be conceived as the ultimate fact, and properties of matter have been explained in terms of it. Thus energy, mass, matter, chemical elements are now expressed as electromagnetic phenomena. The ether is still there for those who like it, but it merely serves to allay the tortures of a metaphysical craving.

But Einstein and Minkowski have gone farther. Hitherto time and space have been treated as separate and independent factors in the scheme of things. They have combined them. This is a complete refashioning of older ideas and is in many ways much more consonant with the Cartesian point of view.

The world as we observe it involves process and extension. Hitherto process has been identified with serial time, and extension with space. But this neglects the fact that there is an extension of time. Conceive any ultimate concrete fact as an extended process. If you have lost process or lost extension, you know that you are dealing with abstraction. What is going on here in this room is extended process. Extension and process are each abstractions. But these abstractions can be made in different ways. The space which we apprehend as extension without process and the time which we apprehend as serial process without spatial extension are not each unique. In different circumstances we affix different meanings to the notion of space, and different meanings to the correlative notion of time. In respect to space there is no paradox in this assertion. For us the space of this room is a definite volume; for a man in the sun the room is sweeping through space. But it is paradoxical to hold that the serial process which we apprehend as time is different from the serial process which the man in the sun apprehends as time. Yet if you do that, you can introduce mathematical formulæ expressing spatio-temporal measurements which at one sweep explain a whole multitude of perplexing scientific observation. In fact the formulæ practically have to be admitted, and the theory is the simplest explanation of them. Also philosophically the closer association of time and space is a great advantage.

We now come back to Descartes. He conceived extension as essentially a quality of matter. Generalize his idea: the ultimate fact is not static matter but the flux of physical existence: call any part of this flux, with all its fullness of content and happening, an event: extension is essentially a quality of events and so is process. But the becomingness of nature is not to be constricted within one serial linear procession of time. It requires an indefinite number of such processions to express the complete vision.

If this line of thought, which is that underlying the modern relativity, be admitted, the whole synthesis of the seventeenth century has to be recast. Its Time, its Space, and its Matter are in the melting-pot—and there we must leave them.

2

PHILOSOPHICAL PROBLEMS OF PHYSICS

Introduction

Einstein's relativity theory and the quantum theory are both products of the twentieth century, and their physical and philosophical consequences are still being explored and exploited in great detail. They are highly sophisticated scientific theories, and the mathematical techniques they utilize are advanced and subtle. Nevertheless, it is possible for a layman to understand these theories, as we shall see, and without the distortion and caricature that occurs in the so-called "popular" presentations of science. I cannot attempt a detailed or exhaustive review of these theories, but I shall try, while staying true to the general sense of the theories, to make clear the points which have the greatest philosophical significance and interest.

1.

Einstein's "theory of relativity" is, in fact, two theories; he first elaborated the *restricted theory* in 1905 and ten years later the *general theory*. I will consider each one in turn, but neither can be understood well without some historical background.

Thomas Young in 1801 revived Christian Huygens' wave theory of light and succeeded in getting it accepted over Newton's corpuscular theory because the latter could not account for certain facts about optical interference. According to the Huygens-Young physical model, light consists of waves which spread out from a center "much like those caused by a stone's falling into a quiet pond except that they were three dimensional – that is, spherical rather than circular." However, if light consists of waves then, like waves of water, they must have some medium in which to be carried. To meet this need, Huygens and Young hypothesized a "luminiferous ether" which is supposedly an invisible substance distributed uniformly throughout space so it can propagate light everywhere and itself moving at right angles to the direction of the light waves. Scientists worried about this concept since it was not mathematically defined and seemed elusive, but, after all, they had got along well with non-observable entities before. But trouble was not slow in coming, and when it arrived could not conveniently be ignored!

The trouble with the ether concept came about in this way. When a body moves through the ether one of two things must happen: either the moving body carries the neighboring ether along with it at its own velocity or else the body moves through the ether at a velocity different from the ether's. Now scientists, for several reasons which we do not need to examine, rejected the notion that the earth, moving in its orbit, carries the neighboring ether along with it at its own velocity. Consequently, they concluded that the earth moves through the ether at a velocity different from the ether's. This hypothesis happily gave rise to a consequence which could be tested experimentally. If an observer on the earth sent out a light signal, it should travel faster when it moves in the direction of the ether's movement than when it moves opposite or at right angles to it. Michelson and Morley decided to test this consequence in their now famous experiment.

> They sent out light-signals in two directions at right angles; each was reflected from a mirror, and came back to the place from which both had been sent out. Now anybody can verify, either by trial or by a little arithmetic, that it takes longer to row a given distance on a river up-stream and then back again, than it takes to row the same distance across the stream and back again. Therefore, if there were an ether wind, one of the two light-signals, which consist of waves in the ether, ought to have travelled to the mirror and back at a slower average rate than the other. Michelson and Morley tried the experiment . . . but not the smallest difference could be observed. The result was a surprise to them as to everybody else; but careful repetitions made doubt impossible.[1]

One could, of course, interpret the Michelson-Morley experiment by saying that the earth must carry the neighboring ether along with it at its own velocity. But this alternative, as I mentioned, scientists already had rejected. Consequently, since the ether apparently neither shares the earth's velocity nor differs from it, the concept had become incomprehensible and had to be abandoned. However, the difficulties were only beginning. The Michelson-Morley experiment suggested that the velocity of light is a constant, independent of the direction of its propagation and the motion of its source. That is, the velocity of light is the same if its source (the earth, say) is moving in the direction of the propagation of light or away from it! It is impossible, in short, to add to the velocity of light. This characteristic of light is puzzling even to common sense. "Everyone knows that if you are on an escalator you reach the top sooner if you walk up than if you stand still. But if the escalator moved with the velocity of light (which it does not do even in New York), you would reach the top at exactly the same moment whether you walked up or stood still."[2] But this characteristic of light was even more disturbing to the physicist since it upset the foundations of mechanics. Galileo's parallelogram principle enables one to combine two forces or motions into a resultant force or motion, but according to this new principle of light propagation one motion added to another, as far as light is concerned, makes no difference whatever! To avoid contradiction between mechanics and light theory, physicists tried persistently to measure a change in the velocity of light with change of motion or direction of the light's source or the observer's position, but they failed so consistently that they began to suspect a "conspiracy of nature" against them! Eventually, however, they had to accept the "conspiracy of nature" as a law of nature — that is, accept the fact of the constancy of the velocity of light and try to reconcile it with the traditional concepts of Galilean mechanics.

H. A. Lorentz in 1893 made the first important attempt at reconciliation. He constructed a new principle for calculating the values of combined motions, which, for relatively low velocities, approximated Galileo's parallelogram principle. But his principle deviated more and more from the old principle as velocities increased until, with the speed of light, added motion caused no further change in velocity at all. This new principle for combining motions became known as the "Lorentz Transformation Principle." To explain this new principle Lorentz took over and developed the Fitzgerald "contraction hypothesis," according to which a body, when in motion, actually be-

[1] Bertrand Russell, *The ABC of Relativity*, revised edition, edited by Felix Pirani (London: George Allen and Unwin, Ltd., 1958), pp. 25–26. In addition to Russell's book I found helpful, and recommend to students, Leopold Infeld's *Albert Einstein: His Work and Its Influence on Our World* (New York: Charles Scribner's Sons, 1950).

[2] Russell, *op. cit.*, p. 28.

comes shorter in the direction of its motion. The greater its velocity the shorter it gets until, with the velocity of light, it would have no length at all! Consequently, since velocity is a function of distance travelled per unit of time, and since at the velocity of light the value of length disappears, there is, of course, no way to determine any further velocity to add to that of light. Unhappily, this contraction hypothesis could not be checked experimentally since presumably all measuring rods would be subject to it. But this sort of strategy will not do in science, for it "resembles nothing so much as the White Knight's plan 'to dye one's whiskers green, and always use so large a fan that they could not be seen' "!

It was at this point that Einstein advanced his radically new theory, his restricted theory of relativity. In this theory, proposed in 1905, Einstein accepted the constancy of the velocity of light as a law of nature and, by re-interpreting Lorentz's transformation formula, squared it with Galileo's parallelogram principle. When Einstein was through, the need for a physical model such as was involved in the contraction hypothesis had vanished.

Einstein argued in the following way. Suppose an observer who is stationary on the ground describes the motion of a rocket, and another observer on a train moving at a constant velocity with respect to the ground also describes the motion of the same rocket. The two observers will find the equations of motion for the rocket to be the same but the values of the spatial and temporal measurements entering the equation at any time will be different. The Lorentz transformation formula, Einstein then showed, can be interpreted not as specifying graduated deviations from the parallelogram principle but as specifying mathematical relationships between the measurements made in the two systems, in which case the values of the measurements can be translated from one system into another.

> [Einstein] accepted Lorentz's transformation principle for the amounts of the changes involved, but said that these occurred in the spatial and temporal units themselves. More accurately, he said that they were to be located not in the spatial and temporal units of any given observer but only in those used for translating his observations of particular motions into statements of how another spectator, moving relative to him, would observe them. . . . One observed in any particular system whatever one observed, and this gave one the true facts; one was not to indulge in any magical juggling of space and time. But calculation of how *the other fellow,* writing up what one saw but putting it in terms of another "system of coordinates," would describe it was another matter. Here Lorentz's transformation equations had to be used.[3]

Numerous consequences follow from this transformation procedure of which, perhaps, the following are the most interesting examples. (1) "The velocity of a motion on a moving body is less when measured by a 'stationary' observer than when measured by an observer on the moving body"; (2) "The mass of a body in motion is greater when measured by a stationary observer than when measured by an observer moving with the body"; and (3) "The length of a moving body (say an airplane) is shorter when measured by a stationary observer than when measured by an observer on the airplane."[4] Consequence (3), note carefully, is Einstein's re-interpretation of the Fitzgerald contraction hypothesis. No longer do physical bodies shrink and grow but the values of the measurements *vary* from one inertial system to another.

In order to transform values from one inertial system to another, Einstein had to introduce the concept of an event being *simultaneous for two separate systems.* Previous

[3] Everett W. Hall, *Modern Science and Human Values,* pp. 246–247.

[4] Marshall J. Walker, "An Orientation Toward Modern Physical Theory," *Scientific Monthly,* 81, 1955, p. 30.

physicists simply had taken for granted the meaningfulness of 'simultaneity' – and, to be sure, it is meaningful in ordinary experience. I say, for example, that I directly experience the simultaneous occurrence of being hungry and wishing for a steak. But the simultaneous occurrence of two events in two separate inertial systems is quite a different matter. In order to say that two events, say one on the earth and the other on Mars, occurred simultaneously, one would need to establish a synchronization of clocks at the two places. In order to do this, one would have to go through this measuring procedure: a light signal would be fired at zero time on the earth clock, and the clock on Mars is set at zero time *when the light signal arrives*. Thus the clocks on earth and Mars are "synchronized." But, of course, you object, they are not *really* synchronized since we must take into account the time it takes the light signal to get from earth to Mars. But, in fact, we *cannot* take it into account, since any effort to calculate it would be circular. The only way to calculate it would be to have the clocks on earth and Mars already synchronized! The conclusion Einstein drew is fascinating and significant indeed. "It had been assumed that an absolute time existed such that any timers anywhere could be synchronized with it. Nature was pointing out most emphatically that such absolute time does not exist. . . . It is as nonsensical to expect to find the same 'time' at two different places as it is to expect to find the same 'point' at two different places." [5]

We have talked a good deal about the restricted theory of relativity without saying in what sense it is restricted – a deficiency we must repair at once since we are now ready to examine several points of philosophical interest in the general theory. Einstein's early theory is "restricted" in the sense that it is limited to inertial systems moving with a *constant relative velocity*. The general theory, on the other hand, concerns systems moving with *variable relative velocity* – that is, where acceleration or change of direction occurs. Here the proper interpretation of gravity is the main problem. (The general theory includes all the postulates of the restricted theory, but not vice-versa; hence their names.)

In order to understand the highlights of the general theory, you should also know something of its historical background. Consider this simple formulation of Newton's law of gravitation: "Any two masses are attracted toward each other by a force directly proportional to the product of the masses and inversely proportional to the square of the distance between their centers." Now this concept of gravitational force, from the very beginning, had some unhappy features. Gravity acted instantaneously over huge distances – say between the earth and sun – so it appeared to act quite independently of spatial separation. Yet, on the other hand, the law itself states that the force is a function of distance – the further away the objects, the less the force. Moreover, when gravitational force acts between two far distant objects it apparently needs a physical medium between the objects through which it can travel. Consequently, the concept of the all permeating ether was again called upon, this time to explain the action-at-a-distance of gravity. But, as we have seen, the concept of the ether, dubious to begin with, had become completely untenable by the end of the nineteenth century.

Einstein, taking his cue from the restricted theory, reinterpreted Newton's law of gravity in a way which resolved these perennial difficulties. Instead of thinking of gravity as a force which, acting at a distance, *causes* acceleration, he conceived of it simply as another way of *describing acceleration* – namely, from another frame of reference taken as stationary. Say an elevator cable

[5] *Ibid.*

breaks and the elevator is falling down its shaft. According to Einstein, if one takes the earth as a stationary frame of reference, then the elevator can be described as accelerating downwards as a result of the gravitational pull of the earth; but if he takes the elevator as a stationary frame of reference, then the objects outside of it can be described as uniformly accelerating upward. 'Gravity,' then, is simply the translation of the acceleration of the elevator frame of reference into that of the earthly one.

Einstein also found in dealing with gravity and its effects that he could better "save the appearances" if he assumed that space had certain non-Euclidean properties instead of the traditional Euclidean ones ascribed to it by Newton. In order to understand this new way of looking at space, consider this imaginary example, in two-dimensional space, of Einstein's procedure. Imagine a being capable of experiencing only two dimensions — call him a Flatlander. He lives on the surface of a big sphere but has traveled such a small area that it seems to him like a Euclidean plane. When he measures a small right triangle he finds, within certain limits, that the Pythagorean theorem holds; and when he measures the angles of his triangle, he discovers that their sum is 180°. All goes well; space apparently is Euclidean. But then he travels and makes measurements over large areas and discovers that the orthodox Euclidean results no longer occur: the Pythagorean theorem breaks down seriously and the angles may add up to anything from 180° to 540°! Then a Flatland mathematician proposes a solution to this theoretical difficulty. Although the lines of the triangles we measure look straight to us Flatlanders, nevertheless we must postulate that they are, in fact, curved. We cannot directly experience this curvature, to be sure, but we must infer it, or postulate it, in order to explain our measurements and relate them in a mathematically coherent way. "This *curvature of space* was nonsense, as any Flatlander could see, but the mathematician used the concept and succeeded in predicting the results already observed"!

Einstein, of course — and this is the crucial point — followed this same procedure for our three-dimensional world: If we are to explain the results of physics already observed, he said, then we must assume that space in the vicinity or "neighborhood" of objects of great mass is *curved* or *distorted.* Let us see quite briefly what this new motion entailed for celestial mechanics.

The shortest distance between two points in any given space varies; on a plane surface it is a straight line, on a sphere it is a great circle, etc. Physicists use the word 'geodesic' to mean 'shortest distance' whatever the space may be. Now using the concept of geodesic Einstein explained celestial movements in the following way: A moving planet moves "naturally" along a geodesic at constant velocity. Thus the earth moves around the sun, for example, because the mass of the sun has curved or deformed space so that the shape of the earth's elliptical orbit is a geodesic. We are now finally in a position to see more clearly just how radically Einstein changed Newton's concept of gravity. No longer is gravity conceived to be a force which operates between masses at great distances but it is rather a local feature of space itself!

2.

I said earlier, you recall, that I would examine only those elements of relativity theory which have some philosophical implications — without, of course, being false to the sense of the theory as a whole. Now, assuming we are reasonably clear about these elements of the theory, we are ready to investigate their philosophical implications. The implications which have actually been drawn are numerous indeed but, as we shall see, not all of them have been drawn legitimately or correctly.

Philosophical Misinterpretations. There are so many misinterpretations of relativity theory that it would be difficult to list all of them, let alone analyze them. Einstein has shown that everything is relative, including moral judgments; he has shown that there is a fourth dimension which, if we look hard enough, we may discover someday; he has introduced a mental element into the description of physical reality itself — these are, perhaps, the most hideous examples of the misrepresentation of relativity theory. Let us take a moment to unravel the last one of these distortions since it is one quite commonly encountered.

According to this view, physical science previous to relativity theory never admitted a mental element in its description of the natural world; the observer himself, so to speak, never figured in the outcome of his observations and calculations. Now, however, the matter is different: in relativity theory we cannot separate the observer from what he observes; consequently, there is a genuine mental element in the very description of physical reality itself. But what does it mean in this argument to say "in relativity theory we cannot separate the observer from what he observes"? Apparently, this sentence refers to the fact that in relativity theory one cannot simply say, "This table has a length of three feet," but must say, "This table has a length of three feet with respect to a frame of reference S." Sometimes, for the sake of convenience and simplicity, one replaces the phrase, 'with respect to a frame of reference S' with 'for observer x,' so that the sentence simply reads, 'This table is three feet long for observer x.' Then it follows that the table has a different length for observer y (in another frame of reference), and the appearance unfortunately is created that the observer "makes a difference" and that a mental element is introduced into physical science. However, consider what the observer in any frame of reference does. He observes coincidences between marks on the yardstick and the edge of the table and, whatever the speed of his system, he or any other observer without sensory impediments will always observe the same coincidences. Since the observer is constant, then, no reference to him is necessary in talking about differences of length; one had better say, to avoid misunderstanding, that the table has a different length for different frames of reference. Consequently, since the observer plays no different role in relativity theory than in traditional physics, relativity does not admit a "mental element" into its physical descriptions and thus is not, contrary to the argument we have examined, a radical departure from ordinary physical science.

The Nature of Scientific Inference. There may appear to be a question whether relativity theory fits the pattern of scientific inference which I sketched at the beginning of Chapter 1, namely, the formation, development, and test of hypotheses. After all, you may argue, relativity theory appears to offer new concepts for traditional ones like absolute time, provide translation formulas, etc., instead of proposing new physical hypotheses; and it appears to be accepted because it eliminates perennial problems about gravity rather than because it has been experimentally confirmed. Such a view, as a matter of fact, would not be false but simply would not tell the whole truth. Relativity theory, to be sure, is a re-interpretation of space and time, but it is also a genuinely new hypothesis about the nature of physical reality since it gives rise to a set of observable consequences which are, in part, different from those of the Newtonian hypothesis.

According to Einstein's theory, a massive object like the sun distorts space in its vicinity. As a result, when a light ray, which travels along a geodesic, passes close to the sun, it will be bent toward the sun in an appreciable amount. This consequence, of course, does not follow from the Newtonian hypothesis which involves no concept of the distortion of space. Moreover, Einstein's theory is not accepted only because it relieves Newtonian mechanics of certain difficulties but also because its consequences which are different from the Newtonian, like the one above, have been tested experimentally and found to hold in fact. The bending effect, as a matter of fact, "has been observed during a total eclipse of the sun as a shift in the apparent position of stars whose light rays pass close to the sun." [6] The conclusion, I take it, is that relativity theory exhibits the same form of scientific inference which Galileo pointed out at the very beginning of modern science.

Furthermore, relativity theory helps to demolish certain "rationalistic" interpretations of scientific inference and the nature of space which philosophers have offered frequently in the past as alternatives to Galileo's view. Since Immanuel Kant perhaps stated this alternative view more clearly than anyone else, let us look for a moment at his work and the way in which relativity theory affects it.

Kant, following Newton, conceived of space as a vast receptacle which includes all of the physical universe – a view supported by ordinary language when, for example, we speak of objects *in space,* not simply as having spatial relations. (This view is sometimes called the *absolute* theory of space, since all objects have an exact, or absolute, location in it independently of its relative location in respect to other physical objects.)

Euclidean geometry, Kant continued, uniquely determines the properties of this space (or, simply, describes its characteristics) in a way which gives us *synthetic a priori knowledge,* by which he meant knowledge of the physical world which is necessarily true, not simply probably true as Galileo held. For example, axioms like "There is only one straight line which connects two points," Kant thought are *self-evidently true,* by which he meant that if one understands the meanings of the concepts in the axioms then he also sees they must be true – and true of our physical world. Further, these self-evidently true axioms, along with definitions of new terms, yield, through deductive manipulation, further truths which are necessary (since all deductive connections are necessary). Now, Kant says, these axioms and theorems constitute a physical system which, in the form of Newtonian mechanics, not simply holds true for our world but, given the necessity peculiar to each type of proposition, *necessarily* holds true for our world – not only probably, as Galileo held.

At this point Kant set himself the most crucial question of all, he thought: namely, *how must we conceive the nature of space in order to explain how this synthetic a priori knowledge of its properties is possible?* Kant argued in the following way. Space, of course, must also be a necessary notion, not simply an empirical one, if we are to explain our necessary knowledge of its properties. But then space can neither be directly perceived nor indirectly conceived as a generalization of, or abstraction from, experience since in either case its origin would be empirical and could lead only to probable knowledge. Consequently, the only alternative, he argued, is that space is an original intuition of the perceiving mind itself, by which he meant "a mental form which molds all possible empirical experience." It is the nature of the perceiving mind, so to speak, to see things *in space* and *in time.* The necessity of the notion of space comes from its non-physical origin; it is a necessary way of perceiving since it is a condition imposed on knowledge by the very nature of the perceiving mind itself. Space, then, Kant concluded, does not exist apart from the knowing or perceiving mind (or, at any rate, if it does, we can never know it!).

Kant reinforced this argument in different ways. For example, he wrote that one

[6] Cf. E. A. Abbott, *Flatland,* seventh edition.

cannot learn the notion of space through experience of external objects and their relations since they are already, and from the first, perceived *in space*. The notion, then, must be *a priori* – that is, exist before, and independently of, any experience of matter of fact – and this is only possible if it is a form of perception of the mind itself. Or, again, he wrote that while one is able to "think away" all objects in space, he cannot think away space itself – it must always be there, so to speak, if anything is. The notion of space, then, must be *necessarily* present in consciousness, in perception, and this, again, is only possible if it is a form of perception of the mind itself and not a result of the objects of perception or their relations.

As you may well see already, the relativity views of geometry and space differ sharply from Kant's. First, the contemporary view of geometry, which distinguishes pure geometry from physical geometry, makes it highly doubtful that geometry provides synthetic *a priori* knowledge – that is, knowledge about the physical world which is necessarily true; and if this view of geometry is the correct one, then the whole foundation of Kant's argument about space collapses, to say nothing of its superstructure. The contemporary view of geometry began to form soon after Kant's death when various non-Euclidean geometries were invented by the mathematicians John Bolyai, N. I. Lobachevski, K. F. Gauss, and B. Riemann. When Euclid's geometry was the only one, it seemed especially clear that it not only did apply to the physical world but must do so. With the advent of non-Euclidean geometries, however, the picture changed: since there were alternative geometries, it became an empirical matter to discover which one applied to our world. Moreover, when Einstein successfully adapted Riemannian geometry to physical theory and introduced the concept of curved space to "save the appearances" better than Newton had done, he showed conclusively not only that Euclidean geometry is not necessarily true of our world but not true at all of the world on an astronomical scale – and only approximately true for small areas and areas of small masses.

Kant's view of geometry and space seems less tenable nowadays for an even more fundamental reason, partly made clear again by Einstein's work. Axioms are no longer conceived to be self-evidently true for the very good reason that they are no longer conceived to be *true* at all! I will only briefly mention this point since Carl Hempel explains and develops it in the following selection, "Geometry and Empirical Science."

Consider the simple deductive argument: All men are mortal; Socrates is a man; Socrates is mortal. The validity of this argument in no way depends upon the factual meaning of the words 'man,' 'mortal,' and 'Socrates'; instead it depends upon the correct use in the argument of the logical words 'all,' 'is,' and 'are' and the proper relations among word positions. As far as the logical development of consequences is concerned, the argument might just as well be,

All x are y
z is x.
―――――
z is y.

The same point holds true for geometry. Axioms can be elaborated deductively without any references to the meanings of the spatial terms which occur in them. Thus, these axioms are like 'All x are y'; they are not sentences at all which are true or false but only sentence *forms* which innumerable sentences can satisfy. The question of the truth or falsity of axioms does not arise until the undefined terms occurring in them are interpreted or defined in some physical way – as when 'All x are y' is interpreted as 'All men are mortal.' Then the axioms have become physical hypotheses which are either true or false and must be confirmed in the old logically invalid way. So Galileo, after all, appears to be right again.

Moreover, relativity theory seems to make Kant's additional arguments for his view of space pointless. If space at large is non-Euclidean, instead of absolute and Euclidean in the way Kant conceived it, then it is neither *a priori* nor *necessary* and the search for the grounds of its apriority and necessity become pointless. The space of relativity is not *a priori* although, to be sure, it is not directly perceived or learned from experience. It is, as Einstein said, a concept freely invented by the mathematical and intellectual imagination to explain what is directly observed. This independence of experience, however, does not make it *a priori* in Kant's sense since, as we have seen, the concept of curved space – whatever its origin – becomes in relativity theory a hypothesis about actual space which must be tested by experience (experiment) to see if it does, in fact, hold true. Nor is the relativity concept of space *necessarily* present whenever one perceives anything at all (because, as Kant said, you can never "think away" space) since the notion of curved space does not occur in any phenomenal way at all, either as itself a matter of perception or as a form which determines the nature of perception. Therefore, if the relativity concept of space at large is correct, and it is neither *a priori* nor necessarily present in perception, then a Kantian apparently loses these reasons, too, for claiming that space must be an original form of perception of the mind itself.

Finally, the relativity notion of space seems directly opposed to the final conclusion toward which all of Kant's arguments point, namely, that space does not exist apart from the perceiving mind (or, at any rate, if it does, we can never know it), since, on this view, space itself has physical properties. The distortions of space, you recall, provide the geodesics which masses like the planets follow; the nature of space, one might say, "determines" the orbits of the planets. Now clearly if space itself has these physical properties, it is indeed difficult to see how space can be interpreted to be a function of the perceiving mind.

Kant presented his "rationalistic" interpretation of science in his famous *Critique of Pure Reason,* of which the major part of the Introduction is reprinted in the following selections. Kant here clearly characterizes the nature of *synthetic a priori* knowledge and indicates why he thinks mathematical propositions, as well as some propositions of physics, must be interpreted as examples of *synthetic a priori* knowledge. The *Critique,* then, is designed to explain how such knowledge, which, Kant believed, we indubitably have, is *possible.* Carl Hempel, in his article on "Geometry and Empirical Science" presents the contemporary empirical viewpoint, namely, that mathematical assertions are not *synthetic a priori* propositions since they are neither true nor false at all! As we saw, if this view of mathematics is true, then the whole foundation of Kant's argument collapses.

Concepts and Meaning. But why, after all, should anyone accept as meaningful such an unobservable concept as 'curved space,' or, for that matter, 'ideal gas,' 'electric field,' 'gene,' 'habit strength,' or any other scientific concept which does not refer to observable objects and events? Obviously because they are related in some way to direct experience. But what is this relationship?

Some empirical philosophers of the nineteenth century suggested that the unobservable or theoretical concepts of physics are either abstractions from, or generalizations of, what is directly experienced. These concepts of physics do not refer to real entities which exist apart from, or independently of, experience but are simply economical ways of expressing the regularities and relationships among our experiences (sensations, perceptions, or whatever). External reality, in short, consists in what it is experienced to be – there is nothing unobservable or hidden behind the observable phenomena. Einstein, in his philosophical writings, strenuously objects to this nineteenth century empirical or positivistic view and thinks it must be mistaken for several reasons. First, the unobservable concepts of physics cannot be abstractions from, or generalizations of, direct experience since it is possible to exhibit two theories with essentially different concepts; namely, Newtonian and relativity physics, which nevertheless both lead in large measure to agreement with direct experience. Second, the theoretical concepts of physics are not simply economic "summaries" of the relations of sensations; they are, rather, free creations of the mathematical imagination which refer to entities that exist even though not directly experienced. External reality, in short, Einstein believed, is whatever it is imagined to be, provided, of course, there is some experiential evidence for accepting it.

Einstein's actual work in relativity theory, however, itself inspired new empirical or positivistic interpretations of the relation between theoretical concepts and direct experience. These two interpretations were the Vienna Circle's logical positivism and P. W. Bridgman's operationism. The decisive part of Einstein's theory, for both views, was his definition of non-local simultaneity. Before Einstein, you recall, physicists simply assumed that it made sense to say that two events in separate inertial systems happened at the same instant. They thought there was an absolute time so that clocks anywhere could be synchronized with it. Einstein showed, however, that this operation could not be carried out; hence the concept of absolute time is meaningless. He discovered an operation, however – using a ray of light, as we saw, for the relative synchronization of clocks; hence the concept of relative time, and relative simultaneity, is meaningful. So the logical positivists, generalizing this procedure, said that a theoretical concept is meaningful if and only if there is an observational criterion for its use. Bridgman, along the same lines, declared that a theoretical concept is meaningful only if there is a public, repeatable operation by which it is established – or, as some people have come to say, only if it is "operationally defined."

The logical positivists and Bridgman originally felt that *every* theoretical concept had to have a criterion of use, or had to have an operation which established it, and that *every* hypothesis using them had to be tested by direct experience. Einstein, however, explicitly rejected this new version of positivism, also. He wrote the following comments in 1949:

> In order to be able to consider a logical system as physical theory it is not necessary to demand that all of its assertions can be independently interpreted and "tested" "operationally"; *de facto* this has never yet been achieved by any theory and can not at all be achieved. In order to be able to consider a theory as a *physical* theory it is only necessary that it implies empirically testable assertions in general.[7]

Any more stringent restriction on the admissibility of concepts, he suggests, would not only give a false view of the logical structure of science but also would be a psychological block for scientists in their imaginative search for new concepts. The logical positivists, also, with Rudolph Carnap leading the way on this problem, came to believe that their original requirement was too stringent. A theoretical concept, he points out, may receive some or all of its meaning from the *system* of concepts in which it occurs (including the implicit restrictions an axiom set puts upon any physical interpretation), and thus the only requirement for the legitimate use of a concept is that *some* of the hypotheses which utilize a system of concepts must be empirically testable.

Einstein apparently had reservations about

[7] Paul Arthur Schilpp, editor, *Albert Einstein: Philosopher-Scientist,* p. 679.

logical positivism on still another ground—although, of course, he would certainly accept this last version of the positivistic requirement for the testability of hypotheses and the legitimate use of theoretical concepts. Einstein felt that the logical positivist, like the nineteenth-century positivist, denied that the freely invented mathematical concepts refer to physical reality—that is, to entities that exist even though not directly experienced. Has not the contemporary positivist told us that metaphysical questions like "What exists independently of perception?" are meaningless ones? But how, Einstein wondered, is this view compatible with what he took to be the programmatic aim of all physics, namely, "the complete description of a real situation as it supposedly exists irrespective of any act of observation or substantiation"? Some logical positivists, however, insist that a statement about "what exists independently of perception" is metaphysical and meaningless only if it has no empirical confirmation whatever. Statements about unobservable entities are perfectly meaningful if they are empirically confirmable; hence the modern positivistic view is compatible with Einstein's view of the aim of all physics. However, some non-positivistic philosophers have wondered if such a liberal view should be called positivism, and so the argument goes.

Albert Einstein and Philipp Frank, in their essays which follow, discuss in detail the problems and arguments of this section. Einstein argues against any rigorous requirement for scientific meaningfulness, and Frank argues that Einstein's claim and the logical positivist's final view are essentially the same. Other writers, however, have claimed that Einstein's position, although it takes elements of both, departs essentially from Kant's *a priori* philosophy and all forms of positivism as well. In your own thinking about this problem, you should try to sort out what may be terminological differences from those which may be real.

3.

The main difficulty in quantum theory is that there are two rival hypotheses about, or physical models of, the nature of matter, neither one of which can fit all the facts nor be combined with the other into a more general hypothesis. In the final two selections of this chapter, Hans Reichenbach and Stephen Körner analyze in detail the origins of this difficulty and the various remedies which have been offered. Therefore, I shall only say enough about this difficulty and the remedies to give you the proper set for reading their essays.

Early in the history of physics the atomic, or particle, hypothesis and the wave hypothesis came into conflict in explaining the nature of light. Newton suggested an atomic theory of light because if one assumes that light consists of small particles, or "corpuscles," which are propagated in straight lines, then he can explain simple facts like shadow casting and many other complex ones. Huygens and Young, as we saw, promoted the wave theory because if one assumes light is a wave, in an ether medium, then he can explain, among other things, what the atomic theory cannot, namely light interference. But in 1924 Louis de Broglie produced a mathematical theory which, he believed, allowed one not only to interpret light as both particle and wave but to interpret matter, too, as particles accompanied by waves, thus inaugurating a dual interpretation in mechanics itself. However, this particle and wave interpretation broke down, and Erwin Schrödinger suggested instead that matter itself consists only of waves. For example, "When a stone is dropped into a still pond a circular group of waves spreads out from the central disturbance. If a narrow ditch opens into the pond, a narrow section of the circular waves will travel up the ditch acting much like a particle moving along the water surface. Here we have a wave group acting like a particle." [8] But this interpretation, too, runs into trouble. The mathematical system which Schrödinger interpreted as a physical wave predicts the *probability,* or percentage-spread, that point events will occur in some specified region of space. But, then, "if we say that these 'waves of probability' are 'real' we use the word 'wave' in the same sense that it is used in expressions like 'wave of suicides' or 'wave of disease,' etc. To speak of a 'wave of flu' as a 'real wave' would be an unusual use of the word 'real.'" [9] Consequently Max Born, Werner Heisenberg, and others interpret matter to be only particles. But these particles, they say, are *indeterminate,* because one cannot specify at one moment both their position and their momentum. Moreover, their behavior is not orderly or causally understandable since their paths do not appear to be continuous! Hence the claim of the breakdown of causality in modern quantum mechanics. But what sense, after all, does it make to interpret matter as particles when these assumed particles do not act like particles should act from what we know of the macroscopic behavior of things?

Nils Bohr, seeing the difficulties of all these views, concludes, in what he calls the "principle of complementarity," that it is possible to interpret waves as real or particles as real but not both. Moreover, we cannot decide between these interpretations because, due to the indeterminate nature of the alleged particles, no crucial experiment is possible. So we seem finally to have returned to the original problem of Newton and Huygens – only this time with matter itself! The incompatible interpretations seem to be a final impasse. (Philosophical arguments have been given why one view is more acceptable than another. See, for example, Henry Morgenau's book, *The Nature of Physical Reality.*) Reichenbach and Körner, in the following selections, not only clarify and explain in detail this impasse but also suggest certain philosophical ways to interpret it.

[8] Walker, *op. cit.,* p. 34.
[9] Philipp Frank, *Philosophy of Science,* p. 244.

Empirical and A Priori Knowledge

IMMANUEL KANT

I. Of the Difference Between Pure and Empirical Knowledge

That all our knowledge begins with experience there can be no doubt. For how is it possible that the faculty of cognition should be awakened into exercise otherwise than by means of objects which affect our senses, and partly of themselves produce representations, partly rouse our powers of understanding into activity, to compare, to connect, or to separate these, and so to convert the raw material of our sensuous im-

From Introduction to 2nd Edition of *Critique of Pure Reason,* Sections I–V. Translated by J. M. D. Meiklejohn.

pressions into a knowledge of objects, which is called experience? In respect of time, therefore, no knowledge of ours is antecedent to experience, but begins with it.

But, though all our knowledge begins with experience, it by no means follows, that all arises out of experience. For, on the contrary, it is quite possible that our empirical knowledge is a compound of that which we receive through impressions, and that which the faculty of cognition supplies from itself (sensuous impressions giving merely the *occasion*), an addition which we cannot distinguish from the original element given by sense, till long practice has made us attentive to, and skilful in separating it. It is, therefore, a question which requires close investigation, and is not to be answered at first sight — whether there exists a knowledge altogether independent of experience, and even of all sensuous impressions? Knowledge of this kind is called *a priori,* in contradistinction to empirical knowledge, which has its sources *a posteriori,* that is, in experience.

But the expression, '*a priori,*' is not as yet definite enough, adequately to indicate the whole meaning of the question above stated. For, in speaking of knowledge which has its sources in experience, we are wont to say, that this or that may be known *a priori,* because we do not derive this knowledge immediately from experience, but from a general rule, which, however, we have itself borrowed from experience. Thus, if a man undermined his house, we say, 'he might know *a priori* that it would have fallen'; that is, he needed not to have waited for the experience that it did actually fall. But still, *a priori,* he could not know even this much. For, that bodies are heavy, and, consequently, that they fall when their supports are taken away, must have been known to him previously, by means of experience.

By the term 'knowledge *a priori,*' therefore, we shall in the sequel understand, not such as is independent of this or that kind of experience, but such as is absolutely so of *all* experience. Opposed to this is empirical knowledge, or that which is possible only *a posteriori,* that is, through experience. Knowledge *a priori* is either pure or impure. Pure knowledge *a priori* is that with which no empirical element is mixed up. For example, the proposition, 'Every change has a cause,' is a proposition *a priori,* but impure, because change is a conception which can only be derived from experience.

II. The Human Intellect, Even in an Unphilosophical State, Is in Possession of Certain Cognitions 'A Priori'

The question now is as to a *criterion,* by which we may securely distinguish a pure from an empirical cognition. Experience no doubt teaches us that this or that object is constituted in such and such a manner, but not that it could not possibly exist otherwise. Now, in the first place, if we have a proposition which contains the idea of necessity in its very conception, it is a judgment *a priori;* if, moreover, it is not derived from any other proposition, unless from one equally involving the idea of necessity, it is absolutely *a priori.* Secondly, an empirical judgment never exhibits strict and absolute, but only assumed and comparative universality (by induction); therefore, the most we can say is — so far as we have hitherto observed, there is no exception to this or that rule. If, on the other hand, a judgment carries with it strict and absolute universality, that is, admits of no possible exception, it is not derived from experience, but is valid absolutely *a priori.*

Empirical universality is, therefore, only an arbitrary extension of validity, from that which may be predicated of a proposition valid in most cases, to that which is asserted of a proposition which holds good in all; as, for example, in the affirmation, 'All bodies are heavy.' When, on the contrary, strict universality characterizes a judgment, it necessarily indicates another peculiar source of knowledge, namely, a faculty of cognition, *a priori.* Necessity and strict universality, therefore, are infallible tests for distinguishing pure from empirical knowledge, and are inseparably connected with each other. But as in the use of these criteria the empirical limitation is sometimes more easily detected than the contingency of the judgment, or the unlimited universality which we attach to a judgment is often a more convincing proof than its necessity, it may be advisable to use the criteria separately, each being by itself infallible.

Now, that in the sphere of human cognition we have judgments which are necessary, and in the strictest sense universal, consequently pure *a priori,* it will be an easy matter to show. If we desire an example from the sciences, we need only take any proposition in mathematics. If we cast our eyes upon the commonest operations of the understanding, the proposition, 'Every change must have a cause,' will amply serve our purpose. In the latter case, indeed, the conception of a cause so plainly involves the conception of a necessity of connection with an effect, and of a strict universality of the law, that the very notion of a cause would entirely disappear, were we to derive it, like Hume, from a frequent association of what happens with that which precedes, and the habit thence originating of connecting representations — the necessity inherent in the judgment being therefore merely subjective. Besides, without seeking for such examples of principles existing *a priori* in cognition, we might easily show that such principles are the indispensable basis of the possibility of experience itself, and consequently prove their existence *a priori.* For whence could our experience itself acquire certainty, if all the rules on which it depends were themselves empirical, and consequently fortuitous? No one, therefore, can admit the validity of the use of such rules as first principles. But, for the present, we may content ourselves with having established the fact, that we do possess and exercise a faculty of pure *a priori* cognition; and, secondly, with having pointed out the proper tests of such cognition, namely, universality and necessity.

Not only in judgments, however, but even in conceptions, is an *a priori* origin manifest. For example, if we take away by degrees from our conceptions of a body all that can be referred to mere sensuous experience — colour, hardness or softness, weight, even impenetrability — the body will then vanish; but the space which it occupied still remains, and this it is utterly impossible to annihilate in thought. Again, if we take away, in like manner, from our empirical conception of any object, corporeal or incorporeal, all properties which mere experience has taught us to connect with it, still we cannot think away those through which we cogitate it as substance, or adhering to substance, although our conception of substance is more determined than that of an object. Compelled, therefore, by that necessity with which the conception of substance forces itself upon us, we must confess that it has its seat in our faculty of cognition *a priori.*

III. Philosophy Stands in Need of a Science Which Shall Determine the Possibility, Principles, and Extent of Human Knowledge 'A Priori'

Of far more importance than all that has been above said, is the consideration that certain of our cognitions rise completely above the sphere of all possible experience, and by means of conceptions, to which there exists in the whole extent of experience no corresponding object, seem to extend the range of our judgments beyond its bounds. And just in this transcendental or supersensible sphere, where experience affords us neither instruction nor guidance, lie the investigations of *Reason,* which, on account of their importance, we consider far preferable to, and as having a far more elevated aim than, all that the understanding can achieve within the sphere of sensuous phenomena. So high a value do we set upon these investigations, that even at the risk of error, we persist in following them out, and permit neither doubt nor disregard nor indifference to restrain us from the pursuit. These unavoidable problems of mere pure reason are GOD, FREEDOM (of will), and IMMORTALITY. The science which, with all its preliminaries, has for its especial object the solution of these problems is named metaphysics—a science which is at the very outset dogmatical, that is, it confidently takes upon itself the execution of this task without any previous investigation of the ability or inability of reason for such an undertaking.

Now the safe ground of experience being thus abandoned, it seems nevertheless natural that we should hesitate to erect a building with the cognitions we possess, without knowing whence they come, and on the strength of principles, the origin of which is undiscovered. Instead of thus trying to build without a foundation, it is rather to be expected that we should long ago have put the question, how the understanding can arrive at these *a priori* cognitions, and what is the extent, validity, and worth which they may possess? We say, this is natural enough meaning by the word natural, that which is consistent with a just and reasonable way of thinking; but if we understand by the term, that which usually happens, nothing indeed could be more natural and more comprehensible than that this investigation should be left long unattempted. For one part of our pure knowledge, the science of mathematics, has been long firmly established, and thus leads us to form flattering expectations with regard to others, though these may be of quite a different nature. Besides, when we get beyond the bounds of experience, we are of course safe from opposition in that quarter; and the charm of widening the range of our knowledge is so great, that unless we are brought to a standstill by some evident contradiction, we hurry on undoubtingly in our course. This, however, may be avoided, if we are sufficiently cautious in the construction of our fictions, which are not the less fictions on that account.

Mathematical science affords us a brilliant example, how far, independently of all experience, we may carry our *a priori* knowledge. It is true that the mathematician occupies himself with objects and cognitions only in so far as they can be represented by means of intuition. But this circumstance is easily overlooked, because the said intuition can itself be given *a priori,* and therefore is hardly to be distinguished from a mere pure conception. Deceived by such a proof of the power of reason, we can perceive no limits to the extension of our knowledge. The light dove cleaving in free flight the thin air, whose resistance it feels, might imagine that her movements would be far more free and rapid in airless space. Just in the same way did Plato, abandoning the world of sense because of the narrow limits it sets to the understanding, venture upon the wings of ideas beyond it, into the void space of pure intellect. He did not reflect that he made no real progress by all his efforts; for he met with no resistance which might serve him for a support, as it were, whereon to rest, and on which he might apply his powers, in order to let the intellect acquire momentum for its progress. It is, indeed, the common fate of human reason in speculation, to finish the imposing edifice of thought as rapidly as possible, and then for the first time to begin to examine whether the foundation is a solid one or no. Arrived at this point, all sorts of excuses are sought after, in order to console us for its want of stability, or rather, indeed, to enable us to dispense altogether with so late and dangerous an investigation. But what frees us during the process of building from all apprehension or suspicion, and flatters us into the belief of its solidity, is this. A great part, perhaps the greatest part, of the business of our reason consists in the analysation of the conceptions which we already possess of objects. By this means we gain a multitude of cognitions, which although really nothing more than elucidations or explanations of that which (though in a confused manner) was already thought in our conceptions, are, at least in respect of their form, prized as new introspections; whilst, so far as regards their matter or content, we have really made no addition to our conceptions, but only disinvolved them. But as this process does furnish real *a priori* knowledge,[1] which has a sure progress and useful results, reason, deceived by this, slips in, without being itself aware of it, assertions of a quite different kind; in which, to given conceptions it adds others, *a priori* indeed, but entirely foreign to them, without our knowing how it arrives at these, and, indeed, without such a question ever suggesting itself. I shall therefore at once proceed to examine the difference between these two modes of knowledge.

IV. Of the Difference Between Analytical and Synthetical Judgments

In all judgments wherein the relation of a subject to the predicate is cogitated (I mention affirmative judgments only here; the application to negative will be very easy), this relation is possible in two different ways. Either the predicate B belongs to the subject A, as somewhat which is contained (though covertly) in the conception A; or the predicate B lies completely out of the conception A, although it stands in connection with it. In the first instance, I term the judgment analytical, in the second, synthetical. Analytical judgments (affirmative) are therefore those in which the connection of the predicate with the subject is cogitated through identity; those in which this connection is cogitated without identity, are called synthetical judgments. The former may be called *explicative*, the latter *augmentative* [2] judgments; because the former add in the predicate nothing to the conception of the subject, but only analyse it into its constituent conceptions, which were thought already in the subject, although in a confused manner; the latter add to our conceptions of the subject a predicate which was not contained in it, and which no analysis could ever have discovered therein. For example, when I say, 'All bodies are extended,' this is an analytical judgment. For I need not go beyond the conception of *body* in order to find extension connected with it, but merely analyse the conception, that is, become conscious of the manifold properties which I think in that conception, in order to discover this predicate in it: it is therefore an analytical judgment. On the other hand, when I say, 'All bodies are heavy,' the predicate is something totally different from that which I think in the mere conception of a body. By the addition of such a predicate, therefore, it becomes a synthetical judgment.

Judgments of experience, as such, are always synthetical. For it would be absurd to think of grounding an analytical judgment on experience, because in forming such a judgment I need not go out of the sphere of my conceptions, and therefore recourse to the testimony of experience is quite unnecessary. That 'bodies are extended' is not an empirical judgment, but a proposition which stands firm *a priori*. For before addressing myself to experience, I already have in my conception all the requisite conditions for the judgment, and I have only to extract the predicate from the conception, according to the principle of contradiction, and thereby at the same time become conscious of the necessity of the judgment, a necessity which I could never learn from experience. On the other hand, though at first I do not at all include the predicate of weight in my conception of

[1] Not synthetical. — *Tr.*

[2] That is, judgments which really add to and do not merely analyse or explain the conceptions which make up the sum of our knowledge. — *Tr.*

body in general, that conception still indicates an object of experience, a part of the totality of experience, to which I can still add other parts; and this I do when I recognize by observation that bodies are heavy. I can cognize beforehand by analysis the conception of body through the characteristics of extension, impenetrability, shape, etc., all which are cogitated in this conception. But now I extend my knowledge, and looking back on experience from which I had derived this conception of body, I find weight at all times connected with the above characteristics, and therefore I synthetically add to my conceptions this as a predicate, and say, 'All bodies are heavy.' Thus it is experience upon which rests the possibility of the synthesis of the predicate of weight with the conception of body, because both conceptions, although the one is not contained in the other, still belong to one another (only contingently, however), as parts of a whole, namely, of experience, which is itself a synthesis of intuitions.

But to synthetical judgments *a priori,* such aid is entirely wanting. If I go out of and beyond the conception A, in order to recognize another B as connected with it, what foundation have I to rest on, whereby to render the synthesis possible? I have here no longer the advantage of looking out in the sphere of experience for what I want. Let us take, for example, the proposition, 'Everything that happens has a cause.' In the conception of *something that happens,* I indeed think an existence which a certain time antecedes, and from this I can derive analytical judgments. But the conception of a cause lies quite out of the above conception, and indicates something entirely different from 'that which happens,' and is consequently not contained in that conception. How then am I able to assert concerning the general conception — 'that which happens' — something entirely different from that conception, and to recognize the conception of cause although not contained in it, yet as belonging to it, and even necessarily? what is here the unknown = X, upon which the understanding rests when it believes it has found, out of the conception A a foreign predicate B, which it nevertheless considers to be connected with it? It cannot be experience, because the principle adduced annexes the two representations, cause and effect, to the representation existence, not only with universality, which experience cannot give, but also with the expression of necessity, therefore completely *a priori* and from pure conceptions. Upon such synthetical, that is augmentative propositions, depends the whole aim of our speculative knowledge *a priori;* for although analytical judgments are indeed highly important and necessary, they are so, only to arrive at that clearness of conceptions which is requisite for a sure and extended synthesis, and this alone is a real acquisition.

V. In All Theoretical Sciences of Reason, Synthetical Judgments 'A Priori' Are Contained as Principles

1. Mathematical judgments are always synthetical. Hitherto this fact, though incontestably true and very important in its consequences, seems to have escaped the analysts of the human mind, nay, to be in complete opposition to all their conjectures. For as it was found that mathematical conclusions all proceed according to the principle of contradiction (which the nature of every apodeictic certainty requires), people became persuaded that the fundamental principles of the science also were recognized and admitted in the same way. But the notion is fallacious; for although a synthetical proposition can certainly be discerned by means of the principle of contradiction, this is possible only when another synthetical proposition precedes, from which the latter is deduced, but never of itself.

Before all, be it observed, that proper mathematical propositions are always judgments *a priori,* and not empirical, because they carry along with them the conception of necessity, which cannot be given by experience. If this be demurred to, it matters not; I will then limit my assertion to *pure* mathematics, the very conception of which implies that it consists of knowledge altogether non-empirical and *a priori.*

We might, indeed, at first suppose that the proposition $7 + 5 = 12$ is a merely analytical proposition, following (according to the principle of contradiction) from the conception of a sum of seven and five. But if we regard it more narrowly, we find that our conception of the sum of seven and five contains nothing more than the uniting of both sums into one, whereby it cannot at all be cogitated what this single number is which embraces both. The conception of twelve is by no means obtained by merely cogitating the union of seven and five; and we may analyse our conception of such a possible sum as long as we will, still we shall never discover in it the notion of twelve. We must go beyond these conceptions, and have recourse to an intuition which corresponds to one of the two – our five fingers, for example, or like Segner in his *Arithmetic* five points, and so by degrees, add the units contained in the five given in the intuition, to the conception of seven. For I first take the number 7, and, for the conception of 5 calling in the aid of the fingers of my hand as objects of intuition, I add the units, which I before took together to make up the number 5, gradually now by means of the material image my hand, to the number 7, and by this process, I at length see the number 12 arise. That 7 should be added to 5, I have certainly cogitated in my conception of a sum $= 7 + 5$, but not that this sum was equal to 12. Arithmetical propositions are therefore always synthetical, of which we may become more clearly convinced by trying large numbers. For it will thus become quite evident, that turn and twist our conceptions as we may, it is impossible, without having recourse to intuition, to arrive at the sum total or product by means of the mere analysis of our conceptions. Just as little is any principle of pure geometry analytical. 'A straight line between two points is the shortest,' is a synthetical proposition. For my conception of *straight* contains no notion of *quantity,* but is merely *qualitative.* The conception of the *shortest* is therefore wholly an addition, and by no analysis can it be extracted from our conception of a straight line. Intuition must therefore here lend its aid, by means of which and thus only, our synthesis is possible.

Some few principles preposited by geometricians are, indeed, really analytical, and depend on the principle of contradiction. They serve, however, like identical propositions, as links in the chain of method, not as principles – for example, $a = a$, the whole is equal to itself, or $(a + b) > a$, the whole is greater than its part. And yet even these principles themselves, though they derive their validity from pure conceptions, are only admitted in mathematics because they can be presented in intuition. What causes us here commonly to believe that the predicate of such apodeictic judgments is already contained in our conception, and that the judgment is therefore analytical, is merely the equivocal nature of the expression. We must join in thought a certain predicate to a given conception, and this necessity cleaves already to the conception. But the question is, not what we must join in thought to the given conception, but what we really think therein, though only obscurely, and then it becomes manifest, that the predicate pertains to these conceptions, necessarily indeed, yet not as thought in the conception itself, but by virtue of an intuition, which must be added to the conception.

2. The science of Natural Philosophy (Physics) contains in itself synthetical judgments *a priori,* as principles. I shall adduce two propositions. For instance, the proposition, 'In all changes of the material world, the quantity of matter remains unchanged'; or, that, 'In all communication of motion,

action and reaction must always be equal.' In both of these, not only is the necessity, and therefore their origin *a priori* clear, but also that they are synthetical propositions. For in the conception of matter, I do not cogitate its permanency, but merely its presence in space, which it fills. I therefore really go out of and beyond the conception of matter, in order to think on to it something *a priori,* which I did not think in it. The proposition is therefore not analytical, but synthetical, and nevertheless conceived *a priori;* and so it is with regard to the other propositions of the pure part of natural philosophy.

3. As to Metaphysics, even if we look upon it merely as an attempted science, yet, from the nature of human reason, an indispensable one, we find that it must contain synthetical propositions *a priori.* It is not merely the duty of metaphysics to dissect, and thereby analytically to illustrate the conceptions which we form *a priori* of things; but we seek to widen the range of our *a priori* knowledge. For this purpose, we must avail ourselves of such principles as add something to the original conception – something not identical with, nor contained in it, and by means of synthetical judgments *a priori,* leave far behind us the limits of experience; for example, in the proposition, 'the world must have a beginning,' and such like. Thus metaphysics, according to the proper aim of the science, consists merely of synthetical propositions *a priori.*

Geometry and Empirical Science

CARL G. HEMPEL

1. Introduction

The most distinctive characteristic which differentiates mathematics from the various branches of empirical science, and which accounts for its fame as the queen of the sciences, is no doubt the peculiar certainty and necessity of its results. No proposition in even the most advanced parts of empirical science can ever attain this status; a hypothesis concerning "matters of empirical fact" can at best acquire what is loosely called a high probability or a high degree of confirmation on the basis of the relevant evidence available; but however well it may have been confirmed by careful tests, the possibility can never be precluded that it will have to be discarded later in the light of new and disconfirming evidence. Thus, all the theories and hypotheses of empirical science share this provisional character of being established and accepted "until further notice," whereas a mathematical theorem, once proved, is established once and for all; it holds with that particular certainty which no subsequent empirical discoveries, however

Originally published in *The American Mathematical Monthly,* Vol. 52, 1945, pp. 7–17. Reprinted by permission of the author and The Mathematical Association of America.

unexpected and extraordinary, can ever affect to the slightest extent. It is the purpose of this paper to examine the nature of that proverbial "mathematical certainty" with special reference to geometry, in an attempt to shed some light on the question as to the validity of geometrical theories, and their significance for our knowledge of the structure of physical space.

The nature of mathematical truth can be understood through an analysis of the method by means of which it is established. On this point I can be very brief: it is the method of mathematical demonstration, which consists in the logical deduction of the proposition to be proved from other propositions, previously established. Clearly, this procedure would involve an infinite regress unless some propositions were accepted without proof; such propositions are indeed found in every mathematical discipline which is rigorously developed; they are the *axioms* or *postulates* (we shall use these terms interchangeably) of the theory. Geometry provides the historically first example of the axiomatic presentation of a mathematical discipline. The classical set of postulates, however, on which Euclid based his system, has proved insufficient for the deduction of the well-known theorems of so-called euclidean geometry; it has therefore been revised and supplemented in modern times, and at present various adequate systems of postulates for euclidean geometry are available; the one most closely related to Euclid's system is probably that of Hilbert.

2. The Inadequacy of Euclid's Postulates

The inadequacy of Euclid's own set of postulates illustrates a point which is crucial for the axiomatic method in modern mathematics: Once the postulates for a theory have been laid down, every further proposition of the theory must be proved exclusively by logical deduction from the postulates; any appeal, explicit or implicit, to a feeling of self-evidence, or to the characteristics of geometrical figures, or to our experiences concerning the behavior of rigid bodies in physical space, or the like, is strictly prohibited; such devices may have a heuristic value in guiding our efforts to find a strict proof for a theorem, but the proof itself must contain absolutely no reference to such aids. This is particularly important in geometry, where our so-called intuition of geometrical relationships, supported by reference to figures or to previous physical experiences, may induce us tacitly to make use of assumptions which are neither formulated in our postulates nor provable by means of them. Consider, for example, the theorem that in a triangle the three medians bisecting the sides intersect in one point which divides each of them in the ratio of 1:2. To prove this theorem, one shows first that in any triangle ABC (see figure) the line segment MN which connects the centers of AB and AC is parallel to BC and therefore half as long as the latter side. Then the lines BN and CM are drawn, and an examination of the triangles MON and BOC leads to the proof of the theorem. In this procedure, it is usually taken for granted that BN and CM intersect in a point O which lies between B and N as well as between C and M. This assumption is based on geometrical intuition, and indeed, it cannot be deduced from Euclid's postulates; to make it strictly demonstrable and independent of any reference to intuition, a special group of postulates has been added to those of Euclid; they

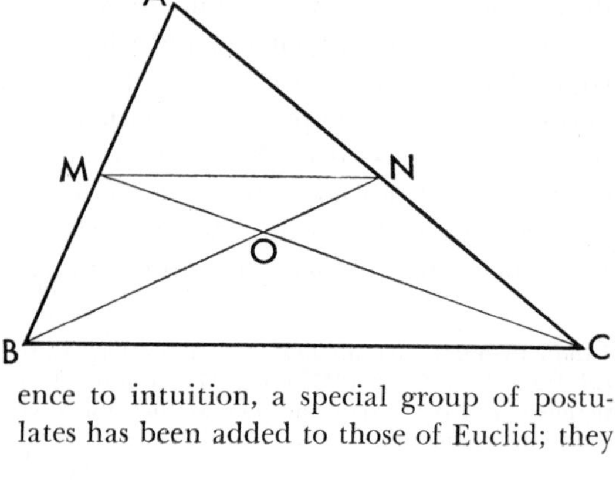

are the postulates of order. One of these — to give an example — asserts that if A, B, C are points on a straight line l, and if B lies between A and C, then B also lies between C and A. — Not even as "trivial" an assumption as this may be taken for granted; the system of postulates has to be made so complete that all the required propositions can be deduced from it by purely logical means.

Another illustration of the point under consideration is provided by the proposition that triangles which agree in two sides and the enclosed angle, are congruent. In Euclid's Elements, this proposition is presented as a theorem; the alleged proof, however, makes use of the ideas of motion and superimposition of figures and thus involves tacit assumptions which are based on our geometric intuition and on experiences with rigid bodies, but which are definitely not warranted by — *i.e.* deducible from — Euclid's postulates. In Hilbert's system, therefore, this proposition (more precisely: part of it) is explicitly included among the postulates.

3. Mathematical Certainty

It is this purely deductive character of mathematical proof which forms the basis of mathematical certainty: What the rigorous proof of a theorem — say the proposition about the sum of the angles in a triangle — establishes is not the truth of the proposition in question but rather a conditional insight to the effect that that proposition is certainly true *provided that* the postulates are true: in other words, the proof of a mathematical proposition establishes the fact that the latter is logically implied by the postulates of the theory in question. Thus, each mathematical theorem can be cast into the form

$$(P_1 \cdot P_2 \cdot P_3 \cdot \cdots \cdot P_N) \rightarrow T$$

where the expression on the left is the conjunction (joint assertion) of all the postulates, the symbol on the right represents the theorem in its customary formulation, and the arrow expresses the relation of logical implication or entailment. Precisely this character of mathematical theorems is the reason for their peculiar certainty and necessity, as I shall now attempt to show.

It is typical of any purely logical deduction that the conclusion to which it leads simply re-asserts (a proper or improper) part of what has already been stated in the premises. Thus, to illustrate this point by a very elementary example, from the premise, "This figure is a right triangle," we can deduce the conclusion, "This figure is a triangle"; but this conclusion clearly reiterates part of the information already contained in the premise. Again, from the premises, "All primes different from 2 are odd" and "n is a prime different from 2," we can infer logically that n is odd; but this consequence merely repeats part (indeed a relatively small part) of the information contained in the premises. The same situation prevails in all other cases of logical deduction; and we may, therefore, say that logical deduction — which is the one and only method of mathematical proof — is a technique of conceptual analysis: it discloses what assertions are concealed in a given set of premises, and it makes us realize to what we committed ourselves in accepting those premises; but none of the results obtained by this technique ever goes by one iota beyond the information already contained in the initial assumptions.

Since all mathematical proofs rest exclusively on logical deductions from certain postulates, it follows that a mathematical theorem, such as the Pythagorean theorem in geometry, asserts nothing that is *objectively* or *theoretically new* as compared with the postulates from which it is derived, although its content may well be *psychologically new* in the sense that we were not aware of its being implicitly contained in the postulates.

The nature of the peculiar certainty of mathematics is now clear: A mathematical theorem is certain *relatively* to the set of postulates from which it is derived; *i.e.* it is necessarily true *if* those postulates are true; and this is so because the theorem, if rigorously proved, simply re-asserts part of what has been stipulated in the postulates. A truth of this conditional type obviously implies no assertions about matters of empirical fact and can, therefore, never get into conflict with any empirical findings, even of the most unexpected kind; consequently, unlike the hypotheses and theories of empirical science, it can never suffer the fate of being disconfirmed by new evidence: A mathematical truth is irrefutably certain just because it is devoid of factual, or empirical content. Any theorem of geometry, therefore, when cast into the conditional form described earlier, is analytic in the technical sense of logic, and thus true *a priori; i.e.* its truth can be established by means of the formal machinery of logic alone, without any reference to empirical data.

4. Postulates and Truth

Now it might be felt that our analysis of geometrical truth so far tells only half of the relevant story. For while a geometrical proof no doubt enables us to assert a proposition conditionally — namely on condition that the postulates are accepted —, is it not correct to add that geometry also unconditionally asserts the truth of its postulates and thus, by virtue of the deductive relationship between postulates and theorems, enables us unconditionally to assert the truth of its theorems? Is it not an unconditional assertion of geometry that two points determine one and only one straight line that connects them, or that in any triangle, the sum of the angles equals two right angles? That this is definitely not the case, is evidenced by two important aspects of the axiomatic treatment of geometry which will now be briefly considered.

The first of these features is the well-known fact that in the more recent development of mathematics, several systems of geometry have been constructed which are incompatible with euclidean geometry, and in which, for example, the two propositions just mentioned do not necessarily hold. Let us briefly recollect some of the basic facts concerning these *non-euclidean geometries.* The postulates on which euclidean geometry rests include the famous postulate of the parallels, which, in the case of plane geometry, asserts in effect that through every point P not on a given line l there exists exactly one parallel to l, *i.e.,* one straight line which does not meet l. As this postulate is considerably less simple than the others, and as it was also felt to be intuitively less plausible than the latter, many efforts were made in the history of geometry to prove that this proposition need not be accepted as an axiom, but that it can be deduced as a theorem from the remaining body of postulates. All attempts in this direction failed, however; and finally it was conclusively demonstrated that a proof of the parallel principle on the basis of the other postulates of euclidean geometry (even in its modern, completed form) is impossible. This was shown by proving that a perfectly self-consistent geometrical theory is obtained if the postulate of the parallels is replaced by the assumption that through any point P not on a given straight line l there exist at least two parallels to l. This postulate obviously contradicts the euclidean postulate of the parallels, and if the latter were actually a consequence of the other postulates of euclidean geometry, then the new set of postulates would clearly involve a contradiction, which can be shown not to be the case. This first non-euclidean type of geometry, which is called hyperbolic geometry, was discovered in the early 20's of the last century almost simultaneously, but independently by the Russian N. I. Lobatschefskij, and by the Hungarian J. Bolyai. Later, Riemann developed an alternative geometry, known as elliptical geometry, in which the axiom of the parallels is replaced by the postulate that no line has any parallels. (The acceptance of this postulate, however, in contradistinction to that of hyperbolic geometry, requires the modification of some further axioms of euclidean geometry, if a consistent new theory is to result.) As is to be expected, many of the theorems of these non-euclidean geometries are at variance with those of euclidean theory; thus, *e.g.*, in the hyperbolic geometry of two dimensions, there exist, for each straight line *l*, through any point *P* not on *l*, infinitely many straight lines which do not meet *l*; also, the sum of the angles in any triangle is less than two right angles. In elliptic geometry, this angle sum is always greater than two right angles; no two straight lines are parallel; and while two different points usually determine exactly one straight line connecting them (as they always do in euclidean geometry), there are certain pairs of points which are connected by infinitely many different straight lines. An illustration of this latter type of geometry is provided by the geometrical structure of that curved two-dimensional space which is represented by the surface of a sphere, when the concept of straight line is interpreted by that of great circle on the sphere. In this space, there are no parallel lines since any two great circles intersect; the endpoints of any diameter of the sphere are points connected by infinitely many different "straight lines," and the sum of the angles in a triangle is always in excess of two right angles. Also, in this space, the ratio between the circumference and the diameter of a circle (not necessarily a great circle) is always less than 2π.

Elliptic and hyperbolic geometry are not the only types of non-euclidean geometry; various other types have been developed; we shall later have occasion to refer to a much more general form of non-euclidean geometry which was likewise devised by Riemann.

The fact that these different types of geometry have been developed in modern mathematics shows clearly that mathematics cannot be said to assert the truth of any particular set of geometrical postulates; all that pure mathematics is interested in, and all that it can establish, is the deductive consequences of given sets of postulates and thus the necessary truth of the ensuing theorems relatively to the postulates under consideration.

A second observation which likewise shows that mathematics does not assert the truth of any particular set of postulates refers to *the status of the concepts in geometry*. There exists, in every axiomatized theory, a close parallelism between the treatment of the propositions and that of the concepts of the system. As we have seen, the propositions fall into two classes: the postulates, for which no proof is given, and the theorems, each of which has to be derived from the postulates. Analogously, the concepts fall into two classes: the primitive or basic concepts, for which no definition is given, and the others, each of which has to be precisely defined in terms of the primitives. (The admission of some undefined concepts is clearly necessary if an infinite regress in definition is to be avoided.) The analogy goes farther: Just as there exists an infinity of theoretically suitable axiom systems for one and the same theory — say, euclidean geometry —, so there also exists an infinity of theoretically possible choices for the primitive terms of that theory; very often — but not always — different axiomatizations of the same theory involve not only different postulates, but also different sets of primitives. Hilbert's axiomatization of plane geometry contains six primitives: point, straight line, incidence (of a point on a line), betweenness (as a relation of three points on a straight line), congruence for line segments, and congruence for angles. (Solid geometry, in Hilbert's axiomatization, requires two further primitives, that of plane and that of incidence of a point on a plane.) All other concepts of geometry, such as those of angle, triangle, circle, *etc.*, are defined in terms of these basic concepts.

But if the primitives are not defined within

geometrical theory, what meaning are we to assign to them? The answer is that it is entirely unnecessary to connect any particular meaning with them. True, the words "point," "straight line," *etc.*, carry definite connotations with them which relate to the familiar geometrical figures, but the validity of the propositions is completely independent of these connotations. Indeed, suppose that in axiomatized euclidean geometry, we replace the over-suggestive terms "point," "straight line," "incidence," "betweenness," etc., by the neutral terms "object of kind 1," "object of kind 2," "relation No. 1," "relation No. 2," *etc.*, and suppose that we present this modified wording of geometry to a competent mathematician or logician who, however, knows nothing of the customary connotations of the primitive terms. For this logician, all proofs would clearly remain valid, for as we saw before, a rigorous proof in geometry rests on deduction from the axioms alone without any reference to the customary interpretation of the various geometrical concepts used. We see therefore that indeed no specific meaning has to be attached to the primitive terms of an axiomatized theory; and in a precise logical presentation of axiomatized geometry the primitive concepts are accordingly treated as so-called logical variables.

As a consequence, geometry cannot be said to assert the truth of its postulates, since the latter are formulated in terms of concepts without any specific meaning; indeed, for this very reason, the postulates themselves do not make any specific assertion which could possibly be called true or false! In the terminology of modern logic, the postulates are not sentences, but sentential functions with the primitive concepts as variable arguments. – This point also shows that the postulates of geometry cannot be considered as "self-evident truths," because where no assertion is made, no self-evidence can be claimed.

5. Pure and Physical Geometry

Geometry thus construed is a purely formal discipline; we shall refer to it also as *pure geometry*. A pure geometry, then, – no matter whether it is of the euclidean or of a non-euclidean variety – deals with no specific subject-matter; in particular, it asserts nothing about physical space. All its theorems are analytic and thus true with certainty precisely because they are devoid of factual content. Thus, to characterize the import of pure geometry, we might use the standard form of a movie-disclaimer: No portrayal of the characteristics of geometrical figures or of the spatial properties or relationships of actual physical bodies is intended, and any similarities between the primitive concepts and their customary geometrical connotations are purely coincidental.

But just as in the case of some motion pictures, so in the case at least of euclidean geometry, the disclaimer does not sound quite convincing: Historically speaking, at least, euclidean geometry has its origin in the generalization and systematization of certain empirical discoveries which were made in connection with the measurement of areas and volumes, the practice of surveying, and the development of astronomy. Thus understood, geometry has factual import; it is an empirical science which might be called, in very general terms, the theory of the structure of physical space, or briefly, *physical geometry*. What is the relation between pure and physical geometry?

When the physicist uses the concepts of point, straight line, incidence, *etc.*, in statements about physical objects, he obviously connects with each of them a more or less definite physical meaning. Thus, the term "point" serves to designate physical points, *i.e.*, objects of the kind illustrated by pinpoints, cross hairs, *etc.* Similarly, the term "straight line" refers to straight lines in the sense of physics, such as illustrated by taut strings or by the path of light rays in a homogeneous medium. Analogously, each of the other geometrical concepts has a concrete physical meaning in the statements of physical geometry. In view of this situation, we can say that physical geometry is obtained by what is called, in contemporary logic, a semantical interpretation of pure geometry. Generally speaking, a semantical interpretation of a pure mathematical theory, whose primitives are not assigned any specific meaning, consists in giving each primitive (and thus, indirectly, each defined term) a specific meaning or designatum. In the case of physical geometry, this meaning is physical in the sense just illustrated; it is possible, however, to assign a purely arithmetical meaning to each concept of geometry; the possibility of such an arithmetical interpretation of geometry is of great importance in the study of the consistency and other logical characteristics of geometry, but it falls outside the scope of the present discussion.

By virtue of the physical interpretation of the originally uninterpreted primitives of a geometrical theory, physical meaning is indirectly assigned also to every defined concept of the theory; and if every geometrical term is now taken in its physical interpretation, then every postulate and every theorem of the theory under consideration turns into a statement of physics, with respect to which the question as to truth or falsity may meaningfully be raised — a circumstance which clearly contradistinguishes the propositions of physical geometry from those of the corresponding uninterpreted pure theory. — Consider, for example, the following postulate of pure euclidean geometry: For any two objects x, y of kind 1, there exists exactly one object l of kind 2 such that both x and y stand in relation No. 1 to l. As long as the three primitives occurring in this postulate are uninterpreted, it is obviously meaningless to ask whether the postulate is true. But by virtue of the above physical interpretation, the postulate turns into the following statement: For any two physical points x, y there exists exactly one physical straight line l such that both x and y lie on l. But this is a physical hypothesis, and we may now meaningfully ask whether it is true or false. Similarly, the theorem about the sum of the angles in a triangle turns into the assertion that the sum of the angles (in the physical sense) of a figure bounded by the paths of three light rays equals two right angles.

Thus, the physical interpretation transforms a given pure geometrical theory — euclidean or non-euclidean — into a system of physical hypotheses which, if true, might be said to constitute a theory of the structure of physical space. But the question whether a given geometrical theory in physical interpretation is factually correct represents a problem not of pure mathematics but of empirical science; it has to be settled on the basis of suitable experiments or systematic observations. The only assertion the mathematician can make in this context is this: If all the postulates of a given geometry, in their physical interpretation, are true, then all the theorems of that geometry, in their physical interpretation, are necessarily true, too, since they are logically deducible from the postulates. It might seem, therefore, that in order to decide whether physical space is euclidean or non-euclidean in structure, all that we have to do is to test the respective postulates in their physical interpretation. However, this is not directly feasible; here, as in the case of any other physical theory, the basic hypotheses are largely incapable of a direct experimental test; in geometry, this is particularly obvious for such postulates as the parallel axiom or Cantor's axiom of continuity in Hilbert's system of euclidean geometry, which makes an assertion about certain infinite sets of points on a straight line. Thus, the empirical test of a physical geometry no less than that of any other scientific theory has to proceed indirectly; namely, by deducing from the basic hypotheses of the theory certain consequences, or predictions, which are amenable to an experimental test. If a test bears out a prediction, then it constitutes confirming evidence (though, of course, no conclusive proof) for the theory; otherwise it disconfirms the theory. If an adequate amount of confirming evidence for a theory has been established, and if no disconfirming evidence has been found, then the theory may be accepted by the scientist "until further notice."

It is in the context of this indirect procedure that pure mathematics and logic acquire their inestimable importance for empirical science: While formal logic and pure mathematics do not in themselves establish any assertions about matters of empirical fact, they provide an efficient and entirely indispensable machinery for deducing, from abstract theoretical assumptions, such as the laws of Newtonian mechanics or the postulates of euclidean geometry in physical interpretation, consequences concrete and specific enough to be accessible to direct experimental test. Thus, *e.g.*, pure euclidean geometry shows that from its postulates there may be deduced the theorem about the sum of the angles in a triangle, and that this deduction is possible no matter how the basic concepts of geometry are interpreted; hence also in the case of the physical interpretation of euclidean geometry. This theorem, in its physical interpretation, is accessible to experimental test; and since the postulates of elliptic and of hyperbolic geometry imply values different from two right angles for the angle sum of a triangle, this particular proposition seems to afford a good opportunity for a crucial experiment. And no less a mathematician than Gauss did indeed perform this test; by means of optical methods — and thus using the interpretation of physical straight lines as paths of light rays — he ascertained the angle sum of a large triangle determined by three mountain tops. Within the limits of experimental error, he found it equal to two right angles.

6. On Poincaré's Conventionalism Concerning Geometry

But suppose that Gauss had found a noticeable deviation from this value; would that have meant a refutation of euclidean geometry in its physical interpretation, or, in other words, of the hypothesis that physical space is euclidean in structure? Not necessarily; for the deviation might have been accounted for by a hypothesis to the effects that the paths of the light rays involved in the sighting process were bent by some disturbing force and thus were not actually straight lines. The same kind of reference to deforming forces could also be used if, say, the euclidean theorems of congruence for plane figures were tested in their physical interpretation by means of experiments involving rigid bodies, and if any violations of the theorems were found. This point is by no means trivial; Henri Poincaré, the great French mathematician and theoretical physicist, based on considerations of this type his famous *conventionalism concerning geometry.* It was his opinion that no empirical test, whatever its outcome, can conclusively invalidate the euclidean conception of physical space; in other words, the validity of euclidean geometry in physical science can always be preserved — if necessary, by suitable changes in the theories of physics, such as the introduction of new hypotheses concerning deforming or deflecting forces. Thus, the question as to whether physical space has a euclidean or a non-euclidean structure would become a matter of convention, and the decision to preserve euclidean geometry at all costs would recommend itself, according to Poincaré, by the greater simplicity of euclidean as compared with non-euclidean geometrical theory.

It appears, however, that Poincaré's account is an oversimplification. It rightly calls attention to the fact that the test of a physical geometry G always presupposes a certain body P of non-geometrical physical hypotheses (including the physical theory of the instruments of measurement and observation used in the test), and that the so-called test of *G* actually bears on the combined theoretical system $G \cdot P$ rather than on *G* alone. Now, if predictions derived from $G \cdot P$ are contradicted by experimental findings, then a change in the theoretical structure becomes necessary. In classical physics, *G* always was euclidean geometry in its physical interpretation, *GE;* and when experimental evidence required a modification of the theory, it was *P* rather than *GE* which was changed. But Poincaré's assertion that this procedure would always be distinguished by its greater simplicity is not entirely correct; for what has to be taken into consideration is the simplicity of the total system $G \cdot P$, and not just that of its geometrical part. And here it is clearly conceivable that a simpler total theory in accordance with all the relevant empirical evidence is obtainable by going over to a non-euclidean form of geometry rather than by preserving the euclidean structure of physical space and making adjustments only in part *P*.

And indeed, just this situation has arisen in physics in connection with the development of the general theory of relativity: If the primitive terms of geometry are given physical interpretations along the lines indicated before, then certain findings in astronomy represent good evidence in favor of a total physical theory with a non-euclidean geometry as part *G*. According to this theory, the physical universe at large is a three-dimensional curved space of a very complex geometrical structure; it is finite in volume and yet unbounded in all directions. However, in comparatively small areas, such as those involved in Gauss' experiment, euclidean geometry can serve as a good approximative account of the geometrical structure of space. The kind of structure ascribed to physical space in this theory may be illustrated by an analogue in two dimensions; namely, the surface of a sphere. The geometrical structure of the latter, as pointed out before, can be described by means of elliptic geometry, if the primitive term "straight line" is interpreted as meaning "great circle," and if the other primitives are given analogous interpretations. In this sense, the surface of a sphere is a two-dimensional curved space of non-euclidean structure, whereas the plane is a two-dimensional space of euclidean structure. While the plane is unbounded in all directions, and infinite in size, the spherical surface is finite in size and yet unbounded in all directions: a two-dimensional physicist, travelling along "straight lines" of that space would never encounter any boundaries of his space; instead, he would finally return to his point of departure, provided that his life span and his technical facilities were sufficient for such a trip in consideration of the size of his "universe." It is interesting to note that the physicists of that world, even if they lacked any intuition of a three-dimensional space, could empirically ascertain the fact that their two-dimensional space was curved. This might be done by means of the method of travelling along straight lines; another, simpler test would consist in determining the angle sum in a triangle; again another in determining, by means of measuring tapes, the ratio of the circumference of a circle (not necessarily a great circle) to its diameter; this ratio would turn out to be less than π.

The geometrical structure which relativity physics ascribes to physical space is a three-dimensional analogue to that of the surface of a sphere, or, to be more exact, to that of the closed and finite surface of a potato, whose curvature varies from point to point. In our physical universe, the curvature of space at a given point is determined by the distribution of masses in its neighborhood; near large masses such as the sun, space is strongly curved, while in regions of low mass-density, the structure of the universe is approximately euclidean. The hypothesis stating the connection between the mass distribution and the curvature of space at a point has been approximately confirmed by astronomical observations concerning the paths of light rays in the gravitational field of the sun.

The geometrical theory which is used to describe the structure of the physical universe is of a type that may be characterized as a generalization of elliptic geometry. It was originally constructed by Riemann as a purely mathematical theory, without any concrete possibility of practical application at hand. When Einstein, in developing his general theory of relativity, looked for an appropriate mathematical theory to deal with the structure of physical space, he found in Riemann's abstract system the conceptual tool he needed. This fact throws an interesting sidelight on the importance for scientific progress of that type of investigation which the "practical-minded" man in the street tends to dismiss as useless, abstract mathematical speculation.

Of course, a geometrical theory in physical interpretation can never be validated with mathematical certainty, no matter how extensive the experimental tests to which it is subjected; like any other theory of empirical science, it can acquire only a more or less high degree of confirmation. Indeed, the considerations presented in this article show that the demand for mathematical certainty in empirical matters is misguided and unreasonable; for, as we saw, mathematical certainty of knowledge can be attained only at the price of analyticity and thus of complete lack of factual content. Let me summarize this insight in Einstein's words:

"As far as the laws of mathematics refer to reality, they are not certain; and as far as they are certain, they do not refer to reality."

The Method of Science

ALBERT EINSTEIN

On the Method of Theoretical Physics

If you wish to learn from the theoretical physicist anything about the methods which he uses, I would give you the following piece of advice: Don't listen to his words, examine his achievements. For to the discoverer in that field, the constructions of his imagination appear so necessary and so natural that he is apt to treat them not as the creations of his thoughts but as given realities.

This statement may seem to be designed to drive my audience away without more ado. For you will say to yourselves, 'The lecturer is himself a constructive physicist; on his own showing therefore he should leave the consideration of the structure of theoretical science to the epistemologist.'

So far as I personally am concerned, I can defend myself against an objection of this sort by assuring you that it was no suggestion of mine but the generous invitation of others which has placed me on this dais,

The first part of this selection was originally published by the Oxford University Press, 1933, in *On the Method of Theoretical Physics* and is reprinted here by permission of the publisher. The second part, "Stratification of the Scientific System," is from "Physics and Reality," *Journal of The Franklin Institute*, Vol. 221, 1936. Reprinted by permission of The Franklin Institute.

which commemorates a man who spent his life in striving for the unification of knowledge.

But even apart from that, I have this justification for my pains, that it may possibly interest you to know how a man thinks about his science after having devoted so much time and energy to the clarification and reform of its principles.

Of course his view of the past and present history of his subject is likely to be unduly influenced by what he expects from the future and what he is trying to realize to-day. But this is the common fate of all who have adopted a world of ideas as their dwelling-place.

He is in just the same plight as the historian, who also, even though unconsciously, disposes events of the past around ideals that he has formed about human society.

I want now to glance for a moment at the development of the theoretical method, and while doing so especially to observe the relation of pure theory to the totality of the data of experience. Here is the eternal antithesis of the two inseparable constituents of human knowledge, Experience and Reason, within the sphere of physics. We honour ancient Greece as the cradle of western science. She for the first time created the intellectual miracle of a logical system, the assertions of which followed one from another with such rigour that not one of the demonstrated propositions admitted of the slightest doubt — Euclid's geometry. This marvellous accomplishment of reason gave to the human spirit the confidence it needed for its future achievements. The man who was not enthralled in youth by this work was not born to be a scientific theorist. But yet the time was not ripe for a science that could comprehend reality, was not ripe until a second elementary truth had been realized, which only became the common property of philosophers after Kepler and Galileo. Pure logical thinking can give us no knowledge whatsoever of the world of experience; all knowledge about reality begins with experience and terminates in it.

Conclusions obtained by purely rational processes are, so far as Reality is concerned, entirely empty. It was because he recognized this, and especially because he impressed it upon the scientific world that Galileo became the father of modern physics and in fact of the whole modern natural science.

But if experience is the beginning and end of all our knowledge about reality, what role is there left for reason in science? A complete system of theoretical physics consists of concepts and basic laws to interrelate those concepts and of consequences to be derived by logical deduction. It is these consequences to which our particular experiences are to correspond, and it is the logical derivation of them which in a purely theoretical work occupies by far the greater part of the book. This is really exactly analogous to Euclidean geometry, except that in the latter the basic laws are called 'axioms'; and, further, that in this field there is no question of the consequences having to correspond with any experiences. But if we conceive Euclidean geometry as the science of the possibilities of the relative placing of actual rigid bodies and accordingly interpret it as a physical science, and do not abstract from its original empirical content, the logical parallelism of geometry and theoretical physics is complete.

We have now assigned to reason and experience their place within the system of theoretical physics. Reason gives the structure to the system; the data of experience and their mutual relations are to correspond exactly to consequences in the theory. On the possibility alone of such a correspondence rests the value and the justifications of the whole system, and especially of its fundamental concepts and basic laws. But for this, these latter would simply be free inventions of the human mind which admit of no *a priori* justification either through the nature of the human mind or in any other way at all.

The basic concepts and laws which are not logically further reducible constitute the indispensable and not rationally deducible part of the theory. It can scarcely be denied that the supreme goal of all theory is to make the irreducible basic elements as simple and as few as possible without having to surrender the adequate representation of a single datum of experience.

The conception here outlined of the purely fictitious character of the basic principles of theory was in the eighteenth and nineteenth centuries still far from being the prevailing one. But it continues to gain more and more ground because of the ever-widening logical gap between the basic concepts and laws on the one side and the consequences to be correlated with our experiences on the other – a gap which widens progressively with the developing unification of the logical structure, that is with the reduction in the number of the logically independent conceptual elements required for the basis of the whole system.

Newton, the first creator of a comprehensive and workable system of theoretical physics, still believed that the basic concepts and laws of his system could be derived from experience; his phrase 'hypotheses non fingo' can only be interpreted in this sense. In fact at that time it seemed that there was no problematical element in the concepts, Space and Time. The concepts of mass, acceleration, and force and the laws connecting them, appeared to be directly borrowed from experience. But if this basis is assumed, the expression for the force of gravity seems to be derivable from experience; and the same derivability was to be anticipated for the other forces.

One can see from the way he formulated his views that Newton felt by no means comfortable about the concept of absolute space, which embodied that of absolute rest; for he was alive to the fact that nothing in experience seemed to correspond to this latter concept. He also felt uneasy about the introduction of action at a distance. But the enormous practical success of his theory may well have prevented him and the physicists of the eighteenth and nineteenth centuries from recognizing the fictitious character of the principles of his system.

On the contrary the scientists of those times were for the most part convinced that the basic concepts and laws of physics were not in a logical sense free inventions of the human mind, but rather that they were derivable by abstraction, i.e. by a logical process, from experiments. It was the general Theory of Relativity which showed in a convincing manner the incorrectness of this view. For this theory revealed that it was possible for us, using basic principles very far removed from those of Newton, to do justice to the entire range of the data of experience in a manner even more complete and satisfactory than was possible with Newton's principles. But quite apart from the question of comparative merits, the fictitious character of the principles is made quite obvious by the fact that it is possible to exhibit two essentially different bases, each of which in its consequences leads to a large measure of agreement with experience. This indicates that any attempt logically to derive the basic concepts and laws of mechanics from the ultimate data of experience is doomed to failure.

If then it is the case that the axiomatic basis of theoretical physics cannot be an inference from experience, but must be free invention, have we any right to hope that we shall find the correct way? Still more – does this correct approach exist at all, save in our imagination? Have we any right to hope that experience will guide us aright, when there are theories (like classical mechanics) which agree with experience to a very great extent, even without comprehending the subject in its depths? To this I answer with complete assurance, that in my opinion there is *the* correct path and, moreover, that it is in our power to find it. Our experience up to date justifies us in feeling sure that in Nature is actualized the ideal of mathematical simplicity. It is my conviction that pure mathematical construction enables us to discover the concepts and the laws connecting them which give us the key to the understanding of the phenomena of Nature. Experience can of course guide us in our choice of serviceable mathematical concepts; it cannot possibly be the source from which they are derived; experience of course remains the sole criterion of the serviceability of a mathematical construction for physics, but the truly creative principle resides in mathematics. In a certain sense, therefore, I hold it to be true that pure thought is competent to comprehend the real, as the ancients dreamed.

Stratification of the Scientific System

The aim of science is, on the one hand, a comprehension, as *complete* as possible, of the connection between the sense experiences in their totality, and, on the other hand, the accomplishment of this aim *by the use of a minimum of primary concepts and relations.* (Seeking, as far as possible, logical unity in the world picture, i.e. paucity in logical elements.)

Science concerns the totality of the primary concepts, i.e. concepts directly connected with sense experiences, and theorems connecting them. In its first stage of development, science does not contain anything else. Our everyday thinking is satisfied on the whole with this level. Such a state of affairs cannot, however, satisfy a spirit which is really scientifically minded; because, the totality of concepts and relations obtained in this manner is utterly lacking in logical unity. In order to supplement this deficiency, one invents a system poorer in concepts and relations, a system retaining the primary concepts and relations of the "first layer" as logically derived concepts and relations. This new "secondary system" pays for its higher logical unity by having, as its own elementary concepts (concepts of the second layer), only those which are no longer directly connected with complexes of sense experiences. Further striving for logical unity brings us to a tertiary system, still poorer in concepts and relations, for the deduction of the concepts and relations of the secondary (and so indirectly of the primary) layer. Thus the story goes on until we have arrived at a system of the greatest conceivable unity, and of the greatest poverty of concepts of the logical foundations, which are still compatible with the observation made by our senses. We do not know whether or not this ambition will ever result in a definite system. If one is asked for his opinion, he is inclined to answer no. While wrestling with the problems, however, one will never give up the hope that this greatest of all aims can really be attained to a very high degree.

An adherent to the theory of abstraction or induction might call our layers "degrees of abstraction"; but, I do not consider it justifiable to veil the logical independence of the concept from the sense experiences. The relation is not analogous to that of soup to beef but rather of wardrobe number to overcoat.

The layers are furthermore not clearly separated. It is not even absolutely clear which concepts belong to the primary layer. As a matter of fact, we are dealing with freely formed concepts, which, with a certainty sufficient for practical use, are intuitively connected with complexes of sense experiences in such a manner that, in any given case of experience, there is no uncertainty as to the applicability or non-applicability of the statement. The essential thing is the aim to represent the multitude of concepts and theorems, close to experience, as theorems, logically deduced and belonging to a basis, as narrow as possible, of fundamental concepts and fundamental relations which themselves can be chosen freely (axioms). The liberty of choice, however, is of a special kind; it is not in any way similar to the liberty of a writer of fiction. Rather, it is similar to that of a man engaged in solving a well designed word puzzle. He may, it is true, propose any word as the solution; but, there is only *one* word which really solves the puzzle in all its forms. It is an outcome of faith that nature — as she is perceptible to our five senses — takes the character of such a well formulated puzzle. The successes reaped up to now by science do, it is true, give a certain encouragement for this faith.

The multitude of layers discussed above corresponds to the several stages of progress which have resulted from the struggle for unity in the course of development. As regards the final aim, intermediary layers are only of temporary nature. They must eventually disappear as irrelevant. We have to deal, however, with the science of today, in which these strata represent problematic partial successes which support one another but which also threaten one another, because today's systems of concepts contain deep seated incongruities which we shall meet later on.

It will be the aim of the following lines to demonstrate what paths the constructive human mind has entered, in order to arrive at a basis of physics which is logically as uniform as possible.

Einstein, Mach, and Logical Positivism

PHILIPP FRANK

Roughly speaking, we may distinguish, according to Max Planck, two conflicting conceptions in the philosophy of science: the metaphysical and the positivistic conception. Each of these regards Einstein as its chief advocate and most distinguished witness. If there were a legal case to be decided, it would be possible to produce satisfactory evidence on behalf of either position by quoting Einstein. We do not, however, intend here to stretch the meaning of words like "positivism" and "metaphysics" as is done — a necessary evil — in legal disputes; we intend, rather, to describe Einstein's position in the philosophy of science and to use some arbitrary but precise meanings of "positivism" and "metaphysics" as points of reference for this description. As a matter of fact, Einstein has always felt the need for describing his position with respect to this frame of reference.

If we mean by "positivism" the philosophy of science which was advocated by Ernst Mach, we may describe it by quoting Ein-

From Paul Arthur Schilpp (Ed.), *Albert Einstein: Philosopher-Scientist,* pp. 271–286. New York: Tudor Publishing Co., 1949. Reprinted by permission of the author, the editor, and the Library of Living Philosophers.

stein's essay of 1916, published as an obituary on Mach in *Physikalische Zeitschrift,* as follows:

Science is nothing else but the comparing and ordering of our observations according to methods and angles which we learn practically by trial and error. . . . As results of this ordering abstract concepts and the rules of their connection appear. . . . Concepts have meaning only if we can point to objects to which they refer and to the rules by which they are assigned to these objects. . . .

He [Mach] conceived every science as the task of bringing order into the elementary single observations which he described as 'sensations.' This denotation was probably responsible for the fact that this sober and cautious thinker was called a philosophical idealist or solipsist by people who had not studied his work thoroughly.[1]

We note here that Einstein obviously does not share a very common misinterpretation of Mach's philosophy. The "idealistic" (mis-)interpretation of Mach's philosophy, which Einstein rightly repudiates, has, as a matter of fact, become of historic importance by virtue of the fact that Lenin took it as the point of departure in this book on *Materialism and Empirio-Criticism,* in which he made a spirited attack on Mach's "idealism." As a result of this pronouncement by the highest Soviet political authority, Mach's philosophy of science has become a target of attack in every textbook and in every classroom in the Soviet Union where philosophy is being taught. Because of the close connection, which obviously exists between Einstein's theory of relativity and Mach's philosophy, Lenin feared that Einstein's theories might become a Trojan horse for the infiltration of idealistic currents of thought among Russian scientists and among educated classes in general. This suspicion accounts for the bittersweet reception which Einstein's theories frequently met in the first years of the Soviet regime in Russia.

In 1916 Einstein himself asserted:

I can say with certainty that the study of Mach and Hume has been directly and indirectly a great help in my work. . . . Mach recognized the weak spots of classical mechanics and was not very far from requireing a general theory of relativity half a century ago [this was written in 1916]. . . . It is not improbable that Mach would have discovered the theory of relativity, if, at the time when his mind was still young and susceptible, the problem of the constancy of the speed of light had been discussed among physicists. . . . Mach's considerations about Newton's bucket experiment show how close to his way of thinking was the search for relativity in a general sense (relativity of acceleration).[2]

It is easy to see which lines of Mach's thought have been particularly helpful to Einstein. The definition of simultaneity in the special theory of relativity is based on Mach's requirement, that every statement in physics has to state relations between observable quantities. The same requirement appeared when Einstein started the theory of gravitation by asking what conditions are responsible for the flattening of a rotating liquid sphere. In this case Mach decided that the cause of flattening does not have to be the rotation in empty space, but the rotations with respect to some material and therefore observable bodies.

There is no doubt that in both cases Mach's requirement, the "positivistic" requirement, was of great heuristic value to Einstein. When Einstein actually developed his general theory, however, he found that it was an oversimplification to require that every statement of physics must be directly translatable into relations between observable quantities. Actually, in Einstein's general theory of relativity, the general statements of physics are relations between sym-

[1] *Physikalische Zeitschrift,* XVII, 1916, 101 ff.

[2] *Ibid.,* 103.

bols (general co-ordinates, gravitational potentials, etc.) from which conclusions can be drawn, which latter are translatable into statements about observable quantities.

The original "positivistic requirement," as advocated by Mach and his immediate followers, had to be replaced by a more general requirement, which allows for any symbols or words in the formulation of the principles, provided that statements about observable quantities can logically be derived from them. In the original "positivistic conception of science," as advocated by Mach, the concepts of which the principles consisted were very near to direct observation and, therefore, very near to possible physical experiments. The road from these experiments to the principles was short and easy to understand.

In his Herbert Spencer Lecture, delivered in London in 1933, Einstein says:

> The natural philosophers of those days [18th and 19th centuries] were . . . most of them possessed with the idea that the fundamental concepts and postulates of physics were not in the logical sense free inventions of the human mind but could be deduced from experience by 'abstraction' — that is to say by logical means. A clear recognition of the erroneousness of this notion really only came with the general theory of relativity, . . . the fictitious character of the fundamental principles is perfectly evident from the fact that we can point to two essentially different principles, both of which correspond with experience to a large extent. . . .

These bases are Newton's and Einstein's principles of gravitation. "This proves," Einstein continues, "that every attempt at a logical deduction of the basic concepts and postulates of mechanics from elementary experiences is doomed to failure." [3]

This logical derivation of laws from experience by "abstraction" was certainly not regarded as possible by Mach. But it was a typical belief of nineteenth century physicists as represented, for instance, in J. Tyndall's famous *Fragments of Science*. It is, however, probable that Mach did not believe that there was a wide gap between the concepts which were used in the description of our physical experiments and the concepts used in the formulation of general laws. Einstein, however, emphasized

> . . . the distance in thought between the fundamental concepts and laws on one side and, on the other, the conclusions which have to be brought into relation with our experience grows larger and larger, the simpler the logical structure becomes — that is to say, the smaller the number of logically independent conceptual elements which are found necessary to support the structure.[4]

Einstein's conception of modern science departs from Mach's "positivistic requirement" in the following point: According to Mach and his immediate followers, the fundamental laws of physics should be formulated so that they would contain only concepts which could be defined by direct observations or at least by a short chain of thoughts connected with direct observations. Einstein, however, recognized that this requirement is an oversimplification. In twentieth-century physics the general principles have been formulated by using words or symbols which are connected with observational concepts by long chains of mathematical and logical argument. Einstein, of course, holds in addition that there must be some consequences of these general principles which can be formulated in terms of observational concepts and which can, therefore, be checked by direct observation. This requirement is "positivistic" in the sense that the "truth" of general principles is ultimately based on a check by direct physical experiment and observation. Einstein does not believe — as Mach's contemporaries did — that the basic principles can be checked directly

[3] "On the Methods of Theoretical Physics," in *The World As I See It*, 35 ff.

[4] *Ibid.*, 34.

or by means of a short chain of conclusions. It had now become clear that the road between principles and observation was a long and arduous one. In the same Herbert Spencer Lecture already quoted, Einstein says that "it is the grand object of all theory to make these irreducible elements as simple and as few in number as possible, without having to renounce the adequate representation of any empirical content whatever." [5]

Einstein requires, accordingly, that two criteria have to be met by a set of basic principles: logical consistency and simplicity, on the one hand, and agreement with the observed facts, on the other – briefly speaking, a logical and an empirical criterion. It is irrelevant by means of what concepts or symbols the principles are formulated. They become, from the purely logical viewpoint, free creations of the human mind. But they also have to meet the empirical criterion; they have to obey the restriction of the free imagination which is necessary to represent the data of experience.

The growing understanding of the general theory of relativity and similar theories accounted for a new development within the views held by Mach's "positivistic" followers. A modification and generalization of Mach's "positivistic requirement" occurred among the scientists who worked in the logic of science after 1920. They tried to adjust their formulations to the methods which had been used successfully in general relativity. Under the name of "logical empiricism" a new school of thought appeared, which can be regarded as an attempt to develop Mach's philosophy of science according to the new developments in theoretical physics. The basic principles of physics were no longer to contain only concepts like "red," "warm," "one spot touching a second spot," etc., which were called "elementary terms" or "observational terms." Instead, the principles themselves were regarded as products of the free human imagination and could contain any "abstract terms" or symbols. But these principles cannot be proved or validated by an appeal to the imagination, to intuition, or even to logical simplicity or beauty. The principles are regarded as "true" only if by logical conclusions statements about observations can be derived which can be confirmed by actual experience.

As an example of this line of thought, I quote from Rudolf Carnap's *Foundations of Logic and Mathematics,* which was published in the *Encyclopedia of Unified Science* in 1939:

> Would it be possible to formulate all laws of physics in elementary terms, admitting more abstract terms only as abbreviations? If so, we would have that ideal of a science in sensationalistic form which Goethe in his polemic against Newton, as well as some positivists, seems to have had in mind. But it turns out – this is an empirical fact, not a logical necessity – that it is not possible to arrive in this way at a powerful and efficacious system of laws. To be sure, historically, science started with laws formulated in terms of a low level of abstractness. But for any law of this kind, one nearly always later found some exceptions and thus had to confine it to a narrower realm of validity. Hence we understand that they [the physicists] are inclined to choose the *second method.* This method begins at the top of the system, . . . It consists in taking a few abstract terms as primitive science and a few fundamental laws of great generality as axioms. . . . If, . . . abstract terms are taken as primitive – according to the second method, the one used in scientific physics – then the semantical rules [which connect the abstract terms with observational terms] have no direct relations to the primitive [abstract] terms of the system but refer to terms introduced by long chains of definitions. The calculus is first constructed floating in the air, so to speak; the construction begins at the top and then adds lower and lower levels. Finally, by the se-

[5] *Ibid.,* 33 ff.

mantical rules, the lowest level is anchored at the solid ground of the observable facts. The laws . . . are not directly interpreted, but only the singular sentences.[6]

This conception of logical empiricism seems to be fairly in accordance with the way Einstein anchored his theory of gravitation in the solid grounds of observable facts by deriving phenomena like the redshift of spectral lines, etc. Whether this generalized conception of the relation between theory and facts is a "positivistic conception" is certainly a question of terminology. Some authors in the United States have given to this conception the name "logical positivism," whereas Charles W. Morris recommends the name "logical empiricism," which I have used in this paper. It is simply a matter of a practical scheme in one's history of thought, whether one includes this conception in his chapter on "positivism" or whether one starts a new chapter.

One thing is certain: the classical authors of "positivism," Ernst Mach and even Auguste Comte, understood very well that to say that the laws of science can be expressed in terms of observational concepts is an oversimplification. They hinted quite pointedly at the necessity of a more general conception; but they did not elaborate this hint at length, because at that time theories of the type of Einstein's theory of gravitation did not exist. But, from the strictly logical viewpoint, it is certain that even Newton's mechanics can not be formulated correctly unless we make use of the Einsteinian type of theory, which Carnap calls "starting from the top" or, in other words, unless we start from relations between symbols and draw conclusions which later can then be interpreted in terms of observable facts.

In 1894 Ernst Mach gave a lecture on the topic, "The Principle of Comparison in Physics" (published in his *Popular Scientific Lectures*), in which he distinguishes between "direct description" and "indirect description." The latter type does not describe facts in observational terms but by comparison with a mathematical scheme. Mach uses the example of the wave theory of light, which describes the optical phenomena by starting from a purely symbolic system of axioms which allows a much more practical description of the observed optical phenomena than a "direct" description in terms of optical sensations.

Auguste Comte, the founder of "positivism," was far from assuming that a physical theory should be expressed in observational terms only. He stresses the point, in fact, that no observation is possible without a theory or, at least, no description of observations is possible without previous acceptance of a conceptual scheme. In 1829 Comte wrote in his *Positive Philosophy:*

> If, on the one hand, every positive theory has to be based on observations, it is, on the other hand, also true that our mind needs a theory in order to make observations. If in contemplating the phenomena we did not link them immediately with some principles, it would not only be impossible to combine the isolated observation and draw any useful conclusions, we would not even be able to remember them, and, for the most part, the facts would not be noticed by our eyes.[7]

Comte was so profoundly convinced of the necessity of having to start from a theory that he regarded man at the beginning of scientific research as being entangled in a vicious circle. He continues:

> Hence, squeezed between the necessity of observing in order to form real theories, and the no less urgent necessity of producing some theories in order to make coherent observations, the human mind had not been able to break this circle if not a natural way

[6] R. Carnap, *Foundations of Logic and Mathematics,* 64 ff.

[7] A. Comte, *Cours de philosophie positive,* Premiére leçon.

out had been opened by the spontaneous growth of theological conceptions.[8]

From these quotations it seems to become clear that even the "classical positivism" of Comte or Mach did not hold the opinion that the laws of nature could be simply "derived" from experience. These men knew very well that there must be a theoretical starting-point, a system of principles constructed by the human imagination in order to compare its consequences with observations. This feeling was so strong that Comte accepted even the theological principles as a starting-point to "get science going."

The principal feature which modern logical empiricism has in common with classical positivism is the requirement that, whatever the basic symbols and the laws of their connection may look like, there must be logical conclusions from these principles which can be confronted with direct experience. A set of principles from which no consequences of this type could be derived were called "meaningless" or "metaphysical" by the logical empiricists, thus giving to the time-honored word "metaphysics" a slightly derogatory meaning.

In order to understand Einstein's attitude toward this conception, we may quote his remarks in the volume on *The Philosophy of Bertrand Russell* in the present series:

> In order that thinking might not degenerate into "metaphysics," or into empty talk, it is only necessary that enough propositions of the conceptual system be firmly enough connected with sensory experience and that the conceptual system, in view of its task of ordering and surveying sense-experience, should show as much unity and parsimony as possible. Beyond that, however, the "system" is (as regards logic) a free play with symbols according to (logical) arbitrarily given rules of the game. . . . The concepts which arise in our thought and in our linguistic expressions are all — when viewed logically — the free creations of thought which can not inductively be gained from sense-experiences.[9]

[8] *Ibid.*

Einstein speaks here almost completely in the line of the logical empiricists; which is not surprising, inasmuch as logical empiricism is, to a considerable extent, a formulation of the very way in which Einstein envisaged the logical structure of his later theories, e.g., the theory of gravitation. Occasionally even Einstein himself uses the term "metaphysics" in exactly the same sense in which it has been used by the logical empiricists. He speaks of "metaphysics or empty talk," meaning by it any set of principles from which no conclusion — i.e., no statement about possible sense-experience — can be derived. Einstein shares the opinion of logical empiricism that the principles of science, e.g., the theories of physics, contain tools which are invented by human ingenuity in order to enable us to survey our sense-experiences in as simple a way as possible. He says, e.g., about the integer numbers: ". . . the series of integers is obviously an invention of the human mind, a self-created tool which simplifies the ordering of certain sensory experiences." [10]

In this context it is instructive to learn how Einstein himself describes the psychology of his creative work. The great French mathematician, Jacques Hadamard, in 1945 published a work on *The Psychology of Invention in the Mathematical Field,* in which he put some questions to prominent scientists concerning their respective way of procedure in mathematical science. Among these was Einstein, who described his work in a letter to Hadamard. Einstein, in this letter, stresses particularly the way in which he finds the symbolic structure which is at the top of every theory:

[9] Albert Einstein in "Remarks on Bertrand Russell's Theory of Knowledge" in Paul A. Schilpp's *The Philosophy of Bertrand Russell,* 1944, 289 and the last part of the quotation, 287.

[10] A. Einstein, *ibid.,* 287.

The words or the language, as they are written or spoken, do not seem to play any role in my mechanism of thought. The psychical entities which seem to serve as elements in thought are certain signs and more or less clear images which can be "voluntarily" reproduced and combined.

There is, of course, a certain connection between those elements and relevant logical concepts. It is also clear that the desire to arrive finally at logically connected concepts is the emotional basis of this rather vague play with the above mentioned elements. But taken from the psychological viewpoint, this combinatory play seems to be the essential feature in productive thought.[11]

According to the conception of logical empiricism the relations between symbols which form the "top" of any scientific theory cannot be produced by any logical method. Their origin can only be explained psychologically. This production is the real nucleus of what one may call "creative thinking." This conception is fairly well confirmed by Einstein's statements. According to his own experience, the "combinatory play with symbols is the essential feature of productive thought."

These relations between symbols are, according to logical empiricism, the first part of any scientific theory. But there is a second part, which connects these symbols with the words of our everyday language: the "semantical rules" or, as P. W. Bridgman puts it, the "operational definitions."

Einstein continues the description of the procedure involved in developing new theories: "Conventional words or other signs have to be sought for laboriously only in a secondary stage, when the mentioned associated play is sufficiently established and can be reproduced at will. . . ." Then starts what Einstein calls "the connection with logical construction in words or other signs which can be communicated to others."[12] This means exactly that "semantical rules" have to be added to the symbolic expressions.

Although Einstein seems to be in considerable agreement with the logical empiricists on a great many points, he speaks occasionally of the "fateful 'fear of metaphysics' . . . which has come to be a malady of contemporary empiricistic philosophizing."[13] It is obvious that in this statement, by which "metaphysics" is being encouraged, he does *not* mean the same type of "metaphysics" which he discouraged in the statement, quoted above, where he uses the phrase, "metaphysics and empty talk." If we read this statement in *The Philosophy of Bertrand Russell* carefully, we see clearly that he disagreed with the belief "that all those concepts and propositions which cannot be deduced from the sensory raw material are, on account of their 'metaphysical' character, to be removed from thinking."[14] Einstein calls here "metaphysical" every concept that cannot be deduced from sensory raw material. But this kind of "metaphysical" concepts have certainly not been rejected by the logical empiricists. The admission of these concepts is exactly the point which distinguishes twentieth century logical empiricism from nineteenth century "positivism" of men like Mach. One could, therefore, give good reasons for not regarding logical empiricism as a kind of "positivism." It has often been called "logical positivism" because it rejected principles, from which, according to their structure, no observable facts could be deduced. But in this rejection there was again agreement with Einstein who called such systems "metaphysics and empty talk" exactly as they have been called by the logical empiricists and, for that matter, already by Hume, Mach, and Comte.

[11] A. Einstein in Jacques Hadamard's *An Essay on the Psychology of Invention in the Mathematical Field* (Princeton, 1945), Appendix II, 142.

[12] *Ibid.*, 143, 142.

[13] Einstein, in *The Philosophy of Bertrand Russell* (Schilpp, ed.), 289.

[14] *Ibid.*, 287–89.

There is even the question, whether Mach, if pinned down, would not have agreed that the general conceptions of science are not "derived" from sensory experience, but constructed by the human imagination to derive observable facts logically from these concepts. This becomes probable if we consider Einstein's personal talk with Mach which occurred in 1913. From this conversation [15] it seems plausible that Mach could be pinned down to admit the usefulness of these constructed concepts in science, although his emphasis and predilection belonged to the direct deduction from sensory material.

Concerning this question the difference between Einstein's approach and that of logical empiricism is only a verbal one. Whereas Einstein would, apparently, not use the term "positivism" for his twentieth century group, they in turn would not use the term "metaphysical" for concepts which are constructed by the human imagination in the process of deriving our sense-perceptions.

The extent of this agreement can best be judged, perhaps, by some of Einstein's statements from his Princeton Lecture of 1921, which do not deal with philosophy but with a presentation of the theory of relativity to physicists. In this lecture occur the following remarks:

> The object of all science, whether natural science or psychology, is to coördinate our experiences and to bring them into a logical system. . . . The only justification for our concepts is that they serve to represent the complex of our experiences; beyond this they have no legitimacy. I am convinced that the philosophers have had a harmful effect upon the progress of scientific thinking in removing certain fundamental concepts from the domain of empiricism, where they are under control, to the intangible heights of the *a priori*. For even if it should appear that the universe of ideas cannot be deduced from experience by logical means, but is, in a sense, a creation of the human mind, without which no science is possible, nevertheless the universe of ideas is just as little independent of the nature of our experiences as clothes are of the form of the human body. This is particularly true of our conceptions of time and space, which physicists have been obliged by the facts to bring down from the Olympus of the *a priori* in order to adjust them and put them in a serviceable condition.[16]

Briefly, I do not see in the question of the origin of the fundamental concepts of science any essential divergence between Einstein and twentieth century logical empiricism. But from the belief that the basic conceptions of science are creations of the human imagination – a belief which is common to both Einstein and the logical empiricists – one could easily draw the conclusion that we shall never reach the definitive basic principles of science. One could even be inclined to believe that such a "correct basis" does not at all exist. Conclusions of this kind have been widely drawn by Henri Poincaré, the godfather of logical empiricism, and by a great many of his followers. Einstein, however, in his Herbert Spencer Lecture of 1933, says:

> If it is true that this axiomatic basis of theoretical physics cannot be extracted from experience but must be freely invented, can we ever hope to find the right way? Nay more, has this right way any existence outside our illusions? . . . I answer without hesitation that there is, in my opinion, a right way, and that we are capable of finding it. . . . I am convinced that we can discover by means of purely mathematical constructions the concepts and the laws connecting them with each other, which furnish the key to the understanding of natural phenomena.[17]

[15] Philipp Frank, *Einstein, His Life and Times* (New York, 1947), 104 ff.

[16] Einstein, *The Meaning of Relativity* (Princeton, 1923), 2 ff.

[17] Einstein, in *The World As I See It,* 36.

By extolling the great heuristic value of mathematics Einstein does not want to suggest that a statement of physics could be proved to be true by this purely logical argument. For he continues: "Experience remains, of course, the sole criterion of the physical utility of a mathematical construction. But the creative principle resides in mathematics."[18] This means that the criterion of truth in physics is experience, but that the method by which the principles are found, or, in other words, produced, is mathematics. Einstein is so convinced of the creative power of mathematics that he says: "In a certain sense . . . I hold it to be true that pure thought can grasp reality, as the ancients dreamed."[19]

This statement could be interpreted as meaning that Einstein agrees with the Platonic belief that a statement of physics could be proved by mathematics. According to Einstein, however, this is true only "in a certain sense." This "certain sense" means "in the sense of heuristic method," but not "in the sense of a criterion of truth."

Nobody would deny the fact that this heuristic method, looking for mathematical simplicity and beauty, has led to successful theories, which have turned out to be "true" in the empirical sense. Everybody, notwithstanding his special philosophic creed, who has had any glimpse of theoretical physics, will agree that this fact is a property of our world. It is itself an empirical fact. It is even – as some people like to express themselves – a "hard fact." The emotional reaction to this "hard fact" can, of course, be of various kinds. Einstein calls this fact the basis of cosmic religion. It is a "mystical experience." As "hard facts" cannot be "explained" but only derived from principles which are themselves "inexplicable hard facts," we can say that the most mystical experience is the experience of hard facts. In his paper "On Physical Reality" (1936) Einstein said: "The most incomprehensible thing about the world is that it is comprehensible."[20]

There are, however, scientists whose personal reaction to this fact is different. As an example we may quote P. W. Bridgman. In his *Logic of Modern Physics* (1927), Bridgman writes:

> With regard to the general question of simple laws, there are at least two attitudes; one is that there are probably simple general laws still undiscovered, the other is that nature has a predilection for simple laws. I do not see how there can be any quarrel with the first of these attitudes. Let us examine the second. We have in the first place to notice that "simple" means simple to us, when stated in terms of our concepts. This is in itself sufficient to raise a presumption against this general attitude. It is evident that our thinking must follow those lines imposed by the nature of our thinking mechanism: does it seem likely that all nature accepts these same limitations? If this were the case, our conceptions ought to stand in certain simple and definite relations to nature. Now if our discussion has brought out any one thing, it is that our concepts are not well defined things, but they are hazy and do not fit nature exactly, and many of them fit even approximately only within restricted range. . . . Considering, then, the nature of our conceptual material, it seems to me that the overwhelming presumption is against the laws of nature having any predisposition to simplicity as formulated in terms of our concepts (which is of course all that simplicity means), and the wonder is that there are apparently so many simple laws. There is this observation to be made about all the simple laws of nature that have hitherto been formulated; they apply only over a certain range. . . . It does not seem so very surprising that over a limited domain, in which the most important phenomena

[18] *Ibid.*, 36 ff.
[19] *Ibid.*, 37.

[20] Einstein, "On Physical Reality," in *Franklin Institute Journal*, Vol. 221, 1936, 349 ff.

are a restricted type, the conduct of nature should follow comparatively simple rules.[21]

Although this interpretation of the simplicity of nature sounds very different from Einstein's, the difference lies not in the assertion of facts or of logical relations but in the emphasis. Einstein stresses the marvelous simplicity and beauty of such symbolic structures as Maxwell's equations of the electromagnetic field or the field equations of the general theory of relativity. This beauty produces, according to Einstein, the feeling of admiration and even of "awe"; whereas Bridgman, in the passage quoted, is simply "wondering" about the existence of so many simple laws. These attitudes do not imply different assertions about the physical world or about the logical system by which this world is scientifically described. The difference is totally within the domain of personal reaction. In his address to the Conference on Science, Philosophy and Religion (1940), Einstein states clearly that the belief in the existence of this regularity in nature belongs to religion.

> To this [sphere of religion] there also belongs the faith in the possibility that the regulations valid for the world of existence are rational, that is comprehensible to reason. I cannot conceive of a genuine scientist without that profound faith. The situation may be expressed by an image: science without religion is lame, religion without science is blind.[22]

Although this personal reaction, which, with Einstein, we may call "cosmic religion," is not implied logically by the facts and principles of physics, it may well be that the kind of reaction which is produced in the mind of the physicist is of relevance for his creative power in science. This is obviously Einstein's opinion. He stresses that this "knowledge, this feeling, is at the center of true religiousness. In this sense, and in this sense only, I belong to the ranks of devoutly religious men."

We see from these words that for Einstein this belief in the "possibility of mathematical physics," if we put it perfunctorily, is almost identical with religion. But, on the other hand, Einstein has never agreed with some contemporary philosophical interpretations of physics, according to which relativity and quantum theory are interpreted as having been a decisive step in the reconciliation between science and religion. He has never agreed with men like Jeans or Eddington, who regarded the Heisenberg principle of indeterminacy in quantum theory as an argument for the freedom of the will and for the moral responsibility of man in contrast to the "iron causality of classical physics." Einstein's cosmic religion has been the belief in the possibility of a symbolic system of great beauty and conceptual simplicity from which the observed facts can be logically derived. Whatever his system may look like and whatever symbols may be used does not matter. Newtonian physics bolsters up cosmic religion in this sense just as well as twentieth century physics does.

Eventually the truly interested student of science should follow Einstein's advice, when he says: "If you want to find out anything from the theoretical physicists about the methods they use, . . . don't listen to their words, fix your attention on their deeds."

21 P. W. Bridgman, *The Logic of Modern Physics* (New York, 1927); 2nd ed., 1946, 201, 203.

22 *Science, Philosophy and Religion*, A Symposium (New York: Harper, 1941), 211.

Are There Atoms?

HANS REICHENBACH

That matter consists of small particles, called atoms, is regarded as an established fact by the educated man of our day. If he has not learned it in school the newspapers have told him so. It seems evident that because there exist atom bombs there must also exist atoms.

The historian of science would display a more critical attitude. He knows that the existence of the atom has been contended since ancient times, but that it has always been controversial and that strong arguments have been adduced both in favor of the atom and against it. If his history of science includes the last twenty-five years, he knows, too, that although during the nineteenth century the theory of the atom had reached a stage at which the existence of the atom appeared unquestionable, recent developments have renewed the controversy and have made the existence of the atom more questionable than ever.

We date the theory of the atom from the philosophy of Democritus (420 B.C.), one of the prominent figures of Greek philosophy. Democritus saw that the physical properties of matter, its compressibility and divisibility, can be well explained when we assume that matter consists of little particles. Compressing a substance then consists in pushing the atoms closer together, while the atoms themselves are perfectly solid and remain unchanged in size. Democritus' theory is a good illustration of what reasoning can achieve and what it cannot do. It can offer possible explanations; whether the explanation is true, however, cannot be found out by reasoning, but must be left to observation. The Greeks were not able to verify the theory of atoms by an empirical test. They attempted to supplement the theory by further theory rather than by observation. They believed that atoms were held together by little hooks; that a finer substance, like the soul or the fire, was composed of very small and smooth atoms; and that larger bodies were formed by the gathering of atoms of equal size, a natural process exemplified in the sorting of pebbles by the surf. But imagination uninhibited by some test through experiment opens the door to empty speculation. For instance, one of the philosophic controversies concerning atomism was the question whether the empty space between the atoms was a logically permissible concept; an empty space is nothing, and if there is nothing between the atoms, they must touch each other and form a solid mass – in which case there would be no atoms.

The theory of the atom was transplanted from the ground of philosophical speculation to the soil of scientific research when, at the eve of the nineteenth century, it was given a foundation by quantitative experiments. J. Dalton measured the ratios of weights by which chemical elements enter into compounds, and discovered that these ratios are fixed and given by simple whole numbers. For instance, the two components of water, hydrogen and oxygen, always combine in the ratio one to eight; if originally

The Rise of Scientific Philosophy, pp. 166–190. Berkeley: University of California Press, 1951. Reprinted by permission of Mrs. Hans Reichenbach and the publisher.

more of one substance is present, it is not included in the compound. Dalton saw that these quantitative ratios call for an atomic explanation. The smallest parts of matter, the atoms combine in fixed ratios; two atoms of hydrogen combine with one atom of oxygen, and the ratio of weights of the atoms is portrayed by the ratio observed in Dalton's measurements.

From the time of Dalton's law the history of the atom has been a march of triumph. Wherever the concept of the atom was employed for the interpretation of observational measurements, it supplied lucid explanation; conversely, such success became overwhelming evidence for the existence of the atom. In the kinetic theory of gases it was possible not only to explain the thermic behavior of gases from atomic conceptions, but also to compute the number of atoms or molecules in one cubic inch. This enormous number, which is written with twenty-one digits, presents a proof of the extreme smallness of the individual atom. The complicated structures of organic bodies could be explained as being built up by molecules composed of hundreds of atoms. The industrial achievements of chemistry would have been impossible without the theory of the atom.

The physicist, furthermore, saw that atomism is not restricted to matter; electricity, too, must be regarded as consisting of atoms. The atoms of electricity were discovered around the end of the nineteenth century and were called electrons; strangely enough they all carried a negative electric charge, and for some decades the physicists believed that the positive atoms of electricity could not be separated from matter. Recent discoveries have shown that there are also positive electrons, usually called positrons. Other recent investigations have revealed the existence of further elementary particles of matter, among which the neutrons play an important part.

While the triumphal march of the atom went on through so many domains of science, it was stopped short in one important domain: in the theory of light. Isaac Newton, known for his theory of gravitation, was also one of the greatest explorers of optics. He saw that the straight-line character of light rays is explainable on the assumption that light consists of small particles ejected at great speed from the light source. Following the laws of motion, such particles will travel along straight paths. Newton thus was the author of the corpuscular theory of light, which remained dominant until the beginning of the nineteenth century. The wave theory of light, the invention of his contemporary C. Huyghens, met with little success at its inception. A full century elapsed before certain decisive experiments were made, which proved the undulatory character of light and thus put an end to the atomistic interpretation of light rays. These experiments were centered around the phenomenon of interference, in which two light rays, superimposed on one another, annihilate each other, a result inconceivable under a corpuscular theory. Two particles moving in the same direction can produce only a stronger impact and provide an increase in light intensity; but two waves moving in the same direction will cancel each other if the crests of the one coincide with the troughs of the other. The phenomenon of interference is known from water waves and accounts for the strange patterns produced by intersecting trains of waves. The medium of propagation of light waves, however, was recognized not to be of the nature of ordinary matter like water or air, but was supposed to be a substance of a peculiar, almost immaterial structure, called ether.

The development of the mathematical means of analyzing waves followed immediately the experimental discoveries. Finally the theory of light waves was connected with that of electricity through the work of James Maxwell; the experimental demonstration of electric waves by Heinrich Hertz removed the last doubts of the possibility of ether waves, and the wave theory of light became "a certainty, humanly speaking," as Heinrich Hertz put it in an address given at a meeting of the German association of scientists in the year 1888.

At about the end of the nineteenth century physics had reached an apparently final stage: light and matter, the two great manifestations of physical reality, seemed to be known in their ultimate structure. Light consisted of waves and matter of atoms. Anyone who dared to question these foundations of the science of physics would have been regarded as a dilettante, or an eccentric, and no serious scientist would have taken the trouble to argue with him.

Physical theories give an account of the observational knowledge of their time; they cannot claim to be eternal truths. Heinrich Hertz had been careful enough to coin the phrase "certainty, humanly speaking." No deeper insight has perhaps ever been documented by a physicist's utterance than is expressed in this modest phrase. The turn which the theory took a decade after Hertz's words is proof of the limits drawn to the certainty of scientific theories.

The year 1900 brought M. Planck's discovery of the quantum; the radical change in our understanding of physical reality which the twentieth century effected, could not be better illustrated than by this coincidence. In order to explain the laws found experimentally for the emission of radiation by hot bodies, Planck introduced the conception that all radiation, including light, is subject to a control by whole numbers, that is, proceeds by whole numbers of an elementary unit of energy, which he called the *quantum*. According to his conception, energy consists of elementary units, the quanta, and whenever energy is emitted or absorbed there will be one or two or one hundred quanta transported, but never will there be a fraction of a quantum. The quantum is the atom of energy, with the qualification, however, that the size of this atom, that is, the amount of the energy unit, depends on the wave length of the radiation through which it is transported; the shorter the wave length, the greater the quantum. Planck's discovery therefore appeared as a new victory of atomism; and when Albert Einstein extended Planck's theory to the idea that light consists of needlelike bunches of waves carrying one quantum of energy, it seemed that the idea of the atom had finally conquered the very domain of physics which so long had been inaccessible to atomistic conceptions. Einstein's equivalence of matter and energy, which in recent years has become so dramatically manifest in the fission of uranium, was another indication that atomism was to include radiation.

The quantum found its most important application in Niels Bohr's theory of the atom. It was in this theory that the two lines of development, of the theory of the atom and of the theory of radiation, were finally united. The study of the atom had made it clear that the atom itself must be regarded as an aggregate of smaller particles, which, however, are so tightly held together that for all chemical reactions the atom behaves as a relatively stable unit. That the atom has an inner structure was first indicated by a discovery of the Russian D. Mendelejeff, who in the middle of the nineteenth century saw that if the atoms of the chemical elements are arranged according to weight, their chemical properties assume a cyclical order. The English physicist E. Rutherford connected these chemical discoveries with the discovery of the electron and constructed the planetary model of the atom, according to which the atom consists of a nucleus around which there revolve, like planets on their orbits, a certain number of electrons. Niels Bohr, at that time a young assistant of Rutherford, discovered in 1913 that Rutherford's model of the atom must be connected with Planck's concept of the quantum of energy. The electrons can only revolve on orbits situated at certain definite distances from the center, so determined that the mechanical energy represented by each orbit is either one, or two, or three quanta, and so forth. Strange as this conception appeared to the physicist in the beginning, it led to an amazing success as far as the presentation of observational data is concerned, since Bohr's theory supplied an interpretation of the highest precision for the data of spectroscopy, that is, for the series of spectral lines that characterize each element. The years from 1913 to 1925 became a period of extensive application and confirmation of Bohr's theory, which was deepened to supply an account of the atomic structure of each individual element.

And yet, in spite of all these successes, the discovery of the quantum turned out to be a gift with strings attached. In exchange for its explanatory power for spectroscopy, inexplicable complications arose on other grounds. The very foundations of the quantum conception appeared incompatible with the classical theory of the generation of electric waves and the phenomenon of interference, known from optics. Thus the new theory imperiled the consistency of physics: some phenomena required a corpuscular conception of light, others required a wave conception, and no way was apparent by which the two contradictory theories could be reconciled.

The strangest phenomenon for the philosophical observer, however, was the fact that physical research was not paralyzed by these contradictions, that the physicist managed somehow to go on with two contradictory conceptions and learned to apply sometimes the one, sometimes the other, with an amazing success as far as observational discoveries are concerned. I do not think this fact proves that contradiction is irrelevant for physical theories and that only the observational success matters; or that, as Hegelians believe, contradiction is immanent in human thought and acts as its propelling force. I rather think it proves that the discovery of new ideas follows other laws than laws of logical order; that knowledge of half the truth can be a sufficient directive for the creative mind on its path to the full truth, and that contradictory theories can be helpful only because there exists, though unknown at that time, a better theory which comprehends all observational data and is free from contradictions. While humans search, truth slumbers; it will be awakened by those who do not stop their search even when their path is obstructed by the brushwood of contradictions.

The decisive turn in the development of the theories of light and matter was a conception put forward by the French physicist Louis de Broglie. While physicists were struggling with the problem of whether light consists *either* of particles *or* of waves, de Broglie ventured the idea that it consists *both* of particles *and* of waves. He even had the boldness to transfer his idea to the atoms of matter, which so far had never required a wave interpretation; he developed a mathematical theory according to which each little particle of matter, too, is accompanied by a wave. The *either–or* was thus replaced by an *and,* and from de Broglie's discovery, therefore, dates the duality of interpretations, which ever since has been confirmed as an inescapable consequence of the structural nature of matter. In an experiment conducted by Davisson and Germer, who used an interference arrangement, de Broglie's waves could be shown to exist for a beam of electrons, so that the existence of waves of matter was insured beyond doubt.

De Broglie's ideas were taken up by E. Schrödinger, who devised a differential equation which has become the mathematical foundation of the modern theory of the quantum, usually called quantum mechanics. His mathematical theory coincided with some other theories, which at first glance looked very different and which were developed independently by W. Heisenberg, M. Born, and P. Jordan on the one hand and

P. Dirac on the other. All these discoveries were made in the years 1925–1926; and in a rather short time a new physics of the elements of matter was developed, which placed in the hands of the physicist a powerful mathematical instrument that he had yet to learn to handle. The difficulties in the manipulations of this instrument derived from the duality of waves and corpuscles. What does it mean to say that matter consists both of waves and of particles? Although the mathematical theory was at hand, its interpretation presented great difficulties. We meet here with a development which manifests the relative independence of a mathematical formalism; the mathematical symbols have a life of their own, so to speak, and lead to the correct result even before the symbol-user understands their ultimate meaning.

De Broglie had interpreted the *and* in its simplest sense; he believed that there were particles accompanied by waves which travel along with the particle and control its motion. Schrödinger, in contrast, believed that he could dispense with the particles, that there were only waves which, however, were accumulated in certain small regions of the space so that something resembling a particle resulted. He spoke of wave packets behaving like particles. After both conceptions had been shown to be untenable, Born suggested the idea that the waves do not constitute anything material at all but represent probabilities. His interpretation gave the problem of the atom an unexpected turn: the elementary entities were assumed to be particles, whose behavior was controlled not by causal laws, but by probability laws of a form resembling waves as far as their mathematical structure was concerned. In this interpretation the waves do not have the reality of material objects, but only that of mathematical quantities.

Carrying on this conception, Heisenberg showed that for the prediction of the path of particles there exists a specific indeterminacy, which makes it impossible to predict that path strictly, a result formulated in his *principle of indeterminacy.* With Born's and Heisenberg's discoveries the step was made that led from a causal interpretation of the microcosm to a statistical interpretation; the individual atomic occurrence was recognized as not being determined by a causal law, but as following only a probability law, and the *if-then* of classical physics was replaced by an *if-then in a certain percentage.* Combining Born's and Heisenberg's results, Bohr finally developed a *principle of complementarity,* according to which Born's interpretation supplies only one aspect of the problem; it is also possible to regard the waves as physically real, a conception for which no particles exist. There is no way of discriminating between the two interpretations, because Heisenberg's indeterminacy makes any *crucial experiment* impossible; that is, it excludes experiments precise enough to tell whether one interpretation is true and the other false.

The duality of interpretations thus assumed its final form: the *and* of de Broglie's discovery does not have the direct meaning that both waves and corpuscles exist at the same time, but has the indirect meaning that the same physical reality admits of two possible interpretations, each of which is as true as the other, although the two cannot be combined into one picture. The logician would say: the *and* is not in the language of physics, but in the *metalanguage,* that is, in a language which speaks about the language of physics. Or, in another terminology, the *and* belongs, not in physics, but in the philosophy of physics; it does not refer to physical objects, but to possible descriptions of physical objects, and thus falls into the realm of the philosopher.

That is, in fact, the final outcome of the controversy between the adherents of waves and of corpuscles, which began with Huyghens and Newton and, after a development of centuries, climaxed in the quantum mechanics of de Broglie, Schrödinger, Born,

Heisenberg, and Bohr: the question *what is matter* cannot be answered by physical experiments alone, but requires a philosophical analysis of physics. Its answer is seen to be dependent on the question *what is knowledge*. The philosophic thought which stood at the cradle of atomism was replaced in the course of the nineteenth century by experimental analysis; but research finally reached a stage of complication which called for a return to philosophical investigation. The philosophy of this investigation, however, could not be supplied by mere speculation; only a scientific philosophy was able to come to the assistance of the physicist. In order to understand this latest development we shall have to inquire into the meaning of statements about the physical world.

Knowledge begins with observation: our senses tell us what exists outside our bodies. But we are not satisfied with what we observe; we want to know more, to inquire into things that we do not observe directly. We reach this objective by means of thought operations, which connect the observational data and account for them in terms of unobserved things. This procedure is applied in everyday life as well as in science; it is at work when we infer from puddles on the road that it rained shortly before, or when the physicist infers from the deflection of a magnetic needle that there is an invisible entity, called electricity, in the wire, or when the physician infers from the symptoms of a disease that there are certain bacteria in the blood stream of the patient. We must study the nature of this inference if we wish to understand the meaning of physical theories.

The inference may look trivial as long as we do not reflect about it; but in deeper analysis it reveals itself as being of a very complicated structure. You say that while you are in your office your house stands unchanged in its place. How do you know? You do not see your house while you are in your office. You will answer that you can easily verify your statement by going home and looking at your house. It is true that you will then see your house; but does that observation verify your statement? What you said was that your house was there when you did not see it; what you verify is that your house is there when you see it. How can you tell whether it was there while you were absent?

I see you are getting indignant. Those philosophers, you say; they are trying to make fools out of everybody. If the house was there in the morning and in the afternoon, how can it have been nonexistent in the forenoon? Does the philosopher think that a contractor could pull down a house in a minute and build it up in another minute? What is such a nonsensical question good for?

The trouble is that unless you can find a better answer to that question than is supplied by the arguments of common sense, you will not be able to solve the problem of whether light and matter consist of particles or waves. That is the point made by the philosopher: common sense may be a good instrument as long as questions of everyday life are concerned; but it is an insufficient instrument when scientific inquiry has reached a certain stage of complication. Science requires a reinterpretation of the knowledge of everyday life, because knowledge is ultimately of the same nature whether it concerns concrete objects or the constructs of scientific thought. We must therefore find better answers to the simple questions of everyday life before we can answer scientific questions.

The Greek philosopher Protagoras, the chief of the Sophists, was known for his principle of subjectivity, which he formulated as follows: "Man is the measure of all things, of things that are what they are, and of things that are not what they are not." We do not know exactly what he meant by this truly sophisticated statement, but let us assume he would have said with respect to our problem: "the house exists only when I look at it, but when I don't look at it, it always vanishes." What can you hold against him? He does not say that it vanishes and reappears in the ordinary way by the hands of bricklayers and carpenters; he means it vanishes in a sort of magical way. He insists that it is the observation by a human observer which produces the house and that therefore unobserved houses do not exist. What arguments do we have against such magical disappearance and creation by a human observer?

You may say that you can call up the janitor from your office and ask whether the house still stands. But the janitor is a human being like you; maybe his observation creates the house like yours. Will the house be there when nobody observes it?

You may say that you can turn your back toward the house and observe its shadow; then the unobserved house must exist because it throws a shadow. But how do you know that unobserved things throw shadows? What you have seen so far is that observed houses throw shadows. You could explain the shadow, which you see while you do not see the house, by assuming that shadows remain when the object has vanished, and that there is a shadow without a house. Do not argue that such shadows of non-existent objects have never been observed. That is true only if you assume what you want to prove, namely, that the house continues to exist while you do not see it. If you assume the contrary, like Protagoras, you have lots of evidence for his statement, because you have seen house-shaped shadows without seeing houses at the same time.

You will defend yourself by resorting to a new appeal to common sense. "Why should I assume," you answer, "that the laws of optics are different for unobserved objects? It is true that these laws were established for observed objects; but do we not have overwhelming evidence that they must hold for unobserved objects, too?" On a little afterthought, however, you will discover that we do not have such evidence at all. We have none because unobserved objects have never been observed.

There remains only one way out of this difficulty. We must regard our statements about unobserved objects not as verifiable statements, but as conventions, which we introduce because of the great simplification of language. What we know is that *if* this convention is introduced it can be carried through without contradictions; that *if* we assume the unobserved objects to be identical with the observed ones, we arrive at a system of physical laws which hold both for observed and unobserved objects. The latter statement, which is an *if* statement, is a matter of fact and verified as true. It proves that our usual language about unobserved objects is an *admissible* language. But it is not the only admissible one. A Protagoras who says that houses vanish when they are unobserved also speaks an admissible language, if he is willing to comply with the consequence that he has to construct two different systems of physical laws, one for observed and one for unobserved objects.

The result of this long discussion is that nature does not dictate to us one specific description; that truth is not restricted to one language. We can measure houses in feet or in meters, temperatures in Fahrenheit or in centigrades; and we can describe the physical world in a Euclidean or a non-Euclidean geometry, as was shown in Chapter 8. We speak different languages when we use different systems of measurement or of geometry, but we say the same thing. The plurality of descriptions repeats itself in a more complicated form when we speak about unobserved objects. There are many ways of saying the truth; they are all equivalent in a logical sense. There are also many ways of saying a falsehood. For instance, it is false to say that ice melts at thirty-two degrees, if we use the centigrade scale. Our philosophy, therefore, does not wipe out the difference between truth and falsehood. But it would be shortsighted to disregard the plurality of true descriptions. Physical reality admits of a class of *equivalent descriptions;* we choose one for the sake of convenience, and this choice rests upon a convention only, that is, on an arbitrary decision. For instance, the decimal system supplies a more convenient description of measurements than other systems. When we speak about unobserved objects, the most convenient language is the one selected by common sense, according to which unobserved objects and their behavior do not differ from observed objects and their behavior. But this language is based upon a convention.

It is the merit of the theory of equivalent descriptions that it allows us to express certain truths which the language of common sense cannot formulate. I refer to the truth formulated by the *if* statement above: it is true that if we assume the unobserved objects to be identical with the observed ones, we arrive at no contradictions, or in other words, that among the admissible descriptions of the physical world there is one in which the unobserved objects are on equal footing with the observed ones. Let me call this description the *normal system*. That the physical world admits of a normal system for its description is one of the most important truths. We have always taken this truth for granted; we did not even formulate it and thus did not know that it was a truth. We saw no problem in it, like the man who sees no problem in the falling of bodies toward the ground because this observation is too general an experience. But scientific mechanics began with the formulation of the law of falling bodies. Similarly, a scientific understanding of the problem of unobserved objects begins with the statement that a description of unobserved objects through a normal system is possible.

How do we know it is possible? All we can say is that the experiences of generations of men have proved it. We should not believe, however, that this possibility could be proved by logical laws. It is a fortunate matter of fact that our world can be so simply described that no difference between observed and unobserved objects results. This is all we can maintain.

Thus far we have spoken of unobserved houses. The particles of matter are also unobserved objects. Let us see how our results can be transferred to them.

As in the world of our daily life, there are observables and unobservables in the world of the atom. What can be observed are collisions between two particles, or between a particle and a light ray; the physicist has devised ingenious instruments that indicate each individual collision. What cannot be observed is what happens during the interval between two collisions, or on the path from the source of radiation to a collision. These occurrences, then, are the unobservables of the quantum world.

But why can they not be observed? Why can we not use a supermicroscope and watch the particles on their path? The trouble is that in order to see a particle we have to illuminate it; and illumination of a particle is something very different from the illumination of a house. A light ray falling on a particle pushes it out of its way; what we observe, therefore, is a collision and not a particle traveling peacefully on its path. Imagine that you wish to watch a bowling ball rolling along its path in a dark hall; that you turn on the light and the moment the light hits the ball it pushes the ball out of its way. Where was the ball before you turned on the light? You would not be able to tell. Fortunately our illustration is not true for bowling balls; they are so large that the impact by a light ray does not disturb them noticeably. It is different with electrons and other particles of matter. When you observe them, you have to disturb them; and therefore you do not know what they did before the observation.

There is some disturbance by the observation even in the macroscopic world. When a police car moves through the traffic of a boulevard, its occupants see all the surrounding cars move slowly within the required speed limits. If the police officer did not sometimes put on civilian clothes and drive an ordinary car, he would infer that all the cars all the time move at such a reasonable speed. In our intercourse with electrons we cannot don civilian clothes; when we watch them we always disturb their traffic.

You will argue: maybe it is true that we cannot observe how an undisturbed particle moves on its path; but can we not figure out, by means of scientific inferences, what they do when we do not look at them? This question returns us to our preceding analysis of unobserved objects. We saw that we can speak about such objects in various ways; that there is a class of equivalent descriptions; and that we shall preferably select a normal system for our description, that is, a system in which the unobserved objects do not differ from the observed ones. Our discussion of the observation of particles, however, has made it clear that for particles we do not have a normal system. The observer of electrons is a Protagoras; he produces what he sees, because seeing electrons means producing collisions with light rays.

Speaking of particles means attributing to them a definite place and a definite velocity for each time point. For instance, a tennis ball occupies at every moment a certain place on its path and has, at this moment, a determinate velocity. Both place and velocity can be measured, at each moment, by suitable instruments. For small particles, however, the disturbance by the observer, as Heisenberg has shown, makes it impossible to measure both values simultaneously. We can measure either the position or the velocity of the particle, but not both. This is the result of Heisenberg's principle of indeterminacy. The question arises whether there do not exist other ways of determining the unmeasured quantity, methods through which the unmeasured quantity is related indirectly to the observed quantities. This would be possible if we could assume that the unobserved quantities follow the same laws as the observed ones. The analysis of quantum mechanics, however, has given a negative answer; the unobserved objects do not follow the same laws as the observed ones in so far as a specific difference arises with respect to causality. The relations controlling unobserved objects violate the postulates of causality; they lead to *causal anomalies*.

This difference results when interference experiments are made, that is, experiments in which a beam of electrons or a light ray passes through a narrow slit and produces an interference pattern on a screen, consisting of black and white stripes. Such experiments have always been explained by the wave nature of light as the result of a superposition of wave crests and troughs. We know, however, that when we use a radiation of a very small intensity, the resulting pattern, although of the same structure when the radiation goes on for a sufficiently long time, is the effect of a great many small impacts on the screen; the stripes are therefore produced by a bombardment resembling machine-gun fire. These individual impacts cannot be reasonably explained as waves. The wave arrives on a large front covering the screen; then there occurs a flash at only one point of the screen, and the whole wave disappears. It is swallowed by the flash, so to speak, an occurrence which is incompatible with the usual laws of causality. This is the point where the wave interpretation leads to unreasonable consequences, or causal anomalies. If we assume, in contrast, that the radiation consists of particles, the impacts on the screen are easily explained. Difficulties arise, however, if two slits are used. Each particle then must pass either through the one or the other slit. The interference pattern is then the result of an interaction of the two slits; but the contribution which each slit makes to the total pattern can be shown to differ from the pattern which the slit would produce if the other slit were closed. This means that the path beyond the slit selected by the particle will be influenced by the existence of the other slit; the particle knows, so to speak, whether or not the other slit is open. This is the point where the particle interpretation arrives at a causal anomaly, that is, a violation of the usual laws of causality. Similar violations occur for all other experimental arrangements and all possible interpretations. This result is formulated in a *principle of anomaly,* which can be derived from the foundations of quantum mechanics.

The violation of the principle of causality in the form of anomalies must be carefully distinguished from the extension expressed in the transition from causal laws to probability laws. That atomic occurrences are controlled by probability laws, and not by causal laws, appears as a relatively harmless result if compared with the causal anomalies just mentioned. These anomalies concern the principle of action by contact, formulating a well-established property of causal transmission: the cause has to spread continuously through space until it reaches the point where it produces a certain effect. If a locomotive starts moving, the individual cars of the train will not follow immediately, but by intervals; the pull of the locomotive has to be transferred from car to car until it finally reaches the last car. When a searchlight is turned on, it will not immediately illuminate the objects to which it is directed; the light has to travel through the space in between, and if it did not move at such a high speed we would notice the time required for the spreading of the illumination. The cause does not affect distant objects instantaneously, but spreads from point to point until it affects the object by contact— this simple fact is one of the most conspicuous features of all known causal transmissions; and the physicist would not easily give up the belief that he holds in this property an indispensable factor of causal interaction. Even the transition to probability laws does not necessarily imply the abandonment of this property. Probability laws can be so constructed that the probability is transferred from point to point, resulting in a probability chain, which is the analogue of a causal action by contact. The fact that the analysis of the unobservables of quantum physics compels us to give up the principle of action by contact, that it leads to a principle of anomaly, is a much heavier blow to the idea of causality than the transition to probability laws. This breakdown of causality makes it impossible to speak of unobserved objects of the microcosm in the same sense as of the macrocosm.

We thus arrive at a specific difference between the world of large things and the world of small things. Both worlds are constructed on the basis of observables by the addition of unobservables. In the world of large things such a supplementation of the observed phenomena involves no difficulties; the unobservables follow the pattern of the observables. In the world of small things, however, a reasonable supplementation of the observables cannot be constructed. The unobservables, whether introduced as particles or as waves, behave unreasonably, violating the established laws of causality. There exists no normal system for the interpretation of the unobservables, and we cannot speak of unobservables in the same sense as is implied for the world of everyday life. We can regard the elementary constituents of matter as particles or waves; both interpretations fit the observations equally well and equally badly.

This, then, is the end of the story. The controversy between the adherents of the wave and the corpuscle interpretation has been transformed into a duality of interpretations. Whether the constituents of matter are waves or particles is a question concerning unobservables; and the unobservables of atomic dimensions, unlike those of the world at large, cannot be uniquely determined by the postulate of a normal system — because there exists no such system.

We should call ourselves fortunate that this indeterminacy is restricted to small objects; for large objects it drops out because Heisenberg's indeterminacy, on account of the small size of Planck's quantum, is not noticeable for them. Even for the atoms as wholes the indeterminacy can be neglected, because they are rather large; and we can treat them as corpuscles, disregarding wave notions. Only the interior structure of the atom, in which lighter particles like electrons play a leading part, requires the quantum mechanical duality of interpretations.

To understand what the duality means, let us imagine a world in which a similar duality holds for large bodies. Assume there is machine-gun fire passing through the windows of a room and we later find the bullets stuck in the walls of the room, so that it seems beyond doubt that the fire consists of bullets. The passage of the fire through the windows, we further assume, follows the laws for waves passing through slits; the fire produces, in the distribution of the bullets in the walls, a pattern of stripes like those of an interference pattern. When we open another window, for instance, the number of bullets hitting a certain place of the wall becomes smaller instead of larger, because the waves interfere at this point. If it were impossible to observe directly a bullet on its path, we then could interpret the fire as consisting of waves or of corpuscles; both interpretations would be true, although each would involve certain unreasonable consequences.

The unreasonableness of such a world will always exist in consequences only, not in what is observed. The individual observations would not be different from what we see in our world; but their totality would determine implications that contradict the fundamentals of causality. It is our good luck that our world of stones and trees and houses and machine guns is not of this type. Indeed, it would be rather unpleasant to live in such an environment, in which things play tricks on us behind our backs, while they behave reasonably as long as we look at them. But we cannot infer that the world of the small things must be of the same simple structure as that of the large ones. The atomic dimensions do not lend themselves to a unique determination of unobservables. We have to learn that their unobservables can be described in various languages, and that there is no question of one being the true language.

It is this characteristic feature of quantum-mechanical occurrences which I would regard as the deeper meaning of Bohr's principle of complementarity. When he calls the wave and the particle description complementary, this means that for questions where one is an adequate interpretation the other is not, and vice versa. For instance, considering the interference pattern on a screen we shall refer to the wave interpretation; but in face of observations with Geiger counters, which show us individual and localized impacts, we shall use the particle interpretation. It should be noticed that the word "complementarity" does not explain, or eliminate, the logical difficulties of quantum-mechanical language; it merely gives them a name. It is a fundamental fact that there is no normal system for the interpretation of quantum-mechanical unobservables and that we have to resort to different languages when we wish to avoid causal anomalies for different occurrences — this is the empirical content of the principle of complementarity. And it should be emphasized that this logical situation has no analogues in our actual macrocosm. I therefore do not think that it clarifies the quantum-mechanical problem when reference is made to such "complementarities" as love and justice, freedom and determinism, and so forth. I would rather speak here of *polarities* and indicate by the change in the name that these macrocosmic relationships have a structure very different from the complementarity of quantum mechanics. They have nothing to do with the extension of language from observables to unobservables and therefore do not bear upon the problem of physical reality.

A different approach has been made by the help of a revision of logic. Instead of a duality or complementarity of languages, a language of a more comprehensive form has been constructed, wide enough in its logical structure to be adaptable to the peculiarities of the quantum-mechanical microcosm. Our usual language is based on a two-valued logic, that is, on the logic of the two truth values "truth" and "falsehood." It is possible to construct a three-valued logic, which possesses an intermediate truth value of indeterminacy; in this logic, statements are either true or false or indeterminate. By the help of such a logic, quantum mechanics can be written in a sort of neutral language, which does not speak of waves or corpuscles, but speaks of coincidences, that is, of collisions, and leaves it indeterminate what happens on the path between two collisions. This logic appears to be the ultimate form of the physics of the quanta – humanly speaking.

It was a long way from Democritus' atoms to the duality of waves and corpuscles. The substance of the universe – in the physicist's sense and not in the metaphoric connotation of the philosopher who identified it with reason – has turned out to be of a rather dubious nature, if compared with the solid particles in which both the philosopher and the scientist believed for some two thousand years. The conception of a corporeal substance, similar to the palpable substance shown by the bodies of our daily environment, has been recognized as an extrapolation from sensual experience. What appeared to the philosophy of rationalism as a requirement of reason – Kant called the concept of substance synthetic a priori – has been revealed as being the product of a conditioning through environment. The experiences offered by atomic phenomena make it necessary to abandon the idea of a corporeal substance and require a revision of the form of the description by means of which we portray physical reality. With the corporeal substance goes the two-valued character of language, and even the fundamentals of logic are shown to be the product of an adaptation to the simple environment into which human beings were born. Speculative philosophy has never exhibited a power of imagination equal to the ingenuity which scientific philosophy has displayed under the guidance of scientific experiments and mathematical analysis. The path of truth is paved with the errors of a philosophy too narrow to envisage the variety of possible experiences.

On Philosophical Arguments in Physics

S. KÖRNER

When the task in hand is not the solution of problems within some established conceptual framework, but rather the construction of the framework, physicists tend to use philosophical arguments. The creators of quantum mechanics, for instance, now and then interrupt their physical and mathematical reasoning by appealing to certain general philosophical principles in order to support positions which they are defending as physicists.

The present paper is an attempt to clarify the relation between these philosophical principles and the physical theories which they are alleged to support; and thus to clarify to some extent the relation between philosophy and physics.

1. Physical Formalisms and Physical Explanations

Although the invention of a particular physical formalism may require rare intellectual gifts and its efficient manipulation long training, the general structure of such formalisms is clear enough and on the whole uncontroversial.[1] A physical formalism consists on the one hand of a mathematical part or calculus. It gives rules for the formation of formulae from given signs and for turning well-formed formulae into new ones which are again well-formed; and it selects some well-formed formulae as postulates. On the other hand it consists of an interpretation, i.e. rules of reference which relate the signs and formulae to possible observations, in such a manner that some of the interpreted formulae express empirical laws of nature. These latter are either causal or statistical correspondences between empirical predicates. Once the general structure of physical formalisms is exhibited, their function in the achievement of conceptual economy, in prediction, and in the technical control of events is easily seen.

The notion of a physical formalism is narrower than the notion of a physical explanation: for a formalism may be reasonably criticized for lacking certain characteristics which it must possess, in addition to those mentioned, if it is to be a satisfactory explanation. Similarly, two physical formalisms which cover the same ground or, more precisely, which imply the same empirical laws of nature, may be reasonably compared

From S. Körner, (Ed.), *Observation and Interpretation.* London: Butterworths Scientific Publications, 1957. Reprinted by permission of the author, the publisher, and the Colston Research Society.

[1] For accounts by physicists see, e.g., Hertz, *Die Prinzipien der Mechanik* etc., Leipzig, 1894, Introduction; and Dirac, *Quantum Mechanics,* 3rd edition, Oxford, 1947, p. 15; for accounts by philosophers, e.g., Duhem, *La Théorie Physique: Son Objet, Sa Structure,* 2nd edition, Paris, 1914; Popper, *Logik der Forschung,* Vienna, 1935; Braithwaite, *Scientific Explanation,* Cambridge, 1953.

with respect to their explanatory power. The distinction between a physical formalism as such, and one which by conforming to additional requirements is qualified to function as an explanation, has also been expressed, among other ways, by saying that only the latter makes the phenomena intelligible. Examples of the distinction being made by physicists come easily to mind and will be given below.

Whereas the notion of a physical formalism is unambiguous, the notion of a physical explanation (of physical intelligibility, etc.) changes from one group of physicists to another. A physicist's statement to the effect that a certain formalism is or is not an explanation, or that it is a better explanation than another, expresses the fact that he has adopted a normative or regulative principle to which he requires physical formalisms to conform. The importance which he attaches to the principle may, of course, vary from individual to individual. But, if it carries any weight at all, its acceptor will, if confronted with the choice between two physical formalisms both of which imply the same empirical laws of nature and of which only one conforms to the principle, prefer that which does so conform.

The regulative principles which express what various physicists require of an explanatory or intelligible formalism are closely related to, if not identical with, propositions of speculative philosophy or metaphysics. The classic instance is the principle of causality – say in its Kantian formulation as the second analogy of experience.[2] Whatever other meaning or function this principle may have for the theoretical physicist who has adopted it, it will function as a principle of conduct – a principle regulating, more or less strictly, his construction of physical formalisms and his choice between them.

The adoption or rejection of any rule by a person is a contingent fact. It is always conceivable, however unlikely it may be, that a physicist should have no adopted regulative principles by which to distinguish intelligible from unintelligible, or more from less intelligible, formalism. If, however, a physicist has adopted a regulative principle it will have a role to play in his reasonings.

2. Arguments Which Operate by Confronting Physical Formalisms with Regulative Principles

Among arguments involving regulative principles we can distinguish roughly two types: those which simply confront a physical formalism with a regulative principle which is assumed to be generally adopted or whose adoption is, at least, not called into question; and those which are intended to influence the adoption or rejection of some regulative principle.

Some of Schrödinger's arguments in favour of his version of wave mechanics are good examples of the simple confrontation of a formalism with regulative principles. In his first paper on *Quantisation as an Eigenvalue-problem*[3] he considers as 'more congenial' (*sympathischer*) the idea that 'in a quantum process energy makes a transition from one form of vibration to another' than the 'idea of jumping electrons.' In his second paper on the subject he declares the suggestion to the effect that 'the events in the atom cannot be subsumed under the spatio-temporal mode of thinking' as being 'from the philosophical point of view . . . an unconditional surrender' (*loc. cit.* p. 36).

These and similar remarks are remarks concerning the explanatory power or intelligibility of formalisms which from the point of view of logic and experimental confirma-

[2] *Kritik der reinen Vernunft,* Akademie edition III. p. 166.

[3] *Gesammelte Abhandlungen zur Wellenmechanik,* Leipzig, 1928, p. 15.

tion are unobjectionable. One therefore at once looks out for some formulation of regulative principles. A very clear statement of such is found in a paper by the same author written twenty years later. 'The *intelligibility* of the picture (namely the world-view of natural science) permits no deviation from the necessity with which in a spatio-temporal process (*im raumzeitlichen Ablauf*) every subsequent stage is determined by the preceding.' [4] The regulative character of this statement is made unmistakeable by the occurrence in it of the term 'permits.'

Again Einstein's dissatisfaction with contemporary quantum mechanics is based quite expressly on his having adopted a regulative principle to which he thinks any wholly intelligible physical formalism must conform. What he finds unsatisfactory in the quantum theory 'is its attitude towards that which appears to be the *programmatic* aim of all physics: the complete description of any (individual) real situation (as it supposedly exists irrespective of any act of observation or substantiation).' [5]

Those who disagree with Einstein and Schrödinger show that they are well aware how largely the dispute is due to the disputing parties having adopted incompatible regulative principles. Their choice of words, one would almost say their tone of voice, suggests disagreements about rules of conduct. Thus Pauli, in a letter quoted by Born, not only predicts that 'the statistical character of the function, and thus of the laws of nature . . . will determine the style of the laws for at least some centuries' but also declares that 'to dream of a way back, back to the classical style of Newton-Maxwell' seems to him 'hopeless, off the way, bad taste.' [6]

[4] *Die Besonderheit des Weltbildes der Naturwissenschaft, Acta Physica Austriaca,* Vol. I, p. 233.

[5] *Albert Einstein: Philosopher-Scientist,* ed. by P. A. Schilpp, Evanston, 1949, p. 667, my italics.

[6] *British Journal for the Philosophy of Science,* Vol. IV, p. 106.

3. Arguments Supporting the Adoption or Rejection of Regulative Principles

Whereas the correctness or otherwise of a logically consistent physical formalism is shown by comparing its empirical laws, statistical or causal, with observation, no such comparison is available in the case of regulative principles. These can be related to observation only indirectly, *via* physical formalisms which conform to them. As examples we may consider the regulative principle of causality, i.e. the rule to the effect that no physical formalism *should* (= no *intelligible* physical formalism *does*) imply irreducibly statistical correspondences; and the contradictory regulative principle of irreducibly statistical correspondences according to which some formalisms, e.g. those relating to atomic events, should imply irreducibly statistical correspondences.

In favour of any one of these principles, the following indirectly empirical, or quasi-inductive, argument may be and has been put forward: since all or most formalisms which have stood up well to experimental tests conform to the regulative principle in question, it is prudent to expect that new successful formalisms will also conform and to act accordingly in one's search for such. Those who argue for the retention of the principle of causality point to all the successful formalisms since Galileo and those who argue for its rejection either consider as alone relevant formalisms relating to atomic phenomena or else they attempt to show that, despite *prima facie* appearance, even the classical formalisms imply irreducibly statistical correspondences.[7]

Logical arguments for adopting any particular regulative principle presuppose some measure of agreement either about other such principles or about the need to preserve some given formalism. An example of a

[7] See, e.g., the paper by M. Fierz in the present volume [i.e., *Observation and Interpretation*].

logical argument of the former kind is that put forward by Dirac [8] in favour of the principle that a formalism which *explains* the constitution of matter would, unlike the classical systems, have to give an absolute meaning to size. His reason is that any classical explanation of the constitution of matter would assume it to be made up of a large number of relatively small parts behaving according to some postulated laws and would thus leave untouched the structure and stability of the constituent parts. The cogency of the argument depends on the assumption that those to whom it is addressed have adopted a further principle, to the effect that any explanation of the constitution of matter must derive the behaviour of it in bulk from laws governing — absolutely or relatively — its small parts. This regulative principle is by no means generally adopted or 'necessary.' It has been rejected e.g. by Leibniz. Indeed Leibniz, as does Dirac, regarded explanation in terms of relatively small parts as incomplete and unsatisfactory. But he considered the adoption of the notion of absolute size as more objectionable than the replacement of atoms by monads.[9]

An example of a logical argument which presupposes the need for preserving the physical formalism of quantum mechanics and which is put forward in favour of the adoption of the principle of irreducibly statistical correspondences is outlined by Heisenberg. He summarizes it by saying that 'the *determinate* propositions (die bestimmten Aussagen) of quantum mechanics . . . imply that a supplementation of the statistical propositions of quantum mechanics is impossible.' [10] In other words, according to Heisenberg it is logically impossible that the *physical* formalism, which as it stands violates the principle of causality, should be embedded in a wider formalism which conforms to it. The question whether this assertion has been formally demonstrated, especially by von Neumann, is still a controversial one. Moreover the demonstration would not show that a causal supplementation of the mathematical formalism only — with changes in its interpretation — is also logically impossible. It is the search for this latter sort of causal supplementation which, for example, Einstein is recommending.[11]

4. On the Relation Between Physics and Metaphysics

If the principle of causality and similar metaphysical principles are regulative, then we must reject some widely held doctrines about the relation between physics and metaphysics. These are, first, the positivistic doctrine, held in various forms by Carnap and others, that metaphysical propositions are irrelevant to physics because they are meaningless; second, the doctrine, held e.g., by Duhem [12] that metaphysical propositions are irrelevant to physics because they are about a different subject-matter which is inaccessible to physics; lastly the view, held in particular by Kant, that those metaphysical propositions which are relevant to physics are true indicative propositions and that their relevance lies in the fact that their denial, though not self-contradictory, would make the construction of any physical formalism, and indeed of any scientific theory, impossible.

The view defended here may be summarized as follows: Some metaphysical propositions are, or function as, regulative principles governing more or less strictly the search for physical formalisms and the choice

[8] *Quantum Mechanics,* 3rd edition, Oxford, 1947, p. 3.

[9] Leibnitz, *Nouveau Système* etc., e.g., §§ 3, 11.

[10] Heisenberg, *Prinzipielle Fragen der Modernen Physik,* Stuttgart, 1948, p. 45.

[11] *Loc. cit.,* pp. 666 ff.

[12] See, e.g., *loc. cit.,* p. 431.

between them. Like other normative propositions they admit of alternatives in the sense that of two mutually incompatible regulative principles both may be satisfiable. (Of two incompatible indicative propositions one, at least, must be false.) They define, again like other normative propositions, standards of excellence, in the present case standards of the intelligibility or explanatory power of physical formalisms. Lastly they share with other normative propositions the capacity of becoming the subject of rational argument.[13]

[13] For a fuller statement see my *Conceptual Thinking*, Cambridge, 1955, chapters XXX–XXXIII.

3

BIOLOGY AND THE SCIENCES OF MAN

Introduction

1.

Biology in its beginnings was not at all a science of the Galilean type. Biologists for centuries spent their time collecting a vast amount of information about the observable properties of plants and animals (an activity eventually aided by microscopic study) and devising various methods of sorting and relating it. Linnaeus began the classification of this vast and ever increasing store of information on an effective basis according to genus and species; but this sort of activity, valuable and necessary as it is, did not make biology a science. This sort of activity—collecting and classifying—instead usually goes under the name "natural history" since it presumably records facts but does not explain them. Biology, then, would be a science only if the biologist could explain why and how plants and animals come to have the characteristics they do, in fact, exhibit.

The break-through from natural history to science came with Darwin's theory of evolution or, more specifically, with his explanation of the fact of evolution by the concept of natural selection. The point is not simply that Darwin offered an explanation of the origin of species or that, unlike Aristotelians, he offered a non-purposive and non-observable mechanism to explain biological fact—although these elements, to be sure, are part of the point—but also that he stimulated a number of specific biological studies out of a classificatory stage (taxonomy) into an explanatory stage that exhibited the same logical structure as the physics of Galileo and Newton. Gregor Mendel, for example, not satisfied with Darwin's account of heredity, advanced the unobservable, theoretical concept of 'gene' which, occurring in complex hypotheses, not only explained the known facts of heredity but also gave rise, through deductive elaboration, to many other consequences which were tested experimentally and found to hold true in fact. Moreover, the concepts of modern genetics, beginning with Mendel, have lent themselves to increasingly sophisticated mathematical formulation, and the hypotheses have lent themselves to similarly impressive mathematical elaboration. In short, the logical structure of biological hypotheses, from quite unlikely beginnings, has come more and more to resemble the structure of Galilean science. Everett W. Hall in his essay on "The Scientific Revolution in Biology" explains this shift in structure in detail and points out how much more impressive this revolution is than the one popularly ascribed to Darwin, namely, that he established the fact of evolution by a vast array of painstaking observations.

Although it is becoming more and more rare, some biologists who call themselves "vitalists" still insist that biology is quite unlike physics in logical structure and must rely for its explanations on purposive concepts which they variously call entelechies, élan vitals, or whatever. Ernest Nagel, in his piece on "Mechanistic Explanation and Organismic Biology," indicates what he takes to be the uselessness of this sort of purposive explanation and suggests, correctly I think, other ways in which the mechanist-vitalist controversy can more profitably be formulated; namely, whether or not an organism has "emergent characteristics," or is "more than the sum of its parts," and whether or not biological concepts and laws can be "reduced" to those of physics.

The notion of reduction is indeed a vague one and often used in an obscure fashion in philosophical literature. It appears clear, though, that both vitalists and mechanists assume that a concept in one science somehow disappears if it is reduced to a concept in another science. The word *reduction* itself suggests that biological concepts, if reduced, would be *nothing but* physical ones, that biological and physical concepts would be identical, that only physical concepts therefore would be ultimately real. The mechanist, holding one type of materialistic metaphysics, finds this consequence desirable and so insists that all biological concepts must be reducible to physical ones. The vitalist, holding other metaphysical views (probably more tenable ones), finds this consequence untenable or undesirable and so insists that biological concepts cannot be reduced to physical ones. However, if one analyzes carefully a case of what mechanists and vitalists both admit to be an example of scientific reduction – namely, the reduction of thermodynamic concepts and laws to those of mechanics – then he sees that the alleged consequence of reduction, the disappearance of the reduced concept, which the mechanist welcomes and the vitalist abhors, does not in fact follow at all, and thus that the issue between them, as far as the nature of science is concerned, is entirely illusory.

In the reduction of thermodynamic concepts and laws to those of mechanics – the famous kinetic theory of gases first suggested by Rumford – the following steps occur. First, the physicist conceives of gas as consisting of a large number of atomic particles which are subject to the laws of mechanics. Then he coordinates every concept of thermodynamics to some mechanical property of these atomic particles: for example, 'gas pressure' corresponds to the total mechanical impulse of the particles; 'temperature' corresponds to some function of their average velocity; and so on for every concept. After these coordinations, the physicist is able to derive the laws of thermodynamics (including our old friend, Boyle's law) as special cases of the laws of mechanics by applying the latter to the atomic particles. But the point which interests us is the relationship between concepts like 'gas pressure' and 'total mechanical impulse of the particles.' Note that 'gas pressure' is not reduced to 'mechanical impulse' in the sense that gas pressure is nothing but mechanical impulse or that gas pressure and mechanical impulse are identical or that only mechanical impulses are ultimately real. On the contrary, 'mechanical impulse,' and all the other mechanical concepts which are coordinated with gas concepts, plus the laws of mechanics simply explain the nature of gas concepts and laws which, of course, do not lose their reality because they are explained! No more, then, would biological concepts lose their reality if and when reduced to physical ones, and thus the respective grounds of the mechanist's insistence that biological concepts *must* be reduced and the vitalist's insistence that they *cannot* be, disappear.

Moreover, an analysis of the kinetic model makes the meaning of 'reduction' a good deal clearer and shows the pointlessness of insisting either that biological concepts can or that they cannot be reduced to physical ones. The reduction of a term, as we saw, is a matter of coordinating it with a concept in another area of science. However, concepts are not coordinated unless there is some body of laws or theory which makes such coordination possible or gives it some point. The question of mechanism and vitalism, then, comes simply to this: Is there any physical theory which makes a coordination of physical and biological concepts possible or fruitful? This question, however, is itself a factual or scientific one, not a speculative or argumentative one; either such a theory exists or it does not. As a matter of fact, some physical theories have made possible a fruitful coordination of biological and physical concepts; thus these biological concepts have been reduced to physical ones. But most biological concepts have not as yet been so coordinated. Will they be in the future? This question, again, is strictly a factual or scientific one, and it is pointless to insist that they will be or will not be. Whether they are or not is a matter of future scientific achievement, or lack of it, not a matter of *a priori* judgment.

2.

Psychology, in its beginnings, was not a Galilean-type science either. According to Wilhelm Wundt, the founder of modern psychology as a study independent of philosophy, physicists investigate the properties of the external world while psychologists examine the properties of consciousness. The psychologist, moreover, uses a method of investigation entirely different from the physicist's; he examines the properties of consciousness by introspectively analyzing the contents of his own conscious experience. The result of introspective analysis was, so to speak, an inventory of the mind. Psychologists discovered, for example, the number of colors and degrees of brightness which can be distinguished, the number of "affective elements" and emotions which can be distinguished, and so on. You can see, then, that psychology, in its beginnings, was a classificatory or taxonomic study just as early biology was; it amounted to a kind of natural history of the mind. This interpretation perhaps is not quite fair since psychologists tried to explain by such laws as 'association by continuity,' 'association by similarity,' etc., how the basic sensory elements become combined into perceptual wholes, how simple affective elements become combined into complex emotions, and so on. Nevertheless, my main point remains the same: the new science of psychology still had a logical structure quite different from the model Galileo first set forth, since the psychologist "explained" complex mental phenomena by qualitative laws relating concepts of direct experience instead of by functional laws relating unobservable, theoretical concepts.

Wundtian psychology declined rapidly at the end of the nineteenth century and was altogether displaced early in the present century. The cause of this decline and fall was intricate indeed, but the most prominent element was, as we saw in Chapter 1, the failure of introspection as a reliable method of investigation. Another element was the fact that many new studies carried out under the name of psychology — studies in animal behavior and aptitude and intelligence testing, to name only two — apparently could not be accommodated within the framework of Wundtian psychology. Eventually, out of the welter of new psychological studies and techniques came a new framework or new conception of the logical structure of science, which, as you may guess, was more akin to the Galilean model than the Wundtian conception was.

According to this new view, the task of the psychologist is not to explain how complex contents of consciousness are built out of elementary ones but to explain why human beings *act* or *behave* the way they do. The behavior to be explained ranges from simple responses like discriminating hues and degrees of brightness or learning how to run a finger maze to complex responses like learning to read a musical score or making neurotic adjustments between conflicting claims. No matter how simple or complex the behavior, however, psychologists, in trying to explain it, have needed recourse to hypotheses which contain all sorts of theoretical concepts like 'habit strength,' 'movement-produced stimuli,' 'sign-Gestalt-expectation,' 'intelligence quotient,' 'id,' and 'super-ego,' to name only a few, some of which are mathematically defined and some of which are qualitatively defined. To be sure, some of the theoretical concepts in psychology are extremely tenuous, and the hypotheses which use them almost barren of any experimental or observational confirmation, while others, even though sound in this respect, have not proved very fruitful. Nevertheless, there are still other concepts and hypotheses in almost every field of psychology which show signs of becoming not only more precise and testable but more fruitful, too; and there is, after all, no necessary or *a priori* reason why these efforts are doomed to fail. At any rate, whatever guess one might hazard about its future prosperity, contemporary psychology, unlike the Wundtian type, does exhibit the same logical structure as any Galilean science, namely, the use of unobservable, theoretical concepts in hypotheses some of which, at least, must give rise to consequences which can be tested experimentally.

Within this modern Galilean framework, however, there are many disagreements about the nature of theoretical concepts. Some psychologists insist that theoretical concepts should be closely tied to observable concepts in order to insure a maximum of empirical meaning. Each such concept, they believe, must be operationally defined or given an observable criterion for use. Other psychologists believe that a system of interconnected theoretical concepts, whose relations are mathematically defined, is necessary in order to relate stimulus variables to a response since those variables are frightfully complex even in the simplest case of a conditioned response.

Another controversy concerns the use of physiological models in the effort to explain human behavior. Some psychologists have claimed that we cannot succeed in this effort if we restrict our theoretical concepts to mathematically or qualitatively defined ones which relate, in however complicated a way, observable stimuli and overt responses, but rather we must supplement them with physiological concepts which, as they say, are not mathematical fictions but refer to "real entities." Other psychologists point out that one needs some purely psychological concepts and some genuine psychological laws before it makes any sense to explain human behavior by physiological concepts and laws.

The most divisive controversy of all centers around the differences in precision and testability of the concepts and hypotheses. Psychologists who specialize in less complex behavior — sensation, perception, and simple learning, for example — criticize the psychologists who deal with whole personality structures because their theoretical concepts are vague and tenuous — witness, for example, the 'id' and 'super-ego' — and their hypotheses generally untestable. They extend this criticism, of course, even more vehemently to clinical psychologists who apply these sketchy notions in actual therapeutic treatment of patients. The personality psychologists and clinical psychologists reply that the work of learning and perceptual theorists, while it may be exact and testable, does not help to further what, after all, is the main purpose of psychology, namely, the understanding of complex human behavior so that the ills of human conflict can be remedied.

Kenneth W. Spence in his essay on "Historic and Modern Conceptions of Psychology" traces out the various steps of the journey from the Wundtian to the modern conception of psychology and points out the various kinds of laws the modern psychologist is seeking. Edward Joseph Shoben, Jr., in his piece on "Psychology and the Psychologist" considers in detail the last, most divisive controversy I mentioned — the one between experimental and clinical psychologists, as it is sometimes put — and suggests, what seems to me, at any rate, a sane way of adjusting the conflicting claims.

3.

Through the years the social sciences, too, have taken on more and more the structure of Galilean science, although I do not have space to discuss this development. Social scientists have their arguments about the nature of theoretical concepts much like those of the psychologists. Can one get along in economics and sociology by operationally defining every theoretical concept, or must one introduce a whole system of concepts? Must one use psychological models in order to explain group behavior, or is it possible to operate with strictly economic concepts, or sociological ones, or anthropological ones, and so on? Will the investigations of simple systems, however precise and testable they may be, ever make it possible to understand the complex interplay of factors in the actual market of today or the complex interplay of social conditions in a Puerto Rican tenement district, in order that these events and conditions can be intelligently controlled?

Social scientists have increasingly used mathematical techniques in analyzing data and forming hypotheses, although one must admit that the results sometimes have been pointless precision and, in some of the "axiomatic" theories of economics, factually empty hypotheses. However, some social scientists are becoming sophisticated enough in mathematics, and in their own subject, not only to use mathematical techniques in appropriate ways but also to see where certain extensions in mathematical theory itself are necessary if they are to have the tools of analysis they need. To those of you who are competent in mathematics and interested in its application to social sciences, I recommend that you read on your own the following two fascinating books: *Mathematical Thinking in the Social Sciences,* edited by Paul F. Lazarsfeld, and *Introduction to Finite Mathematics,* by J. G. Kemeny, J. L. Snell, and G. L. Thompson. In the Lazarsfeld volume, for a summary view, I suggest you read Herbert Simon's essay on "Some Strategic Considerations in the Construction of Social Science Models."

To be sure, not all social scientists interpret the structure of their sciences as primarily Galilean and mathematical in nature. There is a long tradition in all of the social sciences, and psychology too, which insists that concepts, hypotheses, and explanations in the human sciences have a completely different logical structure from those of the physical sciences. This tradition usually claims that explanations in the human sciences occur through *verstehen,* of which the closest English translation, perhaps, is "empathetic understanding."

According to the advocates of this view, the laws used in explanations in physical science are functional relations or statistical correlations between theoretical concepts while the generalizations used in explanations in the human sciences are quite different. Here the explanatory or causal generalizations are themselves a matter of experience and so "understandable." Consider this example. Why did the traveller in a snowstorm suddenly veer from his path and make a long detour to get to an inn which he could have reached more directly by staying on his original course? Well, he saw that what first appeared to be a snow-covered plain was really the frozen surface of Lake Constance. Consequently, since people avoid danger whenever possible, he veered off his course and followed an arc of the shoreline until he reached the inn. Now the generalization used in explaining this piece of human behavior is 'people avoid danger whenever possible.' This generalization quite obviously is not a law; certainly it is not a mathematical or statistical relation between theoretical concepts. Rather the generalization, or "behavior maxim," is a projection of the explainer's own direct experience; he is introspectively aware of the relationship between perception of danger and avoidance responses in his own experience. Hence the generalization of this experience into a "behavior maxim," and its use in explaining another person's behavior, is "understandable" to him. Moreover, generalizations or behavior maxims like the present one "are acceptable to us as propositions even though they have not been established experimentally" since "the relation asserted appears to us as self-evident." [1]

The notion of *verstehen* is quite involved and often far from clear, but Theodore Abel in his essay on "The Operation Called *Verstehen*" throws a good deal of light on the complex meanings of the concept and only then points out what he takes to be its shortcomings. However, there are certain difficulties, I suspect, which should be clear to you already. First, empathetic understanding is not a necessary requirement for explanation in the social sciences since the laws which determine group behavior may contain terms which are not reducible to concepts and relations which individuals are capable of experiencing. Some writers believe that the law of the shifting of consonants in the Indo-European languages, as well as some laws of economics, among others, approach this non-understandable type of regularity. Moreover, empathetic understanding is not a necessary requirement for explanation of individual behavior either. There is a whole series of subjects which are, for most people, increasingly difficult to understand empathetically. At the apex would be a person like Hitler, himself a crucial object of study in social science. If the explanation of his behavior consisted in experiencing hatreds and ambitions like his, then, I hope, he would remain inexplicable for most people. There is, no doubt, at least a partial explanation of Hitler's behavior consisting in causal analyses of abnormal psychology and sociology in which identification with the subject and so "understanding" of the explanatory concepts has diminished to the vanishing point.

So far I have argued quite simply that empathetic understanding is not necessary for an explanation in social science; that is, I have argued that it is perfectly possible to provide explanations of some events in this area which are devoid of it. However, the question is, whenever there *is* empathetic understanding of some individual or group event, does this constitute an adequate or sufficient explanation? This question is even more difficult to answer than the one we have been considering, and you should keep it in mind while reading Abel's article.

Another prominent controversy in the philosophy of the social sciences, and the one which Maurice Mandelbaum considers in his essay, "Societal Facts," is whether or not there are genuinely social facts and laws which are not reducible to facts and laws about the behavior of individuals. Mandelbaum argues that there *are* societal facts which are not resolvable into psychological ones and defends this view against the criticism that a "social fact" would be a highly mysterious sort of fact since you could never point it out as you can any ordinary fact. In thinking about this issue you will want to relate it to the discussion of 'reducibility' in biology, although not all of that discussion is relevant here.

4.

Perhaps the most perplexing philosophical problem of history and the social sciences is this: Can man, after all, achieve *any* sort of objective or verifiable knowledge about human affairs since his thoughts or judgments about its very nature, as well as his explanations of it, seem always to be colored or distorted by his social status and objectives, what he wants and hopes to be the case. Let us see what some prominent philosophers of history, historians, and sociologists have had to say about this problem.

Some idealistic philosophers like Benedetto Croce and R. G. Collingwood, and more recently many existentialist philosophers, have argued in the following fashion.

[1] Maurice Mandelbaum, "Concerning Recent Trends in the Theory of Historiography," *Journal of the History of Ideas,* 16, 1955, p. 511.

The historian deals with data which have meaning for him only insofar as he re-thinks or re-lives them in some empathetic fashion or builds them into his own individual or social experience in some other way. "In short, the past with which the historian actually deals is a living memory which is found in the present and is capable of molding the future; it is not independent of the historian's own thoughts or of his own existential problems." [2] Consequently, the historian does not achieve objective or scientific truth in the determination of facts since he picks and selects only ones that have value or meaning for him and an understanding of which may help him solve his life problems. Moreover, historical interpretations of the facts are myths, not scientific explanations. A myth, of course, is not a falsehood but a value interpretation put upon the facts which has, for the historian who supplies the myth, and for others with his value orientation, the greatest truth possible. But, of course, the same facts can be given many different value interpretations, and thus conflicting myths emerge. Thus history is constantly rewritten for every generation that departs, however slightly, from the value orientations of previous ones. Regarded this way, historical knowledge turns out to be entirely relative. There cannot be in the great Von Ranke's sense a *science* of history by which, of course, is meant simply that history, like science, can reach objective, reliable knowledge — not that history has a logical structure like any Galilean structure replete with theoretical concepts and all. The American historian, Carl Becker, in his famous presidential address to the American Historical Association, "Everyman His Own Historian," which is reprinted in the following pages, presents in a most engaging way the relativistic view of the idealistic philosophers of history. It also stands as an amazing anticipation of the contemporary existentialist way of putting the same point.

Karl Mannheim, eminent proponent of a sociological relativism called the "sociology of knowledge," in his book, *Ideology and Utopia* (1936), classified the patterns of thinking and feeling of all different social and economic classes under two heads: "ideologies" are the thought-patterns of conservatives, those who want a status quo; while "utopias" are the thought-patterns of radicals, those who are bent on changing the existing classes. Now a person who holds a particular ideology — say, a contemporary American who says that his economic system is based on and protects equality of opportunity — believes that he is correctly and objectively describing what is the case; yet his belief in the system, his devotion to it, Mannheim believed, always turns his "description" into an idealization, his reasons into rationalizations. But the person who holds a utopian view, for example, an Italian communist (since, of course, in Russia communism is no utopia but an ideology!), is in no better position. He too, according to Mannheim's views, believes that he has objective knowledge; he thinks he can scientifically predict how economic classes will change, in fact must change, and can explain what changes have occurred already, although in reality, his descriptions, predictions, and explanations are just as much idealizations and rationalizations reflecting his own belief in a particular system as the ideologist's. The final conclusion of this sort of argument appears to be that all ideas, all thinking, must be treated as expressions of life interests determined by particular social conditions; hence none is more true or false than others — they all simply occur.

At first, when a set of ideas was called an ideology, it was in the spirit of condemnation. It was recognized that the group promulgating such ideas had ulterior motives for doing so; the ideas favored the interests

[2] Everett W. Hall, *History of Economic and Social Ideas* (Iowa City, Iowa, 1947), pp. 103–104.

of the group. Hence pointing out that they formed an ideology amounted to unmasking the sinister forces (as Bentham would call them) behind the ideas. That is, 'ideology' . . . was a term of opprobrium. Thus Marx could unmask the capitalist behind such ideas as liberty and equality, parliamentary government, etc. The next stage is reached when it is seen that any set of ideas held by any group is an expression of the social situation and the purpose of that group. Thus Marxism is seen to be proletarian, just as liberal democracy and free enterprise are bourgeois. This gives rise to an objective attitude toward all ideas. They are all determined by the social situations in which they arise. . . . It becomes impossible to extol one ideology as eternally true, all others as false. All we can say is that each arises in its own appropriate time and place, as determined by the life-conditions of those embracing it.[3]

This denouement, you can see, turns out to be embarrassing for Mannheim. If *all* thinking is interpreted to be ideological, all reasons rationalizations, then this view itself – the sociology of knowledge – is simply the ideology of the sociologist and has no claim to truth. The view, in short, is self-destructive: if we have good reason to believe the view is true, then the view itself collapses! Mannheim tried several ways to avoid this difficulty – for example, since the sociologist belongs to the intelligentsia, his class interest determines that he shall be critical of, and unattached to, any particular ideology. But the only way out really is to admit that not *all* thinking is ideological and not all reasons rationalizations.

Ernest Nagel in his article on "Some Issues in the Logic of History" points out what he takes to be the deficiencies of the sort of historical relativism found in Becker's essay, which, as we saw, exhibits both idealistic and existentialist thought, and of Mannheim's sociological relativism too. These criticisms cut deeply and you will want to follow them closely. You would also do well, if time permits, to read Maurice Mandelbaum's extensive criticism of historical and sociological relativism in his *The Problem of Historical Knowledge*.

[3] *Ibid.*

5.

There are many other philosophical problems to which the sciences of man give rise; but none is more interesting, I think, than the question of how history is related to the social sciences. History is not simply another social science, but it is not always clear what it is instead!

To begin with, the social scientist seeks to discover laws of human behavior while the historian tries to explain the occurrence of specific, unique events in the concrete course of human experience. However, even though the historian, and the biographer too, does not *seek* laws, clearly he does *use* laws from psychology and the social sciences in his efforts to explain unique historical events. The fact that the historian uses laws and simple generalizations is often obscured by the fact that he explains his material by using them without explicitly stating them – a process known to the logician as enthymematic reasoning. For example, consider Lytton Strachey's explanation of James Anthony Froude's attachment to Carlyle and his consequent moralizing in *The History of England:*

Old Mr. Froude had drawn a magic circle round his son, from which escape was impossible; and the creature whose life had been almost ruined by his father's moral cruelty . . . remained, in fact, in secret servitude – a disciplinarian, a Protestant, even a churchgoer, to the very end. . . . When his father had vanished, [Froude] submitted himself to Carlyle. The substitution was symptomatic; the new father expressed in explicit dogma the unconscious teaching of the old. . . .[4]

[4] Lytton Strachey, *Portraits in Miniature* (New York, 1931), pp. 193–194.

Strachey, of course, in explaining Froude's behavior depends upon the hypotheses and concepts of psychoanalysis, although he nowhere explicitly mentions or states them. This procedure is standard for biographers and historians; they are not interested in scientific laws or concepts for their own sakes but in using them to explain, as far as possible, concrete events. In this respect the biographer or historian is like the geophysicist who does not seek geophysical laws but tries to apply the laws of physics to the concrete course of physical events, as unique as human ones, and so explain them.

However, it is one thing to say that the biographer and historian use laws, and as often as possible, but quite another thing to say that every explanation of historical events must involve a scientific law or generalization which unhappily falls short of being a genuine law. Part at least of the explanation of biographical and historical events requires pointing out the conscious and reflective motives and ideas which determined individuals to act in a certain way and which, it turned out, produced consequences of enormous historical importance. It is difficult to see why this sort of "rational explanation" should be interpreted as, or cast into the form of, scientific laws; indeed to point out the reasons for certain acts explains them quite as well, although in a different way, as pointing out, say, the unconscious causes of behavior explains them.

It seems likely that the historian depends upon both "causal models" and "motive models" in explaining historical events. Indeed those events are usually so complex and their determining factors so involved that the historian may need to connect up psychological and sociological hypotheses and many "rational explanations" in explaining just one event. However, it is difficult, to say the least, to judge the relative weight and importance of those many different determining factors of an historical event, and the historian often makes completely untestable judgments about which factor is most important or which one has more weight than another. Ernest Nagel, however, in his essay on the logical structure of history, explores several ways in which it would be quite intelligible and testable for an historian to make these judgments.

The Scientific Revolution in Biology

EVERETT W. HALL

Probably the outstanding single event in the history of nineteenth-century science was the publication in 1859 of *The Origin of Species* by Charles Darwin. It had an impact on popular thinking comparable to that of Newton's *Natural Philosophy According to Mathematical Principles.* Indeed, in a sense, it was more striking, for whereas Newton was accepted on all sides and even ex-

From Everett W. Hall, *Modern Science and Human Values: A Study in the History of Ideas,* pp. 221–236.

erted a positive influence on religion (as shown in the spread of Deism), Darwin stirred up violent controversy and was excoriated by a large number of religious thinkers. We shall inquire as to the causes of this presently. In science itself his importance was far below that of Newton; yet it was much greater than is sometimes thought.

The popular view is that Darwin's importance lay in establishing the fact of evolution by accumulating a vast array of observations to substantiate it. His theory of the mechanism of evolution, so it is thought, was something of an aberration on his part — in any case dated and so of antiquarian interest only. What was this "fact" of evolution according to the popular view? That all forms of life on the earth sprang from one or two simple, primitive types; that they can be arranged in a grand hierarchy according to the history of their development; that it is possible and proper to reconstruct this as a majestic story telling how, despite many blind alleys, man, the crowning glory of it all, finally emerged.

This, it seems to me, is quite wrong, almost as wrong as the popular conception of the Copernican revolution. It will be my contention that the basic significance of Darwin lay not in that he wrote or made possible such a history of life but that he brought into biology on a broad basis the concepts and methods of the new kind of science, or perhaps more accurately, that he led biology out of the desert up to the very borders of this promised land. In this journey the notion of the mechanism of evolution was vital, the very guiding beacon.

If our account of it has been correct, the new type of science did not itself aim to reconstruct unique events — not even an event as complex and baffling as that of the development of life on our planet. Such work — and it remained important and probably far more interesting than that of the pure scientist — was to be given to the detective, the historian. It required for its successful pursuit a well filled kit of scientific knowledge. But, inasmuch as its aim was the telling of a story (of unique events in one little corner of the universe), not the formulating of laws (of uniformities in abstract features of events everywhere and everywhen), it was not science.

Interest in the story of life on our planet was characteristic of the nineteenth century. It was, indeed, not without relation to the romantic movement. We have seen how the romanticist, skeptical of the abstractness of the new science which did not "take time seriously," turned to history, to explanation not by reference to scientific laws but by delineation of unique developments culminating in the concrete phenomena to be explained. This kind of approach was not confined to the explanations of peoples and periods in human history but was extended to organic life as a whole and even to physical nature.

The German philosopher, Schelling, devoted his energies as a young man to building a philosophy of nature on this sort of romantic foundation. He saw all things as in some mystical and symbolic sense evolving into the human spirit with its highest development in art and religion. Physical nature was just a low form of this spirit, not yet aware of itself. In the polarity of its forces of attraction and repulsion it everywhere revealed the conflict found in man between his awareness of himself, of his own freedom and creativity, on the one hand, and the outer world and its restrictions upon him, on the other — a conflict overcome only in artistic achievement and religious experience. Starting with the lowest power in nature, gravity, this evolutionary force worked its way up through such manifestations as light, magnetism, electricity and chemical process to organic life, where gradually the distinctive characteristics of spirit emerged. Hegel's dialectic presented another instance of this romantic evolutionism. It portrayed the development of organic life as just one stage in the evolution of the forms of nature, which, as a whole, was in turn simply a step in the over-all unfolding of Everything.

The later romantics in philosophy and literature embraced Darwin's evolutionism with eagerness as giving observational corroboration of their standpoint. True, they did throw out his theory of the mechanism of evolution, Nietzsche, for example, substituting a "will to power" and Bergson an "*élan vital*." In this their instincts were right: it was precisely the *mechanism* that carried the scientific dynamite. It is, of course, undeniable that Darwin contributed to the evolutionary point of view a wealth of confirmatory observations painstakingly accumulated over many years and in so doing helped to lift evolutionism from the disrepute of its association with the wild and uninhibited speculations of the earlier romantics. Nor should this service be underestimated – yet it alone was not science; it could be incorporated in a romantic picture like that drawn in Bergson's *Creative Evolution* without in the least transforming the romanticism into science.

It is my contention that Darwin's contribution to the development of the biological sciences was far more revolutionary than that ascribed to him in the popular view just sketched. Although the new scientific approach had already been adopted in dealing with certain specific biological problems, perhaps most notably by William Harvey in his theory of the circulation of the blood, it was Darwin's work that allowed a thorough reorientation of the sciences of life in conformity with it. These sciences had remained up until his time essentially classificatory and directly descriptive. In the shift from this to the modern experimental basis I think we can distinguish three important services Darwin rendered.

Negatively, his criticism of the tacit presupposition of the traditional approach – the notion of clear-cut, fixed species – was eminently successful in showing that the classification of living forms had to be replaced by something else as the major objective of biological science. Positively, his suggested mechanism of evolution did two things. On the one hand, it directly stimulated the tendency to replace ordinary observation by experimentation. Darwin did not himself use experimental procedures, but one of the cornerstones of his theory of the mechanism of evolution was the work in experimental breeding of domestic animals introduced in the agricultural revolution of the preceding century. Moreover, certain problems connected with "natural selection" but unresolved by Darwin, particularly those associated with the inheritance and variation of characteristics, demanded and soon elicited an experimental approach. The stimulus which Darwin gave to this development can hardly be overestimated. On the other hand, Darwin was able, through the idea of the evolutionary mechanism that he proposed, to save for the biological sciences the concept of organic usefulness while denuding it of its teleological connotation, thereby remaking it, so to speak, from a value concept into a factual one.

The doctrine of the fixity of species went back to Aristotle, who held that offspring were always of the same species as their parents. That this idea dominated the thinking of biologists down into the nineteenth century was due not so much to the weight of Aristotle's authority as to the fact that it was everywhere corroborated by direct observation. Without this basis in experience, the Christian dogma of special creation, that is, that God created each species of life by a separate act, would probably never have been formulated in the first place and certainly would not have displayed the historical tenacity it did.

The recognition of this forces us to put the doctrine of the fixity of species in the wider context of the whole method in biology. Here, as in mechanics, Aristotelian concepts were directly related to observation, being simply abstractive of some feature of everyday experience. It was the objective of biological science to find the natural classes of living beings as these could be observed by anyone, and to construct a system of names and definitions that would mark them out. In this Aristotle had to oppose what might be called the "logical" method of Plato.

Plato's approach was based on the principle that any individual either had or did not have a given property. Thus, an appropriate classification of living forms could be constructed by "dichotomous division." You started with some property and divided up all individuals into two classes – those that possessed it and those that did not – ; then you took the former group and subdivided it with respect to another property and so on. For example, you could divide all animals into those that lived on or in the water and those that did not; you could then subdivide the former into those that breathed water and those that did not; by selecting a further property you could again split up the "left-hand" class and so on. This method of division, obviously, was the expression of a logician-mathematician at work, desiring completeness and symmetry above all else.

In contrast, Aristotle used a more commonsensical classification that took several properties at a time as its basis of definition and tried to follow the divisions of nature as these were open for everyday observation. In so doing he found, he thought, natural classes that were removed from one another by whole groups of properties and whose members were characterized by distinctive systems of organs each of which had a function useful to the individual as a whole. Nature was not interested in illustrating all possible combinations of vital organs, but in putting together and preserving forms that were functionally appropriate to the kinds of life to be lived.

This Aristotelian approach probably reached its apogee in the work of the eighteenth-century Swedish botanist, Linnaeus. He based his classification of plants on characteristics of their sex organs, which he neatly divided into twenty-six parts, allowing him to speak of the "vegetable alphabet." He also invented the modern system of nomenclature which united a generic with a specific name, thus systematically applying the Aristotelian form of definition, *"per genus et differentia."*

This whole classificatory basis of biology was challenged indirectly by the so-called "fact" of evolution, which, by destroying the idea of the fixity of species, took away much of the motivation leading biologists into sheer taxonomy and allowed it to flow into other channels; it was directly opposed by the demonstration of the arbitrary character of its distinctions between genera, species and varieties.

In the first regard, Darwin was anticipated by several men. In biology proper the work of two Frenchmen should be mentioned. Buffon's *Natural History* gave a detailed exposition of eighteenth-century knowledge of living species arranged as a cosmic epic, from the lowest and simplest forms to man. Its author, perhaps due to fear of the church, apparently wavered in his belief between the doctrines of evolution and special creation.

In Lamarck's *Zoological Philosophy,* appearing in the first decade of the nineteenth century, there was no such wavering. Lamarck boldly asserted that the more complex species had evolved from the simpler, and that species were not fixed. He stated, moreover, a definite and consistent theory of the mechanism of evolution which, although not confirmed by experimental results nor even by any very extended accumulation of data of direct observation – Lamarck being satisfied with a few striking yet essentially casual corroborating instances – , was yet capable of being subjected to the most rigorous scientific testing. In outline, his theory was that changed environmental conditions developed new wants in organisms living under them; these new wants gave rise to new habits of action which, in turn, developed new organs from the use of old ones or, contrariwise, atrophied old ones through their disuse; finally, these acquired organic changes were inherited by subsequent generations. It was thus that the giraffe, in need of higher foliage for food, developed its long neck; water birds, stretching the digits of their feet to swim more rapidly, acquired webbed feet; the mole, living for long periods underground, almost lost its eyes. We may, if we wish, smile smugly at this theory, and it must be admitted that Lamarck's notion of empirical verification was rather naïve; yet it might be well to search our own minds to see whether our superiority has not arisen from the fact that it was the Darwinian, not the Lamarckian, theory that, as a matter of historical fact, actually proved successful. For some reason, perhaps not unconnected with the casual and commonsensical character of the corroborating instances Lamarck used, the Lamarckian theory did not have the stimulating effect upon biological experimentation produced by the Darwinian.

In historical geology and paleontology, two English predecessors of Darwin should be mentioned. James Hutton, in his *Theory of the Earth,* did for the geologic past something very similar to what Newton had accomplished for the celestially distant. Just as the earlier thinker had united heavenly motions with terrestrial by assuming the uniformity of nature, so his later compatriot united historically remote processes in the earth's crust with present ones by means of the same assumption. Hutton argued that only those processes presently observable as producing effects upon the earth's surface — such as sedimentation, erosion, volcanic action and earthquakes — should be used to explain the records of the past which the geologist found in the rocks. This view was successful in overthrowing the reigning doctrine that the rock strata were to be interpreted as the signs of a series of extraordinary catastrophes. It helped Darwin combat the allied doctrine of the special creation of each species of life. Charles Lyell's *Principles of Geology* was based on an acceptance of Hutton's principles of uniformity and, by its consistent application, succeeded in working out, in its main outlines, the history of the earth, identifying the main geological eras and establishing their sequence by means of the criterion that an age was nearer our own if, as evidenced by the fossil remains, more species were to be found in it that were extant in the present. This did not presuppose evolution, but it did open a tremendous storehouse of corroborating evidence for it.

Darwin marshaled many arguments in favor of the proposition that existent species had developed from others. Breeders of domestic animals had been able to effect sufficiently great modifications in varieties as to make it plausible that man during his whole history had without intention bred some new species. The very great similarity in the basic processes of life, and the particular likenesses of so-called "homologous structures" — such as wing, foreleg and arm — of different species made it reasonable that different forms of life had had a common origin. Rudimentary organs, of no use to their possessors but similar to useful, fully developed organs of lower species, also seemed to argue for a transformation of species. Fossil records, despite many gaps, offered many instances of forms intermediate between species now distinct.

Perhaps the chief argument Darwin used against the fixity of species was that the distinction between species and variety was arbitrary and vague. Everyone admitted, as indeed the facts of selective breeding demanded, that some varieties of a given species had evolved from others. Darwin showed that in many cases differences, recognized as simply marking out varieties within the same species, were more profound than those admittedly distinguishing different species. Naturalists had never reached agreement on a criterion of species difference; even the widely accepted mark of sterility upon crossing was not accepted universally as separating species difference from variety difference.

By these and similar arguments, bolstered by a wealth of instances, many drawn from his own extensive observations, Darwin combatted the doctrine of the fixity of species and the dogma of special creation. But of more importance for the history of biology and even, as a matter of fact, for the acceptance of the transformation of species was Darwin's account of the mechanism of evolution.

Darwin got his clue from breeders: they did not create variations; they simply selected them for breeding when they spontaneously occurred; the mechanisms of heredity did the rest. The breeder, of course, had to be patient; he had to select small deviations in the direction desired over many generations. But the long history of life on the earth as revealed by the paleontologists indicated that nature had had sufficient time to carry on selective breeding on a grand scale. But here Darwin found himself stopped. What was the mechanism of natural selection? In the case of artificial selection the breeder's purposes and his ability to control mating sufficiently explained the results, but Darwin refused to ascribe design to nature, as this would involve the acceptance of final causes, which, he realized, would be out of harmony with the whole approach of modern science. The solution came to him upon reading Malthus on population. All life, not merely human, tended to reproduce itself beyond the available food supply. This pressure of numbers set up a struggle for existence. On the average only the fittest survived, the unfit being extinguished before they could reproduce themselves. This struggle, then, furnished the means of natural selection. The most fit mated, and the mechanism of heredity could be expected to preserve the characteristics that had been the basis of their selection, and through a repetition of this process over many generations large differences could arise.

Of the many problems Darwin's theory raised, the most immediately pressing centered around the occurrence and inheritance of variations of characters. In this connection I shall mention the work of two men in order to give concrete force to my argument concerning the true significance for biology of Darwin's account of the mechanism of evolution.

The Dutch botanist, Hugo de Vries, found that the small, fluctuating variations between individuals that Darwin thought could, by a sort of cumulative effect over many generations, give rise to new species were not inheritable. On the other hand, he discovered that large variations (or "mutations" as he called them) which occurred very infrequently were inheritable, and that strains exemplifying them showed no signs over many generations of reversion to the primitive forms, as was generally thought to be the case. He argued that the occurrence of such mutations could account for the rise not only of new varieties but even of new species. For the history of biology, however, his methods were more important than his findings. He observed the variations of a single species (Lamarck's evening primrose) under particularly favorable field conditions. Then he transplanted weaker varieties for special cultivation, sowed wild seeds in his garden for more careful observation and, through a sequence of several generations, selected seeds from plants showing some specific variation. In short, he introduced experimentation to solve a biological problem.

As a matter of fact, but not of general knowledge at the time, de Vries had been anticipated in the use of experimental procedures in genetics by the Austrian monk, Gregor Mendel. Mendel was unsatisfied with Darwin's explanation of the formation of new species and set about to study cross-breeding, which Darwin had considered of little significance for evolution, by experimental procedures of rigorous scientific design. He found that when tall edible peas were fertilized by tall, all offspring were tall; when dwarf ones were mated with dwarf, they produced dwarf plants only. When dwarf were crossed with tall, all plants resulting from this union were tall; but when the latter were self-fertilized, individuals in the following generation were tall only in three out of four cases. Continuing with the process of self-fertilization upon this last-mentioned set, he found that the dwarf bred true in all instances, but that only one third of the tall plants had tall offspring which bred true, whereas the remainder produced tall plants only in the ratio of three out of four (this group thereby duplicating the genetic phenomena of the first generation after crossing).

With the help of certain assumptions, Mendel was able to put these data into the framework of a strict scientific law. The assumptions he made were that the inherited characters of an organism were determined by the combination of pollen cells and egg cells producing it; that incompatible characters, such as tallness and dwarfness, were genetically "units," that is, were inherited pure so that the organism had one or the other, not something halfway between; that of such characters one was "dominant" and one "recessive," that is, the union of a pair of egg and pollen cells which individually were hereditary determinants of incompatible unit characters always produced an organism displaying one of the two, namely, the dominant (tallness in his study), but left the hereditary determinants in the egg and pollen cells produced by this organism equally divided, so that, under suitable combination, its offspring could inherit the other or recessive trait; and finally that the combination of a unit determinant with the same unit determinant, whether of a dominant or a recessive character, always bred true. With these assumptions Mendel was able to formulate a very simple genetic law covering his observations to the effect that the combination of hereditary determinants in cross-breeding (that is, breeding from parents themselves possessing incompatible unit characters) was a matter of chance, that is, for large numbers of instances the division of cases according to the various possible combinations of these determinants would approximate an equal distribution. (That his findings, as summarized above, did agree with this law can be easily grasped visually by consulting the diagram on page 128.)

It is important that we appreciate the scientific character of Mendel's law. It was, of course, quantitative, although in the somewhat looser sense of being enumerative rather than mensurational. But this alone, as the reader is now persuaded, would not guarantee its scientific nature. It had the further property of uniting observable, quantitative variables (namely, the numbers of individuals possessing dominant and recessive characters in various generations) in an invariant uniformity, itself not directly observable but calculated from observations made under appropriate conditions. The idea of chance distribution was not one amenable to direct experiential check, for the distribution involved was not one of observed characters but of their determinants through the schema of hereditary dominance and recession: it was, I think, a concept of the Galilean type.

The remarkable stimulus given by Darwin's theory to the adoption of the methods of experimental science in the biological field was not confined to genetics; it rapidly spread to embryology, cytology and related studies. If, perhaps, in these other areas there was no set of problems quite so intimately connected with the mechanism of evolution proposed by Darwin as were those genetics tried to solve, yet the leaven, once introduced, quickly animated the whole mass. Moreover, the mere fact that Darwin

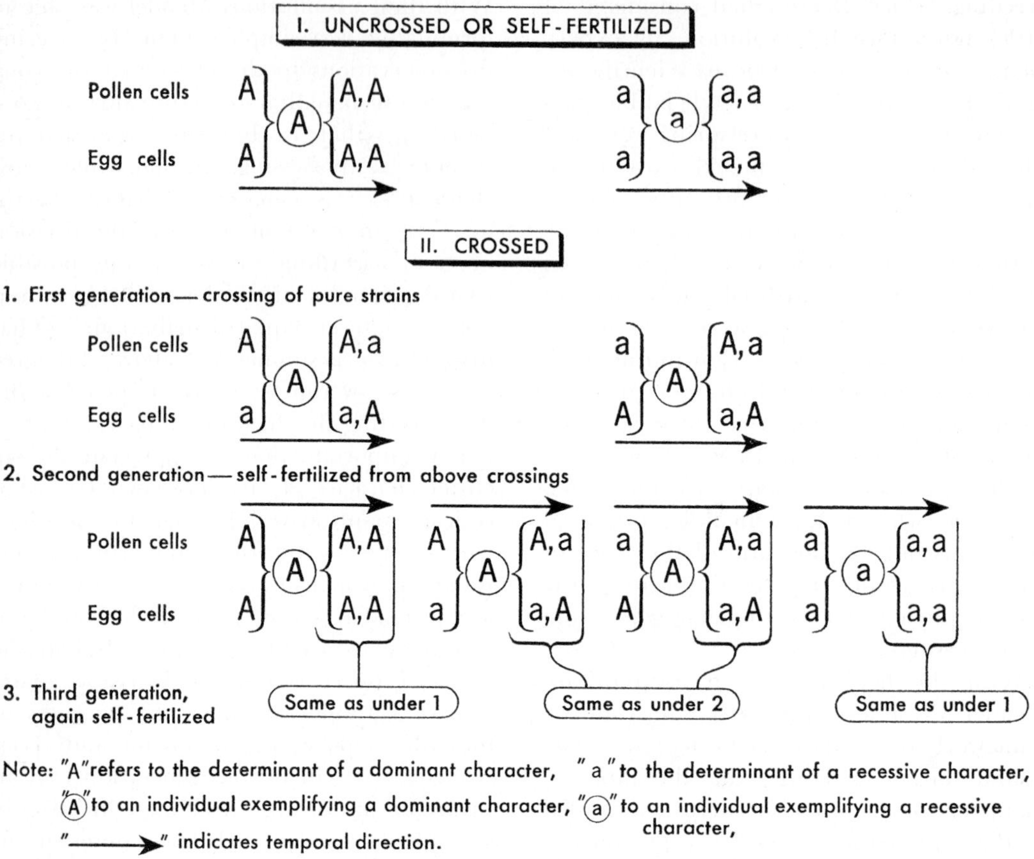

Mendel's Genetic Scheme

had been able to present a plausible theory acted almost like the release of a trigger; the idea of natural selection could replace that of final causes in explaining the apparent purposiveness of biological phenomena. It seemed, indeed, as though Darwin had shown biologists how they could eat their cake and have it, too. They could now use such obviously teleological concepts as "the preservation of the species," "adaptation to the environment" and "organic function" without really committing themselves to any Aristotelian notion of an immanent purpose or a Nature-does-everything-for-the-best, since they were only "as if" (to borrow Hans Vaihinger's pregnant expression). They were just shorter and more picturesque ways of asserting that the process or form involved had been naturally selected through the long eons of evolutionary struggle. By and large, then, it could simply be assumed without special investigation that a given biological phenomenon "served a purpose," and inquiry was increasingly directed toward the mechanism of the phenomenon, toward the discovery of uniformities in its occurrence, especially uniformities of the physico-chemical variety.

It must be admitted that there have been some reactionary movements, the most notable, probably, being the attempt of Hans Driesch to rehabilitate Aristotle's "entelechy" or organic governor; but these have only served to agitate the surface waters and thus contribute to the public turmoil stirred up originally by the Darwinian theory. Indeed, if anything, Newtonianism has been carried too far or, perhaps I should say, has been followed too blindly in biological investigations, so that the overwhelming success that has accompanied the attempt to find the physical and chemical laws exemplified by living phenomena has prejudiced investigators against the possibility that there may be laws of the truly Galilean variety which are irreducibly organic or biologic, that is, which cannot be translated into a complex of merely physical and chemical laws. But the reader will keep in mind that his author is a philosopher and that the warning just issued is in all likelihood merely a philosophic idiosyncrasy. But this, I think, can be accepted without any hesitancy: the biological sciences have adopted the new pattern and will never return to that of Aristotle. This means that in the area of life itself science has abandoned the attempt to give value answers to factual questions and has successfully applied the method of gaining knowledge of nature's regularities instituted by the revolution of the seventeenth century.

As intimated at the beginning of the present section, the analogy between Darwin's work and that of Newton in the history of occidental thought can be pressed further: not only did each give a tremendous stimulus to the adoption of the new scientific method in the areas directly involved, that is, in biology and physics, respectively, but each had an almost overpowering influence upon more distant investigations and, indeed, upon the public mind in general. In illustration of the former, let me mention the spread of Darwinism in anthropology, sociology and psychology in the late nineteenth and early twentieth centuries.

Four years after the appearance of *The Origin of Species* the enthusiastic Darwinian, Thomas Huxley, published his *Man's Place in Nature,* applying, as Darwin himself was to do a little later in *The Descent of Man,* the evolutionary theory to the human species. He argued that man had evolved from an ancestral type from which the anthropoid apes had likewise sprung. Huxley's comparative studies of skulls led to the animated and phenomenally successful search for the "missing links" in this sequence; it also led directly to the establishment of the science of physical anthropology.

The application of the theory of evolution to man brought about a completely new attitude toward primitive peoples. Instead of being treated as superstitious heathen, to be converted to the ways and religions of western Europe, or again as noble savages uncontaminated by the artificialities of civilization, they came to be looked upon as human beings at a lower stage of social evolution than civilized man, their customs, religions and institutions being viewed as the ancestors of our own. Even more specifically, Darwinian concepts were (rather uncritically, it must be admitted) applied to them: for example, William G. Sumner, in his *Folkways,* published at the turn of the century, said that the moral customs and class structures characterizing a given primitive group had been "selected" through their superior "survival value" for the group in its struggle with other groups and with its physical environment and that their persistence was a sort of "social inheritance." Incidentally, this approach easily degenerated into a kind of ethical relativism (present in Sumner's book but more articulately stated in the writings of Edward Westermarck) holding that a custom or institution was morally good or justifiable if it possessed survival value — for example, that infanticide and the killing of the aged were right in conditions of chronic scarcity of food. Such a view, parading as "scientific" in presumably the modern sense, was really a reversion to the medieval confusion of fact and value for it attempted to answer a value question (What institutions and customs are morally justified?) by stating a factual uniformity (groups possessing such and such institutions and customs under such and such conditions tend to survive).

The reigning psychology at the time Darwin published his major work was associationism, which was modeled, as we have seen, upon Newtonian mechanics. The appearance of the evolutionary theory had an enormous effect, amounting to an almost complete change of direction, in this science. In place of sensory elements and the laws of their combination, psychologists came to study the behavior patterns of man considered as an animal trying to survive in and adapt himself to an external environment. Laws of his behavior common to that of other animals were sought and were viewed as having been selected by the evolutionary mechanism much as had the morphological features marking out surviving species. Darwin himself gave great encouragement to this tendency in his *Expression of the Emotions in Man and Animals,* in which he tried to show that normal emotional reactions are the result of natural selection, that, to cite a single illustration, the "freezing" of the frightened rabbit made it more difficult to see and hence less apt to become the prey of one of its natural enemies. This approach furnished direct stimulation to such a physiological psychology as that of W. N. Cannon's *Bodily Changes in Pain, Hunger, Fear, and Rage.* It also spurred the development of animal psychology on the part of such men as G. J. Romanes, Lloyd Morgan and H. S. Jennings. This, in turn, aided by the work of I. P. Pavlov as reported in his *Lectures on the Conditioned Reflex,* gave rise to present-day behaviorism, which insists on "objective" methods in psychology, finding its laws through experimental observations of the external behavior of organisms — "rat psychology" as it has been somewhat unsympathetically designated.

The effect of Darwin's work upon modern philosophy was perhaps second only to that of Newton's. A word must suffice to explain. Two major tendencies were encouraged by Darwin's theory. On the one hand, the idea of evolution was extrapolated from the biological sphere to the cosmic. An instance of this emphasis in its more mechanical form is the rather crude system of Herbert Spencer, "knocked together out of cracked hemlock boards" (as it was appropriately described by William James). Spencer thought he could formulate a single, all-embracing law asserting that everything in the universe has evolved from a simple, unorganized state to a complex, highly organized one. Our solar system on the Laplacean hypothesis was a case in point; a second was life on earth according to the Darwinian theory; a third was the evolution of society from a relatively undifferentiated condition to the complexity of industrial organization. Another instance of this cosmic evolutionism is offered by the more sophisticated views of the emergentists, for example, by those of Samuel Alexander in *Space, Time and Deity* and Lloyd Morgan in *Emergent Evolution.* They insisted that evolution on the cosmic scale required the occurrence of novel developments unpredictable on the basis of knowledge of earlier events — cosmic mutations, so to speak. To illustrate from Alexander's system: the universe at first was composed of colorless, inaudible motions; then there emerged, in sequence, sensory qualities, life and consciousness. Deity was still to come.

The second philosophical current set in motion by Darwin's theory went in an oblique if not contrary direction. Instead of expanding the idea of evolution from a biological theory to a total philosophy, it condensed philosophic systems into biological phenomena that had arisen in the evolutionary process and were selected by their utility in the particular environments (social, of course, as well as physical) in which their proponents lived. Logically, on this account, philosophy was to become a subdivision of biology; its theories were to be judged simply in terms of their biological functions. (The curious fact is to be noted that biologists did not appear to be much taken by this extension of their science; it is possible that they felt that it was not a scientific achievement at all!) The outstanding leader in this movement was John Dewey and, of his many works, perhaps *The Influence of Darwin on Philosophy* might be cited as most relevant to the present point.

Finally, we must glance very hurriedly at the impact of Darwin's thought upon the public mind in general. As already intimated, there is a striking contrast here with the parallel case of Newton. Popular response to Newton's gravitational system in the eighteenth century was uniformly favorable; the like cannot be affirmed of the general reaction in the late nineteenth and early twentieth centuries to Darwin's evolutionary theory. Without for a moment intending to underestimate the force of the favorable response, which by now is overwhelming, I would like, particularly since I believe the answer to be relevant to the main theme of our discussion, to raise the question why there was an immediate and vociferous opposition to his ideas.

As an initial clue, we should note that the opposition was based mainly on religious grounds, secondarily on moral and value considerations generally. There was of course a clash with a specific Christian dogma, the literal inerrancy of the Bible: if the account of creation (or we should say, if either account of creation) given in Genesis had been transcribed verbatim by Moses from the lips of the Creator, then Darwin's theory was blasphemous. There was, by contrast, no such undeniable collision between the Bible and Newtonian mechanics, and so far as the latter did conflict with the Aristotelian position of the Church, the struggle had come to a head with Galileo.

This source of objection should not be underestimated, but it must not be taken as the complete explanation. On the one hand, the literal inerrancy of the Biblical story had been subject to a long and increasingly widespread questioning. Aside from the accumulation of scientific findings incompatible with it and the growth of Biblical criticism applying the same methods to the text of Holy Scriptures as to any other historical documents, there was the tradition of allegorical interpretation which was certainly as ancient and respectable as the doctrine of literal truth. We must, I think, look for some further grounds for the intensely unfavorable reaction to the idea of evolution.

We may perhaps get a lead from the vulgar misapprehension that Darwin held, as against the Christian view that man had been made in God's image, that we were descendants of apes: the theory of evolution belittled man. But again we must remember that man had already been belittled in the scheme of creation; indeed, the Newtonian world picture itself quite successfully accomplished this. So we must press our analysis further still.

I think we come very close to bedrock when, once more turning from the "fact" to the mechanism of evolution as the cardinal matter, we bear in mind that Darwin challenged the appeal to final causes in the last great citadel of its strength – that of life itself. As long as there was still a "Why?" about fact that could be answered by an assertion of some good, the familiar and commonsensical type of explanation, so characteristic of pre-scientific thought, could be retained. If the fact of the possession of such and such organs or the occurrence of such and such physiological processes could be satisfactorily accounted for by reference to the perpetuation of the species or the attainment of the species type by the individual, then there was still at least tacitly present the assumption that "Nature does everything for the best." I think it is not too subtle and strained an interpretation to say that, along with other causes, the negative reaction to Darwinism was motivated by this perhaps largely subconscious attempt to protect the sphere of life from the methods of the new science which required that factual questions be answered factually only, keeping issues of value entirely aside.

Mechanistic Explanation and Organismic Biology

ERNEST NAGEL

Vitalism of the substantival type sponsored by Driesch and other biologists during the preceding and early part of the present century is now a dead issue in the philosophy of biology — an issue that has become quiescent less, perhaps, because of the methodological and philosophical criticism that has been levelled against the doctrine than because of the infertility of vitalism as a guide in biological research and because of the superior heuristic value of alternative approaches for the investigation of biological phenomena. Nevertheless, the historically influential Cartesian conception of biology as simply a chapter of physics continues to meet resistance; and outstanding biologists who find no merit in vitalism believe there are conclusive reasons for maintaining the irreducibility of biology to physics and for asserting the intrinsic autonomy of biological method. The standpoint from which this thesis is currently advanced commonly carries the label of "organismic biology"; and though the label covers a variety of special biological doctrines that are not all mutually compatible, those who fall under it are united by the common conviction that biological phenomena cannot be understood adequately in terms of theories and explanations which are of the so-called "mechanistic type." It is the aim of the present paper to examine this claim.

It is, however, not always clear what thesis organismic biologists are rejecting when they declare that "mechanistic" explanations are not fully satisfactory in biology. In one familiar sense of "mechanistic," a theory is mechanistic if it employs only such concepts which are distinctive of the science of mechanics. It is doubtful, however, whether any professed mechanist in biology would today explicate his position in this manner. Physicists themselves have long since abandoned the seventeenth-century hope that a universal science of nature would be developed within the framework of the fundamental conceptions of mechanics. And no one today, it is safe to say, subscribes literally to the Cartesian program of reducing all the sciences to the science of mechanics and specifically to the mechanics of contact-action. On the other hand, it is not easy to state precisely what is the identifying mark of a mechanistic explanation if it is not to coincide with an explanation that falls within the science of mechanics. In a preliminary way, and for lack of anything better and clearer, I shall adopt in the present paper the criterion proposed long ago by Jacques Loeb, according to whom a mechanist in biology is one who believes that all living phenomena "can be unequivocally explained in physico-chemical terms," — that is, in terms of theories that have been originally developed for domains of inquiry in

Originally published in *Philosophy and Phenomenological Research,* 11, 1951, pp. 327–338. Reprinted by permission of the author and the editor.

which the distinction between the living and nonliving plays no role, and that by common consent are classified as belonging to physics and chemistry.

As will presently appear, this brief characterization of the mechanistic thesis in biology does not suffice to distinguish in certain important respects mechanists in biology from those who adopt the organismic standpoint; but the above indication will do for the moment. It does suffice to give point to one further preliminary remark which needs to be made before I turn to the central issue between mechanists and organismic biologists. It is an obvious commonplace, but one that must not be ignored if that issue is to be justly appraised, that there are large sectors of biological study in which physico-chemical explanations play no role at present, and that a number of outstanding biological theories have been successfully exploited which are not physico-chemical in character. For example, a vast array of important information has been obtained concerning embryological processes, though no explanation of such regularities in physico-chemical terms is available; and neither the theory of evolution even in its current form, nor the gene theory of heredity is based on any definite physico-chemical assumptions concerning living processes. Accordingly, organismic biologists possess at least some grounds for their skepticism concerning the inevitability of the mechanistic standpoint; and just as a physicist may be warranted in holding that some given branch of physics (e.g., electro-magnetic theory) is not reducible to some other branch (e.g., mechanics), so an organismic biologist may be warranted in holding an analogous view with respect to the relation of biology and physico-chemistry. If there is a genuine issue between mechanists and organismic biologists, it is not *prima facie* a pseudo-question.

However, organismic biologists are not content with making the obviously justified observation that only a relatively small sector of biological phenomena has thus far been explained in physico-chemical terms; they also maintain that *in principle* the mode of analysis associated with mechanistic explanations is inapplicable to some of the major problems of biology, and that therefore mechanistic biology cannot be adopted as the ultimate ideal in biological research. What are the grounds for this contention and how solid is the support which organismic biologists claim for their thesis?

The central theme of organismic biology is that living creatures are not assemblages of tissues and organs functioning independently of one another, but are integrated structures of parts. Accordingly, living organisms must be studied as "wholes," and not as the mere "sums" of parts. Each part, it is maintained, has physico-chemical properties; but the interrelation of the parts involves a distinctive organization, so that the study of the physico-chemical properties of the parts taken in isolation of their membership in the organized whole which is the living body fails to provide an adequate understanding of the facts of biology. In consequence, the continuous adaptation of an organism to its environment and of its parts to one another so as to maintain its characteristic structure and activities, cannot be described in terms of physical and chemical principles. Biology must employ categories and a vocabulary which are foreign to the sciences of the inorganic, and it must recognize modes and laws of behavior which are inexplicable in physico-chemical terms.

There is time to cite but one brief quotation from the writings of organismic biologists. I offer the following from E. S. Russell as a typical statement of this point of view:

> Any action of the whole organism would appear to be susceptible of analysis to an indefinite degree — and this is in general the aim of the physiologist, to analyze, to decompose into their elementary processes

the broad activities and functions of the organism.

> But . . . by such a procedure something is lost, for the action of the whole has a certain unifiedness and completeness which is left out of account in the process of analysis. . . . In our conception of the organism we must . . . take into account the unifiedness and wholeness of its activities [especially since] the activities of the organism all have reference to one or other of three great ends [development, maintenance, and reproduction], and both the past and the future enter into their determination. . . .
>
> . . . It follows that the activities of the organism as a whole are to be regarded as of a different order from physico-chemical relations, both in themselves and for the purposes of our understanding. . . .
>
> . . . Bio-chemistry studies essentially the *conditions* of action of cells and organisms, while organismal biology attempts to study the actual modes of action of whole organisms, regarded as conditioned by, but irreducible to, the modes of action of lower unities . . . (*Interpretation of Development and Heredity,* pp. 171–2, 187–8)

Accordingly, while organismic biology rejects every form of substantival vitalism, it also rejects the possibility of physico-chemical explanation of vital phenomena. But does it, in point of fact, present a clear alternative to physico-chemical theories of living processes, and, if so, what types of explanatory theories does it recommend as worth exploring in biology?

(1) At first blush, the sole issue that seems to be raised by organismic biology is that commonly discussed under the heading of "emergence" in other branches of science, including the physical sciences; and, although other questions are involved in the organismic standpoint, I shall begin with this aspect of the question.

The crux of the doctrine of emergence, as I see it, is the determination of the conditions under which one science can be reduced to some other one – i.e., the formulation of the logical and empirical conditions which must be satisfied if the laws and other statements of one discipline can be subsumed under, or explained by, the theories and principles of a second discipline. Omitting details and refinements, the two conditions which seem to be necessary and sufficient for such a reduction are briefly as follows. Let S_1 be some science or group of sciences such as physics and chemistry, hereafter to be called the "primary discipline," to which a second science, S_2, for example biology, is to be reduced. Then (i) every term which occurs in the statements of S_2 (e.g., terms like "cell," "mytosis," "heredity," etc.) must be either explicitly definable with the help of the vocabulary specific to the primary discipline (e.g., with the help of expressions like "length," "electric charge," "osmosis"); or well-established empirical laws must be available with the help of which it is possible to state the sufficient conditions for the application of all expressions in S_2, exclusively in terms of expressions occurring in the explanatory principles of S_1. For example, it must be possible to state the truth-conditions of a statement of the form "x is a cell" by means of sentences constructed exclusively out of the vocabulary belonging to the physico-chemical sciences. Though the label is not entirely appropriate, this first condition will be referred to as the condition of definability. (ii) Every statement in the secondary discipline, S_2, and especially those statements which formulate the laws established in S_2, must be derivable logically from some appropriate class of statements that can be established in the primary science, S_1 – such classes of statements will include the fundamental theoretical assumptions of S_1. This second condition will be referred to as the condition of derivability.

It is evident that the second condition cannot be fulfilled unless the first one is, although the realization of the first condition does not entail the satisfaction of the second one. It is also quite beyond dispute that in the sense of reduction specified by these conditions biology has thus far not been reduced to physics and chemistry, since not even the first step in the process of reduction has been completed – for example, we are not yet in the position to specify exhaustively in physico-chemical terms the conditions for the occurrence of cellular division.

Accordingly, organismic biologists are on firm ground if what they maintain is that all biological phenomena are not explicable thus far physico-chemically, and that no physico-chemical theory can possibly explain such phenomena until the descriptive and theoretical terms of biology meet the condition of definability. On the other hand, nothing in the facts surveyed up to this point warrants the conclusion that biology is *in principle* irreducible to physico-chemistry. Whether biology is reducible to physico-chemistry is a question that only further experimental and logical research can settle; for the supposition that each of the two conditions for the reduction of biology to physico-chemistry may some day be satisfied involves no patent contradiction.

(2) There are, however, other though related considerations underlying the organismic claim that biology is intrinsically autonomous. A frequent argument used to support this claim is based on the fact that living organisms are hierarchically organized and that, in consequence, modes of behavior characterizing the so-called "higher levels" of organization cannot be explained in terms of the structures and modes of behavior which parts of the organism exhibit on lower levels of the hierarchy.

There can, of course, be no serious dispute over the fact that organisms do exhibit structures of parts that have an obvious hierarchical organization. Living cells are structures of cellular parts (e.g., of the nucleus, cytoplasm, central bodies, etc.), each of which in turn appears to be composed of complex molecules; and, except in the case of unicellular organisms, cells are further organized into tissues, which in turn are elements of various organs that make up the individual organism. Nor is there any question but that parts of an organism which occupy a place at one level of its complex hierarchical organization stand in relations and exhibit activities which parts occupying positions at other levels of organization do not manifest: a cat can stalk and catch mice, but though its heart is involved in these activities, that organ cannot perform these feats; again, the heart can pump blood by contracting and expanding its muscular tissues, but no tissue is able to do this; and no tissue is able to divide by fission, though its constituent cells may have this power; and so on down the line. If such facts are taken in an obvious sense, they undoubtedly support the conclusion that behavior on higher levels of organization is not explained by merely citing the various behaviors of parts on lower levels of the hierarchy. Organismic biologists do not, of course, deny that the higher level behaviors occur only when the component parts of an organism are appropriately organized on the various levels of the hierarchy; but they appear to have reason on their side in maintaining that a knowledge of the behavior of these parts when these latter are not component elements in the structured living organism, does not suffice as a premise for deducing anything about the behavior of the whole organism in which the parts do stand in certain specific and complex relations to one another.

But do these admitted facts establish the organismic thesis that mechanistic explanations are not adequate in biology? This does not appear to be the case, and for several reasons. It should be noted, in the first place, that various forms of hierarchical organization are exhibited by the materials of physics and chemistry, and not only by those of biology. On the basis of current theories of matter, we are compelled to regard atoms as structures of electric charges, molecules as organizations of atoms, solids and liquids as complex systems of molecules; and we must also recognize that the elements occupying positions at different levels of the indicated hierarchy generally exhibit traits and modes of activity that their component parts do not possess. Nonetheless, this fact has not stood in the way of establishing comprehensive theories for the more elementary physical particles, in terms of which it has been possible to explain some, if not all, of the physico-chemical properties exhibited by things having a more complex organization. We do not, to be sure, possess at the present time a comprehensive and unified theory which is competent to explain the whole range of physico-chemical phenomena at all levels of complexity. Whether such a theory will ever be achieved is certainly an open question. But even if such an inclusive theory were never achieved, the mere fact that we can now explain some features of relatively highly organized bodies on the basis of theories formulated in terms of relations between relatively more simply structured elements – for example, the specific heats of solids in terms of quantum theory or the changes in phase of compounds in terms of the thermodynamics of mixtures – should give us pause in accepting the conclusion that the mere fact of the hierarchical organization of biological materials precludes the possibility of a mechanistic explanation.

This observation leads to a second point. Organismic biologists do not deny that biological organisms are complex structures of physico-chemical processes, although like everyone else they do not claim to know in minute detail just what these processes are or just how the various physico-chemical elements (assumed as the ultimate parts of living creatures) are related to one another in a living organism. They do maintain, however, (or appear to maintain) that even if our knowledge in this respect were ideally complete, it would still be impossible to account for the characteristic behavior of biological organisms – their ability to maintain themselves, to develop, and to reproduce – in mechanistic terms. Thus, it has been claimed that even if we were able to describe in full detail in physico-chemical terms what is taking place when a fertilized egg segments, we would, nevertheless, be unable to explain mechanistically the fact of segmentation – in the language of E. S. Russell, we would then be able to state the physico-chemical *conditions* for the occurrence of segmentation, but we would still be unable to "explain the *course* which development takes." Now this claim seems to me to rest on a misunderstanding, if not on a confusion. It is entirely correct to maintain that a knowledge of the physico-chemical composition of a biological organism does not suffice to explain mechanistically its mode of action – anymore than an enumeration of the parts of a clock and a knowledge of their distribution and arrangement suffices to explain and predict the mode of behavior of the time piece. To do the latter one must *also* assume some theory or set of laws (e.g., the theory of mechanics) which formulates the way in which certain elementary objects behave when they occur in certain initial distributions and arrangements, and with the help of which we can calculate and predict the course of subsequent development of the mechanism. Now it may indeed be the case that our information at a given time may suffice to describe physico-chemically the constitution of a biological organism; nevertheless, the established physico-chemical theories may not be adequate, even when combined with a physico-chemical description of the initial state of the organism, for deducing just what the course of the latter's development will be. To put the point in terms of the distinction previously introduced, the condition of definability may be realized without the condition of derivability being fulfilled. But this fact must not be interpreted to mean that it is possible under any circumstances to give explanations without the use of some theoretical assumptions, or that because one body of physico-chemical theory is not competent to explain certain biological phenomena it is *in principle impossible* to construct and establish mechanistic theories which might do so.

(3) I must now examine the consideration which appears to constitute the main reason for the negative attitude of organismic biologists toward mechanistic explanations. Organismic biologists have placed great stress on what they call the "unifiedness," the "unity," the "completeness," or the "wholeness" of organic behavior; and, since they believe that biological organisms are complex systems of mutually determining and interdependent processes to which subordinate organs contribute in various ways, they have maintained that organic behavior cannot be analyzed into a set of independently determinable component behaviors of the parts of an organism, whose "sum" may be equated to the total behavior of the organism. On the other hand, they also maintain that mechanistic philosophies of organic action are "machine theories" of the organism, which assume the "additive point of view" with respect to biological phenomena. What distinguishes mechanistic theories from organismic ones, from this perspective, is that the former do while the latter do not regard an organism as a "machine," whose "parts" are separable and can be studied in isolation from their actual functioning in the whole living organism, so that the latter may then be understood and explained as an aggregate of such independent parts. Accordingly, the fundamental reason for the dissatisfaction which organismic biologists feel toward mechanistic theories is the "additive point of view" that allegedly characterizes the latter. However, whether this argument has any merit can be decided only if the highly ambiguous and metaphorical notion of "sum" receives at least partial clarification; and it is to this phase of the question that I first briefly turn.

(i) As is well known, the word "sum" has a large variety of different uses, a number of which bear to each other certain formal analogies while others are so vague that nothing definite is conveyed by the word. There are well-defined senses of the term in various domains of pure mathematics – e.g., arithmetical sum, algebraic sum, vector sum, and the like; there are also definite uses established for the word in the natural sciences – e.g., sum of weights, sum of forces, sum of velocities, etc. But with notable exceptions; those who have employed it to distinguish wholes which are sums of their parts from wholes which supposedly are not, have not taken the trouble to indicate just what would be the sum of parts of a whole which allegedly is not equal to that whole.

I therefore wish to suggest a sense for the word "sum" which seems to me relevant to the claim of organismic biologists that the total behavior of an organism is not the sum of the behavior of its parts. That is, I wish to indicate more explicitly than organismic biologists have done – though I hasten to add that the proposed indication is only moderately more precise than is customary – what it is they are asserting when they maintain, for example, that the behavior of the kidneys in an animal body is more than the "sum" of the behaviors of the tissues, blood stream, blood vessels, and the rest of the parts of the body involved in the functioning of the kidneys.

Let me first state the suggestion in schematic, abstract form. Let T be a definite body of theory which is capable of explaining a certain indefinitely large class of statements concerning the simultaneous or successive occurrence of some set of properties P_1, P_2, . . . P_k. Suppose further that it is possible with the help of the Theory T to explain the behavior of a set of individuals i with respect to their manifesting these properties P when these individuals form a closed system s_1 under circumstances C_1; and that it is also possible with the help of T to explain the behavior of another set of individuals j with respect to their manifesting these properties P when the individuals j form a closed system s_2 under circumstances C_2. Now assume that the two sets of individuals i and j form an enlarged closed system s_3 under circumstances C_3, in which they exhibit certain modes of behavior which are formulated in a set of laws L. Two cases may now be distinguished: (a) It may be possible to deduce the laws L from T conjoined with the relevant initial conditions which obtain in C_3; in this case, the behavior of the system s_3 may be said to be the sum of the behaviors of its parts s_1 and s_2; or (b) the laws L cannot be so deduced, in which case the behavior of the system s_3 may be said *not* to be the sum of the behaviors of its parts.

Two examples may help to make clearer what is here intended. The laws of mechanics enable us to explain the mechanical behaviors of a set of cogwheels when they occur in certain arrangements; those laws also enable us to explain the behavior of freely-falling bodies moving against some resisting forces, and also the behavior of compound pendula. But the laws of mechanics also explain the behavior of the system obtained by arranging cogs, weights, and pendulum in certain ways so as to form a clock; and, accordingly, the behavior of a clock can be regarded as the sum of the behavior of its parts. On the other hand, the kinetic theory of matter as developed during the nineteenth century was able to explain certain thermal properties of gases at various temperatures, including the relations between the specific heats of gases; but it was unable to explain the relations between the specific heats of solids — that is, it was unable to account for these relations theoretically when the state of aggregation of molecules is that of a solid rather than a gas. Accordingly, the thermal behavior of solids is not the sum of the behavior of its parts.

Whether the above proposal to interpret the distinction between wholes which are and those which are not the sums of their parts would be acceptable to organismic biologists, I do not know. But, while I am aware that the suggestion requires much elaboration and refinement to be an adequate tool of analysis, in broad outline it represents what seems to me to be the sole intellectual content of what organismic biologists have had to say in this connection. However, if the proposed interpretation of the distinction is accepted as reasonable, then one important consequence needs to be noted. For, on the above proposal, the distinction between wholes which are and those which are not sums of parts is clearly *relative to some assumed body of theory T;* and, accordingly, though a given whole may not be the sum of its parts relative to one theory, it may indeed be such a sum relative to another. Thus, though the thermal behavior of solids is not the sum of the behavior of its parts relative to the classical kinetic theory of matter, it is such a sum relative to modern quantum mechanics. To say, therefore, that the behavior of an organism is not the sum of the behavior of its parts, and that its total behavior cannot be understood adequately in physico-chemical terms even though the behavior of each of its parts is explicable mechanistically, can only mean that no body of general theory is now available from which statements about the total behavior of the organism are derivable. The assertion, even if true, does *not* mean that it is *in principle* impossible to explain such total behavior mechanistically, and it supplies no competent evidence for such a claim.

(ii) There is a second point related to the organismic emphasis on the "wholeness" of organic action upon which I wish to comment briefly. It is frequently overlooked, even by those who really know better, that no theory, whether in the physical sciences or elsewhere, can explain the operations of any concrete system, unless various restrictive or boundary conditions are placed on the generality of the theory and unless, also, specific initial conditions, relevantly formulated, are supplied for the application of the theory. For example, electro-static theory is unable to specify the distribution of electric charges on the surface of a given body unless certain special information, not deducible from the fundamental equation of the theory (Poisson's equation) is supplied. This information must include statements concerning the shape and size of the body, whether it is a conductor or not, the distribution of other charges (if any) in the environment of the body, and the value of the dialectric constant of the medium in which the body is immersed.

But though this point is elementary, organismic biologists seem to me to neglect it quite often. They sometimes argue that though mechanistic explanations can be given for the behaviors of certain parts of organisms when these parts are studied in abstraction or isolation from the rest of the organism, such explanations are not possible if those parts are functioning conjointly and in mutual dependence as actual constituents of a living organism. This argument seems to me to have no force whatever. What it overlooks is that the initial and boundary conditions which must be supplied in explaining physico-chemically the behavior of an organic part acting in isolation are, in general, *not sufficient* for explaining mechanistically the conjoint functioning of such parts. For when these parts are assumed to be acting in mutual dependence, the environment of each part no longer continues to be what it was supposed to be when it was acting in isolation. Accordingly, a necessary requirement for the mechanistic explanation of the unified behavior of organisms is that boundary and initial conditions bearing on the actual relations of parts as parts of living organisms be stated in *physico-chemical* terms. Unless, therefore, appropriate data concerning the physico-chemical constitution and arrangement of the various parts of organisms are specified, it is not surprising that mechanistic explanations of the total behavior of organisms cannot be given. In point of fact, this requirement has not yet been fulfilled even in the case of the simplest forms of living organisms, for our ignorance concerning the detailed physico-chemical constitution of organic parts is profound. Moreover, even if we were to succeed in completing our knowledge in this respect – this would be equivalent to satisfying the condition of definability stated earlier – biological phenomena might still not be all explicable mechanistically: for this further step could be taken only if a comprehensive and independently warranted physico-chemical theory were available from which, together with the necessary boundary and initial conditions, the laws and other statements of biology are derivable. We have certainly failed thus far in finding mechanistic explanations for the total range of biological phenomena, and we may never succeed in doing so. But, though we continue to fail, then if this paper is not completely in error, the reasons for such failure are not the *a priori* arguments advanced by organismic biology.

(4) One final critical comment must be added. It is important to distinguish the question whether mechanistic explanations of biological phenomena are possible, from the quite different though related problem whether living organisms can be effectively synthesized in a laboratory out of nonliving materials. Many biologists apparently deny the first possibility because of their skepticism concerning the second, even when their skepticism does not extend to the possibility of an artificial synthesis of every chemical compound that is normally produced by biological organisms. But the two questions

are not related in a manner so intimate; and though it may never be possible to create living organisms by artificial means, it does not follow from this assumption that biological phenomena are incapable of being explained mechanistically. We do not possess the power to manufacture nebulae or solar systems, though we do have available physico-chemical theories in terms of which the behaviors of nebulae and solar systems are tolerably well understood; and, while modern physics and chemistry are beginning to supply explanations for the various properties of metals in terms of the electronic structure of their atoms, there is no compelling reason to suppose that we shall one day be able to manufacture gold by putting together artificially its subatomic constituents. And yet the general tenor, if not the explicit assertions, of some of the literature of organismic biology is that the possibility of mechanistic explanations in biology entails the possibility of taking apart and putting together in overt fashion the various parts of living organisms to reconstitute them as unified creatures. But in point of fact, the condition for achieving mechanistic explanations is quite different from that necessary for the artificial manufacture of living organisms. The former involves the construction of factually warranted *theories* of physico-chemical processes; the latter depends on the availability of certain physico-chemical substances and on the invention of effective techniques of control. It is no doubt unlikely that living organisms will ever be synthesized in the laboratory except with the help of mechanistic theories of organic processes — in the absence of such theories, the artificial creation of living things would at best be only a fortunate accident. But, however this may be, these conditions are logically independent of each other, and either might be realized without the other being satisfied.

(5) The central thesis of this paper is that none of the arguments advanced by organismic biologists establish the inherent impossibility of physico-chemical explanations of vital processes. Nevertheless, the stress which organismic biologists have placed on the facts of the hierarchical organization of living things and on the mutual dependence of their parts is not without value. For though organismic biology has not demonstrated what it proposes to prove, it has succeeded in making the heuristically valuable point that the explanation of biological processes in physico-chemical terms is not a necessary condition for the fruitful study of such processes. There is, in fact, no more good reason for dissatisfaction with a biological theory (e.g., modern genetics) because it is not explicable mechanistically than there is for dissatisfaction with a physical theory (e.g., electro-magnetism) because it is not reducible to some other branch of that discipline (e.g., to mechanics). And a wise strategy of research may, in fact, require that a given discipline be cultivated as an autonomous branch of science, at least during a certain period of its development, rather than as a mere appendage to some other and more inclusive discipline. The protest of organismic biology against the dogmatism frequently associated with mechanistic approaches to biology is salutary.

On the other hand, organismic biologists sometimes write as if any analysis of living processes into the behaviors of distinguishable parts of organisms entails a radical distortion of our understanding of such processes. Thus Wildon Carr, one proponent of the organismic standpoint, proclaimed that "Life is individual; it exists only in living beings, and each living being is indivisible, a whole not constituted of parts." Such pronouncements exhibit a tendency that seems far more dangerous than is the dogmatism of intransigent mechanists. For it is beyond serious question that advances in biology occur only through the use of an abstractive method, which proceeds to study various aspects of organic behavior in relative isolation of other aspects. Organismic biologists proceed in this way, for they have no alternative. For example, in spite of his insistence on the indivisible unity of the organism, J. S. Haldane's work on respiration and the chemistry of the blood did not proceed by considering the body as a whole, but by studying the relations between the behavior of one part of the body (e.g., the quantity of carbon dioxide taken in by the lungs) and the behavior of another part (the chemical action of the red blood cells). Organismic biologists, like everyone else who contributes to the advance of science, must be selective in their procedure and must study the behavior of living organisms under specialized and isolating conditions – on pain of making the free but unenlightening use of expressions like "wholeness" and "unifiedness" substitutes for genuine knowledge.

Historical and Modern Conceptions of Psychology

KENNETH W. SPENCE

Psychology as Science

Writing in a textbook in 1892, William James expressed himself as follows concerning the status of psychology as a natural science: "A string of raw facts; a little gossip and wrangle about opinions; a little classification and generalization on the mere descriptive level; a strong prejudice that we *have* states of mind, and that our brain conditions them: but not a single law in the sense in which physics shows us laws, not a single proposition from which any consequence can causally be deduced. We don't even know the terms between which the elementary laws would obtain if we had them. This is no science, it is only the hope of a science" (1892, p. 468). One suspects that the more optimistic psychologists of the period shrugged off this none too complimentary evaluation of their field with a variety of excuses such as, for example, that psychology was, as an experimental endeavor, still very much in its infancy. Indeed, if one measured from the time of founding of the first psychological laboratories in Germany during the seventies, psychology was less than 25 years old. Or, possibly, the defense was based on an appeal to the complexity of the phenomena psychologists sought to investigate and to their relative inaccessibility to observation.

From *Behavior Theory and Conditioning*, pp. 1–13, 15–19. New Haven: Yale University Press, 1956. Reprinted by permission of the author and the publisher.

At the time, the claim that not much could be expected of as young a science as psychology was a reasonable one. After all, there must be a period of purely empirical fact finding in order to provide a sufficiently comprehensive set of low order laws before the more abstract, integrative aspects of science can be expected to appear. A quarter of a century was, perhaps, too short a period to develop much in the way of a widely accepted systematic body of generalizations of any scope.

But what about now, 1956, some 60-odd years later and after almost a century of experimental study of psychological phenomena? Does psychology qualify as a natural science today? While it is probably safe to say that some areas of psychology have attained a respectable level of scientific development, it would nevertheless have to be admitted that much of the field does not qualify. In this connection it is pertinent to note that psychology as such was not included among the fields of natural sciences designated in the Act of Congress establishing the National Science Foundation, although an area of research referred to as general experimental psychology has been included in the division of biological sciences. If we may accept this somewhat dubious criterion of the attainment of sciencehood, then approximately five per cent of current psychologists would qualify as natural scientists, this being the percentage of the total membership of the American Psychological Association that belongs to the Division of Experimental Psychology.

That the process of psychology toward the goal of being a natural science has been slow and, even to some psychologists, disappointing is readily apparent. It is reflected, for example, in a comment that E. G. Boring of Harvard University made in the opening paragraph of his book, *The Physical Dimensions of Consciousness*. After calling attention to the fact that Descartes's dichotomy between body and mind occurred just at the time that science was beginning the development that was to make it the dominating influence in modern civilization, Boring wrote as follows:

> We all know how successful the physical sciences have been and we can also see that biology has prospered in abandoning a vitalism and identifying itself with the physical side of the Cartesian dichotomy. If Descartes was right, if there are these two worlds, then the success of science in attacking the one forms a challenge for the creation of a science of the other. . . Yet, if psychology is coordinate with physics and if the scientific method is applicable to both, then it seems strange that psychology has come such a little way when physics has ramified into many fields and has come so far (1933, p. 3).

While not a historian or methodologist and hence not in a position to base my beliefs on careful comparative study of the developments in psychology during its first hundred years with those in other sciences during a comparable period, I nevertheless share this view that the development of psychology as a natural science has been much slower than might have been expected. Especially does this seem to me to be the case when we consider some of the advantages that a science beginning in the late nineteenth century would have as compared with physics, which, as an experimental science, began some 300 years earlier.

The early physicists, Galileo and his contemporaries, not only had to evolve a new conception of scientific knowledge and a radically new approach to the attainment of this knowledge but also had to face open, even hostile, opposition in the pursuance of this task. Rejection of the dominant Neoplatonic and scholastic conceptions that the observed facts must be deducible from and hence must conform to some existent authoritarian and rational synthesis met the most violent opposition, not only from Church authorities but also from contemporary university professors. Quite in contrast, by the time psychology set out to be an independent experimental discipline the success of the new empirical approach had been so great that such opposition had long since disappeared. Moreover, the success during the intervening period of the application of the methods of physical science in the field of biology helped to create an atmosphere quite favorable to the attempt to extend their use to the study of psychological phenomena.

In addition to starting out in an atmosphere highly supportive of its endeavors, psychology also had the benefit of all that had been learned about the methodology of science in 300 years. Thus it had available many examples of the problems faced by scientists at various stages of development of their field and the manner in which they were approached and solved. The role of measurement and experimental control, the place of concepts and laws, the functions that theories play in the ordering of knowledge had all been revealed many times over. Many of these scientific tools, particularly techniques of measurements and experimentation, were directly applicable to the problems of psychology and could be and were taken over and used. Moreover, the psychologist has recently had the advantage of the analysis of these methods by the philosophers of science whose writings have helped greatly to clarify not only the relations among the different kinds of concepts employed in science but also the relation of the language of science to its empirical basis — the events in the consciousness or sense experience of the individual scientist.

Undoubtedly there are other advantages that psychology has had as a consequence of its late start, not the least of which would be the relatively greater support, financial and otherwise, that all scientific endeavors have received from our society in recent years. But enough has been cited, I believe, to indicate the basis of the great expectations that one might legitimately have held and the consequent disappointment that many have felt in the progress of psychology as a natural science.

As to the factors that have held back psychology during the first century of its existence I should prefer to confine my discussion primarily to those operating in the earlier portion of the period. It would take a person of far more diplomatic skill than I possess to dare go into all of the contemporary obstacles. In turning to the consideration of some of the earlier factors that may account for the slow development of psychology as a natural science, the discussion will be presented in the form of a historical account of what the first self-acknowledged psychologists conceived their task to be and how they proceeded to try to accomplish it. This account will also provide a general historical perspective for the research to be described in the later chapters.

Classical Psychology

Scientific experimental psychology as an independent discipline had its beginning in the work of men whose original training was in the biological sciences, particularly physiology. Thus the immediate forerunners were such well-known physiologists as Johannes Mueller, Fechner, and Helmholtz, while the first acknowledged experimental psychologist, Wilhelm Wundt, obtained a medical degree and taught physiology at Heidelberg for some years prior to turning, in 1870, more specifically to what he regarded as the study of psychological phenomena. While the interests of Wundt and his co-workers were, in part, concerned with the mediating neural processes underlying psychological or mental phenomena, particularly the sensory mechanisms, they considered that a portion of their work called for a uniquely new and independent science, psychology. This aspect of their work, which had to do with the mind or consciousness per se, was dominated by ideas and concepts that had their origins in the writings of such philosophers as Descartes and the early British empiricists, Locke, Berkeley, and Hume, and the later ideas of the British associationists. As Boring (1933) has pointed out the establishment of the dichotomy between mind and body by Descartes provided the raison d'être of an independent science of psychology. Descartes introduced in his method of contemplative "meditation" the basic method of studying the mind, and he himself employed this earliest form of introspection to study the higher forms of cognition and the more complex emotional states. Interest shifted in the subsequent writings of the English empiricists from these central states to the peripherally aroused, simpler mental states known as sensations.

Between the psychological writings of these early philosophers and the beginning of experimental psychology a period of approximately 150 years elapsed, during which there was great interest in the mind and considerable writing and speculation concerning its nature. It was in this period that the conception subsequently known as classical psychology arose. Stemming from the writings of the English empiricists, classical psychology had its beginning in the speculative writings on the human mind of the English physician-philosopher Hartley and the Scottish philosopher Thomas Brown. Its pre-experimental culmination is to be found in the sensationistic-associationistic psychologies of the British associationists, James Mill, his son John Stuart Mill, and Alexander Bain.

Wundt's new experimental psychology was essentially one with this early speculative classical psychology. The main differences were that more precise experimental procedures were introduced and considerable attention was given to the laws connecting the mental phenomena with the environment on the one hand and with their physiological correlates on the other. As such the work of Wundt and his successors in the German laboratories essentially constituted the final, experimental phase of classical psychology. This period came to an end in the first decade of the present century with the rise of functional psychology and behaviorism.

Classical psychology, whether pursued in the armchair of the empiricist-philosopher or in the laboratory of the new experimental psychologist, was conceived as the study of mind or consciousness as revealed through self-observation or introspection. Influenced, undoubtedly, by the atomistic physics of the period and the success of analysis in chemistry, it conceived its problem to be that of analyzing all possible states of consciousness into elements. These elements were regarded as not further decomposable and as providing the materials from which all mental states were compounded. Using himself or another person as a subject, the classical experimental psychologist presented various kinds of stimulation under controlled conditions that included a set to observe and report inner experiences. These situations might consist in the presentation of some visual or auditory stimulus to which the subject was to make some simple response, such as pressing a key in a reaction time experiment, or they might involve some complex problem which he was to solve. Primary interest was not in the overt response made by the subject although it was often recorded. Rather the concern was with the verbal account that the subject gave of the conscious experiences he had during the period of self-observation.

Under the set provided by the instructions these complex states of consciousness, perceptions, images, ideas, thoughts, emotions, and so on, were revealed to consist of such irreducible elements as sensations, feelings, and some kind of relational and thought elements. One of the major sources of disagreement among introspective psychologists during this period was the number of such irreducible elements. Some psychologists, apparently inspired by the chemists' success in finding new elements, sought to find new kinds of mental elements. Indeed a whole new school of psychology was established by Külpe at Würzburg on the claim of having discovered a new thought element. Other psychologists, particularly Titchener, the leading representative of classical psychology in this country, attempted to reduce the number to a single element, sensation.

In addition to this task of analyzing consciousness into its elements, there were two other stated, although somewhat neglected, objectives of classical psychology. One was to discover and formulate the principles of synthesis whereby the mental elements were compounded into the more complex states of consciousness. The main laws here were the so-called laws of association: contiguity in time, contiguity in space and similarity, etc. These laws, describing the conditions whereby conscious experiences become organized into spatial and temporal patterns, Wundt took over directly from the British associationists. Secondly, as was mentioned earlier, the experimental classical psychologists were also interested in discovering the laws relating the states of consciousness to the stimulating conditions (so-called outer psychophysics) and to the functioning of the nervous system (inner psychophysics). The latter laws were regarded as providing for the explanation of the conscious states, whereas the laws of association were supposed to be merely descriptive.

Structuralism and Phenomenalism

In its later phases, classical experimental psychology became subdivided into two main branches, structuralism and phenomenalism. Structuralism represented a later development of the elementarism of Wundt. In its final stages, as represented by the work of Titchener in this country, structuralism belatedly came to the realization that the concept of sensation is a logical, systematic construct and not a raw datum. In its place the structuralist substituted as the end product of introspective analysis, first, the attributes of sensations and, subsequently, the so-called dimensions of consciousness: quality, intensity, extensity, and protensity. The final form of this reconstructed structuralism, as exemplified by Boring (1933), considered its main task to be that of understanding the physiology of these dimensions of consciousness.

The second branch, phenomenalism, or as it has also been called, phenomenology, had its origins in the work of Brentano, one of Wundt's chief rivals. Brentano rejected sensory contents as the materials of psychology and instead proposed that psychical acts such as perceiving, judging, relating, recalling, and so forth were what was revealed by introspection. In his formulation the focus of attention shifted from the peripheral events back to the central regions of the mind. Subsequently the work of the Würzburg group on thinking and the Gestalt psychologists on perception brought out further objections to the type of analytical introspection employed by the Wundtians and the later structuralists.

The Würzburg psychologists were unable, under the particular set their observers employed, to reduce the experiences occurring during thinking to sensory materials as had the Wundtians. Indeed they found it difficult to establish descriptive categories in this area since our vocabulary is woefully inadequate to describe and communicate the contents of experience or processes occurring during such activities. The Gestalt psychologists also attacked the classical notion of perceptual experience as being compounded of sensations and criticized this conception as resulting from the suggestive influence of the knowledge from physiological psychology concerning the structure of the sensory mechanisms. The sensationistic interpretation of perception was suggested, they claimed, by the knowledge of the mosaic structure of the sensory surfaces and the afferent nerves with their bundles of fibers. The Gestaltists pleaded for an unbiased description of immediate experience, one that was free from any systematic preconceptions such as those held by the sensationists. Phenomenological introspection aimed to provide such an initial description of consciousness. It employed terms from everyday language, even slang words. While such pure description has its virtues, especially in a young science, sooner or later some kind of generalization of the initial descriptions must be attempted if the systematic kind of knowledge science seeks is to be obtained. Whereas structuralism tried and failed to formulate a system of constructs and laws of mental analysis and synthesis that gained general acceptance, phenomenalism never succeeded in providing any degree of integration of its observations.

The classical movement in psychology with its emphasis on the method of introspection came to an end with the functionalist-behaviorist revolution in America just after the start of the present century. Looked at in the light of the subsequent conception of psychology as the science of the behavior of living organisms in which the laws sought after state under what environmental and organic conditions organisms behave in the manner they do, this early work of the purely introspective psychologist must be regarded as an unfortunate false start. This is not to say that the problems in which they were interested were of no importance. Rather, as it appears now, their work was less effective because they relied too heavily on an unreliable (i.e., intersubjectively inconsistent) method and because other simpler, although perhaps humanly less interesting, matters had to be investigated first. The laws that these psychologists sought, for the most part, fall into the category of what we shall later refer to as R-R or response-response laws. These R-R laws represent only one small segment of the total framework of a science of behavior, and unfortunately not a very basic one at that. One cannot help but speculate on how much further advanced psychology would be today as a science if the physiologists who started it had been less intrigued by the ideas of the classical speculative psychology of the philosophers and more concerned with the problem of discovering the laws relating mental phenomena, however introspectively reported, to the stimulating conditions and neurophysiological variables.

Functionalism

Not only was a goodly portion of the first 30 years of work thus lost, still another 20 years of polemics were required before psychologists could concentrate their full energies on the task of building an objective science of behavior. The period 1900 to 1920 witnessed the rebellion against the classical orthodoxy. On the Continent the Würzburg group took the lead, questioning the adequacy of the classical type of introspection, while in this country the group of psychologists known as the functionalists was in the vanguard. If this were primarily a book about the history of psychology, which it is not, it would be appropriate at this point to trace the antecedents of functionalism to such influences as the biological theory of evolution, the writings of the early American psychologists, particularly William James, and last but by no means least, the pragmatic temper of America with its interest in success and the practical application of knowledge as a means of assuring it.

Functional psychology, as a formal school, had its birth at the University of Chicago under the guidance of John Dewey and James Rowland Angell. One of the leaders of functionalism, indeed its most effective spokesman, Angell was extremely influential both in his capacity as director of the psychological laboratory at Chicago for 26 years and in his writings. It was in his laboratory that Watson, his student, began his animal studies and developed the ideas that led eventually to behaviorism. Behaviorism is itself, of course, a functional psychology but one that, as we shall see, went beyond the functionalism of Dewey and Angell.

Objecting to the classical psychologist's preoccupation with the structural composition of consciousness, that is, with the question of *what* consciousness *is,* Angell and his group proposed to shift the focus of attention to the problems of how consciousness operates and what uses or functions it serves. The point of view they adopted was a Darwinian one in which the different operations of consciousness, sense perception, imagination, and emotion, were all regarded as different instances of organic adaptation to the environment. Interest was thus directed to the overt behavior of the organism in relation to its environment as well as to the functioning of the mind. However, the functionalists did not propose to neglect consciousness, and they continued to regard introspection, the direct examination of one's own mental processes, as the fundamental method of psychology.

This new functional orientation led to a rapid expansion of the kinds of phenomena that psychologists sought to investigate. Being concerned with the problem of the adjustment of the organism they became interested in the adaptive capacities of the individual and methods of measuring them. Thus was set in motion the development of mental tests and their subsequent use in a variety of situations, particularly in education. Interest in adaptive functions also led to a stressing of research on the genetic and developmental aspects of behavior both in the individual and in the species. Studies of the behavior of children were instituted, and laboratory experimentation with animals, which had just got started with Thorndike's researches at Columbia on cats and dogs in puzzle boxes, was taken up with great enthusiasm at Chicago. Watson established an animal laboratory there and began the series of studies of animal behavior that led him eventually to his behavioristic position.

While functionalism admitted behavior into psychology, consciousness was still its first love. To a considerable extent the behavioral data were considered to possess significance *only* insofar as they were able to throw light upon conscious processes. Thus in animal experiments, after making the behavioral observations, the practice was to infer the animals' consciousness and then show how these processes functioned in the behavioral adjustment to the environment. It was this insistence that behavior data must have analogical reference to consciousness that finally led Watson to rebel against functionalism and to demand that psychology change its viewpoint so as to accept the facts of behavior regardless of whether or not they have any bearings upon the problem of consciousness.

Behaviorism

Watson came to his behavioristic position primarily from his interest in animal research. There he had found that he could pursue quite successfully the study of behavior, even the traditional problems of sensory discrimination, without having to bring in conscious material. He simply proposed to extend the same objective behavioral methods of observation to the study of human behavior.

Watson's declaration of independence from the consciousness-dominated psychology of the period provoked a stormy period of polemical activity which, as it continued, was marked by more and more extreme statements on both sides. If one goes back to Watson's initial formulation, the 1913 *Psychological Review* article entitled "Psychology as the Behaviorist Views It," it may be seen that he did not deny the existence of consciousness, as has sometimes been represented, but simply proposed to use it in the same way that other scientists do. His statement is so clear I should like to quote portions of it:

> Psychology, as the behaviorist views it, is a purely objective, experimental branch of natural science which needs introspection as little as do the sciences of chemistry and physics . . . It can dispense with consciousness in a psychological sense. The separate observation of "states of consciousness" is, on this assumption, no more a part of the task of the psychologist than of the physicist. We might call this the return to a nonreflective and naive use of consciousness. In this sense consciousness may be said to be the instrument or tool with which all scientists work (1913, p. 176).

In other words Watson was arguing that, contrary to the belief of the introspective psychologists, psychology does not, or at least should not, have a unique subject matter, mental or conscious events as contrasted with matter or physical events. Rather, he insisted, the data of the psychologist are of exactly the same kind as those of the physical scientist. That is to say, immediate experience, the initial matrix out of which all sciences develop, is no longer to be conceived as the special province of psychology. The psychologist, like other natural scientists, simply must take consciousness for granted and proceed to his task of describing certain happenings occurring in it and discovering and formulating the nature of the relationships holding among them. The subject matter of psychology is exactly the same *in kind* then as all other sciences; any differentiation among the sciences is merely a matter of convenience, a division of scientific labor resorted to as the amount of detailed knowledge increases beyond the capacity of a single person's grasp.

We shall not attempt to follow the subsequent developments within behaviorism to the present-day forms of objective psychology except to discuss a little further the problem of what in the observable experience of the scientist is to be included as data in psychology. Watson, as we have seen, proposed to include only the observable behavior of living organisms other than the observing individual. He refused to admit the sensations, perceptions, and similar phenomena of the introspective psychologist. In his first article expounding this new behavioristic viewpoint Watson was quite frank in admitting that he was being somewhat arbitrary in rejecting these phenomena. One of the main reasons he gave for doing so was that he was not very optimistic concerning the possibility of any agreement being reached concerning these introspective data among psychologists of different training. Furthermore, he was more interested in getting on with the job of studying behavior.

Logical Empiricism (Operationism)

In later articles Watson attempted to offer other grounds for the rejection of consciousness, as did subsequent defenders of behaviorism. Typically these latter arguments have led into philosophical questions, the answers to which had best be left to the philosophers. From the point of view of the scientist the most important criterion of what aspects of the initial data of observation are to be included is the pragmatic one of which can be reliably made a matter of public record and thus taken out of the realm of private experience. For science is concerned only with such public knowledge.

Recognized today as being needed for this purpose is a language or vocabulary, some of the terms of which may be related in a highly consistent fashion to the direct experiences of the scientist. How these terms and the abstract concepts defined from them are to be introduced so that they are meaningful, precise, and of sufficient scope to provide for explanatory and predictive principles in the form of general laws and theories is an extremely important problem. Fortunately, considerable attention has been given to this problem in recent years, particularly by a group of philosopher-logicians known as logical empiricists. Accepting the requirement that all terms employed by the scientist, no matter how abstract, must ultimately be referable back to some primitive or basic set of terms that have direct experiential reference, these writers have suggested that such a basic vocabulary for science is provided by the terms designating directly observable physical objects such as tables, chairs, and cats, their properties, e.g., green, hard, and loud, and the relations between them such as between, before, and below. Different members within the group refer to this vocabulary of basic terms differently, calling it variously the "observation vocabulary," the "observable-thing language," and so on.[1]

Forming as it does the verification basis of all the scientist's statements, it is essential that this class of basic observables display a high degree of intersubjective agreement among different observers and in the same observer from one occasion to another. As is well known, physicists have depended to a great extent on a subclass of such observations that possess this characteristic in the highest degree, namely, pointer readings involving the observation of the coincidence of points in space or time. Indeed, as historians of science have pointed out, the great advances made in physics at the time of Galileo were largely due to his decision to limit or reduce the extent of eligible experiences that he would admit for study to the small fraction represented by these pointer readings.

For the most part modern objective psychologists have adopted this common-sense approach and have confined their observations to items that can be represented in such a basic scientific language. This does not mean, however, that it is no longer possible for them to deal with the types of problems that interested the classical psychologists. Thus my colleague Gustav Bergmann (1954) has even shown how the classical problem of mental analysis may be treated behavioristically in a manner that gets rid of all the pseudo problems that plagued the introspectionists and brings out whatever genuinely scientific ones they had. Involved in this translation are, roughly speaking, correlations among verbal responses of the subject or, as was indicated earlier, R-R laws.

Similarly, the behavior scientist has made extensive use of verbal responses in the formulation of hypotheses concerning the nature of higher mental processes. To some critics of the modern behavioristic viewpoint this acceptance of verbal reports as part of the data has seemed to represent an abandonment of the strict behavioristic position. Such a contention, however, fails to note a very important difference between the behavioristic treatment of such data and their use by the introspectionist. The introspectionist, it will be recalled, assumed a strict one-to-one relation between verbal responses of his subjects and the inner mental events. Accordingly, he accepted these introspective reports as *facts* or *data* about the inner mental states or processes which they represented. The behavior scientist takes a very different position. He accepts the verbal response as just one more form of observable behavior, and he proposes to use this type of data in exactly the same manner as he does other types of behavior variables. Thus

[1] Actually, the first to acquaint the scientist in a nontechnical manner with the requirements of operational definition of their concepts was the physicist Bridgman (1927). The subsequent technical developments have been mainly the work of the logical empiricists, the statements of it by Carnap (1936, 1937), Bergmann (1943, 1954), and Hempel (1952) probably being among the most important. Attention was first called to the importance of operational analysis in psychology by S. S. Stevens (1939), followed by such technical papers as that of Bergmann and Spence (1941) and the more recent comprehensive analysis of the logical structure of psychology by Bergmann (1953).

he attempts to discover laws relating these verbal responses to environmental events of the past or present, and he seeks to find what relations they have among each other and to other nonverbal types of response. In contrast, then, to the introspectionist's conception of these verbal reports as mirroring directly inner mental events, the behaviorist uses them either as data in their own right to be related to other data or as a base from which to make inferences concerning hypothetical, covert psychological processes.

Modern Objective Psychology

I should like to turn now to an analysis of the general conception of their science that the majority of psychologists in this country hold today. While behavioristic in outlook, this conception is probably better described as objective psychology. As such it does not require adherence to the orthodox doctrines of Watson. Moreover, it provides within its framework not only for alternative theoretical formulations but also for a purely empirical approach such as that espoused by most of the psychologists interested primarily in applied problems. Focusing attention as it does on the behavior of the organism in relation to two other classes of events, the environmental surroundings and the organic conditions of the organism, the concepts or variables of this modern conception fall into three groups or classes: (1) Response (R) variables: qualitative descriptions or measurements of the behavior properties of living organisms. (2) Stimulus (S) variables: qualitative descriptions or measurements of events or properties of the physical and social environment in which the organism behaves. (3) Organic (O) variables: qualitative descriptions or measurements of the anatomical and physiological properties of organisms.

Like every other scientist, the psychologist is interested in discovering and formulating the relations or laws holding among these different classes of variables. The several types of laws with which psychologists have been concerned are as follows: (I) $R = f(R)$; (II) $R = f(S)$; (III) $O = f(S)$; (IV) $R = f(O)$.

The first class, $R = f(R)$ laws, describes relations between different attributes or properties of behavior; they tell us which behavior traits are associated. This type of law is investigated extensively in the fields of intelligence and personality testing, and the laws that have been discovered have formed the basis of much of our technology in the areas of guidance, counseling, and clinical diagnosis. These empirical R-R relations also form the starting point for the theoretical constructs of the factor analysts. Beginning with the intercorrelations among a large number of test (response) scores these theorists have attempted by means of their mathematical methods to discover a minimum set of hypothetical factors that could account for the variance in the behavioral measures. The so-called field theory of Lewin (1935) was also concerned primarily with this R-R type of law, his theoretical concepts being introduced in terms of response variables and eventually returning to other response variables.

The second class of laws, $R = f(S)$, relates response measures as the dependent variable to the determining environmental conditions. There are really two subclasses of laws here, one relating to the environmental events of the present and the second to events of the past. The first subclass includes the traditional laws of psychophysics, perception, reaction time, and emotions. These laws describe how behavior varies with changes in the present physical stimulus. The theories that have been investigated by this kind of law are primarily of the reductionistic type, involving hypotheses as to the nature of the underlying neurophysiological mediating mechanisms.

Insofar as the behavior at any moment is a function of environmental events that occurred prior to the time of observation one is dealing with laws of the second subclass. The most familiar instance of this kind of relation is represented by the so-called learning curve which relates the response variable to previous environmental events of a specified character. Laws of primary and secondary motivation are other examples that fall in this group. These laws have provided the starting point of most theories of learning, although some learning theories have been initiated on the basis of neurophysiological laws.

A survey of the research literature since the beginning of experimental psychology will reveal the extraordinary extent to which the interests of psychologists have turned more and more to the investigation of laws of the first and second class. Less and less interest has been shown in the third and fourth class of relations which involve, as one of the members, physiological and anatomical variables. This trend was apparent even in the early developments in psychophysics. Whereas classical psychophysics was concerned primarily with the mediation problem of tracing the chain of physiological events beginning with the sense organ activity, the later psychophysicists shifted their interest to the correlations between the end terms, the stimulus event and the sensation, or sensory response. With the advent of the functional and behavioristic viewpoints interest in physiological research declined markedly until it now represents a relatively small proportion of the total research activity of psychologists. Presumably as psychology attains a fairly well-developed body of environmento-behavioral laws more and more attention will once again be directed to these physiological variables. In the meantime a number of psychologists, particularly the Gestaltists and those interested in simple sensory phenomena, have continued to investigate the class III type of laws. Mention should also be made of the continuing interest in the central neural mechanisms and their relations to various kinds of behavioral phenomena, including learning and motivation, that Lashley and others have maintained. These investigations have provided us with class IV laws.

The discovery and formulation of these various types of laws in psychology have required, just as in other sciences, three major methodological developments: (1) the specification of operationally defined, quantitative concepts that permit the relations among the variables to be expressed in terms of mathematical functions; (2) the development of instruments and experimental designs that provide for the isolation, control, and systematic variation of the factors in the situation under observation; and (3) the introduction of theories.

The role of the psychologist's theories in this task requires some clarification. The term "theory" as used in an advanced science such as physics typically refers to a system of highly abstract concepts and principles that serves to unify or organize into a single deductive system sets of laws that previously were quite unrelated. The classical example is the Newtonian integration of the previously unconnected laws of planetary motion and mechanics. Other well-known instances are Maxwell's electromagnetic theory of radiation and the kinetic theory of gases. In psychology, on the other hand, the term theory more frequently refers to something quite dissimilar, at least something that serves a very different function. Primarily because of the great complexity of psychological phenomena, the psychologist has often been unable to isolate, experimentally, simple systems of observation in which all of the relevant variables were known to him and under his control. Moreover, even in instances in which this was possible, the determining conditions have usually been so many and so complex in their interrelations that it is extremely difficult to arrive at any comprehensive law or set of laws. In these circumstances the psychologist has introduced what he has called a theory. Essentially such theorizing consists in hazarding hypotheses as to what the unknown factors might be in terms of their possible relations to the known variables and guesses as to the structure of the laws relating the already known variables on the basis of the existing data. In other words, whereas the term theory in modern physics refers to a system of constructs that serves to interrelate sets of already established laws, in psychology the term typically is applied to a device employed to aid in the formulation of the empirical laws describing a realm of observable phenomena.

Most fields of psychology are still in the stage of attempting to identify fruitful concepts that will lead to the formulation of the laws of the system under observation. However, a few areas would appear to have gone beyond this stage of searching for the relevant variables and have reached the point at which the majority of the variables have been specified and fairly precise determinations have been made of the laws relating them. In certain of these more advanced fields, particularly those concerned with some of the sensory functions (e.g., vision and audition), fairly comprehensive theories that attempt to integrate the existing empirical laws have been put forward. In other areas, intermediate in their development, the theories are more limited in scope, being concerned with relatively circumscribed sets of observations.

Psychological Theory Construction and the Psychologist

EDWARD JOSEPH SHOBEN, JR.

As their discipline has come of age, psychologists have concerned themselves more and more with those areas of human activity that have traditionally been the provinces of the priest, the poet, and the philosopher. Both in their rapidly expanding service work and in their investigative efforts, psychologists find themselves dealing increasingly with phenomena of immense complexity and a sometimes frightening degree of human intimacy. Problems in child rearing, the attainment of mental health, the sources of bigotry, the development of intergroup cooperation, the achievement of marital happiness, the reduction of international tensions, the improvement of educational procedures, and the general relief of human fears and misery are not only challenging in their abstract social importance. They profound-

Originally published in the *Journal of General Psychology,* Vol. 52, 1955, pp. 181–188. Reprinted by permission of the author and the editor.

ly touch us all personally and involve us deeply in both our own anxieties and our own value systems.

Further, the welcome that has been accorded psychologists as they have moved into these fields of service and research has not been an unmixed blessing. It has imposed a heavy weight of responsibility and a consequent ego-involvement that hardly makes for dispassionate consideration of intellectual issues. Such a state of affairs is probably quite as it should be, but it does have effects upon the construction of psychological theories, i.e., the systematization of psychological knowledge, and it may be well to try to make these effects somewhat more explicit.

First, let us remind ourselves of what theories essentially are. A theory is a generalized statement of something that we know. It is useful because it allows us to understand a multitude of concrete cases through the application of a general principle. Thus, we can comprehend little Johnny's kicking his mother when she refuses him an ice cream cone and Mr. Smith's swearing volubly if uselessly at his flat tire when he is late for work by means of such a statement as this: If an organism is frustrated, then it will probably respond aggressively.[1]

Second, such generalized statements are inescapable. Learning to understand our world consists substantially in generalizing our experience in particular times and situations to events in other times and other situations. Psychology, like any science, is presumably one of those bodies of generalized statements that help to make sense out of the world, in this case the world of organismic behavior. Theory, then, is the necessary heart of any body of knowledge and of understanding generally.

Third, it might be well to belabor the obvious in pointing out that theories are man made. Consequently, they are subject to the limitations, distortions, and errors that creep into virtually all human products. One of the most useful contributions psychology has made is in the documentation of this particular generalization.[2] It is therefore quite unlikely that any theoretical statement is going to be "true" in any absolute sense or not subject to revision as observation and thinking proceed.

Precisely because we are primarily interested in generalizing knowledge, because we unavoidably use theoretical statements, and because theoretical assertions are subject to the distortions of human construction, we ideally take some pains to minimize sources of error. The chief procedures for accomplishing this purpose are those of controlled observations and the rules of logical inference. By "controlled observation" we simply mean that we try to make the conditions of observation such that comparably trained investigators will obtain the same set of basic data. By the rules of inference we mean the linguistic laws governing the manipulation of symbols in such a way that if we accept any given statement as true (in the probability sense), we can justify the acceptance of some other statement as probably true. In scientific theories, as opposed to theories in the arts or in philosophy, we usually add the requirement that our inferences be testable.

The essence of testability is prediction. Thus, if we observe that a hungry rat fed only in the right arm of a *T*-maze soon comes to take the right turn consistently at the choice point, we may infer that the process that establishes this kind of behavioral consistency is a reduction in some need state. We can begin to test this inference by running our animals under conditions of thirst and with the prediction that a similar behavioral consistency will be established by pro-

[1] J. Dollard, L. Doob, N. E. Miller, O. H. Mowrer, and R. R. Sears, *Frustration and Aggression*. New Haven: Yale Univ. Press, 1939.

[2] F. C. Bartlett, *Remembering: A Study in Experimental and Social Psychology*. Cambridge: Cambridge Univ. Press, 1932. J. G. Miller, "Unconscious Processes and Perception," in R. R. Blake and G. Ramsey, *Perception: An Approach to Personality*. New York: Ronald Press, 1951.

viding water at a predetermined point in the maze. To the extent that our inferred notion of need reduction enables us to predict the behavior of organisms in different situations, it is useful. And this predictive criterion of utility is the test of whether we actually understand the phenomena with which we are concerned.

But the application of the principles of controlled observation, logical inference, and inference testing is most difficult in the very situations that are of deepest significance to us. Suppose we are interested in the effects of parental behavior on child development. We are at once presented with such a welter of observations that we can not possibly record them all, let alone make inferences from them in their raw state. In such a situation, we are likely to resort to highly abstract constructs of varying degrees of utility.

Thus, by abstracting some property from a number of behaviors, we can designate a class. For example, we might interest ourselves in *rejectant* behavior in mothers. By a similar process of abstraction, we might designate a class of child behaviors as *anxious*. We are now approaching a position from which we can study the effects of maternal rejection on children's anxieties, a matter of real interest and tremendous importance.

But complexity and difficulty are still with us. Such notions as those of rejection and anxiety have no genuine meaning apart from the ability of specified observers to agree on their presence or absence in particular subjects. Yet there is the danger that in using such terms we are only deluding ourselves into a semblance of understanding through the magical process of naming, and there is the further danger that by throwing a number of quite different acts into hoppers marked "rejectant" and "anxious," we have increased the chances that comparably trained observers will *not* obtain the same basic set of data. This kind of unreliability, reflecting conceptual inadequacy, is illustrated in virtually any clinical case conference, where people of extensive training dispute with one another as to whether a patient is hostile, dependent, guilty, schizophrenic, or whatever. The point is also illustrated by the difference in the reliability of counts of right turns in T-mazes as against counts of aggressive behavior in children's doll play.

This messiness of observational conditions in situations of crucial social importance is further complicated by inferential difficulties. We encounter a patient who seems to be the soul of gentleness in his social relations but who reports himself as troubled by vague and disturbing anxieties and who tells us of recurrent dreams in which he runs his sainted mother down with a 10-wheel truck or butchers his friends with great merriment. We develop the idea that because of a severe superego this person is repressing his hostility. What do we mean, aside from the fact that our client is gentle but troubled and subject to bad dreams?

This is certainly not the place to tackle the important but difficult problems associated with such constructs as these. For the moment, let's simply note some possibilities. First, such symbols as *superego* and *repressed hostility* hardly refer to entities or things. Likewise, they seem most inadequate as descriptions of behavior sequences. They do seem to have some value in orienting us cognitively in the appalling welter of complex observations that are possible to us.[3] They seem to have some connection, however vague and uncertain, in our experience with lower order symbols that *do* relate to observables. Thus, it is possible that with some hard thinking and some careful observation we could find better, i.e., more predictive, ways of accounting for our unhappy patient's peculiar combination of waking gentleness and dreamy brutality. Proper respect for

[3] J. R. Reid and J. E. Finesinger, "Inference Testing in Psychotherapy," *American Journal of Psychiatry* 1951, Vol. 107, pp. 894–900.

Freud's remarkable and basic insights hardly requires us to follow his language conventions or to refuse to clarify further his generalizations.

But all this brings us to a central point. We have spoken of prediction as the *sine qua non* of understanding and of theories as contributing to understanding through their predictive power. There is another sense, however, in which we can think of comprehending events. Here we are referring to a subjective, *post hoc,* reportable state, the feeling of being able to make sense out of events after they have occurred. An illustration is provided by the man who, after reporting himself as loving his wife, tells his therapist that one night, while sitting in their living room, he looked up at her and experienced a powerful feeling of hatred and revulsion. The therapist nods and says, "I understand." What the therapist means is that he has had some similar experience, either directly or vicariously, and that he therefore believes that such things can happen; or he means that he is willing to listen with a helpful attitude while the patient tells him more about this or similar events. The therapist ordinarily does *not* mean that he could have predicted the patient's revulsion from a knowledge of some set of antecedent conditions and a body of general principles.

Is it not possible that some of the theoretical formulations that we construct are primarily attempts to rationalize this second type of understanding? Faced with extraordinarily complex conditions of observation and forced to use long chains of inferential reasoning, yet committed to their task by virtue of its social importance and burdened by their responsibility for social amelioration, clinical and other applied psychologists often are threatened by severe attacks of doubt. Do we really know enough to make a significant contribution to the healing of the world's ills? Can we really help this patient overcome his anxieties and become a productive member of society? Will we be able to solve the problems of intergroup tensions before we all destroy each other? To answer these questions negatively is to invite an unbearable fit of depression and professional self repudiation.

Two possibilities present themselves as ways out. One is to deny that generalized knowledge of a testable sort is necessary for effective functioning as a psychologist. Instead of rigorous theory, one needs personal sensitivity, a respect for other persons, confidence in oneself, and a certain degree of culture. Since theory is inescapable, this point of view can be developed into a theoretical system itself, complete with constructs and illustrative case reports to "prove" its utility. The consequences of this sort of defense against painful professional self-doubt seem to be, aside from successful reduction of anxiety, a number of things. First, there is a tendency to decry those psychologists who are more concerned with the development of highly limited but relatively rigorous theories as stuffy academics who are totally lacking in social conscience and responsibility. Second, the assertion gains currency that the rigorous investigation of important human phenomena is both destructive of the phenomena themselves and suggestive of a thoroughgoing lack of proper respect for one's fellows. Thus, attempts to specify operationally what is meant by maternal love are charged with missing the spirit of this kind of human relationship, and attempts to account for maternal love in terms, say, of Hullian learning theory are proof positive that the theorist has ice in his veins. Third, the belief is held that the test of theoretical adequacy lies in its immediate practical consequences. The utility of the rigor-is-beside-the-point theory is demonstrated by the fact that its adherents may do effective psychotherapy. And finally, this position furthers fission in psychology, robbing in large degree those interested in more rigorous types of theorizing of the insights and rich hypotheses that come from applied experience and isolating practitioners from their more stringently theoretical confreres.

The second way of escape from the pangs of doubt lies in developing the belief that one's theoretical approximations are final. Instead of taking the notion of repressed hostility induced by a severe superego as the poor best that one can do in this stage of psychology's advancement, one can reify his concepts (always denying that he is doing so) and argue, again with illustrative cases as "proof," that his theory has elegance and power and represents the kind of systematized knowledge that is necessary for effective professional functioning. The consequences seem to be similar to those suggested for our first mechanism of escaping professional doubts.

But on the other hand, clinical and social psychologists currently command the greater degree of social prestige and recognition; they tend to get better salaries; and they tend to be a dominant group within professional organizations. They also are often quite helpful people to have available. These factors tend to enhance a tendency on the part of more rigorously oriented psychologists to become rather defensive about their own efforts and to minimize the efforts of clinicians and other practitioners. Here the point of view seems to be that applied workers are well intentioned folk who talk too much and write too much for ones so deficient in gray matter. Too, the contention seems to be frequently expressed that there is *no* work of value except that which comes out of careful laboratory experimentation and that is rationalized in terms of symbolic logic; all else is superficiality, intellectual sloppiness, and dross. Again, fission is promoted and professional isolation engendered.

Out of this professional split there seems to emerge a number of guiding statements of resolution, some of which are aesthetic and ethical rather than "scientific," that might well be pondered.

First, psychological theory has not caught up to the demands of psychological practice. Perhaps it never will, but it seems likely from the histories of other sciences that improved theory will facilitate improved practice. Moreover, practice is not in opposition to rigorous theorizing. The clinician, for example, may or may not find much benefit in current theories in general psychology, but there is little in his work that seems to justify the claim that such theories are either useless or sins against the state.

Second, in applied psychological work, it would seem that the attributes of the practitioner may constitute some of the most vital variables at work in such areas as psychotherapy or group development. Such variables need serious study. They may even prove to be a basis for appreciable improvements in psychological theory. But they are not substitutes for theory. If being a professional psychologist means something more than being a person whose constitution and experience have endowed him with a particular set of characteristics, it means the possession of generalized knowledge of a relevant kind.

Third, since theory is inescapable and in many ways the hallmark of the professional psychologist, it seems incumbent upon us to try to verify our theoretical contentions as carefully as possible with full acknowledgment of our limitations. Here there are no substitutes for the canons of controlled observation and testable inference, and it should be made quite explicit that successful practice does not demonstrate theoretical validity. Christian Science practitioners seem quite successful with certain types of cases, but their success hardly convinces us of the odd metaphysics in terms of which it is rationalized.

Fourth, it seems quite unlikely that a rigorous approximation to whatever laws govern various types of behavior have any effect on the behavior themselves. If we are ever able to generate a rigorous theoretical formulation of romantic love, for example, it is most probable that lovers will still sigh, that poets will still write odes to their mistress's eyebrow, and that each smitten couple will be fully convinced that never before has there been such ecstasy as theirs. The investigation of events is something different from the direct experience of them. There seems to be no reason why one should preclude the other.

Fifth, the defenders of disembodied rigor in theory construction could profitably learn some humility. At the very least, they could benefit markedly from the hypothesis-forming opportunities provided by applied work and become familiar with a range of problems to which their talents could be profitably applied. The Yale experience of requiring doctoral students in experimental psychology to handle at least one carefully supervised psychotherapy case simply to familiarize a budding research-and-theory man with some of the possible insights to be obtained and problems to be attacked seems to be paying off well in terms of a reduction in intradepartmental fission and the development of a more sophisticated approach to the study of the therapeutic process.

Sixth, defenders of "warmth" in psychological theory construction, i.e., the proponents of theoretical statements which reflect in their language an appreciation for the poignancy, the heartache, the gayety, and the dignity of human life, may be asking both too much and the wrong things of psychology. Almost certainly, such an appreciation is a requirement for effective applied work. If this contention is true, an adequate psychological theory should account for it. But the basic function of a theory in science is to predict phenomena. It is the poet's job rather than the scientist's to describe events in such a way as to evoke a sense of participating in them, of experiencing rather than accounting for experience. It seems most desirable that psychologists should be able to respond to both types of literature and even to fuse them; but they cannot with impunity be *con*fused.

As a corollary of this point, it would seem that those of us whose primary concerns are with complex human behavior are faced with the prospect of living rather tensely, admitting our ignorance as the beginning point in developing wisdom, and maintaining a healthy skepticism about our work while still doing the very best we know how with whatever resources are available. There is no need for apology, but if we are to advance our own culture and improve our services to those to whom we are responsible as professionals, then we are obligated to be as rigorous as we can wherever we can and to admit candidly that psychology has yet a long road to travel. The trip will be more successful if "pure" and "applied" psychologists undertake it together in a spirit of coöperation and mutual aid.

The Operation Called "Verstehen"

THEODORE ABEL

The advocates of *Verstehen*[1] define it as a singular form of operation which we perform whenever we attempt to explain human behavior. The idea behind this claim is by no means of German origin. Long before Dilthey and Weber, Vico acclaimed mathematics and human history as subjects about which we have a special kind of knowledge. This he attributed to the fact that the abstractions and fictions of mathematics are created by us, while history, too, is "made by men." He claimed that human beings can possess a type of knowledge concerning things they themselves produce which is not obtainable about the phenomena of nature.

Comte, too, implied that a special procedure is involved in the interpretation of human behavior. He held that the methods used in sociology embrace not only observation and experiment but a further process of verification which makes use of what he vaguely referred to as "our knowledge of human nature." According to him, empirical generalizations about human behavior are not valid unless they are in accord with our knowledge of human nature. Comte was the first to establish what may be termed "the postulate of *Verstehen*" for sociological research, for he asserted that no sociological demonstration is complete until the conclusions of historical and statistical analyses are in harmony with the "laws of human nature."

In the American sociological field Cooley is the outstanding protagonist of the idea that we understand the human and the social in ways different from those in which we understand the material. His theory is that we can understand the behavior of human beings by being able to share their "state of mind." This ability to share other people's minds is a special knowledge, distinct from the kind of perception gleaned from tests and statistics. Statistical knowledge without "empathic" knowledge is superficial and unintelligent. Between the two, Cooley claims, "there is a difference in kind which it would be fatuous to overlook."[2]

The notion of *Verstehen* is included in

[1] To avoid confusion, we prefer to use the German term instead of its English equivalent, which is "understanding." Understanding is a general term approximating the German *Begreifen* and does not convey the specific meaning intended by the term *Verstehen,* which implies a particular kind of understanding, applicable primarily to human behavior. Understanding is synonymous with comprehension, and Lundberg is perfectly right when he asserts (in *Foundations of Sociology* [New York: Macmillan Co., 1939], p. 51) that "understanding is the end at which all methods aim, rather than a method in itself." In this sense "understanding" is the goal of all sciences. *Verstehen,* on the other hand, is viewed by its proponents as a method by means of which we can explain human behavior. The purpose of this paper is to clarify this point and evaluate its significance.

Originally published in the *American Journal of Sociology,* Vol. 54, 1948–49, pp. 211–218. Reprinted by permission of the author and the editor.

[2] H. E. Cooley, *Sociological Theory and Social Research* (New York: Scribner's, 1930), p. 290.

Znaniecki's concept of the "humanistic coefficient" and particularly in the role he ascribes to "vicarious experience" as a source of sociological data. According to Znaniecki, vicarious experience enables the student of human behavior "to gain a specific kind of information which the natural experimenter . . . ignores altogether."[3]

Similarly, Sorokin stresses the need for *Verstehen* when he insists that the causal-functional method is not applicable to the interpretation of cultural phenomena. He points out that the social sciences must employ the logico-meaningful method which enables us to perceive connections which "are much more intimately comprehensible, more readily perceived, than are causal-functional unities."[4]

MacIver, too, speaks of a special method which must be used whenever we study social causation. He calls this process "imaginative reconstruction." He claims the causal formula of classical mechanics cannot be applied to human behavior. However, the student of human behavior will find this compensated for by "the advantage that some of the factors operative in social causation are understandable as causes; are validated as causal by our own experience."[5]

As these brief references indicate, there is no dearth of tradition and authority behind the idea of *Verstehen*.[6] It is, therefore, surprising to find that, while many social scientists have eloquently discoursed on the existence of a special method in the study of human behavior, none has taken the trouble to describe the nature of this method. They have given it various names; they have insisted on its use; they have pointed to it as a special kind of operation which has no counterpart in the physical sciences; and they have extolled its superiority as a process of giving insight unobtainable by any other methods. Yet the advocates of *Verstehen* have continually neglected to specify how this operation of "understanding" is performed — and what is singular about it. What, exactly, do we do when we say we practice *Verstehen?* What significance can we give to results achieved by *Verstehen?* Unless the operation is clearly defined, *Verstehen* is but a vague notion, and, without being dogmatic, we are unable to ascertain how much validity can be attributed to the results achieved by it.

I. The Operation Illustrated

Our first task is to ascertain the formula according to which the operation of *Verstehen* is performed. To do so, we had best examine a few illustrations of behavior analysis. For this purpose we shall use three examples: the first will deal with a single case; the second, with a generalization; and the third, with a statistical regularity.

Case 1. — Last April 15 a freezing spell suddenly set in, causing a temperature drop from 60 to 34 degrees. I saw my neighbor rise from his desk by the window, walk to the woodshed, pick up an ax, and chop some wood. I then observed him carrying the wood into the house and placing it in the fireplace. After he had lighted the wood, he sat down at his desk and resumed his daily task of writing.

[3] Florian Znaniecki, *The Method of Sociology* (New York: Farrar and Rinehart, 1934), p. 167.

[4] Pitirim Sorokin, *Social and Cultural Dynamics* (New York: American Book Co., 1937), p. 26.

[5] R. M. MacIver, *Social Causation* (Boston: Ginn and Co., 1942), p. 263.

[6] The more important works dealing with *Verstehen* are K. Bühler, *Die Krise der Philosophie* (Jena: Fischer, 1927); W. Dilthey, *Ideen ueber eine beschreibende und zergliedernde Psychologie* (Leipzig: Teubner, 1894); T. Erisman, *Die Eigenart des Geistigen* (Leipzig: Quelle, 1924); P. Häberlin, *Der Geist und die Triebe* (Berlin: Springer, 1924); K. Jaspers, *Allgemeine Psychopathologie* (Berlin: Springer, 1920); H. Rickert, *Die Grenzen der naturwissenschaftlichen Begriffsbildung* (Tübingen: Mohr, 1913); E. Rothacker, *Logik und Systematik der Geisteswissenschaften* (Bonn: Bouvier, 1947); G. Simmel, *Geschichtsphilosophie* (Berlin: Duncan, 1920); E. Spranger, *Lebensformen* (Haile: Niemeyer, 1924); and Max Weber, *Gesammelte Aufsaetze zur Wissenschaftslehre* (Tübingen: Mohr, 1920).

From these observations I concluded that, while working, my neighbor began to feel chilly and, in order to get warm, lighted a fire. This conclusion has all the earmarks of an "obvious fact." Yet it is obvious only because I have fitted the action of my neighbor into a sequential pattern by assuming that the stimulus "drop in temperature" induced the response "making a fire." Since I recognize a relevant connection between the response and the stimulus, I state that I understand the behavior of my neighbor. I may even say that I am certain of it ("The case is obvious"), provided I note carefully to what this certainty refers. I *cannot* be certain that this is the *correct* or true explanation of his conduct. To be sure my explanation is correct, I need additional information. I can go over to him and ask him why he lighted the fire. He may confirm my interpretation. However, I cannot stop there. Suppose he has another, hidden, intention? He may be expecting a guest and wish to show off his fireplace. Or suppose he himself is not aware of the "true" motive? Perhaps he was impelled by a subconscious motive of wanting to burn down his house so as to punish the fellow who harasses him about paying off the mortgage. If so, his lighting the fire would have a symbolic function. Of what, then, am I certain? I am certain only that my interpretation *could* be correct.

Hence, *Verstehen* gives me the certainty that a given interpretation of behavior is a possible one. I *know* that it can happen this way, even though I cannot be certain that such was the case in this instance. My interpretation in itself is not a hypothesis; only its application to the stated case is hypothetical.

Whence comes this certainty that I achieve through *Verstehen?* Since the case is simple, the answer is simple: I have enacted it myself. Feeling chilled, I have gathered wood and lighted a fire; therefore, I *know*. The sense of relevance is the result of personal experience; the connection has been established by me before, so I am *certain* of its possibility.

However, the answer as stated does not give us a clear picture of the operation the act of *Verstehen* involves. It will, therefore, be necessary to schematize the evidence and show the steps taken to perform the operation.

Two sets of observations are given in our example. First, there is a sequence of bodily movement (chopping wood, lighting a fire, etc.); second, there is a thermometer reading of a near-freezing temperature. The act of *Verstehen* links these two facts into the conclusion that the freezing weather was the stimulus which set off the response "making a fire." An elementary examination shows that three items of information are utilized to reach this conclusion:

1. Low temperature (A) reduces the temperature of the body (B).
2. Heat is produced (C) by making a fire (D).
3. A person "feeling cold" (B') will "seek warmth" (C').

Through this interpretation the three items are linked together as follows:

$$\begin{array}{ccc} A - B & & C - D \\ & B' - C' & \end{array}$$

We immediately recognize the third item as the significant element of the interpretation. The two conditions (A–B), together with their known consequences (C–D), are disparate facts. We link them into a sequence and state that C–D is the consequence of A–B by "translating" B and C into feeling-states of a human organism, namely, B' and C'. Introducing these intervening factors enables us to apply a generalization concerning the function of the organism (behavior maxim), from which we deduce the drop in temperature as a possible "cause" of my neighbor's behavior.

By specifying the steps which are implicit in the interpretation of our case, we have brought out two particulars which are characteristic of the act of *Verstehen.* One is the "internalizing" of observed factors in a given situation; the other is the application of a behavior maxim which makes the connection between these factors relevant. Thus we "understand" a given human action if we can apply to it a generalization based upon personal experience. We can apply such a rule of behavior if we are able to "internalize" the facts of the situation.

These propositions require further elucidation, but, before we attempt this, let us consider two other examples of behavior analysis.

Case 2. — In one of Lundberg's articles we find the following generalization:

> Faced by the insecurity of a changing and hostile world, we seek security by creating "eternal verities" in our thoughts. The more inadequate we feel, the more we indulge in this type of wishful thinking. Conversely, as the clergy has always complained, in times of prosperity and security, man tends to neglect his gods. It has been suggested that the Platonic preference for the changeless may be due to the fact that the Greeks did not have a mathematical technique such as the calculus for dealing with modes and rates of change.[7]

The opening sentence of this quotation asserts a relevant connection between "belief in eternal verities" (verbal response) and "a changing and hostile world" (stimulus). The subsequent sentences hint at a possible statistical basis for the generalization and cite two historical examples as illustrations. Clearly there is insufficient evidence to substantiate the validity of the interpretation as a tendency in some of us toward idealistic philosophy. We can recognize, though, that the connection asserted by the generalization is relevant; that is, we "understand" it, and so consider it possible.

The act of *Verstehen* which is implied here involves the same operation we have observed in the first example. We internalize "change and hostility" (*B*), which we observe to be an attribute of "the world" (*A*), into "feeling of inadequacy" (*B′*). The connotation "changeless" (*C*), which the concept "eternal verities" (*D*) implies, we internalize into "feeling of security" (*C′*). Having thus internalized the situation, we can now apply the behavior maxim that a person who feels inadequate (when facing change) will seek security (in something changeless). This procedure provides the mediating links *B′–C′*, which enable us to "understand," or recognize, the relevancy of the causal connection brought out in the generalization.

Case 3. — Competent statistical research has established a high correlation ($r = .93$) between the annual rate of crop production and the rate of marriage in a given year. There are, of course, statistical methods for proving whether or not this correlation is spurious. In this case, however, we feel that we can forego such tests because the correlation as such does not present a problem to us. We regard the connection as relevant; in short, we say we "understand" why the rate of marriage in farming districts closely follows the rate of crop production.

The act of *Verstehen* which this reasoning implies can be shown to involve the same procedure we have observed in the other examples. We use as items of information the fact that failure of crops (*A*) materially lowers the farmer's income (*B*) and the fact that one is making new commitments (*C*) when one marries (*D*). We then internalize *B* into "feeling of anxiety" (*B′*) and *C* — since the behavior in question is "postponement of marriage" — into "fear of new commitments" (*C′*). We are now able to apply the behavior maxim: "People who experience anxiety will fear new commitments"

[7] "Thoughtways of Contemporary Sociology," *American Sociological Review*, Vol. I, 1936, p. 703.

(B'–C'). Since we can fit the fact of fewer marriages when crops fail into this rule, we say we "understand" the correlation.

II. The Operation Analyzed

The examples show that the characteristic feature of the operation of *Verstehen* is the postulation of an intervening process "located" inside the human organism, by means of which we recognize an observed – or assumed – connection as relevant or "meaningful." *Verstehen,* then, consists of the act of bringing to the foreground the inner-organic sequence intervening between a stimulus and a response.

The examples also suggest that there are special conditions which determine the need for making the intervening process explicit. Some connections appear to be obvious; that is, we recognize their relevancy instantaneously and without any awareness of the implicit assumptions upon which the recognition is based. These are usually connections of which we have direct knowledge, because we ourselves established such connections in the past; or they are connections we have previously examined, so that their occurrence is accepted as an expected or familiar happening.

The need for making the intervening process explicit arises whenever behavior is not routine or commonplace. This is clearly the case when we are puzzled. For example, when we were confronted with the evidence that in army units in which promotion was easy there was much more griping about "injustice" than in those units in which very few were promoted, we were puzzled. We would expect the contrary. It is only by internalizing the situation – namely, by introducing the intervening factor of "expectation" – that we are able to understand the connection. If we then assume that in units in which promotion is easy there will be greater expectation of promotion, we can apply the behavior maxim: "The higher one's expectations, the greater one's disappointment if those expectations are not fulfilled." This enables us to "understand" the seemingly paradoxical behavior.

Another condition for making the intervening inner-organic sequence explicit arises whenever we are called upon to explain the reason for asserting a connection between occurrences. This is particularly so when no experimental or statistical data are available and recourse is taken to arguments in support of an interpretation. This happens frequently when interpretations of individual historical events are attempted, as, for example, establishing the cause of a war. Here the behavior in question can be related to earlier events solely on the basis that in terms of assumed feeling-states such a relation is a plausible one.

As has been indicated, the operation of *Verstehen* involves three steps: (1) internalizing the stimulus, (2) internalizing the response, and (3) applying behavior maxims. The questions now arise as to how to go about the process of internalizing and where we get our knowledge of behavior maxims.

1. Internalizing the stimulus. – To the best of my knowledge, no one has yet specified a technique by which we can objectively attribute certain feeling-states to persons faced by a particular situation or event. The arbitrary procedure we employ to internalize a stimulus consists of *imagining* what emotions may have been aroused by the impact of a given situation or event. Sometimes we are able to employ definite clues which we have gathered while observing the impact. These may have been gestures, facial expressions, or exclamations or comments. Where there are no such clues, we note the effect produced by an event or situation. Then we imagine how we would have been affected by such an impact. For example, not being a farmer, I never experienced the consequence of crop failure. However, observing that its effect is a curtailment of income, I attribute to the farmer a feeling of anxiety which I recall having felt — or imagine I might feel — under similar circumstances. Thus the internalizing of a stimulus depends largely upon our ability to describe a situation or event by categorizing it and evoking a personal experience which fits into that category.

2. Internalizing the response. — Here, too, no specific techniques are known which permit a definite association between feeling-states and observed behavior. All that can again be said is that we use our imagination when we ascribe a motive to a person's behavior — for example, "fear of new commitments" as the reason for postponing marriage; or, in another instance, when we view the behavior as expressive of some emotion — namely, when we infer that the "griping" of soldiers over promotions evokes a feeling of disappointment. We generally infer the motive of an act from the known or observed modification it produces. If we express this consequence of an act in general terms, we can utilize our personal experience with motives or feelings we had when we ourselves acted in order to produce a similar result.

In cases where both stimulus and response are stated, imagination is facilitated by the fact that both can be viewed as part of a complete situation. This enables us to relate to each other whatever inferences we make about the stimulus and the response. We then select the inferences which "fit" one another in such a way that the given behavior can be recognized as the "solution" (release of tension) of the "problem" (tension experience) created by the impact of the stated event.

3. Behavior maxims. — The generalizations which we call "behavior maxims" link two feeling-states together in a uniform sequence and imply a functional dependence between them. In the cases cited it can be seen that the functional dependence consists of the fact that the feeling-state we ascribe to a given human action is *directed* by the feeling-state we presume is evoked by an impinging situation or event. Anxiety directs caution; a feeling of cold, the seeking of warmth; a feeling of insecurity, a desire for something that will provide reassurance.

Behavior maxims are not recorded in any textbooks on human behavior. In fact, they can be constructed *ad hoc* and be acceptable to us as propositions even though they have not been established experimentally. The relation asserted appears to us as self-evident.

This peculiarity of behavior maxims can be accounted for only by the assumption that they are generalizations of direct personal experience derived from introspection and self-observation. Such personal experiences appear originally in the form of what Alexander has called "emotional syllogisms." He has this to say about them:

> Our understanding of psychological connections is based on the tacit recognition of certain causal relationships which we know from everyday experience and the validity of which we accept as self-evident. We understand anger and aggressive behavior as a reaction to an attack; fear and guilt as results of aggressiveness; envy as an outgrowth of the feeling of weakness and inadequacy. Such self-evident connections as "I hate him because he attacks me" I shall call emotional syllogisms. The feeling of the self-evident validity of these emotional connections is derived from daily introspective experience as we witness the emotional sequences in ourselves. . . . Just as the logic of intellectual thinking is based on repeated and accumulated experiences of relations in the external world, the logic of emotions is based on the accumulated experiences of our own emotional reactions.[8]

Emotional syllogisms when stated in the form of general propositions are behavior maxims. This explains their familiar ring and accounts for the facility with which they can be formulated. In generalizing emotion-

[8] Franz Alexander, "The Logic of Emotions and Its Dynamic Background," *International Journal of Psychoanalysis,* Vol. XVI, October 1935, p. 399.

al syllogisms we proceed on the assumption that the emotions of others function similarly to our own.

We find, then, that in all its essential features the operation of *Verstehen* is based upon the application of personal experience to observed behavior. We "understand" an observed or assumed connection if we are able to parallel either one with something we know through self-observation does happen. Furthermore, since the operation consists of the application of knowledge we already possess, it cannot serve as a means of discovery. At best it can only confirm what we already know.

III. The Operation Evaluated

From the foregoing description of the operation of *Verstehen* we can draw several inferences as to its limitations and possibilities. The most obvious limitation of the operation is its dependence upon knowledge derived from personal experience. The ability to define behavior will vary with the amount and quality of the personal experience and the introspective capacity of the interpreter. It will also depend upon his ability to generalize his experiences. In some cases it may be possible to secure objective data on the basis of which the verification of an interpretation can be approximated. However, owing to the relative inaccessibility of emotional experiences, most interpretations will remain mere expressions of opinion, subject only to the "test" of plausibility.

Regardless of the relative ability of people to use it, a second limitation to the use of the operation itself lies in the fact that it is *not a method of verification*. This means that what in the realm of scientific research we consider a quality of crucial importance is not an attribute of the operation of *Verstehen*.

When we say we "understand" a connection, we imply nothing more than recognizing it as a possible one. We simply affirm that we have at least once in direct experience observed and established the connection or its equivalent. But from the affirmation of a possible connection we cannot conclude that it is also probable. From the point of view of *Verstehen* alone, any connection that is possible is *equally* certain. In any given case the test of the actual probability calls for the application of objective methods of observation; e.g., experiments, comparative studies, statistical operations of mass data, etc. We do not accept the fact that farmers postpone intended marriages when faced with crop failure because we can "understand" the connection. It is acceptable to us because we have found through reliable statistical operations that the correlation between the rate of marriage and the rate of crop production is extremely high. We would continue to accept the fact even if we could not "understand" it. In this instance the operation of *Verstehen* does no more than relieve us of a sense of apprehension which would undoubtedly haunt us if we were unable to understand the connection.

The postulate of *Verstehen* can now be viewed from a proper perspective. It cannot be made to imply that if we do not "understand" a connection it surely, or most probably, is false. It does, however, imply that our curiosity concerning human behavior does not rest until we have in some way been able to relate it to our personal experience. The satisfaction of curiosity produces subjective increment but adds nothing to the objective validity of a proposition. Thus, all assertions based solely on the evidence of "understandability" can be viewed as cases of "misplaced familiarity."

These limitations virtually preclude the use of the operation of *Verstehen* as a scientific tool of analysis. Still there is one positive function which the operation can perform in scientific investigations: It can serve as an aid in preliminary explorations of a subject. Furthermore, the operation can be particularly helpful in setting up hypotheses, even though it cannot be used to test them.

In dealing with human behavior, we create hypotheses whenever we ask for the "stimulus" which produced a given response, or when we attempt to predict what "response" will follow from a given occurrence. It is an accepted fact that, in formulating hypotheses, we start with some "hunch" or "intuition." Now it appears highly probable that the hunches which lead us to certain hypotheses concerning human behavior originate from the application of the operation of *Verstehen*. This follows from the fact that the operation – in addition to using the stated stimulus or response – allows the use of another item of knowledge (a behavior maxim), which permits us to "reach out" from a given observation to its unknown counterpart. The diagram representing the reasoning about the neighbor seen chopping wood clearly indicates how behavior maxims can serve as a source of "hunches." Suppose *C–D* were given as an item of observation. By internalizing *C*, we obtain *C′*, to which we can then apply a behavior maxim, which gives us *B′*. *B′*, in turn, provides a clue to the nature of the situation or event which may be the possible stimulus (*A–B*) to the behavior in question. Lundberg's generalization (Case 2) is an example of a hypothesis derived in this fashion. By postulating that people who assert "eternal verities" are seeking security, he inferred a strong feeling of anxiety as the counterpart to this motive. He then surmised that the "changing and hostile world" might be the anxiety-producing condition. A "hunch" similarly reached was used by Durkheim in his study of suicide. When he found the rate of suicide varying in different groups, he was confronted by the problem of selecting the most likely determinant from a multitude of attributes of group life. From Merton's statement of the "paradigm of Durkheim's theoretic analysis," we can infer that Durkheim first internalized rates of suicide as "functions of unrelieved anxieties and stresses to which persons are subjected." [9] He then viewed such emotional states as the result of a lack of "psychic support," such as is provided by intimate associations with others. This suggested the possibility of social cohesion being the crucial factor which determines the characteristic rate of suicide in a group. Subsequent investigations established a high degree of probability for this inference because Durkheim was able to show that the rate of suicide varies consistently in inverse ratio with the degree of group coherence.

By reversing the procedure, we arrive at hunches about possible responses to given or expected occurrences. That is, we internalize the situation by projecting it as a problem experience and then, by means of a behavior maxim, infer the problem-solving response (intention). However, to guess the particular form the response will take requires information which the operation of *Verstehen* does not provide. It would not, for example, be of use in trying to conjecture specific ways and means of aggression which may be employed by a group in response to a provocation by another group. The operation gives us "hunches," and it points out the general character of possible factors, but it does not enable us to evaluate probabilities.

The findings with regard to the operation of *Verstehen* may be summarized in the following propositions:

The operation of *Verstehen* is performed by analyzing a behavior situation in such a way – usually in terms of general "feeling-states" – that it parallels some personal experience of the interpreter.

Primarily the operation of *Verstehen* does two things: It relieves us of a sense of appre-

[9] R. K. Merton, "Sociological Theory," *American Journal of Sociology*, Vol. L, May 1945, p. 470.

hension in connection with behavior that is unfamiliar or unexpected and it is a source of "hunches," which help us in the formulation of hypotheses.

The operation of *Verstehen* does not, however, add to our store of knowledge, because it consists of the application of knowledge already validated by personal experience; nor does it serve as a means of verification. The probability of a connection can be ascertained only by means of objective, experimental, and statistical tests.

Societal Facts

MAURICE MANDELBAUM

I. Introduction

If one adopts Broad's distinction between critical and speculative philosophy, the following paper may be regarded as an attempt to deal with one of the major problems of a critical philosophy of the social sciences. Like all such attempts, this paper faces some difficulties which are not encountered in equally acute form by those who deal with the concepts and methods of the natural sciences. In the first place, the concepts and methods utilized in the natural sciences have been more sharply defined than have been those which social scientists employ. In the second place, there is less disagreement among natural scientists than among social scientists as to the purposes which actually do underlie, or which should underlie, their studies. In the third place, the relations among the various branches of natural science seem to be more easily definable and less subject to dispute than is the case among the social sciences. It is with one aspect of the relations among the various social sciences that this paper will be concerned.

There can scarcely be any doubt that there is at present a considerable measure of disagreement among social scientists concerning the relations which obtain among their various disciplines. For example, there is little agreement as to how the province of "social psychology" is related to general psychology on the one hand or to sociology on the other. There is perhaps even less agreement as to how sociology and history are related, or whether, in fact, history is itself a social science. Even the province of cultural anthropology which, in its earlier stages, seemed to be capable of clear definition, is now in a position in which its relations to the other fields of social science have become extremely fluid. This type of fluidity in the boundaries of the various social sciences, and the ease with which concepts employed in one discipline spread to other disciplines, has been quite generally regarded as a promising augury for the future of the social sciences. One notes the frequency with which "integration" is held up as an important programmatic goal for social scientists. But such pleas for integration are ambiguous. On the one hand, they may merely signify a recognition of the fact that attempts to understand some concrete problems call for cooperation between persons trained to use the concepts and methods of different social sci-

Originally published in *The British Journal of Sociology,* Vol. VI, No. 4, pp. 305–317. Reprinted by permission of the author and the editor.

ences, or that workers in one discipline should be aware of the methods and results of those who work in other fields. On the other hand, what some who plead for "integration" in social science seem to demand is that the various disciplines should merge into one larger whole. On such a view the goal of integration would be the achievement of a state in which all persons who work in the field of social science would operate with the same set of concepts and would utilize the same methods of inquiry. If I am not mistaken, it is sometimes assumed that the social sciences will have made their greatest advance when the individual social sciences which now exist will have lost their separate indentities. In so far as this paper has a practical purpose, its purpose is to indicate that "integration," taken in this sense, is a mistaken goal for sociologists and psychologists to pursue.[1]

In stating that I wish to argue against what some social scientists believe to be the most promising path which their sciences can follow, it is clear that this paper has what might be termed an injunctive character. I am attempting to rule in advance that certain modes of procedure should or should not be adopted by practising social scientists. To those trained in the critical philosophy of the natural sciences, such a procedure will doubtless seem both foolhardy and perverse. Yet, it is unavoidable. So long as there are fundamental differences among social scientists with respect to the types of concepts and types of method which they actually use, and so long as the criteria by means of which they measure the adequacy of these concepts and methods differ, every attempt to do more than compile a *corpus* of materials for comparison, will involve that the analyst of the social sciences should take his own stand with respect to the matters under debate. Where one can show reasons for the position adopted, the injunctive element in one's analyses cannot be claimed to be wholly arbitrary. It is in proportion to the strength of these reasons that any particular injunctive proposal is to be judged.

However, any proposal as to the relations which ought to obtain between two or more social sciences will presuppose a belief as to what the goal of the social sciences may be. Concerning this topic there is also a considerable amount of debate. However, I believe it possible to formulate a general statement which might be acceptable to all, leaving unprejudiced those specific issues which have divided social scientists into opposed camps. I submit that the following statement would be quite generally acceptable: it is the task of the social sciences to attain a body of knowledge on the basis of which the actions of human beings as members of a society can be understood. This definition of the aim of the social sciences does not rule out the possibility that an understanding of the actions of human beings as members of a society may be instrumental to some further aim, such as that of attaining the means of controlling human behaviour, or of promoting human welfare. (Nor, of course, does it affirm that this is the case.) Furthermore, it is to be noted that in this statement of the aims of the social sciences I have avoided prejudging this issue as to whether the body of knowledge which is sought can be formulated as a system of laws, and whether an understanding of human actions is equivalent to explaining these actions in the sense in which the term "explanation" is used in the natural sciences. Throughout this paper I wish to avoid raising these questions, and in so far as possible I shall confine my discussion to a neutral terminology which does not prejudge any of these issues. Wherever my language seems to suggest that I am using the model of explanation used in the natural sciences, my point could equally well be phrased in terms which are compatible with the view that the methods and concepts of

[1] In this paper I shall not be concerned with the other social sciences.

the social sciences are utterly different from those employed in the natural sciences. And, conversely, where I use the language of "understanding," my discussion can equally well be rephrased in terms of the language of scientific "explanation."

Having now defined what I take to be the task of the social sciences, I can state the aim of this paper. My aim is to show that one cannot understand the actions of human beings as members of a society unless one assumes that there is a group of facts which I shall term "societal facts" which are as ultimate as are those facts which are "psychological" in character. In speaking of "societal facts" I refer to any facts concerning the forms of organization present in a society. In speaking of "psychological facts" I refer to any facts concerning the thoughts and the actions of specific human beings.

II. An Example of the Irreducibility of Societal Concepts

If it be the case, as I wish to claim, that societal facts are as ultimate as are psychological facts, then those concepts which are used to refer to the forms of organization of a society cannot be reduced without remainder to concepts which only refer to the thoughts and actions of specific individuals.[2] There are many reasons why the type of claim that I am putting forward has been doubted, and we shall note some of these reasons as we proceed. First, however, it will be well to lend some plausibility to the view by means of an example.

Suppose that I enter a bank, I then take a withdrawal slip and fill it out, I walk to a teller's window, I hand in my slip, he gives me money, I leave the bank and go on my way. Now suppose that you have been observing my actions and that you are accompanied by, let us say, a Trobriand Islander. If you wished to explain my behaviour, how would you proceed? You could explain the filling out of the withdrawal slip as a means which will lead to the teller's behaviour towards me, that is, as a means to his handing me some notes and coins; and you could explain the whole sequence of my action as directed towards this particular end. You could then explain the significance which I attached to the possession of these notes and coins by following me and noting how the possession of them led other persons, such as assistants in shops, to give me goods because I gave them the notes and coins which the bank teller had handed to me. Such would be an explanation of my observed behaviour in terms of the behaviour of other specific individuals towards me. And it might at first glance appear as if an explanation couched in terms of these interpersonal forms of behaviour would be adequate to cover all of the aspects of the case.

However, it would also be necessary for you to inform the stranger who accompanies you that it does not suffice for a person to fill out such a slip and hand it to just anyone he may happen to meet. It would also be only fair to inform him that before one can expect a bank teller to hand one money in exchange for a slip, one must have "deposited" money. In short, one must explain at least the rudiments of a banking system to him. In doing so one is, of course, using concepts which refer to one aspect of the institutional organization of our society, and this is precisely the point which I wish to make. (And the same point can be made with reference to how Malinowski has explained to *us* the Trobriand Islanders' system of ceremonial exchanges of gifts.) In all cases of this sort, the actual behaviour of specific individuals towards one another is unintelligible unless one views their behaviour in terms of their status and roles, and the concepts of status and role are devoid of meaning unless one

[2] The term "ultimate" may, of course, have other meanings as well. In the present paper, however, I am taking the irreducibility of a set of concepts to be equivalent to the ultimacy of that set of facts to which these concepts refer.

interprets them in terms of the organization of the society to which the individuals belong.

To this it may be objected that any statement concerning the status of an individual is itself analysable in terms of how specific individuals behave towards other individuals, and how these in turn behave towards them. Thus it might be claimed that while the explanation of an individual's behaviour often demands the introduction of concepts referring to "societal status," such concepts are themselves reducible to further statements concerning actual or probable forms of behaviour. Thus, societal concepts might be held to be heuristic devices, summarizing repeated patterns of behaviour, but they would be nothing more: their real meaning would lie in a conjunction of statements concerning the behaviour of a number of individuals.

However, this view is open to serious objection. We have seen in the foregoing illustration that my own behaviour towards the bank teller is determined by his status. If the attempt is now made to interpret his status in terms of the recurrent patterns of behaviour which others exemplify in dealing with him, then *their* behaviour is left unexplained: each of them – no less than I – will only behave in this way because each recognizes the teller of a bank to have a particular status. Similarly, it is impossible to resolve the bank teller's role into statements concerning his behaviour towards other individuals. If one wished to equate his societal role with his reactions towards those who behave in a particular way towards him, it would be unintelligible that he should hand us money when we present him with a withdrawal slip when he stands in his teller's cage, and yet that he would certainly refuse to do so if we were to present him with such a slip when we met him at a party. Bank tellers as well as depositors behave as they do because they assume certain societally defined roles under specific sets of circumstances. This being the case, it is impossible to escape the use of societal concepts in attempting to understand some aspects of individual behaviour: concepts involving the notions of status and role cannot themselves be reduced to a conjunction of statements in which these or other societal concepts do not appear.

[Precisely the same point may be made with respect to attempts to translate societal concepts into terms of the thoughts of individuals rather than into terms of their overt behaviour. If one should wish to say that I acted as I did towards the teller because I foresaw that through my actions he would be led to give me money, one would still have to admit that my anticipation of his response was based upon my recognition of the fact that he was a bank teller, and that the role of a bank teller demands that he should act as the bank's agent, and the function of a bank (so far as each depositor is concerned) is that of being a custodian of legal tender, etc. etc. Thus, in attempting to analyse societal facts by means of appealing to the thoughts which guide an individual's conduct, some of the thoughts will themselves have societal referents, and societal concepts will therefore not have been expunged from our analysis.]

Now I do not wish to claim that an individual's thoughts or his overt actions are wholly explicable in terms of status and roles. Not only does it seem to be the case that some actions may be explained without introducing these concepts, but it is also the case that two individuals, say two bank tellers, may behave differently towards me in spite of the identity in their roles. Thus, one may be friendly and the other hostile or aloof, and the nature of my own behaviour towards them will then differ. Thus it should be apparent that I am not seeking to explain all facets of individual behaviour by means of statements which only refer to societal facts. What I wish to contend is (*a*) that in understanding or explaining an individual's actions we must often refer to facts concerning the organization of the society in which he lives, and (*b*) that our statements concerning these societal facts are not reducible to a conjunction of statements concerning the actions of individuals. I take it that almost all social scientists and philosophers would grant the first of these contentions, but that many social scientists and most philosophers would reject the second, insisting that societal facts are reducible to a set of facts concerning individual behaviour.

III. The Criterion of "Irreducibility"

It is now necessary to state the criterion of irreducibility which the foregoing illustration has presupposed.

Let us assume that there is a language, *S*, in which sociological concepts such as "institutions," "mores," "ideologies," "status," "class," etc., appear. These concepts all refer to aspects of what we term "a society." That there is a language of this type is clear from the works of sociologists, anthropologists, and historians. It is also clear from the fact that we use such terms as "The President of the United States," or "the unmarried children of X." In order to define the meaning of the latter terms we must make reference to the Constitution of the United States, or to the laws which govern our marriage and kinship systems, and in these references we are employing societal concepts.

There is, of course, also another language, *P*, in which we refer to the thoughts and actions and capabilities of individual human beings. In making statements in this language (which, for want of a better name, I have called our "psychological language") [3] we are not using societal concepts. The differences between these two languages may be illustrated by the fact that the connotation of the term "The present President of the United States" carries implications which do not follow from the personal name "Dwight D. Eisenhower," and statements concerning the personality of Dwight D. Eisenhower carry no implications for our understanding of his societal role. This remains true even though we admit that in this case, as in most others, the status of an individual is often causally connected with the nature of his personality, and even though we also admit that an individual's personality is often connected with the fact that he occupies a particular status, or that he functions within this status as he does.

Put in these terms, my thesis that societal facts are irreducible to psychological facts may be reformulated as holding that sociological concepts cannot be translated into psychological concepts *without remainder*. What is signified by the stipulation "without remainder" must now be made clear.

It would seem to be the case that all statements in the sociological language, *S*, are translatable into statements concerning the behaviour of specific individuals, and thus would be translatable into the language *P*. For example, a statement such as "The institution of monogamous marriage supplanted the polygamous marriage system of the Mormons" could presumably be translated into statements concerning the actions of certain aggregates of individuals. However, it is by no means certain that such translations could be effected without using other concepts which appear in the sociological language. These concepts too might have their translations into *P*, but the translation of the concepts of *S* into *P* would not

[3] It will be noted that what I have termed our psychological language does not include terms such as "neural paths," "brain-traces," etc. My argument aims to show that societal facts are not reducible to facts concerning the thoughts and actions of specific individuals; the problem of whether both societal facts and facts concerning an individual's thoughts and actions are explicable in terms of (or, are in some sense "reducible" to) a set of physical or physiological correlates is not my present concern. It will readily be seen that this is not the point at issue. Those who seek to reduce societal facts to facts concerning individual behaviour are not attempting to speak in physical and physiological terms.

be complete if such translations still had to employ other concepts which appear in *S*. It is with respect to incomplete translations of this type that I speak of translations which cannot be effected "without remainder."

An analogue of this situation was pointed out by Chisholm in his criticism of C. I. Lewis's theory of knowledge.[4] According to Chisholm, thing-statements cannot be completely reduced to statements concerning sense-data because one must specify the conditions of the appearance of these sense-data, and in doing so one must again use thing-statements. And this is precisely the situation which we found to obtain in our illustration of the behaviour of a person withdrawing money from a bank.

Now, it might be argued (as it has sometimes been argued with respect to Chisholm's contention) that our inability to carry out such translations, without remainder, represents a practical and not a theoretical inability. According to those who take this view, the practical difficulty which is present arises from the indefinitely long conjunction of statements which we should have to make in carrying out our analyses, and to the fact that some of these statements would involve a foreknowledge of future events. But it is claimed that no theoretically important consequences follow from our inability to complete a detailed analysis of a particular statement: such partial analyses as we can actually make may not have omitted any theoretically significant aspects of the statements which we wish to analyse. Such a rejoinder would be open to two objections, so far as our present discussion is concerned.

First, we are here concerned with the problem of the relations between two empirical disciplines. Therefore, if it be admitted that it is impossible in practice to reduce statements which contain societal terms to a conjunction of statements which only include terms referring to the thoughts and actions of specific individuals, the rejoinder in question might conceivably be significant from the point of view of a general ontology, but it would not affect my argument regarding the autonomy of the societal sciences.

Second, it is to be noted that whatever may be the case regarding Chisholm's argument concerning the relation of sense-data statements to thing-statements, the problem of reducing statements which include societal terms to statements which only concern specific individuals is not merely a question of how we may *analyse* action statements, but how we may *explain* certain facts. It has been my contention that if we are to explain an individual's behaviour when, say, he enters a bank, we must have recourse to societal concepts and cannot merely employ terms which refer to the fact that this individual makes marks on paper, approaches a specific point, hands the marked paper to another individual, etc. etc. He who knew all of this, and who also knew all of the other actions performed by the members of a society, would possess a series of protocol statements, or biographical "logs." Even though this set of logs included reference to all of the actions performed by all of the members of the society, no societal concepts would appear in it. However, this information would not make it possible for our omniscient collector of data to explain why the depositor fills out a slip in order to withdraw money, or why the teller will exchange notes and coins for such a slip. Such a transaction only becomes explicable when we employ the concept of "a bank," and what it means to speak of "a bank" will involve the use of concepts such as "legal tender" and "contract." Further, what it means to speak of "a contract" will involve reference to our legal system, and the legal system itself cannot be defined in terms of individual behaviour – even the legal realist must distinguish between the behaviour of judges and police-

4 Cf. Chisholm, "The Problem of Empiricism" in *Journal of Philosophy,* V, 45 (1948), pp. 512 ff. (I am indebted to Roderick Firth for calling my attention to this analogue.)

men and the behaviour of "just anyone." Thus, if we are to explain certain forms of individual behaviour we must use societal concepts, and these concepts are not (I have argued) translatable without remainder into terms which only refer to the behaviour of individuals.

Yet it is important to insist that even though societal concepts cannot be translated into psychological concepts without leaving this societal remainder, it is not only possible but is indeed necessary to make the *partial* translation. It is always necessary for us to translate terms such as "ideologies" or "banks" or "a monogamous marriage system" into the language of individual thought and action, for unless we do so we have no means of verifying any statements which we may make concerning these societal facts. Ideologies and banks and marriage systems do not exist unless there are aggregates of individuals who think and act in specific ways, and it is only by means of establishing the forms of their thoughts and their actions that we can apprehend the nature of the societal organization in which they live, or that we can corroborate or disallow statements concerning this organization. Yet, the necessity for this translation of specific sociological concepts into terms of individual behaviour in order that we may verify and refine our sociological statements does not alter the fact that the possibility of making such a translation always involves the necessity for using other societal concepts to define the conditions under which this behaviour takes place. Thus, the translation can never obviate the use of societal concepts and reduce the study of society to a branch of the study of the actions of individuals.

IV. Objections

In the foregoing discussion I have been at pains to state my position in such a way as to avoid the most usual objections to the general type of view which I hold. However, it will be useful to comment on three objections which have frequently been raised against the view that societal facts are irreducible to psychological facts.[5]

The first of these objections may be termed the ontological objection. It consists in holding that societal facts cannot be said to have any status of their own since no such facts would exist if there were not individuals who thought and acted in specific ways. Now, to hold the view which I hold, one need not deny that the existence of a society presupposes the existence of individuals, and that these individuals must possess certain capacities for thought and for action if what we term a society is to exist. Yet, this admission does not entail the conclusion which is thought to follow from it: one need not hold that a society is an entity independent of all human beings in order to hold that societal facts are not reducible to the facts of individual behaviour. The warrant for the latter position is merely this: all human beings are born into a society, and much of their thought and their action is influenced by the nature of the societies in which they live; therefore, those facts which concern the nature of their societies must be regarded as being independent of them. To be sure, these facts are not independent of the ex-

[5] When we consider the type of "irreducibility" which has here been claimed to characterize societal facts, we must be prepared to allow that it may not be the only type of irreducibility to be found among "existential emergents." (On the meaning of this term, which has been borrowed from Lovejoy, cf. my "Note on Emergence," in *Freedom and Reason*, edited by Baron, Nagel, and Pinson; Free Press, Glencoe, Ill., 1951.) I am in fact inclined to believe that there is a stronger form of irreducibility than is here in question. This stronger form may be said to exist between, say, the colour "red" and brain events or light frequencies. In such cases it might be true that even a *partial* translation cannot be effected. All that I have wished to show is that while it is undeniable that we can and do make partial translations of societal concepts by using psychological concepts, these translations cannot be complete: we must always use further societal concepts to specify the conditions under which the observed forms of societally oriented behaviour take place.

istence of *other* individuals, and it will be from the forms of behaviour of these other individuals that any specific individual will have acquired his own societally oriented patterns of behaviour. But these individuals, too, were born into an already functioning societal organization which was independent of them. Thus, their societally oriented behaviour was also conditioned by an already existing set of societal facts, etc. etc.

To be sure, those who wish to press the ontological objection may insist that at some remote time in the history of the human race there were individuals who were not born into an already existing society, and that these individuals must have formed a societal organization by virtue of certain patterns of repeated interpersonal actions. Thus, they would seek to insist that all societal facts have their origins in individual behaviour, and that it is mistaken to argue, as I have argued, that societal facts are irreducible to the facts of individual behaviour. However, this rejoinder is clearly fallacious. Whatever may have been the origin of the first forms of societal organization (a question which no present knowledge puts us in a position to answer), the issue with which we are here concerned is one which involves the nature of societies as they exist at present. To argue that the nature of present societal facts is reducible to the facts of individual behaviour because the origins of a particular social system grew up out of certain repeated forms of behaviour is a clear example of the genetic fallacy. One might as well argue on the basis of our knowledge of the origins of the Greek drama and of the modern drama that every current Broadway play is really to be understood as a religious festival.

However, the above answer to the ontological type of objection is clearly not sufficient.[6] It is, I hope, adequate to show that one usual form of countering my position is untenable; yet, the essential paradox remains. One can still legitimately ask what sort of ontological status societal facts can conceivably possess if it is affirmed that they depend for their existence on the activities of human beings and yet are claimed not to be identical with these activities. There are, it seems to me, two types of answer which might be given to this question. In the first type of answer one might contend that a whole is not equal to the sum of its parts, and a society is not equal to the sum of those individual activities which go to form it. This familiar holistic answer is not the one which I should be inclined to propose. In the first place, it is by no means certain that the principle of holism (as thus stated) is philosophically defensible. In the second place, such an answer assumes that what may be termed the "parts" of a society are to be taken to be individual human beings, and this is an assumption which I should be unwilling to make. All of the preceding argument entails the proposition that the "parts" of a society are specific societal facts, not individuals. If this were not the case, societal concepts could be translated into terms referring to individual behaviour if we had sufficient knowledge of all the interrelations among these individuals. Instead, we have found that an analysis of a statement which concerns a societal fact will involve us in using other societal concepts: for example, that what it means to be a depositor in a bank will involve statements concerning our legal system and our monetary economy. Similarly, what it means to be a college student cannot be defined without recourse to statements concerning our educational system, and such statements cannot be analysed without utilizing concepts which refer to statutory laws as well as to many other aspects of our societal organization. Thus,

[6] In what follows I shall only be discussing human societies. The differences between "animal societies" and human societies are far more striking than are their similarities.

from the arguments which have been given, it follows that the "parts" of a society are not individual human beings, but are the specific institutions, and other forms of organization, which characterize that society. Once this is recognized, it remains an open question as to the extent to which any specific society (or all societies) are to be conceived holistically or pluralistically.

The second method of dealing with the ontological objection is the one which I should myself be inclined to adopt. It consists in holding that one set of facts may depend for its existence upon another set of facts and yet not be identical with the latter. An example of such a relationship would be that which a traditional epiphenomenalist would regard as existing between brain events and the contents of consciousness. Whatever objections one may raise against the epiphenomenalist view of the mind-body relationship, one would scarcely be justified in holding that the position must be false because the content of consciousness could not be different from the nature of brain states and yet be dependent upon the latter. If one has reasons for holding that the content of consciousness *is* different from brain states, and if one also has reason for holding that it *does* depend upon the latter, one's ontology must be accommodated to these facts: the facts cannot be rejected because of a prior ontological commitment. And, without wishing to press my analogy farther than is warranted, I can point out that my statement concerning "the parts" of a society has its analogue in what those who hold to the epiphenomenalist position would say concerning the proper analysis of any statement referring to the content of an individual's field of consciousness. Just as I have claimed that the component parts of a society are the elements of its organization and are not the individuals without whom it would not exist, so the epiphenomenalist would (I assume) say that the parts of the individual's field of consciousness are to be found within the specific data of consciousness and not in the brain events upon which consciousness depends.

These remarks are, I hope, sufficient to dispel the ontological objection to the position which I wish to defend. To be sure, I have not attempted to say what position should be assigned to societal facts when one is constructing a general ontology. To do so, I should have to say much more concerning the nature of societal facts, and I should of course also have to discuss the nature of other types of entity. Here it has only been my concern to suggest that what I have termed the ontological objection to my thesis is by no means as strong as it may at first glance appear to be: the admission that all societal facts depend upon the existence of human beings who possess certain capacities for thought and for action by no means precludes the contention that these facts are irreducible to facts concerning those individuals.

The second of the most usual objections to the thesis that societal facts cannot be reduced to psychological facts is an epistemological objection. This objection may take many forms, depending upon the theory of knowledge which is held by the objector. However, the common core of all such objections is the indubitable fact that societal concepts are not capable of being "pointed to," in the sense in which we can point to material objects, or to the qualities or activities of these objects. Whenever we wish to point to any fact concerning societal organization we can only point to a sequence of interpersonal actions. Therefore, any theory of knowledge which demands that all empirically meaningful concepts must ultimately be reducible to data which can be directly inspected will lead to the insistence that all societal concepts are reducible to the patterns of individual behaviour.

I shall not, of course, seek to disprove this

general theory of knowledge. Yet it is possible to indicate in very brief compass that it is inadequate to deal with societal facts. Since those who would hold this theory of knowledge would presumably wish to show that we can be said to know something of the nature of human societies, and since they would also wish to hold that our means of gaining this knowledge is through the observation of the repeated patterns of activities of individuals, a proof that their theory of knowledge cannot account for our apprehension of the nature of individual action is, in the present context, a sufficient disproof of the epistemological type of objection.

In order to offer such a disproof, let us revert to our illustration of a depositor withdrawing money from a bank. In order to understand his overt actions in entering a bank, filling out a slip, handing it to a teller, receiving notes and coins, and leaving the bank, we must view this sequence of actions as one internally connected series. Yet what connects the elements within the series is the person's intention to withdraw money from his account, and this intention is not itself a directly observable element within the series. Thus, unless it be admitted that we can have knowledge of aspects of human behaviour which are not directly presented to the senses, we cannot understand his behaviour and therefore cannot understand that which we seek to understand; i.e., those societal facts which supposedly are the summations of instances of behaviour of this type. To this, it may of course be objected, that we have learned to attribute certain intentions to agents on the basis of our own experienced intentions, and when this introspective experience is combined with our observation of overt behaviour we learn to interpret human actions. Yet if this enlargement of our modes of knowing is allowed, there is no reason to stop with the facts of individual behaviour as the building-blocks of a knowledge of societal facts. Within our own experience we are no less directly aware of our own names, of our belonging to a particular family, of our status as youngsters or elders, etc., than we are of our own intentions. To be sure, our societal status must, originally, have been learned by us in a sense in which our intentions need not presumably have been learned. Yet, once again, we must avoid the genetic fallacy: the origin of our knowledge is not identical with that knowledge itself. Just as the concept of number has a meaning which need not be identical with the experiences through which it was learned, so the concept of a family, or of differentiated status due to age or sex, need not (even for a child) be identical with the experiences through which this concept was first made manifest. And to these remarks it should be added that once we have grasped the idea of status, or of family, or of authority, we can transfer this concept to situations which are initially alien to our own experience (e.g. to new forms of family organization) no less readily than we can apply a knowledge of our own intentions to the understanding of the intentions of those who act in ways which are initially strange to us. The problem of extending our knowledge from our own experience of others is not, I submit, more impossible in principle in the one case than in the other. And if this be so, there is no epistemological reason why we should seek to reduce societal facts to the facts of individual behaviour. Only if it were true that individual behaviour could itself be understood in terms of the supposedly "hard data" of direct sensory inspection would there be any saving in the reduction of societal facts to facts concerning this behaviour. But, as I have indicated, this is not the case.

The third type of objection to the view which I have been espousing is the objection that such a view interprets individual men as the pawns of society, devoid of initiative, devoid even of a common and socially-unconditioned nature, conceiving of them as mere parts of a self-existing social organism.[7] However, such a view I have in fact already rejected. To hold, as I have held, that societal facts are not reducible without remainder to facts concerning the thoughts and actions of specific individuals, is not to deny that the latter class of facts also exists, and that the two classes may interact. Those who have in the past held to the irreducibility of societal facts have, to be sure, often gone to the extreme of denying that there are any facts concerning individual behaviour which are independent of societal facts. Such has not been my thesis. And it is perhaps worth suggesting that if we wish to understand many of the dilemmas by which individuals are faced, we can do no better than to hold to the view that there are societal facts which exercise external constraints over individuals no less than there are facts concerning individual volition which often come into conflict with these constraints.

[7] It is to be noted that some societally oriented behaviour is only intelligible when interpreted with respect to *both* a societal concept and an individual's intention (e.g. in our case of a person withdrawing money from a bank). However, other instances of societally oriented behaviour (e.g. customary observances of age and sex differences) do not involve a consideration of the agent's intentions.

Everyman His Own Historian

CARL BECKER

I

Once upon a time, long long ago, I learned how to reduce a fraction to its lowest terms. Whether I could still perform that operation is uncertain; but the discipline involved in early training had its uses, since it taught me that in order to understand the essential nature of anything it is well to strip it of all superficial and irrelevant accretions – in short, to reduce it to its lowest terms. That operation I now venture, with some apprehension and all due apologies, to perform on the subject of history.

Originally published in *The American Historical Review*, Vol. 37, 1931–32, pp. 221–236. Reprinted by permission of the editor.

I ought first of all to explain that when I use the term history I mean knowledge of history. No doubt throughout all past time there actually occurred a series of events which, whether we know what it was or not, constitutes history in some ultimate sense. Nevertheless, much the greater part of these events we can know nothing about, not even that they occurred; many of them we can know only imperfectly; and even the few events that we think we know for sure we can never be absolutely certain of, since we can never revive them, never observe or test them directly. The event itself once occurred, but as an actual event it has disappeared; so that in dealing with it the only objective reality we can observe or test is some material trace which the event has left – usually a written document. With these traces of vanished events, these documents, we must be content since they are all we have; from them we infer what the event was, we affirm that it is a fact that the event was so and so. We do not say "Lincoln is assassinated"; we say "it is a fact that Lincoln was assassinated." The event *was,* but is no longer; it is only the affirmed fact about the event that *is,* that persists, and will persist until we discover that our affirmation is wrong or inadequate. Let us then admit that there are two histories: the actual series of events that once occurred; and the ideal series that we affirm and hold in memory. The first is absolute and unchanged – it was what it was whatever we do or say about it; the second is relative, always changing in response to the increase or refinement of knowledge. The two series correspond more or less, it is our aim to make the correspondence as exact as possible; but the actual series of events exists for us only in terms of the ideal series which we affirm and hold in memory. This is why I am forced to identify history with knowledge of history. For all practical purposes history is, for us and for the time being, what we know it to be.

It is history in this sense that I wish to reduce to its lowest terms. In order to do that I need a very simple definition. I once read that "History is the knowledge of events that have occurred in the past." That is a simple definition, but not simple enough. It contains three words that require examination. The first is knowledge. Knowledge is a formidable word. I always think of knowledge as something that is stored up in the *Encyclopædia Britannica* or the *Summa Theologica;* something difficult to acquire, something at all events that I have not. Resenting a definition that denies me the title of historian, I therefore ask what is most essential to knowledge. Well, memory, I should think (and I mean memory in the broad sense, the memory of events inferred as well as the memory of events observed); other things are necessary too, but memory is fundamental: without memory no knowledge. So our definition becomes, "History is the memory of events that have occurred in the past." But events – the word carries an implication of something grand, like the taking of the Bastille or the Spanish-American War. An occurrence need not be spectacular to be an event. If I drive a motor car down the crooked streets of Ithaca, that is an event – something done; if the traffic cop bawls me out, that is an event – something said; if I have evil thoughts of him for so doing, that is an event – something thought. In truth anything done, said, or thought is an event, important or not as may turn out. But since we do not ordinarily speak without thinking, at least in some rudimentary way, and since the psychologists tell us that we can not think without speaking, or at least not without having anticipatory vibrations in the larynx, we may well combine thought events and speech events under one term; and so our definition becomes, "History is the memory of things said and done in the past." But the past – the word is both misleading and unnecessary: misleading, because the past, used in connection with history, seems to imply the distant past, as if history ceased before we were born; unnecessary, because after all everything said or done is already in the past as soon as it is said or done. Therefore I will omit that word, and our definition becomes, "History is the memory of things said and done." This is a definition that reduces history to its lowest terms, and yet includes everything that is essential to understanding what it really is.

If the essence of history is the memory of things said and done, then it is obvious that every normal person, Mr. Everyman, knows some history. Of course we do what we can to conceal this invidious truth. Assuming a professional manner, we say that so and so knows no history, when we mean no more than that he failed to pass the examinations set for a higher degree; and simple-minded persons, undergraduates and others, taken in by academic classifications of knowledge, think they know no history because they have never taken a course in history in college, or have never read Gibbon's *Decline and Fall of the Roman Empire*. No doubt the academic convention has its uses, but it is one of the superficial accretions that must be stripped off if we would understand history reduced to its lowest terms. Mr. Everyman, as well as you and I, remembers things said and done, and must do so at every waking moment. Suppose Mr. Everyman to have awakened this morning unable to remember anything said or done. He would be a lost soul indeed. This has happened, this sudden loss of all historical knowledge. But normally it does not happen. Normally the memory of Mr. Everyman, when he awakens in the morning, reaches out into the country of the past and of distant places and instantaneously recreates his little world of endeavor, pulls together as it were things said and done in his yesterdays, and coördinates them with his present perceptions and with things to be said and done in his to-morrows. Without this historical knowledge, this memory of things said and done, his to-day would be aimless and his to-morrow without significance.

Since we are concerned with history in its lowest terms, we will suppose that Mr. Everyman is not a professor of history, but just an ordinary citizen without excess knowledge. Not having a lecture to prepare, his memory of things said and done, when he awakened this morning, presumably did not drag into consciousness any events connected with the Liman von Sanders mission or the Pseudo-Isidorian Decretals; it presumably dragged into consciousness an image of things said and done yesterday in the office, the highly significant fact that General Motors had dropped three points, a conference arranged for ten o'clock in the morning, a promise to play nine holes at four-thirty in the afternoon, and other historical events of similar import. Mr. Everyman knows more history than this, but at the moment of awakening this is sufficient: memory of things said and done, history functioning, at seven-thirty in the morning, in its very lowest terms, has effectively oriented Mr. Everyman in his little world of endeavor.

Yet not quite effectively after all perhaps; for unaided memory is notoriously fickle; and it may happen that Mr. Everyman, as he drinks his coffee, is uneasily aware of something said or done that he fails now to recall. A common enough occurrence, as we all know to our sorrow — this remembering, not the historical event, but only that there was an event which we ought to remember but can not. This is Mr. Everyman's difficulty, a bit of history lies dead and inert in the sources, unable to do any work for Mr. Everyman because his memory refuses to bring it alive in consciousness. What then does Mr. Everyman do? He does what any historian would do: he does a bit of historical research in the sources. From his little Private Record Office (I mean his vest pocket) he takes a book in MS, volume XXXV, it may be, and turns to page 23, and there he reads: "December 29, pay Smith's coal bill, 20 tons, $1017.20." Instantaneously a series of historical events comes to life in Mr. Everyman's mind. He has an image of himself ordering twenty tons of coal from Smith last summer, of Smith's wagons driving up to his house, and of the precious coal sliding dustily through the cellar window. Historical events, these are, not so important as the forging of the Isidorian Decretals, but still important to Mr. Everyman: historical events which he was not present to observe, but which, by an artificial extension of memory, he can form a clear picture of, because he has done a little original research in the manuscripts preserved in his Private Record Office.

The picture Mr. Everyman forms of

Smith's wagons delivering the coal at his house is a picture of things said and done in the past. But it does not stand alone, it is not a pure antiquarian image to be enjoyed for its own sake; on the contrary, it is associated with a picture of things to be said and done in the future; so that throughout the day Mr. Everyman intermittently holds in mind, together with a picture of Smith's coal wagons, a picture of himself going at four o'clock in the afternoon to Smith's office in order to pay his bill. At four o'clock Mr. Everyman is accordingly at Smith's office. "I wish to pay that coal bill," he says. Smith looks dubious and disappointed, takes down a ledger (or a filing case), does a bit of original research in his Private Record Office, and announces: "You don't owe me any money, Mr. Everyman. You ordered the coal here all right, but I didn't have the kind you wanted, and so turned the order over to Brown. It was Brown delivered your coal: he's the man you owe." Whereupon Mr. Everyman goes to Brown's office; and Brown takes down a ledger, does a bit of original research in his Private Record Office, which happily confirms the researches of Smith; and Mr. Everyman pays his bill, and in the evening, after returning from the Country Club, makes a further search in another collection of documents, where, sure enough, he finds a bill from Brown, properly drawn, for twenty tons of stove coal, $1017.20. The research is now completed. Since his mind rests satisfied, Mr. Everyman has found the explanation of the series of events that concerned him.

Mr. Everyman would be astonished to learn that he is an historian, yet it is obvious, isn't it, that he has performed all the essential operations involved in historical research. Needing or wanting to do something (which happened to be, not to deliver a lecture or write a book, but to pay a bill; and this is what misleads him and us as to what he is really doing), the first step was to recall things said and done. Unaided memory proving inadequate, a further step was essential — the examination of certain documents in order to discover the necessary but as yet unknown facts. Unhappily the documents were found to give conflicting reports, so that a critical comparison of the texts had to be instituted in order to eliminate error. All this having been satisfactorily accomplished, Mr. Everyman is ready for the final operation — the formation in his mind, by an artificial extension of memory, of a picture, a definitive picture let us hope, of a selected series of historical events — of himself ordering coal from Smith, of Smith turning the order over to Brown, and of Brown delivering the coal at his house. In the light of this picture Mr. Everyman could, and did, pay his bill. If Mr. Everyman had undertaken these researches in order to write a book instead of to pay a bill, no one would think of denying that he was an historian.

II

I have tried to reduce history to its lowest terms, first by defining it as the memory of things said and done, second by showing concretely how the memory of things said and done is essential to the performance of the simplest acts of daily life. I wish now to note the more general implications of Mr. Everyman's activities. In the realm of affairs Mr. Everyman has been paying his coal bill; in the realm of consciousness he has been doing that fundamental thing which enables man alone to have, properly speaking, a history: he has been reënforcing and enriching his immediate perceptions to the end that he may live in a world of semblance more spacious and satisfying than is to be found within the narrow confines of the fleeting present moment.

We are apt to think of the past as dead, the future as nonexistent, the present alone as real; and prematurely wise or disillusioned counselors have urged us to burn always with "a hard, gemlike flame" in order to give "the highest quality to the moments as they pass, and simply for those moments' sake." This no doubt is what the glow-worm does; but I think that man, who alone is properly aware that the present moment passes, can for that very reason make no good use of the present moment simply for its own sake. Strictly speaking, the present doesn't exist for us, or is at best no more than an infinitesimal point in time, gone before we can note it as present. Nevertheless, we must have a present; and so we create one by robbing the past, by holding on to the most recent events and pretending that they all belong to our immediate perceptions. If, for example, I raise my arm, the total event is a series of occurrences of which the first are past before the last have taken place; and yet you perceive it as a single movement executed in one present instant. This telescoping of successive events into a single instant philosophers call the 'specious present.' Doubtless they would assign rather narow limits to the specious present; but I will willfully make a free use of it, and say that we can extend the specious present as much as we like. In common speech we do so: we speak of the 'present hour,' the 'present year,' the 'present generation.' Perhaps all living creatures have a specious present; but man has this superiority, as Pascal says, that he is aware of himself and the universe, can as it were hold himself at arm's length and with some measure of objectivity watch himself and his fellows functioning in the world during a brief span of allotted years. Of all the creatures, man alone has a specious present that may be deliberately and purposefully enlarged and diversified and enriched.

The extent to which the specious present may thus be enlarged and enriched will depend upon knowledge, the artificial extension of memory, the memory of things said and done in the past and distant places. But not upon knowledge alone; rather upon knowledge directed by purpose. The specious present is an unstable pattern of thought, incessantly changing in response to our immediate perceptions and the purposes that arise therefrom. At any given moment each one of us (professional historian no less than Mr. Everyman) weaves into this unstable pattern such actual or artificial memories as may be necessary to orient us in our little world of endeavor. But to be oriented in our little world of endeavor we must be prepared for what is coming to us (the payment of a coal bill, the delivery of a presidential address, the establishment of a League of Nations, or whatever); and to be prepared for what is coming to us it is necessary, not only to recall certain past events, but to anticipate (note I do not say predict) the future. Thus from the specious present, which always includes more or less of the past, the future refuses to be excluded; and the more of the past we drag into the specious present, the more an hypothetical, patterned future is likely to crowd into it also. Which comes first, which is cause and which effect, whether our memories construct a pattern of past events at the behest of our desires and hopes, or whether our desires and hopes spring from a pattern of past events imposed upon us by experience and knowledge, I shall not attempt to say. What I suspect is that memory of past and anticipation of future events work together, go hand in hand as it were in a friendly way, without disputing over priority and leadership.

At all events they go together, so that in a very real sense it is impossible to divorce history from life: Mr. Everyman can not do what he needs or desires to do without recalling past events; he can not recall past events without in some subtle fashion relating them to what he needs or desires to do. This is the natural function of history, of history reduced to its lowest terms, of history conceived as the memory of things said and done: memory of things said and done (whether in our immediate yesterdays or in the long past of mankind), running hand in hand with the anticipation of things to be said and done, enables us, each to the extent of his knowledge and imagination, to be intelligent, to push back the narrow confines of the fleeting present moment so that what we are doing may be judged in the light of what we have done and what we hope to do. In this sense all *living* history, as Croce says, is contemporaneous: in so far as we think the past (and otherwise the past, however fully related in documents, is nothing to us) it becomes an integral and living part of our present world of semblance.

It must then be obvious that living history, the ideal series of events that we affirm and hold in memory, since it is so intimately associated with what we are doing and with what we hope to do, can not be precisely the same for all at any given time, or the same for one generation as for another. History in this sense can not be reduced to a verifiable set of statistics or formulated in terms of universally valid mathematical formulas. It is rather an imaginative creation, a personal possession which each one of us, Mr. Everyman, fashions out of his individual experience, adapts to his practical or emotional needs, and adorns as well as may be to suit his æsthetic tastes. In thus creating his own history, there are, nevertheless, limits which Mr. Everyman may not overstep without incurring penalties. The limits are set by his fellows. If Mr. Everyman lived quite alone in an unconditioned world he would be free to affirm and hold in memory any ideal series of events that struck his fancy, and thus create a world of semblance quite in accord with the heart's desire. Unfortunately, Mr. Everyman has to live in a world of Browns and Simths; a sad experience, which has taught him the expediency of recalling certain events with much exactness. In all the immediately practical affairs of life Mr. Everyman is a good historian, as expert, in conducting the researches necessary for paying his coal bill, as need be. His expertness comes partly from long practice, but chiefly from the circumstance that his researches are prescribed and guided by very definite and practical objects which concern him intimately. The problem of what documents to consult, what facts to select, troubles Mr. Everyman not at all. Since he is not writing a book on "Some Aspects of the Coal Industry Objectively Considered," it does not occur to him to collect all the facts and let them speak for themselves. Wishing merely to pay his coal bill, he selects only such facts as may be relevant; and not wishing to pay it twice, he is sufficiently aware, without ever having read Bernheim's *Lehrbuch,* that the relevant facts must be clearly established by the testimony of independent witnesses not self-deceived. He does not know, or need to know, that his personal interest in the performance is a disturbing bias which will prevent him from learning the whole truth or arriving at ultimate causes. Mr. Everyman does not wish to learn the whole truth or to arrive at ultimate causes. He wishes to pay his coal bill. That is to say, he wishes to adjust himself to a practical situation, and on that low pragmatic level he is a good historian precisely because he is not disinterested: he will solve his problems, if he does solve them, by virtue of his intelligence and not by virtue of his indifference.

Nevertheless, Mr. Everyman does not live by bread alone; and on all proper occasions his memory of things said and done, easily enlarging his specious present beyond the narrow circle of daily affairs, will, must inevitably, in mere compensation for the intolerable dullness and vexation of the fleeting present moment, fashion for him a more spacious world than that of the immediately practical. He can readily recall the days of his youth, the places he has lived in, the ventures he has made, the adventures he has had — all the crowded events of a lifetime; and beyond and around this central pattern of personally experienced events, there will be embroidered a more dimly seen pattern of artificial memories, memories of things reputed to have been said and done in past times which he has not known, in distant places which he has not seen. This outer pattern of remembered events that encloses and completes the central pattern of his personal experience, Mr. Everyman has woven, he could not tell you how, out of the most diverse threads of information, picked up in the most casual way, from the most unrelated sources – from things learned at home and in school, from knowledge gained in business or profession, from newspapers glanced at, from books (yes, even history book) read or heard of, from remembered scraps of newsreels or educational films or *ex cathedra* utterances of presidents and kings, from fifteen-minute discourses on the history of civilization broadcast by the courtesy (it may be) of Pepsodent, the Bulova Watch Company, or the Shepard Stores in Boston. Daily and hourly, from a thousand unnoted sources, there is lodged in Mr. Everyman's mind a mass of unrelated and related information and misinformation, of impressions and images, out of which he somehow manages, undeliberately for the most part, to fashion a history, a patterned picture of remembered things said and done in past times and distant places. It is not possible, it is not essential, that this picture should be complete or completely true: it is essential that it should be useful to Mr. Everyman; and that it may be useful to him he will hold in memory, of all the things he might hold in memory, those things only which can be related with some reasonable degree of relevance and harmony to his idea of himself and of what he is doing in the world and what he hopes to do.

In constructing this more remote and far-flung pattern of remembered things, Mr. Everyman works with something of the freedom of a creative artist; the history which he imaginatively recreates as an artificial extension of his personal experience will inevitably be an engaging blend of fact and fancy, a mythical adaptation of that which actually happened. In part it will be true, in part false; as a whole perhaps neither true nor false, but only the most convenient form of error. Not that Mr. Everyman wishes or intends to deceive himself or others. Mr. Everyman has a wholesome respect for cold, hard facts, never suspecting how malleable they are, how easy it is to coax and cajole them; but he necessarily takes the facts as they come to him, and is enamored of those that seem best suited to his interests or promise most in the way of emotional satisfaction. The exact truth of remembered events he has in any case no time, and no need, to curiously question or meticulously verify. No doubt he can, if he be an American, call up an image of the signing of the Declaration of Independence in 1776 as readily as he can call up an image of Smith's coal wagons creaking up the hill last summer. He suspects the one image no more than the other; but the signing of the Declaration, touching not his practical interest, calls for no careful historical research on his part. He may perhaps, without knowing why, affirm and hold in memory that the Declaration was signed by the members of the Continental Congress on the fourth of July. It is a vivid and sufficient image which Mr. Everyman may hold to the end of his days without incurring penalties. Neither Brown nor Smith has any interest in setting him right; nor will any court ever send him a summons for failing to recall that the Declaration, "being engrossed and compared at the table, was signed by the members" on the second of August. As an actual event, the signing of the Declaration was what it was; as a remembered event it will be, for Mr. Everyman, what Mr. Everyman contrives to make it: will have for him significance and magic, much or little or none at all, as it fits well or ill into his little world of interests and aspirations and emotional comforts.

III

What then of us, historians by profession? What have we to do with Mr. Everyman, or he with us? More, I venture to believe, than we are apt to think. For each of us is Mr. Everyman too. Each of us is subject to the limitations of time and place; and for each of us, no less than for the Browns and Smiths of the world, the pattern of remembered things said and done will be woven, safeguard the process how we may, at the behest of circumstance and purpose.

True it is that although each of us is Mr. Everyman, each is something more than his own historian. Mr. Everyman, being but as informal historian, is under no bond to remember what is irrelevant to his personal affairs. But we are historians by profession. Our profession, less intimately bound up with the practical activities, is to be directly concerned with the ideal series of events that is only of casual or occasional import to others; it is our business in life to be ever preoccupied with that far-flung pattern of artificial memories that encloses and completes the central pattern of individual experience. We are Mr. Everybody's historian as well as our own, since our histories serve the double purpose, which written histories have always served, of keeping alive the recollection of memorable men and events. We are thus of that ancient and honorable company of wise men of the tribe, of bards and story-tellers and minstrels, of soothsayers and priests, to whom in successive ages has been entrusted the keeping of the useful myths. Let not the harmless, necessary word 'myth' put us out of countenance. In the history of history a myth is a once valid but now discarded version of the human story, as our now valid versions will in due course be relegated to the category of discarded myths. With our predecessors, the bards and story-tellers and priests, we have therefore this in common: that it is our function, as it was theirs, not to create, but to preserve and perpetuate the social tradition; to harmonize, as well as ignorance and prejudice permit, the actual and the remembered series of events; to enlarge and enrich the specious present common to us all to the end that 'society' (the tribe, the nation, or all mankind) may judge of what it is doing in the light of what it has done and what it hopes to do.

History as the artificial extension of the social memory (and I willingly concede that there are other appropriate ways of apprehending human experience) is an art of long standing, necessarily so since it springs instinctively from the impulse to enlarge the range of immediate experience; and however camouflaged by the disfiguring jargon of science, it is still in essence what it has always been. History in this sense is story, in aim always a true story; a story that employs all the devices of literary art (statement and generalization, narration and description, comparison and comment and analogy) to present the succession of events in the life of man, and from the succession of events thus presented to derive a satisfactory meaning. The history written by historians, like the history informally fashioned by Mr. Everyman, is thus a convenient blend of truth and fancy, of what we commonly distinguish as 'fact' and 'interpretation.' In primitive times, when tradition is orally transmitted, bards and story-tellers frankly embroider or improvise the facts to heighten the dramatic import of the story. With the use of written records, history, gradually differentiated from fiction, is understood as the story of events that actually occurred; and with the increase and refinement of knowledge the historian recognizes that his first duty is to be sure of his facts, let their meaning be what it may. Nevertheless, in every age history is taken to be a story of actual events from which a significant meaning may be derived; and in every age the illusion is that the present version is valid because the related facts are true, whereas former versions are invalid because based upon inaccurate or inadequate facts.

Never was this conviction more impressively displayed than in our own time — that age of erudition in which we live, or from which we are perhaps just emerging. Finding the course of history littered with the *débris* of exploded philosophies, the historians of the last century, unwilling to be forever duped, turned away (as they fondly hoped) from 'interpretation' to the rigorous examination of the factual event, just as it occurred. Perfecting the technique of investigation, they laboriously collected and edited the sources of information, and with incredible persistence and ingenuity ran illusive error to earth, letting the significance of the Middle Ages wait until it was certainly known "whether Charles the Fat was at Ingelheim or Lustnau on July 1, 887," shedding their "life-blood," in many a hard fought battle, "for the sublime truths of Sac and Soc." I have no quarrel with this so great concern with hoti's business. One of the first duties of man is not to be duped, to be aware of his world; and to derive the significance of human experience from events that never occurred is surely an enterprise of doubtful value. To establish the facts is always in order, and is indeed the first duty of the historian; but to suppose that the facts, once established in all their fullness, will 'speak for themselves' is an illusion. It was perhaps peculiarly the illusion of those historians of the last century who found some special magic in the word 'scientific.' The scientific historian, it seems, was one who set forth the facts without injecting any extraneous meaning into them. He was the objective man whom Nietzsche described — "a mirror: accustomed to prostration before something that wants to be known, . . . he waits until something comes, and then expands himself sensitively, so that even the light footsteps and gliding past of spiritual things may not be lost in his surface and film." [1] "It is not I who speak, but history which speaks through me," was Fustel's reproof to applauding students. "If a certain philosophy emerges from this scientific history, it must be permitted to emerge naturally, of its own accord, all but independently of the will of the historian." [2] Thus the scientific historian deliberately renounced philosophy only to submit to it without being aware. His philosophy was just this, that by not taking thought a cubit would be added to his stature. With no other preconception than the will to know, the historian would reflect in his surface and film the "order of events throughout past times in all places"; so that, in the fullness of time, when innumerable patient expert scholars, by "exhausting the sources," should have reflected without refracting the truth of all the facts, the definitive and impregnable meaning of human experience would emerge of its own accord to enlighten and emancipate mankind. Hoping to find something without looking for it, expecting to obtain final answers to life's riddle by resolutely refusing to ask questions — it was surely the most romantic species of realism yet invented, the oddest attempt ever made to get something for nothing!

That mood is passing. The fullness of time is not yet, overmuch learning proves a weariness to the flesh, and a younger generation that knows not Von Ranke is eager to believe that Fustel's counsel, if one of perfection, is equally one of futility. Even the most disinterested historian has at least one preconception, which is the fixed idea that he has none. The facts of history are already set forth, implicitly, in the sources; and the historian who could restate without reshaping them would, by submerging and suffocating the mind in diffuse existence, accomplish the superfluous task of depriving human experience of all significance.

1 *Beyond Good and Evil,* p. 140.

2 Quoted in *English Historical Review,* Vol. 1.

Left to themselves, the facts do not speak; left to themselves they do not exist, not really, since for all practical purposes there is no fact until some one affirms it. The least the historian can do with any historical fact is to select and affirm it. To select and affirm even the simplest complex of facts is to give them a certain place in a certain pattern of ideas, and this alone is sufficient to give them a special meaning. However 'hard' or 'cold' they may be, historical facts are after all not material substances which, like bricks or scantlings, possess definite shape and clear, persistent outline. To set forth historical facts is not comparable to dumping a barrow of bricks. A brick retains its form and pressure wherever placed; but the form and substance of historical facts, having a negotiable existence only in literary discourse, vary with the words employed to convey them. Since history is not part of the external material world, but an imaginative reconstruction of vanished events, its form and substance are inseparable: in the realm of literary discourse substance, being an idea, *is* form; and form, conveying the idea, *is* substance. It is thus not the undiscriminated fact, but the perceiving mind of the historian that speaks: the special meaning which the facts are made to convey emerges from the substance-form which the historian employs to recreate imaginatively a series of events not present to perception.

In constructing this substance-form of vanished events, the historian, like Mr. Everyman, like the bards and story-tellers of an earlier time, will be conditioned by the specious present in which alone he can be aware of his world. Being neither omniscient nor omnipresent, the historian is not the same person always and everywhere; and for him, as for Mr. Everyman, the form and significance of remembered events, like the extension and velocity of physical objects, will vary with the time and place of the observer. After fifty years we can clearly see that it was not history which spoke through Fustel, but Fustel who spoke through history. We see less clearly perhaps that the voice of Fustel was the voice, amplified and freed from static as one may say, of Mr. Everyman; what the admiring students applauded on that famous occasion was neither history nor Fustel, but a deftly colored pattern of selected events which Fustel fashioned, all the more skillfully for not being aware of doing so, in the service of Mr. Everyman's emotional needs – the emotional satisfaction, so essential to Frenchmen at that time, of perceiving that French institutions were not of German origin. And so it must always be. Played upon by all the diverse, unnoted influences of his own time, the historian will elicit history out of documents by the same principle, however more consciously and expertly applied, that Mr. Everyman employs to breed legends out of remembered episodes and oral tradition.

Berate him as we will for not reading our books, Mr. Everyman is stronger than we are, and sooner or later we must adapt our knowledge to his necessities. Otherwise he will leave us to our own devices, leave us it may be to cultivate a species of dry professional arrogance growing out of the thin soil of antiquarian research. Such research, valuable not in itself but for some ulterior purpose, will be of little import except in so far as it is transmuted into common knowledge. The history that lies inert in unread books does no work in the world. The history that does work in the world, the history that influences the course of history, is living history, that pattern of remembered events, whether true or false, that enlarges and enriches the collective specious present, the specious present of Mr. Everyman. It is for this reason that the history of history is a record of the "new history" that in every age rises to confound and supplant the old. It should be a relief to us to renounce omniscience, to recognize that every generation, our own included, will, must inevitably, understand the past and anticipate the future in the light of its own restricted experience, must inevitably play on the dead whatever tricks it finds necessary for its own peace of mind. The appropriate trick for any age is not a malicious invention designed to take anyone in, but an unconscious and necessary effort on the part of 'society' to understand what it is doing in the light of what it has done and what it hopes to do. We, historians by profession, share in this necessary effort. But we do not impose our version of the human story on Mr. Everyman; in the end it is rather Mr. Everyman who imposes his version on us — compelling us, in an age of political revolution, to see that history is past politics, in an age of social stress and conflict to search for the economic interpretation. If we remain too long recalcitrant Mr. Everyman will ignore us, shelving our recondite works behind glass doors rarely opened. Our proper function is not to repeat the past but to make use of it, to correct and rationalize for common use Mr. Everyman's mythological adaptation of what actually happened. We are surely under bond to be as honest and as intelligent as human frailty permits; but the secret of our success in the long run is in conforming to the temper of Mr. Everyman, which we seem to guide only because we are so sure, eventually, to follow it.

Neither the value nor the dignity of history need suffer by regarding it as a foreshortened and incomplete representation of the reality that once was, an unstable pattern of remembered things redesigned and newly colored to suit the convenience of those who make use of it. Nor need our labors be the less highly prized because our task is limited, our contributions of incidental and temporary significance. History is an indispensable even though not the highest form of intellectual endeavor, since it makes, as Santayana says, a gift of "great interests . . . to the heart. A barbarian is no less subject to the past than is the civic man who knows what the past is and means to be loyal to it; but the barbarian, for want of a transpersonal memory, crawls among superstititions which he cannot understand or revoke and among people whom he may hate or love, but whom he can never think of raising to a higher plane, to the level of a purer happiness. The whole dignity of human endeavor is thus bound up with historic issues, and as conscience needs to be controlled by experience if it is to become rational, so personal experience itself needs to be enlarged ideally if the failures and successes it reports are to touch impersonal interests." [3]

I do not present this view of history as one that is stable and must prevail. Whatever validity it may claim, it is certain, on its own premises, to be supplanted; for its premises, imposed upon us by the climate of opinion in which we live and think, predispose us to regard all things, and all principles of things, as no more than "inconstant modes or fashions," as but the "concurrence, renewed from moment to moment, of forces parting sooner or later on their way." It is the limitation of the genetic approach to human experience that it must be content to transform problems since it can never solve them. However accurately we may determine the 'facts' of history, the facts themselves and our interpretations of them, and our interpretation of our own interpretations, will be seen in a different perspective or a less vivid light as mankind moves into the unknown future. Regarded historically, as a process of becoming, man and his world can obviously be understood only tentatively, since it is by definition something still in the making, something as yet unfinished. Unfortunately for the 'permanent contribution' and the universally valid philosophy, time passes; time, the enemy of man as the

[3] *The Life of Reason,* Vol. 68.

Greeks thought; to-morrow and to-morrow and to-morrow creeps in this petty pace, and all our yesterdays diminish and grow dim: so that, in the lengthening perspective of the centuries, even the most striking events (the Declaration of Independence, the French Revolution, the Great War itself; like the Diet of Worms before them, like the signing of the Magna Carta and the coronation of Charlemagne and the crossing of the Rubicon and the battle of Marathon) must inevitably, for posterity, fade away into pale replicas of the original picture, for each succeeding generation losing, as they recede into a more distant past, some significance that once was noted in them, some quality of enchantment that once was theirs.

Some Issues in the Logic of Historical Analysis

ERNEST NAGEL

According to Aristotle, poetry, like theoretical science, is "more philosophic and of graver import" than history, for the former is concerned with the pervasive and universal, and the latter is addressed to the special and the singular. Aristotle's remark is a possible historical source of a widely held current distinction between two allegedly different types of sciences: the nomothetic, which seek to establish abstract general laws for indefinitely repeatable processes; and the ideographic, which aim to understand the unique and nonrecurrent. It is often maintained that the natural sciences are nomothetic, whereas history (in the sense of an account of events) is ideographic; and it is claimed in consequence that the logic and conceptual structure of historical explanations are fundamentally different from those of the natural sciences. It is my aim here to examine this and related issues in the logic of historical analysis.

Scientific Monthly, Vol. 74, 1952, pp. 162–169. Reprinted by permission of the author and the editor.

I

Even a cursory examination of treatises in theoretical natural science and of books on history reveals the prima facie difference between them, that by and large the statements of the former are general in form, and contain few if any references to specific objects, places, and times, whereas the statements of the latter are almost without exception singular and replete with proper names, dates, and geographic specifications. To this extent, at least, the alleged contrast between the natural sciences as nomothetic and history as ideographic appears to be well founded.

It would, however, be a gross error to conclude that singular statements play no role in the theoretical sciences or that historical inquiry makes no use of universal ones.

No conclusions concerning the actual character of specific things and processes can be derived from general statements alone; and theories and laws must be supplemented by initial or boundary conditions when the natural sciences attempt to explain any particular occurrence. Nor does the familiar and often useful distinction between "pure" and "applied" natural science impair the relevance of this point. For, clearly, even the pure natural sciences can assert their general statements as empirically warranted only on the basis of concrete factual evidence, and therefore only by establishing and using a variety of singular statements. And there are branches of natural science, such as geophysics and animal ecology, that are concerned with the spatiotemporal distribution and development of individual systems. It follows, in short, that neither the natural sciences taken as a whole nor their purely theoretical subdivisions can be regarded as being exclusively nomothetic.

Neither can historical study dispense with at least a tacit acceptance of universal statements of the kind occurring in the natural sciences. Thus, although the historian may be concerned with the nonrecurrent and the unique, he selects and abstracts from the concrete occurrences he studies, and his discourse about what is individual and singular requires the use of common names and general descriptive terms. Such characterizations are associated with the recognition of various kinds or types of things and occurrences, and therefore with the implicit acknowledgment of numerous empirical regularities. Again, one phase of a historian's task is to establish the authenticity of documents and other remains from the past, the precise meaning of recorded assertions, and the reliability of testimony concerning past events. For the effective execution of this task of external and internal criticism, the historian must be armed with a wide assortment of general laws, borrowed from one or the other of the natural and social sciences. And, since historians usually aim to be more than mere chroniclers of the past, and attempt to understand and explain recorded actions in terms of their causes and consequences, they must obviously assume supposedly well-established laws of causal dependence. In brief, history is not a purely ideographic discipline.

Nonetheless, there is an important asymmetry between theoretical and historical sciences. A theoretical science like physics seeks to establish both general and singular statements, and in the process of doing so physicists will employ previously established statements of both types. Historians, on the other hand, aim to assert warranted singular statements about the occurrence and interrelations of specific actions; and though this task can be achieved only by assuming and using general laws, historians do not regard it as part of their task to *establish* such laws. The distinction between history and theoretical science is thus somewhat analogous to the difference between medical diagnosis and physiology, or between geology and physics. A geologist seeks to ascertain, for example, the sequential order of geologic formations, and he is able to do so by applying various physical laws to the materials he encounters; it is not the geologist's task, qua geologist, to establish the laws of mechanics or of radioactive disintegration that he may employ.

The fact that historical research is concerned with the singular, and seeks to ascertain the causal dependencies between specific occurrences, does not warrant the widespread contention that there is a radical difference between the logical structure of explanations in the historical and the generalizing sciences. I shall consider only one specific argument to support the claim that there is such a difference. It has been said that there is a demonstrable *formal* difference between the "general concepts" of the theoretical sciences and the "individual concepts" assumed to be the goals of historical inquiry. Concepts of the first kind are alleged to conform to the familiar logical principle of the inverse variation of the extension and intension of terms: when a set of general terms is arranged in order of their increasing extensions, their intensions decrease. But quite the reverse is said to be the case for the individual concepts of historical explanations, since the more inclusive the "scope" of such a concept, the richer and fuller is its "meaning." Thus, the term "French Enlightenment" is claimed to have not only a more inclusive scope than the term "the life of Voltaire," but also to possess a fuller intension.[1]

But this is simply a confusion, derived in part from a failure to distinguish the relation of *inclusion* between the extensions of terms, from some form of *whole-part* relation between an instance of a term and a component of that instance. Thus, the French Enlightenment may be said to "contain" as one of its "components" the life of Voltaire; and it is doubtless correct to maintain that the term "French Enlightenment" is "richer in meaning or content" than the term "the life of Voltaire." But the *extension* of the term "French Enlightenment" does *not* include the *extension* of the term "the life of Voltaire," so that the logical principle under discussion cannot be significantly applied to these terms.

More generally, there appears to be no good reason for claiming that the general pattern of explanations in historical inquiry, or the logical structure of the conceptual tools employed in it, differs from those encountered in the generalizing and the natural sciences. The explanatory premises in history, as in the natural sciences, include a number of implicitly assumed laws, as well as many explicitly (though usually incompletely) formulated singular statements of initial conditions. The tacitly assumed laws may be of various kinds. They may be statements of regularities well attested in some special science, or they may be uncodified assumptions taken from common experience; they may be universal statements of invariable concomitance, or they may be statistical in form; they may assert a uniformity in temperal sequence, or they may assert some relation of coexistent dependence. The singular statements of initial conditions are of comparable variety, and although the truth of many of them is often incontrovertible it is frequently highly conjectural. Indeed, the relevance of such singular statements to the specific problems under investigation, as well as their truth, are questions upon which historians are often undecided or unable to achieve unanimity. There are, in fact, several problems in this connection that are of much concern to historical research, although they are not without relevance to other branches of social science as well. I therefore turn to consider briefly some of the real and alleged difficulties that plague the pursuit of historical knowledge.

II

It is a platitude that research in history as in other areas of science selects and abstracts from the concrete occurrences studied, and that however detailed a historical discourse may be it is never an exhaustive account of what actually happened. Curiously enough, it is the very selectivity of history that generates many of the broader questions relating to the nature of historical inquiry and is sometimes made the occasion for wholesale skepticism concerning the possibility of "objective" explanations in historical matters. Since a historian exercises selection in choosing problems for study, and also in his proposed solutions to them, it will be convenient to examine some of the relevant issues under these two heads.

[1] H. Rickert, *Die Grenzen der naturwissenschaftlichen Begriffsbildung,* p. 281. Tübingen: J. C. B. Mohr, 1921.

1) Historians do not all concern themselves with the same things, and there are undoubtedly many past events that have received attention from no historian. Why does one historian occupy himself with ancient Greece, another with modern Germany, still another with the development of legal institutions in the American colonies, a fourth with the evolution of mathematical notation, and so on? Is there some general feature which differentiates those occurrences that are of concern to historians from those that are not? And, above all, is a historian prevented from giving a warranted or objective account of things because of his initial choice of a limited problem?

It is clear that there is no uniform answer to the first of these queries, for in historical inquiry as in other branches of science a variety of circumstances may determine what problems are to be investigated. It may be individual preference and endowment, controlled by education and the influence of teachers; it may be professional obligation or the desire for financial gain; it may be national pride, social pressure, or a sense of political mission. Historians of ideas have given some attention to this matter, and have uncovered interesting data concerning stimuli to specific investigations. But there is no prima facie reason to believe that, because a historical inquiry begins with a specific problem, or because there are causal determinants for his choice, a historian is in principle precluded – any more than is a natural scientist – from rendering an adequate account of the subjects he is investigating.

Many writers maintain, however, that the selectivity of history is peculiar in that the historian is inescapably concerned with "value-impregnated" subject matter. Thus, according to one influential view, an individual or process can be properly labeled as "historical" only if it is "irreplaceable," either because it unquely embodies some universally accepted cultural value or because it is instrumental to the actualization of such a value. In consequence, the supposition that historical inquiry can ignore theoretical value relations is said by some writers to involve a self-deception,[2] whereas other commentators have concluded that unlike the physical sciences "history is violently personal," since "stars and molecules have no loves and hates, while men do."[3] There is, however, no basis for the claim that historical study is addressed exclusively to value-impregnated occurrences, unless indeed the word "history" is arbitrarily redefined so as to conform with the claim. For, although undoubtedly much historical inquiry is concerned with events that may be so characterized, there are also many investigations commonly called "historical" that are not of this nature – for example, inquiries into the development of the stars, biological species, and much else. More generally, there appears to be no warrant for any of the various claims that the occurrences studied by historians are distinguished by some inherent differentiating feature from those that are not. Moreover, even when a historian is concerned with admittedly value-impregnated subject matter or with occurrences manifesting various passions, it by no means follows that he must himself share or judge those values or passions. It is an obvious blunder to suppose that only a fat cowherd can drive fat kine. It is an equally crude error to maintain that one cannot inquire into the conditions and consequences of values and evalutions without necessarily engaging in moral or aesthetic value judgments.

There is also the broad question whether historical inquiry is inevitably guilty of distorting the facts because it is addressed to limited problems and is concerned only with certain selected materials of the past. The supposition that it is entails the view that

[2] *Ibid.*, p. 254.

[3] A. Nevins, *The Gateway to History*, p. 29. New York: Appleton-Century, 1938.

one cannot have competent knowledge of anything unless one knows everything, and is a corollary to the philosophic doctrine of the "internality" of all relations. It will suffice here to note that, were the doctrine sound, not only would every historical account ever written be condemned as a necessarily mutilated and distorted version of what has happened, but a similar valuation would have to be placed on all science, and indeed on all analytical discourse. In short, the fact that inquiry is selective because it originates in a specific and limited problem places the historian in no worse position than it does other scientists with respect to the possibility of achieving what is commonly characterized as objectively warranted knowledge.

2) Historical inquiry is selective not only in its starting point; it is also selective in proposing solutions to its problems. A variety of skeptical doubts about the possibility of an objective history has been expressed in consequence.

One such expression takes the form that, in view of the inexhaustibly numerous relations in which a given event stands to other events, no account can ever render the "full reality" of what has occurred. Accordingly, since every historical account covers only a few aspects of an occurrence and stops at some point in the past in tracing back its antecedents, every proposed explanation of that occurrence is said to bear the mark of arbitrariness and subjectivity. Part of this objection can be summarily dismissed with the reminder that it is never the task of any inquiry initiated by a specific problem to *reproduce* its subject matter, and that it would be a gratuitous performance were a historian in the pursuit of such a problem to formulate "all that has been said, done, and thought by human beings on the planet since humanity began its long career." Not only is the bare fact that inquiry is selective no valid ground for doubting the objectively warranted character of its conclusions; on the contrary, unless an inquiry were selective it would never come near to resolving the specific question by which it is generated.

However, the objection under discussion also rests on another misconception: it in effect assumes that since every causal condition for an event has its own causal conditions, the event is never properly explained unless the entire regressive series of the latter conditions are also explained. It has been maintained, for example, that

> A Baptist sermon in Atlanta, if we seek to explain it, takes us back through the Protestant Reformation to Galilee – and far beyond in the dim origins of civilization. We can, if we choose, stop at any point along the line of relations, but that is an arbitrary act of will and does violence to the quest for truth in the matter.[4]

But is there any violence to the truth? Is *B* not a cause of *A* simply because *C* is a cause of *B*? When some future position of a planet is predicted with the help of gravitational theory and information about the initial condition of the solar system at some given time, is there ground for skepticism simply because the assumed initial conditions are in turn the outcome of previous ones? These are rhetorical questions, for the answers to all of them are obviously in the negative. Moreover, precisely what is the problem in connection with the Baptist sermon in Atlanta? Is it why a given individual delivered it at a stated time and occasion, or why he chose a particular text and theme, or why that occasion happened to arise, or why Baptists flourish in Atlanta, or why they developed as a Protestant sect, or why the Protestant Reformation occurred, or why Christianity arose in antiquity? These are all quite different questions, and an adequate answer for one of them is not even relevant as a proposed solution for the others. The

[4] C. A. Beard, *The Discussion of Human Affairs*, pp. 68–69. New York: Macmillan, 1936.

supposition that, when a problem is made definite a regressive chain of answers must be sought if any one answer is to be objectively warranted, is patently self-contradictory. On the other hand, the fact that one problem may suggest another, and so lead to a possibly endless series of new inquiries, simply illustrates the progressive character of the scientific enterprise; that fact is no support for the claim that unless the series is terminated, every proposed solution to a given problem is necessarily a mutilation of the truth.

Skepticism concerning the possibility of objectively warranted explanations in human history takes a more empirical turn when it bases its negations on the influence of personal and social bias upon such inquiry. The doubt embodied in the *aperçu* that history is written by the survivors is by no means a novelty; but in recent years it has been deepened and given a radical form by many sociologists of knowledge. According to some of them, all thought is conditioned and controlled by the "existential situation" in which it occurs; and, especially when thinking is directed to human affairs, the interpretation of observed facts, the selection of problems for inquiry and the methods employed for resolving them, and the standards of validity accepted are all functions of the thinker's unconscious value commitments and world outlook, his social position, and his political and class loyalties. Every cognitive claim concerning matters of vital human interest is therefore said to be valid only within the particular social setting in which it emerges; and the belief that it is possible to obtain explanations that are "true" for everyone, irrespective of his position in a given society, is declared to be part of the self-deception (or "ideology") of a culture.

There appear to be four distinct issues raised by this form of skepticism. In the first place, the choice of particular problems for study, especially inquiries into human affairs, is undoubtedly controlled by the character of a given culture, and sometimes by the status of the student in that culture. An investigation of traffic problems is not likely to be made in an agricultural society, and a man's interest in labor history may very well be causally related to his social position. But, as has already been seen, this form of selective activity on the part of an inquirer does not necessarily jeopardize the objectivity of his findings.

In the second place, no inquiry takes place in an intellectual vacuum, and every investigator approaches his task with information and guiding ideas derived in large measure from his culture. But it does not follow from this circumstance alone that the conscious and unconscious value commitments associated with the social status of an investigator inevitably influence his acceptance of one conclusion rather than another. The preconceptions he brings to the analysis of a given problem may be neutral to all differences in social values, even when that problem is concerned with human affairs. And, in point of fact, there are many questions in the social as well as in the natural sciences upon which there is complete agreement among students, despite their different social positions and loyalties.

It is undoubtedly the case, in the third place, that the standards of validity operative in an inquiry are *causally* related to other cultural traits, and that social status, class and national bias, and general world perspectives frequently influence what conclusions a man accepts. For example, the degree of precision currently demanded in experimental work is certainly not independent of the current state of technology; and a comparison of Southern and Northern histories of the period of reconstruction following the American Civil War makes amply clear the force of sectional and race bias. This is an area of study that has not yet been systematically exploited, although sociologists of knowledge have already illuminated the genesis of many ideas and the manner in which social pressures enforce their acceptance. In any event, biased thinking is a perennial challenge to the critical historian of human affairs; and research into the causal determinants of bias is of undoubted value for recognizing its occurrence and for mitigating if not always eliminating its influence. The very fact that biased thinking may be detected and its sources investigated shows that the case for objective explanations in history is not necessarily hopeless. Indeed, the assertion that a historian exhibits bias assumes that there is a distinction between biased and unbiased thinking, and that the bias can be identified – for otherwise the assertion would at best be simply futile name-calling. In consequence, it is possible, even if frequently difficult, to correct the bias and to obtain conclusions in better agreement with the evidence. Accordingly, if doubt concerning the objectivity of a historical explanation is based on considerations relating to the causal influence of various social factors upon the evaluation of evidence, it is often salutary and well taken; but it does not entail a wholesale skepticism concerning the possibility of such explanations.

This brings me to the final issue. It is sometimes argued that the social perspective of a student of human affairs is not only causally influential upon his inquiry, but is *logically* involved both in his standards of validity as well as in the meaning of his statements. And it is also maintained that one must therefore reject the thesis that "the genesis of a proposition is under all circumstances irrelevant to its truth." [5] On the other hand, the radical skepticism concerning objective explanations of human affairs that results is qualified by the further claim that a "relational" type of objectivity can nevertheless be achieved. Thus, students who share the same social perspective and employ the same conceptual and categorical apparatus will allegedly arrive at similar conclusions on any problem when the standards characteristic of their common perspective are correctly applied. And students operating within different social perspectives can attain objectivity in a "roundabout fashion" by construing their inevitable differences in the light of the differences in the structures of their perspectives.

There are, however, grave factual and dialectical difficulties in these several claims. There is no factual evidence to show that the "content and form" of statements, or the standards of validity employed, are *logically* determined by the social perspective of an inquirer. The facts commonly cited establish no more than some kind of causal dependence between these items. For example, the once much-publicized view that the "mentality" or logical operations of "primitive" social groups are different from those typical of European civilization – a difference that was once attributed to institutional differences in the societies compared – is now generally recognized to be without foundation. Moreover, even the most extreme proponents of the sociology of knowledge admit that there are many assertions (those usually mentioned come from mathematics and the natural sciences) which are neutral to differences in social perspective and whose genesis is irrelevant to their validity. Why cannot assertions about human affairs exhibit the same neutrality? If, as no one seems to doubt, the truth of the statement that two horses can in general pull a greater load than either horse alone is logically independent of the social status of the one who asserts it, what inherent social circumstance precludes such independence for the statement that two laborers can in general dig a ditch of given dimensions more quickly than either laborer working alone?

Second, what is the logical status of the

[5] K. Mannheim, *Ideology and Utopia*, pp. 243, 259. New York: Harcourt, Brace, 1936.

claim that social perspectives enter essentially into the content and warrant of all assertions about human affairs? Is the claim itself meaningful and valid only for those occupying a certain social status? In that case, its validity is narrowly self-limited, no student with a different social perspective can properly understand or evaluate it, and it must be dismissed as irrelevant by most inquirers into social questions. Or is the claim peculiarly exempt from what it asserts, so that its meaning and truth are not logically dependent upon the social status of those who assert it? In that case, then, there is at least one conclusion about human affairs which may be "objectively valid" in the usual sense of this phrase; and if there is one such conclusion, there is no clear reason why there may not be others.

Finally, the relational type of objectivity which the claim admits as attainable is nothing other than objectivity in the customary sense, which the claim appears to deny as possible. A translation formula which renders the "common denominator" of seemingly diverse conclusions stemming from differing social perspectives, cannot in turn be "situationally determined" in the sense under dispute. Indeed, the search for such formulas is but a well-known phase of theoretical research in all areas of inquiry. It is a search for objective invariants in numerically and qualitatively distinct processes; and when the quest is successful, as it often is, it terminates in laws of greater or less generality, with whose help what is relevant to the occurrence of an event or to the continuance of a process can be distinguished from what is not.

In brief, therefore, although the historian is undoubtedly selective in the conduct of his inquiries, and although personal and social bias frequently color his judgment and control what conclusions he accepts, none of these facts precludes the possibility of warranted explanations for the events he studies.

III

The elimination of theoretical objections to the possibility of warranted explanations in history obviously does not ensure the realization of that possibility. As a matter of fact, there are serious obstacles, other than those already mentioned, which frequently do obstruct the quest for such explanations.

The search for explanations is directed to the ideal of ascertaining the necessary and sufficient conditions for the occurrence of phenomena. This ideal is rarely achieved, however, and even in the best-developed natural sciences it is often an open question whether the conditions mentioned in an explanation are indeed sufficient. Most historical inquiry is even further removed from this ideal, since the full circumstances are often quite complex and numerous and are usually not known. Historians therefore frequently cite only what they regard as the "main," "primary," "principal," "chief," or "most important" causal factors and cover their ignorance of the others by the convenient phrase "other things being equal." To mention but one example, the "main" cause of America's entrance into the first world war is declared by one careful student to be Germany's adoption of an unrestricted submarine warfare, though the factor cited is not assumed to be sufficient for producing the effect.

The "weighting" of causal factors in respect to their "degree of importance" is sometimes dismissed as essentially "arbitrary" and "meaningless" — partly on the ground that there is no warrant for selecting one occurrence as the cause of a given event rather than some prior cause of that occurrence (for example, since unrestricted submarine warfare was Germany's response to the British blockade, this latter occurrence is allegedly as much the cause of America's entrance into the war as is the former), and partly on the ground that no verifiable sense can be attached to such characterizations as "chief" or "most important" in connection with causal factors. It must be admitted that the natural sciences do not appear to require the imputation of relative importance to the causal variables that occur in their explanations; and it is easy to dismiss the question of whether there is any objective basis for such gradations of variables, with a peremptory denial on the ground that, if a phenomenon occurs only when certain conditions are realized, all these conditions are equally essential, and no one of them can intelligibly be regarded as more basic than the others. And it must also be acknowledged that most historians do not appear to associate any definite meaning with their statements of relative importance, so that the statements often have only a rhetorical intent, from which no clear empirical content can be extracted. Nevertheless, we often do make such claims as that broken homes constitute a more important cause of juvenile delinquency than does poverty, or that the lack of a trained labor force is a more fundamental cause of the backward state of an economy than the lack of natural resources. Many people might be willing to admit that the *truth* of such statements is debatable, but few would be willing to grant that they are totally without *meaning* so that anyone who asserts them is invariably uttering nonsense.

It is desirable, therefore, to make explicit what such statements may be intended to convey. In point of fact, ascriptions of relative importance to determinants of social phenomena appear to be associated with a variety of meanings, some of which I shall try to distinguish. If *A* and *B* are two adequately specified factors upon which the occurrence of a phenomenon *C* is supposed to depend in some fashion, the statements I wish to consider will be assumed to have the schematic form "*A* is a more important (or basic, or fundamental) determinant of *C* than is *B*."

1) *A* and *B* may both be necessary for the occurrence of *C*, though perhaps their joint presence is not sufficient for that occurrence. Then one sense in which *A* might be said to be a more important determinant of *C* than is *B* is simply this: variations in *B* occur infrequently and may be neglected for all practical purposes, whereas variations in *A*, with consequent variations in *C*, are quite frequent and perhaps uncontrollable. Thus, suppose that dislike of foreigners and need for economic markets are both necessary conditions for the adoption of an imperialist policy by some country; but suppose that xenophobia in that country varies little if at all during a given period, whereas the need for foreign markets increases. In this first sense of more important, need for foreign markets is a more important cause of imperialism than is dislike of foreigners.

2) But there is another though more difficult sense of more important. Assume again that *A* and *B* are both necessary for the occurrence of *C*. But suppose that there is some way of specifying the magnitude of variations in *A*, *B*, and *C*, respectively, and that, although changes in one may not be comparable with changes in another, the changes within each item are comparable. Suppose, further, that a greater change in *C* is associated with a given proportional change in *A* than with an equal proportional change in *B*. In that event, *A* might be given a more important rank as a determinant of *C* than is assigned to *B*. For example, assume that a supply of coal and a trained labor force are both necessary for industrial productivity; but suppose that, say, a 10 per cent variation in the labor force produces a greater alteration in the quantity of goods produced (as measured by some convenient index) than does a 10 per cent variation in the coal supply. Accordingly, the availability of a trained labor force could be said to be a more important determinant of productivity than the availability of coal.

3) Suppose now that the joint presence of *A* and *B* is not necessary for the occurrence of *C*, so that *C* can occur under conditions *A*

and *Y*, or under conditions *B* and *Z*, where *Y* and *Z* are otherwise unspecified determinants. In this case, also, there is a sense of more important analogous to the first sense mentioned above. More explicitly, the frequency with which the first condition *B* and *Z* are realized may be small when compared with the frequency of the realization of *A* and *Y;* and this possibility may then be expressed by saying that *A* is a more important determinant of *C* than is *B*. Thus, assume that automobile accidents occur either because of negligence or because of mechanical failure; and suppose that the frequency with which there is such failure that leads to accidents is very much less than the frequency with which carelessness terminates in accidents. In that case, negligence may be said to be a more important cause of accidents than is mechanical failure.

4) Assume, again, that the joint presence of *A* and *B* is not necessary for the occurrence of *C;* and suppose that the relative frequency with which *C* occurs when the condition *A* is realized but *B* is not is greater than the relative frequency of *C*'s occurrence if *B* is realized but *A* is not. It is such a state of affairs which is sometimes intended by the assertion that *A* is a more important determinant of *C* than is *B*. For example, a statement such as that broken homes are a more fundamental cause of juvenile delinquency than is poverty is frequently best interpreted to mean that the relative frequency of delinquency among juveniles coming from broken homes is much greater than among children coming from homes marked by poverty.

5) One final sense of more important must be mentioned. Suppose that a theory *T* is formulated with the help of *A* as a fundamental theoretical term; and suppose that *T* can account for the phenomenon *C* when *T* is supplemented by appropriate data which involve reference to *B*. In consequence, though reference to B is essential for explaining *C* with the help of *T*, reference to *B* is not always necessary when *T* serves to explain phenomena other than *C*. Accordingly, since the range of phenomena which fall within the province of *T* (and therefore within the range of application of *A*) is more inclusive than the phenomena for which *B* is relevant, *A* may be said to be a more basic determinant of *C* than is *B*. Something like this sense of more basic appears to be intended by those who claim that the social relations that govern the production and distribution of wealth constitute a more basic determinant of the legal institutions of a society than do the religious and moral ideals professed in that society.

Other senses of more important or more basic can undoubtedly be distinguished, but the five here mentioned appear to be those most frequently used in discussions of human affairs. It is essential to note that, although a definite meaning may thus be associated with ascriptions of greater importance to assumed determinants of social processes, it does not follow that the available evidence does in fact warrant any given assertion of such a claim. Accordingly, even when a historian does intend to convey a verifiable content by such assertions, it is doubtful whether in most cases they are actually supported by competent evidence. There is next to no statistical material bearing on the relative frequency of occurrence of the phenomena of special concern to students of human affairs. Historians are therefore compelled, willy-nilly, to fall back upon guesses and vague impressions in assigning weights to causal factors. There are often wide divergences in judgment as to what are the main causes of a given event, and one man's opinions may be no better grounded than another's. Whether this defect in current causal imputations in historical research can eventually be remedied is an open question, since the probable cost of remedial measures in terms of labor and money seems staggering. Meanwhile, however, a judicious skepticism concerning the warrant for most if not all judgments of relative importance of causal factors (among those assumed to be relevant to an event) appears to be in order.

Doubtless the basic trouble in this area of inquiry is that we do not possess at present a generally accepted, explicitly formulated, and fully comprehensive schema for weighing the evidence for any arbitrarily given hypothesis so that the logical worth of alternate conclusions relative to the evidence available for each can be compared. Judgments must be formed even on matters of supreme practical importance on the basis of only vaguely understood considerations; and, in the absence of a standard logical canon for estimating the degree in which the evidence supports a conclusion, when judgments are in conflict each often appears to be the outcome of an essentially arbitrary procedure. This circumstance affects the standing of the historian's conclusions in the same manner as the findings of other students. Fortunately, though the range of possible disagreement concerning the force of evidence for a given statement is theoretically limitless, there is substantial agreement among men experienced in relevant matters on the relative probabilities to be assigned to many hypotheses. Such agreement indicates that, despite the absence of an explicitly formulated logic, many unformulated habits of thought embody factually warrantable principles of inference. Accordingly, although there are often legitimate grounds for doubt concerning the validity of specific causal imputations in history, there appears to be no compelling reason for converting such doubt into wholesale skepticism.

4

THE MEANING OF 'CAUSE' AND 'LAW'

Introduction

1.

We use the concepts of cause and effect widely in everyday discourse; in fact, they are among our most familiar terms. Scientists also use these notions in trying to explain how or why things come about as they do, although they use the terms more carefully than we, in the sense that they demand more evidence, and more carefully derived evidence, for their use than we do in ordinary affairs. Some philosophers of science, it is true, insist that scientists do not bother with the notion of cause at all. Cause-and-effect generalizations, they say, hold only within ranges whose limits are unclear and tacitly assume that certain unmentioned factors remain constant; therefore, scientists disregard the concept of causality in favor of the more sophisticated notion of lawfulness or functional connection. In logically sophisticated sciences like physics, to be sure, one infrequently finds the word "cause" used; but the matter is quite otherwise in biological, psychological, and social science where explanation is frequently described as the confirmation of hypotheses of causal connection. Actually, however, it matters little for our purposes whether scientists talk about "causes" or "laws" or whatever, since, as we shall see, the very same difficulties beset one no matter which of these terms he tries to define or clarify.

In the context of everyday language we find many familiar but not altogether clear notions of the meaning of 'cause.' If someone who knew nothing about philosophy or science were asked what he meant when he says "x is the cause of y," whatever 'x' or 'y' may be, he would probably reply that he means x is *responsible for bringing about* y, or x *produces* y, or x *makes* y *happen*. These definitions are not very helpful, however, since it is doubtful if "responsible for bringing about," or "produces," or "makes happen" is any more understandable in this context than "causes." Nevertheless philosophers have not been able to ignore these vague common-sense definitions in their efforts to produce more precise ones.

Let us begin our philosophical analysis of causality with the metaphysical or "necessary connection" viewpoint. This view is called metaphysical since it denies that the concept of cause can be fully understood or defined in terms of experience alone. A proponent of this view agrees readily that part of the meaning of 'cause' is defined in experiential terms; whatever else we mean when we say "x causes y," we mean that x and y are always correlated in our experience, x and y always occur together and never apart. This idea is variously formulated; sometimes it is said that x and y are constantly conjoined, or x and y are functionally related, or, in the symbols of modern logic, $x \supset y$, that is, whenever x, then y. However constant conjunction, or whatever one calls it, is only part of the meaning of cause, the metaphysical proponent says; it is, in a sense, only the symptom of a causal connection. Mere constant conjunction can never give us a complete understanding, or be an adequate definition, of the cause-effect relationship. True, I experience a constant conjunction between willing to raise my arm and the upward movement of my arm, but in such cases of volition I also directly experience the causal relation itself:

I experience the volitional force or energy which *makes* an event — in this case, the movement of the arm — occur. The full meaning of 'cause,' then, is the constant conjunction of x and y, plus a force that necessarily binds x and y together. X and y are not simply conjoined, but connected; they do not simply occur together, they belong together.

In the physical realm, of course, the metaphysical advocate continues, we do not have any direct experience of the causal connection between x's and y's, but nevertheless we must postulate the existence of some unobservable force or ontological tie which binds together the cause and the effect so that we can say the events are connected and not simply conjoined. On the level of commonsense we do feel that a cause and effect are connected in the sense that given the cause, the effect *must* occur; but mere constant conjunction can never explain this notion of *mustness* which we feel intuitively is present in all causal relationships.

In addition, the metaphysical proponent says, constant conjunction cannot be the whole meaning of 'cause' since some constant conjunctions are accidental or, at any rate, not causal in nature, while other constant conjunctions *are* causal. Night follows day, and day follows night universally, but we do not for a moment think that either is the cause of the other. They are both, we say, the effects of a third thing, namely, the illumination of the sun and the rotation of the earth. However, since some constant conjunctions are and some are not causal in nature, constant conjunction cannot be all that is meant by 'cause.' Constant conjunction is only a symptom of causality in the sense that it only provides evidence which makes it reasonable, in some cases, to postulate the existence of a force or tie which insures and explains the universality of that conjunction.

The empirical philosopher, on the other hand, believes that 'cause' means constant conjunction, or lawfulness, and nothing more. To justify this belief he tries to meet, point for point, the metaphysician's reasons for believing in a necessary causal connection and to show, in addition, that this concept is really a nonsensical one, the outgrowth, in short, of a semantical mix-up.

First. — The empiricist denies that we are directly acquainted with causal connections even in volitional experience. As Hume already pointed out, willing to move my arm is not the (complete) cause of the movement since it is only one of a set of many conditions which together make up the cause. Certain physiological conditions must be satisfied also before the movement occurs. If the muscles of my arm are paralyzed, regardless of how much willing I do, the arm will not move. Consequently, since in some cases the movement of the arm does not follow upon the volition, one is not able to say there is a necessary connection between the volition and the movement.

Second. — The empiricist denies that it is *necessary* to presuppose or postulate causal forces or ontological ties between elements or events in the physical world; it is unnecessary since one can make the required distinctions between connected and unconnected events and causal and non-causal constant conjunctions within the ambit of experience itself.

A. — What, after all, do we mean when we say events A and B are *connected* except that there is a chain of intermediate events so that A-a-b-B is perfectly continuous in space and time? However, since there is no gap in space or time between b and B, there is no further connection for these events to exhibit. Consider the example of a doctor administering a drug to his patients. After a reasonable lapse of time, let us say, they invariably recover from their illness. Still, even though we have a constant conjunction between administration of the drug and the recovery of patients, nevertheless we have not succeeded in connecting the events. We would have done the latter only if we knew how the gap between the two types of events is replaced by a continuous series of events which are contiguous in space and time. We would know how this gap is filled, how the events are connected, if we knew for example that the drug is injected into the veins, comes into immediate contact with blood particles, which undergo a chemical change, travel through the body, and come into contact with some organ, thereby changing it in a particular way, etc. The conclusion of the matter, according to one modern empiricist, is this:

> We learn that the causal relation between two separate events is actually explained or understood when we can conceive the two as being connected by a chain of intermediate events. If some of these are still separated, we have to look for new events between them, and so on, until all the gaps are filled out and the chain has become perfectly continuous in space and time. But evidently *we can go no further,* and it would be nonsense to expect more of us. If we look for the causal link that links two events together, we cannot find anything but another event (or perhaps several). Whatever can be observed and shown in the causal chain will be the links, but it would be nonsense to look for the linkage. This shows that we are perfectly right when we think of cause and effect as *connected* by a causal chain, but that we are perfectly wrong when we think that this chain could consist of anything but events, that it could be a kind of mysterious tie called "causality."[1]

B.—The way we distinguish those constant conjunctions which *are* causal from those which are *not,* says the empiricist, is by reference to an overall deductive context, not by invoking an unobservable force. We say that day-night and night-day are not causal correlations because we know that they are both *effects* of a common cause. That is, we know there is a constant conjunction or universal correlation between sources of illumination and the rotation of spheroid bodies from which we can deduce the sequences day-night and night-day as joint effects. If, however, there were no higher-order correlations from which we could deduce this consequence, then one would have to accept, until further notice, the correlation night-day-night as ultimate and so causal. The general conclusion is this: without a deductive context one would not be able to call any universal correlation non-causal.

Moreover, the empiricist asks, is there really a constant conjunction between day and night, albeit not a causal one? He thinks not; rather the higher-order correlation shows that the day and night relation is only an *apparent* or *conditional* constant conjunction, one which occurs only if the conditions specified in the higher-order correlation obtain. But a real constant conjunction, J. S. Mill wrote, is unconditional or exceptionless: a conjunction which occurs no matter what happens. Day and night, of course, would not follow each other no matter what happens. If the sun stopped shining or a screen were obtruded between the sun and earth, or whatever, the conjunction would be destroyed. Of course, we cannot actually destroy this conjunction, but we have good evidence from small scale systems that these conditions would destroy it.

Let us return for a moment to the concept of a deductive hierarchy of correlations in science. The more highly developed a science is, like physics, the more highly articulated is its deductive hierarchy. The important point, however, is that in any science the higher-order correlations necessarily imply the lower-order ones. One is thus able to say: Given the higher-order correlations the lower-order ones *must* follow; given the

1 Moritz Schlick, "Causality in Everyday Life and in Recent Science," *University of California Publications in Philosophy,* 15, 1932. Reprinted in H. Feigl and W. Sellars, editors, *Readings in Philosophical Analysis,* p. 522.

correlation between sources of illumination and the rotation of bodies, the sequences day-night-day etc. *must* follow. However, there is no mustness in the highest-order correlations; unless they contain theoretical terms the only evidence we have finally for their truth is the universality of the correlation of their terms. This analysis has led some empirical philosophers to say we can never be certain that anything is really the cause of something else. Even our highest-order correlations might turn out eventually to be non-causal in the sense that we might discover a still higher correlation from which the terms of the previous correlation could be deduced as joint effects.

Third. – The empiricist claims that the metaphysician's notion of mustness or necessary connection makes no sense in a causal analysis; it is literally the outgrowth of a semantical mix-up. Logic and mathematics are the only contexts in which the notion of necessary connection has any meaning. A conclusion follows as necessarily true from its premises if the premises and the denial of the conclusion are self-contradictory. So, if what the metaphysician means by mustness is logical necessity, then he would have to say that the denial of a causal assertion is self-contradictory. But this position is absurd since if I say "wet feet always cause colds" I am clearly uttering a false sentence and so could not be uttering a self-contradictory one.

The metaphysician might reply that by mustness he does not mean logical connection; rather he means something like the cause *forcing* or *making* the effect occur, or being responsible for the occurrence of the effect. But if this is the case, the metaphysician has confused prescriptive and descriptive laws. A prescriptive law is the statement of a norm, that is, what must be done if one is to avoid sanctions. Of course, it makes perfectly good sense to say that the sanctions of a prescriptive law force a person to accept it or make him follow it, since he might well prefer on other grounds not to accept or follow it. However, this notion of forcing or making is inappropriate in the context of descriptive laws, since this type of law simply describes what is the case, not what must be the case. It is simply a little odd to talk about making or forcing physical objects to act in the required lawful way as if they might really prefer something else.

Some empiricists, trying to make the concept of cause more precise, have offered this string of definitions: 'cause' = 'sufficient condition'; 'sufficient conditions' = 'set of necessary conditions'; 'necessary condition' = 'condition without which the effect would not occur.' Let us use the example of a forest fire to clarify these definitions. A forest fire will occur, one says, if these conditions obtain: some means of ignition, dry underbrush, a prevailing wind, oxygen in the air, etc. Each condition is necessary, not in the metaphysicians' sense, but only in the sense that without it the effect – the forest fire – would not occur. It is, of course, very difficult to find the whole set of necessary conditions, but this whole set, whatever it may be, is the condition sufficient or able to produce the effect and thus is the cause of the effect.

It is doubtful, however, that this analysis of 'cause' carries one any farther than the constant conjunction interpretation. For, after all, the only empirical meaning that can be given to the phrase 'a condition without which the effect would not occur' is this: when C happens (along with other conditions), E also happens; and when C does not happen, E does not happen.

2.

Before we try to discover what the concept of scientific law means, we might be wise to look at several examples of scientific law in order to give a modicum of concreteness to our investigation. (L_1) All metals are conductors of electricity. (L_2) All gases, at constant pressure, expand with increasing temperature. (L_3) All surfaces colder than the surrounding air have moisture condense on them, etc. The aspect about all these laws which strikes one first is their universal form – All x's are y's, or if anything is an x then it is also a y. Some philosophers and most scientists, consequently, have defined scientific law, or simply law, as the universal conjunction of terms, or – since most of them can be given a mathematical formulation – the functional correlation of terms.

Many writers have objected to this straightforward definition of 'law,' and for a reason somewhat similar to an objection advanced against the empirical definition of 'cause.' Universal correlation, they say, is a necessary part of the definition of law but not itself a sufficient definition. There are, after all, many universal correlations which we simply would not consider laws: consider, for example, the statements that all apples in basket *b* at time *t* are red or that all the books on the top shelf of my bookcase are English novels of the nineteenth century. Even though these two sentences assert universal correlations we would not call them laws, since we would not say that any apple, chosen at random, put into basket *b* at time t_1 would be red, or that any book chosen at random from a library shelf and put on the top shelf of my bookcase would be an English novel of the nineteenth century.

However, some empiricists answer, the difficulty with the statements about apples and English novels is simply that their universality refers to a finite class of objects. These statements, to be sure, assert universal correlations, but the items correlated do not belong to an infinite class. So we need to modify the definition of 'law' only slightly: A law is the universal conjunction of terms which belong to a non-finite class. In this way, the sentence 'All metals are conductors of electricity' is a law, since it asserts a universal conjunction between 'metals' and 'conductors of electricity,' each of which can be infinitely exemplified; but 'All apples in basket *b* at time *t* are red' is not, since it asserts a universal conjunction between terms of which an exhaustive inventory can be taken.

At this point, however, a difficulty arises for this amended definition of law. Consider this sentence: 'All sixteen ice cubes in the freezing tray of this refrigerator have a temperature of less than 10° centigrade.' This statement refers to a finite class of objects, sixteen ice cubes in a tray in *this* refrigerator, and so, on this new definition, should not qualify as a law; but nevertheless we are certain intuitively that the correlation it asserts *is* lawful in a way that the correlation between red apples and basket *b* is not. This difficulty can be overcome in a simple way; the statement about ice cubes qualifies as lawful because it is known to be the deductive consequence of more comprehensive laws which contain only terms of an unlimited or non-finite scope. Accordingly the definition of law must be amended slightly again: A law is the universal conjunction of terms which belong to a non-finite class or the universal conjunction of terms which belong to a finite class but are deductively derivable from other universal conjunctions which contain only terms of a non-finite scope.

There is another difficulty with this empirical or Humean type of analysis of 'law' which is not so easily overcome. Let us return to the statement about the apples in basket *b* and the English novels on the top shelf of my bookcase. The trouble with these statements, what keeps them from being lawful universal conjunctions, is not simply that the correlated terms are not infinite in scope but rather that there is no connection, causal or non-artificial or whatever, between basket *b* and the color of apples or between the top shelf of my bookcase and being English novels of the nineteenth century. The correct way for the empiricist to meet this difficulty is to show – in these cases quite easily – that we have a good deal of information from which we can deduce the artificial relationship of the correlations – or, what is the same thing, the accidental relationship of the correlations in *rerum natura.* This account of the problem and its solution, however, quite clearly brings us back to the central problem of causality – that is, is it possible to distinguish between accidental and causal correlations by experiential concepts alone? – and the full circle of our analysis demonstrates the intimacy of the notions of cause and law.

Some philosophers have thought that lawfulness must be analyzed in terms of *counterfactual inference;* that is, a universal statement is a law if and only if it permits a corresponding counterfactual inference. For example, 'All gases at constant pressure expand with increasing temperature' qualifies as a law since it permits this corresponding counterfactual inference, 'If this pencil had the property of being a gas it would expand with increasing temperature.' On the other hand, 'All the books on the top shelf of my bookcase are English novels of the nineteenth century' does not qualify as a law since it does not permit this corresponding counterfactual inference, 'If this chemistry book on my desk had the property of being on the top shelf of my bookcase it would be an English novel of the nineteenth century.' Empiricists or Humeans, however, do not accept this interpretation, since to admit 'what would be the case, but is not' as a basic concept would violate their notion that an unobservable concept must have some relationship, however tenuous, with the concepts of direct experience. Consequently, the empiricist, who offers a regularity view of lawfulness, claims that counterfactual inference must be analyzed in terms of lawfulness rather than the other way around. If one can distinguish between a lawful correlation and an accidental one by the use, say, of a deductive hierarchy of laws, inductively established, then, according to the empiricist, he can legitimately make the corresponding counterfactual inference for the former correlation but not for the latter. But then again in the context of lawfulness we have come to the same problem we had in defining 'cause' – namely, that of distinguishing between lawful and accidental correlations. It is wise to keep in mind, if you continue to explore the concepts of this chapter, that it is this context of lawfulness and counterfactuality in which the identical problem of analyzing lawfulness and causality usually occurs in contemporary philosophical writing.

Laws, at any rate, whatever else one holds, are universal conjunctions of terms or variables. This statement does not tell us enough, however, because variables can exhibit several different kinds of universal conjunctions.

First. – Variables may exemplify either process or syndromatic universal relations. A process law, as its name suggests, consists of a general statement of regularity between variables as a function of time. Given such a law, and the statement of present conditions, one can predict subsequent conditions. There are process laws of varying degrees of generality, from a simple 'If A, then B' sort of generalization to a complicated mathematical formula. A syndromatic law, on the other hand, consists of a statement of coexisting properties of the form 'If x is present, then other specifiable elements y and z co-exist with x.' The laws of physics are primarily process laws, while the taxonomic or classificatory phases of biological science are syndromatic in nature.

Second. – Process laws may be further divided into systematic process laws and historical process laws. In the former, no historical or past information about systems is needed for the formulation of a law. Or, putting it the other way around, when a law is applied to a given case the initial conditions are specifiable from the present state of a system and do not have to be supplemented by historical information. In physics, for example, given the present state of a system of n bodies at t_1, and the laws of mechanics, one can predict the subsequent state of the system at t_2. However, in an historical process law information about past histories is needed for the formulation of a law; and, in any application of it, past information about the initial conditions of that system. The laws or regularities of learning psychology, for example, are historical process laws. We must know how organisms have been affected in the past before we can predict how they will act in the future. That is, the present state of an organism is not open to inspection like physical systems, and can only be inferred through its past experience. However, in principle, it is logically possible that the historical process laws of learning psychology could be explained by the systematic process laws of a perfected physiological psychology. As a matter of factual expectation, however, this perfected psychology is remote indeed.

Third. — Variables may exemplify either causal or statistical relations, where 'causal' is not used in any sense that prejudges its meaning. In the present context, all 'causal law' means is a universal statement which, with a statement of initial conditions, allows one to predict the occurrence or behavior of any particular event or individual. A statistical law, on the other hand, is the statement, say, of the percentage of times a certain item turns up in a whole class of items. It allows one to predict that percentage of occurrences in the group in the future but does not permit one to specify what individuals will be included in the percentage.

Fourth. — Variables may occur in higher-order or lower-order laws; but since we have already seen that this distinction is at the heart of the empiricist analysis of causality and lawfulness we need make nothing more of it here.

Finally, let us qualify the uncontested minimum of meaning in the notion of law — which, you recall, was this: a law is a universal conjunction of terms or variables. The qualification we need to add is 'independently defined terms or variables.' Consider the following sentence: 'Only the fit survive.' It apparently asserts a regular sequence between two terms — if x is fit, then x survives. Yet if there is no other criterion of the occurrence of fitness than survival, then the two concepts are not independently meaningful and consequently they stand in a definitional rather than a lawful relationship.

3.

In the following essays you will find all of the problems I have raised discussed in great detail. A. C. Ewing in his article, "Cause," argues against the Humean view of causality, which he calls the regularity theory, and breaks down what I have called the metaphysical view into two parts, one of which he calls the entailment theory and the other the activity theory. Ewing defends the entailment theory and apparently certain formulations of the activity theory which are entirely compatible with it. David Hume in his classical piece on "The Idea of Necessary Connexion" shows in detail what he takes to be wrong with any view that claims there is a necessary relation, either logical or physical, between cause and effect. After all, he points out, the assertion of a cause and the denial of its effect is not self-contradictory. Curt J. Ducasse, in turn, criticizes Hume's regularity view and offers an alternative interpretation which is quite different, however, from either the entailment or activity theory. 'Cause,' Ducasse writes, means the only change introduced into a situation immediately before an event occurs. You will need to examine this new alternative closely, deciding for yourself what can be said in favor of it and what against it. John Stuart Mill defends the frequency view of causality against one sort of criticism made by Ewing and Ducasse (which had already been made prior to Mill's writing by the Scottish philosopher, Thomas Reid), although he makes certain emendations on the straightforward Humean analysis. Roderick Chisholm in his article on lawfulness suggests that there is no adequate empirical criterion for distinguishing between lawful and accidental universal statements and thus, presumably, that the Humean analysis is not adequate even to define 'lawfulness' — let alone 'causality.'

Finally, in his essay on "Process and Historical Lawfulness," Gustav Bergmann pursues the important problem of distinguishing the different kinds of lawfulness. In his book *Philosophy of Science* he distinguishes, in addition to process and historical laws, also process and syndromatic laws, and statistical and causal laws. The analysis of types of laws, as a matter of fact, is continued in the following chapter, since probability statements can best be understood as statistical laws; thus any helpful analysis of them will be a clarification of the nature of statistical law.

Cause

A. C. EWING

Regularity Theory

Let us consider philosophical theories of what the nature of causation is or, if you prefer to put it that way, what is meant by the term 'cause.' The philosopher who is inclined to be an empiricist will be likely to adopt a view on this topic which identifies or approximates to identifying causation with regular sequence, since regular sequence is something that can be observed empirically. He will indeed have to assume one principle which he cannot justify empirically, namely, that what has succeeded a certain kind of event regularly in the past is also likely to do so in the future, but the regular sequence or 'regularity' view at any rate makes the minimum concessions to the non-empiricist. 'A causes B,' if A and B stand for classes of events, will then mean that B usually or always follows A. This view is by no means identical with the common-sense view of cause, as is shown by the fact that, if it were true, there would be no more special connection between the striking of a match and the flame which followed it than between the striking of the match and an earthquake which might also occur just afterwards. It would merely be that the striking of a match is usually followed by a flame and not usually followed by earthquakes, and that would be all. We could not then say that the striking *made* the flame follow. All intrinsic necessary connection between cause and effect, all active power on the part of the cause is denied. On this view to give a cause is *toto genere* different from giving a reason, it does not in the least help to explain why the effect happened, it only tells us what preceded the effect. So it is clear that the regularity view stands in very sharp contrast to the common-sense view of causation, though this does not necessarily refute the regularity view. Despite this the latter theory, or something very like it, is distinctly popular to-day. It agrees

The Fundamental Questions of Philosophy, Chapter VIII. London: Routledge and Kegan Paul Ltd., 1951. New York: The Macmillan Company, 1951. Reprinted by permission of the author and the publishers.

well with the modern empiricist trend, since it makes causation something that can be empirically observed and goes as far as one can towards eliminating the *a priori*. And it is in accord with one fact about causation. Whether causation is merely regular sequence or not, it is clear that at least in the physical world we cannot see any intelligible connection between cause and effect which explains why the latter must occur if the former does so. The chemist may bring propositions such as that wood burns under more general principles about the nature of matter from which they could be deduced, but these more general propositions themselves are not of such a kind that we can see at all why they should be true, we only find that empirically in fact they are true.

But there are other respects in which the theory is less plausible. First, it presents serious difficulties when we start talking about the causation of single events. 'I caused the flame by striking the match' might be interpreted as meaning: 'Striking a match by me was followed by a flame, and an event of the second class usually does follow an event of the first.' But what about events the causation of which is much more complex such as wars and economic depressions? Nobody has succeeded in discovering a really satisfactory formulation of statements about the causes of these in terms of the regularity view. If we say that Hitler's invasion of Poland caused the second world war to break out when it did we no doubt mean that the war followed it, but the rest of what we mean is not that wars always or usually follow invasions of Poland; it is something much more specific.

Another difficulty about the regularity view is that there are cases of regular sequence which nobody would call cases of causation. For instance, the sounding of a hooter at 8 a.m. in London is regularly followed not only by men going to work at that factory in London but by men going to work at a factory in Manchester which also opens at 8 a.m. Yet everybody would say that, while the arrivals at the factory in London were caused by the hooter in that factory, the arrivals at Manchester were not.

These difficulties might possibly be met by minor amendments of the theory, others are more serious. The theory seems particularly inapplicable in the case of psychology. For instance, when I believe something for a reason, surely my mental state is really determined by the apprehension of the reason and is not merely one of a class of mental states which usually follow the apprehension of similar reasons. If that is all, the belief is not reasonable; for it to be reasonable it must not merely follow on the apprehension of the reason but be determined by the intrinsic character of the reason. Again it is surely incredible that, when I will an action, the action is not determined by my will, or that to say it is 'determined' here merely means something like 'it is a kind of action which follows most or all states of mind like my own at the time in certain specific respects.' Again for memory to be possible one would think that my present state of consciousness must be genuinely determined by, not merely follow on, the past event remembered. There can be no trusting my memory of yesterday's events if it was not really determined by the events said to have been remembered.

Entailment Theory

All this should make one hesitate very much before accepting the regularity theory merely because it is the simplest and keeps closest to what is empirically observed. It seems that besides regularity we must introduce the notion of determination and necessity. There is a sense, it seems, in which the effect not merely does but must follow the cause, and this depends on the specific nature of the cause as such. Can we say anything more to make clearer what it is in which this necessity consists? There is another case of necessity, a clear one, which it is tempting and, I think reasonable, to take as at least an analogy. That is the necessity underlying valid inference. Where a conclusion follows logically from a premise, this must be because the fact expressed by the premise is so connected with the fact expressed by the conclusion that the former could not possibly occur without the latter occurring. This is logical necessity. The theory according to which the connection between cause and effect is the same as or very like that of logical necessity may be called the rationalist or the entailment theory of causation ('entailment' being the relation between the premises and the conclusion in an argument where the latter follows necessarily from the former or between the objective fact expressed by the premises and by the conclusion).

The entailment theory is a theory of philosophers, but it certainly is more closely akin to the common-sense view than is a purely regularity theory, and though one should not say that causation is just entailment, there is a good case for saying that it involves the entailment relation or else something very similar. It is also true of course that an effect does follow regularly its cause; the regularity theory is not mistaken in what it asserts but only in what it denies. The entailment theory was almost universal among philosophers till the nineteenth century (though they did not use that name). The first leading philosopher to question it was David Hume (1711–76), and at the time his views found little favour, though to-day the regularity theory is the one most commonly advocated.

However, it seems to me that there are two strong arguments for the entailment theory. These may be added to the arguments already given against the regularity theory, which did not by themselves suggest another theory to put in its place. The first is that we can after all make legitimate inferences from cause to effect. How could we do this if the cause did not in a very important sense entail the effect? The relation need not be exactly the same as the entailment which occurs in formal logical reasoning, but it must at least be analogous to it in the important respect that it justifies the conclusion. It would be a very odd kind of inference in which we were allowed to draw conclusions from premises which in no way entailed their conclusions. This argument gives the main, though usually unexpressed, reason why philosophers have so often believed in the rationalist (or entailment) theory of causation. I do not of course in using this argument mean to imply that a person must consciously assume the entailment theory before he can see that a particular induction is justified, only that the theory is logically presupposed if induction is to be justified. We do not know the ultimate logical presuppositions of our thinking, at any rate till we become philosophers.

The second argument is as follows. The occurrence of regularities is in any case a fact of experience. For instance, whenever solid objects are left unattached in mid-air they fall to the ground (with certain reservations to cover aeroplanes, etc.). Now, if it were not explained in any way, it would be an incredible coincidence that this should happen so constantly. It would be like having all the trumps in one hand at bridge several times runing, or more improbable even than this. But what explanation could there be except that the nature of the bodies or the nature of the physical universe as a whole somehow entailed their moving in that way? If causation merely means regular sequence, to say that A causes B gives no explanation of the regular sequence of B on A, it merely affirms that B thus succeeds. Only if the cause is a *reason* for the effect, will it explain why this repeated regularity occurs, and the facts surely cry out for an explanation, since the alternative is to leave it as a mere coincidence which would be incredibly unlikely. But how can the cause be a reason for the effect if its nature does not somehow involve the effect? In that case the latter will logically follow from, i.e. be entailed by the former, or at least the relation will be very closely analogous to that of logical entailment.

The following are the main objections brought against the entailment theory. (1) We cannot see any logical connection between cause and effect. This must be admitted as regards the physical world at least. We do not see any ultimate reason why water and not oil should put out a fire or why we should be nourished by bread and not by stones. No doubt a scientist could in a sense give reasons for these laws by explaining, e.g. that stones are too hard to digest and that bread contains nitrogenous matter in an organized form in which it is not present in stones; but the reasons of the scientist only amount either to interpolating intermediate causes so that he explains how A causes B by pointing to an intermediate link C, i.e. something which appears between A and B, or to showing that the generalization to be explained is just an instance of a wider generalization itself founded on experience, e.g. that no animals can extract nutriment direct from inorganic matter. In neither case does he tell us anything which amounts to more than a statement that events of a certain kind occur under certain circumstances; he does not explain why they occur. This is made clearer by comparing the conclusions of other sciences with those of mathematics. In the latter alone do we see not merely as an empirical fact that the conclusion is true but why it must be true. No causal law about the physical world even appears to us as logically necessary like the laws of mathematics; we cannot prove any such law *a priori,* but only establish it as an empirical generalization. However the fact that we cannot see any necessary *a priori* connection behind causal laws is no proof that there is not any. Till comparatively recently most of the logically necessary connections of mathematics had not been discovered by any human being, but they no doubt held all the same in prehistoric days as much as to-day. We cannot set limits to what is in nature by our ignorance. It would be very different if we were not only unable to see any necessary connection between cause and effect but were able to see positively that there is no such connection. Some philosophers think that they can see this, and if so they are justified in ruling out the entailment theory, but in the absence of this positive insight the negative argument is only of light weight.

(2) The relation between cause and effect is in one respect at least different from that holding in any generally recognized case of necessary connection, i.e. cause and effect are not, normally at least, simultaneous, but occur at different times. This of course again does not prove that necessary causal connection cannot occur, but only somewhat lessens the plausibility of the contention that it does. But if there are good positive reasons to suppose it occurs, the fact that it is unlike what happens in other cases is no adequate ground for rejecting the reasons in question.

(3) It is objected that in cases of *a priori* reasoning we attain certainty, but in cases of causal reasoning only probability. This may, however, be explained compatibly with the entailment theory. In the first place we never know the whole cause. What common sense calls the cause is only the most striking part of a vast complex of conditions all of which are relevant to the exact manner in which the effect occurs. But, even if the whole cause entails the whole effect, this gives no reason to suppose that a part of it, which is all we know, will do so. The best we can do is to conclude on the ground of previous experience that the factors in the cause of which we are not aware are unlikely to be of such a kind as to counteract the others and prevent the occurrence of something like the expected effect. Secondly, since we cannot see the necessary connection directly even if it is there, we are in any case bound to proceed by employing the recognized methods of induction, which can logically only yield probability not certainty. For in

the absence of direct insight into it, we can only arrive at conclusions as to when it occurs indirectly by considering what regularities normally occur and inferring from those what are most likely to be the laws underlying them, as on any other view of causation.

The entailment theory is of course incompatible with the view which we earlier rejected that all logically necessary propositions are verbal or analytic in a sense which would make what is entailed part of what entails. Since the effect is a different event from and not part of the cause, the two cannot be necessarily connected unless some propositions not analytic in this sense are *a priori*. Propositions about causation may be analytic in some cases, where something has been defined in terms of its causal properties, but this cannot always be so. If we define a species of thing in terms of one causal property, it will be a synthetic proposition that members of the species have any other causal property they may possess.

So far I have spoken as if it were common ground that we could never have insight into causal entailments, but I should not be ready to admit this. It seems to me true of the physical world, not of the world of psychology. Our insight that the death of a beloved person will tend to cause grief or that insults will tend to cause annoyance does not seem to be based merely on experience. We seem also to see *a priori* that the cause will tend to produce these effects. There is surely something in the thwarting of a desire which entails a tendency to produce pain. Even apart from experience it would not be as reasonable to expect that the death of a beloved person would cause the lover to jump from joy. We must indeed admit that we can at the best only see a causal *tendency* in these cases. If A loves B now, it is not certain that he will grieve if B dies, for by the time this has happened he may have gone mad or quarrelled with B so violently as to rejoice at his death. But we can see, it seems, that the nature of love is such as to tend strongly in the direction mentioned and not in the opposite one. That we can only say what its tendency is and not predict with certainty that this will be fulfilled on a given occasion is presumably because the situation is always very complex and we cannot know that there will not be factors which counteract the tendency in question. It may further be argued that we can easily explain why we should not see entailments in the physical world even if they are really there. For, firstly it is generally held that the internal nature of matter is quite unknown to us, and how can we tell whether what is quite unknown to us does or does not entail something? In psychology alone are we immediately aware of the internal nature of the object with which we are dealing, namely mind, and here we can reasonably claim to see that certain causal entailments hold, as we have just noted. Secondly, we never are in a position to give the whole cause, and it would be the whole cause that entailed the effect, not a part of it. . . .

Whether we are to maintain or reject the entailment theory depends largely on our attitude to the problem of induction. Modern logicians generally have tried to solve the problem of the validity of induction without assuming the entailment theory of causation and generally admit that they have failed. They have not, even according to themselves, shown why we are entitled to make inductive predictions in advance of experience. The main trouble is that there is no reason why we should think that A will be followed by B in the future merely because it has been so in the past. But if we suppose that the repeated experience in the past is an indication of something in the nature of A which entails B, that will be a good reason for expecting B to follow on future occasions also, even if we do not see why the assumed entailment should hold. No detailed theory of induction has been worked out on this basis, but it is significant that modern logicians who will not admit the entailment theory of causation have (usually according to their own admission) failed to produce any rational justification of induction. Nevertheless it has seemed so odd to many philosophers that there should be a relation of logical entailment between different events that they would rather admit all our induction to be irrational than save its rationality in such a fashion. Yet we cannot really suppose it irrational to believe that if we jump from a height we shall fall; and even if we say that all induction is in some sense irrational, it will still be incumbent on us to explain the distinction between scientific inductions and those inductions which would be accepted by no sensible person. What is the difference between the two kinds if they are both irrational?

It has been said that inductive arguments, though not rational in the same way as deductive arguments, are rational in some other way. It is easy enough to say this, but difficult to grasp what this sense of 'rational' could be. Inductive arguments are after all inferences, and for an inference to be valid the conclusion must follow from the premises. But for this to be so the premises must entail the conclusion, or at the very least be connected with it by a relation closely analogous to that of logical entailment. It is difficult to escape this argument. Nor have those who try to meet the difficulty by saying that induction is rational but rational in a different sense from deduction succeeded in defining the sense in which induction is rational. They have either left it undefined or defined it in terms of practical utility. In the latter case an inductive inference is rational if it is of a kind which is practically useful. But this seems hardly to solve the problem. It is clear that in order to act in a practically useful way it is not enough to do what has proved useful in the past unless this is an indication that it is likely to be useful also in the future, and it is just as much an induction to infer that something will have good practical results in the future from the results it has had in the past as it is to infer that something will be true of future events because it has been true of past.

It seems to me therefore that there is a strong case for the entailment theory of causation. But I must admit that this is not the opinion of the majority of contemporary philosophers. It is in any case a very important issue metaphysically. One of the most fundamental differences there are in philosophy is between those who think of the world as a rationally connected system and those who regard it as a mere collection of brute facts externally related, and which side we take in this controversy will depend chiefly on whether we, consciously or unconsciously, assume the entailment view of causation or not. One of the chief issues in philosophy through the ages has been that between monism and pluralism, between those who look on the unity of things as more important and those who give a more fundamental position to their plurality; and we shall certainly regard the world as much more of a unity if we adopt than if we do not adopt the entailment view of causation. If that view is true, everything in the world will be united in a logical system, since everything is causally connected with everything else either directly or indirectly. If that view is true, everything in the world will be a unity in a very important sense, for the very nature of a thing will also involve the other things with which it is causally connected.

Activity Theory

There is a third view of causation which is now generally known as the *activity view*. We are certainly apt to think of cause as a kind of depersonalized will, and some philosophers have thought that the key to the philosophical conception of causation lay in the notion of will. This view was taken by Berkeley. He argued that for a cause to produce something it must be 'active' and assumed that activity involved willing. He therefore contended that the only possible cause was a being possessed of will and used this as his chief argument for the existence of God, whom he, denying the material world in a realist sense, made the direct cause of everything which could not be attributed to the causation of human minds. Other philosophers, e.g. Locke, while admitting that material things could be proximate causes, insisted that, since causation ultimately involved will, the only ultimate cause must be mind or spirit. They could argue that, though a physical object once started in motion might move and otherwise affect other physical objects, it could not itself originate motion. We cannot think of a chair as getting up and moving about the room of its own accord, and if it apparently did we should feel forced to suppose either that it was moved in an unknown way by some mind external to it or that it was itself animated by some sort of rudimentary mind. In this fashion the activity view of cause has often been used as the basis for an argument to the existence of God in order to get the motion started originally. There are however forms of the activity view which would not involve such an argument. It might be held that the activity presupposed by causation was not conscious rational volition, but some kind of semi-conscious striving such as we commonly suppose to occur in the lower animals and which we might then extend in a still more rudimentary form to what we call inanimate objects. The activity theory of causation would then involve panpsychism but not necessarily theism. Or we might go further still in the direction of attenuating the idea of activity, and say what is involved in causation is a quality which we experience consciously when we will but which can exist without being experienced in any way. It might in that case occur in objects which are in the full sense inanimate and might be supposed to constitute the essence also of their totally unconscious causality.

Again, the activity view has sometimes been combined with and sometimes given as an alternative to the entailment view. In modern times Prof. Stout has first argued for the entailment view and then argued that the only instances in which we can conceive how the cause could entail the effect are instances where will or at least some sort of conation (striving or aiming at ends) is present, not necessarily in what we call the cause itself but in or behind the whole process. This then becomes an argument either for theism or panpsychism. The chief difficulty about this argument is to be sure whether it is really the case that the cause can entail the effect only if conation is present or merely that we can conceive how it could only if conation is supposed to be present. The cases I have mentioned in which we did seem to see causal connection directly and any other instances I could have given are cases in which conation is in some way present, but the fact that we can see causal connection only in such cases does not necessarily prove that it is only present in such cases. Others would oppose the activity view to the entailment view as providing an alternative account of the causal necessity which the regularity view errs in denying. They think of the effect as following necessarily in the sense of being forced by the cause but not in the sense of being logically entailed by it. This notion of forcing is certainly involved in the usual common-sense view of causation, but the common-sense view also involves the notion of explanation or reason, which can only be interpreted in terms of the entailment view as far as I can see. That the entailment view is, however, not a complete account of the common-sense view can easily be seen in the following way. Entailment, if it occurs, works both ways: it is just as true that the cause can be inferred from the effect as that the effect can be inferred from the cause, and so if inference presupposes entailment it will be just as true that the effect entails the cause as that the cause entails the effect. But there is certainly a sense in which we think of the cause as necessitating or determining the effect but do not think of the effect as necessitating or determining the cause. Causation is regarded as a one-sided or irreversible relation. If I hit somebody in the face and gave him a black eye, the black eye would be produced by my blow in a sense in which the black eye certainly did not produce the blow, and we think of the future as necessitated by the past in a sense in which we should never think of the past as necessitated by the future. But it is impossible to give arguments to show that this element in our ordinary conception of causation applies to the real world, so the activity view must remain inadequately grounded.

It may be further asked how we form the idea of causation at all. On the regularity view the answer is simple: all that causation means is regular sequence, and it is obvious that we can observe regular sequence. On the entailment view the situation is more complex. If it can be claimed that we even occasionally see some causal entailments, we might derive our idea from those we see and then could easily apply it also in cases where we do not ourselves see an entailment but suppose there must be some cause. Or it might be held that the entailment element in our common-sense view of causation was derived from the analogy of non-causal arguments, where we do admittedly see entailments. On the activity view of causation the idea of cause is usually held to be derived from the experience of volition. It is supposed that, when we voluntarily move a part of our body, we are, at least in some cases, immediately aware of our will causing our body to move. (The common objection that an act of will does not always produce motion, since we may be struck with paralysis, might be met by saying that we could still be aware in some cases of our will as at least *tending* to produce motion.) The chief objection to this is constituted by the circumstance that an act of will never moves a part of the body by direct causation, but only by means of a number of intermediate links in the nervous system. Now it is difficult to hold that we can see directly C to cause E where C does not cause E directly, but only causes an intermediate term D (a set of vibrations in the nervous system), which then produces E without our being aware of D in the least, for we have only learnt of D not through the experience of willing in ourselves but through the reports of physiologists. It is less difficult, however, to hold that we can be immediately aware of our will as cause not of physical motion but of changes in our mental states, as when we will to attend to something. If we reject the regularity view but cannot explain how our idea of what there is in causation beyond regularity is derived, we can still fall back on the theory that it is an innate idea, but we should avoid this if possible.

The Idea of Necessary Connexion

DAVID HUME

Part I

There are no ideas, which occur in metaphysics, more obscure and uncertain, than those of *power, force, energy* or *necessary connexion,* of which it is every moment necessary for us to treat in all our disquisitions. We shall, therefore, endeavour, in this section, to fix, if possible, the precise meaning of these terms, and thereby remove some part of that obscurity, which is so much complained of in this species of philosophy.

It seems a proposition, which will not admit of much dispute, that all our ideas are nothing but copies of our impressions, or, in other words, that it is impossible for us to *think* of any thing, which we have not antecedently *felt,* either by our external or internal senses. I have endeavoured to explain and prove this proposition, and have expressed my hopes, that, by a proper application of it, men may reach a greater clearness and precision in philosophical reasonings, than what they have hitherto been able to attain. . . .

To be fully acquainted, therefore, with the idea of power or necessary connexion, let us examine its impression; and in order to find the impression with greater certainty, let us search for it in all the sources, from which it may possibly be derived.

When we look about us towards external objects, and consider the operation of causes, we are never able, in a single instance, to discover any power or necessary connexion; any quality, which binds the effect to the cause, and renders the one an infallible consequence of the other. We only find, that the one does actually, in fact, follow the other. The impulse of one billiard-ball is attended with motion in the second. This is the whole that appears to the *outward* senses. The mind feels no sentiment or *inward* impression from this succession of objects: Consequently, there is not, in any single, particular instance of cause and effect, any thing which can suggest the idea of power or necessary connexion.

From the first appearance of an object, we never can conjecture what effect will result from it. But were the power or energy of any cause discoverable by the mind, we could foresee the effect, even without experience; and might, at first, pronounce with certainty concerning it, by mere dint of thought and reasoning.

In reality, there is no part of matter, that does ever, by its sensible qualities, discover any power or energy, or give us ground to imagine, that it could produce any thing, or be followed by any other object, which we could denominate its effect. Solidity, extension, motion; these qualities are all complete in themselves, and never point out any other event which may result from them. The scenes of the universe are continually shifting, and one object follows another in an

From Hume: *An Enquiry Concerning Human Understanding,* Sect. 7.

uninterrupted succession; but the power or force, which actuates the whole machine, is entirely concealed from us, and never discovers itself in any of the sensible qualities of body. We know, that, in fact, heat is a constant attendant of flame; but what is the connexion between them, we have no room so much as to conjecture or imagine. It is impossible, therefore, that the idea of power can be derived from the contemplation of bodies, in single instances of their operation; because no bodies ever discover any power, which can be the original of this idea.

Since, therefore, external objects as they appear to the senses, give us no idea of power or necessary connexion, by their operation in particular instances, let us see, whether this idea be derived from reflection on the operations of our own minds, and be copied from any internal impression. It may be said, that we are every moment conscious of internal power; while we feel, that, by the simple command of our will, we can move the organs of our body, or direct the faculties of our mind. An act of volition produces motion in our limbs, or raises a new idea in our imagination. This influence of the will we know by consciousness. Hence we acquire the idea of power or energy; and are certain, that we ourselves and all other intelligent beings are possessed of power. This idea, then, is an idea of reflection, since it arises from reflecting on the operations of our own mind, and on the command which is exercised by will, both over the organs of the body and faculties of the soul.

We shall proceed to examine this pretension; and first with regard to the influence of volition over the organs of the body. This influence, we may observe, is a fact, which, like all other natural events, can be known only by experience, and can never be foreseen from any apparent energy or power in the cause, which connects it with the effect, and renders the one an infallible consequence of the other. The motion of our body follows upon the command of our will. Of this we are every moment conscious. But the means, by which this is effected; the energy, by which the will performs so extraordinary an operation; of this we are so far from being immediately conscious, that it must for ever escape our most diligent enquiry.

For *first;* is there any principle in all nature more mysterious than the union of soul with body; by which a supposed spiritual substance acquires such an influence over a material one, that the most refined thought is able to actuate the grossest matter? Were we empowered, by a secret wish, to remove mountains, or control the planets in their orbit; this extensive authority would not be more extraordinary, nor more beyond our comprehension. But if by consciousness we perceived any power or energy in the will, we must know this power; we must know its connexion with the effect; we must know the secret union of soul and body, and the nature of both these substances; by which the one is able to operate, in so many instances, upon the other.

Secondly, We are not able to move all the organs of the body with a like authority; though we cannot assign any reason besides experience, for so remarkable a difference between one and the other. Why has the will an influence over the tongue and fingers, not over the heart or liver? This question would never embarrass us, were we conscious of a power in the former case, not in the latter. We should then perceive, independent of experience, why the authority of will over the organs of the body is circumscribed within such particular limits. Being in that case fully acquainted with the power or force, by which it operates, we should also know, why its influence reaches precisely to such boundaries, and no farther.

A man, suddenly struck with palsy in the leg or arm, or who had newly lost those members, frequently endeavours, at first to move them, and employ them in their usual offices. Here he is as much conscious of power to command such limbs, as a man in perfect health is conscious of power to actuate any member which remains in its natural state and condition. But consciousness never deceives. Consequently, neither in the one case nor in the other, are we ever conscious of any power. We learn the influence of our will from experience alone. And experience only teaches us, how one event constantly follows another; without instructing us in the secret connexion, which binds them together, and renders them inseparable.

Thirdly, We learn from anatomy, that the immediate object of power in voluntary motion, is not the member itself which is moved, but certain muscles, and nerves, and animals spirits, and, perhaps, something still more minute and more unknown, through which the motion is successively propagated, ere it reach the member itself whose motion is the immediate object of volition. Can there be a more certain proof, that the power, by which this whole operation is performed, so far from being directly and fully known by an inward sentiment or consciousness, is, to the last degree, mysterious and unintelligible? Here the mind wills a certain event: Immediately another event, unknown to ourselves, and totally different from the one intended, is produced: This event produces another, equally unknown: Till at last, through a long succession, the desired event is produced. But if the original power were felt, it must be known: Were it known, its effect also must be known; since all power is relative to its effect. And *vice versa,* if the effect be not known, the power cannot be known nor felt. How indeed can we be conscious of a power to move our limbs, when we have no such power; but only that to move certain animal spirits, which, though they produce at last the motion of our limbs, yet operate in such a manner as is wholly beyond our comprehension?

We may, therefore, conclude from the whole, I hope, without any temerity, though with assurance; that our idea of power is not copied from any sentiment or consciousness of power within ourselves, when we give rise to animal motion, or apply our limbs to their proper use and office. That their motion follows the command of the will is a matter of common experience, like other natural events: But the power or energy by which this is effected, like that in other natural events, is unknown and inconceivable. . . .

The generality of mankind never find any difficulty in accounting for the more common and familiar operations of nature — such as the descent of heavy bodies, the growth of plants, the generation of animals, or the nourishment of bodies by food: But suppose that, in all these cases, they perceive the very force or energy of the cause, by which it is connected with its effect, and is for ever infallible in its operation. They acquire, by long habit, such a turn of mind, that, upon the appearance of the cause, they immediately expect with assurance its usual attendant, and hardly conceive it possible that any other event could result from it. It is only on the discovery of extraordinary phaenomena, such as earthquakes, pestilence, and prodigies of any kind, that they find themselves at a loss to assign a proper cause, and to explain the manner in which the effect is produced by it. It is usual for men, in such difficulties to have recourse to some invisible intelligent principle as the immediate cause of that event which surprises them, and which, they think, cannot be accounted for from the common powers of nature. But philosophers, who carry their scrutiny a little farther, immediately perceive that, even in the most familiar events, the energy of the cause is as unintelligible as in the most unusual, and that we only learn by experience the frequent *Conjunction* of objects, without being ever able to comprehend anything like *Connexion* between them.

Part II

But to hasten a conclusion of this argument, which is already drawn out to too great a length: We have sought in vain for an idea of power or necessary connexion in all the sources from which we could suppose it to be derived. It appears that, in single instances of the operation of bodies, we never can, by our utmost scrutiny, discover any thing but one event following another, without being able to comprehend any force or power by which the cause operates, or any connexion between it and its supposed effect. The same difficulty occurs in contemplating the operations of mind on body — where we observe the motion of the latter to follow upon the volition of the former, but are not able to observe or conceive the tie which binds together the motion and volition, or the energy by which the mind produces this effect. The authority of the will over its own faculties and ideas is not a whit more comprehensible: So that, upon the whole, there appears not, throughout all nature, any one instance of connexion which is conceivable by us. All events seem entirely loose and separate. One event follows another; but we never can observe any tie between them. They seem *conjoined,* but never *connected.* And as we can have no idea of any thing which never appeared to our outward sense or inward sentiment, the necessary conclusion *seems* to be that we have no idea of connexion or power at all, and that these words are absolutely without any meaning, when employed either in philosophical reasonings or common life.

But there still remains one method of avoiding this conclusion, and one source which we have not yet examined. When any natural object or event is presented, it is impossible for us, by any sagacity or penetration, to discover, or even conjecture, without experience, what event will result from it, or to carry our foresight beyond that object which is immediately present to the memory and senses. Even after one instance or experiment where we have observed a particular event to follow upon another, we are not entitled to form a general rule, or foretell what will happen in like cases; it being justly esteemed an unpardonable temerity to judge of the whole course of nature from one single experiment, however accurate or certain. But when one particular species of event has always, in all instances, been conjoined with another, we make no longer any scruple of foretelling one upon the appearance of the other, and of employing that reasoning, which can alone assure us of any matter of fact or existence. We then call the one object, *Cause;* the other, *Effect.* We suppose that there is some connexion between them; some power in the one, by which it infallibly produces the other, and operates with the greatest certainty and strongest necessity.

It appears, then, that this idea of a necessary connexion among events arises from a number of similar instances which occur of the constant conjunction of these events; nor can that idea ever be suggested by any one of these instances, surveyed in all possible lights and positions. But there is nothing in a number of instances, different from every single instance, which is supposed to be exactly similar; except only, that after a repetition of similar instances, the mind is carried by habit, upon the appearance of one event, to expect its usual attendant, and to believe that it will exist. This connexion, therefore, which we *feel* in the mind, this customary transition of the imagination from one object to its usual attendant, is the sentiment or impression from which we form the idea of power or necessary connexion. Nothing farther is in the case. Contemplate the subject on all sides; you will never find any other origin of that idea. This is the sole difference between one instance, from which we can never receive the idea of connexion, and a number of similar instances, by which it is suggested. The first time a man saw the communication of motion by impulse, as by the shock of two billiard balls, he could not pronounce that the one event was *connected:* but only that it was *conjoined* with the other. After he has observed several instances of this nature, he then pronounces them to be *connected.* What alteration has happened to give rise to this new idea of *connexion?*

Nothing but that he now *feels* these events to be *connected* in his imagination, and can readily foretell the existence of one from the appearance of the other. When we say, therefore, that one object is connected with another, we mean only that they have acquired a connexion in our thought, and give rise to this inference, by which they become proofs of each other's existence: A conclusion which is somewhat extraordinary, but which seems founded on sufficient evidence. Nor will its evidence be weakened by any general diffidence of the understanding, or sceptical suspicion concerning every conclusion which is new and extraordinary. No conclusions can be more agreeable to scepticism than such as make discoveries concerning the weakness and narrow limits of human reason and capacity.

And what stronger instance can be produced of the surprising ignorance and weakness of the understanding than the present? For surely, if there be any relation among objects which it imports to us to know perfectly, it is that of cause and effect. On this are founded all our reasonings concerning matter of fact or existence. By means of it alone we attain any assurance concerning objects which are removed from the present testimony of our memory and senses. The only immediate utility of all sciences, is to teach us, how to control and regulate future events by their causes. Our thoughts and enquiries are, therefore, every moment, employed about this relation: Yet so imperfect are the ideas which we form concerning it, that it is impossible to give any just definition of cause, except what is drawn from something extraneous and foreign to it. Similar objects are always conjoined with similar. Of this we have experience. Suitably to this experience, therefore, we may define a cause to be *an object, followed by another, and where all the objects similar to the first are followed by objects similar to the second.* Or in other words, *where, if the first object had not been, the second never had existed.* The appearance of a cause always conveys the mind, by a customary transition, to the idea of the effect. Of this also we have experience. We may, therefore, suitably to this experience, form another definition of cause, and call it, *an object followed by another, and whose appearance always conveys the thought to that other.* But though both these definitions be drawn from circumstances foreign to the cause, we cannot remedy this inconvenience, or attain any more perfect definition, which may point out that circumstance in the cause, which gives it a connexion with its effect. We have no idea of this connexion, nor even any distinct notion what it is we desire to know, where we endeavour at a conception of it. We say, for instance, that the vibration of this string is the cause of this particular sound. But what do we mean by that affirmation? We either mean *that this vibration is followed by this sound, and that all similar vibrations have been followed by similar sounds: Or, that this vibration is followed by this sound, and that upon the appearance of one the mind anticipates the senses, and forms immediately an idea of the other.* We may consider the relation of cause and effect in either of these two lights; but beyond these, we have no idea of it.

To recapitulate, therefore, the reasonings of this section: Every idea is copied from some preceding impression or sentiment; and where we cannot find any impression, we may be certain that there is no idea. In all single instances of the operation of bodies or minds, there is nothing that produces any impression, nor consequently can suggest any idea of power or necessary connexion. But when many uniform instances appear, and the same object is always followed by the same event; we then begin to entertain the notion of cause and connexion. We then *feel* a new sentiment or impression, to wit, a customary connexion in the thought or imagination between one object and its usual attendant; and this sentiment is the original of that idea which we seek for. For as this idea arises from a number of similar instances, and not from any single instance, it must arise from that circumstance, in which the number of instances differ from every individual instance. But this customary connexion or transition of the imagination is the only circumstance in which they differ. In every other particular they are alike. The first instance which we saw of motion communicated by the shock of two billiard balls (to return to this obvious illustration) is exactly similar to any instance that may, at present, occur to us; except only, that we could not, at first, *infer* one event from the other; which we are enabled to do at present, after so long a course of uniform experience. . . .

What, then, is the conclusion of the whole matter? A simple one; though, it must be confessed, pretty remote from the common theories of philosophy. All belief of matter of fact or real existence is derived merely from some object, present to the memory or senses, and a customary conjunction between that and some other object. Or in other words; having found, in many instances, that any two kinds of objects — flame and heat, snow and cold — have always been conjoined together; if flame or snow be presented anew to the senses, the mind is carried by custom to expect heat or cold, and to *believe* that such a quality does exist, and will discover itself upon a nearer approach. This belief is the necessary result of placing the mind in such circumstances. It is an operation of the soul, when we are so situated, as unavoidable as to feel the passion of love, when we receive benefits; or hatred, when we meet with injuries. All these operations are a species of natural instincts, which no reasoning or process of the thought and understanding is able either to produce or to prevent.

Causality: Critique of Hume's Analysis

CURT J. DUCASSE

A variety of opinions are current today as to the nature and the role of the causal relation. One finds accounts of what science now means by causal connection, but also statements that the notion of cause is not employed in science at its maturity, but only appears at the crude, early stages of its development. Again, many philosophers are dissatisfied with Hume's analysis of causality, upon which Mill's failed to improve. Yet, in default of some definite and more acceptable positive analysis, Hume's probably remains still the most influential. Inasmuch as the analysis of causality I shall offer diverges sharply from Hume's, I shall now first set forth the reasons I see for rejecting his account.

From *Nature, Mind, and Death,* pp. 91–100. La Salle, Illinois: The Open Court Publishing Co., 1951. Reprinted by permission of author and publisher.

1. Hume's Skepticism

Hume's famous skepticism is not, like that of some of the ancients, a doctrine he propounds, but rather the acknowledgment by him of "a malady, which can never be radically cur'd, but must return upon us every moment, however we may chace it away, and sometimes may seem entirely free from it." [1] This malady, as Hume observes it in himself, consists in the fact that although reflection shows certain ones and certain others of our beliefs to be mutually incompatible, yet we cannot give up either the ones or the others. The self-stultification which is noticeable at so many points in Hume's writings, and which so baffles the reader who would extract from them a consistent doctrine, is rooted in that malady. Again and again, especially in the *Treatise,* Hume disregards at one place conclusions he had reached earlier, and he could not without doing so proceed to say what he next wants to say. The *Treatise,* I believe, is thus to be regarded not as an attempt to set forth one consistent doctrine, but much rather only as an account of the philosophical sights to be seen from the road one travels under the guidance of certain principles which Hume accepts from the outset – one of the chief of these being that nothing exists or is known to us except "perceptions." Hume simply follows these principles remorselessly wherever they seem to him to lead; and when the conclusions to which they bring him are mutually incompatible or incompatible with firm natural beliefs, he just admits the fact as he would admit having gout or a cold in the head and similarly calls it a malady. His great service to philosophy thus is not that he solved, but much rather that he raised, important philosophical problems. There is perhaps no philosophical book more intellectually irritating – nor therefore more thought-provoking – than his *Treatise.* This is true in particular of what he has to say in it concerning causation.

2. Hume's Analysis of Causality

Hume's "official" view on this subject may perhaps be summarized as follows: To be is to be perceived. No connection is ever perceived between a cause and its effect. Therefore there is none. An "object" of kind *A* is called the cause of one of kind *B* if, in our experience, objects of kind *A* have always been followed each by an object of kind *B*. But such following of one object upon a certain other is not "necessary." In logic and mathematics, that is necessary the contradictory of which is self-contradictory. But no self-contradiction is ever involved in supposing an object we call a cause to exist without its effect following, or one we call an effect to exist without having been preceded by one such as we call its cause. Where objects are concerned, "necessity" is the name not of a relation among them, but only of the felt "propensity, which custom produces, to pass from an object to the idea of its usual attendant." Necessity, then, is "but an internal impression of the mind"; it is a relation between certain ideas, something "that exists in the mind, not in objects." Hume accordingly offers two definitions of cause. According to one, formulated in purely objective terms, "we may define a cause to be *an object, followed by another, and where all the objects similar to the first are followed by objects similar to the second.*" According to the other we may say, in subjective terms, that a cause is *"an object followed by another, and whose appearance always conveys the thought to that other."* [2] The first of these is the basic one, since unless we had experience of causation as there described, the "conveying of the thought," in terms of

[1] Hume, *A Treatise of Human Nature,* Selby-Bigge ed., p. 218.

[2] Hume, *An Enquiry Concerning Human Understanding,* Open Court ed., p. 79.

which the second definition is worded, would not occur.

3. Hume's Analysis Fails To Fit Some of the Facts

As stated at the outset, I believe that this account of the nature of causation – simply as succession *de facto* regular – represents an incorrect analysis of the ordinary notion of cause – of the notion, that is to say, in the light of which our ordinary judgments of causation actually are made. To make evident the incorrectness of that analysis it will be sufficient to show, on the one hand, that there are cases which conform to Hume's definition but where we judge the events concerned not to be related as cause to effect; and on the other hand, that there are cases which do not conform to Hume's definition but which we nevertheless judge to be cases of causation.

As to the first, if a man were so situated as always to have heard two clocks striking the hours, one of which always struck immediately before the other, he would according to Hume's definition of cause have to say that the strokes of the first cause the strokes of the second; whereas in fact they do not. Of course, the relation he observes between the strokes of the two clocks is the effect of a common remote cause of the strokes of the two clocks. But although this is true, it is irrelevant; for to say that *B* is caused by *A* is one thing, and to say that both *B* and *A* are caused by *C* is quite another thing. The example thus shows that Hume's definition of the relation of cause and effect fits some cases where the relation between the two events concerned is in fact not that of cause to effect but a different one.

Other examples of sequences which are regular, and yet the terms of which are not related as cause to effect, are not hard to find. Thomas Reid mentioned the succession of day and night; and we may add to the list the fact, for instance, that in infants the growth of hair is regularly followed by the growth of teeth; or that in human beings birth regularly follows the tenth return of the moon since conception.[3]

In connection with such cases, it should be noted that what observation of *de facto* regular succession or correlation of two events does is not to *answer* the question whether one of the two events causes the other, but much rather to *raise* the question as to whether one causes the other, or whether some antecedent third causes both, or whether the conjunction of the two is simply accidental. For although causation of *B* by *A* entails constancy of their conjunction (*i.e.*, recurrence of *B* as often as *A* recurs), the converse does not hold: constancy of conjunction, far from itself being the relation of cause to effect, is not sure evidence even of indirect or of as yet hidden causal connection between the events concerned.

To show now, on the other hand, that there are cases which do not conform to Hume's definition, but which we nevertheless judge to be cases of causation, I shall mention a simple experiment I have sometimes performed with students. I bring into the room and place on the desk a paper-covered parcel tied with string in the ordinary way, and ask the students to observe closely what occurs. Then, proceeding slowly so that observation may be easy, I put my hand on the parcel. The end of the parcel the students face then at once glows. I then ask them what caused it to glow at that moment, and they naturally answer that the glowing was caused by what I did to the parcel immediately before.

[3] A striking instance, in the case of which the relation between the events concerned is patently neither that of cause to effect nor that of joint effects of a common cause, is quoted by Morris Cohen (*Reason and Nature,* p. 92) from an unpublished study by George Marshall at the Brookings Institute. It is that, for a number of years, the membership in the International Association of Machinists shows a very high correlation (86%) with the death rate in the Indian state of Hyderabad.

In this case it is clear that what the spectators observed, and what they based their judgment of causation upon, was not repetition of a certain act of mine followed each time by the glow, but *one single case* of sequence of the latter upon the former. The case, that is to say, does not conform to Hume's definition of causation as constant conjunction but is nevertheless judged by unprejudiced observers to be a case of causation.

If I then further ask: What makes you think that my having done what I did caused the parcel to glow? they answer: Because nothing else happened to the parcel at the time. Thus, by the *cause* of the observed glowing they do not mean some event having repeatedly preceded it. They mean *the only change introduced into the situation immediately before the glowing occurred.*

It may be said truly, of course, that the change they observed was perhaps not the only change which actually occurred in that situation, and that their judgment as to the cause of the observed glowing was thus perhaps mistaken. To urge this, however, is to question not their conception of the meaning of "causation," but their claim that what they observed was a true case of what they meant and still mean by that word. For what indicates what they meant when they called what I did the cause of the observed glowing is not whether what I did *really* was the only change that occurred in the situation immediately before, but whether they *believed* it to have been the only change. So long as they do believe it to have been the only change, they continue to describe it as having been the cause of that glowing — even if a glowing should never again occur on repetition of my act.

4. Hume on Ascertainment of Causation by a Single Experiment

In this connection, it is interesting to note that Hume himself asserts that "we may attain the knowledge of a particular cause merely by one experiment, provided it be made with judgment, and after a careful removal of all foreign and superfluous circumstances." But how a *single* experiment, in which a case of *B* was observed to have followed a case of *A*, can assure us that *every* case of *A* is followed by a case of *B* is anything but obvious. One would expect, rather, that, once causation has been defined merely as *de facto* constant conjunction, the only way to observe its presence or absence would be to observe *many* cases of *A* and note whether or not a case of *B* follows constantly, *i.e.*, each time.

Hume perceives this difficulty, or rather the difficulty corresponding to it when his second definition of causation is the one considered — the difficulty, namely, how the customary expectation of *B* upon the occurrence of *A*, which he has stated before is the result of having *repeatedly* observed *B* following after *A*, can be present when the sequence, *A,B* has been observed not repeatedly but only once. He attempts to meet this difficulty by saying that even then we have had millions of experiments "to convince us of this principle, *that like objects placed in like circumstances, will always produce like effects,*" and that this principle then "bestows an evidence and firmness on any opinion, to which it can be applied." [4]

By itself, however, this principle would support equally the generalizing of *any* sequence observed — of one which is accidental as well as of one which turns out to be causal. The possibility of its being useful therefore rests on the stipulated preliminary "careful removal of all foreign and superfluous circumstances." But the principle does not tell us how to discover by one experiment which these are; for obviously the "foreign and superfluous circumstances" are those which are not the cause, *i.e.*, on his view, those which are not *constantly* followed by *B*.

[4] Hume, *Treatise*, pp. 104–105.

Preliminary removal of the circumstances which are "foreign and superfluous" therefore amounts to preliminary discovery of the circumstance which *is* the cause! Thus, the principle is good not for discovering the cause in a single experiment, but *only for generalizing it* if we have already managed somehow to discover it by a single experiment. If, however, causation can be ascertained by a single experiment, then causation does not consist in constancy of conjunction even if it entails such constancy.

5. Hume's "Rules by Which To Judge of Causes and Effects"

Hume appears to have been obscurely conscious of this. For one thing, he introduces the two definitions of cause quoted above by the remark: "So imperfect are the ideas which we form concerning [the relation of cause and effect] that it is impossible to give any just definition of cause, except what is drawn from something extraneous and foreign to it." And, after the second definition, he repeats that both definitions are "drawn from circumstances foreign to the cause." Again, in his "Rules by which to judge of causes and effects," which are rules for discovering a cause by a single experiment and therefore, as pointed out above, really concern causation in a sense other than that of empirically constant conjunction, Hume at first refers to causation as "that constant conjunction, on which the relation of cause and effect *totally* depends"; but in the third rule, he no longer says "totally" but instead "chiefly"; and in the fourth rule he describes "constant repetition" only as that "from which the *first* idea of [the causal relation] is derived." [5]

Of the rules given by Hume for discovering a cause by a single experiment, the fifth, sixth, and seventh are the clearest statements not only up to Hume's time, but until the appearance of Herschel's *Discourse* nearly a hundred years later, of what Mill afterwards called the experimental methods of Agreement, Difference, and Concomitant Variations. Hume's fourth, fifth, and sixth rules, which are the most important theoretically, are as follows:

> 4. The same cause always produces the same effect, and the same effect never arises but from the same cause. This principle we derive from experience, and is the source of most of our philosophical reasonings. For when by any clear experiment we have discovered the causes or effects of any phenomenon, we immediately extend our observation to every phenomenon of the same kind, without waiting for that constant repetition, from which the first idea of this relation is derived.
>
> 5. There is another principle, which hangs upon this, *viz.* that where several different objects produce the same effect, it must be by means of some quality, which we discover to be common amongst them. For as like effects imply like causes, we must always ascribe the causation to the circumstance, wherein we discover the resemblance.
>
> 6. . . . The difference in the effects of two resembling objects must proceed from that particular, in which they differ. For as like causes always produce like effects, when in any instance we find our expectation to be disappointed, we must conclude that this irregularity proceeds from some difference in the causes.

It will be noticed that in the fourth rule the principle mentioned earlier (same cause, same effect) is supplemented by its converse (same effect, same cause), but is now presented explicitly as a principle not for discovering causal relations but only for generalizing them once we have managed to discover them somehow in a single case by a "clear experiment." But the fifth and sixth rules might be thought to give us just what we need for such discovery, *viz.*, the criteria by

[5] Hume, *Treatise*, pp. 173 ff. (Italics mine.)

which to decide which circumstances are "foreign and superfluous" to the cause.

Scrutiny of them, however, reveals that they do not do this, for they are presented by Hume as corollaries of the principle mentioned in the fourth rule (*viz.*, same cause, same effect; same effect, same cause), and this principle is not as he there asserts derived from experience, nor is it derivable from it. As he himself has shown earlier with admirable clearness,[6] neither reason nor experience gives us anything which would warrant us in assuming (as the principle in his fourth rule does assume and has to assume if the fifth and sixth rules are to be corollaries of it) that those instances, of which we have had as yet no experience, resemble those of which we have had experience. A principle, which experience might conceivably have yielded, would be that like antecedents placed in like circumstances *have always been observed to have had* like sequents, and that like sequents have always been observed to have had like antecedents. But this principle not only does not yield his fifth and sixth rules as corollaries, but indeed is itself *invalidated by every situation to which Hume would apply these two rules.* For (to quote from rule 5) "where several different objects produce the same effect" what obviously follows is that, as a strict matter of experience, an *exception* to the principle "same effect, same cause" is then confronting us and the principle is thereby invalidated. Just this is what follows, and not, as Hume asserts, that these different objects must have some hidden common quality; for either such a common quality is itself observed, and then the objects are experienced as alike rather than, as supposed, different; or else a common quality is not observed, and then, to know that it exists nonetheless we should need to know that the same effect has the same cause in all cases, future as well as past; and, as recalled above, Hume himself has shown that neither experience nor reason can give us this knowledge.

6 Hume, *Treatise,* pp. 87 ff.

Invariable and Unconditional Antecedents

J. S. MILL

When we define the cause of any thing (in the only sense in which the present inquiry has any concern with causes) to be "the antecedent which it invariably follows," we do not use this phrase as exactly synonymous with "the antecedent which it invariably *has* followed in our past experience." Such a mode of conceiving causation would be liable to the objection very plausibly urged by Dr. Reid, namely, that according to this doctrine night must be the cause of day, and day the cause of night; since these phenomena have invariably succeeded one another from the beginning of the world. But it is neces-

A System of Logic, Book III, Chapter V, Section 6.

sary to our using the word cause, that we should believe not only that the antecedent always *has* been followed by the consequent, but that, as long as the present constitution of things endures, it always *will* be so. And this would not be true of day and night. We do not believe that night will be followed by day under all imaginable circumstances, but only that it will be so *provided* the sun rises above the horizon. If the sun ceased to rise, which, for aught we know, may be perfectly compatible with the general laws of matter, night would be, or might be, eternal. On the other hand, if the sun is above the horizon, his light not extinct, and no opaque body between us and him, we believe firmly that unless a change takes place in the properties of matter, this combination of antecedents will be followed by the consequent, day; that if the combination of antecedents could be indefinitely prolonged, it would be always day; and that if the same combination had always existed, it would always have been day, quite independently of night as a previous condition. Therefore is it that we do not call night the cause, nor even a condition, of day. The existence of the sun (or some such luminous body), and there being no opaque medium in a straight line between that body and the part of the earth where we are situated, are the sole conditions; and the union of these, without the addition of any superfluous circumstance, constitutes the cause. This is what writers mean when they say that the notion of cause involves the idea of necessity. If there be any meaning which confessedly belongs to the term necessity, it is *unconditionalness*. That which is necessary, that which *must* be, means that which will be, whatever supposition we may make in regard to all other things. The succession of day and night evidently is not necessary in this sense. It is conditional on the occurrence of other antecedents. That which will be followed by a given consequent when, and only when, some third circumstance also exists, is not the cause, even though no case should ever have occurred in which the phenomenon took place without it.

Invariable sequence, therefore, is not synonymous with causation, unless the sequence, besides being invariable, is unconditional. There are sequences, as uniform in past experience as any others whatever, which yet we do not regard as cases of causation, but as conjunctions in some sort accidental. Such, to an accurate thinker, is that of day and night. The one might have existed for any length of time, and the other not have followed the sooner for its existence; it follows only if certain other antecedents exist; and where those antecedents existed, it would follow in any case. No one, probably, ever called night the cause of day; mankind must so soon have arrived at the very obvious generalization, that the state of general illumination which we call day would follow from the presence of a sufficiently luminous body, whether darkness had preceded or not.

We may define, therefore, the cause of a phenomenon, to be the antecedent, or the concurrence of antecedents, on which it is invariably and *unconditionally* consequent. Or if we adopt the convenient modification of the meaning of the word cause, which confines it to the assemblage of positive conditions without the negative, then instead of "unconditionally," we must say, "subject to no other than negative conditions."

To some it may appear, that the sequence between night and day being invariable in our experience, we have as much ground in this case as experience can give in any case, for recognizing the two phenomena as cause and effect; and that to say that more is necessary – to require a belief that the succession is unconditional, or, in other words, that it would be invariable under all changes of circumstances, is to acknowledge in causation an element of belief not derived from experience. The answer to this is, that it is experience itself which teaches us that one uniformity of sequence is conditional and another unconditional. When we judge that the succession of night and day is a derivative sequence, depending on something else, we proceed on grounds of experience. It is the evidence of experience which convinces us that day could equally exist without being followed by night, and that night could equally exist without being followed by day. To say that these beliefs are "not generated by our mere observation of sequence," is to forget that twice in every twenty-four hours, when the sky is clear, we have an *experimentum crucis* that the cause of day is the sun. We have an experimental knowledge of the sun which justifies us on experimental grounds in concluding, that if the sun were always above the horizon there would be day, though there had been no night, and that if the sun were always below the horizon there would be night, though there had been no day. We thus know from experience that the succession of night and day is not unconditional. Let me add, that the antecedent which is only conditionally invariable, is not the invariable antecedent. Though a fact may, in experience, have always been followed by another fact, yet if the remainder of our experience teaches us that it might not always be so followed, or if the experience itself is such as leaves room for a possibility that the known cases may not correctly represent all possible cases, the hitherto invariable antecedent is not accounted the cause; but why? Because we are not sure that it *is* the invariable antecedent.

Such cases of sequence as that of day and night not only do not contradict the doctrine which resolves causation into invariable sequence, but are necessarily implied in that doctrine. It is evident, that from a limited number of unconditional sequences, there will result a much greater number of conditional ones. Certain causes being given, that is, certain antecedents which are unconditionally followed by certain consequents; the mere co-existence of these causes will give rise to an unlimited number of additional uniformities. If two causes exist together, the effects of both will exist together; and if many causes co-exist, these causes (by what we shall term hereafter the intermixture of their laws) will give rise to new effects, accompanying or succeeding one another in some particular order, which order will be invariable while the causes continue to co-exist, but no longer. The motion of the earth in a given orbit round the sun, is a series of changes which follow one another as antecedents and consequents, and will continue to do so while the sun's attraction, and the force with which the earth tends to advance in a direct line through space, continue to co-exist in the same quantities as at present. But vary either of these causes, and this particular succession of motions would cease to take place. The series of the earth's motions, therefore, though a case of sequence invariable within the limits of human experience, is not a case of causation. It is not unconditional.

Law Statements and Counterfactual Inference

RODERICK M. CHISHOLM

The problems I have been invited to discuss arise from the fact that there are two types of true synthetic universal statement: statements of the one type, in the context of our general knowledge, seem to warrant counterfactual inference and statements of the other type do not. I shall call statements of the first type "law statements" and statements of the second type "nonlaw statements." Both law and nonlaw statements may be expressed in the general form, "For every x, if x is S, x is P." Law statements, unlike nonlaw statements, seem to warrant inference to statements of the form, "If *a*, which is not S, *were* S, *a* would be P" and "For every x, if x *were* S, x would be P." I shall discuss (I) this distinction between law and nonlaw statements and (II) the related problem of interpreting counterfactual statements.[1]

Originally published in *Analysis*, Vol. 15, 1955, pp. 97–105. Reprinted by permission of the author and the editor.

[1] Detailed formulations of this problem are to be found in the following works: W. E. Johnson, *Logic*, Vol. III, chapter I; C. H. Langford, review of W. B. Gallie's "An Interpretation of Causal Laws," *Journal of Symbolic Logic*, Vol. VI, 1941, p. 67; C. I. Lewis, *An Analysis of Knowledge and Valuation*, Part II; Roderick M. Chisholm, "The Contrary-to-fact Conditional," *Mind*, Vol. 55, 1946, pp. 289–307 (reprinted in H. Feigl and W. S. Sellars, *Readings in Philosophical Analysis*); Nelson Goodman, "The Problem of Counterfactual Conditionals," *Journal of Philosophy*, Vol. 44, 1947, pp. 113–128 (reprinted in L. Linsky, *Semantics and the Philosophy of Language*); F. L. Will, "The Contrary-to-fact Conditional," *Mind*, Vol. 56, 1947, pp. 236–249; and William Kneale, "Natural Laws and Contrary to Fact Conditionals," *Analysis*, Vol. 10, 1950, pp. 121–125. See further references below and in Erna Schneider, "Recent Discussion of Subjunctive Conditionals," *Review of Metaphysics*, Vol. VI, 1953, pp. 623–647. My paper, referred to above, contains some serious errors.

I

Let us consider the following as examples of law statements:

L1. Everyone who drinks from this bottle is poisoned.

L2. All gold is malleable.

And let us consider the following as examples of nonlaw statements:

N1. Everyone who drinks from —— bottle wears a necktie.

N2. Every Canadian parent of quintuplets in the first half of the twentieth century is named 'Dionne.'

Let us suppose that L1 and N1 are concerned with the same bottle (perhaps it is one of short duration and has contained only arsenic.) Let us suppose, further, that the blank in N1 is replaced by property terms which happen to characterize the bottle uniquely (perhaps they describe patterns of fingerprints). I shall discuss certain philosophical questions which arise when we make the following "preanalytic" assumptions. From L1 we can infer

L1.1 If Jones had drunk from this bottle, he would have been poisoned.

and from L2 we can infer

L2.1 If that metal were gold, it would be malleable.

But from N1 we cannot infer

N1.1 If Jones had drunk from —— bottle, he would have worn a necktie.

and from N2 we cannot infer

N2.1 If Jones, who is Canadian, had been parent of quintuplets during the first half of the twentieth century, he would have been named 'Dionne."

I shall not defend these assumptions beyond noting that, in respects to be discussed, they correspond to assumptions which practically everyone does make.

There are two preliminary points to be made concerning the interpretation of counterfactual statements. (1) We are concerned with those counterfactuals whose antecedents, "if *a* were S," may be interpreted as meaning the same as "if *a* had property S." There is, however, another possible interpretation: "if *a* were S" could be interpreted as meaning the same as "if *a* were identical with something which in fact does have property S." [2] Given the above assumptions, N2.1 is false according to the first interpretation, which is the interpretation with which we are concerned, but it is true according to the second (for if Jones were identical with one of the Dionnes, he would be named 'Dionne'). On the other hand, the statement

N2.2 If Jones, who is Canadian, had been parent of quintuplets during the first half of the twentieth century, there would have been at least two sets of Canadian quintuplets.

is true according to the first interpretation and false according to the second. (2) It should be noted, secondly, that there is a respect — to be discussed at greater length below — in which our counterfactual statements may be thought of as being elliptical. If we assert L1.1, we might, nevertheless, accept the following qualification: "Of course, if Jones had emptied the bottle, cleaned it out, filled it with water, and *then* drunk from it, he might not have been poisoned." And, with respect to L2.1, we might accept this qualification: "If that metal were gold it would be malleable — provided, of course, that what we are supposing to be contrary-to-fact is that statement 'That metal is not gold' and *not* the statement 'All gold is malleable.' "

Can the relevant difference between law and nonlaw statements be described in familiar terminology without reference to counterfactuals, without use of modal terms such as "causal necessity," "necessary condition," "physical possibility," and the like, and without use of metaphysical terms such as "real connections between matters ot fact"? I believe no one has shown that the relevant difference *can* be so described. I shall mention three recent discussions.

(1) It has been suggested that the distinction between law statements and nonlaw statements may be made with respect to the universality of the nonlogical terms which appear in the statements. A term may be thought of as being universal, it has been suggested, if its meaning can be conveyed without explicit reference to any particular object; it is then said that law statements, unlike nonlaw statements, contain no nonlogical terms which are not universal.[3]

[2] Compare K. R. Popper, "A Note on Natural Laws and so-called 'Contrary-to-fact Conditionals,'" *Mind,* Vol. 58, 1949, pp. 62–66.

[3] Compare C. G. Hempel and Paul Oppenheim, "Studies in the Logic of Explanation," *Philosophy of Science,* Vol. 15, 1948, pp. 135–175 (reprinted in H. Feigl and M. Brodbeck, *Readings in the Philosophy of Science*). It should be noted that these authors (i) attempt to characterize laws with respect only to formalized languages, (ii) concede that "the problem of an adequate definition of purely qualitative (universal) predicates remains open," and (iii) propose a distinction between "derived" and "fundamental" laws. The latter distinction is similar to a distinction of Braithwaite, discussed below. See also Elizabeth Lane Beardsley, "Non-Accidental and Counterfactual Sentence," *Journal of Philosophy,* Vol. 46, 1949, pp. 573–591; review of the latter by Roderick M. Chisholm, *Journal of Symbolic Logic,* Vol. XVI, 1951, pp. 63–64.

(These points can be formulated more precisely.) This suggestion does not help, however, if applied to what we have been calling "law statements" and "nonlaw statements," for L1 is a law statement containing the *non*universal nonlogical term "this bottle" and N1 (we have supposed) is a nonlaw statement all of whose nonlogical terms *are* universal. It may be that, with respect to ordinary usage, it is incorrect to call L1 a "law statement"; this point does not affect our problem, however, since we are assuming that L1, whether or not it would ordinarily be called a "law statement," does, in the context of our general knowledge, warrant the inference to L1.1.

(2) It has been suggested that the two types of statement might be distinguished epistemologically. P. F. Strawson, in his *Introduction to Logical Theory,* suggests that in order to *know,* or to have good evidence or good reason for believing, that a given nonlaw statement is true, it is necessary to know that all of its instances have in fact been observed; but in order to know, or to have good evidence or good reason for believing, that a given law statement is true, it is *not* necessary to know that all of its instances have been examined. (We need not consider the problem of defining "instance" in this use.) "An essential part of our grounds for accepting" a nonlaw statement must be "evidence that there will be no more" instances and "that there never were more than the limited number of which observations have been recorded" (p. 199). Possibly this suggestion is true, but it leaves us with our problem. For the suggestion itself requires use of a modal term; it refers to what a man *needs* to know, or what it is *essential* that he know, in order to know that a law statement is true. But if we thus allow ourselves the use of modal terms, we could have said at the outset merely that a law statement describes what is "physically necessary," etc., and that a nonlaw statement does not.

(3) R. B. Braithwaite, in *Scientific Explanation,* suggests that a law statement, as distinguished from a nonlaw statement is one which "appears as a deduction from higher-level hypotheses which have been established independently of the statement" (p. 303). "To consider whether or not a scientific hypothesis would, if true, be a law of nature is to consider the way in which it could enter into an established scientific deductive system" (Ibid). In other words, the question whether a statement is law-like may be answered by considering certain logical, or epistemological, relations which the statement bears to certain *other* statements. Our nonlaw statement N2, however, is deducible from the following two statements: (i) "Newspapers which are generally reliable report that all parents of quintuplets during the first half of the twentieth century are named 'Dionne,'" and (ii) "If newspapers which are generally reliable report that all parents of quintuplets during the first half of the twentieth century are named 'Dionne,' then such parents are named 'Dionne.'" Statements (i) and (ii) may be considered as "higher level" parts of a "hypothetical-deductive system" from which the nonlaw statement N2 can be deduced; indeed (i) and (ii) undoubtedly express the grounds upon which most people accept N2. It is not enough, therefore, to describe a nonlaw statement as a statement which "appears as a deduction from higher level hypotheses which have been established independently." (I suggest, incidentally, that it is only at an advanced stage of inquiry that one regards a synthetic universal statement as being a *non*law statement.)

II

Even if we allow ourselves the distinction between law statements and nonlaw statements and characterize the distinction philosophically, by reference, say, to physical possibility (e.g. "All S is P" is a law statement provided it is not physically possible that anything be both S and not P, etc.), we find that contrary-to-fact conditionals still present certain difficulties of interpretation.[4] Assuming that the distinction between law statement and nonlaw statement is available to us, I shall now make some informal remarks which I hope will throw light upon the ordinary use of these conditionals.

Henry Hiz has suggested that a contrary-to-fact conditional might be interpreted as a metalinguistic statement, telling us something about what can be inferred in a given system of statements. "It says that, if something is accepted in this system to be true, then something else can be accepted in this system to be true."[5] This suggestion, I believe, can be applied to the ordinary use of contrary-to-fact conditionals, but it is necessary to make some qualifying remarks concerning the relevant "systems of statements."

Let us consider one way of justifying the assertion of a contrary-to-fact conditional, "If *a* were S, *a* would be P." The antecedent of the counterfactual is taken, its indicative form, as a *supposition* or *assumption*.[6] One says, in effect, "Let us *suppose* that *a* is S," even though one may believe that *a* is not S. The indicative form of the consequent of the counterfactual – viz., "*a* is P" – is then shown to follow logically from the antecedent taken with certain other statements already accepted. This demonstration is then taken to justify the counterfactual. The point of asserting the counterfactual may be that of *calling attention to, emphasizing,* or *conveying,* one or more of the premises which, taken with the antecedent, logically imply the consequent.

In simple cases, where singular counterfactuals are asserted, we may thus think of the speaker: (i) as having deduced the consequences of a singular supposition, viz., the indicative form of the counterfactual antecedent, taken with a statement he interprets as a law statement; and (ii) as being concerned in part to call attention to, emphasize, or convey, the statement interpreted as a law statement. We can usually tell, from the context of a man's utterance, what the supposition is and what the other statements are with which he is concerned. He may say, "If that were gold, it would be malleable"; it is likely, in this case, that the statement interpreted as a law statement is L2, "All gold is malleable"; it is also likely that this is the statement he is concerned to emphasize.

F. H. Bradley suggested in his *Principles of Logic,* that when a man asserts a singular counterfactual "the real judgment is concerned with the individual's *qualities,* and asserts no more than a connection of adjectives."[7] Bradley's suggestion, as I interpret it, is that the *whole* point of asserting a singular counterfactual, normally, is to call attention to, emphasize, or convey the statement interpreted as a law statement. It might be misleading, however, to say that the man is *affirming* or *asserting* what he takes to be a law statement, or statement describing a "connection of adjectives," for he has not formulated it explicitly. It would also be misleading to say, as Bradley did (p. 89), that the man is merely *supposing* the law statement to be true, for the law statement is something he *believes,* and not merely supposes, to be true. If he were merely supposing "All gold is malleable," along with

[4] Modal analyses of law statements are suggested by Hans Reichenbach, *Elements of Symbolic Logic,* Ch. VIII and Arthur Burks, "The Logic of Causal Propositions," *Mind,* Vol. LX, 1951, pp. 363–382.

[5] Henry Hiz, "On the Inferential Sense of Contrary-to-fact Conditionals," *Journal of Philosophy,* Vol. 48, 1949, pp. 586–587.

[6] Compare S. Jaskowski, "On the Rules of Suppositions in Formal Logic," *Studia Logica,* No. 1 (Warsaw, 1934), and A. Meinong, *Über Annahmen,* concerning this use of "assumption."

[7] *Op. cit.,* p. 90. Compare D. J. O'Connor, "The Analysis of Conditional Sentences," *Mind,* Vol. LX, 1951, p. 360; Robert Brown and John Watling, "Counterfactual Conditionals," *Mind,* Vol. LXI, 1952, p. 226.

"That is gold," then it is likely he would include this supposition in the antecedent of his counterfactual and say "If that were gold and if all gold were malleable, then that would be malleable." Let us say he is *presupposing* the law statement.

We are suggesting, then, that a man in asserting a counterfactual is telling us something about what can be deduced from some "system of statements" when the indicative version of the antecedent is added to this system as a *supposition.* We are referring to the statements of this system (other than the indicative version of the antecedent) as the *presuppositions* of his assertion. And we are suggesting that, normally, at least part of the point of asserting a counterfactual is to *call attention to, emphasize,* or *convey,* one or more of these presuppositions.

The statements a man presupposes when he asserts a counterfactual will, presumably, be statements he accepts or believes. But they will not include the denial of the antecedent of his counterfactual (even if he believes this denial to be true) and they will not include any statements he would treat as nonlaw statements.[8] And normally there will be many other statements he believes to be true which he will deliberately exclude from his presuppositions. The peculiar problem of interpreting ordinary counterfactual statements is that of specifying which, among the statements the asserter believes, he intends to *exclude* from his presuppositions. What statements he will exclude will depend upon what it is he is concerned to call attention to, emphasize, or convey.

Let us suppose a man accepts the following statements, taking the universal statements to be law statements: (1) All gold is malleable; (2) No cast-iron is malleable; (3) Nothing is both gold and cast-iron; (4) Nothing is both malleable and not malleable; (5) That is cast-iron; (6) That is not gold; and (7) That is not malleable. We may contrast three different situations in which he asserts three different counterfactuals having the same antecedents.

First, he asserts, pointing to an object his hearers don't know to be gold and don't know not to be gold, "If that *were* gold, it would be malleable." In this case, he is supposing the denial of (6); he is excluding from his presuppositions (5), (6), and (7); and he is concerned to emphasize (1).

Secondly, he asserts, pointing to an object he and his hearers agree to be cast-iron, "If *that* were gold, then some gold things would not be malleable." He is again supposing the denial of (6); he is excluding (1) and (6), but he is no longer excluding (5) or (7); and he is concerned to emphasize either (5) or (2).

Thirdly, he asserts, "If that were gold, then some things would be both malleable and not malleable." He is again supposing the denial of (6); he is now excluding (3) and no longer excluding (1), (5), (6), or (7); and he is now concerned to emphasize (1), (2), or (5).

Still other possibilities readily suggest themselves.

If, then, we were to ask "What if that were gold?" our question would have a number of possible answers – e.g., the subjunctive forms of the denial of (7), the denial of (1), and the denial of (4). Any one of these three answers might be appropriate, but they would not *all* be appropriate in conjunction. Which answer is the appropriate one will depend upon what we wish to know. If, in asking "What if that were gold?", we wish to know of some law statement describing gold, the denial of (7) is appropriate; if we wish to know what are the properties of the thing in question, the denial of (1) is appropriate; and if we wish

[8] Instead of saying his presuppositions include no statement he treats as a law statement, it might be more accurate to say this: if his presuppositions include any statement N he would interpret as a nonlaw statement, then N and the man's supposition cannot be so formulated that the supposition constitutes a substitution-instance of N's antecedent.

to know whether the thing has properties such that a statement saying nothing gold has those properties is a law statement, the denial of (4) is appropriate. The counterfactual question, "What if that were gold?", is, therefore, clearly ambiguous. But in each case, the question could be formulated clearly and unambiguously.

Counterfactuals are similar to *probability* statements in that each type of statement is, in a certain sense, elliptical. If we ask, "What is the probability that this man will survive?", our question is incompletely formulated; a more explicit formulation would be, "With respect to such-and-such-evidence, what is the probability that this man will survive?" Similarly, if we ask, "What would American policy in Asia be if Stevenson were President?" our question is incompletely formulated; a more explicit formulation would be, "Supposing that Stevenson were President, and presupposing so-and-so, but not so-and-so, what would be the consequences with respect to American policy in Asia?" But there is an important respect in which counterfactual statements *differ* from such probability statements. If a man wishes to know what is the probability of a certain statement, i.e., if he wishes to know the truth of a categorical probability statement, then, we may say, he should take into consideration *all* the relevant evidence available to him; the premises of his probability inference should omit no relevant statement which he is justified in believing.[9] But this "requirement of total evidence" cannot be assumed to hold in the case of counterfactual inference. If a man asks, "What would American policy in Asia be if Stevenson were President?", and if his question may be interpreted in the way in which it ordinarily would be interpreted, then there are many facts included in his store of knowledge which we would expect him to *overlook,* or *ignore,* in answering his question; i.e., there are many facts which we would expect him deliberately to *exclude* from his presuppositions. Normally we would expect him to exclude the fact that Eisenhower's program is the one which has been followed since 1953; another is the fact that Mr. Dulles is Secretary of State. But there are other facts, which may also be included in the man's store of knowledge, whose status is more questionable. Does he intend to exclude the fact that Congress was Republican; does he intend to exclude those Asiatic events which have occurred as a result of Eisenhower's policies; does he intend to exclude the fact that Stevenson went to Asia in 1953? There is no point in insisting either that he consider or that he exclude these facts. But, if he wishes to be understood, he should tell us which are the facts that he is considering, or presupposing, and which are the ones he is excluding.

Bradley suggested the ambiguity of some counterfactual statements may be attributed to the fact that "the supposition is not made evident" (*op. cit.*, p. 89). In our terminology, it would be more accurate to say that the *presupposition* is not made evident; for the supposition is usually formulated explicitly in the antecedent of the counterfactual statement. (But when a man says, "If that thing, which is not S, were S. . . . ," the subordinate indicative clause expresses neither a supposition nor a presupposition.) Ideally it might be desirable to formulate our counterfactuals in somewhat the following way: "Supposing that that is S, and presupposing so-and-so, then it follows that that is P." In practice, however, it is often easy to tell from the context in which a counterfactual is asserted, just what it is that is being presupposed and what it is that is being excluded.[10]

[9] Compare Rudolf Carnap, *Logical Foundations of Probability,* pp. 211 ff.

[10] "The Contrary-to-fact Conditional" (pp. 303–304; Feigl-Sellars, p. 494). I discuss what I take to be certain conventions of ordinary language pertaining to this point.

Although I have been using the terms "counterfactual" and "contrary-to-fact" throughout this discussion, it is important to note that, when a man arrives at a conditional statement in the manner we have been discussing, his supposition – and thus also the antecedent of his conditional – need *not* be anything he believes to be false. For example, a man in deliberating will consider the consequences of a supposition, taken along with certain presuppositions, and he will also consider the consequences of its denial, taken along with the same presuppositions. It is misleading to say, therefore, that the conditionals he may then affirm are "counterfactual," or "contrary-to-fact," for he may have no beliefs about the truth or falsity of the respective antecedents and one of these antecedents will in fact be true.[11] A better term might be "suppositional conditional" or, indeed, "hypothetical statement."

[11] Compare Alan Ross Anderson, "A Note on Subjunctive and Counterfactual Conditionals," *Analysis,* Vol. 12, 1951, pp. 35–38; Roderick M. Chisholm, review of David Pears' "Hypotheticals," *Journal of Symbolic Logic,* Vol. 15, 1950, pp. 215–216.

Historical Laws

GUSTAV BERGMANN

A plant physiologist undertakes a quantitative growth study of a certain species. The result he expects is a so-called growth curve. He hopes to discover how the two parameters of this curve, the one that determines the rate of growth of the plant and the one that determines its eventual size, say, specifically, its height, depend on such factors as amounts of humidity, irradiation, certain chemicals in the soil, and so on. These are therefore the factors he systematically varies in his numerous experimental plots. So far the story is rather conventional; I must now give it the twist that makes it the vehicle of a new group of ideas. Imagine that our scientist obtains not one growth curve but, in a perfectly clear-cut fashion, two. Assume further that, to increase his puzzlement, he finds that for each of these two curves the arithmetical form of the dependency of its two parameters on the experimental variables is the same. The only difference is that certain constants in this function have different values with the result that, say, one-half of the seedlings grow more slowly and less tall than the others. Our man sets out in search of the overlooked relevant variable (or variables) whose different values for the two groups of plants, call them *A* and *B,* might account for the difference. This is still routine, just as is the "deterministic" assumption that there is such a variable. Yet he finds no clues of a routine nature. The only difference he discovers is that the seeds he planted came from two different bags, which he had bought at a store. Thereupon our scientist, lest he miss any

From Bergmann, *Philosophy of Science,* pp. 124–129. Madison: The University of Wisconsin Press, 1957. Reprinted by permission of the author and of the copyright owners, the Regents of the University of Wisconsin.

chance, somewhat reluctantly considers the possibility that the seeds for group *A* all came from one of the bags, while those for group *B* all came from the other. He kept no records from which he could learn whether this is actually the case; fortunately, though, enough seeds of both kinds are left to repeat the experiment. (This time, some seeds of each kind are deliberately saved.) The second experiment confirms the hunch. The next step, again routine, is a careful examination of the seeds that were saved. The seeds from the two bags are found to be alike in many respects. Eventually an elaborate microbiological test uncovers in those that produced the slow-growing and stunted plants the "traces" of a disease from which their ancestors had suffered. Further experimentation confirms that this is the difference that made the difference.

Logically, all this is just another case in which a few steps led a scientist to add to his S^0 a new variable, namely, the trace or scar certain past events have left on some of the seeds but not on the others. Whatever fancy there is lies in the story I made up. So let me now give it another twist. Imagine that at the time the experiments were performed those microbiological tests were as yet unknown. Assume, furthermore, that in the absence of any laboratory clues our persistent scientist engages in a different kind of investigation. He learns from the merchant who sold him the two bags that they came from different parts of the country and eventually, after further inquiry, that a certain disease has long plagued the species in the region from which one of the bags came. For the disease is well known; what is unknown is the microbiological test. From there on we may imagine the experiment to proceed as before. Roughly speaking, it leads to the same law. Yet there is an important difference between the two situations and the two laws. Everything I shall say in this section turns on this difference.

Let me for brevity's sake speak of the earlier and the later law. The later law fits, however roughly, into the process schema. S^0 or, generally, S^t consists of the set of values certain variables have at the time 0 or, generally, at the time *t*. The additional variable, call it the trace variable, is no exception. What makes the difference is the "present" value of this variable or, less elaborately speaking, the presence or absence of the microscopic scar. But I do for once want to speak elaborately. In the earlier situation the additional information consists of a statement or statements describing an earlier or "past" state or states of the system. Again I am speaking elaborately, but by now I trust my purpose is clear. I want to construct the schema of laws that predict the "future" not from the "present" alone but from the present in conjunction with some information about the "past." Such laws, however perfect or imperfect they may be, are no longer process laws. (Yet I shall in describing them continue to use, somewhat inaccurately, the letters *C* and *S*.) Let $\pi\ S^0$ and $\pi\ S^t$ stand for some information, either partial or complete, about either a state or states in which the system was either at one or at some or at all moments preceding time 0 or time *t* respectively. Briefly, the prefix 'π' indicates some information about the "past." Then the schema of the earlier law can be diagrammed as follows:

(H) $$(C \,\&\, S^0 \,\&\, \pi S^0) \longrightarrow S^t, \quad t > 0,$$

which contrasts with the familiar diagram of the process schema

$$(C \,\&\, S^0) \longrightarrow S^t.$$

Instances of schema (H) I call *historical laws.*

The tale I told makes it in a sense harder for me to make my point. Such self-imposed handicaps have their advantages. The difficulty I deliberately created for myself is that the story seems to confirm the unexamined "assumptions" of a "frame of reference." The earlier law is "merely" a historical law. The later law, the one we can state after the "trace" has been discovered, is "no longer" a historical law. Moreover, after it has been stated, the earlier, historical law becomes, in an obvious sense, expendable. The unexamined assumption to which I wish to draw attention is that there "must" be a trace and that a historical law is therefore "necessarily" an item of imperfect knowledge that will eventually become expendable. Very probably this is so. The point is that it is merely a matter of fact, one of those broad "facts" of which "frames of reference" are made. That we take this particular "fact" for granted is one ingredient of the frame of reference that stems from the Newtonian process schema. It is well worth while to understand this ingredient accurately. A few comments should help. I shall devote one paragraph to each, numbering them consecutively.

1. In many cases we have found the trace. The story I told is in this respect quite realistic. This shows clearly that 'historical,' as I use it, is the name of a certain structure or form with respect to time which a law may or may not exemplify. Also, a historical law may become expendable long before we have reached process knowledge in its area. Without further explanation it makes no sense therefore to say that an area (not a law), e.g., psychology or physics, is or is not historical. One thing one could mean is that *at a particular time* our actual knowledge in the area is, was, or will be either partly or, perhaps, predominantly historical. To another, more recondite meaning I shall attend presently. (I find myself again using 'area' before I have explicated it; but again I think this will do no harm.)

2. Aristotle's observations on memory are probably the earliest articulate attempt to state psychological laws. They are historical. So are the various laws of association the classical British psychologists proposed. So are very many of the laws of contemporary psychology, the laws of learning as well as the more ambitious and therefore more elusive generalizations of the psychoanalysts. Small wonder, then, that in Volumes Two and Three we shall have to make use of the notion of historical lawfulness again and again. This is why we must grasp it firmly and see clearly its place among the possible patterns of lawfulness.

3. Like virtually every ordinary word that is made into a technical term, 'historical' has unwanted associations. At the moment it is for us still an open question whether there are any laws of the "social process" or, as it is sometimes put, whether there are any laws of "history." Certainly, I do not wish to hint or to appear to hint that such laws, if there are any, are necessarily historical. To these questions I shall attend much later, in Volume Two. Still with respect to the word, two things may come to mind if one is guided by its ordinary uses; I do not mean either when I call a law historical. For one thing, every law is arrived at by generalization (induction), either directly, or indirectly by deduction from laws so arrived at; and the instances on which the generalization is based, or at least some of these instances, will as a rule lie in the past. In this obvious and entirely nonspecific sense all laws would be "historical." For another thing, in one of the meanings of 'cause,' any earlier state of a system may be said to be the cause of any later one. In this sense every dynamic law would be "historical." When I call a law historical I mean neither of these two things but, to repeat, a certain structure of the law itself with respect to time.

4. A developmental law is not a historical law, nor conversely. To understand the difference it suffices to consider a three-stage developmental law (*A*, *B*, *C*) anchored at the intermediate stage (*B*). For our purposes it may be schematized by 'If (*B* now) then (*A* earlier *and* *C* later).' The schema of the "corresponding" historical law is 'If (*B* now and *A* earlier) then (*C* later)' or, what

amounts to the same thing, 'If (*B* now) then (*if A* earlier *then C* later).' The difference comes out in the difference between the two logical connectives, 'and' and 'if-then,' which I italicized.

5. In the first chapter I introduced the notion of historical concepts. Among the examples I gave was 'tempered,' as said of steel, and 'hungry_1,' which means by definition 'having been deprived of food during a certain time interval.' The notion of a historical concept is closely connected with that of a historical law. Though the connection is obvious, I shall be tedious rather than too concise and state it explicitly. To have had a certain character in the past is a historical character of the present. Thus πS^0 can be considered as a conjunction of statements attributing historical characters to objects mentioned in the antecedent of the law. It follows that every historical law contains at least one historical concept. Let us also cast another glance at the hunger example. We encountered two further notions of hunger, one defined in terms of stomach contractions (hungry_2), one defined in terms of a disposition to approach and consume food (hungry_3). Any law connecting hunger_1 with either hunger_2 or hunger_3 is a historical law.

6. Let me describe accurately what happens when a historical law becomes "expendable." Perhaps the most common historical concept, much used in the biological as well as in the behavior sciences, is age. In the case of trees we can replace 'age' by 'number of rings.' Consider a lawful connection between some property of (a kind of) trees and their age. Call the "two" laws that state this connection L' and L'' respectively; L' being the one mentioning age, L'' the one that mentions instead of age the number of rings. Call L the law that states the connection between a tree's age and the number of its rings. L is historical. L'' follows deductively from the conjunction of L and L', but neither L nor L' follows deductively from L''. It would seem, then, that L is not expendable and that instead of having got rid of historicity in this case we have merely limited its scope. In a sense this is indeed so. But there is also the presumption that (1) L will eventually be superseded by a process law that "grinds out" the number of rings as a function of time (notice that I say time, not age), and (2) we are approaching this ideal if we replace L and L' by L and L''. It is instructive to compare this situation with the case of 'red' and 'red_1' (p. 104). If I may so express myself, 'red' is as we saw not expendable in an analytical account of what we know. Nor are statements of individual fact about the past (either inferred or memory). This is not so for historical laws and historical concepts. Whether or not we need them depends on the kind of lawfulness (if any) which we discover.

A historical law may be an item of incomplete knowledge; many have in fact turned out to be just that. Nor is it difficult to show schematically how a historical law may be deduced from a process law. Again, I shall not bother to write down the schema. But again, one could not possibly show that every historical law can thus be "projected" against an eventual "ahistorical" process. There remains another possibility, the one our ahistorical frame of reference excludes. Probably it is no more than a possibility. Yet to be aware of it not only helps to understand one's own frame of reference; such awareness is also the best safeguard against the temptation to hypostatize it. There is a further advantage to this awareness, if one wishes to examine the behavior sciences, an area that is at present in fact largely historical. Notice that I said behavior science is at present historical. I did not say that it is "still" historical. Not that I hesitate to commit myself or, perhaps better, to make a prognosis. The point is that an intelligent forecast requires some further distinctions. To these questions I shall attend in Volume Two. Then it will also appear that, when the analytical job has been done, forecasting loses much of its interest. As often happens, the urge to "commit" one's self on matters of this sort is greatly reduced after analysis has, incidentally, bared its ideological sources.

The possibility we must not overlook is a law or theory which, though historical, is in all other respects perfect in exactly the same sense in which a process law is perfect. In this case one would not inappropriately speak of a *historical process*. It could be that the comprehensive theory of some area actually is a historical process. Or, to go even further, since, as we saw, the thesis of determinism makes sense (though, as I put it, only very broadly and therefore not very excitingly), so would its historical variant. In the notation I use it is not at all difficult to write down the schema, call it (P_h), of a historical process law. One merely needs to double the number of "state variables," replacing each of them say, $x_i{}^0$ by the pair $x_i{}^0, \pi x_i{}^0$, whose second member represents some information about the past values of $x_i{}^0$. I write down only the first line of (P_h):

$$x_1{}^t = f_1(c_1, c_2, \ldots, c_m; x_1{}^0, \pi x_1{}^0, \ldots, x_n{}^0, \pi x_n{}^0; t)$$

Mathematicians have for some time investigated the form a historical process law might reasonably be expected to exemplify. For (P_h), like (P), is not the schema of the equations in which the law itself is stated but, rather, that of their solution. Fully articulated process laws are, as we saw, differential equations. Historical process laws of this kind would be so-called integro-differential equations.

A "historical" world would probably have some peculiar features. Their exploration may safely be left to the mathematical students of integro-differential equations. One comment, though, I shall not suppress. Assume a process that is totally historical, i.e., a historical process such that each πS^t comprehends the complete value course of S^t for all moments earlier than t. A little reflection shows that what I just said must not be taken too literally. By the nature of the schema, any S^t in conjunction with its πS^t would determine the process, no matter how remote in the past t happens to be. Thus there is no single past event and, even, no event in any preselected past interval one would have to know in order to predict the future.

In conclusion a few words about the role of time — still, as always, prerelativistically. As I mentioned earlier, the way time enters into the process schema explicates what could be meant by saying that time as such is not causally efficacious. Nor would it be if the fundamental process were historical, though in this case we would probably speak about action over distance in time. This, too, I mentioned earlier. But it would still be the "content" of a cross section or an interval rather than "time as such" that we would consider as causally efficacious.

Imagine that our physicists discover a "trend" in some of the fundamental constants, say, the gravitational constant and the charge of the electron. Assume, for instance, that these constants are found to increase very slowly though, to be sure, at a rate ten or twenty times the error of measurement. Or they may be found to change periodically, with a period of 20,000 years and a mild but equally clear-cut amplitude. It is safe to predict that in this most unlikely event our physicists would very stubbornly try either to derive the changes from their fundamental process law or to modify it so that they could be derived. Only as a last resort would they add to it the three equations, without further trying to deduce these equations, which represent the three constants as functions of time. For if they did this they would not only abandon the process idea; they would also make time as such causally efficacious. The main purpose of this tale is, of course, to explain what it could mean to say that time as such is causally efficacious. Needless to add that if this possibility were actually realized, the departure from our frame of reference would be even more radical than in the case of action over distance in time.

5

PROBABILITY NOTIONS

Introduction

It is difficult to know where best to place a chapter on probability since, as we shall see, it is closely related to many topics in the philosophy of science. There are good reasons, however, for its present location between chapters on the nature of 'law' and the riddle of induction. Probability statements which have the form '90% of x's are also y's' can best be interpreted as statistical laws, and certain problems about the nature of these laws lead into the riddle of induction.

The word 'probable' has many uses in everyday life and science and it is difficult to disentangle and properly relate them, or — as some writers say — to find a common meaning among them. Consider these examples of probability statements:

1) The probability of a thrown die turning up face 3 is 1/6.
2) The probability of a thirty-year-old person living in the United States surviving his thirty-first birthday is .945.
3) The probability of the general theory of relativity is greater than it was thirty-five years ago.

We must be clear, of course, that these three examples are *types* of probability statements; we would have little difficulty in thinking up three equally good examples to mark off the three-way distinction we are beginning to make: for example, 1′) the probability of a tossed coin turning up heads is 1/2; 2′) The probability of a thirty-year-old person living in Florida surviving his thirty-first birthday is .999; 3′) The theory of evolution has a much higher probability than the theory of special creation. But what differences do these types of examples signify? Everything I have to say below will help explain this three-way difference in one way or another, but let us note several points by way of a beginning. First, the examples in 1) and 1′) are taken from games of chance; 2) and 2′) from insurance statistics and 3) and 3′) from science. Now these three types of examples have given rise to the three most influential views about the meaning of 'probable' and 'probability'; they are called, respectively, the classical, the frequency, and the inductive theories of probability — although you must realize that 'theory' here refers to the meaning of a word, not to a scientific theory about the physical world. In what follows I will examine these three views in turn, pointing out along the way their many conflicts and relationships.

The Classical Theory. Pierre Simon, Marquis de Laplace, in the early part of the nineteenth century wrote *Théorie analytique des probabilités* in which he propounded, in its most complete form, the "classical" view of probability. Recall the example of a thrown die. 'The probability of a thrown die turning up face 3 is 1/6.' Laplace analyzed this sort of statement in the following way. When a die is thrown, any one of the six faces of the die might turn up, and each of these events is *equiprobable.* By 'equiprobable' Laplace meant that any face of the die, as far as we know, has just as much chance to turn up as any other. We know certainly that one of the six faces will turn up but since our knowledge, or ignorance, of which one it will be is equally divided, we have no more or less reason for expecting one rather than another. Thus, as far as we know, they are equiprobable. With the introduction of this key notion of equiprobability, Laplace was able to state his view in a simple way: The probability of an event is a fraction whose numerator is the event in question and whose denominator is the total number of equiprobable events. Hence, in our example, the probability of a thrown die turning up face 3 is $\frac{1}{6}$. Or, "if the letters of the word *Roma* be thrown down casually in a row, what is the probability that they will form a significant Latin word? The possible arrangements of four letters are $4 \times 3 \times 2 \times 1$, or 24 in number, and if all the arrangements be examined, seven of these will be found to have meaning, namely, *Roma, ramo, oram, mora, maro, armo,* and *amor*. Hence the probability of a significant result is $\frac{7}{24}$." [1]

Several corollaries of particular interest follow from this classical definition of probability. First, this theory is *a priori,* by which I mean that one calculates the probability of an event without collecting any factual information of a statistical sort about how often the event has occurred in the past. I do not need to know how often face 3 turns up in a long series of throws in order to calculate its chances of turning up on any given one; I need to know only a few antecedent facts, that the die has six faces and each one has an equal chance to turn up.

Second, according to this view, 'probable' does not refer to an objective property of events themselves but is a measure of the degree of rational belief. Take any specific throw. There is nothing probable about the event itself; either a 3 will turn up or not. 'Probable' refers, rather, to our rational expectation that it has $\frac{1}{6}$ of a chance to come up on this throw.

Third, according to this view, a probability judgment is *relative* to some specifiable set of evidence or knowledge; when the set changes, the probability judgment changes. If I know a die is loaded in favor of face 4, I will expect the chance of face 3 turning up to be much less than $\frac{1}{6}$. Or, say, a steamship is missing; some people think she has sunk in mid-ocean, others not. Now the probability of the event's having occurred will vary from day to day, and from mind to mind, as the evidence changes or increases, with the addition of the slightest information regarding vessels met at sea, prevailing weather, condition of vessel, sign of wreck, etc.

Numerous criticisms have been advanced through the years against the classical view, but we will examine only a few of them here. First, it is difficult to see how most probability statements can be analyzed in terms of 'equiprobable events.' If a die is loaded, it is no longer possible to specify the total number of equiprobable events in the denominator of the required ratio. Even more apparent, it is impossible to specify the equiprobable events in any statistical probability statement like 'the probability of a thirty-year-old man living another year is .945.' "It is absurd to interpret such a statement as meaning that there are a thousand possible eventuations to a man's career, 945 of which are favorable to his surviving at least another year. Moreover, the Laplacian definition requires a probability coefficient to be a rational number. But irrational numbers frequently occur as values for such coefficients, and there is no way of interpreting them as ratios of a number of alternatives." [2]

Second, a paradox results from considering probability judgments as *a priori*. Consider the possibility that a person should always throw a coin head uppermost and appear unable to get a tail by chance. On the

1 W. S. Jevons, *The Principles of Science* (London: Macmillan and Co., 1924), p. 203.

2 Ernest Nagel, *Principles of the Theory of Probability,* Vol. I (No. 6 of *International Encyclopedia of Unified Science* (Chicago: University of Chicago Press, 1939), p. 45.

classical view the probability judgment would remain steadfastly ½; experience does not change it. This *a priori* judgment, Jevons wrote, would not be falsified, "because the classical theory contemplates the possibility of the most extreme runs of luck. Our actual experience might be counter to all that is probable; the whole course of events might seem to be in complete contradiction to what we should expect." [3] Jevons, however, wished to minimize this paradox; coincidences of this sort are so "unlikely," he wrote, "that the whole duration of history . . . does not give any appreciable probability of their being encountered."

> The probability that any extreme runs of luck will occur is so excessively slight, that it would be absurd seriously to expect their occurrence. It is almost impossible, for instance, that any whist player should have played in any two games where the distribution of the cards was exactly the same, by pure accident. Such a thing as a person always losing at a game of chance, is wholly unknown. Coincidences of this kind are not impossible, as I have said, but they are so unlikely that the lifetime of any person, or indeed the whole duration of history, does not give any appreciable probability of their being encountered. Whenever we make any extensive series of trials of chance results, as in throwing a die or coin, the probability is great that the results will agree nearly with the predictions yielded by theory.[4]

Unfortunately, however, Jevons' use of 'unlikely' and 'probability' in the minimizing of the paradox cannot be given a classical interpretation and appears to be a poorly concealed concession to the fundamental role of empirical information and a consequent abandonment of pure *a priorism*.

Finally, the classical view that 'probable' always refers to the degree of rational belief and never to an objective property of the event in question runs into difficulty again with statistical probability statements. The statement, 'The probability of a thirty-year-old man living at least another year is .945' apparently refers to an empirical fact, a statistical one, to be sure, namely that out of the whole class of thirty-year-olds 945 of every 1000 have been found to survive their next birthday.

The Frequency Theory. This view, as I suggested at the beginning, grew out of statistical probability statements like the one we just considered. John Venn and Charles Peirce, two nineteenth-century authors, were primarily responsible for this view, while Richard Von Mises and Hans Reichenbach, among others in the present century, have made the viewpoint more precise and acceptable.

These men regarded probability as the measure of the relative frequency with which the members of a specified class of objects or events exhibit a certain property. In our example, an actuary observes the *class* of thirty-year-old men in the United States and discovers that for every 1000 men in this class, 945 exhibit the *property* of surviving their next birthday. The value .945 indicates, then, the precise numerical frequency which the property of surviving exhibited *relative to* the class of thirty-year-old American males. This numerical value, however, must not be determined on a small amount of evidence. The value, after many instances are investigated, may still fluctuate considerably; but when our evidence mounts into the thousands and millions, then fluctuations become fewer and fewer until in the long run the value tends to become fixed. But these notions of "long run" and "tend to become fixed" are exceedingly vague and imprecise. Peirce was one of the first to replace them by the precise notion of a mathematical limit.

> I will limit myself to a single needful explanation that, so far as I know, the reader

[3] Jevons, *op. cit.*, p. 207.

[4] *Ibid.*

could not find definitely stated in any of the books. It is that when we say that a certain ratio will have a certain value in "the long run," we refer to the *probability-limit* of an endless succession of fractional values; that is, to the only possible value from 0 to ∞, inclusive, about which the values of the endless succession will never cease to oscillate; so that, no matter what place in the succession you may choose, there will follow both values above the probability-limit and values below it; while if V be any *other* possible value from 0 to ∞, but *not* the probability-limit, there will be some place in the succession beyond which all the values of the succession will agree, either in all being greater than V, or else in all being less.[5]

Several corollaries of particular interest follow from the frequency view. First, the theory is *empirical,* by which I mean that one calculates the probability of an event by collecting factual information about how often it has occurred in the past. To be sure, one might, in some cases, deduce from certain information what the relative frequency of an event will be; but even here the actual empirical count is necessary to *test* the deduction – perhaps the premises from which it was drawn are false. For example, knowing that pennies are symmetrical, and having a knowledge of mechanics, I might infer that the forces which make a head or a tail turn up will eventually cancel each other out, and hence infer that in the long run the relative frequency of either head or tail will approximate .5. But if pennies never *did* approximate this value, I would have to conclude that something was false about my premises, not ignore the value of the actual series.

Second, 'probable' refers to an objective property of events themselves, not to a degree of rational belief. The numerical values of probability statements refer to the number of times *the members of a specified class of objects or events exhibit a certain property.* Third, a probability judgment is *relative* to some specified set of objects or events. The frequency with which the property 'swarthy' occurs is much greater relative to the class of Spaniards than to the class of Swedes. Fourth, to talk, except in an elliptical fashion, of the probability of an *individual* event is meaningless, for frequency judgments refer only to the relative occurrence of a property in a class of events. Consequently a statement like 'The probability of getting a head on this toss is .5' must be interpreted as an elliptical way of saying, 'The relative frequency with which the property heads occurs in the class of coin tosses approximates, in the long run, .5.'

Numerous criticisms have been leveled against the frequency view, some of which will be discussed in detail in the selections. I shall only say enough about them here to acquaint you with certain types of recurring criticisms. First, the concepts of 'long run' and 'limit' have not gone unchallenged. Consider this situation. Suppose we throw a die a hundred times and get one hundred 3's. Since the relative frequency of 3's is 1 instead of approximating $\frac{1}{6}$, should we conclude the die is loaded? Not necessarily, since the frequency theory simply states that the correct frequency will occur in the long run, and apparently one hundred throws is not long enough. But how long must the series be? Well, of course, we can never know for certain, some philosophers say, since a radical variation is always *logically* possible. And this fact leads to a further difficulty. If no series, however long, can falsify an expected ratio, then no series can confirm an expectation either. If, in a thousand throws, the series approximates $\frac{1}{6}$ for 3's, this fact does not confirm our expectation since 1000 throws need not be considered a "long run"; and so it is possible in subsequent series that the ratio will

[5] *Collected Papers,* edited by Charles Hartshorne and Paul Weiss (Cambridge: Harvard University Press, 1931–35), Vol. 2, 758.

change significantly, and so on for any length of series. These puzzles are not unique to the frequency view of probability, however; they occur in any inductive context. Essentially the problem, wherever it occurs, is the same: what is the justification for extrapolating 'X *is* always the case' or 'X *is* the case 90% of the time' into 'X *will be* the case always or 90% of the time' or 'X is the case always or 90% of the time in *unobserved instances*'? This puzzle is the famous "problem of induction" and I will say no more about it now since the following chapter is devoted entirely to it.

Second, the inability to explain probability statements which are clearly about individual events certainly restricts the frequency theory. Some probability statements about individual events, to be sure, can be interpreted simply as elliptical ways of referring to relative frequencies. But this sort of analysis hardly applies to a statement like this, 'It is probable that even if Napoleon had been victorious at Waterloo, he would have been unable to remain Emperor of France for much longer,' since Napoleon and the battle of Waterloo are events which are unique and not repeatable. True, one might say there is a class of generals and a class of battles, to which Napoleon and Waterloo belong, etc., but you want to ask yourself seriously if this sort of reply does not strain the statistical concept at the heart of the frequency theory.

The Inductive Theory. This theory can be either a simple straightforward notion or a highly complex one. According to the simple version, the meaning of 'probability' is 'weight or amount of evidence confirming a hypothesis, theory, or statement.' Thus, a theory with much evidence is 'highly probable'; a theory with some evidence is 'more or less probable'; and a theory with little evidence is 'improbable.' On this version, the use of 'probable' is qualitative and unanalyzable but nonetheless important for that. It coincides simply with the logic of the confirmation of hypotheses which we examined in the first chapter. The probability of a hypothesis increases, but not in any quantitative way, when each additional consequence is confirmed and alternative hypotheses eliminated; decreases under the opposite condition; and remains constant while no new consequences are deduced from any of the rival hypotheses.

Some writers, however, have tried to make "weight" of evidence more than a metaphor; they have advanced an inductive theory of probability in which weight or amount of evidence of a theory receives a numerical value (in a way which Carnap discusses in his essay which follows), although this numerical value has a meaning quite different from the numerical ratios of the frequency theory. For example, "If the weather man were to venture to say that the probability of rain tomorrow was 4/10, he would not be describing a statistical fact but would simply mean that, should you bet on it raining tomorrow, you had better ask for odds of 4 to 6." [6]

Some scientists and philosophers, both in the past and in the present, have tried strenuously to eliminate, in one way or another, the logical theory of probability, whether it be conceived in a qualitative or quantitative way. All through the history of science and philosophy, people like Aristotle, Aquinas, Hobbes, Descartes, and Kant have insisted that scientific inference, contrary to our analysis in Chapter 1, is strictly valid, and hence scientific knowledge is not probable at all but *certainly true.* And through the nineteenth and twentieth centuries, philosophers like John Venn, Karl Popper, and Hans Reichenbach have insisted that any inductive theory of probability is gratuitous since the frequency theory already accounts for the use of 'probability' in statements like 'The probability of the

[6] Cf. Carnap, "Statistical and Inductive Probability," reprinted this volume, p. 269.

general theory of relativity is greater than it was thirty-five years ago.' Let us look, for a moment, at these two interesting claims.

Aristotle is a good example of one who insists that scientific inference is strictly valid and hence certainly true. We can reason about the stars and planets, he says, in the following way. Since we know that a light source at a great distance twinkles and a light source nearby is steady, and since we know that stars twinkle and planets do not, we know the stars are far away and the planets relatively nearby. We can, then, make this formal inference:

If the light of the planets is steady, then they are relatively near.
The light of the planets is steady.
___
The planets are relatively near.

This inference, unlike the confirmation of a hypothesis which we studied in Chapter 1, is valid. But Aristotle was no more satisfied with this inference than we would be. The trouble is this: the statement, 'If the light of the planets is steady, then they are relatively near,' is not a scientific hypothesis which is deductively elaborated. The hypothesis is 'The planets are relatively near' and its deductive consequence is 'so the light of the planets is steady.' So, Aristotle says, we must take as the first statement in this inference 'If the planets are relatively near, then their light is steady.'

If the planets are relatively near, then their light is steady.
Their light is steady.
___
The planets are relatively near.

This inference, however, is the pattern we displayed in Chapter 1; and since it is invalid it does not lead to certain truth and Aristotle thus needs to avoid it. The correct alternative, he believed, is this inference:

If the planets are relatively near, then their light is steady.
They are relatively near.
___
Their light is steady.

Unhappily, however, while this inference is valid and certainly true it is completely idle, since we need information not directly ascertainable — the nearness of the planets — in order to prove in the conclusion what was never in doubt, what is an obvious fact of direct experience, namely that the light of the planets is steady! Aristotle is left with a dilemma, indeed. If one has a valid inference either the 'If-then' statement is not the deductive elaboration of a hypothesis; or, if it is, then the conclusion is entirely pointless or gratuitous. Apparently, then, one must give up the idea that science is necessarily true and accept the logic of scientific inference presented in Chapter 1 and speak about the *probability* of scientific hypothesis.

The second move to eliminate the inductive theory of probability, you recall, was this: the theory is gratuitous since the frequency theory already accounts for the use of 'probability' in statements like 'The probability of the general theory of relativity is greater than it was thirty-five years ago.' Numerous ingenious methods have been used to prove this claim; yet, I think, for several reasons it is false. Peirce made one of these points quite nicely. We cannot, after all, pick universes out of a grab-bag and find in what proportion of them a law or theory holds good! Peirce, however, concluded that since the frequency theory cannot explain the use of 'probable' in reference to scientific theories, then this use is nonsense. But clearly we do so talk, and it is not apparent nonsense; in fact, it is only nonsense if one insists on stretching the frequency view to cover all the uses of 'probable.' But why do this? We had better restrict the theory to what it explains and admit that there are other legitimate meanings of 'probable.'

Another reason for insisting on the separateness of frequency and inductive statements of probability, it seems to me, is that evidence affects the two types of statements in very different ways. In inductive probability statements, evidence increases or decreases the probability, while in frequency statements evidence either confirms or changes the probability. For example, if a physicist should deduce a new consequence from the general theory of relativity, test it, and find it to hold in fact, we would say that this new confirming evidence increases the probability of the theory, while dis-confirming evidence – that is, a negative result – would decrease the probability. On the other hand, recall the frequency statement, 'The probability of a man surviving his thirty-first birthday is .945.' Here further statistical evidence about how many men live beyond their thirty-first birthdays does not increase or decrease the probability in question but simply either confirms or changes it. If the further evidence still approximates .945, then this evidence confirms the statement; if the evidence approximates, say, .900 instead, then the value of the original statement *changes* to this new number.

Conclusion. Out of this welter of claims and criticisms, what *can* one conclude? Well, of course, you will have to decide your own position after weighing what I have written and carefully reading the following essays – and even then you will have barely started on what is indeed a very complex topic. You may find it helpful, however, in doing your own thinking to know the climate of opinion of experts in this field. They have, by and large, dismissed the classical theory (except for several elements which have passed over into Carnap's inductive theory). Some of them accept the frequency theory only; some accept an inductive theory only; but others, not the least in number, accept both of the views, insisting that neither of these senses of 'probable' is reducible to the other.

In the following essays you will meet some of these experts. Pierre Simon, Marquis de Laplace, presents the *a priori* or classical theory in its most precise and definitive form. In addition to his definition of 'probability' he presents the first simple elements of the mathematical theory of probability (that is, how individual propositions are combined into more complex ones) which any philosophical theory of probability accepts. John Venn, one of the earliest proponents of the frequency theory, criticizes the classical view, while John W. Lenz points up some of the difficulties of the frequency view, particularly the problem of the individual case. Rudolph Carnap presents, in outline, his quantitative version of the inductive theory, and finally A. J. Ayer criticizes this quantitative version. In several of the essays, you will discover, Carnap's inductive theory of probability is sometimes called the "logical" theory, and the point of this latter designation is that the relationship between the evidence and the conclusion of a hypothesis, as Carnap conceives it, is analytical or "logical" – not empirical or factual.

Even after reading these essays, however, you may still have to reserve your opinion on the meaning of 'probability.' One of the criticisms of the frequency theory, you will recall, involved us in the problem of induction, and you will need to read the next chapter in order to judge the value of this criticism. That is, by the way, the habit of philosophical problems: they are forever running together in the most intimate fashion.

Probability and Its Principles

PIERRE SIMON, MARQUIS DE LAPLACE

Concerning Probability

All events, even those which on account of their insignificance do not seem to follow the great laws of nature, are a result of it just as necessarily as the revolutions of the sun. In ignorance of the ties which unite such events to the entire system of the universe, they have been made to depend upon final causes or upon hazard, according as they occur and are repeated with regularity, or appear without regard to order; but these imaginary causes have gradually receded with the widening bounds of knowledge and disappear entirely before sound philosophy, which sees in them only the expression of our ignorance of the true causes.

Present events are connected with preceding ones by a tie based upon the evident principle that a thing cannot occur without a cause which produces it. This axiom, known by the name of *the principle of sufficient reason,* extends even to actions which are considered indifferent; the freest will is unable without a determinative motive to give them birth; if we assume two positions with exactly similar circumstances and find that the will is active in the one and inactive in the other, we say that its choice is an effect without a cause. It is then, says Leibnitz, the blind chance of the Epicureans. The contrary opinion is an illusion of the mind, which, losing sight of the evasive reasons of the choice of the will in indifferent things, believes that choice is determined of itself and without motives.

We ought then to regard the present state of the universe as the effect of its anterior state and as the cause of the one which is to follow. Given for one instant an intelligence which could comprehend all the forces by which nature is animated and the respective situation of the beings who compose it – an intelligence sufficiently vast to submit these data to analysis – it would embrace in the same formula the movements of the greatest bodies of the universe and those of the lightest atom; for it, nothing would be uncertain and the future, as the past, would be present to its eyes. The human mind offers, in the perfection which it has been able to give to astronomy, a feeble idea of this intelligence. Its discoveries in mechanics and geometry, added to that of universal gravity, have enabled it to comprehend in the same analytical expressions the past and future states of the system of the world. Applying the same method to some other objects of its knowledge, it has succeeded in referring to general laws observed phenomena and in foreseeing those which given circumstances ought to produce. All these efforts in the search for truth tend to lead it back continually to the vast intelligence which we have just mentioned, but from which it will al-

From *A Philosophical Essay on Probabilities,* translated from the Sixth French Edition by F. W. Truscott and F. L. Emory, Chapters II and III.

ways remain infinitely removed. This tendency, peculiar to the human race, is that which renders it superior to animals; and their progress in this respect distinguishes nations and ages and constitutes their true glory.

Let us recall that formerly, and at no remote epoch, an unusual rain or an extreme drought, a comet having in train a very long tail, the eclipses, the aurora borealis, and in general all the unusual phenomena were regarded as so many signs of celestial wrath. Heaven was invoked in order to avert their baneful influence. No one prayed to have the planets and the sun arrested in their courses: observation had soon made apparent the futility of such prayers. But as these phenomena, occurring and disappearing at long intervals, seemed to oppose the order of nature, it was supposed that Heaven, irritated by the crimes of the earth, had created them to announce its vengeance. Thus the long tail of the comet of 1456 spread terror through Europe, already thrown into consternation by the rapid successes of the Turks, who had just overthrown the Lower Empire. This star after four revolutions has excited among us a very different interest. The knowledge of the laws of the system of the world acquired in the interval had dissipated the fears begotten by the ignorance of the true relationship of man to the universe; and Halley, having recognized the identity of this comet with those of the years 1531, 1607, and 1682, announced its next return for the end of the year 1758 or the beginning of the year 1759. The learned world awaited with impatience this return which was to confirm one of the greatest discoveries that have been made in the sciences, and fulfil the prediction of Seneca when he said, in speaking of the revolutions of those stars which fall from an enormous height: "The day will come when, by study pursued through several ages, the things now concealed will appear with evidence; and posterity will be astonished that truths so clear had escaped us." Clairaut then undertook to submit to analysis the perturbations which the comet had experienced by the action of the two great planets, Jupiter and Saturn; after immense calculations he fixed its next passage at the perihelion toward the beginning of April, 1759, which was actually verified by observation. The regularity which astronomy shows us in the movements of the comets doubtless exists also in all phenomena.

The curve described by a simple molecule of air or vapor is regulated in a manner just as certain as the planetary orbits; the only difference between them is that which comes from our ignorance.

Probability is relative, in part to this ignorance, in part to our knowledge. We know that of three or a greater number of events a single one ought to occur; but nothing induces us to believe that one of them will occur rather than the others. In this state of indecision it is impossible for us to announce their occurrence with certainty. It is, however, probable that one of these events, chosen at will, will not occur because we see several cases equally possible which exclude its occurrence, while only a single one favors it.

The theory of chance consists in reducing all the events of the same kind to a certain number of cases equally possible, that is to say, to such as we may be equally undecided about in regard to their existence, and in determining the number of cases favorable to the event whose probability is sought. The ratio of this number to that of all the cases possible is the measure of this probability, which is thus simply a fraction whose numerator is the number of favorable cases and whose denominator is the number of all the cases possible.

The preceding notion of probability supposes that, in increasing in the same ratio the number of favorable cases and that of all the cases possible, the probability remains the same. In order to convince ourselves let us take two urns, A and B, the first containing four white and two black balls, and the second containing only two white balls and one black one. We may imagine the two black balls of the first urn attached by a thread which breaks at the moment when one of them is seized in order to be drawn out, and the four white balls thus forming two similar systems. All the chances which will favor the seizure of one of the balls of the black system will lead to a black ball. If we conceive now that the threads which unite the balls do not break at all, it is clear that the number of possible chances will not change any more than that of the chances favorable to the extraction of the black balls; but two balls will be drawn from the urn at the same time; the probability of drawing a black ball from the urn A will then be the same as at first. But then we have obviously the case of urn B with the single difference that the three balls of this last urn would be replaced by three systems of two balls invariably connected.

When all the cases are favorable to an event the probability changes to certainty and its expression becomes equal to unity. Upon this condition, certainty and probability are comparable, although there may be an essential difference between the two states of the mind when a truth is rigorously demonstrated to it, or when it still perceives a small source of error.

In things which are only probable the difference of the data, which each man has in regard to them, is one of the principal causes of the diversity of opinions which prevail in regard to the same objects. Let us suppose, for example, that we have three urns, A, B, C, one of which contains only black balls while the two others contain only white balls; a ball is to be drawn from the urn C and the probability is demanded that this ball will be black. If we do not know which of the three urns contains black balls only, so that there is no reason to believe that it is C rather than B or A, these three hypotheses will appear equally possible, and since a black ball can be drawn only in the first hypothesis, the probability of drawing it is equal to one third. If it is known that the urn A contains white balls only, the indecision then extends only to the urns B and C, and the probability that the ball drawn from the urn C will be black is one half. Finally this probability changes to certainty if we are assured that the urns A and B contain white balls only.

It is thus that an incident related to a numerous assembly finds various degrees of credence, according to the extent of knowledge of the auditors. If the man who reports it is fully convinced of it and if, by his position and character, he inspires great confidence, his statement, however extraordinary it may be, will have for the auditors who lack information the same degree of probability as an ordinary statement made by the same man, and they will have entire faith in it. But if some one of them knows that the same incident is rejected by other equally trustworthy men, he will be in doubt and the incident will be discredited by the enlightened auditors, who will reject it whether it be in regard to facts well averred or the immutable laws of nature.

It is to the influence of the opinion of those whom the multitude judges best informed and to whom it has been accustomed to give its confidence in regard to the most important matters of life that the propagation of those errors is due which in times of ignorance have covered the face of the earth. Magic and astrology offer us two great examples. These errors inculcated in infancy, adopted without examination, and having for a basis only universal credence, have maintained themselves during a very long time; but at last the progress of science has destroyed them in the minds of enlightened men, whose opinion consequently has caused them to disappear even among the common people, through the power of imitation and habit which had so generally spread them abroad. This power, the richest resource of the moral world, establishes and conserves in a whole nation ideas entirely contrary to those which it upholds elsewhere with the same authority. What indulgence ought we not then to have for opinions different from ours, when this difference often depends only upon the various points of view where circumstances have placed us! Let us enlighten those whom we judge insufficiently instructed; but first let us examine critically our own opinions and weigh with impartiality their respective probabilities.

The difference of opinions depends, however, upon the manner in which the influence of known data is determined. The theory of probabilities holds to considerations so delicate that it is not surprising that with the same data two persons arrive at different results, especially in very complicated questions. Let us examine now the general principles of this theory.

The General Principles of the Calculus of Probabilities

First Principle. — The first of these principles is the definition itself of probability, which, as has been seen, is the ratio of the number of favorable cases to that of all the cases possible.

Second Principle. — But that supposes the various cases equally possible. If they are not so, we will determine first their respective possibilities, whose exact appreciation is one of the most delicate points of the theory of chance. Then the probability will be the sum of the possibilities of each favorable case. Let us illustrate this principle by an example.

Let us suppose that we throw into the air a large and very thin coin whose two large opposite faces, which we will call heads and tails, are perfectly similar. Let us find the probability of throwing heads at least one time in two throws. It is clear that four equally possible cases may arise, namely, heads at the first and at the second throw; heads at the first throw and tails at the second; tails at the first throw and heads at the second; finally, tails at both throws. The first three cases are favorable to the event whose probability is sought; consequently this probability is equal to $3/4$; so that it is a bet of three to one that heads will be thrown at least once in two throws.

We can count at this game only three different cases, namely, heads at the first throw, which dispenses with throwing a second time; tails at the first throw and heads at the second; finally, tails at the first and at the second throw. This would reduce the probability to $2/3$ if we should consider with d'Alembert these three cases as equally possible. But it is apparent that the probability of throwing heads at the first throw is $1/2$, while that of the two other cases is $1/4$, the first case being a simple event which corresponds to two events combined: heads at the first and at the second throw, and heads at the first throw, tails at the second. If we then, conforming to the second principle, add the possibility $1/2$ of heads at the first throw to the possibility $1/4$ of tails at the first throw and heads at the second, we shall have $3/4$ for the probability sought, which agrees with what is found in the supposition when we play the two throws. This supposition does not change at all the chance of that one who bets on this event; it simply serves to reduce the various cases to the cases equally possible.

Third Principle. — One of the most important points of the theory of probabilities and that which lends the most to illusions is the manner in which these probabilities increase or diminish by their mutual combination. If the events are independent of one another, the probability of their combined existence is the product of their respective probabilities. Thus the probability of throwing one ace with a single die is $1/6$; that of throwing two aces in throwing two dice at the same time is $1/36$. Each face of the one being able to combine with the six faces of the other, there are in fact thirty-six equally possible cases, among which one single case gives two aces. Generally the probability that a simple event in the same circumstances will occur consecutively a given number of times is equal to the probability of this simple event raised to the power indicated by this number. Having thus the successive powers of a fraction less than unity diminishing without ceasing, an event which depends upon a series of very great probabilities may become extremely improbable. Suppose then an incident be transmitted to us by twenty witnesses in such manner that the first has transmitted it to the second, the second to the third, and so on. Suppose again that the probability of each testimony be equal to the fraction $9/10$; that of the incident resulting from the testimonies will be less than $1/8$. We cannot better compare this diminution of the probability than with the extinction of the light of objects by the interposition of several pieces of glass. A relatively small number of pieces suffices to take away the view of an object that a single piece allows us to perceive in a distinct manner. The historians do not appear to have paid sufficient attention to this degradation of the probability of events when seen across a great number of successive generations; many historical events reputed as certain would be at least doubtful if they were submitted to this test.

In the purely mathematical sciences the most distant consequences participate in the certainty of the principle from which they are derived. In the applications of analysis to physics the results have all the certainty of facts or experiences. But in the moral sciences, where each inference is deduced from that which precedes it only in a probable manner, however probable these deductions may be, the chance of error increases with their number and ultimately surpasses the chance of truth in the consequences very remote from the principle.

Fourth Principle.—When two events depend upon each other, the probability of the compound event is the product of the probability of the first event and the probability that, this event having occurred, the second will occur. Thus in the preceding case of the three urns A, B, C, of which two contain only white balls and one contains only black balls, the probability of drawing a white ball from the urn C is $2/3$, since of the three urns only two contain balls of that color. But when a white ball has been drawn from the urn C, the indecision relative to that one of the urns which contains only black balls extends only to the urns A and B; the probability of drawing a white ball from the urn B is $1/2$; the product of $2/3$ by $1/2$, or $1/3$, is then the probability of drawing two white balls at one time from the urns B and C.

We see by this example the influence of past events upon the probability of future events. For the probability of drawing a white ball from the urn B, which primarily is $2/3$, becomes $1/2$ when a white ball has been drawn from the urn C; it would change to certainty if a black ball had been drawn from the same urn. We will determine this influence by means of the following principle, which is a corollary of the preceding one.

Fifth Principle.—If we calculate *a priori* the probability of the occurred event and the probability of an event composed of that one and a second one which is expected, the second probability divided by the first will be the probability of the event expected, drawn from the observed event.

Here is presented the question raised by some philosophers touching the influence of the past upon the probability of the future. Let us suppose at the play of heads and tails that heads has occurred oftener than tails. By this alone we shall be led to believe that in the constitution of the coin there is a secret cause which favors it. Thus in the conduct of life constant happiness is a proof of competency which should induce us to employ preferably happy persons. But if by the unreliability of circumstances we are constantly brought back to a state of absolute indecision; if, for example, we change the coin at each throw at the play of heads and tails, the past can shed no light upon the future and it would be absurd to take account of it. . . .

Difficulties of the Classical View of Probability

JOHN VENN

[Critique of the Concept of Equiprobability]

If Probability were only concerned with the kind of events which in practice are commonly made subjects of insurance, probably no other view than the [empirical] would ever have obtained credence. But the fact of most of its examples having been chosen from such things as dice and cards has infected the whole science with an *a priori* tendency, which has biassed the minds of its followers in other applications.

An opinion prevails that in certain cases we are able to determine beforehand what the series will be, and this with such certainty that the real basis of our calculation is not the series itself, but some *a priori* conditions on which the series depends. As I consider this opinion to be erroneous in fact, and likely to cause confusion in the theory of the subject, I will proceed to a detailed examination of it; first in its stronghold of games of chance, and then in some of its other places of occasional resort. From the celebrity of the writers who have maintained this view it could not be passed over in silence.

From *The Logic of Chance,* 1st edition, 1866, pp. 27–33, 60–75.

*4. Let us take a very simple example, that of tossing up a penny. Suppose that I am contemplating beforehand a succession of two throws; I clearly know that the only possible events are . . . H.H. H.T. T.H. T.T. So much is quite certain. We are moreover tolerably well convinced from experience that these events occur, in the long run, about equally often. This is admitted on all hands. But on the view against which I am contending it is asserted that we might have known the fact beforehand by principles which are applicable to an indefinite number of other and more complex cases. The form in which this view would generally be advanced is, that we are enabled to know beforehand that the four throws above mentioned are *equally likely*. This is asserted by almost every writer on the subject. To this I would ask, What is the meaning of the expression 'equally likely'? To such a question I think but two forms of reply are possible. The one of these would seek an explanation in the state of mind of the observer, the other would seek it in some characteristic of the things observed. (1) It might, for instance, be said on the one hand that what is meant is that

* [Paragraph numbers from original text. – *Ed.*]

the two events contemplated are equally easy to imagine, or, more accurately, that our expectation or belief in their occurrence is equal. We could hardly be content with this reply, for the further enquiry would then be urged, On what grounds do we believe this? What are the characteristics of events of which our expectation is equal? If we consented to give an answer to this further enquiry we should be led, I think, to the second form of reply to be noticed directly; if we did not consent we should be admitting that Probability was only a portion of Psychology, confined therefore to considering states of mind and not the external events to which they referred. We should be ceasing to make it a science of inference about things. (2) In the other form of reply the explanation of the phrase in question would be sought, not in a state of mind but in a quality of the things contemplated. It might give the following as the meaning, viz. that the events really would occur with equal frequency in the long run. The ground of this assertion would probably be found in past experience, and it would doubtless be impossible so to frame the answer as to exclude the notion of our belief altogether. But still there is a broad distinction between seeking the equality in the amount of our belief, as before, and in the frequency of occurrence of the events, as here; I am convinced that this second form of reply is the correct one, but it may easily be shewn that it is tantamount to abandoning the *a priori* theory, for it involves the admission that the real starting point of Probability is a sequence of events.

5. For *can* the assertion in this reply be made *a priori?* Those who say it can, have never, I think, fairly faced the difficulties which meet them. For the moment we begin to enquire seriously whether the penny will really do what is expected of it, we shall find that restrictions have to be introduced. In the first place the penny must be an ideal one, with its sides equal and fair. This restriction is perfectly intelligible; the study of solid geometry has enabled me to idealize a penny into a circular or cylindrical lamina. This restriction is always admitted, but it is the only one that is admitted, although it is only one condition out of several that combine towards the result. But this is not sufficient; there are other conditions. We must also idealize the 'randomness' of the throwing of the penny, which is a process that one feels rather at a loss to know how to set about performing. This is no idle subtlety; for will it be asserted that the heads and tails would get their fair chances supposing that, in the act of throwing, I were always to start the same side uppermost? Scarcely, I think; the difference, slight as it is, might become at last appreciable. Or if I persisted in starting with the two sides upwards alternately, would the long repetitions of the same side get *their* fair chance? Perhaps it will be replied that we are to think nothing at all about these matters, and all will come right. It may, and doubtless will, but this is falling back upon experience. For suppose, lastly, that the circumstances of nature or my bodily or mental constitution were such that the same side always *is* started uppermost; well, it will be replied, it would not then be a fair trial. I am convinced that if we press in this way for an answer to such enquiries, we shall find that these tacit restrictions on the *a priori* plan are really nothing else than a mode of securing an experimental result. They are only a way of saying, Let a series of actions be performed in such a way as to secure a sequence of a particular kind, viz. of the kind described in the last chapter.

The remarks above made will apply, of course, to most of the other common examples of chance; the throwing of dice, drawing of cards, of balls from bags, &c. In all these cases, if we scrutinize our language carefully, we shall find that the supposed *a priori* mode of stating the problem is little else than a compendious way of saying, Let means be taken for obtaining a given result.

Since, then, it is upon this result that our inferences ultimately rest, it seems to me simpler and more philosophical to appeal to it at once as the groundwork of our science.

6. It will be seen, by this time, how very narrow is the range of cases which the so-called *a priori* plan can be supposed to embrace. It is confined to games of chance, and can only be introduced there by the aid of many tacit restrictions. This alone would be conclusive against the theory of the subject being based upon it. The experimental plan, on the other hand, is of universal application. It would include the ordinary problems of games of chance, as well as those where the dice are loaded and the pence are not ideal, and also the indefinitely numerous applications of statistics to social phenomena and the facts of inanimate nature.

7. I quite admit the advantages of the *a priori* plan where it can be used. Without it chance problems could scarcely be set in examinations, and the science would be deprived of a certain neatness and independence which the common mode of treatment confers upon it. Moreover, in many cases it would be a real hardship to be debarred from appealing to it. We are often enabled, by geometrical and other considerations, to ascertain with tolerable accuracy what kind of a sequence of events we may look for, at a time when we are either without specific experience or should find it tedious to obtain it. Against this as a practical measure not a word of objection can be raised; I am only contending that it is not the simplest and most consistent way of studying the theory of the subject. We may use an artifice for obtaining the series, but it would be a great mistake to take anything but the series as the foundation of our rules.

[Critique of Probability as a Measure of Belief]

3. Let a penny be tossed up a very great many times; we may then be supposed to know for certain this fact (amongst many others) that in the long run head and tail will occur equally often. But suppose we consider only a moderate number of throws, or fewer still, and so continue limiting the number until we come down to three or two, or even one? We have as the extreme cases certainty or something undistinguishably near it, and utter uncertainty. Have we not, between these extremes, all gradations of belief? There is a large body of writers, including some of the most eminent authorities upon this subject, who reply that we are distinctly conscious of such a variation of the amount of our belief, and that this state of our minds can be measured and determined with almost the same accuracy as the external events to which they refer. The principal mathematical supporter of this view is Professor De Morgan, who has insisted strongly upon it in all his works on the subject. The clearest exposition of his opinions will be found in his Formal Logic, in which work he has made the view which we are now discussing the basis of his system. He holds that we have a certain amount of belief of every proposition which may be set before us, an amount which in its nature admits of determination, though we may practically find it difficult in any particular case to determine it. He considers, in fact, that Probability is a sort of sister science to Formal Logic, speaking of it in the following words: "I cannot understand why the study of the effect, which partial belief of the premises produces with respect to the conclusion, should be separated from that of the consequences of supposing the former to be absolutely true." In other words, there is a science — Formal Logic — which investigates the rules according to which one proposition can be necessarily inferred from another; corresponding with this there is a science which investigates the rules according to which the amount of our belief of one proposition varies with the amount of our belief of other propositions with which it is connected.

4. If this were the opinion of Professor De Morgan only, or even of mathematicians generally (and I believe that substantially the same opinion is adopted by all who have treated the subject mathematically), it might be objected that their peculiar studies had given them a bias towards discovering the distinctions and accuracy of numbers in matters into which these qualities are not commonly supposed to enter. But it must be observed that a professed logician, Archbishop Thomson, has to a considerable extent adopted the same opinion. In his work on the Laws of Thought he gives a distinct section to the treatment of what he calls 'Syllogisms of Chance.' He prefaces it with a statement that the substance of the section is extracted from the works of Professor De Morgan, and others who agree with Professor De Morgan; he also makes a quotation from Professor Donkin, with which he seems to agree, which declares that the subject matter of the science of Probability is 'quantity of belief.' I must confess, with all respect to the Archbishop, that this chapter has always appeared to me less acute than the rest of his work. I refer to it here only in order to show that the opinion now under discussion is by no means confined to mathematicians, but has been recognized and adopted by men who certainly cannot be charged with being subject to a mathematical bias.

5. Before proceeding to criticise this opinion I would make one remark upon it which has been constantly overlooked. It should be borne in mind that, even were this view of the subject not actually incorrect, it would nevertheless be insufficient for the purpose of a definition, inasmuch as variation of belief is not confined to Probability. It is a property with which that science is concerned, no doubt, but it is a property which meets us in many other directions as well. In every case in which we extend our inferences by Induction or Analogy, or depend upon the witness of others, or trust to our own memory of the past, or come to a conclusion through conflicting arguments, or even make a long and complicated deduction by mathematics or logic, we have a result of which we can scarcely feel as certain as of the premises from which it was obtained. In all these cases then we are conscious of varying quantities of belief, but are the laws according to which the belief is produced and varied the same? If they cannot be reduced to one harmonious scheme, if in fact they can be brought to nothing but a number of different schemes each with its own body of laws and rules, then it is in vain to endeavour to force them into one science.

This opinion is strengthened by observing that most of the writers who adopt the definition in question do practically dismiss from consideration most of the above-mentioned examples of diminution of belief, and confine their attention to classes of events which have the property . . . 'ignorance of the few, knowledge of the many.' It is quite true that considerable violence has to be done to some of these examples, by introducing exceedingly arbitrary suppositions into them, before they can be forced to assume a suitable form. But still I have little doubt that, if we carefully examine the language employed, we shall find that in almost every case assumptions are made which virtually imply that our knowledge of the individual is derived from propositions given in the typical form . . . [of a series]. This will be more fully proved when we come to consider some common misapplications of the science.

6. Even then, if the above-mentioned view of the subject were correct, it would yet be insufficient for the purpose of a definition; but it is at least very doubtful whether it is correct. Before we could properly assign to the belief side of the question the prominence given to it by Professor De Morgan and others, certainly before the science could be defined from that side, it would be necessary, I think, to establish the two following positions, against both of which strong objections can be brought.

(1) That our belief of every proposition is a thing which we can, strictly speaking, be said to measure. There must be a certain amount of it in every case, which we can realize somehow in consciousness and refer to some standard so as to pronounce upon its value.

(2) That the value thus apprehended is the correct one according to the theory, viz. that it is the exact fraction of full conviction that it should be. This statement will perhaps seem somewhat obscure at first; it will be explained presently.

7. (I) Now, in the first place, as regards the difficulty of obtaining any measure of the amount of our belief. One source of this difficulty is too obvious to have escaped notice; this is the disturbing influence produced on the quantity of belief by any strong emotion or passion. A deep interest in the matter at stake, whether it excite hope or fear, plays great havoc with the belief-meter, so that we must assume the mind to be quite unimpassioned in weighing the evidence. This is noticed and acknowledged by Laplace and others; but these writers seem to assume it to be the only source of error, and also to be of comparative unimportance. Even if it were the only source of error I cannot see that it would be unimportant. We experience hope or fear in so very many instances, that to omit such influences from consideration would be almost equivalent to saying that whilst we profess to consider the whole quantity of our belief we will in reality consider only a portion of it. Very strong feelings are, of course, exceptional, but we should nevertheless find that the emotional element, in some form or other, makes itself felt on almost every occasion. It is very seldom that we cannot speak of our surprise or expectation in reference to any particular event. Both of these expressions, but especially the former, seem to point to something more than mere belief. I know that the word 'expectation' is generally defined in treatises on Probability as equivalent to belief; but I doubt whether any one who attends to the popular use of the terms would admit that they were exactly synonymous. Be this however as it may, the emotional element is present upon almost every occasion, and its disturbing influence therefore is constantly at work.

8. Another cause, which co-operates with the former, is to be found in the extreme complexity and variety of the evidence on which our belief of any proposition depends. Hence it results that our belief is one of the most fugitive and variable things possible, so that we can scarcely ever get sufficiently clear hold of it to measure it. This is not confined to the times when our minds are in a turmoil of excitement through hope or fear. In our calmest moments we shall find it no easy thing to give a precise answer to the question, how firmly do I hold this or that belief? There may be one or two prominent arguments in its favour, and one or two corresponding objections against it, but this is far from comprising all the causes by which our state of belief is produced. Because such reasons as these are all that can be practically introduced into oral or written controversies, we must not conclude that it is by these only that our conviction is influenced. On the contrary, our conviction generally rests upon a sort of chaotic basis composed of an infinite number of inferences and analogies of every description, and these moreover distorted by our state of feeling at the time, dimmed by the degree of our recollection of them afterwards, and probably received from time to time with varying force according to the way in which they happen to combine at the moment. To borrow a striking illustration from Abraham Tucker, the substructure of our convictions is not so much to be compared to the solid foundations of an ordinary building, as to the piles of the houses of Rotterdam which rest somehow in a deep bed of soft mud. They bear their weight securely enough, but it would not be easy to point out accurately the dependence of the different

parts upon one another. Directly we begin to think of the amount of our belief, we have to think of the arguments by which it is produced – in fact, these arguments will intrude themselves without our choice. As each in turn flashes through the mind, it modifies the strength of our conviction; we are like a person listening to the confused hubbub of a crowd, where there is always something arbitrary in the particular sound we choose to listen to. There may be reasons enough to suffice abundantly for our ultimate choice, but on examination we shall find that they are by no means apprehended with the same force at different times. The belief produced by some strong argument may be very decisive at the moment, but it will often begin to diminish when the argument is not actually before the mind. It is like being dazzled by a strong light; the impression still remains, but begins almost immediately to fade away. I think that this is the case, however we try to limit the sources of our conviction.

9. (II) But supposing that it were possible to strike a sort of average of this fluctuating state, should we find this average to be of the amount assigned by theory? In other words, is our natural belief in the happening of two different events in direct proportion to the frequency with which those events happen in the long run? There is a lottery with 100 tickets and ten prizes; is a man's belief that he will get a prize fairly represented by one-tenth of certainty? The mere reference to a lottery should be sufficient to disprove this. Lotteries have flourished at all times, and have never failed to be abundantly supported, in spite of the most perfect conviction, on the part of many of those who put into them, that in the long run all will lose. Deductions should undoubtedly be made for those who act from superstitious motives, from belief in omens, dreams, &c. But apart from these, and supposing any one to come fortified by all that mathematics can do for him, I cannot believe that his natural impressions about single events would be always what they should be according to theory. Are there many who can honestly declare that they would have no desire to buy a single ticket? They would probably say to themselves that the sum they paid away was nothing worth mentioning to lose, and that there was a chance of gaining a great deal; in other words, they are not apportioning their belief in the way that theory assigns.

What bears out this view is, that the same persons who would act in this way in single instances, would often not think of doing so in any but single instances. In other words, the natural tendency is to attribute too great an amount of belief where it is or should be small; i.e. to disparage the risk in proportion to the contingent advantage. They would very likely, when argued with, attach disparaging epithets to this state of feeling by calling it an unaccountable fascination, or something of that kind, but of its existence there can be little doubt. I am speaking now of what is the natural tendency of our minds, not of that into which they may at length be disciplined by education and thought. If, however, educated persons have succeeded for the most part in controlling this tendency in games of chance, the 'spirit of reckless speculation' has scarcely yet been banished from commerce. On examination, this tendency will be found, I think, so universal in all ages, ranks, and dispositions, that it would be inadmissible to neglect it in order to bring our supposed instincts more closely into accordance with the commonly received theories of Probability.

10. There is another aspect of this question which has been often overlooked, but which seems to deserve some attention. Granted that we have an instinct of credence, why should it be assumed that it must be just of that intensity which subsequent experience will justify? Our instincts are implanted in us by our Creator, and are intended to act immediately and unconsciously.

They are, however, subject to control, and have to be brought into accordance with what we believe to be true and right. In other departments of psychology we do not assume that every spontaneous prompting of nature is to be left just as we find it, or even that on the average, omitting individual variations, it is set at that pitch that will be found in the end to be the best when we come to think about it and assign it its rules. Take, for example, the case of resentment. Here we have an instinctive tendency, and one that on the whole is good in its results. But moralists are agreed that almost all our efforts at self-control are to be directed towards subduing it and keeping it in its right direction. It is assumed to be given as a sort of rough protection, and to be set, if one might so express oneself, at too high a pitch to be deliberately and consciously acted on in society. May not something of this kind be the case also with our belief? I only make a passing reference to this point here, as on the theory of Probability adopted in this work it does not seem to be at all material to the science. But it seems a strong argument against the expediency of commencing the study of the science from the subjective side, or even of assigning any great degree of prominence to this side.

That men *do* not believe in exact accordance with this theory must have struck almost every one, but this has probably been considered as mere exception and irregularity; the assumption being made that on the average, and in far the majority of cases, they do so believe. As stated above, I think it very doubtful whether the tendency which has just been discussed is not so universal that it might with far more propriety be called the law than the exception. And it may be better that it should be so: many good results may follow from that cheerful disposition which induces a man sometimes to go on trying after some great good, the chance of which he overvalues. He will keep on through trouble and disappointment, without serious harm perhaps, when the cool and calculating bystander sees plainly that his 'measure of belief' is much higher than it should be. So, too, the tendency also so common, of underrating the chance of a great evil may also work for good. To many men death might be looked upon as an almost infinite evil, at least they would so regard it themselves; suppose they kept this contingency constantly before them at its right value, how would it be possible to get through the practical work of life? Men would be stopping indoors because if they went out they might be murdered or bitten by a mad dog. I am not advocating a return to our instincts; when we have once reached the critical and conscious state, it is not possible to do so; but it should be noticed that the advantage gained by correcting them is at best but a balanced one. What is most to our present purpose, it suggests the inexpediency of attempting to found an exact theory on what may afterwards prove to be a mere instinct, unauthorized in its full extent by experience.

11. It may be replied, that though people, as a matter of fact, do not apportion belief in this exact way, yet they *ought* to do so. The purport of this remark will be examined presently; I will only say here that it grants all that I am contending for. For it admits that the degree of our belief is capable of modification, and may need it. But in accordance with what is the belief to be modified? obviously in accordance with experience; it cannot be trusted to by itself, but the fraction at which it is to be rated must be determined by the comparative frequency of the events to which it refers. Experience, then, furnishing the standard, it is surely most reasonable to start from this experience, and to found the theory of our process upon it.

If we do not do this it should be observed that we are detaching Probability altogether from the study of things external to us, and making it nothing else in effect than a portion of Psychology. If we refuse to be controlled by experience, but confine our attention to the laws according to which belief is naturally or instinctively compounded and distributed in our minds, we have no right then to appeal to experience afterwards even for illustrations, unless under the express understanding that we do not guarantee its accuracy. Our belief in some single events, for example, might be correct, and yet that in a compound of several (if derived merely from our instinctive laws of belief) very possibly might not be correct, but might lead us to error if we determined to act upon it. Even if the two were in accordance, this accordance would have to be proved, which would lead us round, by what I cannot but think a circuitous process, to the point which has been already chosen for commencing with.

12. Professor De Morgan seems to imply that the doctrine criticized above finds its justification from the analogy of Formal Logic. I confess I cannot see much force in the analogy. Formal Logic is based upon the assumption that there are laws of mind as distinguished from laws of things, and that these laws of mind can be ascertained and studied without taking into account their reference to any particular object. But to support this assumption a postulate has to be claimed, or else a consequence faced. The postulate is, that the laws of the things are so far in harmony with those of our minds that we may be certain that any exercise of our minds will not lead us into contradictions in practice. If this postulate be not granted we must then be prepared to brave any consequences that may follow from a want of such harmony. It is supposable, as some logicians seem ready to admit, that the laws of matter should be defiantly at variance with those of mind. So much the worse for us, but we cannot help it; we must go on thinking in accordance with our laws, for they are unhappily fixed for ever and invariable, and we must be content to take the consequences. But, as was briefly stated in § 11, no such distinction can be drawn in the case of laws of belief as we find them in Probability. Our instincts of credence are unquestionably in frequent hostility with experience; and what do we do then? We simply modify the instincts into accordance with the things. We are constantly performing this practice, and no cultivated mind would find it possible to do anything else. No man would think of divorcing his belief from the things on which it was exercised, or of thinking that the former had anything else to do than to follow the lead of the latter. Whatever then may be the claims of Formal Logic to rank as a separate science, it cannot, I think, furnish any support to the theory of Probability as conceived by some mathematicians.

13. I have examined the doctrine in question with a minuteness which may seem tedious, but in consequence of the eminence of its supporters it would have been presumptuous to have rejected it without the strongest grounds. The objections which have just been urged might be summarized as follows; — the amount of our belief of any given proposition, supposing it to be in its nature capable of determination (which is extremely doubtful), depends upon a great variety of causes, of which statistical frequency, — the subject of Probability — is but one. That even if we confine our attention to this one cause, the natural amount of our belief is not necessarily what theory would assign, but has to be checked by appeal to experience. The subjective side of Probability therefore, though very interesting and well deserving of examination, seems a mere appendage of the objective, and affords in itself no safe ground for a science of inference.

The Frequency Theory of Probability

JOHN W. LENZ

The frequency interpretation of probability is far from new. It is already suggested by Aristotle's remarks that probable events are those which happen for the most part. Only in recent times, however, has a succession of writers (for example, Venn, v. Mises, and Reichenbach) developed this interpretation into a systematic theory.[1] Since Reichenbach has carried this development the furthest, I shall usually refer to his views in the critical discussion that follows.

1. The Frequency Interpretation

The essence of the frequency interpretation can be easily seen from a consideration of the following simple example. Suppose that a sympathetic nurse attempts to calm a prospective father by remarking, "The probability of twins is only $\frac{1}{87}$." The frequentist interprets the nurse as asserting that one birth in 87 results in twins. More generally, the frequentist interprets the probability of A's being B's as the relative frequency with which things that are A are also B. The numerical value of such probabilities is m/n, where n is the number of A's and m is the number of A's that are B's.

A more precise indication of the frequency interpretation can be obtained from noting what would verify or refute one's claim that the probability of A's being B's is, say, $\frac{1}{2}$. The observation of 10 A's, of which only three were B's, would certainly not refute this claim, for the claim is that "in the long run" the relative frequency with which A's are B's is $\frac{1}{2}$. On the other hand, if in the long run, that is, as one observed more and more A's, the frequency with which A's are B's differs less and less from the value $\frac{1}{2}$, one would regard the above claim as established. However, such phrases as "in the long run" are imprecise, and any definition employing them would not be subject to exact mathematical treatment. Accordingly frequentists such as Reichenbach "idealize" the definition as follows: the probability of A's being B's is defined as the limit of the fraction m/n (where n is the number of A's and m the number of A's that are B's) as m approaches infinity. The non-mathematical reader can be assured that nothing philosophically important hangs on the exact "mathematical" way of putting this definition.[2]

It is important, rather, that we note the essential features of probability statements when interpreted along frequentist lines. 1) Probability statements assert the relative

[1] John Venn, *The Logic of Chance* (London, 1866). Richard von Mises, *Probability, Statistics, and Truth* (New York, 1939). Hans Reichenbach, *Theory of Probability* (Berkeley, 1949). *Experience and Prediction* (Chicago, 1938).

[2] A more complete but still simple explanation of the frequency interpretation can be found in Ernest Nagel, *Principles of the Theory of Probability* (Chicago, 1939), pp. 19–26.

frequency of the members of two *classes* of things. 2) Probability statements are, therefore, factual claims. 3) Probability statements are, moreover, predictive in their force, for a statement about "long run" relative frequencies must be based upon the "shorter run" relative frequencies that have been observed. In all three ways they differ from probability statements as interpreted by a logical theorist such as Carnap.[3]

Before turning our attention to the merits of the frequency interpretation I want to point out one more thing. Frequentists need not, as Venn did, limit themselves to speaking about the relative frequency of two classes of *events.* Very significantly they can talk about the frequency with which certain statements are true. They may, for example, speak about the relative frequency with which hypotheses based upon certain methodological rules are true, and thus be able to speak of the probable reliability of these methods. To take just one example, they may speak of the relative frequency with which statistical hypotheses made on the basis of small samples are true. Since statistical hypotheses are probability statements, the frequentist can in this way speak about the probability of probability statements being true. He can allow a whole "hierarchy" of probabilities of different levels. As we shall see, this is extremely important to remember when we consider some of the standard objections against the frequency interpretation.

2. Types of Criticism

The frequency interpretation has many virtues. It has enabled frequentists to give a complex and useful mathematical treatment of the subject of probability. Reichenbach is able to show that given the frequency interpretation, the commonly accepted axioms of the probability calculus are all logically true. Nonetheless, the frequentist faces many serious objections.[4]

These objections may be divided into two types. One type challenges the frequentist's claim to be explicating the concept of probability as actually employed in science and daily life. Another challenges what may be called the assertability of probability statements when given the frequency interpretation. These two kinds of objection are not unrelated, as we shall see, but I shall make use of this convenient distinction in ordering the many objections we shall consider. I shall first discuss objections of type one.

It must be said immediately that Reichenbach, at least to some extent, does not claim to be analyzing "probability" in all its many uses. He claims, rather, to be saying how "probability" *should* be employed in any "rational reconstruction" of human knowledge. Thus, he is ready to challenge the force of objections of the first kind. My own view is that we need neither over-emphasize nor under-emphasize the importance of such objections. It is surely important to see to what extent the frequency interpretation does or does not fit the ordinary employment of "probability" in science and every day living. However, two additional points must also be made. First, we must be careful to see whether certain uses of "probability" which, prima facie, the frequency interpretation does not fit can in fact be assimilated to it. Secondly, we must ascertain if those uses it does not fit are themselves defensible.

3 Cf. Rudolf Carnap, "The Two Concepts of Probability," contained in *Readings in Philosophical Analysis,* ed. H. Feigl and W. Sellars (New York, 1949).

4 A good discussion of the frequency theory can be found in "A Symposium on Probability," *Philosophy and Phenomenological Research,* 1945 and 1946. This contains comments on the frequency interpretation by D. Williams, E. Nagel, H. Margenau, G. Bergmann, and F. Kaufman, among others. The articles by Nagel are especially important. Another good critical discussion of the frequency interpretation is Nagel's "Probability and the Theory of Knowledge," contained in *Sovereign Reason* (Glencoe, Illinois, 1954), pp. 225–265.

3. Short Run Frequencies

There is an obvious objection to Reichenbach's definition of probability. I do not regard it as a crucial one, but since many critics have offered it, I shall consider it right off. The objection is that in many, if not most cases, one does not wish to talk about relative frequencies in the very long run. (In technical terms, one does not wish to speak of the limit of the relative frequency in an infinite series of events.) For example, suppose two insurance company executives wish, in order to set insurance rates, to determine the probability of healthy male Americans of the age 32 surviving to the age 60. Here it would be fanciful to suppose that the insurance executives are concerned with the limit of m/n as n approaches infinity (where n would be the number of healthy male Americans 32 years old and m would be the number of healthy male Americans 32 years old who survive to the age 60). The insurance executives are only concerned with the relative frequency m/n where n is fairly large, perhaps the number of healthy male Americans who reach the age 32 within the next 50 years or so.

Two points can be made in reply to this objection. First, it is not true that this objection is of unlimited applicability. It is plausible to suppose that physicists, in their formulation of statistical laws, use the term "probability" in a way that exactly fits Reichenbach's definition. Physicists, after all, are concerned to state laws "that hold for all time." Second, Reichenbach's definition can easily be amended to fit examples like that involving the insurance executives. One could define the probability of A's being B's as m/n (where n is the number of A's and m is the number of A's that are B's) where n is large enough for our purposes. However, it must be pointed out that, while this emendation is easily made, it is made at the price of destroying the mathematical simplicity and elegance of the frequency theory. This, however, does not seem to me to be too serious; one could regard Reichenbach's definition as simply an "idealization" of our more usual employment of the concept of probability. Accordingly, I conclude that this first objection to the frequency interpretation can be answered satisfactorily.

4. Probabilities Do Not Refer to Relative Frequencies

A second more serious objection to the frequency interpretation has also been made by many writers. I shall consider Toulmin's most recent version of it. Toulmin claims that "probability" (and its cognates "probably," "probable," etc.) [5] are never used to speak about relative frequencies. Toulmin claims that, on the contrary, "probability" and its cognates are used to *guard* predictions, as when the weather man says, "probably it will rain tomorrow."

The extreme claim of Toulmin's that "probability" never refers to relative frequencies must, as our previous discussion already shows, be rejected. It is perfectly respectable for a biologist to say, "The probability of twins is 1/87" and mean by this that in the long run approximately 1 out of 87 births results in twins.

However, rejecting Toulmin's extreme claim does not refute more modest objections to the frequency interpretation. It may be that this interpretation does not fit all justifiable uses of "probability." It is an interesting question, for example, whether the frequentist can in fact assimilate the use Toulmin emphasizes, that of guarding our predictions. It must be pointed out, however, that if it turns out, as we examine such questions, that the frequency interpretation does not fit all justifiable uses of "probability" it does not follow that it is a completely worthless interpretation. As we have already seen, it

[5] Stephen Toulmin, *The Uses of Argument* (Cambridge, 1958), p. 79.

does fit at least one very important type of probability statement. Sophisticated logical theorists such as Carnap would be the first to point this out.

5. The Single Case

Another traditional objection to the frequency interpretation is its alleged inability to speak of probabilities of single events. An example will make this objection clear. When the frequentist speaks of the probability of American marriages ending in divorce as 1/7, he is speaking about the relative frequency of the members of two classes of events. He does not speak specifically about the probability of this or that particular marriage breaking up, as, it seems, we often do. The question in general is: can the frequency interpretation assimilate such statements?

The logical theory advocated by Carnap has no difficulty in speaking about "probabilities of single events." It allows one to say that the hypothesis, "This particular marriage will end in divorce" is, on the given evidence, confirmed to such and such a degree. The frequency theory must deny that it makes sense to speak of the probability of single events unless this is an elliptical way of speaking about the relative frequency of the members of two classes of events. Here, it would seem, the logical theorist has the nod over the frequentist.

However, the frequentist can attempt to show how in an indirect way one can in fact speak about the probability of a single event. This answer takes us into an extremely important aspect of Reichenbach's theory of probability, his concept of weight. Suppose that an insurance company must decide whether to insure a relatively healthy American man who is 32 years old. Suppose further that the insurance company believes that the probability of such men living to the age 60 is 9/10. It may then predict, says Reichenbach, that this man will survive to the age 60. It could add, Reichenbach says further, that the weight of this prediction, or wager, is 9/10, meaning by this that 9/10 of such predictions will be true. Thus weight here is interpreted essentially as the frequency with which predictions of a certain type are true, and thus the concept of weight is given a frequency interpretation. Reichenbach's reply to the single case objection is that, while we cannot directly speak of the probability of a single event, we can make predictions concerning single events and then speak of the weight of such predictions. Reichenbach claims that this answer is sufficient in view of our actual purposes.

This answer to the problem of the single case raises many issues, some of which I shall discuss in connection with another objection. At this point I shall discuss only one difficulty that is especially relevant here. This is the so-called problem of choosing the best "reference class" in which to place the single event in question. Let us go back to the insurance company that is trying to decide whether it ought to insure a particular man, say John Jones, who is a relatively healthy American male 32 years old. Now the probability of American males living to the age 60 no doubt differs from the probability of 32 year old American males living to the age 60, and both of these probabilities will in turn differ from the probability of relatively healthy American males aged 32 living to the age 60. The question is: which of these probabilities shall we make use of in making our wagers about John Jones' surviving till the age 60? The frequentist will answer that we should choose the last mentioned probability since it makes use of the most information we have about Jones. However, the frequentist cannot say that in general we should make use of the most information we have about Jones. Let us assume that John Jones has only 9 fingers. We cannot make use of this information because we have no reliable statistics about the relative frequency with which nine fingered men survive to the age 60. The general rule must be, therefore, to make use of the most information about a single event so long as we are able to make reliable probability statements. The general lines of this answer are undoubtedly correct; at least it is the best answer that the frequentist can give. But it is important to note that what will be the best predictions we can make concerning single events will vary with the state of our knowledge.[6]

6. Guarding Predictions

Let us now examine Toulmin's claim that words such as "probably," "likely" are used to guard predictions. I think it is evident that from what was said concerning the objection of the single case that Reichenbach can, in all essential ways, assimilate this use to the frequency interpretation. Consider, for example, Toulmin's favorite case, the weather man's saying, "Probably it will rain tomorrow." The frequentist could say that the weather man was not only predicting rain but saying that this prediction had a relatively high weight. In saying the latter the weather man would not be telling us to expect that all such predictions are correct, but only a high percentage of them. Surely this is the direct way of guarding one's predictions.[7]

7. Probability as Degree of Evidential Support

We come now to what I consider to be the most crucial objection to Reichenbach's claim that all probability statements can be interpreted along frequentist lines. We often say such things as, "On the basis of the present evidence, the hypothesis that Shakespeare wrote Hamlet is highly probable," "Relative to the evidence then available, Newton's law of universal gravitation was highly probable," "In the light of new evidence, the theory of probability is more probable than before." Writers such as Carnap have suggested that such probability statements assert a certain relation between a hypothesis and given evidence, namely, the degree to which the evidence supports or confirms the hypothesis. Carnap has further claimed that the concept of probability employed here is essentially different from that given by the frequency interpretation. This objection, in my opinion, must be handled very carefully.[8]

In a sense this objection is but a generalized version of the objection that the frequency interpretation cannot handle probabilities about single events, and much of what was said concerning that objection is again relevant here. We saw, for example, that while the frequentist could not speak directly about probabilities of single events, he could speak about the weight of predictions concerning single events, where weight was interpreted as the truth frequency of such predictions. The frequentist's reply to this latest objection would be simply that "degree of evidential support" is to be equated with this notion of weight. His reply would be that to speak of certain evidence highly confirming a hypothesis about a single event is to speak about the frequency with which such hypotheses based upon such evidence are true.

The frequentist could generalize this claim to say that whenever we speak about the degree to which evidence confirms a hypothesis, we are saying that this hypothesis has a certain weight. Let us consider another example. Suppose that we are considering the general hypothesis that all smokers will contract lung cancer. And suppose that our

6 Reichenbach, *Theory of Probability*, pp. 366–378; *Experience and Prediction*, pp. 297–319. A good discussion of Reichenbach's concept of weight and its application to the problem of the single case can be found in Nagel's "Probability and the Theory of Knowledge," contained in *Sovereign Reason*, pp. 228–248.

7 Toulmin admits that we expect a weather man who repeatedly predicts "Probably it will rain tomorrow" to be right a high proportion of times.

8 Cf. Carnap's "Two Concepts of Probability."

evidence is that we have observed three smokers from Los Angeles and have found that all three have contracted lung cancer. Relative to this evidence, surely, the general hypothesis is confirmed only to a small degree. The frequentist would take this to mean that the truth frequency of general hypotheses made on the basis of small "biased" samples was very low.

To what extent the frequentist can assimilate all such statements about evidential support is, in my opinion, a very complex question. I surely cannot settle the matter in this paper. It must be pointed out, however, that so far no frequentist has shown that this is possible in all cases. And it must be pointed out, too, that in principle it seems implausible to suppose that it is. Consider the statement, "Upon the latest evidence, the theory of relativity is highly confirmed." Does the frequentist really believe that this statement asserts that the truth frequency of such hypotheses based upon such evidence is very high? How shall we delineate the class of such hypotheses, and where shall we find reliable statistics upon which we could establish the truth frequency of such hypotheses? Here the frequentist's way of trying to assimilate statements asserting a degree of confirmation seems little more than an *ad hoc* suggestion with no ring of plausibility.

In any case Carnap can point out that there remains a radical difference between *his* concept of degree of confirmation and the concept of weight. On his interpretation statements asserting a degree of confirmation are logically true and, thus, do not predict anything at all, whereas statements asserting weights predict something, namely, the truth frequency of predictions or hypotheses. I myself think that so interpreted statements asserting a degree of confirmation cannot be assimilated to the frequency view. Let me say more cautiously, that *given* a good definition of "degree of confirmation" statements asserting degrees of evidential support can be obtained purely logically, whereas statements asserting that a prediction has a certain weight are themselves predictions and thus must be established inductively. However, two things more must be said. First, there is the difficult question as to how such a definition of degree of confirmation can be established.[9] Secondly, there is the further difficult question as to whether statements that are established purely logically can ever be good guides to life. But to discuss these questions would take us into a full discussion of the logical theory itself.

8. The Assertability of Probability Statements

All the objections so far have concerned the degree to which the frequency interpretation can assimilate "probability" as actually employed in science and daily life. We turn now to the question of the assertability of probability statements when given the frequency interpretation. On the frequentist's own admission, this is a very serious problem confronting him.

The problem as to whether we are ever justified in asserting probability statements when interpreted along frequentist lines arises in this way. Such probability statements are always factual statements, purporting to describe the world. They are, moreover, predictive in character; they assert that certain relative frequencies will obtain. While such predictions are based upon empirical evidence, namely, observed relative frequencies, they "go beyond" that evidence. The question is: what justification do we have for making such statements?

Frequentists have at times seemed to think

[9] Cf. Carnap's "Statistical and Inductive Probability," the next article in this volume; see p. 269. For a more thorough statement of the problem see Rudolf Carnap, *Continuum of Inductive Methods* (Chicago, 1952). For a critical examination of Carnap's solution and a further amplification of my point here see John Lenz, "Carnap on Defining 'Degree of Confirmation'," *Philosophy of Science,* July, 1956, pp. 230–236.

that this problem can be solved by the use of second order probabilities. As we have seen, the frequentist can speak of the probability of a probability statement being true. Frequentists have at times seemed to say that, therefore, while we cannot give any assurance of the truth of probability statements, we can always assess the probability of their being true. This answer, however, does not solve the problem; it only postpones having to raise it. As we have seen, "second order" probability statements are themselves predictive; while based upon observed evidence, namely, the observed truth frequency of predictions, they go beyond it. Thus, the problem of the assertability of probability statements simply occurs at the higher level.

The logical theorist is ready to step in at this point to say that the frequentist needs to supplement his theory with the notion of degree of confirmation. In that case we could say that probability statements, while not known to be true, are at least confirmed to such and such a degree. This answer involves difficulties of its own, but in any case it cannot be given by the thoroughgoing frequentist who has denied the need or validity of the concept of degree of confirmation.

The frequentist has another way out, one which Reichenbach himself takes, but this solution only raises further difficulties. Reichenbach, unlike many other frequentists, agrees that the frequency theory of probability must postulate some inductive rule, by means of which one can make predictions about long run relative frequencies on the basis of the short run relative frequencies that are observed. Reichenbach admits, furthermore, that such a rule of induction stands in need of justification.[10] Thus, Reichenbach solves the problem of the assertability of frequency probability statements only at the cost of facing a more difficult one, the infamous problem of justifying induction.

[10] Reichenbach's own "pragmatic" justification of induction is contained in *Theory of Probability,* pp. 469–482. For a critical examination of this justification see John Lenz, "The Pragmatic Justification of Induction," printed in this volume.

Statistical and Inductive Probability

RUDOLF CARNAP

If you ask a scientist whether the term 'probability' as used in science has always the same meaning, you will find a curious situation. Practically everyone will say that there is only one scientific meaning; but when you ask that it be stated, two different answers will come forth. The majority will refer to the concept of probability used in mathematical statistics and its scientific applications. However, there is a minority of those who regard a certain non-statistical

Pamphlet published by The Galois Institute of Mathematics and Art, Brooklyn, N.Y., 1955. Reprinted by permission of the author and the publisher.

concept as the only scientific concept of probability. Since either side holds that its concept is the only correct one, neither seems willing to relinquish the term 'probability.' Finally, there are a few people — and among them this author — who believe that an unbiased examination must come to the conclusion that both concepts are necessary for science, though in different contexts.

I will now explain both concepts — distinguishing them as 'statistical probability' and 'inductive probability' — and indicate their different functions in science. We shall see, incidentally, that the inductive concept, now advocated by a heretic minority, is not a new invention of the twentieth century, but was the prevailing one in an earlier period and only forgotten later on.

The *statistical concept of probability* is well known to all those who apply in their scientific work the customary methods of mathematical statistics. In this field, exact methods for calculations employing statistical probability are developed and rules for its application are given. In the simplest cases, probability in this sense means the relative frequency with which a certain kind of event occurs within a given reference class, customarily called the "population." Thus, the statement "The probability that an inhabitant of the United States belongs to blood group A is p" means that a fraction p of the inhabitants belongs to this group. Sometimes a statement of statistical probability refers, not to an actually existing or observed frequency, but to a potential one, i.e. to a frequency that would occur under certain specifiable circumstances. Suppose, for example, a physicist carefully examines a newly made die and finds it is a geometrically perfect and materially homogeneous cube. He may then assert that the probability of obtaining an ace by a throw of this die is $1/6$. This means that *if* a sufficiently long series of throws with this die were made, the relative frequency of aces would be $1/6$. Thus, the probability statement here refers to a potential frequency rather than to an actual one. Indeed, if the die were destroyed before any throws were made, the assertion would still be valid. Exactly speaking, the statement refers to the physical microstate of the die; without specifying its details (which presumably are not known), it is characterized as being such that certain results would be obtained if the die were subjected to certain experimental procedures. Thus the statistical concept of probability is not essentially different from other disposition concepts which characterize the objective state of a thing by describing reactions to experimental conditions, as, for example, the I.Q. of a person, the elasticity of a material object, etc.

Inductive probability occurs in contexts of another kind; it is ascribed to a hypothesis with respect to a body of evidence. The hypothesis may be any statement concerning unknown facts, say, a prediction of a future event, e.g., tomorrow's weather or the outcome of a planned experiment or of a presidential election, or a presumption concerning the unobserved cause of an observed event. Any set of known or assumed facts may serve as evidence; it consists usually in results of observations which have been made. To say that the hypothesis h has the probability p (say, $3/5$) with respect to the evidence e, means that for anyone to whom this evidence but no other relevant knowledge is available, it would be reasonable to believe in h to the degree p or, more exactly, it would be unreasonable for him to bet on h at odds higher than p: (1—p) (in the example, 3:2). Thus inductive probability measures the strength of support given to h by e or the *degree of confirmation* of h on the basis of e. In most cases in ordinary discourse, even among scientists, inductive probability is not specified by a numerical value but merely as being high or low or, in a comparative judgment, as being higher than another probability. It is important to recognize that every inductive probability judgment is relative to some evidence. In many cases no explicit reference to evidence is made; it is then to be understood that the totality of relevant information available to the speaker is meant as evidence. If a member of a jury says that the defendant is very probably innocent or that, of two witnesses A and B who have made contradictory statements, it is more probable that A lied than that B did, he means it with respect to the evidence that was presented in the trial plus any psychological or other relevant knowledge of a general nature he may possess. Probability as understood in contexts of this kind is not frequency. Thus, in our example, the evidence concerning the defendant, which was presented in the trial, may be such that it cannot be ascribed to any other person; and if it could be ascribed to several people, the juror would not know the relative frequency of innocent persons among them. Thus the probability concept used here cannot be the statistical one. While a statement of statistical probability asserts a matter of fact, a statement of inductive probability is of a purely logical nature. If hypothesis and evidence are given, the probability can be determined by logical analysis and mathematical calculation.

One of the basic principles of the theory of inductive probability is the *principle of indifference.* It says that, if the evidence does not contain anything that would favor either of two or more possible events, in other words, if our knowledge situation is symmetrical with respect to these events, then they have equal probabilities relative to the evidence. For example, if the evidence e_1 available to an observer X_1 contains nothing else about a given die than the information that it is a regular cube, then the symmetry condition is fulfilled and therefore each of the six faces has the same probability $\frac{1}{6}$ to appear uppermost at the next throw. This means that it would be unreasonable for X_1 to bet more than one to five on any one face. If X_2 is in possession of the evidence e_2 which, in addition to e_1, contains the knowledge that the die is heavily loaded in favor of one of the faces without specifying which one, the probabilities for X_2 are the same as for X_1. If, on the other hand, X_3 knows e_3 to the effect that the load favors the ace, then the probability of the ace on the basis of e_3 is higher than $\frac{1}{6}$. Thus, inductive probability, in contradistinction to statistical probability, cannot be ascribed to a material object by itself, irrespective of an observer. This is obvious in our example; the die is the same for all three observers and hence cannot have different properties for them. Inductive probability characterizes a hypothesis relative to available information; this information may differ from person to person and vary for any person in the course of time.

A brief look at the historical development of the concept of probability will give us a better understanding of the present controversy. The mathematical study of problems of probability began when some mathematicians of the sixteenth and seventeenth centuries were asked by their gambler friends about the odds in various games of chance. They wished to learn about probabilities as a guidance for their betting decisions. In the beginning of its scientific career, the concept of probability appeared in the form of inductive probability. This is clearly reflected in the title of the first major treatise on probability, written by Jacob Bernoulli and published posthumously in 1713; it was called *Ars Conjectandi,* the art of conjecture, in other words, the art of judging hypotheses on the basis of evidence. This book may be regarded as marking the beginning of the so-called classical period of the theory of probability. This period culminated in the great systematic work by Laplace, *Theorie analytique des probabilités* (1812). According to Laplace, the purpose of the theory of probability is to guide our judgments and to protect us from illusions. His explanations show clearly that he is mostly concerned, not with actual frequencies, but with methods for judging the acceptability of assumptions, in other words, with inductive probability.

In the second half of the last century and still more in our century, the application of statistical methods gained more and more ground in science. Thus attention was increasingly focussed on the statistical concept of probability. However, there was no clear awareness of the fact that this development constituted a transition to a fundamentally different meaning of the word 'probability.' In the nineteen twenties the first probability theories based on the frequency interpretation were proposed by men like the statistician R. A. Fisher, the mathematician R. von Mises, and the physicist-philosopher H. Reichenbach. These authors and their followers did not explicitly suggest to abandon that concept of probability which had prevailed since the classical period, and to replace it by a new one. They rather believed that their concept was essentially the same as that of all earlier authors. They merely claimed that they had given a more exact definition for it and had developed more comprehensive theories on this improved foundation. Thus, they interpreted Laplace's word 'probability' not in his inductive sense, but in their own statistical sense. Since there is a strong, though by far not complete analogy between the two concepts, many mathematical theorems hold in both interpretations, but others do not. Therefore these authors could accept many of the classical theorems but had to reject others. In particular, they objected strongly to the principle of indifference. In the frequency interpretation, this principle is indeed absurd. In our earlier example with the observer X_1, who knows merely that the die has the form of a cube, it would be rather incautious for him to assert that the six faces will appear with equal frequency. And if the same assertion were made by X_2, who has information that the die is biased, although he does not know the direction of the bias, he would contradict his own knowledge. In the inductive interpretation, on the other hand, the principle is valid even in the case of X_2, since in this sense it does not predict frequencies but merely says in effect, that it would be arbitrary for X_2 to have more confidence in the appearance of one face than in that of any other face and therefore it would be unreasonable for him to let his betting decisions be guided by such arbitrary expectations. Therefore it seems much more plausible to assume that Laplace meant the principle of indifference in the inductive sense rather than to assume that one of the greatest minds of the eighteenth century in mathematics, theoretical physics, astronomy, and philosophy chose an obvious absurdity as a basic principle.

The great economist John Maynard Keynes made the first attempt in our century to revive the old but almost forgotten inductive concept of probability. In his *Treatise on Probability* (1921) he made clear that the inductive concept is implicitly used in all our thinking on unknown events both in every-day life and in science. He showed that the classical theory of probability in its application to concrete problems was understandable only if it was interpreted in the inductive sense. However, he modified and restricted the classical theory in several important points. He rejected the principle of indifference in its classical form. And he did not share the view of the classical authors that it should be possible in principle to assign a numerical value to the probability of any hypothesis whatsoever. He believed that this could be done only under very special, rarely fulfilled conditions, as in games of chance where there is a well determined number of possible cases, all of them alike in their basic features, e.g., the six possible results of a throw of a die, the possible distributions of cards among the players, the possible final positions of the ball on a roulette table, and the like. He thought that in all other cases at best only comparative judgments of probability could be made, and even these only for hypotheses which belong, so to speak, to the same dimension. Thus one might come to the result that, on the basis of available knowledge, it is more probable that the next child of a specified couple will be male rather than female; but no comparison could be made between the probability of the birth of a male child and the probability of the stocks of General Electric going up tomorrow.

A much more comprehensive theory of inductive probability was constructed by the geophysicist Harold Jeffreys (*Theory of Probability*, 1939). He agreed with the classical view that probability can be expressed numerically in all cases. Furthermore, in view of the fact that science replaces statements in qualitative terms (e.g., "the child to be born will be very heavy") more and more by those in terms of measurable quantities ("the weight of the child will be more than eight pounds"), Jeffreys wished to apply probability also to hypotheses of quantitative form. For this reason, he set up an axiom system for probability much stronger than that of Keynes. In spite of Keynes' warning, he accepted the principle of indifference in a form quite similar to the classical one: "If there is no reason to believe one hypothesis rather than another, the probabilities are equal." However, it can easily be seen that the principle in this strong form leads to contradictions. Suppose, for example, that it is known that every ball in an urn is either blue or red or yellow but that nothing is known either of the color of any particular ball or of the numbers of blue, red, or yellow balls in the urn. Let B be the hypothesis that the first ball to be drawn from the urn will be blue, R, that it will be red, and Y, that it will be yellow. Now consider the hypotheses B and non-B. According to the principle of indifference as used by Laplace and again by Jeffreys, since nothing is known concerning B and non-B, these two hypotheses have equal probabilities, i.e., one half. Non-B means that the first ball is not blue, hence either red or yellow. Thus "R or Y" has probability one half. Since nothing is known concerning R and Y, their probabilities are equal and hence must be one fourth each. On the other hand, if we start with the consideration of R and non-R, we obtain the result that the probability of R is one half and that of B one fourth, which is incompatible with the previous result. Thus Jeffreys' system as it stands is inconsistent. This defect cannot be eliminated by simply omitting the principle of indifference. It plays an essential role in the system; without it, many important results can no longer be derived. In spite of this defect, Jeffreys' book remains valuable for the new light it throws on many statistical problems by discussing them for the first time in terms of inductive probability.

Both Keynes and Jeffreys discussed also the statistical concept of probability, and both rejected it. They believed that all probability statements could be formulated in terms of inductive probability and that therefore there was no need for any probability concept interpreted in terms of frequency. I think that in this point they went too far. Today an increasing number of those who study both sides of the controversy which has been going on for thirty years, are coming to the conclusion that here, as often before in the history of scientific thinking, both sides are right in their positive theses, but wrong in their polemic remarks about the other side. The statistical concept, for which a very elaborate mathematical theory exists, and which has been fruitfully applied in many fields in science and industry, need not at all be abandoned in order to make room for the inductive concept. Both concepts are needed for science, but they fulfill quite different functions. Statistical probability characterizes an objective situation, e.g., a state of a physical, biological or social system. Therefore it is this concept which is used in statements concerning concrete situations or in laws expressing general regularities of such situations. On the other hand, inductive probability, as I see it, does not occur *in* scientific statements, concrete or general, but only in judgments *about* such statements; in particular, in judgments about the strength of support given by one statement, the evidence, to another, the hypothesis, and hence about the acceptability of the latter on the basis of the former. Thus, strictly speaking, inductive probability belongs not to science itself but to the methodology of science, i.e., the analysis of concepts, statements, theories, and methods of science.

The theories of both probability concepts must be further developed. Although a great deal of work has been done on statistical probability, even here some problems of its exact interpretation and its application, e.g., in methods of estimation, are still controversial. On inductive probability, on the other hand, most of the work remains still to be done. Utilizing results of Keynes and Jeffreys and employing the exact tools of modern symbolic logic, I have constructed the fundamental parts of a mathematical theory of inductive probability or inductive logic (*Logical Foundations of Probability*, 1950). The methods developed make it possible to calculate numerical values of inductive probability ("degree of confirmation") for hypotheses concerning either single events or frequencies of properties and to determine estimates of frequencies in a population on the basis of evidence about a sample of the population. A few steps have been made towards extending the theory to hypotheses involving measurable quantities such as mass, temperature, etc.

It is not possible to outline here the mathematical system itself. But I will explain some of the general problems that had to be solved before the system could be constructed and some of the basic conceptions underlying the construction. One of the fundamental questions to be decided by any theory of induction is, whether to accept a principle of indifference and, if so, in what form. It should be strong enough to allow the derivation of the desired theorems, but at the same time sufficiently restricted to avoid the contradictions resulting from the classical form.

The problem will become clearer if we use a few elementary concepts of inductive logic. They will now be explained with the help of the first two columns of the accompanying diagram. We consider a set of four individuals, say four balls drawn from an urn. The individuals are described with respect to a given division of mutually exclusive properties; in our example, the two properties black (B) and white (W). An *individual distribution* is specified by ascribing to each individual one property. In our example, there are sixteen individual distributions; they are pictured in the second column (e.g., in the individual distribution No. 3, the first, second, and fourth ball are black, the third is white). A *statistical distribution,* on the other hand, is characterized by merely stating the number of individuals for each property. In the example, we have five statistical distributions, listed in the first column (e.g., the statistical distribution No. 2 is described by saying that there are three B and one W, without specifying *which* individuals are B and which W).

By the *initial probability* of a hypothesis ("probability a priori" in traditional termi-

	STATISTICAL DISTRIBUTIONS		INDIVIDUAL DISTRIBUTIONS	METHOD I	METHOD II	
	Number of Blue	Number of White		Initial Probability of Individual Distributions	Initial Probability of Statistical Distributions	Initial Probability of Individual Distributions
1.	4	0	1. ● ● ● ●	1/16	1/5	1/5 = 12/60
2.	3	1	2. ● ● ● ○	1/16	1/5	1/20 = 3/60
			3. ● ● ○ ●	1/16		1/20 = 3/60
			4. ● ○ ● ●	1/16		1/20 = 3/60
			5. ○ ● ● ●	1/16		1/20 = 3/60
3.	2	2	6. ● ● ○ ○	1/16	1/5	1/30 = 2/60
			7. ● ○ ● ○	1/16		1/30 = 2/60
			8. ● ○ ○ ●	1/16		1/30 = 2/60
			9. ○ ● ● ○	1/16		1/30 = 2/60
			10. ○ ● ○ ●	1/16		1/30 = 2/60
			11. ○ ○ ● ●	1/16		1/30 = 2/60
4.	1	3	12. ● ○ ○ ○	1/16	1/5	1/20 = 3/60
			13. ○ ● ○ ○	1/16		1/20 = 3/60
			14. ○ ○ ● ○	1/16		1/20 = 3/60
			15. ○ ○ ○ ●	1/16		1/20 = 3/60
5.	0	4	16. ○ ○ ○ ○	1/16	1/5	1/5 = 12/60

Inductive Probability Methods. (From Rudolf Carnap, "What Is Probability?" *Scientific American*, September, 1953.)

nology) we understand its probability before any factual knowledge concerning the individuals is available. Now we shall see that, if any initial probabilities which sum up to one are assigned to the individual distributions, all other probability values are thereby fixed. To see how the procedure works, put a slip of paper on the diagram alongside the list of individual distributions and write down opposite each distribution a fraction as its initial probability; the sum of the sixteen fractions must be one, but otherwise you may choose them just as you like. We shall soon consider the question whether some choices might be preferable to others. But for the moment we are only concerned with the fact that any arbitrary choice constitutes one and only one *inductive method* in the sense that it leads to one and only one system of probability values which contain an initial probability for any hypothesis (concerning the given individuals and the given properties) and a relative probability for any hypothesis with respect to any evidence. The procedure is as follows. For any given statement we can, by perusing the list of individual distributions, determine those in which it holds (e.g., the statement "among the first three balls there is exactly one W" holds in distributions No. 3, 4, 5, 6, 7, 9). Then we assign to it as initial probability the sum of the initial probabilities of the individual distributions in which it holds. Suppose that an evidence statement e (e.g., "The first ball is B, the second W, the third B") and a hypothesis h (e.g., "The fourth ball is B") are given. We ascertain first the individual distributions in which e holds (in the example, No. 4 and 7), and then those among them in which also h holds (only No. 4). The former ones determine the initial probability of e; the latter ones determine that of e and h together. Since the latter are among the former, the latter initial probability is a part (or the whole) of the former. We now divide the latter initial probability by the former and assign the resulting fraction to h as its relative probability with respect to e. (In our example, let us take the values of the initial probabilities of individual distributions given in the diagram for methods I and II, which will soon be explained. In method I the values for No. 4 and 7 — as for all other individual distributions — are $1/16$; hence the initial probability of e is $2/16$. That of e and h together is the value of No. 4 alone, hence $1/16$. Dividing this by $2/16$, we obtain $1/2$ as the probability of h with respect to e. In method II, we find for No. 4 and 7 in the last column the values $3/60$ and $2/60$ respectively. Therefore the initial probability of e is here $5/60$, that of e and h together $3/60$; hence the probability of h with respect to e is $3/5$.)

The problem of choosing an inductive method is closely connected with the problem of the principle of indifference. Most authors since the classical period have accepted some form of the principle and have thereby avoided the otherwise unlimited arbitrariness in the choice of a method. On the other hand, practically all authors in our century agree that the principle should be restricted to some well-defined class of hypotheses. But there is no agreement as to the class to be chosen. Many authors advocate either method I or method II, which are exemplified in our diagram. Method I consists in applying the principle of indifference to individual distributions, in other words, in assigning equal initial probabilities to individual distributions. In method II the principle is first applied to the statistical distributions and then, for each statistical distribution, to the corresponding individual distributions. Thus, in our example, equal initial probabilities are assigned in method II to the five statistical distributions, hence $1/5$ to each; then this value $1/5$ or $12/60$ is distributed in equal parts among the corresponding individual distributions, as indicated in the last column.

If we examine more carefully the two ways of using the principle of indifference, we find that either of them leads to contradictions if applied without restriction to all divisions of properties. (The reader can easily check the following results by himself. We consider, as in the diagram, four individuals and a division D_2 into two properties; blue (instead of black) and white. Let h be the statement that all four individuals are white. We consider, on the other hand, a division D_3 into three properties: dark blue, light blue, and white. For division D_2, as used in the diagram, we see that h is an individual distribution (No. 16) and also a statistical distribution (No. 5). The same holds for division D_3. By setting up the complete diagram for the latter division, one finds that there are fifteen statistical distributions, of which h is one, and 81 individual distributions (viz., 3x3x3x3), of which h is also one. Applying method I to division D_2, we found as the initial probability of h $1/16$; if we apply it to D_3, we find $1/81$; these two results are incompatible. Method II applied to D_2 led to the value $1/5$; but applied to D_3 it yields $1/15$. Thus this method likewise furnishes incompatible results.) We therefore restrict the use of either method to one division, viz. the one consisting of all properties which can be distinguished in the given universe of discourse (or which we wish to distinguish within a given context of investigation). If modified in this way, either method is consistent. We may still regard the examples in the diagram as representing the modified methods I and II, if we assume that the difference between black and white is the only difference among the given individuals, or the only difference relevant to a certain investigation.

How shall we decide which of the two methods to choose? Each of them is regarded as *the* reasonable method by prominent scholars. However, in my view, the chief mistake of the earlier authors was their failure to specify explicitly the main characteristic of a reasonable inductive method. It is due to this failure that some of them chose the wrong method. This characteristic is not difficult to find. Inductive thinking is a way of judging hypotheses concerning unknown events. In order to be reasonable, this judging must be guided by our knowledge of observed events. More specifically, other things being equal, a future event is to be regarded as the more probable, the greater the relative frequency of similar events observed so far under similar circumstances. This *principle of learning from experience* guides, or rather ought to guide, all inductive thinking in everyday affairs and in science. Our confidence that a certain drug will help in a present case of a certain disease is the higher the more frequently it has helped in past cases. We would regard a man's behavior as unreasonable if his expectation of a future event were the higher the less frequently he saw it happen in the past, and also if he formed his expectations for the future without any regard to what he had observed in the past. The principle of learning from experience seems indeed so obvious that it might appear superfluous to emphasize it explicitly. In fact, however, even some authors of high rank have advocated an inductive method that violates the principle.

Let us now examine the methods I and II from the point of view of the principle of learning from experience. In our earlier example we considered the evidence e saying that of the four balls drawn the first was B, the second W, the third B; in other words, that two B and one W were so far observed. According to the principle, the prediction h that the fourth ball will be black should be taken as more probable than its negation, non-h. We found, however, that method I assigns probability $1/2$ to h, and therefore likewise $1/2$ to non-h. And we see easily that it assigns to h this value $1/2$ also on any other evidence concerning the first three balls. Thus method I violates the principle. A man following this method sticks to the initial probability value for a prediction, irrespective of all observations he makes. In spite of this character of method I, it was proposed as the valid method of induction by prominent philosophers, among them Charles Sanders Peirce (in 1883) and Ludwig Wittgenstein (in 1921), and even by Keynes in one chapter of his book, although in other chapters he emphasizes eloquently the necessity of learning from experience.

We saw earlier that Method II assigns, on the evidence specified, to h the probability 3/5, hence to non-h 2/5. Thus the principle of learning from experience is satisfied in this case, and it can be shown that the same holds in any other case. (The reader can easily verify, for example, that with respect to the evidence that the first three balls are black, the probability of h is 4/5 and therefore that of non-h 1/5.) Method II in its modified, consistent form, was proposed by the author in 1945. Although it was often emphasized throughout the historical development that induction must be based on experience, nobody as far as I am aware, succeeded in specifying a consistent inductive method satisfying the principle of learning from experience. (The method proposed by Thomas Bayes (1763) and developed by Laplace – sometimes called "Bayes' rule" or "Laplace's rule of succession" – fulfills the principle. It is essentially method II, but in its unrestricted form; therefore it is inconsistent.) I found later that there are infinitely many consistent inductive methods which satisfy the principle (*The Continuum of Inductive Methods*, 1952). None of them seems to be as simple in its definition as method II, but some of them have other advantages.

Once a consistent and suitable inductive method is developed, it supplies the basis for a *general method of estimation,* i.e., a method for calculating, on the basis of given evidence, an estimate of an unknown value of any magnitude. Suppose that, on the basis of the evidence, there are n possibilities for the value of a certain magnitude at a given time, e.g., the amount of rain tomorrow, the number of persons coming to a meeting, the price of wheat after the next harvest. Let the possible values be x_1, x_2, . . . , x_n, and their inductive probabilities with respect to the given evidence p_1, p_2, . . . , p_n, respectively. Then we take the product p_1x_1 as the expectation value of the first case at the present moment. Thus, if the occurrence of the first case is certain and hence $p_1 = 1$, its expectation value is the full value x_1; if it is just as probable that it will occur as that it will not, and hence $p_1 = 1/2$, its expectation value is half its full value ($p_1x_1 = x_1/2$), etc. We proceed similarly with the other possible values. As estimate or total expectation value of the magnitude on the given evidence we take the sum of the expectation values for the possible cases, that is, $p_1x_1 + p_2x_2 + \ldots + p_nx_n$. (For example, suppose someone considers buying a ticket for a lottery and, on the basis of his knowledge of the lottery procedure, there is a probability of 0.01 that the ticket will win the first prize of $200 and a probability of 0.03 that it will win $50; since there are no other prizes, the probability that it will win nothing is 0.96. Hence the estimate of the gain in dollars is $0.01 \times 200 + 0.03 \times 50 + 0.96 \times 0 = 3.50$. This is the value of the ticket for him and it would be irrational for him to pay more for it.) The same method may be used in order to make a rational decision in a situation where one among various possible actions is to be chosen. For example, a man considers several possible ways for investing a certain amount of money. Then he can – in principle, at least – calculate the estimate of his gain for each possible way. To act rationally, he should then choose that way for which the estimated gain is highest.

Bernoulli and Laplace and many of their followers envisaged the idea of a theory of inductive probability which, when fully developed, would supply the means for evaluating the acceptability of hypothetical assumptions in any field of theoretical research and at the same time methods for determining a rational decision in the affairs of practical life. In the more sober cultural atmosphere of the late nineteenth century and still more in the first half of the twentieth, this idea was usually regarded as a utopian dream. It is certainly true that those audacious thinkers were not as near to their aim as they believed. But a few men dare to think today that the pioneers were not mere dreamers and that it will be possible in the future to make far-reaching progress in essentially that direction in which they saw their vision.

The Conception of Probability as a Logical Relation

A. J. AYER

There is a fairly widespread view that, at least in one important sense of the term, probability is most properly attributed to statements: and that what is being asserted when it is said that a statement is probable, in this sense, is that it bears a certain relation to another statement, or set of statements, which may also be described as confirming, or supporting, or providing evidence for it. There are some, indeed, who maintain that this is the only sense in which it is correct to speak of probability; that what we 'really mean' when we assert anything to be probable is always that some statement bears the requisite relation to such and such a piece of evidence. Thus Keynes [1] assumes that every significant probability statement can be fitted into his formula '$a/h = p$,' where a is the proposition which is said to be probable, h is the evidence on which it is probable, and p is the degree of probability that h confers on a, a quantity which may or may not be numerically measurable. And Kneale [2] takes it for granted that probability is relative to evidence: if this is often overlooked, it is because in talking about probability we seldom bother to specify the evidence on which we are relying: 'our probability statements are commonly elliptical.' [3] Other writers, like Carnap,[4] distinguish this sense of probability from one in which to speak of the probability of an event is to attribute a numerical frequency to the distribution of some property among events of a given class. Carnap himself allows that we have a use for this conception of probability in terms of observed frequencies, or of the limits towards which they are supposed to tend. He calls it probability$_2$ to differentiate it from the other, logical, conception of probability, what he calls probability$_1$. It is, however, on the basis of probability$_1$ that he develops his inductive logic.[5]

Not all the advocates of this conception of probability agree with Keynes in regarding probability as an unanalysable logical rela-

From S. Körner (Ed.), *Observation and Interpretation,* pp. 12–17. London: Butterworths Scientific Publications, 1957. Reprinted by permission of the author, the publisher, and the Colston Research Society.

[1] J. M. Keynes, *A Treatise on Probability.*

[2] W. Kneale, *Probability and Induction.*

[3] *Op. cit.,* p. 10.

[4] R. Carnap, 'The Two Concepts of Probability,' *Philosophy and Phenomenological Research,* Vol. V, No. 4.

[5] Vide, *The Logical Foundations of Probability.*

tion. Certainly Carnap does not suppose his probability$_1$ to be unanalysable. But he does recognize that, on this interpretation of them, probability statements come to resemble statements of formal logic in the sense that if they are true they are analytic. This might, indeed, be disputed by philosophers like Kneale who wish to hold on to the synthetic *a priori,* and so to confine analyticity within more narrow limits: but they would at least allow that statements of probability, in this sense, are not empirical. They are necessarily true, if they are true at all. For it is characteristic of any view of this type that the existence of a probability relation between statements is made to depend, not on any contingent matter of fact, but solely on the meaning of the statements concerned. And this is my ground for saying that the advocates of such views treat probability as a logical relation, whether they assent to this form of words or not.

Now it seems to me that there is a very simple objection to theories of this type, which has strangely escaped the notice of their supporters [6] and even of their critics. Let us suppose that a disciple of Keynes has decided to bet upon a horse-race and that he is considering the chances of a horse named 'Eclipse.' He is determined to be rational and so to bring his degree of belief in the horse's victory into exact accordance with the objective probabilities. He assembles the evidence: h_1 that Eclipse will be ridden by the champion jockey; h_2 that the going will be hard; h_3 that Eclipse is suited by the distance; h_4 that it went lame after its last race; h_5 that it has previously beaten the more fancied of its competitors; h_6 that it has recently dropped in the betting, and so forth. Assume that he evaluates all the relevant evidence that he can acquire, or, in other words, that, so far as his knowledge goes, he has not omitted any true proposition which, if it were conjoined with his other data, would make any difference to the resultant probability. So, taking a to be the proposition that Eclipse will win, he decides that the probability of a on $h_1 = p_1$, $a/h_2 = p_2$, $a/h_3 = p_3$, $a/h_1h_2 = p_x$, $a/h_{1\text{-}4} = P_y$, . . . ; and finally that a/h_{1-n}, where h_{1-n} represents the totality of the relevant evidence at his command, $= p_z$. How is he to place his bet?

To common sense the answer is obvious. If his degree of belief in the proposition that Eclipse will win is to be rational, it must correspond to the probability p_z. He must find a means of comparing this with the odds that he is offered and bet accordingly. But what reason can he have, on his principles, for accepting the common-sense answer? In what way is the probability p_z better than the other probabilities, p_1, p_2n, . . . , p_x, p_y, which he has also estimated? If his estimates are correct, all these statements of probability are necessary truths. And in that case how can any one of them be superior to the others? What one wants to say is that the probability p_z, since it is the only one that is estimated on the basis of all the relevant evidence, provides the best appraisal of what is actually likely to happen. But what can this mean to Keynes? An event will happen, or it will not. To say that it is likely to happen is, on his theory, only a misleading way of saying that the statement that it will happen is probable on the basis of certain other statements. But this leaves us free to choose these other statements in any way we like, provided only that we have sufficient warrant for accepting them. It may seem, indeed, that even this proviso sets a problem; for to say that we have sufficient warrant for accepting a given statement must mean, for Keynes, that it follows from, or is made probable by, another statement, or set of statements, which we have sufficient warrant for accepting: and

[6] Professor Braithwaite reminds me that Keynes does notice the point which I am about to raise when he discusses the Weight of Arguments in Chapter VI of his Treatise. But, since he concludes that probabilities are unaffected by the weight of evidence, he misses the force of the objection.

then one appears to be threatened with an infinite regress. Keynes meets this difficulty, however, by assuming that there are certain statements which we can know directly to be true: and it is on statements of this sort that all rational judgments of probability must finally depend. This assumption may be questioned; but even if it be admitted, our original objection still holds. Once we have assembled some trustworthy data by these means, there can be no reason, on Keynes's system, why we should trouble to carry our investigations any further. The addition of more evidence may, indeed, yield a higher or lower probability for the statement in which we are interested. But unless we have made some logical mistake, this probability cannot be said to be more, or less, correct than the one that was yielded by the evidence with which we started. Neither can any sense be given to the claim that it is a better estimate of what is likely to happen.

Carnap has seen that there is a difficulty here, and he has tried to meet it by introducing what he calls 'the principle of total evidence.' 'Let $c(h, e)$,' he says, 'be the degree of confirmation of the hypothesis h with respect to the evidence e. Let us suppose that we have a definition of the function c and, based upon this definition, a theorem "$c(h, e) = q$," which states the value q of c for given h and e. A principle which seems generally recognized, although not always obeyed, says that if we wish to apply such a theorem of the theory of probability to a given knowledge situation, then we have to take as evidence e the *total evidence* available to the person in question at the time in question, that is to say, his total knowledge of the results of his observations.' [7]

But why *have* we to take as evidence the total evidence available to us, whatever that may mean? What sort of principle is this? It can hardly be a *moral* principle. So far as morality goes, we might equally well choose to rely on the evidence which yielded the highest degree of confirmation for the hypothesis in which we were interested, or on that which yielded the lowest, or on whatever evidence we found most pleasing. Unless we miscalculate, the result at which we arrive will in each case be a necessary truth; and there can surely be no moral reason for preferring any one of these necessary truths to any other. It might, however, be thought that there was a practical reason: and indeed one may suppose that Carnap intended his principle of total evidence to be pragmatic. The suggestion would seem to be that we should trust hypotheses to the degree to which they are confirmed; and that by taking all the available evidence into account, we diminish the risk of falling foul of the facts, that is, of over- or under-estimating the likelihood of the actual occurrence of the event to which our hypothesis refers. Once again, this is in accordance with common sense: but how can it possibly be justified on Carnap's principles? The event will occur or it will not. To say that there is a probability, of a given degree, that it will occur is to say only that the hypothesis that it will occur is confirmed to that degree by such and such evidence. If this proposition is true, it is necessarily true: but so are all the other true propositions which, on the basis of greater, or less, or partly, or wholly different evidence, assign to the hypothesis a different degree of confirmation. There is no sense, therefore, in which the proposition which brings in all the available evidence can be superior to any of the others as a measure of probability. And this being so, there can be no practical reason why we should take it as a guide.

So far as I can see, the only way in which Carnap might hope to meet this objection would be to make his principle of total evidence a part of the definition of probabil-

[7] R. Carnap, 'On the Application of Inductive Logic,' *Philosophy and Phenomenological Research*, Vol. VIII, No. 1.

ity$_1$. He might claim that what we must be understood to mean by saying that a hypothesis is probable, in this sense, to a certain degree is just that it is confirmed, to this degree, by the totality of the evidence which is available to us. But what is this totality? If it be only 'the total knowledge of the results of our observations,' then the difficulty will not be met. For, to revert to my example of the horse race, it may well be that the only information I have bothered to acquire, which is in any way relevant to the hypothesis that Eclipse will win, is that it is to be ridden by the champion jockey; and in that case I shall be justified in regarding the hypothesis as probable to the extent that this single piece of evidence confirms it, and betting accordingly. No doubt if I were to investigate further, as any sensible punter would, I should find evidence which would lead me to revise my estimate of Eclipse's chances. But why should I take the trouble? If what I mean by saying that it is probable to such and such a degree that Eclipse will win is that the hypothesis that it will win is confirmed to this degree by the totality of the relevant observations that I have actually made, then the fact that the probability might be different if I had extended my observations need not concern me. For, on this view, if I do not miscalculate, there is no sense in which this second estimate of probability could be any better than the first.

The answer to this might seem to be that the probability is to be defined by reference not to the results of all the relevant observations that one happens to have made, but to those of all the relevant observations that one could make if one chose. The totality of evidence that is available to me will not as a rule be limited to the evidence that I actually have. But then what are its limits? What means is there of deciding which are the observations that it is possible for me to make? Presumably, in the case of the horse race, the condition of the horse's lungs is relevant. Is this within the range of evidence that is available to me? Well, I could use X-rays to find it out. But what if I have not the skill? Then, I can employ a radiologist to do it for me. But what if I cannot discover a radiologist who is willing? What if he asks more money than I can afford to pay? Then, perhaps, I can find some way of forcing him to do it: perhaps I can steal the money. But will this always be possible? I do not see how there can be a general answer to such questions; nor, therefore, how there can be a rule for determining what is the totality of the available evidence. But in default of such a rule, this definition of probability would seem to be both vague in principle, and of little practical use.

Furthermore, it makes judgements of probability at least partly subjective. If the stable guards its secrets well, the totality of the evidence that is available to me will fall short of the totality of the evidence that is available to the horse's trainer. Let us make the implausible assumption that both he and I are in fact possessed of all the relevant evidence that is respectively available to us, and that we correctly calculate the degree of confirmation of the hypothesis that Eclipse will win, arriving naturally at different results. Both results will be valid, but the one that is valid for him will not be valid for me. If I take over his estimate I shall fall into error, for I shall then be asserting that the hypothesis is confirmed to the degree he says by the totality of the evidence that is available to *me,* when it is not in fact confirmed to that degree by the totality of the evidence that is available to me but only by the different totality of the evidence that is available to *him.* It follows also, on this view, that there is no such thing as *the* probability of a hypothesis: there are as many different probabilities as there are persons who have access to different quantities of evidence. This conclusion may or may not be objectionable in itself; but I think it would be regarded as disturbing at least by some of those who wish us to look upon probability as a logical relation.

It may be suggested that they can avoid this conclusion by assuming that everyone has access, in principle, to all the evidence that there is. Then to say that a statement is probable to such and such a degree will be to say that it is confirmed to that degree by the totality of true statements. There is no need to put in the proviso that these statements must all be relevant, since the inclusion of irrelevant truths will make no difference to the result. This does indeed yield an objective definition of probability, but it has the fatal disadvantage that the probability of every hypothesis becomes either 0 or 1. For the totality of true statements must include either the negation of the hypothesis in question, or the hypothesis itself.

To escape from this predicament, one would have to restrict the range of the available evidence in such a way that it excluded any statement, or set of statements, which entailed either the hypothesis or its negation. And then one might equate the probability of the hypothesis with the degree to which it was confirmed by the totality of true statements that satisfied this condition. One objection to this would be that in assessing probabilities we could never draw on any universal statement of law. For if the event, to which our hypothesis referred, were subject to causal laws, the relevant statements of law, when combined with the statements affirming the appropriate initial conditions, would always entail the hypothesis or its negation. We could indeed keep the statements of law if we excluded the singular statements which joined with them in producing the entailments; but this would be an absurd proceeding, since it is only through establishing singular statements that we ever acquire any evidence at all. And just for this reason, it may be said, we can afford to forgo the universal statements of law; for they draw all their support from the singular statements which are derivable from them; and these we shall have. Moreover, statistical laws, with frequencies of less than a hundred per cent, will not be excluded, though it may well be argued that they too will be superfluous, if all true singular statements are to be comprised in the available evidence.

A more serious objection to this definition of probability is that it allows us to have very little confidence in any of the judgements of probability that we actually make. For it can very seldom be the case that we in fact know every true singular statement that is relevant to the hypothesis in which we are interested. But in so far as the evidence at our disposal falls short of the total evidence, we cannot infer that the hypotheses which it is supposed to confirm are at all likely to be true. For all that is meant by their being likely to be true is that they are confirmed, to whatever degree, by the total evidence; and this is not in our possession. What we want to say is that, even if we can never be sure of having all the requisite evidence, nevertheless by acquiring more evidence, and incorporating it into our calculations, we bring our estimates of probability nearer to the truth. And clearly this is the view that Carnap holds. But I am not at all sure that he, or anyone else who conceives of probability as a logical relation, is entitled to hold it. For, as we have already remarked, each necessary truth to the effect that a given hypothesis is confirmed by some collection of evidence to such and such a degree is in itself as good as every other: we can pick out a special set of these propositions and say that they alone are to be regarded, by definition, as statements of probability; but then it will follow that the others, which fall outside this privileged set, are not statements of probability at all; there will be no justification for treating them even as approximations to the measures of objective probability for which we are in search.

Perhaps this difficulty could be met by introducing the concept of second-order probabilities. They might then be defined in such a way that one could assign a probability to the hypothesis that a given statement of confirmation was a statement of probability: and this probability would be made to increase, as one added to the evidence on which the statement of confirmation was based.

It seems to me, however, that such devices do not, in the end, remove the fundamental weakness of the logical theory. It has been well remarked by Kneale that 'no analysis of the probability relation can be accepted as adequate, i.e. as explaining the ordinary usage of the word "probability," unless it enables us to understand why it is rational to take as a basis for action a proposition which stands in that relation to the evidence at our disposal.' [8] And, even if the other objections to it can be met, I maintain that the view which we have been considering fails this test. For, if we are presented only with a stock of necessary facts to the effect that certain statements, or groups of statements, bear logical relations to each other in virtue solely of their meaning, I do not see what reason there could be for differentiating between the items of this stock as bases for action. I am not clear even what could be meant within the terms of this theory, by saying that one of them was a better basis for action than another. It is true that one may select a subclass of these necessary propositions and decide to *call* its members statements of probability; but in so doing one will beg the question. For the use of the word 'probability,' in this connexion, itself implies that it is most rational to act on the basis of the propositions which have thus been selected: and this has not been proved.

In conclusion, I do not wish to say that probability, in the sense which here concerns us, is in no way relative to evidence. It seems clear that an appeal to evidence is needed to justify the belief that such and such an event is more or less likely to happen; and also that it is rational in such cases to take all the evidence at our disposal into account, the ground for this being, I suppose, that experience has shown us that our forecasts are more often right when this is done than when it is not. It does not follow, however, that statements of probability, in this sense, are statements *about* the relations of hypotheses to their evidence; and I do not think that they are. Nor, in the sense in which probability is the guide of life, do I think that statements of probability can be logically true.

8 *Probability and Induction,* p. 20.

6

THE RIDDLE OF INDUCTION

Introduction

Whenever one observes gas being heated while kept at constant pressure, he sees that it expands. Repeated observations of this phenomenon provide an evidential base, and from this base we infer that this event will always happen. But the evidential base – this event has always happened up to now – is much weaker or narrower in scope than the conclusion – this event will always happen – ; and since the conclusion goes beyond the scope or range of the evidential base, philosophers usually say that inductive inference involves an "inductive leap." The question which naturally arises is this: what reason justifies this inductive leap, or what reason justifies the belief that something will happen simply because it has happened? It is not justified, certainly, in the sense that the conclusion is a logical consequence of the evidence. It involves no self-contradiction to assert that an event will not happen in the future even though it has happened many times in the past. And the conclusion is not justifiable in the sense that one has inductive evidence for its truth since the validity of the inductive procedure is the point in doubt. David Hume, who first offered this type of analysis, concluded that inductive inference, since it cannot be justified either deductively or inductively, has no rational foundation at all and rests only on habit and animal faith.

The case of heating gas at constant pressure is an example of causal inductive inference. But the problem of induction can be stated just as easily in the framework of statistical inductive inference. Statistical inference does not yield a prediction about the occurrence or nature of an individual or particular event but yields a percentage-wise prediction. If a sample of a population (that is, the class of objects or events being investigated) shows a certain percentage of x and a certain percentage of y, we infer that the entire population has the same percentages. To the question, "What reason do we have for extrapolating from the sample to the whole lot sampled?", the usual answer is, "Because the sample is a fair or representative one."

To illustrate what is meant by a fair sample let us suppose we are presented with a wagon load of wheat containing a mixture of two distinguishable types of grain and asked to determine the percentage of each type in the entire wagon load. Now being good scientists we would thoroughly stir the wheat before we took a sample – consisting, say, of several handfuls of wheat scooped from various parts of the wagon. Thoroughly stirring the wheat, we would say, insures the random distribution of the grains, so that each grain has as good a chance as any other of turning up in the sample. In this way, the sample is not "biased" or "prejudiced"; and an unbiased or unprejudiced sample is precisely what we mean by a fair or representative sample. And, finally, because it is a fair sample we are justified in extrapolating the ratio of grain types found in our sample to the whole wagon load of wheat.

However, a sceptical philosopher like Hume would be unmoved by this argument. True, if we *know* the wheat was thoroughly – that is, sufficiently – stirred, then we would know we had a fair sample and there would be no problem of induction. But how do we *know* that the wheat is sufficiently stirred to insure randomness? When the sceptical philosopher looks at the scientist's attempt to obtain a fair sample, he replies, "In the case of the carload of wheat, even though the wheat was thoroughly stirred, how can you know that there is not some pocket of unstirred wheat, the presence of which would destroy the validity of your calculation?" The sceptic would readily agree that the scientist has made a meritorious effort to ascertain the true percentages of grain types in the entire lot but would argue that the scientist cannot *know* his sample is fair since he cannot know there are no unstirred pockets without extending the sample until it coincides with the whole population sampled – in which case, of course, the possibility of any inductive inference at all vanishes. The sceptic concludes that since we can never know we have a fair sample, we have no rational foundation for making the inference at all. So statistical inductive inference, like causal inductive inference, rests ultimately only on habit and animal faith.

In their attempts to solve the problem of induction and avoid Hume's scepticism, philosophers have put forward three essentially different types of answers: 1) metaphysical justifications of induction, 2) pragmatic vindications of induction, and 3) dismissals or dissolutions of the problem as itself unreasonable.

The Justification of Induction. Metaphysical justifications are efforts to show, despite the objections mentioned above, that an inductive inference follows logically or necessarily from inductive premises. If one supplements the empirical evidence with the metaphysical assumption or presupposition that *nature is uniform,* then the inductive inference – the extrapolation of what the evidence tells us to all cases – follows logically or is necessarily true. That is, 'x and y have always occurred together' plus 'nature is uniform' implies 'x and y (will) always occur together.' It is not always clear, however, what philosophers mean when they say nature is uniform, although frequently they have meant something like the following. Nature is uniform in the specific sense that the regularities of nature are independent of space and time. 'Nature is uniform' asserts the irrelevance of mere position in space and time to the correlations or laws of science. It does not matter where or when gas at constant pressure is heated, it still expands. Now if the laws of science are independent of spatial and temporal location, then the fact that empirical evidence – all observed x's are y's – is by the nature of the case always *past* in no way makes it awkward to infer all x's in the future, too, are y's.

Some philosophers prefer to state the principle of uniformity thus: 'Same cause, same effect.' But this formulation is equivalent to the one we have been discussing since 'same cause, same effect' only means that if a cause occurs ten years ago, today, tomorrow, or ten years in the future, it will still have the same effect. If it did not, we would not call it a cause.

But what is meant by calling the statement, 'nature is uniform,' a metaphysical assumption or presupposition of science? The principle is metaphysical in the sense that it purports to state a factual feature of our universe and yet is not empirically or experientially verifiable. Some philosophers call this type of statement a *synthetic a priori* statement. J. S. Mill, however, did think the principle was empirically verifiable. He claimed that 'nature is uniform' is a higher-order empirical generalization resulting from the observation of past and present specific uniformities in nature. Many philosophers have objected to this view of the uniformity principle. Since the validity of each individual induction presupposes the principle, the principle itself cannot be established as a final inductive conclusion of these specific inductions. Such a procedure would be, of course, circular and so pointless. So the principle is not empirically verifiable; it is a metaphysical principle in the simple sense that it must be assumed or pre-supposed in order to make empirical inference itself rational and justifiable. While the principle is not a part of experience, it is not divorced from experience either; it must be assumed in order to make experience count for something.

There are several telling difficulties with the metaphysical doctrine of the uniformity of nature, interpreted as a logical justification of induction. First, it is utterly fatuous, proving not too little but always too much, justifying any inductive inference whatever. If one gives our wagon load of wheat a few quick turns and takes the ratio of grain types in a sample, then, assuming the uniformity of nature, we have succeeded in justifying the extrapolation of this ratio to the whole lot sampled. If, however, after giving the load ten good turns, this ratio changes, then, assuming the uniformity of nature, we have succeeded in justifying the extrapolation of *this* ratio. But, of course, what one wants to do is justify the latter extrapolation only. The uniformity-of-nature principle, then, completely obscures, and is helpless in making, what, after all, is the crucial distinction – namely, the distinction between lawful and non-lawful universal statements, one of which can and one of which cannot legitimately be extrapolated.

Second, the principle of uniformity itself needs more justification than the claim that it is necessary to assume it in order to make induction reasonable. Perhaps induction is not reasonable. But how can this principle be further justified? The claim that nature is uniform is not a logical truth since its denial is not self-contradictory. The only other grounds for accepting the principle would be empirical ones; but we have already seen, in talking about Mill, that an empirical or inductive justification of uniformity is circular. R. B. Braithwaite sums up this difficulty: "The overwhelming objection to the assimilation of all induction to deduction is that this would require that one should reasonably believe a very general empirical major premiss [the uniformity of nature], the reasonableness of belief in which would have to be justified by another inductive argument." [1]

The Vindication of Induction. The proponents of this position agree that there is no logical justification of induction, even if the empirical evidence is supplemented with a metaphysical principle of uniformity; and they insist there is no inductive justification of inductive inference since this procedure is always circular. However, they do not accept Hume's scepticism either. True, they say, we cannot show that inductive techniques are adequate to produce knowledge of future events but we can show that they will produce such knowledge *if it is to be had at all.* In a terminology we used previously we could say that induction cannot be shown to be a sufficient condition of knowledge of the future, but it can be shown to be a necessary one. Thus, since inductive techniques are at least a necessary condition for knowledge of the future, it is reasonable to adopt and follow them. The proponents of this type of argument call it a practical vindication of induction in order to contrast it with the logical justifications that try to show that induction is a sufficient condition for knowledge of the future. Let us examine the vindication view in detail.

The proponents of vindication say that there is not and cannot be any guarantee that inductive techniques will achieve reliable knowledge about future events; but if these techniques fail, so will all other ways of finding out about the future since all other ways are dependent upon induction. Clairvoyance, prevision, soothsaying, and, for that matter, omniscience are all, to be sure, logically possible non-inductive ways of knowing about the future. However, we would find these unusual ways of knowing the fu-

[1] *Scientific Explanation,* p. 259.

ture acceptable only if they correctly predicted future events over a long period of time. But the only way to discover whether or not these methods correctly predict the future over a long period of time, of course, is through induction. So all these non-inductive ways of knowing the future depend ultimately on induction. Thus, if induction itself is not warranted, there is no possibility of knowing the future at all. We have succeeded, then, in vindicating induction by showing it is a necessary condition for knowledge of the future: if the future is to be known at all, inductive techniques must be used. (There are, you will discover, several variations or versions of this "necessary condition" vindication of induction.)

Induction is further vindicated, some philosophers believe, because it is *self-corrective* in nature. Charles Sanders Peirce made this point frequently. He wrote, for example, "The true guarantee of the validity of induction is that it is a method of reaching conclusions which, if it be persisted in long enough, will assuredly correct any error concerning future experience into which it may temporarily lead us." What Peirce had in mind is this: sampling enables us to make inferences about future experience; but if, when that experience comes, it is not what we expect – that is, if it does not conform to our inference – then this experience itself becomes part of the enlarged data of sampling and corrects our previous expectations. Since inductive inference avails itself eventually of every sort of experience, any inductive inference, since it is only provisional, corrects itself at last.

These practical vindications of induction, while they are attractive and persuasive in many ways, are not without difficulties. First, the view that induction is a necessary condition for reliable knowledge of the future is not much of a consolation. We can never know that induction is an adequate way to know the future; we only know that if it is not, nothing else is either. This position is scarcely any advance over Hume's scepticism. But we can criticize this vindication in a more straightforward and direct fashion. Suppose a clairvoyant claims to have knowledge of future events through his own private techniques, and suppose further that he successfully foretells what will happen in the future. His very success, then, on the vindication view, is an inductive warrant or certificate of his clairvoyant powers. But the clairvoyant might well answer thus: "To be sure, the grounds an outsider would have for believing me to be clairvoyant are the successes of my powers. I, however, who possess the powers, have an explanation of my very success; namely, I directly apprehend the future so that I avoid entirely the perils of the inductive leap. Indeed, I can tell you beforehand, when you use inductive techniques, whether your inference coincides with the future I directly apprehend!"

Of course, clairvoyants, we feel, are not successful, at least over a long period of time, but what then? On the vindication view, we say that their lack of success is good inductive evidence for rejecting their claim of knowing the future; but if this is so, the success of the inductive techniques of science should be good inductive evidence for accepting induction as a reliable way of knowing the future. But if the success of inductive procedure is good evidence for accepting inductive inference as a reliable method, then we are giving an inductive justification of induction which the proponents of vindication, as we have seen, following Hume, explicitly reject.

Moreover, there are several difficulties with the self-corrective vindication of induction. The inductive method, we are told, "must avail itself of every sort of experience; and our inference, which was only provisional, corrects itself at last." 'At last,' unfortunately, can only mean when the need for any inference has passed, because there is nothing left to infer to. That is to say, the more nearly certain we become of the accuracy of the ratio of grain types in our sample, the less use we have for it, for the more nearly exhaustive is our examination of the whole wagon load of wheat. For any practical purposes, and this is the crux of the whole matter, there is a line to be drawn between the process of investigation and the application of its results. What we seek is something that can be regarded as knowledge of the future, in the sense that we have good reasons *now* for believing it, and not merely something to be regarded always as provisional and itself only one step in an indefinite process of inductive investigation. A promissory note isn't any good if you cannot ever collect it.

Finally, the notion of self-correction is itself misleading in the context of the problem of induction. All that one can say legitimately about subsequent changes or differences in ratios is simply that they are changes, or modifications, or alterations; the changing or altering process could be called self-corrective only if one knew a ratio, accepted it as correct, and discovered that the distance between this ratio and the empirically discovered ratios tended to diminish. But, of course, this knowledge necessary for calling induction self-corrective is precisely what we do not have.

Dismissal or Dissolution of the Problem. Is there not a simple recourse for one who cannot accept either metaphysical justification or practical vindication of induction? After all, is it not perfectly reasonable or justifiable to accept the inductive inference about the wheat, or any like it, precisely because it exemplifies 'normal inductive procedure,' that is, careful "stirring," holding variables constant, varying factors systematically, and whatever else one can do along these lines, and observing under these conditions many instances of a relationship that always holds? Some common-sense or "ordinary language" philosophers do claim that it is perfectly reasonable or justifiable to do so, and that the sceptic's denial of this obvious truth is either self-contradictory, mistaken, or vacuous. The ways in which they try to establish these conclusions are quite various and cannot easily be lumped together as critics of this type of analysis are wont to do. These analysts emphasize their individuality; although it cannot be denied that there are certain recurring types of thrusts designed to unseat the sceptic. Let us examine one of them.

Why, after all, *should* anyone claim that anything more than normal inductive procedure is necessary for the justification of an induction? Upon looking at the scientist's effort to obtain a fair sample, the sceptic, as we have seen, regardless of the success of the predictions, might say, "How can you really be certain that you have a truly representative sample? In the case of the wagon load of wheat, even though the wheat was stirred and stirred, how can you *know* that there is not some latent pocket of unstirred wheat which would destroy the validity of your calculation? But if you can never *know* the sample is really fair, what justification do you have for calling inductive inference *knowledge* at all?" The first ordinary language thrust at this sceptic might be: The terms 'fair sample' and 'representative sample' in 'real fair sample' and 'true representative sample' in your argument occur either in a self-contradictory or vacuous way. 'Fair sample' in its ordinary usage is *defined* in terms of its capacity to satisfy the requirements of careful "stirring," stratification, and whatever else can be done along these lines. The phrase, 'whatever else can be done along these lines,' of course, keeps the definition open so it can include future refinements and new techniques which have arisen and no doubt will continue to arise in science and everyday life. In fact, to say that 'fair sample,' in the sense in which it is ordinarily used, is *defined* by these requirements does not imply that the requirements are definite and precise. "What is meant is that the use of the term is learned by taking note of the *kind* of thing which is evidence for that term's exemplification. We teach a child or a foreigner the *meaning* of the word . . . by showing him situations in which the use of the term would be appropriate."[2] Nevertheless, the term may be introduced into discourse by a formal explanation of its meaning — in which case 'fair sample' is defined in terms of its capacity to satisfy the specified vague requirements. Now, to return to the sceptic's argument, if he uses 'fair sample' initially in the way people commonly do (which he does apparently since we understood him at the outset), he is referring to a kind of sample revealed by one of the vague requirements, or some refinement thereof. If he does utilize this meaning, but also talks about a "real fair sample" which one can never know he has, or have good reason to believe he has, no matter how many or refined the requirements it meets, then his use of the term is self-contradictory, meaning that at once it both does and does not satisfy the ordinary requirements of a fair sample. If the use of the term is to avoid being self-contradictory, it must function in some new sense. Since no new sense is provided, however, if it is not self-contradictory, it is vacuous.

The decisive difficulty with this maneuver, it seems likely, is this: By identifying the meanings of 'fair sample' and 'sample that is stirred, stratified, etc.' a person is unable to give as a reason why a given sample is a fair one, the fact that it has been stirred, stratified, etc.; but this, of course, is precisely what one wants to be able to do. I cannot give as a reason why something is what it is, a synonymous phrase. I have given no support to my statement, 'John is my brother,' by saying, 'John is my male-sibling.' And if one asks, "Why is this a fair sample?" or "Is this a fair sample?", I have not answered him at all if, having asserted the equivalence of 'fair sample' and 'sample that is stirred . . . ,' I reply, "Because it has been stirred, stratified, etc." All I would have managed to say, making the proper substitutions, is, "This sample is fair because it is a fair sample."

By way of summary: To the question, "What are the rational foundations of induction?," Hume replied, "There are none." We examined three ways of avoiding his scepticism — metaphysical justification, practical vindication, and ordinary-language dissolution — and found certain difficulties with all three ways. Should the reader return to Hume's scepticism? Not necessarily. There are many other justifications, vindications, and dissolutions besides the ones we have considered, some of which you will find in the following essays; and it may well be that you will find one of them quite compelling and acceptable as an answer to Hume.

John Stuart Mill, in his discussion, "Of the Ground of Induction," insisting in his own way on a uniformity-of-nature principle, represents the metaphysical justification type of analysis. Charles Sanders Peirce presents the self-corrective sort of pragmatic vindication in his essay, and John W. Lenz, in "The Pragmatic Justification of Induction," states clearly Reichenbach's influential pragmatic vindication — *if success is possible,* the inductive method will bring success — and indicates in detail what he takes to be wrong with it. P. F. Strawson in his "The 'Justification' of Induction" represents the ordinary-language type of analysis; he tries to show in many ingenious ways not only that the sceptic about induction is mistaken but also how he was led into making his mistake. In the next selection I criticize all three types of replies to Hume's scepticism, although I do not intend by this any defense of the sceptical position. I try to show that the sceptic's question and claim, while not meaningless, are pointless and that while they cannot be refuted, they can be attenuated and thus safely ignored.

[2] Max Black, *Language and Philosophy* (Ithaca, New York: Cornell University Press, 1949), p. 13.

The essay by Bertrand Russell requires special comment. Through much of his philosophical career Russell believed that inductive inference requires some principle of uniformity if the inference is to be valid or justifiable. Later, however, becoming convinced that a uniformity principle is demonstrably false, he decided that certain requirements must be met by non-demonstrative statements in order for them to have an antecedent probability and thus admit of inductive test. These antecedent requirements, not any uniformity principle, Russell concludes, provide the grounds which justify non-demonstrative inference. In the selection, "Non-demonstrative Inference and Induction," the first part represents Russell's earlier view; the second part, which has not previously been published, presents his present view.

Whatever position you finally adopt as your own, by the time you finish reading these selections you should have a good understanding of the problem of induction and a feeling for the twists and turns of its philosophical analysis.

Of the Ground of Induction

J. S. MILL

Induction properly so called, as distinguished from those mental operations, sometimes, though improperly, designated by the name, may, then, be summarily defined as Generalization from Experience. It consists in inferring from some individual instances in which a phenomenon is observed to occur, that it occurs in all instances of a certain class; namely, in all which *resemble* the former, in what are regarded as the material circumstances.

In what way the material circumstances are to be distinguished from those which are immaterial, or why some of the circumstances are material and others not so, we are not yet ready to point out. We must first observe, that there is a principle implied in the very statement of what Induction is; an assumption with regard to the course of nature and the order of the universe; namely, that there are such things in nature as parallel cases; that what happens once, will, under a sufficient degree of similarity of circumstances, happen again, and not only again, but as often as the same circumstances recur. This, I say, is an assumption, involved in every case of induction. And, if we consult the actual course of nature, we find that the assumption is warranted. The universe, so far as known to us, is so constituted, that whatever is true in any one case, is true in all cases of a certain description; the only difficulty is, to find what description.

This universal fact, which is our warrant for all inferences from experience, has been described by different philosophers in different forms of language: that the course of nature is uniform; that the universe is governed by general laws; and the like. One of the most usual of these modes of expression,

A System of Logic, Book III, Chapter III, Sections 1, 2. 8th edition. New York: Harper and Brothers, 1895.

but also one of the most inadequate, is that which has been brought into familiar use by the metaphysicians of the school of Reid and Stewart. The disposition of the human mind to generalize from experience – a propensity considered by these philosophers as an instinct of our nature – they usually describe under some such name as "our intuitive conviction that the future will resemble the past." Now it has been well pointed out by Mr. Bailey, that (whether the tendency be or not an original and ultimate element of our nature), Time, in its modifications of past, present, and future, has no concern either with the belief itself, or with the grounds of it. We believe that fire will burn to-morrow, because it burned to-day and yesterday; but we believe, on precisely the same grounds, that it burned before we were born, and that it burns this very day in Cochin-China. It is not from the past to the future, as past and future, that we infer, but from the known to the unknown; from facts observed to facts unobserved; from what we have perceived, or been directly conscious of, to what has not come within our experience. In this last predicament is the whole region of the future; but also the vastly greater portion of the present and of the past.

Whatever be the most proper mode of expressing it, the proposition that the course of nature is uniform, is the fundamental principle, or general axiom, of Induction. It would yet be a great error to offer this large generalization as any explanation of the inductive process. On the contrary, I hold it to be itself an instance of induction, and induction by no means of the most obvious kind. Far from being the first induction we make, it is one of the last, or at all events one of those which are latest in attaining strict philosophical accuracy. As a general maxim, indeed, it has scarcely entered into the minds of any but philosophers; nor even by them, as we shall have many opportunities of remarking, have its extent and limits been always very justly conceived. The truth is, that this great generalization is itself founded on prior generalizations. The obscurer laws of nature were discovered by means of it, but the more obvious ones must have been understood and assented to as general truths before it was ever heard of. We should never have thought of affirming that all phenomena take place according to general laws, if we had not first arrived, in the case of a great multitude of phenomena, at some knowledge of the laws themselves; which could be done no otherwise than by induction. In what sense, then, can a principle, which is so far from being our earliest induction, be regarded as our warrant for all the others? In the only sense, in which (as we have already seen) the general propositions which we place at the head of our reasonings when we throw them into syllogisms, ever really contribute to their validity. As Archbishop Whately remarks, every induction is a syllogism with the major premise suppressed; or (as I prefer expressing it) every induction may be thrown into the form of a syllogism, by supplying a major premise. If this be actually done, the principle which we are now considering, that of the uniformity of the course of nature, will appear as the ultimate major premise of all inductions, and will, therefore, stand to all inductions in the relation in which, as has been shown at so much length, the major proposition of a syllogism always stands to the conclusion; not contributing at all to prove it, but being a necessary condition of its being proved; since no conclusion is proved, for which there can not be found a true major premise.

The statement, that the uniformity of the course of nature is the ultimate major premise in all cases of induction, may be thought to require some explanation. The immediate major premise in every inductive argument, it certainly is not. Of that, Archbishop Whately's must be held to be the correct account. The induction, "John, Peter, etc., are mortal, therefore all mankind are mortal," may, as he justly says, be thrown into a syllogism by prefixing as a major premise (what is at any rate a necessary condition of the validity of the argument), namely, that what is true of John, Peter, etc., is true of all mankind. But how came we by this major premise? It is not self-evident; nay, in all cases of unwarranted generalization, it is not true. How, then, is it arrived at? Necessarily either by induction or ratiocination; and if by induction, the process, like all other inductive arguments, may be thrown into the form of a syllogism. This previous syllogism it is, therefore, necessary to construct. There is, in the long run, only one possible construction. The real proof that what is true of John, Peter, etc., is true of all mankind, can only be, that a different supposition would be inconsistent with the uniformity which we know to exist in the course of nature. Whether there would be this inconsistency or not, may be a matter of long and delicate inquiry; but unless there would, we have no sufficient ground for the major of the inductive syllogism. It hence appears, that if we throw the whole course of any inductive argument into a series of syllogisms, we shall arrive by more or fewer steps at an ultimate syllogism, which will have for its major premise the principle, or axiom, of the uniformity of the course of nature.

It was not to be expected that in the case of this axiom, any more than of other axioms, there should be unanimity among thinkers with respect to the grounds on which it is to be received as true. I have already stated that I regard it as itself a generalization from experience. Others hold it to be a principle which, antecedently to any verification by experience, we are compelled by the constitution of our thinking faculty to assume as true. Having so recently, and at so much length, combated a similar doctrine as applied to the axioms of mathematics, by arguments which are in a great measure applicable to the present case, I shall defer the more particular discussion of this controverted point in regard to the fundamental axiom of induction, until a more advanced period of our inquiry. . . .

In order to obtain a better understanding of the problem which the logician must solve if he would establish a scientific theory of Induction, let us compare a few cases of incorrect inductions with others which are acknowledged to be legitimate. Some, we know, which were believed for centuries to be correct, were nevertheless incorrect. That all swans are white, can not have been a good induction, since the conclusion has turned out erroneous. The experience, however, on which the conclusion rested, was genuine. From the earliest records, the testimony of the inhabitants of the known world was unanimous on the point. The uniform experience, therefore, of the inhabitants of the known world, agreeing in a common result, without one known instance of deviation from that result, is not always sufficient to establish a general conclusion.

But let us now turn to an instance apparently not very dissimilar to this. Mankind were wrong, it seems, in concluding that all swans were white: are we also wrong, when we conclude that all men's heads grow above their shoulders, and never below, in spite of the conflicting testimony of the naturalist Pliny? As there were black swans, though civilized people had existed for three thousand years on the earth without meeting with them, may there not also be "men whose heads do grow beneath their shoulders," notwithstanding a rather less perfect unanimity of negative testimony from observers? Most persons would answer No; it was more credible that a bird should vary in its color, than that men should vary in the relative position of their principal organs. And there is no doubt that in so saying they would be right: but to say why they are right, would be impossible, without entering more deeply than is usually done, into the true theory of Induction.

Again, there are cases in which we reckon with the most unfailing confidence upon uniformity, and other cases in which we do not count upon it at all. In some we feel complete assurance that the future will resemble the past, the unknown be precisely similar to the known. In others, however invariable may be the result obtained from the instances which have been observed, we draw from them no more than a very feeble presumption that the like result will hold in all other cases. That a straight line is the shortest distance between two points, we do not doubt to be true even in the region of the fixed stars. When a chemist announces the existence and properties of a newly-discovered substance, if we confide in his accuracy, we feel assured that the conclusions he has arrived at will hold universally, though the induction be founded but on a single instance. We do not withhold our assent, waiting for a repetition of the experiment; or if we do, it is from a doubt whether the one experiment was properly made, not whether if properly made it would be conclusive. Here, then, is a general law of nature, inferred without hesitation from a single instance; a universal proposition from a singular one. Now mark another case, and contrast it with this. Not all the instances which have been observed since the beginning of the world, in support of the general proposition that all crows are black, would be deemed a sufficient presumption of the truth of the proposition, to outweigh the testimony of one unexceptionable witness who should affirm that in some region of the earth not fully explored, he had caught and examined a crow, and had found it to be gray.

Why is a single instance, in some cases, sufficient for a complete induction, while in others, myriads of concurring instances, without a single exception known or presumed, go such a very little way toward establishing a universal proposition? Whoever can answer this question knows more of the philosophy of logic than the wisest of the ancients, and has solved the problem of induction.

Induction as Experimental and Self-Corrective

CHARLES S. PEIRCE

Suppose a ship arrives at Liverpool laden with wheat in bulk. Suppose that by some machinery the whole cargo be stirred up with great thoroughness. Suppose that twenty-seven thimblefulls be taken equally from the forward, midships, and aft parts, from the starboard, center, and larboard parts, and from the top, half depth, and lower parts of her hold, and that these being

Reprinted by permission of the publishers from Charles Hartshorne and Paul Weiss, editors, *Collected Papers of Charles Sanders Peirce,* Vol. VI, *Scientific Metaphysics,* Cambridge, Mass.: Harvard University Press, mixed and the grains counted, four-fifths of the latter are found to be of quality *A*. Then we infer, experientially and provisionally, that approximately four-fifths of all the grain in the cargo is of the same quality. I say we infer this *experientially* and *provisionally*. By saying that we infer it *experientially,* I mean that our conclusion makes no pretension to knowledge of wheat-in-itself, our ἀλήθεια, as the derivation of that word implies, has nothing to do with *latent* wheat. We are dealing only with the matter of possible experience – experience in the full acceptation of the term as something not merely affecting the senses but also as the subject of thought. If there be any wheat hidden on the ship, so that it can neither turn up in the sample nor be heard of subsequently from purchasers – or if it be half-hidden, so that it may, indeed, turn up, but is less likely to do so than the rest – or if it can affect our senses and our pockets, but from some strange cause or causelessness cannot be reasoned about – all such wheat is to be excluded (or have only its proportional weight) in calculating that true proportion of quality *A,* to which our inference seeks to approximate. By saying that we draw the inference *provisionally,* I mean that we do not hold that we have reached any assigned degree of approximation as yet, but only hold that if our experience be indefinitely extended, and if every fact of whatever nature, as fast as it presents itself, be duly applied, according to the inductive method, in correcting the inferred ratio, then our approximation will become indefinitely close in the long run; that is to say, close to the experience *to come* (not merely close by the exhaustion of a finite collection) so that if experience in general is to fluctuate irregularly to and fro, in a manner to deprive the ratio sought of all definite value, we shall be able to find out approximately within what limits it fluctuates, and if, after having one definite value, it changes and assumes another, we shall be able to find that out, and in short, whatever may be the variations of this ratio in experience, experience indefinitely extended will enable us to detect them, so as to predict rightly, at last, what its ultimate value may be, if it have any ultimate value, or what the ultimate law of succession of values may be, if there be any such ultimate law, or that it ultimately fluctuates irregularly within certain limits, if it do so ultimately fluctuate. Now our inference, claiming to be no more than thus experiential and provisional, manifestly involves no [uniformity] postulate whatever.

For what is a postulate? It is the formulation of a material fact which we are not entitled to assume as a premiss, but the truth of which is requisite to the validity of an inference. Any fact, then, which might be supposed postulated, must either be such that it would ultimately present itself in experience, or not. If it will present itself, we need not postulate it now in our provisional inference, since we shall ultimately be entitled to use it as a premiss. But if it never would present itself in experience, our conclusion is valid but for the possibility of this fact being otherwise than assumed, that is, it is valid as far as possible experience goes, and that is all that we claim. Thus, every postulate is cut off, either by the provisionality or by the experientiality of our inference. For instance, it has been said that induction postulates that, if an indefinite succession of samples be drawn, examined, and thrown back each before the next is drawn, then in the long run every grain will be drawn as often as any other, that is to say, postulates that the ratio of the numbers of times in which any two are drawn will indefinitely approximate to unity. But no such postulate is made; for if, on the one hand, we are to have no other experience of the wheat than from such drawings, it is the ratio that presents itself in those drawings and not the ratio which belongs to the wheat in its latent existence that we are endeavoring to determine; while if, on the other hand, there is some other mode by which the wheat is to come under our knowledge, equivalent to another kind of sampling, so that after all our care in stirring up the wheat some experiential grains will present themselves in the first sampling operation more often than others in the long run, this very singular fact will be sure to get discovered by the inductive method, which must avail itself of every sort of experience; and our inference, which was only provisional, corrects itself at last. Again, it has been said, that induction postulates that under like circumstances like events will happen, and that this postulate is at bottom the same as the principle of universal causation. But this is a blunder, or *bévue,* due to thinking exclusively of inductions where the concluded ratio is either 1 or 0. If any such proposition were postulated, it would be that under like circumstances (the circumstances of drawing the different samples) different events occur in the same proportions in all the different sets – a proposition which is false and even absurd. But in truth no such thing is postulated, the experiential character of the inference reducing the condition of validity to this, that if a certain result does not occur, the opposite result will be manifested, a condition assured by the provisionality of the inference. But it may be asked whether it is not conceivable that every instance of a certain class destined to be ever employed as a datum of induction should have one character, while every instance destined not to be so employed should have the opposite character. The answer is that, in that case, the instances excluded from being subjects of reasoning would not be experienced in the full sense of the word, but would be among these *latent* individuals of which our conclusion does not pretend to speak.

To this account of the rationale of induction I know of but one objection worth mention: it is that I thus fail to deduce the full degree of force which this mode of inference in fact possesses; that according to my view, no matter how thorough and elaborate the stirring and mixing process had been, the examination of a single handful of grain would not give me any assurance, sufficient to risk money upon, that the next handful would not greatly modify the concluded value of the ratio under inquiry, while, in fact, the assurance would be very high that this ratio was not greatly in error. If the true ratio of grains of quality A were 0.80 and the handful contained a thousand grains, nine such handfuls out of every ten would contain from 780 to 820 grains of quality A. The answer to this is that the calculation given is correct when we know that the units of this handful and the quality inquired into have the normal independence of one another, if for instance the stirring has been complete and the character sampled for has been settled upon in advance of the examination of the sample. But in so far as these conditions are not known to be complied with, the above figures cease to be applicable. Random sampling and predesignation of the character sampled for should always be striven after in inductive reasoning, but when they cannot be attained, so long as it is conducted honestly, the inference retains some value. When we cannot ascertain how the sampling has been done or the sample-character selected, induction still has the essential validity which my present account of it shows it to have.

The Pragmatic Justification of Induction

JOHN W. LENZ

The purpose of this paper is to examine critically the so-called pragmatic justification of induction. This defense was first given by Peirce, but I shall restrict my discussion to Reichenbach's more thorough statement of it.[1] I shall, first, explain Reichenbach's formulation of the rule of induction; second, explain his pragmatic justification of this rule; and, third, assess the significance of his defense. Nowhere in this paper shall I discuss the much larger question whether induction needs some kind of justification, though, in my opinion, the answer is yes. And though I shall be highly critical of Reichenbach's pragmatic vindication, I shall leave aside the residual question of how induction should be justified.

1. Reichenbach's Rule of Induction

The rule of induction has been formulated in many ways, some of which are none too precise: "when predicting, assume that the future will be like the past," "make one's predictions on the assumption that nature is uniform," etc. To understand Reichenbach's justification we must first see what specific formulation of the inductive rule he is defending.

Reichenbach's rule of induction can be illustrated by the following simple application of it. Suppose that we have tossed a coin 200 times, and that it has turned up heads 98 times. Suppose, that is, that in an initial part of the series of coin tosses the relative frequency with which it has turned up heads is $98/200$. Reichenbach's rule of induction tells us to predict that, if the coin is tossed long enough, the relative frequency with which heads occurs remains approximately $98/200$. More exactly and more generally, his rule is: if in an initial segment of a series of events the relative frequency with which A's have been B's is m/n (where n is the number of A's and m is the number of A's that are B's), predict that in the long run, that is, as the number of A's gets larger and larger, the relative frequency will at some point continue to be approximately m/n. Those who are familiar with Reichenbach's frequency interpretation of probability will see that his rule of induction tells us to predict that the limit of the relative frequency in an infinite series of events is identical with, or close to, the relative frequency in an initial segment of the series.[2]

[1] Charles S. Peirce, "Induction as Experimental and Self-corrective," reprinted in this volume. Hans Reichenbach, *Theory of Probability* (Berkeley, 1949), pp. 429–482. A less technical account may be found in his *Experience and Prediction* (Chicago, 1938), pp. 339–363.

[2] Here as elsewhere in this paper I am trying to avoid technicalities. Reichenbach's exact formulation is: "If an initial section of n elements of a sequence x_i is given, resulting in the frequency f^n, and if, furthermore, nothing is known about the probability of the second level for the occurrence of a certain limit p, we posit that the frequency f^i $(i > n)$ will approach a limit p within $f^n \pm \delta$ when the sequence is continued." *Theory of Probability*, p. 446.

It is necessary to always keep in mind that it is *this* rule of induction alone which Reichenbach tries to justify. Certainly there are many other formulations of the rule of induction to which his pragmatic justification is irrelevant. We must note too that while in one sense Reichenbach's formulation of the rule of induction is fairly broad, in another sense it is extremely narrow. It is broad in the sense that the usual inductive rule: "when all observed A's have been B's, predict that all A's will continue to be B's" is simply a particular case of Reichenbach's more general rule. It is a particular case in that here the observed relative frequency with which A's have been B's is 1. Reichenbach's rule has the virtue of allowing us to make not only universal generalizations but statistical generalizations as well.

On the other hand Reichenbach's rule of induction is narrow in at least two ways. It is narrow, first of all, in that it is only one among many inductive rules that are actually employed in science and everyday life. For example, it is also a rule of science and of common sense that we should not make predictions on the basis of small samples. Reichenbach's reply here, however, would be that all other such rules can be established by using his inductive rule.[3] The conclusion that we should "avoid predicting on the basis of small samples" is itself inductively inferred from our having observed that in the past such predictions have been very unreliable. Whether Reichenbach's general claim here is valid is a complex question into which I cannot enter in this paper.

In any case Reichenbach's rule of induction is narrow in a more crucial sense. It is narrow in that the predictions it advises concern only what will happen in the long run (for example, that, as the coin is tossed more and more, the relative frequency with which heads occurs will after some point remain approximately $^{98}\!/_{200}$). His rule of induction does not enable us to predict what will happen in the short run (for example, to predict that in the next 100 tosses of the coin, the frequency with which heads occurs is $^{98}\!/_{200}$). This means that even if Reichenbach succeeds in justifying his rule of induction, it does not follow that he will have succeeded in justifying a rule of induction enabling us to predict what happens in the short run.

[3] *Theory of Probability*, pp. 442–444.

2. Reichenbach's Justification of Induction

The problem of induction is easily formulated. In any inductive inference employing Reichenbach's rule the conclusion asserts more than the evidence upon which it is based. The problem of induction is simply to justify such inferences in which "the conclusion goes beyond the premises," or more exactly, to justify the rule which such inferences employ.

Reichenbach points out that obviously the conclusion of an inductive inference does not logically follow from a statement of the evidence; it is not contradictory to affirm the evidence and deny the conclusion. Hence, he concludes that it is not possible to justify induction "logically" in the sense of demonstrating that all, or even some, inductive conclusions are correct. He insists, moreover, that one cannot inductively justify the rule of induction, that is, infer that because in the past it has been more or less successful it will continue to be successful. Such a justification, Reichenbach agrees, would be circular. In denying that one can give such *a priori* or *a posteriori* justifications of induction Reichenbach follows Hume completely.

Nonetheless Reichenbach assures us that we need not despair, for some other kind of justification of induction is possible. This justification can best be explained in terms of the simple example we used in explaining his rule of induction. Suppose, again, that we have tossed a coin 200 times, and that it has turned up heads 98 times. Reichenbach's rule, we will remember, tells us to predict that in the long run the relative frequency with which heads occurs will remain $98/200$. Reichenbach admits that no guarantee can be given that this particular prediction is correct. It might be that as the coin is tossed more and more the frequency with which heads occurs remains $1/4$. Reichenbach admits, furthermore, that we cannot guarantee that even the repeated use of his rule of induction will ever lead to a successful prediction. Suppose, that is, that as we toss the coin more and more we use the "latest" observed relative frequency with which heads occurs in making our predictions of the relative frequency in the long run. Reichenbach admits that no guarantee can be given that a single one of these predictions is correct. It might be the case that as the coin is tossed more and more the relative frequency with which heads occurs continues to oscillate violently.

Reichenbach's justification of induction rests upon a different claim. Reichenbach shows that if it is the case that, as the coin is tossed more and more, there is some point after which the relative frequency with which heads occurs remains more or less constant, then the *repeated* use of the rule of induction will discover that relative frequency. One can easily generalize his claim here: if, as the number of A's gets larger and larger, there is some point after which the relative frequency with which A's are B's remains fairly constant, then the repeated use of his rule of induction will lead to correct predictions of that relative frequency. This, Reichenbach shows, is demonstrably true.

Several points are important here. First, Reichenbach's claim is hypothetical in form. It says that *if success is possible* (where success is interpreted narrowly to mean correctly predicting long run relative frequencies) then the repeated use of the inductive method will bring success. Second, Reichenbach does not really defend any particular use of the rule of induction but only its *repeated* use. The rule of induction is self-corrective in the precise sense that its repeated use will eventually lead to success, if success is possible. Thirdly, Reichenbach admits that one cannot know *at what point* the repeated use of the inductive method will bring success, if success is possible. Fourthly, Reichenbach shows that we can *know,* prior to any inductive evidence, that the rule of induction is self-corrective in the above sense.

So far Reichenbach's defense consists simply in stating certain properties which his rule of induction has. We must now turn to Reichenbach's further claim that, in comparison with other methods of predicting, the rule of induction is the *best* means we have of attaining our end of successful prediction.

At times Reichenbach makes the very misleading statement that the method of induction is a necessary condition of successful prediction. This is surely misleading in that it suggests that only the inductive method will lead to successful prediction. This cannot be Reichenbach's claim. Indeed, he does agree that other methods, say that of the clairvoyant, could be successful. Reichenbach agrees, even, that other methods, say that of the soothsayer, might be successful more quickly than the inductive method. Reichenbach's claim is, first, that if any other method of prediction is successful then the repeated use of the inductive method will eventually lead to success. In other words, the eventual success of the repeated use of the inductive method is a necessary condition of any successful prediction. His claim is, second, that only the inductive method can be known in advance, and without any prior inductive inference, to lead to success if success is possible. This is enough, Reichenbach claims, to justify our use of the inductive method.

3. Criticism

To deny that Reichenbach has justified induction would be, I think, to enter into a fruitless quarrel concerning the word "justify." [4] However, a clear understanding of Reichenbach's pragmatic justification of induction will show how very weak it is. In this section I shall content myself simply with underlining the insignificance of Reichenbach's defense.

First of all, it must never be forgotten that since his rule of induction speaks only about relative frequencies in the long run his justification leaves entirely aside the problem of justifying predictions of short run relative frequencies. And surely in science and everyday life we are most concerned with the latter. An insurance company does not care to know the long run relative frequency with which American males of age 32 die before reaching 60. They are, after all, concerned only with the next 50 years or so. Of course, if we could assume that the short run relative frequencies will approximate those of the long run, Reichenbach's rule of induction would be helpful. But of the truth of this assumption Reichenbach's pragmatic justification gives no assurance.

In the second place, it must always be remembered that Reichenbach in his pragmatic justification of induction gives us no assurance that any of the predictions one actually makes using his rule are correct or even probably correct. He does show, it is true, that the repeated use of the inductive rule will lead to success (in his narrow sense of success) if success is possible. However, as he readily admits, he gives no reason for believing success is possible. Furthermore, even if success is possible, it may be achieved too late for all of us. It hardly helps to be assured that the repeated use of the inductive method will eventually lead to success. That eventuality may come too late for every member of the human race.[5] Still further, even if success is achieved by using his rule of induction, one will never know it on the strength of Reichenbach's justification. As Reichenbach admits, we do not know how many tries with the inductive method we must make before success comes.

My third point is one that cannot be easily explained, but since it is an extremely crucial one, I shall outline it here. Actually, one can show that there are other inductive methods which are known to be self-corrective in Reichenbach's sense. Reichenbach not only "justifies" his rule of induction but also a whole class of inductive rules. It is true that the predictions made on the basis of any of these rules converge towards the limit of the relative frequency in an infinite series of events, if there is such a limit. That is, as the evidence gets larger and larger the predictions these rules lead to vary less and less. But before this happens, the predictions we make will vary tremendously depending upon which rule is used. Since we have, on Reichenbach's own terms, no decisive reason for choosing between these rules, our predictions will accordingly be almost entirely arbitrary. We simply shall not know what predictions to make.

One of these rules may lead to the best predictions, as a simple illustration will show. Suppose that the long run relative frequency with which A's are B's is $\frac{3}{5}$. Suppose further that the observed relative frequency with which A's have been B's is $\frac{40}{60}$. There exists an inductive rule, justified in Reichenbach's sense, which would predict, on the basis of this evidence, that the long run relative frequency is $\frac{3}{5}$. This rule, if

[4] One could, perhaps, charge Reichenbach with using words like "justify," "success," "self-corrective," etc. in an unusual and, therefore, potentially misleading way. Cf. Max Black, *Problems of Analysis* (Ithaca, N.Y., 1954), p. 187.

[5] This point is mitigated somewhat by Reichenbach's at times putting his defense in terms of a "practical limit," that is, a limit of a series whose convergence is rapid enough to be discovered by humans. None-the-less, Reichenbach gives us no more assurance that such a limit exists than he does that there is a limit of any kind.

used in this case, would, therefore, actually be superior to Reichenbach's own rule of induction, which would predict that the long run relative frequency was 2/3. It would be superior to Reichenbach's rule of induction in that by using it, we would achieve success earlier. The trouble is, of course, that we do not know in advance what the actual long run relative frequency is, and accordingly we do not know which rule to use, which predictions to make.

4. Conclusion

In conclusion I want to make just two points. First, nowhere have I denied that Reichenbach has done valuable service in clarifying the logical properties of his rule of induction. Pragmatic considerations aside, it is worthwhile having shown that his rule of induction is "self-corrective" in at least one precise sense. Second, I want to suggest why any such "justification" as Reichenbach's must remain pragmatically insignificant. In so doing I shall simply repeat a principle that was the keystone of Hume's original formulation of the problem of induction. The heart of Reichenbach's vindication is a bare tautology, namely, that his rule of induction is in his sense "self-corrective." [6] Hume's well known point is that no tautology can by itself lead to "useful" conclusions, and the one Reichenbach gives us is no exception.

[6] The following example will bring out the tautological character of Reichenbach's justification. When one understands Reichenbach's formulation of the principle of induction one sees that all it asserts is that there is a limit of the relative frequency in an infinite series. Reichenbach's justification of this principle is that it is true if there is a limit. Thus his justification of the principle of induction reduces to the bare logical truth that if there is a limit, there is a limit.

The 'Justification' of Induction

P. F. STRAWSON

[1] We have seen something of the nature of inductive reasoning; of how one statement or set of statements may support another statement, S, which they do not entail, with varying degrees of strength, ranging from being conclusive evidence for S to being only slender evidence for it; from making S as certain as the supporting statements, to giving it some slight probability. We have seen too, how the question of degree of support is complicated by consideration of relative frequencies and numerical chances.

There is, however, a residual philosophical question which enters so largely into discussion of the subject that it must be dis-

Introduction to Logical Theory, Chapter 9. London: Methuen and Co., Ltd., 1952; New York: John Wiley & Sons, Inc., 1952. Reprinted by permission of the author and the publishers.

cussed. It can be raised, roughly, in the following forms. What reason have we to place reliance on inductive procedures? Why should we suppose that the accumulation of instances of *A*s which are *B*s, however various the conditions in which they are observed, gives any good reason for expecting the next *A* we encounter to be a *B?* It is our habit to form expectations in this way; but can the habit be rationally justified? When this doubt has entered our minds it may be difficult to free ourselves from it. For the doubt has its source in a confusion; and some attempts to resolve the doubt preserve the confusion; and other attempts to show that the doubt is senseless seem altogether too facile. The root-confusion is easily described; but simply to describe it seems an inadequate remedy against it. So the doubt must be examined again and again, in the light of different attempts to remove it.

If someone asked what grounds there were for supposing that deductive reasoning was valid, we might answer that there were in fact no grounds for supposing that deductive reasoning was always valid; sometimes people made valid inferences, and sometimes they were guilty of logical fallacies. If he said that we had misunderstood his question, and that what he wanted to know was what grounds there were for regarding deduction in general as a valid method of argument, we should have to answer that his question was without sense, for to say that an argument, or a form or method of argument, was valid or invalid would *imply* that it was deductive; the concepts of validity and invalidity had application only to individual deductive arguments or forms of deductive argument. Similarly, if a man asked what grounds there were for thinking it reasonable to hold beliefs arrived at inductively, one might at first answer that there were good and bad inductive arguments, that sometimes it was reasonable to hold a belief arrived at inductively and sometimes it was not. If he, too, said that his question had been misunderstood, that he wanted to know whether induction in general was a reasonable method of inference, then we might well think his question senseless in the same way as the question whether deduction is in general valid; for to call a particular belief reasonable or unreasonable is to apply inductive standards, just as to call a particular argument valid or invalid is to apply deductive standards. The parallel is not wholly convincing; for words like 'reasonable' and 'rational' have not so precise and technical a sense as the word 'valid.' Yet it is sufficiently powerful to make us wonder how the second question could be raised at all, to wonder why, in contrast with the corresponding question about deduction, it should have seemed to constitute a genuine problem.

Suppose that a man is brought up to regard formal logic as the study of the science and art of reasoning. He observes that all inductive processes are, by deductive standards, invalid; the premises never entail the conclusions. Now inductive processes are notoriously important in the formation of beliefs and expectations about everything which lies beyond the observation of available witnesses. But an *invalid* argument is an *unsound* argument; an *unsound* argument is one in which *no good reason* is produced for accepting the conclusion. So if inductive processes are invalid, if all the arguments we should produce, if challenged, in support of our beliefs about what lies beyond the observation of available witnesses are unsound, then we have no good reason for any of these beliefs. This conclusion is repugnant. So there arises the demand for a justification, not of this or that particular belief which goes beyond what is entailed by our evidence, but a justification of induction in general. And when the demand arises in this way it is, in effect, the demand that induction shall be shown to be really a kind of deduction; for nothing less will satisfy the doubter when this is the route to his doubts.

Tracing this, the most common route to the general doubt about the reasonableness of induction, shows how the doubt seems to escape the absurdity of a demand that induction in general shall be justified by inductive standards. The demand is that induction should be shown to be a rational process; and this turns out to be the demand that one kind of reasoning should be shown to be another and different kind. Put thus crudely, the demand seems to escape one absurdity only to fall into another. Of course, inductive arguments are not deductively valid; if they were, they would be deductive arguments. Inductive reasoning must be assessed, for soundness, by inductive standards. Nevertheless, fantastic as the wish for induction to be deduction may seem, it is only in terms of it that we can understand some of the attempts that have been made to justify induction.

[2] The first kind of attempt I shall consider might be called the search for the supreme premise of inductions. In its primitive form it is quite a crude attempt; and I shall make it cruder by caricature. We have already seen that for a particular inductive step, such as 'The kettle has been on the fire for ten minutes, so it will be boiling by now,' we can substitute a deductive argument by introducing a generalization (e.g., 'A kettle always boils within ten minutes of being put on the fire') as an additional premise. This maneuver shifted the emphasis of the problem of inductive support on to the question of how we established such generalizations as these, which rested on grounds by which they were not entailed. But suppose the maneuver could be repeated. Suppose we could find one supremely general proposition, which taken in conjunction with the evidence for any accepted generalization of science or daily life (or at least of science) would entail that generalization. Then, so long as the status of the supreme generalization could be satisfactorily explained, we could regard all sound inductions to unqualified general conclusions as, at bottom, valid deductions. The justification would be found, for at least these cases. The most obvious difficulty in this suggestion is that of formulating the supreme general proposition in such a way that it shall be precise enough to yield the desired entailments, and yet not obviously false or arbitrary. Consider, for example, the formula: 'For all f, g, wherever n cases of f and g, and no cases of f and not g, are observed, then all cases of f are cases of g.' To turn it into a sentence, we have only to replace 'n' by some number. But what number? If we take the value of 'n' to be 1 or 20 or 500, the resulting statement is obviously false. Moreover, the choice of any number would seem quite arbitrary; there is no privileged number of favourable instances which we take as decisive in establishing a generalization. If, on the other hand, we phrase the proposition vaguely enough to escape these objections – if, for example, we phrase it as 'Nature is uniform' – then it becomes too vague to provide the desired entailments. It should be noticed that the impossibility of framing a general proposition of the kind required is really a special case of the impossibility of framing precise rules for the assessment of evidence. If we could frame a rule which would tell us precisely when we had *conclusive* evidence for a generalization, then it would yield just the proposition required as the supreme premise.

Even if these difficulties could be met, the question of the status of the supreme premise would remain. How, if a non-necessary proposition, could it be established? The appeal to experience, to inductive support, is clearly barred on pain of circularity. If, on the other hand, it were a necessary truth and possessed, in conjunction with the evidence for a generalization, the required logical power to entail the generalization (e.g., if the latter were the conclusion of a hypothetical syllogism, of which the hypothetical premise was the necessary truth in question), then the evidence would entail the generalization independently, and the problem would not arise: a conclusion unbearably paradoxical. In practice, the extreme vagueness with which candidates for the role of supreme premise are expressed prevents their acquiring such logical power, and at the same time renders it very difficult to classify them as analytic or synthetic: under pressure they may tend to tautology; and, when the pressure is removed, assume an expansively synthetic air.

In theories of the kind which I have here caricatured the ideal of deduction is not usually so blatantly manifest as I have made it. One finds the 'Law of the Uniformity of Nature' presented less as the suppressed premise of crypto-deductive inferences than as, say, the 'presupposition of the validity of inductive reasoning.' I shall have more to say about this in my last section.

[3] I shall next consider a more sophisticated kind of attempt to justify induction: more sophisticated both in its interpretation of this aim and in the method adopted to achieve it. The aim envisaged is that of proving that the probability of a generalization, whether universal or proportional, increases with the number of instances for which it is found to hold. This clearly is a realistic aim: for the proposition to be proved does state, as we have already seen, a fundamental feature of our criteria for assessing the strength of evidence. The method of proof proposed is mathematical. Use is to be made of the arithmetical calculation of chances. This, however, seems less realistic: for we have already seen that the prospect of analysing the notion of support in these terms seems poor.

I state the argument as simply as possible; but, even so, it will be necessary to introduce and explain some new terms. Suppose we had a collection of objects of different kinds, some with some characteristics and some with others. Suppose, for example, we had a bag containing 100 balls, of which 70 were white and 30 black. Let us call such a collection of objects a *population;* and let us call the way it is made up (e.g., in the case imagined, of 70 white and 30 black balls) the *constitution* of the population. From such a population it would be possible to take *samples* of various sizes. For example, we might take from our bag a sample of 30 balls. Suppose each ball in the bag had an individual number. Then the collection of balls numbered 10 to 39 inclusive would be one sample of a given size; the collection of balls numbered 11 to 40 inclusive would be another and different sample of the same size: the collection of balls numbered 2, 4, 6, 8 . . . 58, 60 would be another such sample; and so on. Each possible collection of 30 balls is a different sample of the same size. Some different samples of the same size will have the same constitutions as one another; others will have different constitutions. Thus there will be only one sample made up of 30 black balls. There will be many different samples which share the constitution: 20 white and 10 black. It would be a simple matter of mathematics to work out the number of possible samples of the given size which had any one possible constitution. Let us say that a sample *matches* the population if, allowing for the difference between them in size, the constitution of the sample corresponds, within certain limits, to that of the population. For example, we might say that any possible sample consisting of, say, 21 white and 9 black balls matched the constitution (70 white and 30 black) of the population, whereas a sample consisting of 20 white and 10 black balls did not. Now it is a proposition of pure mathematics that, given any population, the proportion of possible samples, all of the same size, which match the population, increases with the size of the sample.

We have seen that conclusions about the ratio of a subset of equally possible chances to the whole set of those chances may be expressed by the use of the word 'probability.' Thus of the 52 possible samples of one card from a population constituted like an orthodox pack, 16 are court-cards or aces. This fact we allow ourselves to express (under the conditions, inductively established, of equipossibility of draws) by saying that the probability of drawing a court-card or an ace was $4/13$. If we express the proposition referred to at the end of the last paragraph by means of this use of 'probability' we shall obtain the result: The probability of a sample matching a given population increases with the size of the sample. It is tempting to try to derive from this result a general justification of the inductive procedure: which will not, indeed, show that any given inductive conclusion is entailed by the evidence for it, taken in conjunction with some universal premise, but will show that the multiplication of favourable instances of a generalization entails a proportionate increase in its probability. For, since *matching* is a symmetrical relation, it might seem a simple deductive step to move from

I. The probability of a sample matching a given population increases with the size of the sample

to

II. The probability of a population matching a given sample increases with the size of the sample.

II might seem to provide a guarantee that the greater the number of cases for which a generalization is observed to hold, the greater is its probability; since in increasing the number of cases we increase the size of the sample from whatever population forms the subject of our generalization. Thus pure mathematics might seem to provide the sought-for proof that the evidence for a generalization really does get stronger, the more favourable instances of it we find.

The argument is ingenious enough to be worthy of respect; but it fails of its purpose, and misrepresents the inductive situation. Our situation is not in the least like that of a man drawing a sample from a given, i.e., fixed and limited, population from which the drawing of any mathematically possible sample is equiprobable with that of any other. Our only datum is the sample. No limit is fixed beforehand to the diversity, and the possibilities of change, of the 'population' from which it is drawn: or, better, to the multiplicity and variousness of different populations, each with different constitutions, any one of which might replace the present one before we make the next draw. Nor is there any *a priori* guarantee that different mathematically possible samples are equally likely to be drawn. If we have or can obtain any assurance on these points, then it is assurance derived inductively from our data, and cannot therefore be assumed at the outset of an argument designed to justify induction. So II, regarded as a justification of induction founded on purely mathematical considerations, is a fraud. The important shift of 'given' from qualifying 'population' in I to qualifying 'sample' in II is illegitimate. Moreover, 'probability,' which means one thing in II (interpreted as giving the required guarantee) means something quite different in I (interpreted as a proposition of pure mathematics). In I probability is simply the measure of the ratio of one set of mathematically possible chances to another; in II it is the measure of the inductive acceptability of a generalization. As a mathematical proposition, I is certainly independent of the soundness of inductive procedures; and as a statement of one of the criteria we use in assessing the strength of evidence of a generalization, II is as certainly independent of mathematics.

It has not escaped the notice of those who have advocated a mathematical justification of induction, that certain assumptions are required to make the argument even seem to fulfil its purpose. Inductive reasoning would be of little use if it did not sometimes enable us to assign at least fairly high probabilities to certain conclusions. Now suppose, in conformity with the mathematical model, we represented the fact that the evidence for a proposition was conclusive by assigning to it the probability figure of 1; and the fact that the evidence for and against a proposition was evenly balanced by assigning to it the probability figure $\frac{1}{2}$; and so on. It is a familiar mathematical truth that, between any two fractions, say $\frac{1}{6}$ and $\frac{1}{5}$, there is an infinite number of intermediate quantities; that $\frac{1}{6}$ can be indefinitely increased without reaching equality to $\frac{1}{5}$. Even if we could regard II as mathematically established, therefore, it fails to give us what we require; for it fails to provide a guarantee that the probability of an inductive conclusion ever attains a degree at which it begins to be of use. It was accordingly necessary to buttress the purely mathematical argument by large, vague assumptions, comparable with the principles designed for the role of supreme premise in the first type of attempt. These assumptions, like those principles, could never actually be used to give a deductive turn to inductive arguments; for they could not be formulated with precision. They were the shadows of precise unknown truths, which, if one did know them, would suffice, along with the data for our accepted generalizations, to enable the probability of the latter to be assigned, after calculation, a precise numerical fraction of a tolerable size. So this theory represents our inductions as the vague sublunary shadows of deductive calculations which we cannot make.

[4] Let us turn from attempts to justify induction to attempts to show that the demand for a justification is mistaken. We have seen already that what lies behind such a demand is often the absurd wish that induction should be shown to be some kind of deduction – and this wish is clearly traceable in the attempts at justification which we have examined. What other sense could we give to the demand? Sometimes it is expressed in the form of a request for proof that induction is a *reasonable* or *rational* procedure, that we have *good grounds* for placing reliance upon it. Consider the uses of the phrases 'good grounds,' 'justification,' 'reasonable,' etc. Often we say such things as 'He has *every justification* for believing that *p*'; 'I have *very good* reasons for believing it'; 'There are *good grounds* for the view that *q*'; 'There is *good evidence* that *r*.' We often talk, in such ways as these, of justification, good grounds or reasons or evidence for certain beliefs. Suppose such a belief were one expressible in the form 'Every case of *f* is a case of *g*.' And suppose someone were asked what he meant by saying that he had good grounds or reasons for holding it. I think it would be felt to be a satisfactory answer if he replied: 'Well, in all my wide and varied experience I've come across innumerable cases of *f* and never a case of *f* which wasn't a case of *g*.' In saying this, he is clearly claiming to have *inductive* support, *inductive* evidence, of a certain kind, for his belief; and he is also giving a perfectly proper answer to the question, what he meant by saying that he had ample justification, good grounds, good reasons for his belief. It is an analytic proposition that it is reasonable to have a degree of belief in a statement which is proportional to the strength of the evidence in its favour; and it is an analytic proposition, though not a proposition of mathematics, that, other things being equal, the evidence for a generalization is strong in proportion as the number of favourable instances, and the variety of circumstances in which they have been found, is great. So to ask whether it is reasonable to place reliance on inductive procedures is like asking whether it is reasonable to proportion the degree of one's convictions to the strength of the evidence. Doing this is what 'being reasonable' *means* in such a context.

As for the other form in which the doubt

may be expressed, viz., 'Is induction a justified, or justifiable, procedure?', it emerges in a still less favourable light. No sense has been given to it, though it is easy to see why it seems to have a sense. For it is generally proper to inquire *of a particular belief,* whether its adoption is justified; and, in asking this, we are asking whether there is good, bad, or any, evidence for it. In applying or withholding the epithets 'justified,' 'well founded,' etc., in the case of specific beliefs, we are appealing to, and applying, inductive standards. But to what standards are we appealing when we ask whether the application of inductive standards is justified or well grounded? If we cannot answer, then no sense has been given to the question. Compare it with the question: Is the law legal? It makes perfectly good sense to inquire of a particular action, of an administrative regulation, or even, in the case of some states, of a particular enactment of the legislature, whether or not it is legal. The question is answered by an appeal to a legal system, by the application of a set of legal (or constitutional) rules or standards. But it makes no sense to inquire in general whether the law of the land, the legal system as a whole, is or is not legal. For to what legal standards are we appealing?

The only way in which a sense might be given to the question, whether induction is in general a justified or justifiable procedure, is a trivial one which we have already noticed. We might interpret it to mean 'Are all conclusions, arrived at inductively, justified?', i.e., 'Do people always have adequate evidence for the conclusions they draw?' The answer to this question is easy but uninteresting: it is that sometimes people have adequate evidence, and sometimes they do not.

[5] It seems, however, that this way of showing the request for a general justification of induction to be absurd is sometimes insufficient to allay the worry that produces it. And to point out that 'forming rational opinions about the unobserved on the evidence available' and 'assessing the evidence by inductive standards' are phrases which describe the same thing, is more apt to produce irritation than relief. The point is felt to be 'merely a verbal' one; and though the point of this protest is itself hard to see, it is clear that something more is required. So the question must be pursued further. First, I want to point out that there is something a little odd about talking of 'the inductive method,' or even 'the inductive policy,' as if it were just one possible method among others of arguing from the observed to the unobserved, from the available evidence to the facts in question. If one asked a meteorologist what method or methods he used to forecast the weather, one would be surprised if he answered: 'Oh, just the inductive method.' If one asked a doctor by what means he diagnosed a certain disease, the answer 'By induction' would be felt as an impatient evasion, a joke, or a rebuke. The answer one hopes for is an account of the tests made, the signs taken account of, the rules and recipes and general laws applied. When such a specific method of prediction or diagnosis is in question, one can ask whether the method is justified in practice; and here again one is asking whether its employment is inductively justified, whether it commonly gives correct results. This question would normally seem an admissible one. One might be tempted to conclude that, while there are many different specific methods of prediction, diagnosis, etc., appropriate to different subjects of inquiry, all such methods could properly be called 'inductive' in the sense that their employment rested on inductive support; and that, hence, the phrase 'non-inductive method of finding out about what lies deductively beyond the evidence' was a description without meaning, a phrase to which no sense had been given; so that there could be no question of justifying our selection of one method, called 'the inductive,' of doing this.

However, someone might object: 'Surely

it is possible, though it might be foolish, to use methods utterly different from accredited scientific ones. Suppose a man, whenever he wanted to form an opinion about what lay beyond his observation or the observation of available witnesses, simply shut his eyes, asked himself the appropriate question, and accepted the first answer that came into his head. Wouldn't this be a non-inductive method?' Well, let us suppose this. The man is asked: 'Do you usually get the right answer by your method?' He might answer: 'You've mentioned one of its drawbacks; I never do get the right answer; but it's an extremely easy method.' One might then be inclined to think that it was not a method of finding things out at all. But suppose he answered: Yes, it's usually (always) the right answer. Then we might be willing to call it a method of finding out, though a strange one. But, then, by the very fact of its success, it would be an inductively supported method. For each application of the method would be an application of the general rule, 'The first answer that comes into my head is generally (always) the right one'; and for the truth of this generalization there would be the inductive evidence of a long run of favourable instances with no unfavourable ones (if it were 'always'), or of a sustained high proportion of successes to trials (if it were 'generally').

So every successful method or recipe for finding out about the unobserved must be one which has inductive support; for to say that a recipe is successful is to say that it has been repeatedly applied with success; and repeated successful application of a recipe constitutes just what we mean by inductive evidence in its favour. Pointing out this fact must not be confused with saying that 'the inductive method' is justified by its success, justified because it works. This is a mistake, and an important one. I am not seeking to 'justify the inductive method,' for no meaning has been given to this phrase. *A fortiori,* I am not saying that induction is justified by its success in finding out about the unobserved. I am saying, rather, that any successful method of finding out about the unobserved is necessarily justified by induction. This is an analytic proposition. The phrase 'successful method of finding things out which has no inductive support' is self-contradictory. Having, or acquiring, inductive support is a necessary condition of the success of a method.

Why point this out at all? First, it may have a certain therapeutic force, a power to reassure. Second, it may counteract the tendency to think of 'the inductive method' as something on a par with specific methods of diagnosis or prediction and therefore, like them, standing in need of (inductive) justification.

[6] There is one further confusion, perhaps the most powerful of all in producing the doubts, questions, and spurious solutions discussed in this Part. We may approach it by considering the claim that induction is justified by its success in practice. The phrase 'success of induction' is by no means clear and perhaps embodies the confusion of induction with some specific method of prediction, etc., appropriate to some particular line of inquiry. But, whatever the phrase may mean, the claim has an obviously circular look. Presumably the suggestion is that we should argue from the past 'successes of induction' to the continuance of those successes in the future; from the fact that it has worked hitherto to the conclusion that it will continue to work. Since an argument of this kind is plainly inductive, it will not serve as a justification of induction. One cannot establish a principle of argument by an argument which uses that principle. But let us go a little deeper. The argument rests the justification of induction on a matter of fact (its 'past successes'). This is characteristic of nearly all attempts to find a justification. The desired premise

of Section 2 was to be some fact about the constitution of the universe which, even if it could not be used as a suppressed premise to give inductive arguments a deductive turn, was at any rate a 'presupposition of the validity of induction.' Even the mathematical argument of Section 3 required buttressing with some large assumption about the make-up of the world. I think the source of this general desire to find out some fact about the constitution of the universe which will 'justify induction' or 'show it to be a rational policy' is the confusion, the running together, of two fundamentally different questions: to one of which the answer is a matter of non-linguistic fact, while to the others it is a matter of meanings.

There is nothing self-contradictory in supposing that all the uniformities in the course of things that we have hitherto observed and come to count on should cease to operate to-morrow; that all our familiar recipes should let us down, and that we should be unable to frame new ones because such regularities as there were were too complex for us to make out. (We may assume that even the expectation that all of us, in such circumstances, would perish, were falsified by someone surviving to observe the new chaos in which, roughly speaking, nothing foreseeable happens.) Of course, we do not believe that this will happen. We believe, on the contrary, that our inductively supported expectation-rules, though some of them will have, no doubt, to be dropped or modified, will continue, on the whole, to serve us fairly well; and that we shall generally be able to replace the rules we abandon with others similarly arrived at. We might give a sense to the phrase 'success of induction' by calling this vague belief the belief that induction will continue to be successful. It is certainly a factual belief, not a necessary truth; a belief, one may say, about the constitution of the universe. We might express it as follows, choosing a phraseology which will serve the better to expose the confusion I wish to expose:

I. (The universe is such that) induction will continue to be successful.

I is very vague: it amounts to saying that there are, and will continue to be, natural uniformities and regularities which exhibit a humanly manageable degree of simplicity. But, though it is vague, certain definite things can be said about it. (1) It is not a necessary, but a contingent, statement; for chaos is not a self-contradictory concept. (2) We have good inductive reasons for believing it, good inductive evidence for it. We believe that some of our recipes will continue to hold good because they have held good for so long. We believe that we shall be able to frame new and useful ones, because we have been able to do so repeatedly in the past. Of course, it would be absurd to try to use I to 'justify induction,' to show that it is a reasonable policy; because I is a conclusion inductively supported.

Consider now the fundamentally different statement:

II. Induction is rational (reasonable).

We have already seen that the rationality of induction, unlike its 'successfulness,' is not a fact about the constitution of the world. It is a matter of what we mean by the word 'rational' in its application to any procedure for forming opinions about what lies outside our observations or that of available witnesses. For to have good reasons for any such opinion is to have good inductive support for it. The chaotic universe just envisaged, therefore, is not one in which induction would cease to be rational; it is simply one in which it would be impossible to form rational expectations to the effect that specific things would happen. It might be said that in such a universe it would at least be rational to refrain from forming specific expectations, to expect nothing but irregularities. Just so. But this is itself a higher-order induction: where irregularity is the rule, expect further irregularities.

Learning not to count on things is as much learning an inductive lesson as learning what things to count on.

So it is a contingent, factual matter that it is sometimes possible to form rational opinions concerning what specifically happened or will happen in given circumstances (I); it is a non-contingent, *a priori* matter that the only ways of doing this must be inductive ways (II). What people have done is to run together, to conflate, the question to which I is answer and the quite different question to which II is an answer; producing the muddled and senseless questions: 'Is the universe such that inductive procedures are rational?' or 'What must the universe be like in order for inductive procedures to be rational?' It is the attempt to answer these confused questions which leads to statements like 'The uniformity of nature is a presupposition of the validity of induction.' The statement that nature is uniform might be taken to be a vague way of expressing what we expressed by I; and certainly this fact is a condition of, for it is identical with, the likewise contingent fact that we are, and shall continue to be, able to form rational opinions, of the kind we are most anxious to form, about the unobserved. But neither this fact about the world, nor any other, is a condition of the necessary truth that, if it is possible to form rational opinions of this kind, these will be inductively supported opinions. The discordance of the conflated questions manifests itself in an uncertainty about the status to be accorded to the alleged presupposition of the 'validity' of induction. For it was dimly, and correctly, felt that the reasonableness of inductive procedure was not merely a contingent, but a necessary, matter; so any necessary condition of their reasonableness had likewise to be a necessary matter. On the other hand, it was uncomfortably clear that chaos is not a self-contradictory concept; that the fact that some phenomena do exhibit a tolerable degree of simplicity and repetitiveness is not guaranteed by logic, but is a contingent affair. So the presupposition of induction had to be both contingent and necessary: which is absurd. And the absurdity is only lightly veiled by the use of the phrase 'synthetic *a priori*' instead of 'contingent necessary.'

The Riddle of Induction

EDWARD H. MADDEN

I believe there is something wrong with "ordinary language" replies to the critic of induction in general, only particular prob- suggest some alternative ways of answering him.

Originally published in *The Journal of Philosophy*, Vol. LV, No. 17, 1958. Reprinted by permission of the editor.

I.

It is indeed difficult to criticize "ordinary language" analysts in a sweeping fashion since they are highly individualistic and use various techniques to achieve similar ends. Nevertheless, it seems to me that these analysts, in their work on the problem of induction, invariably fail in one of two ways:

either they do not eliminate the critic's demand or, if they do, they use notions of 'meaning,' either implicitly or explicitly, which are no more acceptable than the views about induction which they would eliminate.[1]

Consider, first, the ubiquitous contextual argument: there *is* no problem of justifying induction in general, only particular problems of justifying particular inductions.[2] It is sensible to talk about justifying particular scientific tests and techniques, since there are significant alternatives among which a choice must be made. However, it is queer to talk about "justifying" induction since there is no significant alternative. Clairvoyance, soothsaying, and oracular pronouncement are not *possible,* albeit not scientifically accredited, ways of non-inductively finding out about the future, as one might think, since these methods are vitiated if unsuccessful and are warranted by simple enumerative induction if successful. Again, since there is no significant alternative to induction as a way of finding out the future, as there are significant alternatives to a particular inductive procedure, it is pointless to talk about the justification of induction while it is not at all pointless to talk about the justification of a particular inductive procedure.

One might deny the correctness of this contextual argument by insisting there *are* possible non-inductive ways of knowing the future. The only grounds an outsider would ever have for believing another person to be clairvoyant or possessed of prevision would be, indeed, the success of these procedures. The clairvoyant or "previewer," however, after he became convinced he was one, through induction, perhaps, would have an explanation of his very success; namely, that he directly apprehends the future and so avoids the perils of the inductive leap. And one must admit, despite its many shortcomings, that the notion of celestial omniscience is not self-inconsistent; and granting this much, it would seem more than queer to talk about checking this prevision inductively. More to the point, however, one might allow the correctness of the contextual argument but insist that it leaves the critic unscathed. The contextual argument proves only that induction itself cannot be justified in the way a particular induction can; it does not prove that induction itself cannot be justified in any way. But since the critic is not demanding for induction itself the kind of justification it is possible to give particular inductions but demands a logically conclusive justification of inductive inference – i.e., a demonstration that inductive evidence entails the inductive conclusion, – he is not touched by the contextual argument. Now the demand for a deductive justification may well be an unreasonable one, but the contextual argument does not show that it is. This type of argument, therefore, must be accompanied, as it usually is, by some meaning analysis in terms of which this demand is shown to be unreasonable.

The *ignoratio elenchi* argument, it seems to me, has a similar weakness. According to this argument,[3] the critic of induction does the unremarkable thing of refuting the view that positive observation, or stratification, etc., is a good reason for accepting an inductive conclusion when 'good reason' means 'logically conclusive reason.' But, of course, he certainly has not refuted the claim that positive observations do constitute a good reason for accepting an inductive conclusion where 'good reason' is used in its ordinary sense. The *ignoratio elenchi* which the critic of induction commits, because he is heedless of his redefinition, consists of re-

[1] I am not including in this generalization, of course, those analysts who confine themselves to an empirical study of language in use without trying thereby to nullify "philosophical" assertions.

[2] Cf. P. F. Strawson, *Introduction to Logical Theory,* pp. 256–263.

[3] Cf. Paul Edwards, "Bertrand Russell's Doubts About Induction," *Logic and Language* (First Series), ed. by Anthony Flew, pp. 55–79.

futing the former claim when allegedly he is refuting the latter one. I do not wish to argue, of course, whether or not critics of induction ever do make this mistake but I do wish to insist that if they do they are completely off the track of what, in their explicit moments, they have to say or, at any rate, what they need to say. The critic of induction willingly concedes that in the ordinary sense of 'good reason' there are perfectly good reasons for accepting inductive inferences as valid but argues – for reasons by now quite familiar – that the ordinary sense of 'good reason' is an insufficient sense of 'good reason' for justifying inductive inference. The sense of 'good reason' sufficient for this justification, one more "fundamental" than the ordinary sense, is, to be sure, 'logically conclusive reason.' Now, again, this demand for a logically conclusive reason may well be an unreasonable one, but the *ignoratio elenchi* argument does not show that it is. This type of argument, therefore, must be supplemented by some meaning analysis which shows the unreasonableness of the demand.[4]

"Ordinary language" analysts, both implicitly and explicitly, have committed themselves to numerous views of 'meaning' which supposedly show the meaningless, self-contradictory, or incorrect nature of the critic's demand. Notice, first, the words that the critic of induction characteristically uses: How can you know that you have a *truly representative sample?* In Peirce's case of the boatload of wheat, even though the wheat is stirred and stirred, how can you know that there is not some latent pocket of unstirred wheat which would destroy the validity of the calculation? But if you can never know the sample is *really fair,* what justification do you have for calling inductive inference knowledge at all? One retort might be: The terms 'fair sample' and 'representative sample' in 'real fair sample' and 'true representative sample' in this argument occur either in a self-contradictory or vacuous way. 'Fair sample,' in its ordinary usage, is defined in terms of its capacity to satisfy the requirements of careful "stirring," stratification, or whatever else can be done along these lines. 'Whatever else can be done along these lines,' of course, keeps the definition open so it can include future refinements and new techniques which have arisen and no doubt will continue to arise in science and everyday life. In fact, however, to say that 'fair sample,' in the sense in which it is ordinarily used, is defined by these requirements does not imply that the requirements are definite and precise. Nevertheless, for some "restricted purposes" – apparently for refuting the critic! – the term might be introduced into discourse by a formal explanation of its meaning – in which case 'fair sample' is *defined* in terms of its capacity to satisfy the specified vague requirements. Now, to return to the critic's argument, if he uses 'fair sample' initially in the way people commonly do (which he apparently does, since we understood him at the outset), he is referring to a kind of sample revealed by one of the vague requirements, or some refinement thereof. If he does utilize this meaning, but also talks about a 'real fair sample' which one can never know he has or have good reason to believe he has no matter how many or how refined are the requirements it meets, then his use of the term is self-contradictory, meaning that at once it both does and does not satisfy the ordinary requirements of a fair sample. If the use of the term is to avoid being self-contradictory, it must function in some new sense. Since no new sense is provided, however, if it is not self-contradictory it is vacuous. (Sometimes the concept 'use' is involved in

[4] There are, of course, other techniques to unravel the "confusions" which lead to "paradoxical" assertions which could, with a little ingenuity, be applied to our problem, but similar criticisms, I suspect, would apply to them.

this type of argument,[5] but I shall attend later to this notion.)

The decisive difficulty with this maneuver, it seems to me, is this: By identifying the meanings of 'fair sample' and 'sample that is stirred, stratified, etc.,' a person is unable to give as a reason why a given sample is a fair one the fact that it has been stirred, stratified, etc.; but this, of course, is precisely what one wants to be able to do. I cannot give as a reason why something is what it is, a synonymous phrase. I have given no support to my statement 'John is my brother' by saying, "John is my male-sibling." And if one asks, "Why is this a fair sample?" or "Is this a fair sample?" I have not answered him at all if, having asserted the equivalence of 'fair sample' and 'sample that is stirred, . . . ,' I reply, "Because it has been stirred, stratified, etc." All I would have managed to say, making the proper substitutions, is, "This sample is fair because it is a fair sample."

Another retort to the critic of induction might be: Since the critic's claim that the ordinary sense of 'good reason' is insufficient to justify inductive inference and the justifier's claim that a "uniformity of nature" principle is required are not "factual" or "empirical" in nature, they must be construed as statements about language, albeit the critic and justifier mistakenly believe that they are not talking about language at all. The critic and justifier, impressed by the incorrigibility of logical and mathematical reasoning, can only be interpreted as wanting (or proposing or recommending) to use 'good reason' and 'warranted inference' only in reference to these paradigms, thereby abandoning the ordinary senses in which these words are used. Then, in order to refute them, one shows it is unnecessary or incorrect to abandon the ordinary uses (the ordinary distinctions will still have to be made all over again in the new terminology, etc.). Let me add that this type of analysis, although it has, of course, been used as stated,[6] is not monolithic (indeed, none of them are). Every part of it (e.g., 'Philosophical assertions are really about language') is still used separately and in conjunction with other concepts already examined and to be examined; [7] but my criticisms, as far as I can see, accompany them wherever they go.

I have kept 'factual' and 'empirical' in double quotes because it is not always clear what the proponents of this type of analysis mean when they say philosophical assertions are not factual or empirical.[8] Sometimes they apparently mean that philosophical assertions are not factual because the same facts are available to philosophical disputants who nevertheless reach opposite conclusions. Moreover, no further fact could possibly resolve their dispute. The truth or falsity of "philosophical" statements, in short, cannot, even theoretically, be determined by recourse to "actual" or "possible" facts. This claim, I take it, amounts to saying that "philosophical" assertions, since they do not make any difference in either actual or possible experience, are not verifiable, and what is not verifiable cannot be factual. But, of course, one who says that nature is uniform is insisting that although this assertion is not a matter of experience it is a factual assumption about the universe which one must make in order to account for things which are experienced. He would, in short, reject the present analysis because it amounts to an (unguarded) equivalent of the verifiability theory and so exhibits the

[5] Cf. Max Black, *Language and Philosophy*, p. 13. Cf. also pp. 3–22, 65–68.

[6] For analysis and criticism of this technique, cf. Roderick M. Chisholm, "Comments on the 'Proposal Theory' of Philosophy," *Journal of Philosophy*, Vol. XLIX, 1952, pp. 301–306.

[7] Sometimes, in current analyses, '*x* is not factual' appears as '*x* has no test procedures for its application.'

[8] Chisholm, *op. cit.*, pp. 302 ff.

well-known deficiencies in consistency and adequacy. Analysts, to be sure, sometimes interpret 'Philosophical assertions are not factual' differently; e.g., 'Sceptical assertions, with their redefinitions of ordinary terms, are *necessary* propositions.' However, assume one can show 'Ordinary evidence is insufficient to justify inductive inference' is a necessary proposition (since, for the critic, 'sufficient evidence' means 'logically conclusive evidence'), does it follow that the critic's assertion is "about language," a proposal or whatever, albeit he mistakenly thinks it is about something else? Not at all, since the analysts (or "elucidators") are unable to offer any criterion for deciding when a sentence ostensibly about something else is "really" about language (as paradoxical a claim as any paradox it would help eliminate). And they cannot operate on the assumption that any sentence *must* be about language if it is not empirical, for this operating principle would be, simply, another variant of the verifiability theory, different, certainly, in numerous ways from the positivistic version but identical with it in eliminating the possibility of unverifiable factual assertions. Moreover, one cannot *refute* linguistic proposals or recommendations, or show they are incorrect; [9] all one can do is to offer reasons for not accepting them. But the proponents of the proposals will offer counter reasons for *accepting* them with the result that all the old philosophical assertions and disputes will occur in a new context, and, as we have seen, numerous ideal languages will flourish as "competitors" of ordinary language – justifiably for anything this argument shows to the contrary.

The most ubiquitous notion of meaning, and one which can be applied in numerous ways to the critic of induction, concerns the concept 'use.' Unfortunately the use of 'use' is often far from explicit.[10] Sometimes analysts, when they say of an expression that it has no use, apparently mean that it is *meaningless* in one or more of the senses already analyzed, or in one or more parts of these senses; or that it has no "test procedures" which can be specified for its application; or that, like 'unextended material body,' it is self-contradictory; or that, irrelevantly, a philosophical redefinition of an ordinary word has no application to ordinary situations – and, conversely, of course, that it has a use if it is meaningful in one or more of the senses already analyzed, etc., or has "test procedures," or is unlike 'unextended material body,' or has an application to ordinary situations. Sometimes analysts, when they say of an expression that it has a use, mean that there are typical situations to which anyone who understands a certain descriptive expression would be prepared to apply it unhesitatingly. The expression acquires its meaning from its regular application to, and its meaning is usually taught by reference to, these typical situations (paradigm cases). That an expression has a use in this sense implies, of course, that it has a denotation; consequently the critic's claim that 'fair sample' can never be known to be exemplified is necessarily incorrect or mistaken since one can show that 'fair sample' is an expression that *does* have a use in this sense. (The recent controversy between Flew and Watkins centers around the application of this type of argument, used in many contexts, to the concept 'acting of his own free-will.' [11])

(i) References like 'the meaning of an expression is usually taught' or 'can be taught' cannot play any significant role in this analysis since the critic of induction has at his disposal many plausible hypotheses about ways in which certain concepts are learned,

[9] Cf. Morris Lazerowitz, "Moore's Paradox," in *The Philosophy of G. E. Moore* (Library of Living Philosophers), p. 376.

[10] Cf. J. W. N. Watkins, "Farewell to the Paradigm-Case Argument," *Analysis,* Vol. 18, No. 2, 1957, p. 28.

[11] *Analysis,* Vol. 18, No. 2, 1957, pp. 25–42.

even though on his view there are no genuine instances of these concepts. (ii) If the regular application of 'fair sample' to paradigm cases of careful "stirring," stratification, etc., ostensively *defines* it, then careful "stirring," stratification, etc., cannot be used, as we have seen, as reasons why a sample is fair. (The same difficulty, of course, can be worked out with 'free-will.') (iii) No reason is given why philosophical concepts like 'fair sample' and 'free-will' cannot be considered compound descriptive terms and so not necessarily ostensively definable.[12] (iv) When the critic says that 'fair sample' can never be known to be exemplified, or that there is never any good reason for accepting an inductive inference, he uses the terms 'fair sample' and 'good reason' in his extended or unusual senses. However, since the present refutation depends on interpreting him as using these concepts *correctly* (i.e., in their ordinary senses) and denying that these ordinary senses are ever exemplified, it misses its mark.

Moreover, most ordinary language analysts themselves, while agreeing that the over-all strategy of this type refutation is sound, would insist that this refutation is *inadequate.* One never does enough simply to point out *that* an expression has a use but must explicate *what* this use is in order to avoid the application of the expression to *prima facie* but not genuine exemplifications of it. Flew, I take it, in his reply to Watkins,[13] has realized just this deficiency in his earlier arguments. He writes that examples used in explaining the use of a word must satisfy a certain "general specification," which, in fact, distinguishes between *prima facie* and genuine paradigm cases. It is simply not enough, e.g., to say 'freewill' is exemplified when a man marries without any social pressure or duress; in view of psychoanalytic knowledge it is necessary to add, say, that he did what he did after rejecting possible alternative courses of action, etc. Again, it simply would not be enough to say 'fair sample' is exemplified by any sample the elements of which have been selected randomly; in view of well-known inductive problems, it is necessary to add that the population and sample be stratified, etc. However, whenever one has (adequately!) specified a *paradigm,* then one proceeds, on Flew's account, essentially as before. One shows of a specific case that it fits, *as a matter of fact,* the specification of the paradigm, and thus just *is,* tautologically, an instance of 'fair sample,' 'free-will,' or whatever the paradigm is that is specified. And since the critic, when he says that one never acts of free-will or never has good reason for accepting an inductive inference, is denying this tautology he is caught up in a self-contradiction. Flew's reformulation, however, while it avoids criticism (iii), *still does not avoid (iv)*. And it does not avoid (ii) either, since this criticism, phrased in the context of ostensive definition, can be rephrased in the context of "general specification" of 'fair sample.'

Finally, analysts would insist that elucidation of the use of a term, in addition to the assertion that it has a use, is also insufficient. The analyst, in addition, must discover, and by clarification remove, the misleading analogies and arguments which lead philosophers to make their "paradoxical" assertions.[14] At this point, however, casuistic analysis has gone full circle, since these techniques are usually of the contextual, *ignoratio elenchi,* and presuppositional types. There are, of course, other "ordinary language" techniques which I have not examined at all – and, no doubt, there are more to come – but all too frequently they turn out to be, on counter-analysis, simply variations on the examined themes.

12 Cf. Watkins, *ibid.,* p. 29.
13 *Analysis,* Vol. 18, No. 2, 1957, pp. 34–40.
14 Norman Malcolm, "Philosophy for Philosophers," *Philosophical Review,* Vol. 60, 1951, p. 340.

II.

If one denies 'It is possible to justify induction' is meaningless or self-contradictory he does not need to believe, on the other hand, as if it were the only alternative, that he must meet the critic's demand for a justification of induction. It does not follow that because a demand is meaningful it is also significant and requires to be met. If one shows that a demand is meaningless or self-contradictory then he has *eliminated* it and precludes anyone from making it. On the other hand, if one shows that a demand is pointless or trivial then he has *attenuated* it and so may dissuade others from making it or, at any rate, persuade himself that he can safely ignore it. Now any demand which could not in principle ever be met because any answer to it is bound to fail, or, if not bound to fail, doomed to prove too much, etc., while not self-contradictory is *pointless* (not trivial), and while it cannot be eliminated it can be attenuated (by pointing out these deficiencies) and thus safely ignored. However, can one show that the critic's demand for a conclusive defense of induction (whether his intent be remedial or sceptical) cannot in principle ever be met since any answer to it is bound to fail, or must prove too much, and thus attenuate the demand?

The first attenuation has long been with us. A principle of the uniformity of nature type or limited variety type is not a logical principle since its denial is not self-contradictory – and, indeed, it must be contingent if it is to do the job of justification required of it; but, then, of course, *it* requires some inductive grounds for acceptance and so the original difficulty inevitably reappears and a conclusive defense inevitably fails. Or, in terms of 'reasonableness': "The overwhelming objection to the assimilation of all induction to deduction is that this would require that we should reasonably believe a very general empirical major premiss, the reasonableness of belief in which would have to be justified by another inductive argument." [15] To be sure, this type of principle might be said to have an initial probability in the sense of subjective expectancy – in which case, however, one has not got beyond Hume's analysis in terms of custom or habit. And any objective concept of probability, whether degree of confirmation or statistical, "would presuppose a principle of induction by means of which we could ascertain the probability of such world hypotheses in comparison with the (infinite) range of their alternatives." [16] But cannot 'degree of confirmation' assimilate induction to deduction without reference to any principle of this type? [17] Apparently not, since "a deductive system of probability statements will only give the probability of an inductive hypothesis on the basis of its confirmation in a set of instances (its 'posterior probability') as an arithmetical product one of whose factors is its probability before it has been confronted with experience (its 'prior probability'); and a supreme major premiss is necessary to insure that this prior probability should be greater than zero." [18] (I shall return to 'degree of confirmation' in a subsequent context.)

Recently some philosophers,[19] trying to avoid these difficulties and salvage a deductive justification of induction, have said that the entailment view of causality yields the deductive grounds of inductive inference. A term is defined, in part, by its causal relations; so if "*a*" turned out, in the future, not to exhibit the required and expected causal relations, it would be necessary only to say it was not therefore a genuine instance of *a*.

[15] R. B. Braithwaite, *Scientific Explanation*, p. 259.

[16] Herbert Feigl, "De Principiis Non Disputandum . . . ?" *Philosophical Analysis*, ed. by Max Black, p. 136.

[17] Cf. John W. Lenz, "Carnap on Defining 'Degree of Confirmation,'" *Philosophy of Science*, Vol. 23, 1956, pp. 230–236.

[18] Braithwaite, *op. cit.*, p. 259.

[19] A. C. Ewing, e.g., in *The Fundamental Questions of Philosophy*, Chapter VIII.

This stratagem, however, successfully insures only that if one knows he has a genuine instance of *a,* then he knows that *x* must necessarily follow in the future, or simply, in the unobserved; but unfortunately it simply shifts the critic's doubts from the inductive inference to the empirical question of whether or not one really has a genuine instance of *a.* Some philosophers, too, still take Kant's principle of causality, conceived as a *pre-condition of knowledge,* as a justification of induction: the human understanding itself impresses the causal order upon the data of the senses. Unfortunately, however, if this principle is to do the job required of it, it would have to include the assumption that human understanding can be relied upon to continue without fail to impress its forms on future data. And, in any case, one could not be certain for any specific effect that he really had the correct cause; and so he could never know certainly that any extrapolation is justified.[20] But, in a Kantian vein, could we not call a major premise of the uniformity or limited variety type a *pre-condition* of knowledge – a principle which is neither directly knowable nor inductively or deductively related to propositions directly knowable but a principle which has to be *postulated,* or assumed to be true, in order to justify other knowledge or reasonable belief? However, this view does not avoid the difficulty inherent in any deductive justification of induction since, on this view, the principle is still a contingent one and "to call an empirical generalization a *postulate* . . . does not make it any the less an empirical generalization; nor does renaming a proposition provide a new method for getting to know it." [21]

There are, of course, other ways to attenuate the critic's demand. E.g., it is pointless to make the demand since, even if it could be met, an answer either presupposes confidence in careful inductive procedures or else justifies any inductive inference whatever. Assume, in the case of the boatload of wheat, that one gives the cargo a few "quick turns," takes samples, and hits upon a ratio. No one would suggest that we justify the extrapolation of this ratio by including a uniformity principle, or whatever, among the premises, since the ratio would likely be upset by further more careful and controlled investigation. However, after giving the cargo one hundred "good turns," taking samples, and hitting upon a ratio, then one might suggest that we justify the extrapolation of this ratio by including a uniformity premise, since the ratio is less likely to be upset by further investigation. In this case, however, one reason, at least, in the conclusive justification of any given inference is confidence in careful inductive procedures. And if one denies completely any confidence in careful inductive procedures, then he must necessarily invoke the uniformity principle in any inductive inference whatever, the one resulting from a few quick turns as well as the one resulting from the careful hundred (since he no longer has any reason for discriminating between them), and so he justifies any inductive inference whatever – the trap, in fact, always waiting for philosophers, of proving or justifying too much rather than too little.

The critic of induction, of course, could reply: Even if you attenuate my demand, *you* must produce some reason for using or adopting inductive procedures since you admit 'It is possible to justify induction' is not meaningless or self-contradictory and have allowed indirectly, by arguing against the contextualist, that there is some general problem of defending induction. I accede to this new demand (for a *justificatio actionis*) although I would insist that answering it amounts to an attenuation of *this* demand, since the answers are so thoroughly simple and obvious. (The obviousness of the answers reflects the *triviality* of the demand.)

[20] Cf. G. H. von Wright, *The Logical Problem of Induction* (Second Revised Edition), pp. 27 ff.

[21] Braithwaite, *op. cit.,* p. 259, footnote.

To ask a person, in all seriousness, what reason he has for using or adopting inductive procedures is like asking a miner with a going claim why he continues to work it. The answer is extremely simple: Gold makes getting through life easier and less hazardous. To be sure, I don't know the claim will last indefinitely; indeed I may be on a short "run of luck," but, of course, the only way to discover that is to keep mining and in the meantime getting the gold and getting through life easier! And, certainly, if the gold gives out I'll drop working the claim. So it is with induction: Induction makes getting through life easier and less hazardous. To be sure, we don't know that it will always continue to be a successful guide; indeed we may be on a short run of luck (or the universe may suffer a breakdown—Peirce in reverse), but, of course, the only way to discover that is to keep on using inductive procedures and in the meantime making inductive inferences and getting through life easier. And, certainly, if inductive procedures give out I'll stop using them (and give out too!). There are other reasons, of course, for using inductive procedures—including the sort of thing one would say to a child who was unconvinced that he would get burned *next* time—but they are all equally simple and obvious and so would continue the attenuation of the demand. And one must not run the psychological risk of marshaling many answers since this might suggest the demand is difficult to meet.

It might appear plausible to interpret the current "vindications" of induction as attenuations of the demand for a *justificatio actionis*. Some writers,[22] e.g., call their vindications "simple tautologies" or "trivial" as if to attenuate the demand for them, but that they do not intend them so appears from additional comments like "But nevertheless they are illuminating" or "They are necessary for the sake of philosophical clarification." Notice the vindicator's reply to this criticism, "Vindications, even if correct, prove so little"—namely, "A weak defense of the use of inductive procedures is better than nothing at all" or "Philosophers do not seem grateful for small mercies." If, however, the question is simply, Why use inductive procedures?, the correct answer would be, "Because there is so little to prove!" The authors of "means-ends" vindications, however, believe that they can prove something, albeit little, about the *success* of inductive procedures, namely, that if any way of knowing the future works induction does, or if there is any order in nature induction will reveal it. However, these vindications which "concern the choice of means for the attainment of an end" have serious deficiencies. Consider this vindication. The end desired in the use of inductive procedures is "successful prediction, [or] more generally, true conclusions of nondemonstrative inference"[23]; and the question is whether these means are adequate to achieve this end. While one cannot prove they *must* be successful, he can prove that if there is an order in nature not too deeply hidden, then a consistent application of the rule of induction will reveal it—and this proof vindicates the use of the rule. More specifically, Feigl writes that Carnap has shown "there is a large class, in fact a continuum, of inductive rules (or what is tantamount: of definitions of degree of confirmation), of which Reichenbach's rule is an element, which all share the following significant feature: If the world has some degree of order at all, predictions made according to any one of the inductive rules will in the long run (strictly speaking, in the limit) not only converge with the others, but can also be shown (de-

[22] Herbert Feigl, "Philosophy of Science of Logical Empiricism," *Minnesota Studies in the Philosophy of Science,* Vol. I, p. 30; "De Principiis . . . ," *loc. cit.,* p. 138; "Validation and Vindication: An Analysis of the Nature and Limits of Ethical Arguments," *Readings in Ethical Theory,* ed. by W. Sellars and J. Hospers, p. 675.

[23] Feigl, "De Principiis . . . ," *loc. cit.,* p. 136.

ductively!) to be the only type of predictions that utilize evidence methodically and are capable of anticipating that order of nature." [24]

There is, however, a crucial difficulty in Carnap's method of vindication. The fundamental problem in Carnap's logical theory of probability is how one can choose an adequate *c*-function. Questions of economy and aesthetic satisfaction aside, an adequate *c*-function is one in which the degree of confirmation of hypotheses corresponds with the actual truth frequency of these hypotheses. "The more clearly these two values, one a logically ascertained value, the other an empirically ascertained value, correspond, the more successful as a guide for predictions will the *c*-function be. The more closely these two values correspond the better will be the performance of the *c*-function." [25] However, it should be recalled, if one chooses for future use the *c*-function which has met this requirement most closely in the past (say Carnap's *c**-function rather than the straight rule or the Keynes-Wittgenstein *c*-function), then he is assuming that this function will continue to be successful in the future. But at this point, of course, the whole problem of induction, Feigl's assertion notwithstanding, reasserts itself. Moreover, as Lenz remarks, "Carnap is right when he calls the adoption of a certain *c*-function a practical decision which is not true or false. The objection is that the decision is based upon a synthetic hypothesis which is true or false but whose truth value is not known. Calling the choice of a *c*-function a practical decision in no way avoids the above difficulty." [26]

Certain "self-corrective" vindications,[27] which again concern the success of induction in meeting ends and only *prima facie* resemble part of my simple argument, also have certain difficulties. According to this argument, sampling enables us to make inferences about future experience; but, when that experience comes, if it does not conform to the inference it is at once seen to constitute part of the enlarged corrected data of sampling, since the inductive method must avail itself of every kind of experience. Thus the inference, which was only provisional, corrects itself at last or in the long run. "At last," in cases like the boatload of wheat, unfortunately, can only be when the need for any inference has passed because there is nothing left to infer to. That is to say, the more nearly certain we become of the accuracy of our ratio, the less use we have for it, for the more nearly exhaustive is our examination of the class. On the other hand, when the class is inexhaustible, then the long run is an indefinitely "long run" and so there is no corrective "at last." [28]

Not all vindications apparently consist in judgments about means and ends, although it is difficult to decide the question since the relationships among the various vindications are frequently obscure and sometimes conflict.[29] Moreover, the 'validation,' the correlate of 'vindication,' is not without difficulty.[30] Validating principles – i.e., locutions which determine whole systems of justification (as distinct from vindication) – are construed to be stipulations, definitions, or conventions; but these principles, since they allegedly provide grounds or reasons for other assertions, could hardly be definitions or conventional rules of substitution. (Cf. my criticism of the first ordinary language meaning analysis.) They must, in short, have some categorial status to do the job required of them.

There are, needless to say, types of de-

[24] Feigl, *Minnesota Studies . . .* , p. 29.

[25] Lenz, *loc. cit.*, p. 233.

[26] *Ibid.*, p. 234.

[27] Cf. Black, *Problems of Analysis,* pp. 169, 170–171.

[28] 'Limit,' 'practical limit,' etc., I believe, defer but do not avoid the difficulty.

[29] Cf. Black, *Problems of Analysis,* pp. 167–168, and Feigl, *Minnesota Studies . . .* , p. 30.

[30] Cf. footnote 22.

mands and answers in the complex riddle of induction which we have not even mentioned let alone analyzed,[31] some of which need to be met in different ways while others, I suspect, can be met by pointing out difficulties similar to the ones examined.

[31] E.g., self-supporting and probability justifications.

Non-Demonstrative Inference and Induction

BERTRAND RUSSELL

A horse who has been driven always along a certain road expects to be driven along that road again; a dog who is always fed at a certain hour expects food at that hour and not at any other. Such expectations, as Hume pointed out, explain only too well the common-sense belief in uniformities of sequence, but they afford absolutely no logical ground for beliefs as to the future, not even for the belief that we shall continue to expect the continuation of experienced uniformities, for that is precisely one of those causal laws for which a ground has to be sought. If Hume's account of causation is the last word, we have not only no reason to suppose that the sun will rise to-morrow, but no reason to suppose that five minutes hence we shall still expect it to rise to-morrow.

It may, of course, be said that all inferences as to the future are in fact invalid, and I do not see how such a view could be disproved. But, while admitting the legitimacy of such a view, we may nevertheless inquire: If inferences as to the future *are* valid, what principle must be involved in making them?

The principle involved is the principle of induction, which, if it is true, must be an *a priori* logical law, not capable of being proved or disproved by experience. It is a difficult question how this principle ought to be formulated; but if it is to warrant the inferences which we wish to make by its means, it must lead to the following proposition: "If, in a great number of instances a thing of a certain kind is associated in a certain way with a thing of a certain other kind, it is probable that a thing of the one kind is always similarly associated with a thing of the other kind; and as the number of instances increases, the probability approaches indefinitely near to certainty." It may well be questioned whether this proposition is true; but if we admit it, we can infer that any characteristic of the whole of the observed past is likely to apply to the future and to the unobserved past. This proposition, therefore, if it is true, will warrant the inference that causal laws probably hold at all times, future as well as past; but without

From *Our Knowledge of the External World,* pp. 240–242. New York: W. W. Norton and Company, Inc., 1929. Reprinted by permission of the author and the publisher. The material following the ellipsis was written March 20, 1959 (Plas Penrhyn) and has not previously been published.

this principle, the observed cases of the truth of causal laws afford no presumption as to the unobserved cases, and therefore the existence of a thing not directly observed can never be validly inferred.

It is thus the principle of induction, rather than the law of causality, which is at the bottom of all inferences as to the existence of things not immediately given. With the principle of induction, all that is wanted for such inferences can be proved; without it, all such inferences are invalid. This principle has not received the attention which its great importance deserves. Those who were interested in deductive logic naturally enough ignored it, while those who emphasized the scope of induction wished to maintain that all logic is empirical, and therefore could not be expected to realise that induction itself, their own darling, required a logical principle which obviously could not be proved inductively, and must therefore be *a priori* if it could be known at all. . . .

My beliefs about induction underwent important modifications in the year 1944, chiefly owing to the discovery that induction used without common sense leads more often to false conclusions than to true ones. Put briefly, my views since 1944 have been:

Non-demonstrative inference plays a larger part than is usually realized both in science and in common sense. Most of us do not remember anything that happened to us before the age of two, but none of us doubt that we existed before that age. If you walk in the evening with the sun behind you, a shadow marches in front of you and you do not for a moment doubt that it has a causal connection with your own body. It has been usual to suppose that non-demonstrative inferences depend upon induction. This, however, is not true except in a carefully limited sense. The inductions that scientists are inclined to accept are such as commend themselves to what may be called scientific common sense. If common sense is ignored, induction is much more likely to lead to false conclusions than to true ones. Crude induction argues that, if all known instances of A are also instances of B, it is probable, if the instances are sufficiently numerous, that all A's are B's. As a general statement, this is obviously false. Given two classes, A and B, which have a certain number of members in common, there will be infinitely more classes B to which not all A's belong than classes B to which all A's belong. Induction as a general principle is, therefore, demonstrably false, and if it is to be used, it must be used with stated limitations. Take, for instance, the following illustration: You have, let us suppose, a growing boy whose height you measure on the first of every month. You may find that, for a certain period, his rate of growth is constant. If you knew nothing about human growth, you might infer by induction that he would continue to grow at this rate until his head strikes the stars. There are, in fact, an infinite number of formulae which will fit any finite set of facts as to your boy's growth. Pure induction, if valid, would lead you to regard all these formulae as probable, although they contradict each other. Keynes, in his *Treatise on Probability,* shows that under certain circumstances an induction is valid if the generalization in question has a finite probability before any instances of its correctness are known. Accepting this view, I conclude that induction, in so far as it can be validly employed, is not an indemonstrable premiss, but that other indemonstrable premisses are necessary in order to give the necessary finite probability to inductions which we wish to test. The conclusion is that scientific inference demands certain extra-logical postulates of which induction is not one. What seem to me sufficient postulates for the purpose are given in Part VI, chapter IX, of my *Human Knowledge*. These postulates should, in my opinion, replace induction as what is needed in non-demonstrative inference.

7

SCIENCE AND VALUES

Introduction

In everyday life we use two radically different kinds of sentences which we can distinguish as "descriptive" and "prescriptive." Descriptive sentences announce that something *is* the case, like 'This table is brown' or 'The traffic on the boulevard is fast.' Prescriptive sentences assert what *ought* to be the case whether it is in fact or not, like 'You ought not to beat your wife' or 'You ought to tell the truth.' Scientific sentences, of course, are descriptive although they vary greatly in content and structure – 'The pointer is between 9 and 10,' 'There is an electric current in this wire,' 'Space at large is curved.' Now the problem of this chapter is this: What relationship, if any, holds between scientific descriptive sentences and prescriptive ones? I do not wish to suggest, however, that we are interested only in "verbal" or "terminological" relations. I could just as well suggest our problem with another question; namely, what is the relation between scientific fact and moral judgment? Or, more specifically, in what way, if any, does science enter into, or affect, moral judgments and arguments about moral judgments?

Philosophers and scientists have answered this question in numerous ways, some of which have been strained and misleading to say the least. On the other hand, other answers are clear and very interesting; we shall examine several of these in some detail. First, we shall look into some of the ways in which science has been brought into the traditional philosophical problem of determinism and moral responsibility, the suggestions being either that science supports "free will" or that it supports "determinism." I shall argue that scientific matters are irrelevant to this philosophical problem and that efforts to show that they are relevant tend to obscure the real import of a science like psychoanalysis for moral philosophy. Second, we shall look into the claim which some philosophers make that factual considerations, arrived at by checking the consequences of different types of actions, are competent to provide the grounds for making moral judgments or decisions in the same way that factual considerations in science, arrived at by checking consequences of rival hypotheses, provide the grounds for making a theoretical judgment or decision. I shall argue that in one sense this claim may very well be true but that in another sense it is clearly false. Finally, I must make a concluding remark about what value science itself may have.

1.

The problem concerning determinism and moral responsibility arises in the following way. Modern science seems to provide a notion of cause, quite distinct from Aristotle's final cause, which implies that if something is caused then it could not be other than it is. If I have a genuine instance of a cause (that is, if I am not mistaken), then a certain effect *must* occur. It could not be otherwise, for if something else *could* occur then the cause is still unknown. If the concepts of cause and determinism applied only to physical objects there would be no trouble, but these concepts also apply to human behavior and here the perplexities begin to arise. If human behavior, too, is caused or determined, then *it* could not be other than it is. But moral judgments of behavior, on the other hand, are meaningful only if it *is* possible for behavior to be other than it is. If I say, "You ought not to beat your wife," I presume, if this judgment is to be sensible, that you could either beat or not beat her, that you chose the former course, and that I am morally condemning you for making the wrong choice. Apparently, then, science and moral philosophy come into headlong conflict. If human behavior is caused, then it could not be other than it is; if human behavior is morally judgeable, then it could have been other than it is. Hence, either human behavior is not caused, or else it is not morally responsible. Or, putting the point positively, either human behavior is caused, or it is morally responsible – but not both.

This traditional way of formulating the problem of determinism and moral responsibility is still accepted by many scientists and philosophers, although, as you may guess, it has serious flaws. Accepting this formulation, a person apparently has only two choices: he may either say that behavior is morally judgeable so not caused, in which case he is an "indeterminist," or he may say that behavior is caused so not morally judgeable, in which case he is a "determinist." Indeterminists do not in fact generally hold that all human behavior is uncaused; on the contrary, psychology, sociology, and all the other human sciences tell us a great deal about what causes personality traits, group behavior, and so on. Nevertheless, in choice situations there is, finally, a decision of will, freely made, for which the moral agent is responsible and, hence, judgeable.

Now many indeterminists feel that modern science, far from showing that moral judgments are impossible or senseless, actually justifies the indeterminist position. After all, they point out, in quantum mechanics itself physicists no longer talk about particles in a causal way. As we have seen, it is not simply that both position and momentum of a single particle cannot be determined but rather that particles do not appear to have continuous orbits; that is, they are causally anomalous. But, the argument goes, if causality "breaks down" already in physics, certainly it is reasonable to believe that it also breaks down in human behavior, at the choice point at least, and thus behavior is morally responsible.

However, there seems to be a difficulty with this claim independently of whether its description of quantum theory is adequate. If the indeterminist strictly means that choices are not caused at all then he must admit that the agent who acted one way under certain conditions may subsequently act in an entirely different way under the same conditions, even though he himself has not changed at all. But this way out of the deterministic dilemma is no help, for it does not introduce moral responsibility but simply straightforward caprice. Ernst Cassirer in his essay on "The Implications of Physics for Ethics" shows in detail why he believes that the indeterminist's trust in quantum mechanics as a support for his position is mistaken. Moral responsibility demands the presence of something positive, not simply the absence of determinism.

Determinism, on the other hand, seems equally as untenable as indeterminism. There are a number of reasons why this is so, but the simplest and most convincing is that determinism is self-destructive. If determinism were correct, "then our thoughts and the conclusions to which they lead would in every last detail be conditioned by factors which wholly antedated the thinking processes themselves. Evaluation or discrimination between better and worse, true and false, would be inexplicable and futile. Hence no rational defense of determinism would be possible. In short, if determinism is true, it is undemonstrable." [1]

[1] Lucius Garvin, *A Modern Introduction to Ethics* (Boston: Houghton Mifflin Co., 1953), p. 75.

Since there is something artificial and untenable about both indeterminism and determinism, philosophers have come to suspect that the very formulation of the determinism issue which spawned them is confused. They have suggested that perhaps a further analysis of 'cause' and 'determinism' will dispel the whole problem with its strained alternatives. After all, behavior can be caused or determined in two radically different ways. Heredity and early environment are "external causes" over which we had no control but which nevertheless made us, in some sense, the way we are. To the extent that these factors control behavior — "by mechanisms behind the scenes" — a person indeed is not "free" and morally responsible. On the other hand, reason, imagination, and insight, along with a host of other subtle factors, are "internal causes" over which I have control and which quite obviously also determine my behavior. To the extent that these factors control behavior, a person is indeed morally responsible. In fact, this notion of a reasonable being who can consider the consequences of his acts, unlike that of 'uncaused choice,' is the ordinary meaning of 'morally responsible.' Therefore, according to the present argument, while it is true that all behavior is caused, nevertheless some behavior is morally responsible, namely, that which is self-caused. This concept of self-cause can depend either on a complicated Kantian transcendental self or on a simple common-sense view that man is capable of acting on reasons rather than simply using them as rationalizations.

At this point in the dialectic of the determinism issue the cry has once again arisen that science — this time psychoanalysis — shows that moral judgments are impossible or nonsense. According to this view, psychoanalysis annihilates the concept of self-cause, and thus this new way of salvaging moral responsibility comes to naught. The psychoanalyst, after all, tells us that our behavior, including our so-called reasonable behavior, is really unconsciously determined and that conscious, reasonable life is merely a façade of rationalizations. "The unconscious is the master of every fate and the captain of every soul." However, it seems clear that this attempt to bolster determinism through psychoanalysis will not do. Psychoanalysts do not in fact usually claim that all *prima facie* reasonable behavior is unconsciously determined, for this view, of course, would deny that there are any objective or rational grounds for accepting the tenets of psychoanalysis itself — it would be self-destructive in the same way that traditional determinism is. In my essay, "Psychoanalysis and Moral Judgeability," I argue that the psychoanalyst's point is, rather, that much less behavior than anyone dreamed possible is free or responsible in the ordinary sense that it is consciously and reasonably shaped. However, this point is clearly irrelevant to the traditional determinism puzzle; for this puzzle simply disappears with the acceptance of the qualified statement, 'Most behavior is not free' or 'Very little behavior is free.' The puzzle only arises if all behavior is said to be determined in a way which implies it could not have been otherwise.

Some philosophers, on the other hand, have argued that psychoanalysis, far from annihilating the common-sense concept of self-determinism, actually provides the very techniques for deciding when and how much "freedom" a person has. In my essay I argue against this view, too, showing why I believe it is equally irrelevant, along with the former claim, to the traditional determinism issue. Philosophical argument and analysis, not scientific fact, is needed to defend the ordinary notion of self-cause and moral responsibility. Nevertheless, I argue, psychoanalysis does have crucially important moral implications which are often unhappily obscured when philosophers mix up psychoanalysis with the traditional determinism issue. The crucial moral import, which forensic psychiatrists have long pointed out, is that neurotic behavior is non-responsible since it "could not be otherwise." If this view is genuinely defensible and tenable, then its implications for penology, law, and our whole social fabric are important indeed.

2.

Numerous scientists and philosophers have claimed that factual considerations arrived at by checking the consequences of different types of actions are competent to provide the grounds for making moral judgments and decisions in the same way that factual considerations provide the grounds for theoretical decisions in science. This view is not unambiguous; it might mean that basic moral imperatives along with factual considerations provide the ground for further more specific moral judgments or it might mean that factual considerations alone provide the ground for all moral judgments. Let us examine these two possibilities in some detail as a preparation for reading John Dewey's essay on "Reconstruction in Moral Conceptions" and Melvin Rader's "Comments on Dewey's Ethics."

Some moral philosophers called "teleologists" believe that acts can be determined to be right and wrong only by examining their consequences. If an act gives rise to "good" consequences, it is a right act; if it gives rise to "bad" consequences, it is a wrong one. But how are we, then, to interpret 'good' and 'bad'? Some teleologists called "utilitarians" reply that only happiness is intrinsically good and misery intrinsically bad. Therefore, they say, a right act is one which produces consequences conducive to happiness – not to any particular person's happiness, to be sure, but to the happiness of the greatest number of people involved. The moral imperative of the utilitarian, then, reads like this: "In any moral situation choose that act which will bring the greatest amount of happiness to the greatest number of people."

Neither scientific nor common-sense factual knowledge can justify this moral imperative or convince anyone not already persuaded of its validity. How could it, since it announces how people ought to act independently of whether or not they do so in fact? However, the teleologist continues, even though this supreme or final moral imperative cannot be justified by knowledge of facts, nevertheless its application to specific moral problems is completely dependent upon knowledge of scientific and common-sensical matters of fact. To see that this is so let us consider a specific problem.

Moral rules like "You ought to tell the truth" or "You ought to help preserve human life whenever possible" should be followed, according to the utilitarian, since we have found, as a matter of fact, that acting on them tends in the long run to increase general welfare, even though acting on them in some cases produces dreadful consequences (the cancer patient, for example). Moreover, what happens when moral rules come into conflict? Suppose that a doctor has a patient with a very serious disease and he believes, knowing the psychological makeup of the patient, that the patient's knowledge of the seriousness of the disease may itself prevent recovery. When the patient asks him about the seriousness of his illness, should he tell him the truth or not? Here the moral rules, "Tell the truth" and "Preserve life," come into conflict, and the decision between them, contrary to appearances, is not an easy matter; it requires a careful inquiry into matters of fact both scientific and common-sensical. How good is the psychological evidence that knowledge of the seriousness of the illness will preclude recovery? May not the patient be led to act in ways detrimental to his health out of ignorance of his true condition? Moreover, what are the psychological effects of the lie on the doctor, however noble his intentions?

And what about the ill effects for medicine itself if patients learn not to rely on their doctor's word? And so on. In any specific case, then, the utilitarian concludes, we cannot know what we ought to do without having factual information about probable consequences of acts, and this information might better be scientific than common-sensical, whenever possible, if this means it is better confirmed and is more trustworthy. Yet, again, the ultimate moral imperative itself cannot be justified on any scientific or factual ground.

John Dewey's moral philosophy is teleological in nature, too, directed toward consequences, but it is relativistic in a way in which other teleological systems like the utilitarian are not. Valuation, according to Dewey, is stimulated when a person has specific conflicts, tensions, and unsatisfied needs. Recall the situation of the doctor; he was confronted with conflicting courses of action both of which made urgent claims. What should he do? Dewey wrote,

> The practical meaning of the situation – that is to say the action needed to satisfy it – is not self-evident. It has to be searched for. There are conflicting desires and alternative apparent goods. What is needed is to find the right course of action, the right good. Hence, inquiry is exacted: observation of the detailed makeup of the situation; analysis into its diverse factors; clarification of what is obscure; discounting the more insistent and vivid traits; tracing the consequences of the various modes of action that suggest themselves; regarding the decision reached as hypothetical and tentative until the anticipated or supposed consequences which led to its adoption have been squared with actual consequences.[1]

Here then is an example of Dewey's teleological orientation, specifically modeled after the pattern of scientific inference, as you will discover from his essay. But his relativistic viewpoint is closely interwoven with this teleological one. If our chosen course of action does resolve our conflict or relieve some need, then, to be sure, Dewey wrote, we have discovered or constructed a value. But it will not be an ultimate or absolute value, since conflicts and needs change continuously and we have to construct new values as intelligently as we can for each new situation as it arises. We never have, in short, a final Value; only relative values.

Since Dewey did not allow an ultimate moral imperative of any sort, and since he believed that intelligent inquiry, modeled after the pattern of scientific inference, is competent to justify all the relative ends or values of life, he was apparently committed to the view that factual inquiry is competent to justify all the ends of life. At any rate, whether or not he was finally committed to this view – an untenable one, I suggested at the beginning of our discussion – you will want to keep this problem of interpretation in mind as you read Dewey's stimulating essay and Rader's insightful comments on it.

Finally, I want to pose the question about the relation of science and value in a completely different way. So far we have talked a good deal about the import of science for moral philosophy. But no account of the relation between science and value would be complete without asking the reverse question, "Are there any specifically moral aspects in the making of scientific decisions themselves?" Richard Rudner, in the last selection, answers this question with a straightforward "yes," and you will do well to master completely the reasons underlying this answer.

[1] See Dewey's essay which follows.

Implications of Physics for Ethics

ERNST CASSIRER

Our earlier considerations have moved exclusively within the circles of physics and epistemology. Without looking to right or left, without any speculative side glances or concerns about ethical implications, we have attempted to pursue our goal, which consisted of no more than the logical clarification of the problems of modern physics. Only at the end do we turn to ask what the significance of these problems might be for the whole of philosophical knowledge, for our *Weltanschauung* as a whole.

But if we look back to the results of our analysis of the basic concepts of physics, we realize that we must not expect too much. For the essence of these results consists precisely in this, that they exhort us to methodological restraint and moderation. Kant always insisted on the principle that no augmentation but only a distortion of the fields of knowledge results when we permit their boundaries to run into each other. Such a running together of boundaries occurs when statements about indeterminism in quantum theory are directly connected with metaphysical speculations about the freedom of the will. It is imagined that thus a greater unity between physics and ethics can be achieved and the gulf separating them can be bridged. But does this gulf really present a danger for critically schooled thought? Are we to yield here to the facile tendency of unifying and simplifying all problems — or is it necessary to perceive each set of problems in sharp isolation and to see in each set its own characteristic uniqueness?

It is precisely this uniqueness that lies at the basis of the problem of ethics. There is no competition between physics and ethics in the sense that they both presuppose the same realm of being but fight with each other about its explanation and significance. Ethics would certainly be in a bad way — it would lose all its dignity — if it could maintain its authority and fulfill its particular function in no other way than by keeping a lookout for gaps in the scientific explanation of nature and taking shelter, so to speak, in these gaps. There it could lead a shadowy existence; ethical freedom would somehow be tolerated in the world but it could not exert any effect, any true power; it could not move anything outward. Yet for the problem of ethics everything depends on this outward influence. Moral freedom must not be limited in its meaning to a mere possibility, an empty potentiality; its meaning and significance consist in its actualization, in its constantly progressing self-realization. For this act of self-realization the merely negative concept of indeterminacy or indeterminability is inadequate; other positive forces, characteristic principles and grounds of determination, are required. These grounds are not to be found on the level of physical explanations of nature,

From *Determinism and Indeterminism in Modern Physics,* pp. 197–207. New Haven: Yale University Press, 1956. Reprinted by permission of the publisher.

whether those of classical physics or those of quantum mechanics; they cannot even be envisaged on this level. They demand in every case a μετάβασις εἰς ἄλλο γένος, a shift to another realm. No physical indeterminism, however far it is pursued, can save us the transition that is here expected and demanded of us. The problem is not how to break through or in any way to lessen the force of strict laws of nature in the realm of empirical events. The problem is to discover and develop a new viewpoint, to set up a new standard which cannot be reduced to that of empirical causality but which on the other hand is in no sense in conflict with it. Ethics demands that human actions are to be capable of and accessible to a double judgment; they are to be determined as events in time, but their content and meaning is not to be exhausted by this determinism. The insight into the course of these actions, no matter how strictly these may be determined, should not blind us to the other yardstick with which we have to measure them – to the question of their *quid juris,* their ethical value and dignity. This requirement of evaluation can never be grasped and justified in a merely negative way; it must be secured positively. We are not dealing here with an attempt to discover some exceptions to certain general rules; we are dealing with the far more serious and difficult problem of discovering a new rule, a new type of conformity to law, which is to underlie all action that we designate as moral action.

If the history of ethics is followed from its first beginnings, it can be seen that it has always been this basic problem that has occupied and deeply concerned all students of philosophical ethics. Philosophical, as contrasted with religious, systems of ethics are not satisfied with teaching morality; they aim to base morality on rational grounds. But in this attempt at supplying a rational basis (λόγον διδόναι), philosophical thought is immediately faced with two types of causes. In classical pregnancy and clarity this duality is described at one point in Plato's *Phaedo,* which can justly be considered the true origin of philosophical ethics. What is the reason, Socrates asks in the *Phaedo,* for my sitting here in prison, awaiting the execution of the death sentence, when I was at liberty to escape?

> Should I say first that I am now sitting here because my body is composed of bones and sinews, and the bones are hard and have joints which divide them and the sinews can be contracted and relaxed and, with the flesh and the skin which contains them all, are laid about the bones; and so, as the bones are hung loose in their ligaments, the sinews, by relaxing and contracting, make me able to bend my limbs now, and that is the cause of my sitting here with my legs bent? . . . [But this] should fail to mention the real causes, which are, that the Athenians decided that it was best to condemn me, and therefore I have decided that it was best for me to sit here and that it is right for me to stay and undergo whatever penalty they order. For, by Dog, I fancy these bones and sinews of mine would have been in Megara or Boeotia long ago, carried thither by an opinion of what was best, if I did not think it was better and nobler to endure any penalty the city may inflict rather than to escape and run away. . . . If any one were to say that I could not have done what I thought proper if I had not bones and sinews and other things that I have, he would be right. But to say that those things are the cause of what I do, and that I act with intelligence but not from the choice of what is best, would be an extremely careless way of talking. Whoever talks in that way is unable to make a distinction and to see that in reality a cause is one thing, and the thing without which the cause would never be a cause is quite another thing. (ἄλλο μέν τί ἐστι τὸ αἴτιον τῷ ὄντι, ἄλλο δὲ ἐκεῖνο, ἄνευ οὗ τὸ αἴτιον οὐκ ἄν ποτ' εἴη αἴτιον.) And so it seems to me that most people, when they give the name of cause to the latter, are groping in the dark, as it

were, and are giving it a name that does not belong to it.[1]

What from purely physical considerations, from the standpoint of pre-Socratic philosophy of nature, was commonly designated as a cause sinks for Socrates to the level of being merely the occasion (*Veranlassung*) or condition. And Plato intensified this distinction. The true ground of moral or free action cannot be found in the current physical situation, or in what immediately preceded the action in time. It demands a new direction of outlook, a new form of viewing things. That man acts freely who acts with regard to the world of Ideas; and a free subject is the one who is aware of these Ideas and in virtue of them can survey the whole realm of phenomena, of spatiotemporal appearances, and can recognize it in all its determinateness. Thus this type of freedom does not limit or declare invalid a single relation or a particular form of determination within the physical world – instead it aims to go beyond the totality of the physical world, which is to be ethically transcended. According to Plato the specifically moral bearing is only attained through such a transcendence, for the Idea of the good lies "beyond being" (ἐπέκεινα τῆς οὐσίας).

But even if this Platonic transcendence is abandoned, if a solution of the ethical problem is sought strictly within the boundaries of scientific knowledge, the twofold aspect remains. Even within a strictly naturalistic ethic, the dualism between freedom and natural necessity cannot be evaded. Spinoza is the first who demanded and carried through this naturalistic justification within modern philosophy. The leading methodological principle on which the structure of his ethics rests demands that we no longer treat human actions as a state within a state. There is only one order and one law underlying happening, as truly as there exists only one being, one all-embracing substance. The concept of purpose must, therefore, be excluded not only from science but also from ethical considerations. It proves in both cases to be merely an *asylum ignorantiae*. Human actions are not to be judged differently from the way we judge mathematical figures such as triangles or circles. We may not make judgments about them by an assumed anthropomorphic standard. They must merely be described, and understood in virtue of this description. But even this purely descriptive method does not abandon the concept of freedom within Spinoza's system. Even Spinoza cannot evade the admission that it is a "different kind of cause" to which we are led when considering human actions. We cannot nor do we wish to withdraw from the dominion of general laws of nature; but these take on a different character when they refer not to the motions of bodies but to our self-conscious activity, to our representing, desiring and willing. Ethical laws are natural laws but they are laws of our rational nature. This expression of the rational nature represents for Spinoza the unification and reconciliation of nature and freedom – the only one there is, and the only one that can rightfully and meaningfully be demanded by ethics. To act freely does not mean to act arbitrarily or without prior decision; it means rather to act in accordance with a decision which is in harmony with the essence of our reason. This essence and with it the specific priority of reason consists of the knowledge of the whole. Reason does not deal with particular things and events; its concern is to understand the whole in its form and essence. Its realm is not that of mere existence but of pure essence. Out of this essential knowledge springs the true and deepest form of the moral will and moral behavior. It is the *amor dei intellectualis* that is the inner connection between the two. He who is filled with love for and in-

[1] Plato, *Phaedo*, 98c ff.; English trans., H. N. Fowler (London, 1917), pp. 339 ff.

sight into the whole does not succumb to the illusions of the imagination or the incitements of passing and momentary motives. He is "free" insofar as he does not live in the moment and himself does not suffer alteration with the changing moments. He grasps the norm of the universe and determines his actions by this norm as by an unchanging and eternal rule. To act "freely" means for Spinoza merely to act in accordance with this rule. The aim is not to elude all determination but to realize in one's action a quite definite, qualitatively designated form of determination: that one which is derived from the rational law as such. *Libere agere* and *ex ductu rationis agere* are one and the same. It is a waste of effort to seek another concept of freedom and a different concept of morality. The power and compulsion of all merely external particular causes break down in the face of this highest and all embracing form of human willing and human knowledge: "nothing is given in nature which is contrary to this intellectual love, or which could destroy it."

We face a completely different systematic formulation of the relation between freedom and necessity in Kant's development of ethics. Kant directs us back to Plato. His doctrine of morality rests entirely on that distinction which he himself called "classic," the "division of all objects whatsoever into phenomena and noumena." But it is clear to Kant from the start that this division cannot be carried through in a dogmatic-metaphysical sense but only in a "transcendental" sense. The "sensuous world" and the "intellectual world" are thus not posited as two opposing absolute forms of being, and for that reason the necessity for this opposition must be derived from principles of knowledge. It is the particular form of practical knowledge and practical judgment which leads to this opposition as its necessary correlate. Every human action has a double connection with being, since it can and must be subsumed under different norms of judgment. By its temporal origin and its temporal course it is a link in the chain of causes and effects – an element of that nexus which we designate as nature. But its determination within this totality of nature never exhausts its true content and meaning. As our actions belong to the realm of nature, so they also belong to the realm of purposes and must be referred to the systematic unity of this realm and judged in accordance with it. This judgment is governed by entirely different concepts and rules from those on which the intuition of the phenomenon "nature" rests. Though for the latter we may be satisfied to "spell out appearances that we may be able to read them as experience," we must in the former case take the step into the intelligible. An action may in all its aspects be spatiotemporally conditioned and therefore determined as a phenomenon of nature. Yet it is never merely the connection with the empirical world of things and facts which comes to expression in it. It points at the same time to the moral subject that plays its part in it and whose character and essence are revealed in it. It is this revelation of the person that Kant designates by the expression of "intelligible character," an expression which summarizes for him the essential aspects of the problems of freedom and ethics. By virtue of this doctrine Kant can remain a strict empirical determinist and can nevertheless assert that precisely this empirical determination leaves the way open for another determination, different in principle, which he calls the determination through the moral law or the pure autonomy of the will. The two are not mutually exclusive in the Kantian system but rather require and condition each other – a situation that can of course only be understood and justified if we strictly hold fast to the position that we are here dealing not with a metaphysical but with a critical-transcendental antithesis. It does not refer to absolute being as such, independent of all conditions of our empirical and our ethical knowledge. It merely establishes the aspect and the horizon of our reality from the standpoint of our basic theoretical concepts and ethical demands. Every rational being, according to Kant, has two points of view from which he can regard himself and recognize laws governing his actions.

First, so far as he belongs to the world of sense, he finds himself subject to laws of nature (heteronomy); secondly, as belonging to the intelligible world, under laws which being independent of nature have their foundation not in experience but in reason alone. . . . The conception of a world of the understanding is then only a point of view which reason finds itself compelled to take outside the appearances, in order to conceive itself as practical, which would not be possible if the influences of the sensibility had a determining power on man, but which is necessary unless he is to be denied the consciousness of himself as an intelligence, and consequently as a rational cause, energizing by reason – that is, operating freely.[2]

Within the limits of this investigation it is neither possible nor necessary to pursue further the history of the concept of freedom and its systematic significance. The examples quoted are only to prove one thing, that none of the great thinkers who were deeply conscious of the problems connected with this concept and continuously wrestled with them, ever yielded to the temptation to master them simply by denying the general causal principle and equating freedom with causelessness. Such an attempt is not to be found in Plato or Spinoza or Kant. For all of them freedom did not mean indeterminateness but rather a certain form of determinability: determinability through the pure intuition of Ideas, determinability through a universal law of reason that at the same time is the highest law of being, determinability through the pure concept of duty in which autonomy, the will's self-ordering according to law, expresses itself; these are the basic criteria to which the problem of freedom is brought back. That other form of determination, which occurs in the general laws of nature, is here neither denied nor discarded, but rather presupposed. The new mode of determination which is to be established is not built on the ruins of nature's conformity to law; rather it joins the latter as a correlative and complement. For this reason alone it is most questionable whether, or in what manner, a relaxation or dissolution of scientific determinism can be made useful for the solution of the fundamental problem of ethics. A "freedom" emanating from such a source and based on such a foundation would be a fatal gift to ethics. For it would contradict the characteristic and positive meaning of ethics; it would not leave room for that moral responsibility the possibility and necessity of which ethics aims to prove. Whenever something is "ascribed" to a person in the ethical sense, it presupposes, and is connected with, some type of prior determination on the part of that person. An action which should simply fall out of the causal nexus, which should take place at random without reasons, would stand entirely alone and could not be referred or ascribed to a persisting ethical subject. Only an action "grounded" in some way can be considered a responsible action, and the value ascribed to it depends on the type, on the quality of these grounds and not on their absence. Thus the question of free will cannot and must not be confused with the question of physical indeterminism. The free will whose establishment concerns ethics is incompatible with a dogmatic fatalism; but it is by no means incompatible with a critically conceived and developed determinism. We have seen time and again that quantum mechanics has also by no means

[2] *Grundlegung zur Metaphysik der Sitten* (1st ed. 1797); English trans., T. K. Abbott, *Fundamental Principles of the Metaphysics of Ethics* (4th ed. London, 1889), pp. 72, 78.

abandoned the idea of natural order according to law, but has rather lent it a new form. Thus if the idea of ethical freedom is threatened by natural order, it could not expect any help from quantum mechanics. For the problem under consideration, it makes no difference whether we think of natural events as being governed by strict dynamical laws, or whether we merely presuppose a statistical regularity. For from the latter standpoint they would also remain determined to such an extent that the supposed "freedom," a *liberum arbitrium indifferentiae,* would not find any refuge there. An action which from a physical standpoint is branded as not entirely impossible but in the highest degree improbable is not an action we can count on in any way in the realm of the decisions of our will. Our ethical decisions would be in a sad state if we had to count on such improbabilities and had to make our decisions dependent on them. The extremely improbable is practically the same as the impossible; the degree of predictability which is left us by quantum mechanics would be entirely sufficient to destroy ethical freedom if the latter, in its conception and its essential meaning, were inconsistent with predictability.

But one of the essential tasks of the philosophical ethics consists of showing why such an opposition does not exist, why freedom does not need to be upheld against physical causality, but instead maintains and asserts itself on its own grounds. "Persistence" is not only a physical but also and at the same time an ethical category, although in an entirely different sense. For all truly ethical actions must spring from the unity and persistence of a definite ethical character. This in itself shows us that it would be fatal for ethics to tie itself to and, as it were, fling itself into the arms of a limitless indeterminism. From such a standpoint we would have to evaluate an action more highly, the more it bears the earmark of the arbitrary, the unforeseen, the unpredictable. Yet true ethical judgment runs in exactly the opposite direction. It does not value behavior highly which is capricious, "uncontrollable," and changing from moment to moment; rather it values a course of action that springs from the basic substratum of the personality and is firmly anchored in it. Ethical character is distinguished by the fact that it is not completely determined from the outside, that in its decisions it is not thrown hither and thither by the changing conditions of the moment but remains itself and persists in itself. By virtue of this persistence we can count on such a person; we rely on his remaining true to himself and on his arriving at his decision not by mood and arbitrariness but by an autonomous law, by that which he himself recognizes and acknowledges as right. Schiller sets the foundation of his doctrine of moral freedom on the postulate that there exist ultimately two fundamental theoretical and ethical concepts, before which analysis must come to a halt and acknowledge its limitations. The one is the concept of person, the other the concept of state (*Zustand*). In man, as finite being, the two determinations must necessarily remain different and cannot be reduced to each other. "The person must be his own ground, for the permanent cannot arise out of change; and thus we have in the first place the idea of the absolute being, grounded in itself – that is, freedom. A state must have a cause; it must follow something, since it does not exist through the person, and it is therefore not absolute; and thus we have in the second place the condition of all dependent being or becoming, viz. time." Accordingly, causality and freedom are as little opposed as are being and time; the structure of our theoretical as well as ethical world depends on the permeation and correct complementation of each by the other.

This complementation is of course not to be understood as suggesting that the two factors are simply to be put side by side, or regarded as parts which may be added together and which, by this addition, produce a homogeneous whole. The synthesis here sought and demanded is entirely a synthesis of different elements, which, however, are not incapable of union, though they are qualitatively disparate. This disparity cannot be overcome or eliminated in any way. Thus it becomes clear from this side as well, that a possible change of the physical "causality concept" cannot directly touch ethics. For however physics may change its internal structure, by abandoning, for example, the concept of the simple mass point or the possibility of strict predictions, the opposition in principle between the physical and ethical world, between the realm of nature and the realm of ethics cannot be bridged. These realms will always confront each other in the same manner, no matter to what immanent transformations of their form we consider them subjected. The problem of freedom and nature remains the same, whether we formulate the general laws constituting nature as dynamic or statistical laws. We are concerned here not with a difference in their thing-content, but with a formal difference, or more precisely a difference in category. We cannot do away with the guiding concept of determination in either case, in the structure of the physical world or of the ethical world. But determination follows different categories in the realm of being and in that of duty (*Sollen*). These categories do not conflict because they belong to entirely different dimensions of consideration. Thus they can never meet in one point; they cannot become identical, nor do they disturb or destroy each other. Equally, they are not distributed over separate special realms of being, but always demand the whole of being, though each from a special "aspect."

The methodological problem here before us is by no means restricted to the relation between "nature" and "ethics"; it has a far more general character. It recurs wherever different determinations and interpretations of meaning confront each other. For instance in the case of religion, its philosophical interpretation was again and again faced with the basic problem, whether, and in what manner, the religious explanation of events can be brought into harmony with the other, humanly "natural" one. Again and again at this point the conflict between faith and knowledge sprang up; and for faith the miracle seemed to be "faith's dearest child." An event was more securely understood and established in a religious sense; the more it was documented as a miracle, the more it constituted a breach of the general laws of nature. However, in the modern philosophy of religion since Leibniz and Schleiermacher, this interpretation has undergone a considerable change. It no longer questions the validity of a strict and general order according to law in nature; rather it lends the latter a religious character; it sees in it a proof of the divine nature of being. "A miracle," Schleiermacher maintains, "is nothing but the religious term for an event"; it does not contradict the concept of regularity; rather it elevates this regularity as such into the sphere of religion and expresses it in religious terminology.

The aesthetic "sense" is constituted in an analogous manner. Art is not an "imitation of nature," nor does it add something entirely foreign to nature by transforming it according to aesthetic ideals. Rather it *discovers* the beautiful in nature by measuring it with a new and independent standard. An idol revered in a shrine can be described according to purely scientific principles, and can be represented according to the concepts and categories of science. In this way it becomes a "piece of nature," subject like any other to physicochemical laws. Yet we know that with all these determinations we do not penetrate to its full meaning. The latter is not exhausted by the mere enumeration of scientific data. It demands other criteria, different in principle. No matter from how many viewpoints we may observe and analyze the marble as a natural object, the result will never divulge anything about its form and the beauty of this form, or about its significance in religious worship as an object of religious reverence. And it is just as impossible to arrive at the characteristic content of the problem of freedom if we strictly adhere to the realm of statements of scientific knowledge. This problem also is a problem *sui generis,* a question which cannot be solved by simple reduction to natural laws but has to be based on an independent type of orderliness according to law, the autonomous orderly structure of the will. If this is kept in mind, it becomes understandable why ethics has nothing to fear and little to hope from the changes in the basic concepts of science which have taken place in modern physics. Now as always it will have to seek and find its own way, a way on which physics can neither confuse nor greatly assist it. Even where, as with Spinoza, ethics was bound to a strict naturalism, this situation was not changed in principle. The distinctive methodological character of its approach always broke through at some point or other. Regardless then of how the conflict between determinism and indeterminism will ultimately be decided in the realm of physics, one thing is certain, that the decision of ethics cannot be anticipated by it. For ethics, the cry *Hic Rhodus, hic salta* [3] will always be valid at this point. Ethics must pass judgment in its own right on the problem of freedom. It cannot refer the problem to another court, nor can it acknowledge any prejudice in this its most proper basic question. The student of ethics who inquires after the possibility of freedom cannot expect any essential help from physics, as long as he poses his question in the only sense significant for ethics. Even if a solution to the riddle could be offered in the form of some physical indeterminism, he would have to reject it with the words Queen Christina of Sweden is said to have used when she renounced crown and kingdom: *non mi bisogna e non mi basta.*[4] . . .

[3] Cf. T. James, *Aesop's Fables* (New York, 1848), p. 209. Fable 199, "The Boasting Traveller": "A man who had been travelling in foreign parts, on his return home was always bragging and boasting of the great feats he had accomplished in different places. In Rhodes for instance, he said he had taken such an extraordinary leap, that no man could come near him, and he had witnesses there to prove it. 'Possibly,' said one of his hearers, 'but if this be true, just suppose this to be Rhodes, and then try the leap again.'" *Translator.*

[4] Cf. Leibniz, "Theodicee": "As a comment on the explanations of such mysteries which appear from time to time, one might cite what the queen of Sweden had inscribed on a medal, with reference to the crown she had abandoned: 'I don't need it, and it's not enough anyway.'" *Philosophische Schriften,* ed. Gerhardt, *6,* 81.

Psychoanalysis and Moral Judgeability

EDWARD H. MADDEN

I

Psychoanalysis, moralists generally have come to see, does not reinforce traditional determinism. The psychoanalyst's point is that much less behavior than anyone ever dreamed possible is free or responsible in the ordinary sense that it is consciously and reasonably shaped. This point is clearly irrelevant to the traditional puzzle; for this puzzle simply disappears when the qualified statements "Most behavior is not free" or "Very little behavior is free" occur. The determinist's puzzle is how any behavior can be shown to be free if it is caused, since this implies it could not have been otherwise (or, if it is not caused, since this implies caprice). This "dilemma of responsibility" undercuts James's "dilemma of determinism."

Psychoanalysis does not help establish the possibility of human freedom either, although this corresponding incompetence is not so clearly recognized nowadays. Numerous recent interpreters of psychoanalysis [1] have tried to show that it is not only compatible with freedom but provides the very techniques for deciding when and how much freedom is attained. The analyst's techniques establish what behavior is obsessive, non-obsessive but unconscious, and rational — and, consequently, the argument goes, these techniques establish what behavior is nonresponsible and what responsible. And, after all, the point and frequent result of therapy is to produce freedom and responsibility where it did not exist before. More generally, some writers [2] argue that psychoanalysis, far from destroying the possibility of freedom, re-emphasizes the distinction between "reasons for action" and "causes of action" in its own employment of the "reason" or "motive" model of explanation rather than the efficient cause model. The analyst sometimes is misled by his hydraulic metaphors into thinking he has found efficient causes but only the physiologist with his palpable neurons can find the efficient causes of mental phenomena. (A strange view methodologically, certainly; for it would legislate learning psychology out of existence!)

The common strain in all these views is that psychoanalysis reinforces or even establishes common sense self-determinism and

Originally published in *Philosophy and Phenomenological Research,* Vol. XVIII, No. 1, 1957. Reprinted by permission of the editor.

[1] Herbert Fingarette, "Psychoanalytic Perspectives on Moral Guilt and Responsibility: A Re-evaluation," *Philosophy and Phenomenological Research,* XVI, September 1955, pp. 18–36; Stephen Toulmin, "The Logical Status of Psycho-analysis," in Margaret Macdonald (Editor), *Philosophy and Analysis* (Oxford: Basil Blackwell, 1954), pp. 132–139; and Antony Flew, "Psycho-analytic Explanation," in *Philosophy and Analysis,* pp. 139–148. Toulmin and Flew follow F. Waismann's distinction in "Language Strata," in A. G. N. Flew (Editor), *Logic and Language, Second Series* (Oxford: Basil Blackwell, 1953), pp. 1–13.

[2] Toulmin and Flew.

so salvages the notion of moral responsibility. This type of argument, however, misses the heart of the determinist's puzzle. Its irrelevance to the core of the puzzle is pointed up by imagining how a determinist would reply to it. He would say that he knows perfectly well there are common sense tests which one uses to show a person could have done otherwise (by showing that he has the ability, displayed on other occasions, to do the alternate type of act and was under no duress to do the act he did) and scientific tests which one applies for distinguishing obsessive, non-obsessive but unconscious, and rational behavior; so that it makes sense both commonsensically and scientifically to make the distinction between free and unfree, responsible and nonresponsible acts; but nevertheless what he wants is proof that even in allegedly free acts we are not, without knowing it, being determined by neurotic or normal unconscious motivation beyond the range of our most careful tests to detect. This problem is the philosophical core of the determinist's position, since self-determinism, whether idealistic or commonsensical, plus the existentialist insight (namely, that in normal or non-neurotic behavior the point is not that man *is* responsible but that he *becomes* responsible as the price of maturity, of no longer being a child, and thus that he does *accept* responsibility for the consequences of his personality and character even though he had no control over their formation), easily avoids the original dilemma of the determinist. The determinist's real puzzle is the isomorph of a number of other philosophical puzzles. Even though there are accepted techniques for distinguishing veridical and illusory perception, how can I prove, or (Descartes' evil genius?) how can I be sure, that the allegedly veridical ones are not illusory or hallucinatory beyond the range of the accepted techniques – a crucial step in the dialectic of the issue over our knowledge of the external world. From this paradigm of philosophical puzzles, which includes science in its scope, psychoanalysis clearly cannot rescue us.

To be sure, one might argue that the issue which the determinist raises is spurious and the proof he demands nonsensical. He might try to show that the determinist's use of "free" in "For all we know we are really never free" is self-contradictory because the ordinary sense of "freedom," which he is apparently using (for otherwise the word is vacuous because he does not specify another meaning), is defined by the kind of thing which is evidence for the term's exemplification. Or one may cast his lot with common sense on other grounds, namely, that a property and predicate are "meaningful" over and above the tests of presence or applicability. In either case, however, the dialectic of determinism has eventuated in the dialectic of meaningfulness, which obviously antedates, logically, any empirical findings. Consequently, whether the issue the determinist raises is real or spurious psychoanalysis has nothing to do with solving or dissolving it.

In this problem, psychology does not have philosophical results but philosophy has psychological results. When one realizes the true nature of the determinist's position (demand) his original perplexity is attenuated. What I have in mind is this. If one believes that the determinist's demand has not been parried successfully, he will admit, nevertheless, if he is honest with himself, that as a result of the dialectical drift he does not worry about the issue in the way that he did originally. He worried that the determinist had shown his ordinary views on freedom to be wrong, but it turns out simply that he has not proved they are right. But this ubiquitous problem, How can I be sure what I naïvely think to be true really is so?, is the paradigm of philosophical puzzles, and is not peculiar to a moral context, is not dependent on it for its formation. So the original perplexity and worry loses its force and urgency. A paradoxical way of saying the same thing is that a person worries less about determinism because he has to worry about the same problem everywhere. I think one could defend the view that therapeutic and casuistic positivists frequently confuse the attenuation of a philosophical problem with its dissolution and that the obvious fact that there is at least one philosophical problem that cannot be attenuated reflects the existence of the unannounced meaning criterion of the philosophical therapists and casuists.

II

There are numerous other ways in which psychoanalysis and morality get mixed together to the benefit of neither and the obscuration of the real import of the former for the latter; all that one can do is be alert to the danger and concentrate steadily on the real import, which is the view, long defended by most forensic psychiatrists, that neurotic behavior is nonresponsible. Some philosophers, along with the forensic psychiatrists, have defended this view; and the argument usually relied on is, roughly, the following: Neurotic behavior is nonresponsible because childhood neuroses cause adult neuroses, which, in turn, eventuate in criminal or queer behavior. But since a person has no control over the formation of his childhood neurosis, and no control over what follows inevitably from it, he cannot be held responsible for these consequences. The point of therapy, of course, is to make it possible for the neurotic to accept responsibility in the ordinary sense of the word; but *prior* to therapy, or where therapy has not occurred or is unsuccessful, the "malevolent" nature of the neurotic's unconscious makes him nonresponsible for his behavior. One must be careful, at this point, not to extend the claim of nonresponsibility to normal unconscious behavior because this extension brings in a host of additional issues and usually culminates in the old confusion of making the general determinist claim that one is nonresponsible because he had no control over the formation of his personality, to which claim the existentialist position is again applicable.

The juristic view of legal and moral responsibility, however, is far from hospitable to the psychiatrist's claim that neurotic behavior is nonresponsible; indeed the struggles in court between lawyer and psychiatrist even in the rare cases where the medical psychopathologist represents the court and not the plaintiff or defendant, have become notorious.

On the juristic view of the matter, a person is legally and presumably morally responsible if, or because, he is able, or has the capacity, "to tell the difference between right and wrong"; if, or because, he "knows the consequences, both legal and moral, of his act." This rule is the famous McNaghten Rule the jurist relies on, the legal definition of sanity and insanity; but it simply incorporates what is apparently obvious common sense. In criminal law this view is again reflected in the concept of *mens rea*. Jurists speak of the mental element in criminal liability (*mens rea*) and by this phrase they mean knowledge of consequences, foresight, intention, voluntariness, etc. One can disallow the presence of *mens rea*, or mitigate it, or simply defeat the allegation of responsibility, only if he can present defenses or exceptions like duress, provocation, infancy, or insanity. However, since the neurotic person meets the requirement of knowing consequences, etc., and is not under duress, or provoked, or insane, he cannot be judged otherwise by the court than as legally and morally responsible for his acts.

The McNaghten Rule, it should be noted at the outset, not only prevents the psychiatrist from making a case for the nonresponsibility of a neurotic individual but even makes it extremely difficult for him to establish the nonresponsibility of the psychotic. A person plans his own death; he murders another intending to get caught so he will be executed. The judge in the case, applying the McNaghten Rule, held the man clearly sane and responsible because he deliberately acted in terms of consequences![3] This consequence of the McNaghten Rule amounts to a *reductio ad absurdum* and clearly points up the psychological naïveté of the legalistic view; a naïveté which, as we shall see, is again reflected in the deterrence theory of punishment; but it remains to give direct reasons why this view is naïve, and to present counter-stimuli which may help carry the day over deep-seated fears and anxieties. The forensic psychiatrists, I believe, are more successful in these endeavors than philosophical interpreters of psychoanalysis because they do not rest content, the way the latter do, with establishing the nonresponsibility of neurotic behavior by pointing to the way such behavior originates. A number of remarks would be necessary for complete clarity but two fundamental ones must suffice for now.

1) The McNaghten type rule is psychologically unrealistic because the criminal's consideration of consequences, even when it is present, which is usually not the case, is impotent to prevent his acting out his wishes because of the compulsive nature of some motivation. This realization, to be sure, has filtered into legal concepts, albeit inadequately since the determination of this motivation is still the layman's task, and is a step in the right direction; but it is far from reaching psychological bedrock. The most important "disorder of emotion" is the flattening or dulling of the emotional tone of a person or its complete absence; this disorder is important because it is the one least understood empathically and so misunderstood as mere callousness.

> [A criminal] may speak as if he understands "the nature and consequences of his act," but if he does not feel it all adequately he is like a man who is awake, normal, rational — but totally anesthetic. . . . The considerable diminution or absence of emotion, or "affect" as we say, is probably the most virulent phenomenon leading to the paralysis of moral judgment and of will. Our laws have no provision for taking into account this extremely important psychological phenomenon, yet it has been observed and recognized for a long time.[4]
>
> The flattening of emotion, the "failure to feel," results from many severe psychopathological reactions, and it plays an important role in many different kinds of criminal personalities. Within these personality types, a person understands emotional life only in the way a blind man "understands" color; he may know things *about* it, what causes it, what effects it has, etc., but does not *experience* it.
>
> Under the circumstances, the aggressive drives would break through, since the barrier of feeling fails to arrest the action; the will cannot step in, as it were, and assert its control. The will can act only if that which is reason and that which is feeling are integrated. If they split off from one another even partially, the door to aggression opens to the extent of the diminution of affect. That which has become known in present-day psycho-analytic psychology as the ego — the very substance of the human personality — cannot function either in the direction of conscience or in the direction of virtue, unless it is fully integrated with adequate feeling tones. . . .[5]

This emotional indifference of many criminals is generally assessed as moral indifference, callousness, incorrigibility, and depravity, and opens the floodgates to all sorts of feelings of counter-aggression by members of

[3] Gregory Zilboorg, *The Psychology of the Criminal Act and Punishment* (London: Hogarth Press, 1955), pp. 25–27. Other men whose work is particularly important in this area, and from whom I have profited greatly, are Winfred Overholser and Walter Bromberg.

[4] *Ibid.*, pp. 71–72.

[5] *Ibid.*, p. 72.

society, and to an eventual vindictively motivated retribution.

This set of feelings is as frequent among people as it is natural, but it offers us no understanding of the event, it provides really no answer to the inevitable question: Why? This 'why' is uttered with desperation by the public, and the immediate answer is 'never mind, destroy the criminal, the human animal.' This 'why?' is uttered by the law in a tone of indignant objectivity, but actually it is but the echo of the hollow voice of 'the man in the street' who, knowing nothing about human motives, 'sees' the true answer only in the logic of acquiring easy money. This 'why' is asked by the sociologist, but his answer is but a number of statistics and generalizations, among which the person who committed the crime is lost, and with him the secret of the true answer. This 'why' is asked rather anxiously and almost desperately by the psychiatrist, but the world and/or the law offer him the obscurities of the McNaghten rule for a guide, or merely an electrocuted or hanged or gassed corpse.[6]

2) Rules of the McNaghten type are psychologically unrealistic and, in their effects, pernicious because they utilize formal, universal criteria where individual analysis and insight is needed, and depend on fragmentary criteria where understanding of the whole personality is needed. They are rules which, technically, are non-vague; they either apply or do not apply to every individual; but the psychological facts are such that make this application wholly arbitrary and itself immoral. The analyst needs to know the *whole historical background* of an individual case in order to "diagnose" psychosis, neurosis, etc., and whether and what therapy is applicable and might successfully rehabilitate; and he finds that each individual case is not simply different but unique. Psychiatry by its very nature cannot be formalized either as a clinical system or as a therapeutic method.

When a formalistic clinical attitude is assumed in psychiatry, the psychiatrist loses his usefulness as a healer; but strange as it may seem, he may gain in stature as a psychiatric expert. For if he feels that he can classify mental diseases with precision, and if he feels he can look upon the individual as the sum total of so many logical categories, and formal principles, he can fit himself and his opinions perfectly into the mold of the verbal metaphysics of certain aspects of the law.[7]

The crucial point for us is that if law is to make judgments about responsibility which are themselves moral each case must be judged in terms of its specific circumstances, the statement but not judgment of which the Qualified Psychiatrist is alone competent to make. One must be careful, however, not to identify the "uniqueness" view with the methodological view that sometimes goes by the name of "idiographic" explanation as distinct from ordinary "nomothetic" scientific explanation; there is no necessary connection between the two views and it only courts confusion to reinforce the one by the other as some analysts have done.[8] Finally it is a matter of more than passing importance that the emphasis on specificity of circumstances makes it necessary to interpret the claim that neurotic behavior is nonresponsible as only a heuristic slogan and not itself universally true or acceptable. Indeed psychiatrists, in contrast to philosophers, have urged this point.

Further, judgments of responsibility under the McNaghten Rule are based on fragmentary, abstracted criteria, overlook whole personality frames, and are thereby psycho-

[6] *Ibid.*, p. 32.

[7] *Ibid.*, p. 126.

[8] *Ibid.*, pp. 57–58; 125–126.

logically meaningless and themselves morally condemnable. In a case previously mentioned, a man murdered a youth because he wished to be apprehended and hanged. The judge in the case declared that since he knew the *consequences* of his act quite well, he knew the "*nature and quality of the act,*" the usual terminology of McNaghten type rules, and was thus responsible for the act. He was hanged accordingly, before which, however, the prisoner happily expressed his appreciation! Cases like this one, some of which are more refined and accordingly less dramatic, more than formal analysis, make it abundantly clear that one cannot infer that another understands "the nature and quality of an act," where this means its moral import, because he manipulated it or used it in a utilitarian fashion, or because he reacted to it with any other isolated rational or emotional response. The only way to understand how an individual construes "the nature and quality of an act" is in terms of the harmony of his total personality – particularly when it is the insane harmony of a pathological mind or the queer harmony of a neurotic one.

The above analyses make understandable the difficult and untenable role of the psychiatrist in present-day court procedure. The untenability arises, it is evident, because the psychiatrist is asked to determine the applicability of legal, common sense concepts by psychological methods which not only do not accommodate these concepts but repudiate them.[9] The psychiatrist wishes to impress on law and legal philosophy that it has no criterion for legal sanity and insanity and, in fact, believes the term refers to a wholly fictitious property.

The present interpretation of psychiatry implies a rehabilitative "theory of punishment," the relation of which to the rival Kantian and utilitarian "theories" is usually far from clear. This traditional three-way classification, unfortunately, has more than one basis of division. If behavior is responsible, then Kantian and utilitarian theories are the significant alternatives (there is no rehabilitation to be achieved in non-neurotic behavior) ; but if behavior is nonresponsible, then rehabilitation and utilitarianism are the significant alternatives. Utilitarianism, unlike Kantian penology, is still a meaningful theory if behavior is nonresponsible because on this view punishment, and the pain it inflicts, is not intrinsically good but instrumentally good in preventing further more intense and overall greater pain. Punishment (preferably simple incarceration) achieves this end, the utilitarian believes, by protecting society and acting as an example that is effective in deterring not only the criminal himself from further criminal acts but also the potential criminal from acting out his wishes. Kantian and utilitarian theories are mutually exclusive theories of punishment if behavior is responsible. Protection and deterrence, for Kant, could never be legitimate reasons for punishing a person, but only desirable consequences of punishment. (One can, of course, try to show that both deontological and teleological justifications of punishment are exaggerations of different strands of common sense and that each in its own way is a "good reason" for punishment.) However, rehabilitation and utilitarianism are not mutually exclusive theories of punishment if behavior is nonresponsible; they are related in oblique ways, competitive in a sense but not mutually exclusive. For the person who believes that neurotic behavior is nonresponsible, the clarification of this oblique, and generally misunderstood relationship, is the most urgent need of penological theory.

The difficulty with the utilitarian example or deterrence view, the analyst feels, is not in principle, but simply that it does not do what it is supposed to do. Pickpockets plied

[9] *Ibid.*, pp. 119 ff.

their trade most avidly at executions, when all eyes were focused on the gallows, at a time when robbery itself was punishable by death! [10] And comparisons among states which do and do not have capital punishment seem to indicate a lack of deterrence by harsh example (although there is sensible counter-evidence on this point).[11] This deterrence view is psychologically naïve because it does not take into account the neurotic roots of much crime which renders rational deterrence irrelevant. And without the techniques of rehabilitation which do take these factors into account, straightforward punishment simply does not deter the criminal from repeating his behavior. "What the law . . . fails to see is that punishment alone inflicted from outside produces only a hostile response, an intensification of hatred, and consequently the diminution of those healthy, auto-punitive, restorative trends in man, which alone make man capable of inwardly accepting punishment and making salutary use of it." [12]

Rehabilitation and utilitarian social protection are in one sense obviously compatible. During rehabilitation the criminal is incarcerated and society is duly protected. However it follows that if the rehabilitation process appears successful the patient then has the *right* to be returned to society. Psychiatrists, however, meet great public indignation at either the idea or fact of the criminal's return. Analysts explain the vehement hostility of this objection in the following way. People identify themselves with the criminal's own impulses (who has not had them?) and are tempted to give way to the impulses. They become anxious and feel guilty, and are quieted by a sudden, unconscious denial of similarity with the criminal – and so react with great destructive hostility toward him. These causal analyses are usually justified but nevertheless one must not overlook the rational basis which underlies nonhysterical objections to returning the criminal to society – namely, a lack of confidence in the success and permanency of psychoanalytic therapy. Since psychiatry and psychoanalysis are not developed and certain sciences and psychiatrists and analysts differ much among themselves on theoretical concepts, one must proceed cautiously, for the protection of society, in the return of rehabilitated criminals. One psychiatrist, in meeting the criticism of theoretic disagreement, writes that after all there is considerable disagreement in all areas of science, including the most rigorous – witness the disagreements of Einstein, Heisenberg, and De-Broglie – without impugning their reliability.[13] This type of defense, completely ignoring levels of disagreement, can only heighten the critic's suspicion that analysts are not always clear about what they are doing!

There is, finally, a regrettable tendency among certain forensic psychiatrists to sentimentalize their antagonism to utilitarian views in a position they call "individualistic humanism." They condemn "legal utilitarianism" because it submerges the rights of the individual in a metaphysical entity, society, etc. A utilitarian, of course, is astonished at *this* sort of criticism because his notion of the greatest good is individualistic to the core – the largest amount of mutually compatible experienced goods. The psychiatrist's quarrel with utilitarian morality is a matter of detail, not principle.

III

Several recent papers on psychoanalysis and responsibility illustrate the pitfalls, always waiting to be stepped into, which I

[10] *Ibid.*, pp. 28–29.

[11] Jerome Hall, "Science and Reform in Criminal Law," in Philip Wiener (Editor), *Readings in Philosophy of Science* (New York: Charles Scribner's Sons, 1953), pp. 297–309. Text and footnotes.

[12] Zilboorg, *op. cit.*, pp. 112–113.

[13] *Ibid.*, pp. 118–119.

have discussed in Sections I and II. John Hospers has claimed [14] that one cannot legitimately be held responsible for the inevitable consequences of uncontrollable events (i.e., for the queer or criminal behavior which results from adult neuroses, which result from childhood neuroses, over the formation of which the individual obviously had no control). Herbert Fingarette denies [15] this claim and, in addition, attacks what he takes to be another blunder in the philosophical interpretation of psychoanalysis, namely, that neurotic guilt is not real guilt. I suspect this conflict results mainly from confusions to which each author, perhaps, has contributed a share.

Therapy, Herbert Fingarette says,[16] often consists, first, in making the patient aware that he feels intensely guilty. The second step is to find the ground of the guilt feeling which, in neurosis, is unconscious. The analyst tries to reduce, only *temporarily,* the burden of felt guilt so that the wish, to which the guilt is attached, finally comes into consciousness. The crucial point is that the patient rightly feels guilt over the wish. The guilt feeling is not disproportionate; the wish merits it. In the cases where the wish looks trivial it is, by and large, a mask that a fundamentally evil wish, which is unconscious, wears. And it is fruitless to say that the person is not really guilty because after all he did not *act* on his wish; for the wish itself is *morally,* albeit not consequentially, equivalent to the act. Consequently, the first step in therapy, when the guilt feeling becomes conscious, can be described morally by saying "the patient is enabled to face his guilt rather than to run away from it as he has in the past." [17] And when the ground of the guilt, the evil wish, emerges into consciousness one can say, from the moral perspective, that the person has been forced to face not only his guilt but in addition the evil within him which is the basis of his guilt.

At this point in therapy the patient is able to reflect upon his evil wish in the context of his life circumstances and ideals, which context, through therapy, he sees more realistically than before. Appraising his wish within this context, he is at last able to reject the wish, modify it, or retain it, and even sometimes modify one of his fundamental ideals. As a result of therapy, then, the patient *accepts* responsibility; i.e., accepts as *his* the task of doing something about his wishes or suffering the moral and psychological consequences. "In spite of Hospers' assumption that we cannot be held responsible for the inevitable consequences of uncontrollable events, we seem to see in therapy an acceptance of responsibility for just such events." [18] And this result unexpectedly lends support to the existentialist analysis of moral responsibility. It is not that we *were* or *are* responsible, as the existentialist says, but we must *accept* responsibility, by an act of will, of deliberate choice, as the price of maturity. True, it is hard to be responsible in the future for some of the things we are when we had no hand in so becoming, but nevertheless we must accept the hard reality that the world is not fair and just and assume responsibility in order sensibly to go about the business of living. Stop complaining; you are paying the price of no longer being a child. We can reach true humanity only by accepting the challenge to *make* the world just.

1) *Guilt.* Clearly, I think, it is one thing to say an agent's wish or act is guilty in the sense that it is condemnable or morally wrong and another to say that the agent is guilty in the sense that *he* is condemnable.

[14] John Hospers, "Free-Will and Psychoanalysis," in W. Sellars and J. Hospers (Editors), *Readings in Ethical Theory* (New York: Appleton-Century-Crofts, Inc., 1952), pp. 560–575.

[15] Fingarette, *op. cit.*

[16] *Ibid.,* pp. 26 ff.

[17] *Ibid.,* p. 27.

[18] *Ibid.,* p. 30.

The second sense of "guilty" is the usual one, the sense which presupposes responsibility, and occurs in legal sentences like "not guilty by reason of insanity." Fingarette realizes that his use of "guilty" does not presuppose responsibility – we can be guilty when not responsible, he says, because guilt occurs very early in life, while responsibility occurs later [19] – yet he blurs the distinction by going from "guilty wish" to "guilty agent" before responsibility occurs. The first step in therapy, when the guilt feeling becomes conscious, he writes, can be described morally by saying "the patient is enabled to face his guilt rather than to run away from it as he has in the past." [20] This type of blur occurs frequently; but it is not the confusion which leads to his dissent from Hospers' view.

2) *Responsibility.* I can see no objection whatever in saying man *becomes* responsible or *accepts* responsibility as the price of maturity; and consequently that he does accept responsibility for the inevitable consequences of his personality and character even though they were not under his formative control. As I said in Section I, this claim effectively helps to meet the determinist's original dilemma. The point is, however, that in neurotic behavior this result only occurs after therapy. The forensic psychiatrist, on the other hand, is claiming that prior to therapy, or where therapy has not occurred or is unsuccessful, the "malevolent unconscious" makes an agent nonresponsible for his behavior; and we have seen above the type of reason he gives to defend this view. Hospers in some places in his article seems to be making the same point. However, if this is the case then his and Fingarette's views could not conflict because they do not even meet on the same ground; yet Fingarette offers his view as a devastating criticism of Hospers'. The only way to explain this state of affairs is that Fingarette interprets Hospers' view as if it were the traditional determinist's point that all behavior is nonresponsible because it is determined by our character but we did not have any control over *its* formation. That Fingarette interprets Hospers thusly is again suggested when Fingarette says that Hospers' analysis of psychoanalysis is not necessary or needed to make the point.

It is interesting to note that we would indeed have a paradox, if we accept Hospers' assumption about moral responsibility. For in that case, even if we did not consider psychoanalytic doctrine but simply granted that, in some way or other, our present nature and behavior are the causal consequences of earlier states of the world, we would be faced with the problem of explaining how we could *ever* be responsible for *any* of our adult behavior.[21]

In view of some of Hospers' statements, Fingarette's interpretation seems legitimate; or understandable, at any rate, even if Hospers did not intend to hold the view. Hospers writes, for example: "An act is free when it is determined by the man's character, say moralists; but what if the most decisive aspects of his character were already irrevocably acquired before he could do anything to mold them?" [22] "The unconscious is the master of every fate and the captain of every soul." [23] Also Fingarette's interpretation is suggested in the way in which Hospers presents his analysis of psychoanalysis as if it were a necessary refutation of the Schlick-Russell type of dissolution of the determinism-responsibility issue when it is an (elaborate?) sufficient one. And bringing in the issue of the nonresponsibility of non-neurotic unconscious behavior I suspect is misleading, too, because it brings up additional issues to which Fingarette's and existential analyses are highly pertinent.

Hospers and Fingarette, it seems to me,

19 *Ibid.*, p. 33.

20 *Ibid.*, p. 27.

21 *Ibid.*, p. 31.

22 Hospers, *op. cit.*, p. 563.

23 *Ibid.*, p. 572.

each in his own way, slide psychiatry into the traditional determinism-responsibility issue; Hospers suggesting, in one way or another, that psychoanalysis reinforces determinism and Fingarette unequivocally holding that it reinforces commonsensical self-determinism and so moral responsibility. This manoeuvre, I believe, is unfortunate either way; and the real import of psychoanalysis for morality – namely, that neurotic behavior is not morally judgeable – is likely to be lost in the resulting confusion. The forensic psychiatrist cannot be anything but dismayed at this turn of events.

Reconstruction in Moral Conceptions

JOHN DEWEY

The impact of the alteration in methods of scientific thinking upon moral ideas is, in general, obvious. Goods, ends are multiplied. Rules are softened into principles, and principles are modified into methods of understanding. Ethical theory began among the Greeks as an attempt to find a regulation for the conduct of life which should have a rational basis and purpose instead of being derived from custom. But reason as a substitute for custom was under the obligation of supplying objects and laws as fixed as those of custom had been. Ethical theory ever since has been singularly hypnotized by the notion that its business is to discover some final end or good or some ultimate and supreme law. This is the common element among the diversity of theories. Some have held that the end is loyalty or obedience to a higher power or authority; and they have variously found this higher principle in Divine Will, the will of the secular ruler, the maintenance of institutions in which the purpose of superiors is embodied, and the rational consciousness of duty. But they have differed from one another because there was one point in which they were agreed: a single and final source of law. Others have asserted that it is impossible to locate morality in conformity to law-giving power, and that it must be sought in ends that are goods. And some have sought the good in self-realization, some in holiness, some in happiness, some in the greatest possible aggregate of pleasures. And yet these schools have agreed in the assumption that there is a single, fixed and final good. They have been able to dispute with one another only because of their common premise.

The question arises whether the way out of the confusion and conflict is not to go to the root of the matter by questioning this common element. Is not the belief in the single, final and ultimate (whether conceived as good or as authoritative law) an intellectual product of that feudal organization which is disappearing historically and of that belief in a bounded, ordered cosmos, wherein rest is higher than motion, which has disappeared from natural science? It has been repeatedly suggested that the pres-

From *Reconstruction in Philosophy* (Enlarged Ed.), pp. 161–186. Boston: The Beacon Press, 1948. Reprinted by permission of the publisher.

ent limit of intellectual reconstruction lies in the fact that it has not as yet been seriously applied in the moral and social disciplines. Would not this further application demand precisely that we advance to a belief in a plurality of changing, moving, individualized goods and ends, and to a belief that principles, criteria, laws are intellectual instruments for analyzing individual or unique situations?

The blunt assertion that every moral situation is a unique situation having its own irreplaceable good may seem not merely blunt but preposterous. For the established tradition teaches that it is precisely the irregularity of special cases which makes necessary the guidance of conduct by universals, and that the essence of the virtuous disposition is willingness to subordinate every particular case to adjudication by a fixed principle. It would then follow that submission of a generic end and law to determination by the concrete situation entails complete confusion and unrestrained licentiousness. Let us, however, follow the pragmatic rule, and in order to discover the meaning of the idea ask for its consequences. Then it surprisingly turns out that the primary significance of the unique and morally ultimate character of the concrete situation is to transfer the weight and burden of morality to intelligence. It does not destroy responsibility; it only locates it. A moral situation is one in which judgment and choice are required antecedently to overt action. The practical meaning of the situation – that is to say the action needed to satisfy it – is not self-evident. It has to be searched for. There are conflicting desires and alternative apparent goods. What is needed is to find the right course of action, the right good. Hence, inquiry is exacted: observation of the detailed makeup of the situation; analysis into its diverse factors; clarification of what is obscure; discounting of the more insistent and vivid traits; tracing the consequences of the various modes of action that suggest themselves; regarding the decision reached as hypothetical and tentative until the anticipated or supposed consequences which led to its adoption have been squared with actual consequences. This inquiry is intelligence. Our moral failures go back to some weakness of disposition, some absence of sympathy, some one-sided bias that makes us perform the judgment of the concrete case carelessly or perversely. Wide sympathy, keen sensitiveness, persistence in the face of the disagreeable, balance of interests enabling us to undertake the work of analysis and decision intelligently are the distinctively moral traits – the virtues or moral excellencies.

It is worth noting once more that the underlying issue is, after all, only the same as that which has been already threshed out in physical inquiry. There too it long seemed as if rational assurance and demonstration could be attained only if we began with universal conceptions and subsumed particular cases under them. The men who initiated the methods of inquiry that are now everywhere adopted were denounced in their day (and sincerely) as subverters of truth and foes of science. If they have won in the end, it is because, as has already been pointed out, the method of universals confirmed prejudices and sanctioned ideas that had gained currency irrespective of evidence for them; while placing the initial and final weight upon the individual case stimulated painstaking inquiry into facts and examination of principles. In the end, loss of eternal truths was more than compensated for in the accession of quotidian facts. The loss of the system of superior and fixed definitions and kinds was more than made up for by the growing system of hypotheses and laws used in classifying facts. After all, then, we are only pleading for the adoption in moral reflection of the logic that has been proved to make for security, stringency and fertility in passing judgments upon physical phenomena. And the reason is the same.

The old method in spite of its nominal and esthetic worship of reason discouraged reason, because it hindered the operation of scrupulous and unremitting inquiry.

More definitely, the transfer of the burden of the moral life from following rules or pursuing fixed ends over to the detection of the ills that need remedy in a special case and the formation of plans and methods for dealing with them, eliminates the causes which have kept moral theory controversial, and which have also kept it remote from helpful contact with the exigencies of practice. The theory of fixed ends inevitably leads thought into the bog of disputes that cannot be settled. If there is one *summum bonum,* one supreme end, what is it? To consider this problem is to place ourselves in the midst of controversies that are as acute now as they were two thousand years ago. Suppose we take a seemingly more empirical view, and say that while there is not a single end, there also are not as many as there are specific situations that require amelioration; but there are a number of such natural goods as health, wealth, honor or good name, friendship, esthetic appreciation, learning and such moral goods as justice, temperance, benevolence, etc. What or who is to decide the right of way when these ends conflict with one another, as they are sure to do? Shall we resort to the method that once brought such disrepute upon the whole business of ethics: Casuistry? Or shall we have recourse to what Bentham well called the *ipse dixit* method: the arbitrary preference of this or that person for this or that end? Or shall we be forced to arrange them all in an order of degrees from the highest good down to the least precious? Again we find ourselves in the middle of unreconciled disputes with no indication of the way out.

Meantime, the special moral perplexities where the aid of intelligence is required go unenlightened. We cannot seek or attain health, wealth, learning, justice or kindness in general. Action is always specific, concrete, individualized, unique. And consequently judgments as to acts to be performed must be similarly specific. To say that a man seeks health or justice is only to say that he seeks to live healthily or justly. These things, like truth, are adverbial. They are modifiers of action in special cases. How to live healthily or justly is a matter which differs with every person. It varies with his past experience, his opportunities, his temperamental and acquired weaknesses and abilities. Not man in general but a particular man suffering from some particular disability aims to live healthily, and consequently health cannot mean for him exactly what it means for any other mortal. Healthy living is not something to be attained by itself apart from other ways of living. A man needs to be healthy *in* his life, not apart from it, and what does life mean except the aggregate of his pursuits and activities? A man who aims at health as a distinct end becomes a valetudinarian, or a fanatic, or a mechanical performer of exercises, or an athlete so one-sided that his pursuit of bodily development injures his heart. When the endeavor to realize a so-called end does not temper and color all other activities, life is portioned out into strips and fractions. Certain acts and times are devoted to getting health, others to cultivating religion, others to seeking learning, to being a good citizen, a devotee of fine art and so on. This is the only logical alternative to subordinating all aims to the accomplishment of one alone — fanaticism. This is out of fashion at present, but who can say how much of distraction and dissipation in life, and how much of its hard and narrow rigidity is the outcome of men's failure to realize that each situation has its own unique end and that the whole personality should be concerned with it? Surely, once more, what a man needs is to live healthily, and this result so affects all the activities of his life that it cannot be set up as a separate and independent good.

Nevertheless the general notions of health, disease, justice, artistic culture are of great importance: Not, however, because this or that case may be brought exhaustively under a single head and its specific traits shut out, but because generalized science provides a man as physician and artist and citizen, with questions to ask, investigations to make, and enables him to understand the meaning of what he sees. Just in the degree in which a physician is an artist in his work he uses his science, no matter how extensive and accurate, to furnish him with tools of inquiry into the individual case, and with methods of forecasting a method of dealing with it. Just in the degree in which, no matter how great his learning, he subordinates the individual case to some classification of diseases and some generic rule of treatment, he sinks to the level of the routine mechanic. His intelligence and his action become rigid, dogmatic, instead of free and flexible.

Moral goods and ends exist only when something has to be done. The fact that something has to be done proves that there are deficiencies, evils in the existent situation. This ill is just the specific ill that it is. It never is an exact duplicate of anything else. Consequently the good of the situation has to be discovered, projected and attained on the basis of the exact defect and trouble to be rectified. It cannot intelligently be injected into the situation from without. Yet it is the part of wisdom to compare different cases, to gather together the ills from which humanity suffers, and to generalize the corresponding goods into classes. Health, wealth, industry, temperance, amiability, courtesy, learning, esthetic capacity, initiative, courage, patience, enterprise, thoroughness and a multitude of other generalized ends are acknowledged as goods. But the *value* of this systematization is intellectual or analytic. Classifications *suggest* possible traits to be on the lookout for in studying a particular case; they suggest methods of action to be tried in removing the inferred causes of ill. They are tools of insight; their value is in promoting an individualized response in the individual situation.

Morals is not a catalogue of acts nor a set of rules to be applied like drugstore prescriptions or cook-book recipes. The need in morals is for specific methods of inquiry and of contrivance: Methods of inquiry to locate difficulties and evils; methods of contrivance to form plans to be used as working hypotheses in dealing with them. And the pragmatic import of the logic of individualized situations, each having its own irreplaceable good and principle, is to transfer the attention of theory from preoccupation with general conceptions to the problem of developing effective methods of inquiry.

Two ethical consequences of great moment should be remarked. The belief in fixed values has bred a division of ends into intrinsic and instrumental, of those that are really worth while in themselves and those that are of importance only as means to intrinsic goods. Indeed, it is often thought to be the very beginning of wisdom, of moral discrimination, to make this distinction. Dialectically, the distinction is interesting and seems harmless. But carried into practice it has an import that is tragic. Historically, it has been the source and justification of a hard and fast difference between ideal goods on one side and material goods on the other. At present those who would be liberal conceive intrinsic goods as esthetic in nature rather than as exclusively religious or as intellectually contemplative. But the effect is the same. So-called intrinsic goods, whether religious or esthetic, are divorced from those interests of daily life which because of their constancy and urgency form the preoccupation of the great mass. Aristotle used this distinction to declare that slaves and the working class though they are necessary *for* the state — the commonweal — are not constituents *of* it. That which is regarded as *merely* instrumental must approach drudgery; it cannot command either intellectual, artistic or moral attention and respect. Anything becomes *unworthy* whenever it is thought of as intrinsically lacking worth. So men of "ideal" interests have chosen for the most part the way of neglect and escape. The urgency and pressure of "lower" ends have been covered up by polite conventions. Or, they have been relegated to a baser class of mortals in order that the few might be free to attend to the goods that are really or intrinsically worth while. This withdrawal, in the name of higher ends, has left, for mankind at large and especially for energetic "practical" people the lower activities in complete command.

No one can possibly estimate how much of the obnoxious materialism and brutality of our economic life is due to the fact that economic ends have been regarded as *merely* instrumental. When they are recognized to be as intrinsic and final in their place as any others, then it will be seen that they are capable of idealization, and that if life is to be worth while, they must acquire ideal and intrinsic value. Esthetic, religious and other "ideal" ends are now thin and meagre or else idle and luxurious because of the separation from "instrumental" or economic ends. Only in connection with the latter can they be woven into the texture of daily life and made substantial and pervasive. The vanity and irresponsibility of values that are merely final and not also in turn means to the enrichment of other occupations of life ought to be obvious. But now the doctrine of "higher" ends gives aid, comfort and support to every socially isolated and socially irresponsible scholar, specialist, esthete and religionist. It protects the vanity and irresponsibility of his calling from observation by others and by himself. The moral deficiency of the calling is transformed into a cause of admiration and gratulation.

The other generic change lies in doing away once for all with the traditional distinction between moral goods, like the virtues, and natural goods like health, economic security, art, science and the like. The point of view under discussion is not the only one which has deplored this rigid distinction and endeavored to abolish it. Some schools have even gone so far as to regard moral excellencies, qualities of character, as of value only because they promote natural goods. But the experimental logic when carried into morals makes every quality that is judged to be good according as it contributes to amelioration of existing ills. And in so doing, it enforces the moral meaning of natural science. When all is said and done in criticism of present social deficiencies, one may well wonder whether the root difficulty does not lie in the separation of natural and moral science. When physics, chemistry, biology, medicine contribute to the detection of concrete human woes and to the development of plans for remedying them and relieving the human estate, they become moral; they become part of the apparatus of moral inquiry or science. The latter then loses its peculiar flavor of the didactic and pedantic; its ultra-moralistic and hortatory tone. It loses its thinness and shrillness as well as its vagueness. It gains agencies that are efficacious. But the gain is not confined to the side of moral science. Natural science loses its divorce from humanity; it becomes itself humanistic in quality. It is something to be pursued not in a technical and specialized way for what is called truth for its own sake, but with the sense of its social bearing, its intellectual indispensableness. It is technical only in the sense that it provides the technique of social and moral engineering.

When the consciousness of science is fully impregnated with the consciousness of human value, the greatest dualism which now weighs humanity down, the split between the material, the mechanical, the scientific and the moral and ideal will be destroyed. Human forces that now waver because of this division will be unified and reinforced. As long as ends are not thought of as individualized according to specific needs and opportunities, the mind will be content with abstractions, and the adequate stimulus to the moral or social use of natural science and historical data will be lacking. But when attention is concentrated upon the diversified concretes, recourse to all intellectual materials needed to clear up the special cases will be imperative. At the same time that morals are made to focus in intelligence, things intellectual are moralized. The vexatious and wasteful conflict between naturalism and humanism is terminated.

These general considerations may be amplified. First: Inquiry, discovery take the same place in morals that they have come to occupy in sciences of nature. Validation, demonstration become experimental, a matter of consequences. Reason, always an honorific term in ethics, becomes actualized in the methods by which the needs and conditions, the obstacles and resources, of situations are scrutinized in detail, and intelligent plans of improvement are worked out. Remote and abstract generalities promote jumping at conclusions, "anticipations of nature." Bad consequences are then deplored as due to natural perversity and untoward fate. But shifting the issue to analysis of a specific situation makes inquiry obligatory and alert observation of consequences imperative. No past decision nor old principle can ever be wholly relied upon to justify a course of action. No amount of pains taken in forming a purpose in a definite case is final; the consequences of its adoption must be carefully noted, and a purpose held only as a working hypothesis until results confirm its rightness. Mistakes are no longer either mere unavoidable accidents to be mourned or moral sins to be expiated and forgiven. They are lessons in wrong methods of using intelligence and instructions as to a better course in the future. They are indications of the need of revision, development, readjustment. Ends grow, standards of judgment are improved. Man is under just as much obligation to develop his most advanced standards and ideals as to use conscientiously those which he already possesses. Moral life is protected from falling into formalism and rigid repetition. It is rendered flexible, vital, growing.

In the second place, every case where moral action is required becomes of equal moral importance and urgency with every other. If the need and deficiencies of a specific situation indicate improvement of health as the end and good, then for that situation health is the ultimate and supreme good. It is no means to something else. It is a final and intrinsic value. The same thing is true of improvement of economic status, of making a living, of attending to business and family demands — all of the things which under the sanction of fixed ends have been rendered of secondary and merely instrumental value, and so relatively base and unimportant. Anything that in a given situation is an end and good at all is of equal worth, rank and dignity with every other good of any other situation, and deserves the same intelligent attention.

We note thirdly the effect in destroying the roots of Phariseeism. We are so accustomed to thinking of this as deliberate hypocrisy that we overlook its intellectual premises. The conception which looks for the end of action within the circumstances of the actual situation will not have the same measure of judgment for all cases. When one factor of the situation is a person of trained mind and large resources, more will be expected than with a person of backward mind and uncultured experience. The absurdity of applying the same standard of moral judgment to savage peoples that is used with civilized will be apparent. No individual or group will be judged by whether they come up to or fall short of some fixed result, but by the direction in which they are moving. The bad man is the man who no matter how good he *has* been is beginning to deteriorate, to grow less good. The good man is the man who no matter how morally unworthy he *has* been is moving to become better. Such a conception makes one severe in judging himself and humane in judging others. It excludes that arrogance which always accompanies judgment based on degree of approximation to fixed ends.

In the fourth place, the process of growth, of improvement and progress, rather than the static outcome and result, becomes the significant thing. Not health as an end fixed once and for all, but the needed improvement in health – a continual process – is the end and good. The end is no longer a terminus or limit to be reached. It is the active process of transforming the existent situation. Not perfection as a final goal, but the ever-enduring process of perfecting, maturing, refining is the aim in living. Honesty, industry, temperance, justice, like health, wealth and learning, are not goods to be possessed as they would be if they expressed fixed ends to be attained. They are directions of change in the quality of experience. Growth itself is the only moral "end."

Although the bearing of this idea upon the problem of evil and the controversy between optimism and pessimism is too vast to be here discussed, it may be worth while to touch upon it superficially. The problem of evil ceases to be a theological and metaphysical one, and is perceived to be the practical problem of reducing, alleviating, as far as may be removing, the evils of life. Philosophy is no longer under obligation to find ingenious methods for proving that evils are only apparent, not real, or to elaborate schemes for explaining them away or, worse yet, for justifying them. It assumes another obligation: – That of contributing in however humble a way to methods that will assist us in discovering the causes of humanity's ills. Pessimism is a paralyzing doctrine. In declaring that the world is evil wholesale, it makes futile all efforts to discover the remediable causes of specific evils and thereby destroys at the root every attempt to make the world better and happier. Wholesale optimism, which has been the consequence of the attempt to explain evil away, is, however, equally an incubus.

After all, the optimism that says that the world is already the best possible of all worlds might be regarded as the most cynical of pessimisms. If this is the best possible, what would a world which was fundamentally bad be like? Meliorism is the belief that the specific conditions which exist at one moment, be they comparatively bad or comparatively good, in any event may be bettered. It encourages intelligence to study the positive means of good and the obstructions to their realization, and to put forth endeavor for the improvement of conditions. It arouses confidence and a reasonable hopefulness as optimism does not. For the latter in declaring that good is already realized in ultimate reality tends to make us gloss over the evils that concretely exist. It becomes too readily the creed of those who live at ease, in comfort, of those who have been successful in obtaining this world's rewards. Too readily optimism makes the men who hold it callous and blind to the sufferings of the less fortunate, or ready to find the cause of troubles of others in their personal viciousness. It thus co-operates with pessimism, in spite of the extreme nominal differences between the two, in benumbing sympathetic insight and intelligent effort in reform. It beckons men away from the world of relativity and change into the calm of the absolute and eternal.

The import of many of these changes in moral attitude focusses in the idea of happiness. Happiness has often been made the object of the moralists' contempt. Yet the most ascetic moralist has usually restored the idea of happiness under some other name, such as bliss. Goodness without happiness, valor and virtue without satisfaction, ends without conscious enjoyment – these things are as intolerable practically as they are self-contradictory in conception. Happiness is not, however, a bare possession; it is not a fixed attainment. Such a happiness is either the unworthy selfishness which moralists have so bitterly condemned, or it is, even if labelled bliss, an insipid tedium, a millennium of ease in relief from all struggle and labor. It could satisfy only the most delicate of molly-coddles. Happiness is found only in success; but success means succeeding, getting forward, moving in advance. It is an active process, not a passive outcome. Accordingly it includes the overcoming of obstacles, the elimination of sources of defect and ill. Esthetic sensitiveness and enjoyment are a large constituent in any worthy happiness. But the esthetic appreciation which is totally separated from renewal of spirit, from re-creation of mind and purification of emotion is a weak and sickly thing, destined to speedy death from starvation. That the renewal and re-creation come unconsciously not by set intention but makes them the more genuine.

Upon the whole, utilitarianism has marked the best in the transition from the classic theory of ends and goods to that which is now possible. It had definite merits. It insisted upon getting away from vague generalities, and down to the specific and concrete. It subordinated law to human achievement instead of subordinating humanity to external law. It taught that institutions are made for man and not man for institutions; it actively promoted all issues of reform. It made moral good natural, humane, in touch with the natural goods of life. It opposed unearthly and other worldly morality. Above all, it acclimatized in human imagination the idea of social welfare as a supreme test. But it was still profoundly affected in fundamental points by old ways of thinking. It never questioned the idea of a fixed, final and supreme end. It only questioned the current notions as to the nature of this end; and then inserted pleasure and the greatest possible aggregate of pleasures in the position of the fixed end.

Such a point of view treats concrete activities and specific interests not as worth while in themselves, or as constituents of happiness, but as mere external means to getting pleasures. The upholders of the old tradition could therefore easily accuse utilitarianism of making not only virtue but art, poetry, religion and the state into mere servile means of attaining sensuous enjoyments. Since pleasure was an outcome, a result valuable on its own account independently of the active processes that achieve it, happiness was a thing to be possessed and held onto. The acquisitive instincts of man were exaggerated at the expense of the creative. Production was of importance not because of the intrinsic worth of invention and reshaping the world, but because its external results feed pleasure. Like every theory that sets up fixed and final aims, in making the end passive and possessive, it made all active operations *mere* tools. Labor was an unavoidable evil to be minimized. Security in possession was the chief thing practically. Material comfort and ease were magnified in contrast with the pains and risk of experimental creation.

These deficiencies, under certain conceivable conditions, might have remained merely theoretical. But the disposition of the times and the interests of those who propagated the utilitarian ideas, endowed them with power for social harm. In spite of the power of the new ideas in attacking old social abuses, there were elements in the teaching which operated or protected to sanction new social abuses. The reforming zeal was shown in criticism of the evils inherited from the class system of feudalism, evils economic, legal and political. But the new economic order of capitalism that was superseding feudalism brought its own social evils with it, and some of these ills utilitarianism tended to cover up or defend. The emphasis upon acquisition and possession of enjoyments took on an untoward color in connection with the contemporary enormous desire for wealth and the enjoyments it makes possible.

If utilitarianism did not actively promote the new economic materialism, it had no means of combating it. Its general spirit of subordinating productive activity to the bare product was indirectly favorable to the cause of an unadorned commercialism. In spite of its interest in a thoroughly social aim, utilitarianism fostered a new class interest, that of the capitalistic property-owning interests, provided only property was obtained through free competition and not by governmental favor. The stress that Bentham put on security tended to consecrate the legal institution of private property provided only certain legal abuses in connection with its acquisition and transfer were abolished. *Beati possidentes* – provided possessions had been obtained in accord with the rules of the competitive game – without, that is, extraneous favors from government. Thus utilitarianism gave intellectual confirmation to all those tendencies which make "business" not a means of social service and an opportunity for personal growth in creative power but a way of accumulating the means of private enjoyments. Utilitarian ethics thus afford a remarkable example of the need of philosophic reconstruction which these lectures have been presenting. Up to a certain point, it reflected the meaning of modern thought and aspirations. But it was still tied down by fundamental ideas of that very order which it thought it had completely left behind: The idea of a fixed and single end lying beyond the diversity of human needs and acts rendered utilitarianism incapable of being an adequate representative of the modern spirit. It has to be reconstructed through emancipation from its inherited elements.

If a few words are added upon the topic of education, it is only for the sake of suggesting that the educative process is all one with the moral process, since the latter is a continuous passage of experience from worse to better. Education has been traditionally thought of as preparation: as learning, acquiring certain things because they will later be useful. The end is remote, and education is getting readv, is a preliminary to something more important to happen later on. Childhood is only a preparation for adult life, and adult life for another life. Always the future, not the present, has been the significant thing in education: Acquisition of knowledge and skill for future use and enjoyment; formation of habits required later in life in business, good citizenship and pursuit of science. Education is thought of also as something needed by some human beings merely because of their dependence upon others. We are born ignorant, unversed, unskilled, immature, and consequently in a state of social dependence. Instruction, training, moral discipline are processes by which the mature, the adult, gradually raise the helpless to the point where they can look out for themselves. The business of childhood is to grow into the independence of adulthood by means of the guidance of those who have already attained it. Thus the process of education as the main business of life ends when the young have arrived at emancipation from social dependence.

These two ideas, generally assumed but rarely explicitly reasoned out, contravene the conception that growing, or the continuous reconstruction of experience, is the only end. If at whatever period we choose to take a person, he is still in process of growth, then education is not, save as a by-product, a preparation for something coming later. Getting from the present the degree and kind of growth there is in it is education. This is a constant function, independent of age. The best thing that can be said about any special process of education, like that of the formal school period, is that it renders its subject capable of further education: more sensitive to conditions of growth and more able to take advantage of them. Acquisition of skill, possession of knowledge, attainment of culture are not ends: they are marks of growth and means to its continuing.

The contrast usually assumed between the period of education as one of social dependence and of maturity as one of social independence does harm. We repeat over and over that man is a social animal, and then confine the significance of this statement to the sphere in which sociality usually seems least evident, politics. The heart of the sociality of man is in education. The idea of education as preparation and of adulthood as a fixed limit of growth are two sides of the same obnoxious untruth. If the moral business of the adult as well as the young is a growing and developing experience, then the instruction that comes from social dependencies and interdependencies is as important for the adult as for the child. Moral independence for the adult means arrest of growth, isolation means induration. We exaggerate the intellectual dependence of childhood so that children are too much kept in leading strings, and then we exaggerate the independence of adult life from intimacy of contacts and communication with others. When the identity of the moral process with the processes of specific growth is realized, the more conscious and formal education of childhood will be seen to be the most economical and efficient means of social advance and reorganization, and it will also be evident that the test of all the institutions of adult life is their effect in furthering continued education. Government, business, art, religion, all social institutions have a meaning, a purpose. That purpose is to set free and to develop the capacities of human individuals without respect to race, sex, class or economic status. And this is all one with saying that the test of their value is the extent to which they educate every individual into the full stature of his possibility. Democracy has many meanings, but if it has a moral meaning, it is found in resolving that the supreme test of all political institutions and industrial arrangements shall be the contribution they make to the all-around growth of every member of society.

Comment on Dewey's Ethical Views

MELVIN RADER

Main Emphases in Dewey's Ethics

. . . When Dewey takes up the subject of ethics, he shifts his emphasis from *value* to *valuation,* being more concerned with the process of appraisal than with the qualities appraised. Valuation, he maintains, should be in accordance with the methods of experimental logic. No one has insisted more strenuously than Dewey upon scientific study of the actual needs of human beings

From *The Enduring Questions,* by Melvin Rader. By permission of Henry Holt and Company, Inc., Copyright 1956.

and the concrete, experimental means of satisfying these needs. "Not all who say Ideals, Ideals," he remarks, "shall enter into the kingdom of the ideal, but those who know and respect the roads that conduct to the kingdom." [1] His main contribution to ethical theory has been to explore the roads rather than to describe the destination. Indeed, he does not believe in a fixed destination but rather, in a never-ending and exploratory journey. Since conditions are constantly changing, rules cannot be made nor goals ascertained in advance. Living well is an experiment, and there should be flexible reappraisal and reorientation as the experiment progresses.

Valuation is stimulated by tension, conflict, unsatisfactoriness; and successful valuation points to ways of resolving the tensions and releasing the pent-up energies. In regard to ethics, as in pragmatist theory in general, inquiry is conceived to be instrumentalist – a tool for controlling experience. Values are not passively "given," without intelligent effort, but are actively constructed. There is a fundamental difference between what is merely "liked" and what is genuinely "likable," merely "desired" and really "desirable," merely "admired" and truly "admirable," merely "satisfying" and dependably "satisfactory." Only the latter are *values* in the sense that they have been *validated*. They can be achieved only if we know the conditions and consequences of our desires, affections, and enjoyments, and if we learn intelligently to coordinate and control them. The idea of a *good* should be treated as a hypothesis, to be tested like any other.

In the testing, we must see ends and means as "continuous" – the ends as means to future satisfactions, and the means as not merely instrumentally but intrinsically valuable or disvaluable. Kant, for example, was fundamentally mistaken in exalting virtue as an end apart from being a means, for the very qualities that make it good as end make it good as means also. Dewey believes that experience is most satisfactory when the instrumental and the consummatory are closely linked – when action and contemplation fructify each other. We should neither subordinate growth and spontaneity to static contemplation nor concentrate merely upon activity to the neglect of rational goals. Life should combine both repose and stimulation – the sense of achievement and the sense of adventure. In thus insisting upon "the continuity of means and ends," Dewey is exhibiting the anti-dualistic tendency that pervades his entire philosophy. He protests strongly against the inveterate tendency to think in terms of hard-and-fast distinctions between, for example, facts and values, experience and nature, freedom and organization, learning and doing; and he seeks to resolve all such sharp dualisms by insisting upon the continuity and interpenetration of "opposites." Values are to be studied as natural facts, and facts are to be evaluated; experience is to be regarded as inseparable from nature, and nature is to be interpreted in terms of experience; freedom is to be secured by organization, and organization is to be liberalized by freedom; learning is to be achieved by doing, and doing is to be directed by learning. His whole philosophy can thus be regarded as a "revolt against dualism," of almost every kind and description. The fruit of this philosophy is the perfecting of experience by the elimination of conflicts.

There is no sense, according to Dewey, in talking about *the* end of life – as if there were a single end or final consummation. Life is simply an on-going process, with a plurality of ends which function also as means. His stress is upon the dynamic rather than the static, the specific rather than the general, the concrete and plural rather than the abstract and monistic. "Faith in

1 "The Pragmatic Acquiescence," *New Republic*, Vol. 49, Jan. 5, 1927, p. 189.

the varied possibilities of diversified experience," he declares, "is attended with the joy of constant discovery and constant growing."[2] Growth provides its own sufficient criterion, and it is a mistake to seek anything more fixed and constant.

On the Distinction Between Science, Technology, and Morals

According to some critics, Dewey's ethical philosophy is strong in method but weak in vision; strong in delineating the variety of experience but weak in revealing the unity of life; strong in its awareness of novelty but weak in its blindness to universal and enduring values; strong in opposing static absolutism but weak in yielding to mercurial relativism; strong in realizing the need for growth but weak in criticizing the direction of growth; strong in relating science, technology, and morals, weak in failing to distinguish them. Whether this estimate is justified we shall leave to the readers of this book to decide. The last point of criticism, however, calls for more detailed comment.

The heart of Dewey's ethical philosophy is the attempt to link science, technology, and morals, and it is therefore important to consider their interrelations. We can begin by noting three realms of discourse, as illustrated by the following sentences:

"That is a strong poison."

"You ought to use a strong poison" (said to a would-be murderer).

"You ought not to murder."

The first sentence is *descriptive;* it simply indicates a matter of fact, with no commendation or disparagement. The second sentence is *evaluative,* but in what Kant would call a *hypothetical* rather than a categorical sense. The "ought" here simply means that, *if* you want to murder this man, you ought to use a poison strong enough to accomplish your purpose. It does not express a *duty* to use a strong poison. The third sentence is also *evaluative,* but in what Kant would call a *categorical* rather than a hypothetical sense. It expresses a duty to refrain from murdering. Sentences of the first type are characteristic of pure science; sentences of the second type are characteristic of technology; and sentences of the third type are characteristic of morals. (To accept these distinctions, we would not have to agree with Kant's formulae for determining categorical imperatives. If we were utilitarians, for example, our formula might read: "So act that in every case there shall be no better results." If our duty is to achieve the best results possible, it is still our *duty.*)

The charge that can be made against Dewey is that he has failed to distinguish clearly among science, technology, and morals. In his laudable effort to relate them, he has obscured their differences. We shall not discuss the adequacy of his distinction between pure science and technology — this question is relevant to the issues presented in Chapter 5 and might well be debated in that connection. At present, we are concerned only with the relation between morals and science and between morals and technology.

1. *Morals and science.* "Experience," Dewey notes, "actually presents esthetic and moral traits."[3] These stand on "the same level" as the redness of a rose or the absentmindedness of a professor — they are matters of fact which can be studied like any other. There is a valid point here that should not be denied. Human beings do exhibit esthetic and moral traits and experience satisfactions and enjoyments. These can be described like any other natural facts. Moral theories that try to exclude consideration of human nature and its environment are hopelessly unrealistic. If this is all that Dewey means, we need not disagree

[2] "What I Believe," *Forum,* March 1930, p. 179.

[3] *Experience and Nature* (Chicago: Open Court, 1929), p. 2.

with him. But it is still the case that a psychologist bent upon *describing* human nature has a different task than the moralist bent upon *evaluating* moral alternatives. Such words as "good," "right," "ought," as used by the moralist, are nouns and adjectives of commendation, not of description. How can we make the leap from description to evaluation? How can we get, for example, from "desired" to *ethically* "desirable"? The latter does not mean *psychologically* desirable, in the sense that someone *can* desire it. It means *worth* desiring – desiring in the sense that it *ought* to be desired. A naturalistic theory of ethics, such as that of Dewey, seems to overlook the nondescriptive, purely ethical character of the moral *ought.*

Dewey could reply that "desirable" means that which one desires *after* one has seen all its conditions and consequences. But this does not solve the problem, because it is perfectly possible for a malevolent person to desire something that is morally evil after he has thoroughly understood its connections with other things. Dewey could also reply that the ethically desirable is that which is desired by a fair and impartial judge. But this definition is circular; it amounts to saying that something is ethically desirable (good or right) when it is approved by somebody who approves only what *is* ethically desirable. The only solution, Dewey's critics would say, is to admit a clear-cut distinction between facts and norms, morals and science – and this he fails to do.

2. *Morals and technology.* Dewey often appears to be identifying morality with technology, or to be thinking of it as a kind of super-technology. There would seem to be much to support this point of view. The language of technological discourse, as we have already noted, is distinguished by normative terms, such as "ought" or "ought not," or by imperatives, such as "do this" or "do not do that." Such language is intended to direct choice among alternative possibilities. There are different kinds of norms and normative statements belonging to different levels of technological discourse. Many technological imperatives are mere counsels of skill, as when a carpenter says to his helper, "You ought to sharpen the teeth of that saw." He means, "*If* you want to use your saw effectively for the purpose at hand, you ought to sharpen its teeth." At a somewhat higher and more general level, the norms have a quasi-ethical or esthetic character, as in the case of the artistic norm of "beauty," the legal norm of "justice," the medical norm of "health," and the economic norm of "prosperity." Finally, there are highest level norms that pertain to a total economy of values. They are invoked when there is a conflict between lower-level oughts, and may be thought of as decidedly ethical. Morality will then be conceived as a technology of technologies, the function of which is to coordinate all the various techniques that a society has at its disposal.

This view of morality is by no means new. Aristotle had a similar conception of the art of arts, the technology of technologies. In the opening paragraphs of his *Ethics,* as we have seen, he pointed out that the arts are to be distinguished by the ends which they serve. Health is the aim of medicine, vessels of shipbuilding, victory of military strategy, and wealth of economics. The ends and the corresponding arts form a hierarchy, some being subservient to others. Bridle-making is subservient to horsemanship, horsemanship to strategy, and so on. Finally we arrive at some ultimate end and the art corresponding to it. This is the art of arts – the art whose function it is to harmonize and control all the other arts and whose end, therefore, is not this or that particular good but the good for man. Aristotle calls this highest art the art of politics, of which ethics, since it defines the ultimate good, is an integral part. Here the word "art" is being used in the same sense as we intend by "technology," and Aristotle's conception of politics as an "art of arts" is analogous to the conception of morality as a "technology of technologies."

Up to a point, this way of looking at morality seems sound, but there are important qualifications that need to be made. It is important to recognize that morality, as a kind of supreme technology, is fundamentally different from ordinary technology – so different, indeed, that we should perhaps not call it a technology at all. An ordinary technological norm is an *instrument* of a decision-maker, not a *control* over him; and, therefore, to interpret moral norms as ordinary technological norms would imply that technology needs no control or is somehow self-regulating. Such a view is exceedingly mischievous, especially in this age of nuclear fission, when bombs threaten to blow all of us, even the technologists and all their works, to smithereens. Consequently, there must be norms controlling the decision-maker rather than norms which are merely his instruments. The right use of instrumental norms presupposes some non-instrumental criteria.

In the case of ordinary technology, in other words, it is not the right motivation of the agent that is in question but the skill to be used in carrying out a motivation that is taken for granted. In the case of morality, on the other hand, it is precisely the motivation that is most in question, and the problem of finding the right means is secondary. The norms of ordinary technology usually prescribe how to perform some action. The moral question, on the other hand, is not simply *how* to do something, but *what* to do.

Pragmatists, such as John Dewey, are prone to exaggerate the similarity between ordinary technology and morality. They are so intent upon the fluidity and instrumentality of norms that they neglect or even deny the question of *ultimate* motivation. They are inclined to take "the problematic situation" as it arises and to interpret right action as "problem-solving" within the context of this situation. The problem, as they see it, is "solved" when the diverse competing interests in the situation are brought into some kind of moving equilibrium, which leads to new "problematic situations" and thus to new and revised norms. So understood, morality is closely akin to ordinary technology. But morality cannot afford merely to implement and reconcile interests that are taken for granted. Its task is more radical. It criticizes interests in the light of ultimate norms; and, in exercising this sort of stubborn and very radical criticism, it differentiates itself from technology.

The question that we have posed is whether Dewey has sufficiently realized this fact, and whether he has also realized the clear-cut difference between morality (or ethics, as its theoretical basis) and natural science.

Value Judgments in Scientific Validation

RICHARD RUDNER

An important underlying point . . . is the manner in which, if at all, value judgments impinge on the process of validating scientific hypotheses and theories.

I think that such validations do *essentially* involve the making of value judgments in a typically ethical issue. And I emphasize *essentially* to indicate my feeling that not only do scientists, as a matter of psychological fact, make value judgments in the course of such validations – since as human beings they are so constituted as to make this virtually unavoidable – but also that the making of such judgments is *logically* involved in the validation of scientific hypotheses; and consequently that a logical reconstruction of this process would entail the statement that a value judgment is a requisite step in the process.

My reasons for believing this may be set forth briefly, but before presenting them I should like to distinguish my thesis as clearly as I can from apparently similar ones that have traditionally been offered.

Traditionally, the involvement of value judgments (in some typically ethical sense) in science has ordinarily been argued on three grounds: (i) Our having a science at all, or, at any rate, our voluntary engagement in such activities, in itself presupposes a value judgment. (ii) To be able to select among alternative problems, or, at any rate, among alternative foci of his interests, the scientist must make a value judgment. (iii) The scientist cannot escape his quite human self. He is a "mass of predilections," and these predilections must inevitably influence all his activities – not excepting his scientific ones. These traditional arguments have never seemed entirely adequate, and the responses that some empirically oriented philosophers and some scientists have made to them have been telling. These responses have generally had the following import.

If it is necessary to make a value decision to have a science before we can have one, then this decision is literally prescientific and has not, therefore, been shown to be any part of the *procedures* of science. Similarly, the decision that one problem is more worth while as a focus of attention than another is an extraproblematic decision and forms no part of the procedures involved in dealing with the problem *decided* upon. Since it is these procedures that constitute the method of science, the value judgment has not thus been shown to be involved in the scientific method as such.

With respect to the presence of our predilections in the laboratory, most empirically oriented philosophers and scientists agree that this is "unfortunately" the case; but, they hasten to add, if science is to progress toward objectivity, the influence of our personal feelings or biases on experimental results must be minimized. We must try not to let our personal idiosyncrasies affect our

Originally published in *Scientific Monthly*, 79, 1954.

scientific work. The perfect scientist – the scientist *qua* scientist – does not allow this kind of value judgment to influence his work. However much he may find doing so unavoidable, *qua* father, *qua* lover, *qua* member of society, *qua* grouch, *when* he does so he is not behaving *qua* scientist. Consequently, a logical reconstruction of the scientific method would not need, on this account, to include a reference to the making of value judgments. From such considerations it would seem that the traditional arguments for the involvement of value judgments in science lack decisiveness.

But I think a different and somewhat stronger argument can be made. I assume that no analysis of what constitutes the method of science would be satisfactory unless it comprised some assertion to the effect that the scientist validates – that is, accepts or rejects – hypotheses. But if this is so, then clearly the scientist does make value judgments. Since no scientific hypothesis is ever completely verified, in accepting a hypothesis on the basis of evidence, the scientist must make the decision that the evidence is *sufficiently* strong or that the probability is *sufficiently* high to warrant the acceptance of the hypothesis. Obviously, our decision with regard to the evidence and how strong is "strong enough" is going to be a function of the *importance,* in the typically ethical sense, of making a mistake in accepting or rejecting the hypothesis. Thus, to take a crude but easily manageable example, if the hypothesis under consideration stated that a toxic ingredient of a drug was not present in lethal quantity, then we would require a relatively high degree of confirmation or confidence before accepting the hypothesis – for the consequences of making a mistake here are exceedingly grave by our moral standards. In contrast, if our hypothesis stated that, on the basis of some sample, a certain lot of machine-stamped belt buckles was not defective, the degree of confidence we would require would be relatively lower. *How sure we must be before we accept a hypothesis depends on how serious a mistake would be.*

The examples I have chosen are from scientific inferences in industrial quality control. But the point is clearly quite general in application. It would be interesting and instructive, for example, to know how high a degree of probability the Manhattan Project scientists demanded for the hypothesis that no uncontrollable pervasive chain reaction would occur before they proceeded with the first atomic bomb detonation or even first activated the Chicago pile above a critical level. It would be equally interesting and instructive to know how they decided that the chosen probability value (if one was chosen) was high enough rather than one that was higher; on the other hand, it is conceivable that the problem, in this form, was not brought to consciousness at all.

In general, then, before we can accept any hypothesis, the value decision must be made in the light of the seriousness of a mistake, and the degree of probability must be *high enough* or the evidence must be *strong enough* to warrant its acceptance.

Some empiricists, confronted with the foregoing considerations, agree that *acceptance* or *rejection* of hypotheses essentially involves value judgments, but they are nonetheless loath to accept the conclusion; instead they have denied the premise that it is the business of the scientist *qua* scientist to validate hypotheses or theories. They have argued that the scientist's task is *only to determine the strength of the evidence* for a hypothesis and not, as scientist, to accept or reject the hypothesis.

But a little reflection shows that the plausibility of this as an objection is merely apparent. The determination that the degree of confirmation is, say, p or that the strength of the evidence is such and such, which is on this view the indispensable task of the scientist *qua* scientist, is clearly nothing more than *the acceptance, by the scientist, of the hypothesis that the degree of confidence is p or that the strength of the evidence is such and such;* and, as these men have conceded, acceptance of hypotheses does require value decisions.

If the major point I have tried to establish is correct, then we are confronted with a first-order crisis in science and methodology. The positive horror with which most scientists and philosophers of science view the intrusion of value considerations into science is wholly understandable. Memories of the conflict, now abated but to a certain extent still continuing, between science and, for example, the dominant religions over the intrusion of religious value considerations into the domain of scientific inquiry are strong in many reflective scientists. The traditional search for objectivity exemplifies science's pursuit of one of its most precious ideals. For the scientist to close his eyes to the fact that scientific method *intrinsically* requires the making of value decisions, and for him to push out of his consciousness the fact that he does make them, can in no way bring him closer to the ideal of objectivity. To refuse to pay attention to the value decisions that *must* be made, to make them intuitively, unconsciously, and haphazardly, is to leave an essential aspect of scientific method scientifically out of control.

What seems necessary (and no more than the sketchiest indications of the problem can be given here) is nothing less than a radical reworking of the ideal of scientific objectivity. The naive conception of the scientist as one who is cold-blooded, emotionless, impersonal, and passive, mirroring the world perfectly in the highly polished lenses of his steel-rimmed glasses is no longer, if it ever was, adequate.

What is proposed here is that objectivity for science lies at least in becoming precise about what value judgments are being made and might have been made in a given inquiry – and, stated in the most challenging form, what value decisions ought to be made.

Epilogue

No discussion of the relation between science and value would be complete without asking, and answering to one's own satisfaction, this most fundamental question: What is, after all, the value of science itself? Immediately the answer comes: Its value lies in the enormous technological advances it has made possible, of course! Look at the advances in preventive and curative medicine, the production of greater food supplies, the opening of new worlds through better transportation, and the control over nature's caprices science has made possible – and all these only a small fraction of the ways in which it has contributed to the greater comfort and happiness of mankind. Yet one thinks also of Hiroshima and atomic fallout and suddenly science seems something less than beneficent, to say the least. The truth of the matter is plain to see: technological "advancements" are neither good nor bad in themselves but instruments of dreadful import for evil and great import for good depending upon what we do with them. And we are learning slowly but sadly that even apparently outright beneficial "advances" are not unmixed with unhappy consequences. At any rate, even if all the technological applications of science were beneficial, its positive value would still be instrumental only. Science would be valuable because it led via technology to desirable consequences. But we want to know what is the intrinsic value, if any, of science itself. Why study it except as a technological means? The answer I want to insist on is that science, like any other study, is intrinsically valuable because it produces *knowledge* – something which is valuable in and of itself independently of what we can do with it. Science, when seen in this light, is an exciting adventure of the imagination bent on discovering the nature of our physical, social, and psychological worlds; bent on discovering, if you please, the secrets of nature and the human mind. But this concept of the value of science is less and less put before us. Bertrand Russell writes,

> Science in its beginnings was due to men who were in love with the world. They perceived the beauty of the stars and the sea, of the winds and the mountains. Because they loved them their thoughts dwelt upon them, and they wished to understand them more intimately than a mere outward contemplation made possible. . . . But step by step, as science developed, the impulse of love which gave it birth has been increasingly thwarted, while the impulse of power [control through knowledge], which was at first a mere camp-follower, has gradually usurped command in virtue of its unforeseen success. The lover of nature has been baffled, the tyrant over nature has been rewarded.[1]

It is unlikely, however, that the drift away from a realization of the intrinsic merit of science is due solely to the dramatic successes of applied science. The drift away has been largely caused, I suspect, by the unfortunate way science is taught and talked about in university classes and public lectures. How is it possible, indeed, to find science an exciting adventure of the imagination when scientists themselves present their results like ex-

[1] *The Scientific Outlook* (New York: W. W. Norton and Co., 1931), pp. 271–272.

hibits in a museum, out of context and out of touch with the methods by which they came into being? And the results often are so specialized that they do not exhibit the slightest relation to a significant body of knowledge. And the experiments in our laboratories, by which students are supposed to learn the scientific method, are notorious failures; students, knowing the results they should get, piously make corrections so the great structure of science will go unchallenged! Studies in the philosophy and history of science were supposed to correct these difficulties; they were to clarify the methods and structures of all the sciences and exhibit science as an ongoing, cumulative enterprise full of great advances but not without many blind alleys too. Unhappily these studies have not always or frequently succeeded in the task of humanizing science; instead they have often created concepts and problems which needed as much explication as the concepts of science itself. Nor has the talk about science in the traditional humanistic studies been helpful in understanding science either. There is a lot of talk, and perfectly good talk in its own way, about the implications of science for art and literature, about the way science influences society, and about the way society influences science; but in all this talk, I submit, there is nothing which illuminates the nature of science itself. And I am not certain we can be clear about these other questions until we are clear about the nature of science.

On the other hand, some scientists like Erwin Schrödinger, along with an increasing number of philosophers of science, have, happily, done much good work in presenting science in its true light — as itself a humanistic enterprise of the highest order and not simply a bag of minutiae, technological tricks, and social implications. I hope this book and this course in the philosophy of science have helped in their own way to demonstrate this great truth. If not, your study, after all, avails nothing; if it does, your adventures in the world of scientific ideas have just begun.

Selected Bibliography

1. Making Sense of Science

A. GENERAL

Benjamin, A. C., *An Introduction to the Philosophy of Science.* New York: The Macmillan Co., 1937.

Bergmann, Gustav, "An Empiricist's System of the Sciences," *Scientific Monthly,* 59, 1944.

Bergmann, Gustav, "The Logic of Measurement," *State University of Iowa Studies in Engineering,* 1956.

Bergmann, Gustav, *Philosophy of Science.* Madison: University of Wisconsin Press, 1957.

Braithwaite, R. B., *Scientific Explanation.* Cambridge: Cambridge University Press, 1953.

Broad, C. D., *Scientific Thought.* London: Kegan Paul, Trench, Trubner & Co., 1927.

Burtt, E. A., *The Metaphysical Foundations of Modern Physical Science.* Revised Edition. New York: Doubleday and Co., 1955.

Campbell, N. R., *Physics; the Elements.* Cambridge: Cambridge University Press, 1920.

Campbell, N. R., *What Is Science?* London: Methuen, 1921.

Cassirer, Ernst, *The Problem of Knowledge.* New Haven: Yale University Press, 1950.

Churchman, C. W., *Theory of Experimental Inference.* New York: The Macmillan Co., 1948.

Clifford, William Kingdon, *The Common Sense of the Exact Sciences.* New York: Alfred A. Knopf, 1946.

Clifford, William Kingdon, *Lectures and Essays.* London: The Macmillan Co., 1886.

Conant, James Bryant, ed., *Harvard Case Histories in Experimental Science.* Cambridge: Harvard University Press, 1957.

Conant, James B., *Modern Science and Modern Man.* New York: Columbia University Press, 1952.

Conant, James B., *On Understanding Science.* New Haven: Yale University Press, 1947.

Dewey, John, *Logic, the Theory of Inquiry.* New York: Henry Holt, 1939.

Dingle, Herbert, *The Scientific Adventure.* New York: Philosophical Library, 1953.

Ducasse, C. J., "Science: Its Nature, Method, and Scope," *David Wight Prall Memorial Lecture,* Vol. III, No. 1, 1947.

Eddington, Arthur, *The Philosophy of Physical Science.* New York: The Macmillan Co., 1939.

Feigl, Herbert and May Brodbeck, eds., *Readings in the Philosophy of Science.* New York: Appleton-Century-Crofts, Inc., 1953.

Feigl, H. and M. Scriven, eds., *Minnesota Studies in the Philosophy of Science,* Vols. I and II. Minneapolis: University of Minnesota Press, 1956, 1958.

Feigl, H. and W. Sellars, eds., *Readings in Philosophical Analysis.* New York: Appleton-Century-Crofts, 1949.

Frank, Philipp, *Modern Science and Its Philosophy.* Cambridge: Harvard University Press, 1949.

Frank, Philipp, *Philosophy of Science.* Englewood Cliffs, N.J.: Prentice-Hall, Inc., 1957.

Gamow, George, *The Creation of the Universe.* New York: Viking Press, 1952.

Herschel, John F. W., *Preliminary Discourse on the Study of Natural Philosophy.* London: Longman, Brown, Green and Longmans, 1842.

Hoyle, Fred, *The Nature of the Universe.* New York: Harper and Brothers, 1950.

Hutten, Ernest H., *The Language of Modern Physics.* London: George Allen and Unwin, Ltd., 1956.

Kemeny, John G., *A Philosopher Looks at Science.* Princeton, N.J.: D. Van Nostrand Co., 1959.

Mach, Ernst, *The Analysis of Sensations.* Chicago: Open Court, 1914.

Madden, Edward H., ed., *Theories of Scientific Method from the Renaissance to the Nineteenth Century.* Seattle: University of Washington Press, 1959.

Newton, Isaac, *The Mathematical Principles of Natural Philosophy,* ed. Motte. New York: 1846.

Northrop, F. S. C., *The Logic of the Sciences and the Humanities.* New York: The Macmillan Co., 1947.

Pearson, Karl, *Grammar of Science.* London: Dent, 1937.

Poincaré, Henri, *The Foundations of Science.* New York: Science Press, 1929.

Schlick, Moritz, *Philosophy of Nature.* New York: Philosophical Library, 1949.

Smart, J. J. C., "Theory Construction," *Philosophy and Phenomenological Research,* 2, 1950–51.

Watson, W. H., *On Understanding Physics.* Cambridge: Cambridge University Press, 1938.

Werkmeister, W. H., *A Philosophy of Science.* New York: Harper and Brothers, 1940.

Whewell, William, *Philosophy of Discovery.* London: John W. Parker and Son, 1860.

Whitehead, A. N., *Science and the Modern World.* New York: The Macmillan Co., 1925.

Wiener, Philip P., *Readings in Philosophy of Science.* New York: Charles Scribner's Sons, 1953.

Woodger, J. H., *The Technique of Theory Construction,* Vol. II, No. 5, of *The International Encyclopedia of Unified Science.* Chicago: University of Chicago Press, 1939.

Woodruff, L. L., ed., *The Development of the Sciences,* Second Series. New Haven: Yale University Press, 1941.

B. HISTORY OF SCIENCE

Brunet, P., *Histoire des sciences antiquité.* Paris: Payot, 1935.

Butterfield, H., *The Origins of Modern Science 1300–1800.* London: G. Bell and Sons, 1950.

Crombie, A. C., *Augustine to Galileo.* London: Falcon Press, 1952.

D'Abro, A., *The Evolution of Scientific Thought from Newton to Einstein,* 2nd ed. New York: Dover, 1950.

Duhem, Pierre, *Le systeme du Monde: histoire des doctrines cosmologiques de Platon à Copernic.* Paris: A. Herman et fils, 1913–1954.

Duhem, Pierre, *The Aim and Structure of Physical Theory,* Tr. Philip P. Wiener. Princeton, N.J.: Princeton University Press, 1954.

Hall, A. R., *The Scientific Revolution 1500–1800.* New York: Longmans, Green and Co., 1954.

Haskins, Charles H., *Studies in the History of Medieval Science.* Cambridge: Harvard University Press, 1927.

Hull, L. W. H., *History and Philosophy of Science.* London: Longmans, Green and Co., 1959.

Mason, S. F., *Main Currents of Scientific Thought.* New York: Henry Schuman, 1953.

Sarton, George, *A History of Science.* Cambridge: Cambridge University Press, 1952.

Thorndike, Lynn, *A History of Magic and Experimental Science.* New York: The Macmillan Co., 1929–1941.

Wiener, Philip P. and Aaron Noland, eds., *Roots of Scientific Thought.* New York: Basic Books, 1957.

Wolf, A., *A History of Science, Technology, and Philosophy in the Eighteenth Century.* New York: The Macmillan Co., 1939.

Wolf, A., *A History of Science, Technology, and Philosophy in the Sixteenth and Seventeenth Centuries.* London: George Allen and Unwin, 1950.

2. Problems of Modern Physics

A. THE NATURE OF LOGIC AND MATHEMATICS

Carnap, Rudolph, *Foundations of Logic and Mathematics,* Vol. I, No. 3, *The International Encyclopedia of Unified Science.* Chicago: University of Chicago Press, 1939.

Carnap, Rudolph, *Meaning and Necessity.* Chicago: University of Chicago Press, 1947.

Carnap, Rudolph, *Philosophy and Logical Syntax.* London: Kegan Paul, 1935.

Frege, G., *The Foundations of Arithmetic,* tr. J. L. Austin. New York: Philosophical Library, 1950.

Kleene, S. C., *Introduction to Metamathematics.* Princeton, N.J.: D. Van Nostrand Co., 1952.

Nicod, J., *Foundations of Geometry and Induction.* New York: Harcourt, Brace and Co., 1930.

Quine, Willard Van Orman, *Mathematical Logic.* New York: W. W. Norton Co., 1940.

Quine, Willard Van Orman, "Truth by Convention," in O. H. Lee, ed., *Philosophical Essays for A. N. Whitehead.* New York: Longmans, Green and Co., 1936.

Ramsey, F. P., *The Foundations of Mathematics and Other Logical Essays.* New York: Harcourt, Brace and Co., 1931.

Rosser, J. B., *Logic for Mathematicians.* New York: McGraw-Hill Book Co., 1953.

Russell, Bertrand, *Introduction to Mathematical Philosophy*. London: G. Allen, 1948.

Tarski, Alfred, *Introduction to Logic and to the Methodology of the Deductive Sciences*. London: Oxford University Press, 1941.

Waismann, F., *Introduction to Mathematical Thinking*. New York: Ungar, 1951.

Weyl, Herman, *Philosophy of Mathematics and Natural Science*. Princeton, N.J.: Princeton University Press, 1949.

Whitehead, A. N., and Bertrand Russell, *Principia Mathematica*, Vols. I–III. 2nd ed., Cambridge: Cambridge University Press, 1925.

B. SPACE, TIME, AND RELATIVITY

Alexander, H. G., ed., *The Leibniz-Clarke Correspondence*. New York: Philosophical Library, 1956.

Broad, C. D., "Is Space Euclidean?", *Mind*, 24, 1915.

Cassirer, Ernst, *Substance and Function and Einstein's Theory of Relativity*. New York: Dover Publications, Inc., 1953.

Einstein, Albert. *Ideas and Opinions*. New York: Crown Publishers, Inc., 1954.

Einstein, A., and L. Infeld, *The Evolution of Physics*. New York: Simon and Schuster, 1938.

Frank, Philipp, *Einstein, His Life and Times*, tr. G. Rosen, ed. S. Kusaka. New York: Alfred A. Knopf, 1947.

Frank, Philipp, *Relativity, A Richer Truth*. Boston: The Beacon Press, 1950.

Greene, T. M., Introduction to *Kant Selections*. New York: Charles Scribner's Sons, 1929.

Grünbaum, Adolf, "The Clock Paradox in the Special Theory of Relativity," *Philosophy of Science*, 21, 1954.

Infeld, Leopold, *Albert Einstein*. New York: Charles Scribner's Sons, 1950.

Jammer, Max, *Concepts of Space*. Cambridge: Harvard University Press, 1954.

Kant, Immanuel, *Critique of Pure Reason*, tr. Max Muller, 2nd Ed., Revised. New York: The Macmillan Co., 1927.

Margenau, Henry, "Can Time Flow Backwards?", *Philosophy of Science*, 21, 1954.

Margenau, Henry and Richard A. Mould, "Relativity: An Epistemological Appraisal," *Philosophy of Science*, 24, 1957.

Martin, Seymour G., *et al.*, "Immanuel Kant," Ch. 11 of *A History of Philosophy*. New York: F. S. Crofts and Co., 1947.

Reichenbach, Hans, *Philosophie der Raum-Zeitlehre*. Berlin and Leipzig: Gruyter, 1928.

Russell, Bertrand, *The ABC of Relativity*, Rev. Ed., ed. F. Pirani. London: George Allen and Unwin, Ltd., 1958.

Schlick, Moritz, *Space and Time in Contemporary Physics*, tr. H. L. Brose. London: Oxford University Press, 1920.

Whitehead, A. N., *The Principle of Relativity*. Cambridge: Cambridge University Press, 1922.

C. OPERATIONISM AND LOGICAL EMPIRICISM

Bergmann, Gustav, "Sense and Nonsense in Operationism," *Scientific Monthly*, 79, 1954.

Boring, E. G., "Temporal Perception and Operationism," *American Journal of Psychology*, 48, 1936.

Bridgman, P. W., *The Logic of Modern Physics*. New York: The Macmillan Co., 1927.

Bridgman, P. W., *The Nature of Physical Theory*. Princeton, N.J.: Princeton University Press, 1936.

Bridgman, P. W., *The Nature of Some of Our Physical Concepts*. New York: Philosophical Library, 1952.

Frank, Philipp, ed., *The Validation of Scientific Theories*. Boston: The Beacon Press, 1956.

Ginsberg, Arthur, "Operational Definitions and Theories," *Journal of General Psychology*, 52–53, 1955.

Hempel, C. G., *Fundamentals of Concept Formation in the Empirical Sciences*, Vol. II, No. 7 of *The International Encyclopedia of Unified Science*. Chicago: University of Chicago Press, 1952.

Hempel, Carl G., "A Logical Appraisal of Operationism," *Scientific Monthly*, 79, 1954.

Hempel, C. G., "Problems and Changes in the Empiricist Criterion of Meaning," *Revue Internationale de Philosophie*, 4, 1950.

Kaplan, Abraham, "Definition and Specification of Meaning," *Journal of Philosophy*, 43, 1946.

Stevens, S. S., "The Operational Basis of Psychology," *American Journal of Psychology*, 47, 1935.

Stevens, S. S., "The Operational Definition of Psychological Concepts," *Psychological Review*, 42, 1935.

Stevens, S. S., "Psychology: The Propaedeutic Science," *Philosophy of Science*, 3, 1936.

Underwood, Benton J., "Operational Definitions," in *Psychological Research*. New York: Appleton-Century-Crofts, 1957.

D. QUANTUM THEORY

Bergmann, Gustav, "The Logic of Quanta," *American Journal of Physics,* 15, 1947.

Birkhoff, G. D., and J. von Neumann, "The Logic of Quantum Mechanics," *Annals of Mathematics,* 37, 1936.

Bohr, Niels, "On Atoms and Human Knowledge," *Daedalus,* 87, 1958.

Born, Max, *The Restless Universe*. New York: Harper and Brothers, 1936.

Heisenberg, Werner, *Philosophic Problems of Nuclear Science*. London: Faber and Faber Limited, 1952.

Heisenberg, Werner, "The Representation of Nature in Contemporary Physics," *Daedalus,* 87, 1958.

Körner, S., "On Philosophical Arguments in Physics," *Observation and Interpretation*. London: Butterworths Scientific Publications, 1957.

Landé, Alfred, *Foundations of Quantum Theory*. New Haven: Yale University Press, 1955.

Margenau, Henry, "The Meaning of 'Elementary Particle'," *American Scientist,* 39, 1951.

Margenau, Henry, *The Nature of Physical Reality*. New York: McGraw-Hill Book Co., 1950.

Reichenbach, Hans, *Philosophic Foundations of Quantum Mechanics*. Berkeley: University of California Press, 1944.

Schrödinger, Erwin, "What Is an Elementary Particle?", *Endeavour,* 9, 1950.

Walker, Marshall J., "An Orientation Toward Modern Physical Theory," *Scientific Monthly,* 81, 1955.

3. Biology and the Sciences of Man

A. BIOLOGY AND REDUCTIONISM

Bertalanffy, L. von, *Problems of Life – An Evolution of Modern Biological Thought*. New York: John Wiley and Sons, 1952.

Darwin, Charles and Alfred Russell Wallace, *Evolution by Natural Selection*. Cambridge: Cambridge University Press, 1958.

Dobzhansky, T., "A Critique of the Species Concept in Biology," *Philosophy of Science,* 2, 1935.

Dobzhansky, T., *Genetics and the Origin of Species,* 3rd Edition Revised. New York: Columbia University Press, 1951.

Ducasse, C. J., "Explanation, Mechanism, and Teleology," *Journal of Philosophy,* 22, 1925.

Goudge, T. A., "The Concept of Evolution," *Mind,* LXIII, NS, 1954.

Goudge, T. A., "Is Evolution Finished?", *University of Toronto Quarterly,* 26, 1957.

Goudge, T. A., "Some Philosophical Aspects of The Theory of Evolution," *University of Toronto Quarterly,* 23, 1954.

Henle, Paul, "The Status of Emergence," *Journal of Philosophy,* 39, 1942.

Huxley, Julian, *Evolution: The Modern Synthesis*. London: 1942.

Ingle, Dwight J., *Principles of Research in Biology and Medicine*. Philadelphia: J. B. Lippincott Co., 1958.

Kemeny, John G. and Paul Oppenheim, "On Reduction," *Philosophical Studies,* 7, 1956.

Mandelbaum, Maurice, "The Scientific Background of Evolutionary Theory in Biology," *Journal of the History of Ideas,* 18, 1957.

Nagel, Ernest, "The Meaning of Reduction in the Natural Sciences" in Robert C. Stauffer, ed., *Science and Civilization*. Madison: University of Wisconsin Press, 1949.

Nagel, Ernest, "Mechanistic Explanation and Organismic Biology," *Philosophy and Phenomenological Research,* 11, 1950–51.

Simpson, G. G., *The Meaning of Evolution*. New Haven: Yale University Press, 1949.

Woodger, J. H., *Biology and Language*. Cambridge: Cambridge University Press, 1952.

Woodger, J. H., *Physics, Psychology, and Medicine*. Cambridge: Cambridge University Press, 1956.

B. PSYCHOLOGY

Beck, S. J., "The Science of Personality: Nomothetic or Idiographic?", *Psychological Review,* 60, 1953.

Bergmann, Gustav, "The Logic of Psychological Concepts," *Philosophy of Science,* 18, 1951.

Bergmann, Gustav, "Psychoanalysis and Experimental Psychology," *Mind,* 53, 1944.

Bergmann, Gustav, "Theoretical Psychology," *Annual Review of Psychology,* 4, 1953.

Boring, E. G., "The Role of Theory in Experimental Psychology," *American Journal of Psychology,* 57, 1953.

Dennis, Wayne, *et al., Current Trends in Psychological Theory.* Pittsburgh: University of Pittsburgh Press, 1951. (Particularly Herbert Feigl, "Principles and Problems of Theory Construction in Psychology.")

Falk, J. L., "Issues Distinguishing Idiographic from Nomothetic Approaches to Personality Theory," *Psychological Review,* 63, 1956.

Freud, Sigmund, "A Note on the Unconscious in Psychoanalysis" from *A General Selection from the Works of Sigmund Freud,* ed. John Rickman. London: Hogarth Press, 1937.

Ginsberg, Arthur, "Hypothetical Constructs and Intervening Variables," *Psychological Review,* 61, 1954.

Hull, Clark L., *A Behavior System.* New Haven: Yale University Press, 1952.

Hull, Clark L., *Principles of Behavior.* New York: Appleton-Century-Crofts, 1943.

James, William, *Principles of Psychology.* New York: Henry Holt and Co., 1896.

Jessor, Richard, "The Problem of Reductionism in Psychology," *Psychological Review,* 65, 1958.

Koffka, Kurt, *Principles of Gestalt Psychology.* New York: Harcourt, Brace and Co., 1935.

Köhler, Wolfgang, *Gestalt Psychology.* New York: Liveright Publishing Corporation, 1947.

Madden, Edward H., "A Logical Analysis of 'Psychological Isomorphism'," *The British Journal for the Philosophy of Science,* 8, 1957.

Madden, Edward H., "The Nature of Psychological Explanation," *Methodos,* 9, 1957.

Madden, Edward H., "The Philosophy of Science in Gestalt Theory," *Philosophy of Science,* 19, 1952.

Madden, Edward H., "Science, Philosophy and Gestalt Theory," *Philosophy of Science,* 20, 1953.

Madden, Marian and Edward H. Madden, "Chauncey Wright and the Logic of Psychology," *Philosophy of Science,* 9, 1952.

Mandelbaum, Maurice, "Professor Ryle and Psychology," *The Philosophical Review,* 67, 1958.

Marx, Melvin, ed., *Psychological Theory: Contemporary Readings.* New York: The Macmillan Co., 1951.

Pratt, C. C., *The Logic of Modern Psychology.* New York: The Macmillan Co., 1939.

Rescher, Nicholas and Paul Oppenheim, "Logical Analysis of Gestalt Concepts," *The British Journal for the Philosophy of Science,* 6, 1955.

Ryle, Gilbert, *The Concept of Mind.* London: Hutchinson's University Library, 1949.

Skinner, B. F., "Are Theories of Learning Necessary?", *Psychological Review,* 57, 1950.

Skinner, B. F., *Science and Human Behavior.* New York: The Macmillan Co., 1953.

Snygg, Donald, "Scientific Method in Psychology," *Journal of General Psychology,* 52–53, 1955.

Spence, Kenneth W., "The Empirical Basis and Theoretical Structure of Psychology," *Philosophy of Science,* 24, 1957.

Spiker, C. C., and B. R. McCandless, "The Concept of Intelligence and the Philosophy of Science," *Psychological Review,* 61, 1954.

Watson, John, "Psychology as the Behaviorist Views It," *Psychological Review,* 1913.

C. SOCIAL SCIENCE

Acton, H. B., "The Marxist Outlook," *Philosophy,* 22, 1947.

Brodbeck, May, "On the Philosophy of the Social Sciences," *Philosophy of Science,* 21, 1954.

Brown, Robert, "Explanation by Laws in Social Science," *Philosophy of Science,* 21, 1954.

Gewirth, Alan, "Subjectivism and Objectivism in the Social Sciences," *Philosophy of Science,* 21, 1954.

Gurvitch, G., and W. E. Moore, eds., *Twentieth Century Sociology.* New York: Philosophical Library, 1945.

Hayek, F. A., *The Counter-Revolution of Science.* Glencoe, Ill.: The Free Press, 1952.

Hinshaw, Virgil G., Jr., "The Epistemological Relevance of Mannheim's Sociology of Knowledge," *Journal of Philosophy,* 40, 1943.

Hook, Sidney, *From Hegel to Marx.* New York: John Day Co., 1936.

Hook, Sidney, *Marx and the Marxists: The Ambiguous Legacy.* Princeton, N.J.: D. Van Nostrand Co., 1955.

Hook, Sidney, *Reason, Social Myths, and Democracy.* New York: John Day Co., 1940.

Kaplan, Abraham, "Sociology Learns the Language of Mathematics," *Commentary,* 14, 1952.

Kemeny, J. G., J. L. Snell, and G. L. Thompson, *Introduction to Finite Mathematics.* Englewood Cliffs, N.J.: Prentice-Hall, 1957.

Lazarsfeld, Paul F., ed., *Mathematical Thinking in the Social Sciences.* Glencoe, Ill.: The Free Press, 1954.

Lazarsfeld, Paul F., and Morris Rosenberg, eds., *The Language of Social Research, A Reader In the Methodology of Social Research.* Glencoe, Ill.: The Free Press, 1955.

Lenin, V. I., "The Teachings of Karl Marx" in *Handbook of Marxism,* ed. Emile Burns. New York: International Publishers, 1935, pp. 537–570.

Lerner, D., and H. Lasswell, eds., *The Policy Sciences.* Stanford: Stanford University Press, 1951.

Mandelbaum, Maurice, "Societal Facts," *The British Journal of Sociology,* 6, 1955.

Mandelbaum, Maurice, "Societal Laws," *The British Journal for the Philosophy of Science,* 8, 1957.

Mannheim, Karl, *Ideology and Utopia.* New York: Harcourt, Brace and Co., 1936.

Mannheim, Karl, *Man and Society in An Age of Reconstruction.* New York: Harcourt, Brace and Co., 1948.

Marshall, Alfred, *Principles of Economics,* 8th ed. New York: The Macmillan Co., 1953.

Marx, Karl, *Capital,* Vol. I, Revised and Amplified according to 4th German Edition by Ernest Untermann. Chicago: Charles H. Kerr & Co., 1919.

Merton, Robert K., "The Sociology of Knowledge," *Isis,* 26–27, 1936–1937.

Metzger, Walter P., "Ideology and The Intellectual: A Study of Thorstein Veblen," *Philosophy of Science,* 16, 1949.

Nagel, Ernest and Carl Hempel, "Problems of Concepts and Theory in the Social Sciences," a symposium, in *Language, Science, and Human Rights.* Philadelphia: University of Pennsylvania Press, 1952.

Papandreou, Andreas G., *Economics As a Science.* Chicago: J. B. Lippincott Co., 1958.

Popper, K. R., *The Open Society.* Revised edition, Princeton, N.J.: Princeton University Press, 1950.

Rudner, Richard S., "Philosophy and Social Science," *Philosophy of Science,* 21, 1954.

Von Schelting, Alexander, "Review of Mannheim's *Ideologie und Utopie,*" *American Sociological Review,* 1, 1936.

Weber, Max, *The Methodology of the Social Sciences.* Tr. and ed. E. A. Shils and H. A. Finch. Glencoe, Ill.: The Free Press, 1949.

D. HISTORY

Bergmann, Gustav, "Holism, Historicism and Emergence," *Philosophy of Science,* 11, 1944.

Cohen, Morris R., *The Meaning of Human History.* Chicago: Open Court, 1947.

Collingwood, R. G., *The Idea of History.* London: Oxford University Press, 1946.

Croce, Benedetto, *History as the Story of Liberty.* New York: W. W. Norton and Co., 1941.

Danto, Arthur C., "On Explanations in History," *Philosophy of Science,* 23, 1956.

Danto, A. C., "More Chronicle and History Proper," *Journal of Philosophy,* 50, 1953.

Dray, W. H., "Historical Understanding as Re-Thinking," *University of Toronto Quarterly,* 27, 1958.

Dray, William, *Laws and Explanation in History.* London: Oxford University Press, 1957.

Gardiner, P., *The Nature of Historical Explanation.* London: Oxford University Press, 1952.

Hempel, Carl, "The Function of General Laws in History," *Journal of Philosophy,* 39, 1942.

Hinshaw, Virgil, Jr., "The Objectivity of History," *Philosophy of Science,* 25, 1958.

Hook, Sidney, *The Hero in History.* New York: John Day Co., 1943.

Jaspers, Karl, *The Origin and Goals of History.* London: Routledge and Kegan Paul, 1953.

Lee, Dwight E. and Robert N. Beck, "The Meaning of 'Historicism'," *The American Historical Review,* 59, 1954.

Mandelbaum, Maurice, *The Problem of Historical Knowledge.* New York: Liveright Publishing Corporation, 1938.

Mandelbaum, Maurice, "Recent Trends in the Theory of Historiography," *Journal of the History of Ideas,* 16, 1955.

Niebuhr, Reinhold, *Faith and History.* New York: Charles Scribner's Sons, 1949.

Reis, Lincoln and P. O. Kristeller, "Some Remarks on the Method of History," *Journal of Philosophy,* 40, 1943.

Smith, Charlotte W., *Carl Becker: On History and the Climate of Opinion.* Ithaca, N.Y.: Cornell University Press, 1956.

Walsh, W. H., *An Introduction to Philosophy of History.* London: Hutchinson, 1951.

White, M. G., "The Attack on the Historical Method," *Journal of Philosophy,* 42, 1945.

White, M. G., "Historical Explanation," *Mind,* 12, 1943.

4. The Meaning of 'Cause' and 'Law'

Bohr, Niels, "Causality and Complementarity," *Philosophy of Science,* 4, 1937.

Born, Max, *Natural Philosophy of Cause and Chance.* London: Oxford University Press, 1949.

Chisholm, Roderick M., "The Contrary-to-Fact Conditional," *Mind,* 55, 1946.

Ducasse, C. J., *Causation and the Types of Necessity.* Seattle: University of Washington Press, 1924.

Ewing, A. C., "A Defense of Causality," *Proceedings of the Aristotelian Society,* 33, 1932–1933.

Goodman, Nelson, *Fact, Fiction, and Forecast.* Cambridge: Harvard University Press, 1955.

Hartshorne, Charles, "Causal Necessities: An Alternative to Hume," *Philosophical Review,* 63, 1954.

Körner, Stephen, "On Laws of Nature," *Mind,* 62, 1953.

Pap, Arthur, *Elements of Analytic Philosophy.* New York: The Macmillan Co., 1949.

Russell, Bertrand, "The Notion of Cause," from *Our Knowledge of the External World.* New York: W. W. Norton and Co., 1929.

Sellars, W. S., "Concepts as Involving Laws and Inconceivable Without Them," *Philosophy of Science,* 15, 1948.

Simon, H. A., "On the Definition of the Causal Relation," *Journal of Philosophy,* 49, 1952.

Stebbing, L. S., *Modern Introduction to Logic,* Ch. 15. London: Methuen, 1930.

Stout, G. F., *Mind and Matter,* Bk. 1, Ch. 2. Cambridge: Cambridge University Press, 1931.

"Symposium on the Conception of Law in Science," *Journal of Philosophy,* 50, 1953.

Ushenko, A. P., "The Principle of Causality," *Journal of Philosophy,* 49, 1952.

Weinberg, J. R., "The Idea of Causal Efficacy," *Journal of Philosophy,* 47, 1950.

Whitehead, Alfred North, Ch. II of *Symbolism: Its Meaning and Effect.* New York: The Macmillan Co., 1927.

5. Probability Notions

Bergmann, Gustav, "The Logic of Probability," *American Journal of Physics,* 9, 1941.

Brown, G. Spencer, *Probability and Scientific Inference.* London: Longmans, Green and Co., 1957.

Carnap, Rudolph, *Logical Foundations of Probability.* Chicago: University of Chicago Press, 1950.

Copeland, A. H., "Predictions and Probabilities," *Erkenntnis,* 6, 1936.

Hay, W. H., "Carnap's *Continuum of Inductive Methods,*" *Philosophical Review,* 62, 1953.

Hay, W. H., "Professor Carnap and Probability," *Philosophy of Science,* 19, 1952.

Jeffreys, H., "The Present Position in Probability Theory," *The British Journal for the Philosophy of Science,* 5, 1955.

Jeffreys, H., *Theory of Probability.* Oxford: The Clarendon Press, 1939.

Jevons, W. S., *The Principles of Science.* New York: The Macmillan Co., 1905.

Keynes, J. M., *Treatise on Probability.* London: The Macmillan Co., 1921.

Kneale, W. C., *Probability and Induction.* Oxford: The Clarendon Press, 1949.

Laplace, P. S., *Theorie analytique des probabilités.* Paris, 1812.

Lenz, John W., "Carnap on Defining 'Degree of Confirmation'," *Philosophy of Science,* 23, 1956.

Margenau, Henry, "On the Frequency Theory of Probability," *Philosophy and Phenomenological Research,* 6, 1945–46.

Mises, Richard von, *Probability, Statistics, and Truth.* New York: The Macmillan Co., 1939.

Nagel, Ernest, "The Meaning of Probability," *Journal of American Statistical Association,* 31, 1936.

Nagel, Ernest, *Principles of the Theory of Probability.* Chicago: University of Chicago Press, 1939.

Reichenbach, Hans, *Theory of Probability.* Berkeley: University of California Press, 1949.

Wright, G. H. von, *A Treatise on Induction and Probability.* London: Routledge and Kegan Paul, 1951.

6. The Riddle of Induction

Black, Max, *Language and Philosophy,* Ch. 3. Ithaca, N.Y.: Cornell University Press, 1949.

Black, Max, *Problems of Analysis* (Part 3). Ithaca, N.Y.: Cornell University Press, 1954.

Burks, A. W., "Presupposition Theory of Induction," *Philosophy of Science,* 20, 1953.

Edwards, Paul, "Russell's Doubts about Induction," *Mind,* 58, 1949.

Feigl, Herbert, "Scientific Method Without Metaphysical Presuppositions," *Philosophical Studies,* 5, 1954.

Kyburg, Henry E. Jr., "The Justification of Induction," *The Journal of Philosophy,* 53, 1956.

Peirce, Charles S., *Collected Papers,* eds. Charles Hartshorne and Paul Weiss. Cambridge: Harvard University Press, 1931–1935.

Reichenbach, Hans, *Experience and Prediction,* Ch. 5. Chicago: University of Chicago Press, 1938.

Russell, Bertrand, *Human Knowledge,* (Part 6). New York: Simon and Schuster, 1948.

Salmon, Wesley, "Should We Attempt to Justify Induction?", *Philosophical Studies,* 8, 1957.

Smart, H. R., "The Problem of Induction," *Journal of Philosophy,* 25, 1928.

Stace, W. T., *The Theory of Knowledge and Existence,* Ch. 11. Oxford: The Clarendon Press, 1932.

Wang, H., "On Scepticism about Induction," *Philosophy of Science,* 17, 1950.

Will, Frederick, "Is There a Problem of Induction?", *Journal of Philosophy,* 39, 1942.

Will, Frederick, "Will the Future Be Like the Past?", *Mind,* 55, 1946.

Williams, Donald, *The Ground of Induction.* Cambridge: Harvard University Press, 1947.

Williams, Donald, "Induction and the Future," *Mind,* 57, 1948.

Wisdom, J. O., *Foundations of Inference in Natural Science.* London: Methuen, 1952.

Wright, G. H. von, *The Logical Problem of Induction,* 2nd Revised Edition. New York: The Macmillan Co., 1957.

7. Science and Values

Bergmann, Gustav, "Ideology," *Ethics,* 61, 1951.

Biggs, John, Jr., *The Guilty Mind.* New York: Harcourt, Brace and Co., 1955.

Brown, Harcourt, ed., *Science and the Creative Spirit.* Toronto: University of Toronto Press, 1958.

Dewey, John, "Science and Society," from *Philosophy and Civilization.* New York: Minton, Balch and Co., 1931, pp. 318–330.

Ewing, A. C., *The Definition of Good.* New York: The Macmillan Co., 1947.

Fingarette, Herbert, "Blame: Its Motive and Meaning in Everyday Life," *The Psychoanalytic Review,* 44, 1957.

Hall, Everett W., *Modern Science and Human Values.* Princeton, N.J.: D. Van Nostrand Co., 1956.

Hook, Sidney, ed., *Determinism and Freedom.* New York: New York University Press, 1958.

Hospers, John, *An Introduction to Philosophical Analysis,* Chs. 4, 7. Englewood Cliffs, N.J.: Prentice-Hall, 1953.

Köhler, Wolfgang, *The Place of Value in a World of Fact.* New York: Liveright Publishing Corporation, 1938.

Lewis, C. I., *An Analysis of Knowledge and Valuation.* La Salle, Illinois: Open Court, 1946.

Margenau, Henry, "The New View of Man in His Physical Environment," *The Centennial Review of Arts and Science,* 1, 1957.

Moore, G. E., *Principia Ethica.* Cambridge: Cambridge University Press, 1903.

Russell, Bertrand, "Science and Values" (Ch. XVII) of *The Scientific Outlook.* London: George Allen & Unwin, 1931, pp. 269-279.

Schlick, Moritz, *Problems of Ethics.* Englewood Cliffs, N.J.: Prentice-Hall, 1939.

Schrödinger, Erwin, *Science and Humanism.* Cambridge: Cambridge University Press, 1951.

Stevenson, C. L., *Ethics and Language.* New Haven: Yale University Press, 1945.

Waddington, C. H., *The Scientific Attitude,* Revised Ed. West Drayton: Pelican Books, 1948.

Zerby, L. K., "Some Remarks on the Philosophy of Law," *Journal of Philosophy,* 46, 1949.

Zilboorg, Gregory, *The Psychology of the Criminal Act and Punishment.* London: The Hogarth Press, 1955.

Index